D0162699

Managing Human Resources

SEVENTH EDITION

Herbert J. Chruden
Professor of Business Administration
California State University, Sacramento

Arthur W. Sherman, Jr.
Professor of Psychology
California State University, Sacramento

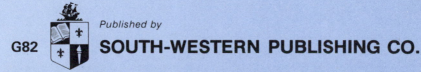

G82 *Published by*
SOUTH-WESTERN PUBLISHING CO.

CINCINNATI   WEST CHICAGO, ILL.   DALLAS   PELHAM MANOR, N.Y.   PALO ALTO, CALIF.

Copyright © 1984

Philippine Copyright 1984

by South-Western Publishing Co.
Cincinnati, Ohio

ALL RIGHTS RESERVED

The text of this publication, or any part thereof, may not be reproduced or transmitted in any form or by any means, electronic or mechanical, including photocopying, recording, storage in an information retrieval system, or otherwise, without the prior written permission of the publisher.

ISBN: 0-538-07820-0

Library of Congress Catalog Card Number: 81-51892

3 4 5 6 7 8 **D** 0 9 8 7 6 5 4

Printed in the United States of America

CONTENTS

Cases

PREFACE

For this 7th Edition we have adopted a new title: *Managing Human Resources*. The title is in keeping with the growing recognition that one of an organization's most valuable resources is its personnel. This title also acknowledges the growing participation of human resources managers in strategic planning and decision making and the importance of their contributions to the achievement of organizational objectives. Moreover, it is consistent with the more recent systems orientation of human resources management which recognizes the interrelationships of the personnel functions that are performed. In our discussion of the personnel functions, the focus is upon these interrelationships throughout the book. Furthermore, in the appropriate chapters pertaining to a particular function, models are presented to provide examples of some of the interrelationships existing between each function and the other functions.

As in the previous edition, we have attempted to define more precisely the impact of the internal and external environments upon the activities of human resources managers. We emphasize that the management of human resources occurs in a culture that is highly dynamic. You are, therefore, advised at many points to be alert for changing conditions that will present new problems which require new solutions.

We have attempted to show wherever possible the contributions that human resources management can make to productivity. Discussions of ethics, career development, professionalization of human resources practitioners, and the rights and responsibilities of employers and employees are among the topics which have received special emphasis.

We are continuing the orientation that we have had since the first edition in 1959 of having a balanced approach to human resources management that melds the principles of behavioral science with traditional personnel and labor relations philosophies and practices. In the process of bringing the material up to date, we have recognized the growing body of laws and regulations that influence the daily activities of human resources managers and their staffs. Obviously, in the limited space available, it is possible to cite only the federal laws and some of the decisions of the Supreme Court of the United States. We have endeavored, however, to remind you of the role of state and local laws. In this edition we have expanded the discussions of affirmative action and equal employment opportunity requirements. Rather than devoting a single chapter to these important topics, we have chosen to include them wherever they apply to the personnel function being described in a particular chapter.

Now, as in the past, we have tried to use the language of the human resources practitioner and to emphasize current issues and problems of the "real world" with which managements must be concerned. To do this we must depend upon reported experiences and the published works of many authors. We have tried to cite those articles and books that we believe are both timely and authoritative. To make these references readily available to you and to provide the recognition to the authors whose works are cited, we have presented them as footnotes on the pages containing the information which is cited.

The material in this book is divided into seven parts. In Part 1 we endeavor to show why and how the various personnel functions have evolved. The various environments that must be considered in managing human resources and organizational considerations are examined. In Part 2 we emphasize the importance of meeting human resources requirements by establishing job requirements, planning for and recruiting personnel to staff the organization, analyzing the qualifications of job candidates, and making valid selection decisions. In Part 3 we are concerned with developing human resources through training programs, career development programs, and evaluating and improving performance.

Part 4, "Creating a Productive Work Environment," emphasizes employee motivation, communication, group behavior, and supervision. For some students Part 4 will serve as a valuable review of organizational behavior principles from the standpoint of human resources management. Part 5 contains three chapters devoted to various aspects of labor relations, including union recognition, collective bargaining, and disciplinary actions and appeal procedures. Part 6, "Compensation and Security," covers compensation programs, employee benefits, and safety and health. The concluding part, Part 7, is concerned with auditing the human resources management program and with the career opportunities in human resources management.

Additional opportunities to apply the theories and principles presented in this textbook may be found in *Practical Study Experiences in Managing Human Resources*, 7th Edition. This is a project book designed to give students a variety of experiences similar to those they are likely to find on the job. It also contains review questions that can be used to check the student's understanding of each chapter in this textbook. Finally, our *Readings in Managing Human Resources*, 6th Edition, contains a selection of journal articles that elaborate on the theories and principles discussed in the text. Both the project book and the readings book have been designed to correlate closely with the material in the textbook.

Suggestions for Studying the Book

To gain maximum value from studying this textbook, we recommend that you first review the table of contents in order to acquire a perspective of the material that will be covered. Before reading each chapter, study the objectives, then scan through its pages to familiarize yourself with how the information is presented. Look at the headings as you go. Return to the beginning of the chapter and begin your reading. Look for the main ideas. Also give special attention to words that are printed in *boldface* type. These are important concepts. Make brief notes or mark the printed page as you prefer. When you have finished reading the chapter, look at the list of terms to identify. Check your understanding of them. Also refer back to the objectives at the beginning of the chapter to determine your comprehension of what you have read. Then answer the discussion questions at the end of the chapter. Finally, study the problem or problems at the end of the chapter to determine if you can apply what you have learned to a practical problem in human resources management. Review each chapter frequently in order to make what you have learned more permanent. From time to time your instructor will probably assign cases at the end of this textbook. These cases cover situations that a particular organization has encountered in managing its human resources. Generally they are broader in scope than the problems at the end of the chapter.

Acknowledgments

In preparing the manuscript for this 7th Edition, we have drawn not only upon the current literature but also upon the current practices of organizations that have furnished information and illustrations relating to their human resources programs. We are indebted to the leaders in the field who have developed the available heritage of information and practices of human resources management and who have influenced us through their writings and personal associations. We have also been aided by students in our classes, by former students of ours, by the participants in the management development programs with whom we have been associated, by human resources managers, and by our colleagues. In particular, we would like to express our appreciation to the following individuals for their various contributions:

Richard H. Crossman	Dr. Robert F. Mager
Pallo Deftereos	Dr. E. C. Miller
Dr. Austin J. Gerber	Midge Moore
Cynthia Gorton	Francis G. Stoffels
Dr. Irving Herman	Robert B. Wall
Robert E. Hill	Charles J. Wong
Dr. Irl A. Irwin	

Our greatest indebtedness is to our wives—Marie Chruden and Leneve Sherman—who have contributed in so many ways to the development of this book over the past 30 years. Through their active participation in the preparation of the manuscript for this edition, as in the past, they have been a source of invaluable guidance and assistance. Furthermore, by their continued enthusiasm and support, they have made the process a more pleasant and rewarding experience. We are most grateful to them for their many contributions to this publication, to our lives, and to our families.

Herbert J. Chruden

January, 1984

Arthur W. Sherman, Jr.

Human Resources Management in Perspective

part 1

- To describe the concept and approach underlying human resources management.
- To trace the early development of the field of human resources management.
- To cite the leaders and movements that contributed significantly to the field, as well as the nature of their contributions.
- To describe the principal functions performed in human resources management and how these functions evolved.
- To cite the origin and characteristics of behavioral science and its contribution to human resources management.
- To identify the organizations, publications, and the code of ethics that are contributing to the professional status of human resources management.

1

The Development of Human Resources Management

Employees and the public at large increasingly are demanding that employers demonstrate greater social responsibility in managing their human resources. Complaints that many jobs are debilitating the lives and injuring the health of employees are not uncommon. Charges of discrimination against women, minorities, the physically handicapped, and the aged with respect to hiring, training, advancement, and compensation also are being leveled against some employers. Other demands that employers are being forced to face include those involving comparable pay for comparable work, equal employment access to all jobs, and more compensation for less work. Where employees are organized, employers can encounter costly collective bargaining proposals, strike threats, and charges of unfair labor practices. Court litigation, demands for corrective action by governmental agencies, and sizable damage awards in response to employee complaints are still other hazards that contemporary employers must try to avoid.

It is estimated that "human resources executives—whether they carry the title or not—now hold key manpower planning responsibilities in almost all of the nation's 500 largest industrial companies, compared with only a handful of companies five years ago."[1] Top managers increasingly are depending upon the contributions of their human resources managers to organizational planning and strategy formulation.[2] Human resources managers, Meehan concludes, are being accorded a role comparable to that of the chief financial planning officer.[3] The function of human resources management, therefore, is being recognized for the contributions it can render to profit achievement on the "bottom line." As the president of Horn/Ferry International has stated, "Today corporations recognize that the right executive in human resources can add to profits."[4] Having thus outgrown their previous office manager roles, human resources managers are gaining vice-presidential rank and are being accepted as a part of the top management team. Here they can have a definite impact upon operating policy.

Although human resources managers have the responsibility for coordinating and enforcing policies relating to personnel functions, all supervisors and managers within an enterprise are responsible for performing these functions in their relations with subordinates. It is in such positions of authority that the majority of students using this book eventually will be employed. The material in this book, therefore, is intended to help them in managing subordinates more effectively. References in the book concerning the role of the human resources department, however, can serve to provide them with a better understanding and perception of the functions performed by this department. These references, furthermore, should be of particular interest to students planning a career in this department. However, for those who will be managing other employees, a familiarity with the role of the human resources department should help them to cooperate more closely with the department's staff and to utilize more fully the assistance and services that are available from this source.

1. "Personnel Widens Its Franchise," *Business Week* (February 26, 1979), p. 116.
2. Lena B. Prewitt, "The Emerging Field of Human Resources Management," *Personnel Administrator*, Vol. 27, No. 5 (May, 1982), pp. 81–87.
3. Robert H. Meehan, "The Future Personnel Executive," *Personnel Administrator*, Vol. 26, No. 1 (January, 1981), p. 25.
4. "Personnel Widens Its Franchise," *loc. cit.*

THE CONCEPT OF HUMAN RESOURCES MANAGEMENT

Traditionally **personnel management** was viewed largely as involving the performance of certain basic personnel functions such as selection, training, and compensation. These functions often were performed without much regard for their interrelationships or intended contributions to organizational objectives. In contrast, **human resources management** as it is currently perceived represents the extension rather than the rejection of the traditional requirements for managing personnel effectively. Required still is an understanding of human behavior and the skill to utilize it. Also required is a knowledge and understanding of the various personnel functions performed in managing human resources, as well as the ability to perform them in accordance with organizational objectives. An awareness of existing economic, social, and legal constraints upon the performance of these functions is most essential.

Human resources management as it is practiced today represents a systems approach. This approach recognizes the dynamic interaction of personnel functions with each other and with the objectives of the organization. Most important, it recognizes that human resources planning must be coordinated closely with the organization's strategic and related planning functions.[5] As a result, efforts in human resources management are being directed toward providing more support for the achievement of the organization's operating goals.[6]

The present status of the field of human resources management has been achieved only after years of progress involving an evolutionary development. We hope this chapter will help readers not only to better understand the forces that have contributed to this progress, but also to become more aware of the forces that may have an effect upon it today and in the future. This chapter also will provide a frame of reference upon which to better understand the role of the various personnel functions that human resources management currently entails. In addition, it will alert readers to the governmental regulations and other elements of an organization's environment that can affect the management of this most important resource.

EARLY STAGES OF DEVELOPMENT

Personnel management, at least in a primitive form, has existed since the dawn of group effort. Certain personnel functions, even though informal in nature, have been performed whenever people came together for a common purpose. During the course of this century, however, the processes of managing people have become more formalized and specialized. As a result, a growing body of knowledge concerning these processes has been accumulated by practitioners and scholars. An understanding of the events (see Figure 1–1) contributing to this growth of the personnel field,

---

5. Joyce D. Ross, ''A Definition of Human Resources Management,'' *Personnel Journal*, Vol. 60, No. 10 (October, 1981), p. 781.
6. Deborah J. Cornwall, ''Human Resource Programs: Blue Sky or Operating Priority?'' *Business Horizons*, Vol. 23, No. 1 (April, 1980), p. 49.

Figure 1–1   Important Events in the Development of Human Resources Management

1786	Earliest authenticated strike in America by Philadelphia printers to gain minimum weekly wage of $6.00
1794	First profit-sharing plan in the United States established by Albert Gallatin at his glass works in Pennsylvania
1842	*Commonwealth v. Hunt* decision in which the conspiracy doctrine restricting collective bargaining was overturned by the Massachusetts Supreme Court
1848	Passage of a law in Philadelphia setting a minimum wage for workers in commercial occupations
1868	Passage by Congress of the first federal 8-hour day covering laborers, workers, and mechanics employed by or in behalf of the government
1875	Initiation by the American Express Company of the first employer-sponsored pension plan
1881	Beginning of Frederick W. Taylor's work in scientific management at the Midvale Steel Plant
1883	Establishment of the United States Civil Service Commission
1886	Founding of the American Federation of Labor (AFL)
1888	Passage of the Arbitration Act of 1888 to help resolve disputes in the railway industry, thus constituting the first federal labor law
1912	Passage in Massachusetts of the first minimum wage law
1913	Establishment of the United States Department of Labor
1913	Publication of Hugo Münsterberg's book, *Psychology and Industrial Efficiency*
1914	Congressional hearings on interstate commerce helped Taylor to publicize scientific management
1915	First course in personnel management offered at Dartmouth College for employment managers
1917	First large-scale use of group intelligence tests—the Army *Alpha* and *Beta* tests
1920	First text in personnel administration published by Tead, Ordway, & Metcalf
1924	Point-method of job evaluation first developed by the National Electric Manufacturers' Association and the National Metal Trades Association
1927	Hawthorne Studies begun by Mayo, Roethlisberger, and Dickson
1935	Establishment of Congress of Industrial Organizations (CIO) by several unions previously affiliated with the AFL
1939	Publication of the first *Dictionary of Occupational Titles*
1941	Beginning of World War II which created sudden needs to train large numbers of supervisors and workers
1955	Merger of the AFL and CIO unions
1976	Beginning of professional accreditation program by the Personnel Accreditation Institute of the American Society for Personnel Administration (ASPA)
1978	Passage of the Civil Service Reform Act which established the Office of Personnel Management (OPM), the Merit Systems Protection Board (MSPB), and the Federal Labor Relations Authority (FLRA)

therefore, can help to improve the reader's perception of practices in contemporary human resources management.

The Guild System

The **guild system** of the Middle Ages provides the beginning of efforts to regulate the apprentice training and employment of workers who had certain craft skills. Craftsmen who were also entrepreneurs were able to organize and exercise some degree of control over their respective trades through their guilds. These guilds were the forerunners of contemporary employer associations. In turn, the journeymen who worked for these craftsmen-entrepreneurs organized into **yeomanry guilds**, which were the counterpart of today's craft unions.

The Factory System

During the 19th century, the development of mechanical power made possible a factory system of production. Power-driven equipment and improved production techniques enabled products to be manufactured more cheaply than had been possible previously in small shops and in homes. However, this process also created many jobs that were monotonous, unchallenging, and often unhealthy and hazardous. Moreover, factory workers lacked salable skills with which to bargain for improved working conditions or for economic security. This meant that they could be replaced by other individuals who could be trained quickly to perform their jobs. (Even today the quality of work life and employment security are issues of concern for many factory workers).

The concentration of workers in factories served to focus public attention upon their conditions of employment. It also enabled workers to act collectively to achieve better conditions. Therefore, during the late 1880s, laws were passed in some states to regulate hours of work for women and children, to establish minimum wages for male labor, and to regulate working conditions that affect employee health and safety. It was also at this time that laws began to be initiated to provide indemnity payments for injuries suffered through industrial accidents. Eventually, as the result of state legislation and collective bargaining, employment conditions began to improve. Even today, however, labor organizations believe there still is room for further improvement.

The Mass Production System

Mass production was made possible by designing parts that were standardized and interchangeable for assembly-line production. With it came improvements in production techniques and the use of laborsaving machinery and equipment. The accompanying increases in overhead costs and wage rates, however, forced companies to seek ways of using production facilities and labor more efficiently.

Contributions of Scientific Management.   The use of **scientific management** involved a more objective and systematic approach to improving worker efficiency

based upon the collection and analysis of data. Frederick W. Taylor, whose contributions stimulated the scientific management movement, is often referred to as the father of scientific management. Among his contemporaries in this movement were Frank and Lillian Gilbreth, Henry L. Gantt, Harrington Emerson, and Harry Kopf.[7] Lillian Gilbreth deserves special recognition as being one of the first women to gain an international reputation as a management consultant. She combined a career as an industrial psychologist (Ph.D. degree) with that of being a homemaker and the mother of twelve children—whom her husband alleged were "cheaper by the dozen."[8]

Taylor believed that work could be systematically analyzed and studied by using the same scientific approach of researchers in the laboratory. In his words, scientific management constituted "the substitution of exact scientific investigation and knowledge for the old individual judgment or opinion, either of the workman or the boss, in all matters relating to the work done in the establishment."[9] Taylor regarded accurate performance standards, based upon objective data gathered from time studies and other sources, as important personnel management tools. These standards provided a basis for rewarding the superior workers financially and for eliminating the unproductive ones. According to Taylor, scientific management offered the best means for increasing workers' productivity and earnings and for providing higher profits to owners and lower prices to customers. His approach was in sharp contrast to the then prevailing practice of attempting to gain more work from employees by threatening them with the loss of their jobs. However, it also differs from current concepts of motivation which recognize that most employees seek psychological, as well as financial, rewards from their work.

Contributions of Industrial Psychology.   By the early 1900s some of the knowledge and research from the field of psychology was beginning to be applied to the management of personnel. One of the best known pioneers in industrial psychology was Hugo Münsterberg. His book, *Psychology and Industrial Efficiency*, called attention to the contributions that psychology could render in the areas of employment testing, training, and efficiency improvement.[10]

Other psychologists, whose work up to that time had been largely theoretical and experimental in nature, followed Münsterberg's lead in making practical contributions to the personnel field. For example, Walter Dill Scott received acclaim for his early work dealing with the rating of sales personnel and for his classic book

7. Harrington Emerson, *The Twelve Principles of Efficiency* (New York: The Engineering Magazine Co., 1913). *See also* Alex W. Rathe (ed.), *Gantt on Management* (New York: American Management Associations, 1961).

8. Frank B. Gilbreth, Jr. and Ernestine Gilbreth Carey, *Cheaper by the Dozen* (New York: Grosset and Dunlap, 1948).

9. Frederick W. Taylor, "What Is Scientific Management?" as reprinted in Harwood F. Merrill (ed.), *Classics in Management* (New York: American Management Associations, 1960), p. 80. *See also* Edwin A. Locke, "The Ideas of Frederick W. Taylor: An Evaluation," *Academy of Management Review*, Vol. 7, No. 1 (January, 1982), pp. 14–24.

10. Hugo Münsterberg, *Psychology and Industrial Efficiency* (Boston: Houghton Mifflin, 1913).

in personnel management.[11] J. McKeen Cattell, another pioneer, is noted for his test-development activities and his leadership in establishing the Psychological Corporation (1921)—an organization which still offers personnel services. A contemporary, Walter Van Dyke Bingham, gained prominence as an author of books in interviewing and aptitude testing and as chief psychologist for the War Department.[12]

CONTEMPORARY DEVELOPMENTS

The contemporary era of human resources management began in the late 1920s. It was characterized by an increased concern for the human element in management. With this era came research in the area of human behavior and the development of new tools and techniques for managing people. It was also during this period that employer-employee relations began to become the subject of governmental regulations.

The Hawthorne Studies

Begun in the 1920s, the **Hawthorne Studies** represented an effort to determine what effect hours of work, periods of rest, and lighting might have upon worker fatigue and productivity. These experiments comprised one of the first cooperative industry/university studies. As the studies progressed, however, it was discovered that the social environment could have an equal if not a greater effect upon productivity than the physical environment. Conducted by Mayo, Roethlisberger, and Dickson, these studies were a pioneering endeavor in what eventually evolved into the present-day field of behavioral science.[13] The Hawthorne Studies revealed the influence that the informal work group can have upon the productivity of employees and upon their response to financial incentives. Also, these studies popularized the use of nondirective counseling with employees.

The Human Relations Movement

Along with the work of Kurt Lewin at the National Training Laboratories, the Hawthorne Studies helped to give rise to the **human relations movement** by providing new insights concerning human behavior. This movement focused attention on individual differences among employees and on the influence that informal groups may have upon employee performance and behavior. It focused

11. Walter Dill Scott and Robert C. Clothier, *Personnel Management: Practices and Point of View* (New York: A.W. Shaw, Co., 1923). *See also* Edmund C. Lynch, *Walter Dill Scott, Pioneer in Personnel Management* (Austin, TX: Bureau of Business Research, The University of Texas at Austin, 1968), pp. 22–23.

12. Walter Van Dyke Bingham and Bruce Victor Moore, *How to Interview* (New York: Harper and Brothers, 1931). *See also* Walter Van Dyke Bingham, *Aptitudes and Aptitude Testing* (New York: Harper and Brothers, 1937).

13. F. J. Roethlisberger and W.J. Dickson, *Management and the Worker* (Cambridge, MA: Harvard University Press, 1939).

attention also on the need for managers to gain improved communication and greater sensitivity concerning employee behavior and the reactions of others to it. Furthermore, the movement emphasized the need for providing a more participative and employee-centered form of supervision.

Emergence of the Behavioral Sciences

As the human relations movement evolved, it became broader in scope. The understanding of human behavior was enhanced by contributions not only from the traditional disciplines of psychology, sociology, and anthropology, but also from social economics, political science, linguistics, and education. More important, the interrelationships of these various disciplines became more widely recognized so that they are now referred to as the **behavioral sciences**. Although the behavioral science approach recognizes the need to promote employee efficiency, it focuses upon behavior in the total organizational environment rather than solely on the behavioral effects of interpersonal relations. Behavioral science does not ignore the value of high morale, but it rejects the insincere and manipulative tactics that sometimes characterized the human relations approach. Some of the principal characteristics of the behavioral sciences, according to Rush, are listed in Figure 1-2.[14]

One of the major contributions of the behavioral sciences has been its application to **organizational behavior (O.B.)** which is concerned with employee behavior in work organizations. The focus of O.B. is upon the interrelations involving individuals, groups, and the environment within an organization and their impact upon employee behavior. Efforts to create an organizational environment that will enlist cooperation and teamwork among employees has encouraged the growth of what has become known as **organizational development (O.D.)**. The goal of O.D. is to bring about a change in the attitudes, values, and behavioral patterns of individuals and of the organizational environment in which they work. The reduction

Figure 1–2 **Characteristics of a Contemporary Behavioral Science**

1. It is an applied science.
2. It is normative and value centered.
3. It is humanistic and optimistic.
4. It is oriented toward economic objectives.
5. It is concerned with the total climate or milieu.
6. It stresses the use of groups.
7. It is aimed at participation.
8. It is concerned with development of interpersonal competence.
9. It views the organization as a total system.
10. It is an ongoing process to manage change.

14. Harold M.F. Rush, *Behavioral Science: Concepts and Management Application,* Personnel Policy Study No. 216 (New York: National Industrial Conference Board, 1969), p. 2.

of mistrust and conflict within the organization, the encouragement of greater participation and productivity, and operating flexibility within the organization are among the specific outcomes sought from O.D. programs.

The High Technology Explosion

The most significant development of the past decade has been the rapid advancements in the field of technology. The invention of semiconductors has made possible the miniaturization of computers with greatly increased capabilities. Advancements in computer technology have enabled organizations to cope with another explosion—the information explosion. Through the use of computers, unlimited amounts of data can be stored, retrieved, and used as a basis of decision making. Computers can provide printouts of virtually any stored information concerning an individual employee, a characteristic of the work force, or the activities of a particular function within the human resources program. Advancements in computer technology also have permitted their use in controlling electronically the production work of robots and similar automated devices. Furthermore, in what is being referred to as the "second computer age," computers are starting to reason, make judgments, and to learn.[15] The impact of these advancements upon future production operations, as well as upon society as a whole, at this point in time is difficult even to imagine.

Growth of Functional Specialization

Initially the management of personnel was the exclusive responsibility of each departmental supervisor. This responsibility was limited largely to the functions of hiring, firing, and record keeping. Eventually clerical personnel were employed to assist in keeping records related to hours worked, to payroll, and ultimately to other personnel data, as Figure 1–3 indicates. Unfortunately these record-keeping activities created an image for personnel managers that has been difficult to erase. Even today, in a few organizations, what is referred to as personnel management still is considered to be an upgraded clerical function.

Employee Welfare.   One of the first jobs involving actual personnel work was that of **welfare secretary**. The welfare secretary's responsibility was to assist workers and their families in coping with personal problems of a financial, medical, housing, or other nature.[16] Many of the persons who were appointed welfare secretaries had gained previous experience in philanthropic or social work. As the benefits to be derived from a formal personnel program became more widely recognized and accepted, personnel work expanded far beyond record-keeping, hiring, and employee-welfare functions.

---

15. "Artificial Intelligence—The Second Computer Age Begins," *Business Week* (March 8, 1982), p. 66.

16. Henry Eilbirt, "The Development of Personnel Management in the United States," *Business History Review*, Vol. 33, No. 3 (Autumn, 1959), pp. 345–364.

Figure 1–3 **Evolution of the Personnel Manager**

Recruitment.   In the past, recruitment efforts often varied with the supply of qualified applicants available to fill position openings. If there was a lineup of applicants actively seeking work, recruitment often was accomplished at the entrance to company premises. Furthermore, the grapevine within the community usually served to alert those seeking work of impending job openings. For jobs requiring some degree of skill or training, advertisements or private agencies were used to contact applicants.

Selection.   Employee selection was based initially upon subjective decisions reached through face-to-face contact. With the establishment of the Civil Service Commission in 1883, the federal government became one of the first employers to attempt to select and promote employees on an objective basis. By developing competitive examination procedures for hiring job applicants, the Commission provided a foundation for various types of employment tests in the decades that ensued. However, it was not until a critical need for more effective selection tools developed during World War I that tests for selection purposes began to be utilized. The Army *Alpha* and *Beta* tests, which measured the intelligence of army recruits, were the first tests to be used on a mass basis as a selection tool. The use of these military tests encouraged the construction of other types of tests to measure such attributes as job knowledge, aptitudes, interests, and personalities.

Training and Development.   Personnel training was emphasized by both industry and government during World Wars I and II. The most important innovation during World War II was the creation of the **Training Within Industry (TWI)** program for helping supervisors to become more effective in their positions. Experience and knowledge gained during both wars helped to make companies aware of the potential contributions of formal training programs. In recent years training programs have been broadened to include developmental activities and career planning for personnel at all levels.

Performance Evaluation.   One of the first systems of performance evaluation was that developed by Walter Dill Scott to rate salespersons, as mentioned earlier in this chapter. At that time it was referred to as the man-to-man rating scale. Under this system the performance of salespersons was compared against the performance levels of selected individuals which provided the benchmarks on the rating scale. Contemporary graphic-type rating scales have evolved from this system. More recently, graphic rating systems in many organizations have been replaced by a newer system for evaluating managers called Management by Objectives (MBO). Under MBO, performance is judged on the basis of ability to achieve performance objectives reached through conference between the individual and his or her superior. This system of evaluation is a part of the trend toward enlisting employee participation in decisions affecting them.

Compensation Management.   It was not until the middle 1920s that an objective system was developed for determining hourly wage rates based upon the worth of jobs. One such system of job evaluation was the point system. Another was the factor comparison system. At about that time more employers also began to provide, as a part of their compensation programs, certain benefits and services for their employees. These included health and recreation services, paid holidays, vacations, sick leave, and life insurance. Unfortunately these benefits often were initiated as an act of paternalism rather than in return for something employees had earned or gained through collective bargaining. Although these benefits were reduced drastically during the Great Depression, they were restored on an even greater scale beginning with World War II.

Labor Relations. The National Labor Relations Act of 1935 (Wagner Act) offered encouragement for employees in the private sector to unionize and bargain collectively. More recently, employees in the public sector have been receiving similar encouragement. Once unionized, employees in both sectors have bargained and even gone on strike for improved employment conditions. Labor relations, therefore, is now a vital function of human resources management in virtually every type of organization. How effectively an organization is able to control labor costs often is contingent upon how successfully its management bargains with union representatives. Consequently, top management is recognizing the importance of labor relations and is assuming a more active role in this area. Some employers also have utilized the services of consultants to advise them on how to avoid unionization.

Growth of Governmental Regulations

Prior to the 1930s, employer relations with employees and with their labor organizations were subject to very few federal or state regulations. However, political pressures for social reform created by the Great Depression gave rise to both state and federal legislation affecting these relations. These regulations are a major cause for the increase in paperwork, as is being observed in Figure 1–4. Starting with the National Labor Relations Act, federal regulations have expanded to the point where they govern the performance of virtually every personnel function. Similar regulations exist in many of our states. Some of the major federal regulations and the functional areas they affect are listed in Figure 1–5. These regulations will be discussed at greater length, where appropriate, throughout the text.

HUMAN RESOURCES MANAGEMENT AS A PROFESSION

Due to changes occurring in the work force and its environment, human resources managers no longer can function primarily as technical specialists who merely perform the various personnel functions. Instead they must be concerned with the total scope of human resources management and its role within the organization and in society as a whole. Therefore, human resources managers today should be professionals with respect to both their qualifications and their performance.

One of the characteristics of a profession is the development through research and experimentation of an organized body of knowledge. This knowledge is exchanged through conferences, seminars, and workshops sponsored by professional

Figure 1–4   **Increasing Paperwork**

"I guess the rumors about the
increase in paperwork are true!"

SOURCE: *Supervision* (August, 1977). Reproduced with permission.

associations of persons who pursue this field. The latest information in the field is communicated through the literature published by the professional associations, as well as by various types of nonprofit organizations and educational institutions. Other characteristics of a profession include the establishment of a code of ethics and of accreditation requirements for its members. Human resources management exhibits all these characteristics.

Professional Associations

Presently a number of professional organizations represent general, as well as specialized, areas of interest in human resources management. The professional association with the largest membership—more than 31,000—is the American Society for Personnel Administration (ASPA). Affiliated with it are local chapters in major cities throughout the United States. Many of these local chapters sponsor student chapters at neighboring colleges and universities. The ASPA conducts regional conferences, seminars and workshops, and annual national meetings. It also publishes the monthly *Personnel Administrator* and other bulletins.

Other leading professional associations in the field include the International Personnel Management Association, the International Personnel Management Association for Personnel Women, the American Management Associations (AMA), and

Figure 1–5 **Important Federal Legislation Governing Human Resources Management**

1926	Railway Labor Act supporting the premise of collective bargaining in the railroad industry
1935	National Labor Relations Act (Wagner Act) giving workers the right to organize and bargain collectively
1937	Social Security Act which initially provided only for retirement benefits
1938	Fair Labor Standards Act (FLSA) establishing a federal minimum wage with time and a half for overtime
1947	Labor Management Relations Act (Taft-Hartley Act) placing curbs on union activities
1959	Labor-Management Reporting and Disclosure Act (Landrum-Griffin Act) designed to eliminate improper activities toward union members by unions and managements
1963	Equal Pay Act, amendment to the FLSA, prohibiting wage differentials based upon sex
1964	Civil Rights Act of 1964 barring discrimination on the basis of race, color, religion, sex, or national origin
1967	Age Discrimination in Employment Act barring discrimination against employment of persons 40 to 70 years of age
1970	Occupational Safety and Health Act (OSHA) establishing and enforcing safety and health standards
1972	Equal Employment Opportunity Act strengthening the Civil Rights Act of 1964 and providing for affirmative-action programs
1973	Rehabilitation Act aiding handicapped workers
1974	Vietnam Era Veterans Readjustment Act requiring federal contractors to undertake affirmative-action program for veterans
1974	Employee Retirement Income Security Act (ERISA) reforming and regulating private pension systems
1978	Pregnancy Discrimination Act prohibiting discrimination against employment of pregnant women

the National Industrial Conference Board (NICB). The AMA and the NICB are prominent nonprofit organizations that provide publications and educational services relating to human resources management and other functional areas. Organizations that represent specialized areas of interest include the American Compensation Association, the American Society for Training and Development, the Association for Industrial Research, and the Society for Industrial and Organizational Psychology of the American Psychological Association. For professors in the field, there is the Personnel and Human Resources Division of the Academy of Management.

Human resources managers are also very active in other countries. In Canada, the Council of Canadian Personnel Associations helps to further interests of the profession. Mexico has a number of active personnel organizations. In Europe and Great Britain, personnel managers have formed local and national associations in their respective countries. Many of them also participate in the European Association for Personnel Management.

Research Organizations

Throughout this book many of the findings from the research efforts of a number of different research organizations will be reported. The primary function of these organizations is to conduct research and to make their findings available to all who are interested in them. Many such organizations may be found at universities. Probably the largest university research center in the behavioral sciences is the Institute for Social Research at the University of Michigan. Its two main divisions—the Survey Research Center and the Research Center for Group Dynamics—have published well over 2,000 articles, reports, and books as a result of their research activities. A number of state universities have centers for the study of labor and industrial relations including those in California, Minnesota, Illinois, and New York. Organizations sponsored by industry, such as the American Management Associations and the National Industrial Conference Board, publish research studies that benefit managers in their personnel relations. The Bureau of National Affairs, Commerce Clearing House, and Prentice-Hall also conduct surveys relating to personnel policies and practices. Agencies of the federal government conduct research or contract with private research organizations for a wide variety of projects, the results of which are generally available to the public.

Professional Literature

Personal development in any profession requires keeping abreast of current literature in the field. A number of periodicals publish articles on general or specialized areas of interest in human resources management. Among some of the more important periodicals with which students and practitioners should be familiar are:

1. *Academy of Management Journal*
2. *Academy of Management Review*
3. *Compensation Review*
4. *Human Resource Management*
5. *Industrial and Labor Relations Review*
6. *Industrial Relations*
7. *Journal of Applied Psychology*
8. *Labor Law Journal*
9. *Monthly Labor Review*
10. *Personnel*
11. *Personnel Administrator*
12. *Personnel Journal*
13. *Personnel Psychology*
14. *Public Personnel Management*
15. *Supervision*
16. *Supervisory Management*
17. *Training and Development Journal*

Other periodicals that cover the general field of business and management also may contain articles pertaining to personnel and industrial relations. Among these are the *Harvard Business Review, Management Review, Business Week,* and *The Wall Street Journal.* Most of the large universities also publish journals containing articles of similar interest.

The vast number of books and articles being published makes it impossible even to scan, let alone read, all of the literature in the field. Consequently, students and practitioners will find two references invaluable in locating the limited books and articles they may have time to read. One is *Personnel Management Abstracts*, which contains abstracts from journals and books and an index of periodical literature.[17] The other is *Work Related Abstracts*, which is organized into broad categories with a cumulative guide to specific subjects, organizations, and individuals.[18]

Code of Ethics

A typical contribution of many professional associations is the development of a **code of ethics** which members are expected to observe. The code shown in Figure 1–6 was developed for human resources managers by the American Society for Personnel Administration (ASPA). Many large corporations have their own code of ethics which governs corporate relations with their employees and the public at large. In general, these guides of conduct encourage managers to provide cooperative, equitable, and nondiscriminatory treatment which respects the dignity and privacy of the individual.

Professional Accreditation

The professionalization of a field generally leads to some form of **accreditation** for practitioners to enhance their status and to recognize their competency levels. The Personnel Accreditation Institute sponsored by the ASPA has developed an accreditation program for professionals in the field of human resources management. The program offers four types of accreditation, each of which reflects the number of specialties and amount of experience and/or academic training possessed by the recipient. Briefly, these accreditations and the requirements for achieving them are:

1. Accredited Personnel Specialist (APS)—Demonstrated competency in one functional area with six years of college and/or experience.
2. Accredited Personnel Diplomate (APD)—Demonstrated competency in one functional area with ten years of college and/or experience.
3. Accredited Personnel Manager (APM)—Demonstrated competency in three functional areas with six years of college and/or experience.
4. Accredited Executive in Personnel (AEP)—Demonstrated competency in four functional areas with ten years of college and/or experience.

Since these accreditations are relatively new, they serve largely to indicate the qualifications of recipients and encourage others to qualify for accreditation. However, as the reputation of the accreditation program grows and becomes more widely recognized among the ranks of top management, it can become an important qualification for individuals seeking positions in human resources management. Furthermore, if the medical, legal, and accounting professions are to serve as a precedent, accreditation may some day become a basis for licensing human resources practitioners.

---

17. Published quarterly by the Bureau of Industrial Relations, Graduate School of Business Administration, University of Michigan.
18. Published monthly by Information Coordinators, Inc., 1435-37 Randolph Street, Detroit, MI 48226.

Figure 1–6 **Code of Ethics of the ASPA**

American Society for Personnel Administration

Code of Ethics

Each member of the American Society for Personnel Administration shall acknowledge his or her personal responsibility to strive for growth in the field of human resources management, and will pledge to carry out the following Society objectives, to the best of his or her ability:

- Support the goals and objectives of the Society in order to reflect the highest standards of the human resource management profession.

- Support the personal and professional development programs of the Society in Personnel Administration and Industrial Relations to help create an environment of recognition and support of human values in the workplace.

- Support the self-enforcement provisions in the codes of other associations to achieve the overall goal of development of each person to his/her full human potential.

- Display a unity of spirit and cohesiveness of purpose in bringing fair and equitable treatment of all people to the forefront of employers' thought; transmit that cohesive-ness to academia by actively cooperating to instill the PAIR ethic into the curricula of accredited institutions.

- Practice respect and regard for each other as a paramount personal commitment to a lifestyle exemplary in its motivation toward making business profitable in both human and monetary values.

- Express in the workplace through corporate codes the basic rules governing moral conduct of the members of the organization in order to provide employees and the public with a sense of confidence about the conduct and intentions of management.

- Personally refrain from using their official positions (regular or volunteer) to secure special privilege, gain or benefit for themselves, their employers or the Society.

SOURCE: American Society for Personnel Administration. Reproduced with permission.

Academic Training

With primary attention focused upon the behavioral sciences during the 1960s and early 1970s, the subject of personnel management in some universities suffered from benign neglect. More recently, however, affirmative action and other developments involving human resources management have rekindled interest in personnel courses. For example, affirmative action has forced practitioners to make certain that the personnel functions for which they are responsible are not performed in a manner that discriminates against women, minorities, older persons, and the physically handicapped. Furthermore, human resources managers also must be able to prove that their decisions on such personnel functions as selection, development, and compensation are made on an objective and valid basis. As noted earlier, personnel functions have had to be integrated more closely with other functions of an organization by means of a systems approach to management.

Reflecting these developments, college and university curricula are providing more course offerings in human resources management. For example, two of the nation's leading graduate schools of business—Stanford University and Harvard University—have recently initiated a course in human resources management. Other universities are demonstrating similar interest in this area. These courses, like this textbook, are intended to help students become more aware of the role of the personnel functions within an organization. They are intended also to provide the foundation needed to perform these functions more effectively in managing subordinates.

In the last chapter we will discuss the opportunities for students who may choose a career in the field of human resources management. However, it should be emphasized at this point that formal course work in the personnel/industrial relations area is becoming an important qualification for such a career. According to one survey, when hiring young persons to assist them in their personnel work, respondents indicated a preference for a university graduate with formal academic training in the major areas of personnel. They were almost unanimous in stating that personnel/industrial relations was a professional vocation for which there should be a prescribed academic training. In addition to this academic background, some practical experience in line management and in personnel-industrial relations was an essential qualification for holding the position of human resources manager.[19] An introductory course, such as one in which this text may be used, can provide a good foundation for further course work leading to an academic major in human resources management.

RÉSUMÉ

Human resources management represents a new concept and a systems approach in performing personnel functions. It still requires the performance of those

---

19. **Pradeep Kumar, "Professionalism in Canadian Personnel and Industrial Relations,"** *Canadian Personnel and Industrial Relations Journal*, Vol. 17, No. 5 (October, 1980), pp. 35–37.

personnel functions that have evolved over the years in response to emerging needs. But, instead of being treated as being separate and distinct, these functions are being performed as interrelated parts of a management system. Human resources management recognizes that human resources planning must be integrated closely with strategic organizational planning. Accordingly, human resources managers are becoming more involved in the decision making of top management.

The contemporary field of human resources management is the product of evolutionary development reflecting the concepts of scientific management and the human relations movement. The most recent conceptual development has been the emergence of behavioral science, which is contributing to a better understanding of organizational behavior and to programs for organizational development.

The evolution of the field of human resources management also is characterized by a growth in its professional status. This status is evinced by the code of ethics developed by the American Society for Personnel Administration. It is further seen in the programs initiated by the Personnel Accreditation Institute for accrediting generalists and specialists in the field of human resources management. Additional indicators of this rising status are the increases in the rank and pay of human resources managers and the growth of literature and research efforts within the field.

TERMS TO IDENTIFY

personnel management
human resources management
guild system
yeomanry guilds
scientific management
Hawthorne Studies
human relations movement

behavorial sciences
organizational behavior (O.B.)
organizational development (O.D.)
welfare secretary
Training Within Industry (TWI)
code of ethics
accreditation

DISCUSSION QUESTIONS

1. In what respects does human resources management differ from the traditional approach to personnel management?
2. What were some of the conditions that helped to bring about the scientific management movement?
3. How did Taylor's concept of employee motivation differ from current concepts?
4. What improvements does the behavorial science approach offer over the human relations approach?

5. Of those functions that are performed in human resources management, which do you consider to be the most and the least important?
6. Cite some of the more recent federal laws governing human resources management and their areas of impact.
7. What are some of the contributions of the American Society for Personnel Administration to human resources management?
8. What are the primary purposes of a course in which this text is likely to be used?

_____ SUGGESTED READINGS _____

Chruden, Herbert J., and Arthur W. Sherman, Jr. *Readings in Managing Human Resources*, 6th ed. Cincinnati: South-Western Publishing Co., 1984, Part I.

Desatnick, Robert L. *The Expanding Role of the Human Resources Manager*. New York: American Management Associations, 1979.

Gilbreth, Lillian Moller. *The Quest for the One Best Way: A Sketch of the Life of Frank Bunker Gilbreth*. Easton, PA: Hive Publishing Co., 1975.

Kakar, Subhir. *Frederick Taylor: A Study in Personality and Innovation*. Cambridge, MA: MIT Press, 1970.

Roethlisberger, F. J. *The Elusive Phenomena: An Autobiographical Account of My Work in the Field of Organizational Behavior at the Harvard Business School*. Boston: Graduate School of Business Administration, Harvard University, 1977.

Spriegel, William R., and Clark E. Meyers (eds.). *The Writings of the Gilbreths*. Homewood, IL: Richard D. Irwin, 1953.

Stockard, James G. *Rethinking People Management: A New Look at the Human Resources Function*. New York: American Management Associations, 1980.

- To recognize the various elements comprising an organization's external and internal environments and their possible impact upon the management of human resources.
- To identify demographic and cultural changes occurring within society and their implications for human resources management.
- To describe the possible reasons for the success of Japanese companies in managing their human resources.
- To understand the philosophy underlying job enrichment and the methods by which it may be achieved.
- To describe some of the modifications being made in traditional work schedules and their possible advantages and disadvantages.

2

The Contemporary Environment: Changes and Challenges

The growing recognition being accorded to human resources management reflects the increasingly important role it is serving in most organizations. This recognition also reflects the current challenges that confront employers in managing human resources. Such challenges, to a large extent, are the result of the rapid changes occurring within society and in the environment in which organizations must operate. Changes occurring in this environment and in the work force also are having an impact upon the work environment that exists within these organizations. The nature of these changes and their implication for human resources management will be the subject of this chapter.

ELEMENTS OF AN ORGANIZATION'S ENVIRONMENT

The **environment** of an organization consists of the conditions, circumstances, and influences that affect the organization's ability to achieve its objectives. Figure 2-1 shows that every organization exists in an environment that is both external and internal in nature. It also indicates that both the external and the internal environment are comprised of five elements: physical, technological, political, economic, and social.

A major challenge for employers today is not only to understand and cope with their dual-natured environment, but also to influence it. As the president of the Conference Board of Canada has so aptly stated:

> For an increasing number of human resource executives, their role goes beyond the sensing and interpreting of the impact of the environment on the organization. For them it is equally important to participate in and influence the environment.[1]

The External Environment

The environment that exists outside the organization is its **external environment**. The external environment can have a significant impact upon the policies and practices governing human resources management. It helps determine the values, attitudes, and behavior that employees bring to their jobs. This is why many organizations are engaging in **environmental scanning**, which involves analyzing the environment and changes occurring within it. Their purpose is to determine its possible impact on organizational policies and practices. Another closely related practice is **issue management** by which managers attempt to keep abreast of current issues which may affect their organization's position with respect to these issues. This includes bringing their policies in line with prevailing public opinion.

Physical Element.   The physical element of the external environment includes the climate, topography, and other physical characteristics of the area in which the organization is located. It can be a positive or a negative factor in helping

---

1. James R. Nininger, "Human Resource Priorities in the 1980s," *The Canadian Business Review*, Vol. 7, No. 4 (Winter, 1980), p. 11.

Figure 2–1 **The Environments for Managing Human Resources**

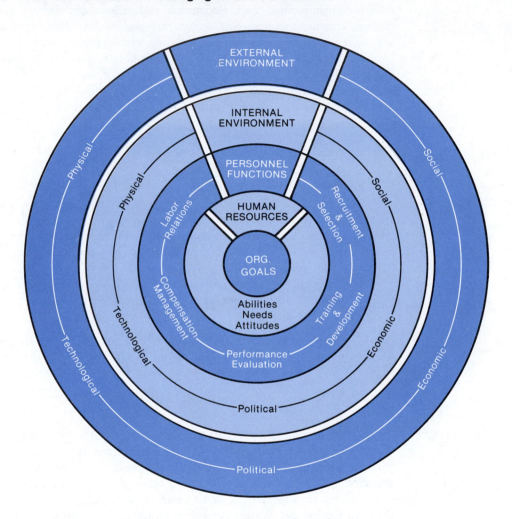

organizations to attract and retain employees. Housing, commuting, and living costs can vary from one location to another and can have a significant impact upon the compensation employees are to be paid. Recent population shifts to the Sun Belt and to small towns and rural areas can be attributed, at least in part, to the desire of the migrants to work and live in what they perceive to be a more favorable physical environment. Ironically this movement has created the congestion, pollution, and other problems of population growth that have had an undesirable effect upon the environment in the areas to which people are moving.

Technological Element. Currently we live in an extremely competitive age. It is only through technological innovation that new products and services can be developed and existing ones improved to meet competition. Technology also provides a basis for attaining the productivity and quality needed to gain a competitive advantage. The introduction of computer-operated equipment and robots represents one of the most significant innovations of this century.

Technology and Employment Opportunity. In every country of the free world, political leaders are under pressures to provide jobs for their unemployed—not just jobs, but "decent jobs" that will provide the standard of living to which their citizens aspire. These jobs can be created only if employers are able to compete successfully in the domestic and foreign markets. Unfortunately many of the largest companies in the United States, including those in the steel, automobile, and rubber industries, have been losing out to foreign competition. The failure of our steel companies to adopt more technologically advanced steel-making processes has helped contribute to their competitive decline. The reluctance of the automobile and tire companies to meet consumer demand for smaller, fuel-efficient cars and steel-belted radial tires, respectively, contributed to their competitive decline and the loss of jobs for their workers.

A major fear of workers is that technological improvements will cause their jobs to be eliminated. To the contrary, however, such improvements also can serve to reduce costs and increase sales and, in the long run, create more jobs within the organization. Nevertheless, many union leaders complain that, in the long run, their members no longer will be needed.

Technology and Job Requirements. Technological advancements have tended to reduce the number of jobs that require little skill and increase the number of jobs that require considerable skill. We thus experience a paradox of having pages of newspaper advertisements for applicants with technical or scientific training while several million job seekers without such training register for work with employment agencies.

Social Element. Increasingly employers are being expected to demonstrate a greater sense of social responsibility toward society and toward employees. Employees, furthermore, are expecting the same freedom, rights, and benefits on the job that they enjoy as members of society. Employers who fail to recognize and adjust to this fact are encountering difficulties with their employees. In addition, employers are being subjected to adverse legislation and court decisions.

Many employees are concerned less with the acquisition of more wealth than with the pursuit of happiness. They are seeking life-styles that are less complicated but more meaningful. These new life-styles cannot help but have an impact upon the way employees must be motivated and supervised. Consequently, human resources management has become more complex than it was when employees were concerned primarily with economic survival.

Political Element. Governments at various levels are having a significant impact upon human resources management. Each of the functions performed in the management of human resources—from employee recruitment and selection to termination—is in some way affected by policies or regulations promulgated at the state and federal levels.

Federal regulations in particular are made more complex by different interpretations placed upon them. The federal agency charged with administering a particular law typically develops guidelines for its interpretation which are published in the *Federal Register*. Unfortunately this interpretation may differ from congressional intent in passing the law. Furthermore, subsequent court decisions provide still a different interpretation of a particular law. In order to keep abreast with the latest interpretations, most human resources managers find it advisable to utilize one of the principal labor services.[2] Figure 2–2 illustrates the penalties some employers are encountering in the equal employment opportunity/affirmative action area when they neglect to conform to this area of federal laws and the current interpretations of them.

Economic Element.   Closely interrelated with the political element is the economic element. Many of the nation's economic ills today are of political origin. It has been typical of our lawmakers to appropriate funds to support generous programs and benefits for their constituents without levying the necessary taxes to cover the entire cost of them. In the process, this deficit spending, coupled with the monetary and fiscal policies of the federal government, has created more and more inflation. By eroding purchasing power, inflation has constituted a form of taxation in disguise. Unfortunately the burden of it has fallen most heavily upon people in the lower- and the fixed-income groups.

The Impact of Inflation.   Inflation has had a significant impact upon personnel programs. It has made necessary periodic upward adjustments in employee

Figure 2–2   Penalties Being Encountered by Employers

1. A public utility company to pay $2.2 million in settlement with blacks and women.
2. A tire manufacturer agrees to pay $5.2 million in settlement of sex discrimination charges.
3. Judge approves $1.24 million against an airline company in settlement of pregnancy dispute.
4. Twenty-seven female janitors in a school district were awarded $197,000 for being paid less than male janitors.
5. Firm agrees to $225,000 in handicapped bias case.
6. Airline company assessed $52,000 in jury trial of sex harassment case.
7. Minnesota Supreme Court holds employer liable for employee harassment.
8. An electronics firm agrees to $15 million job bias settlement.

NOTE: The names of the employers have been omitted purposely.

SOURCE: *Fair Employment Digest.*

2. Prentice-Hall, the Commerce Clearing House, and The Bureau of National Affairs are the leading publishers of such services.

compensation and benefit payments. Unions, which are an important part of the economic environment, seek through collective bargaining to keep abreast of inflation. Their efforts may lead to severe strikes for which they and the public may have to pay a high price. Some employees who possess strong bargaining power have been able to keep up with inflation at the expense of others. Unfortunately economic disparities within our society have thereby been widened in the process. Efforts to control inflation usually create recessions, which increase unemployment and business failures. These conditions then precipitate political pressure for corrective action that leads to more inflation.

When inflation pushes employees up into higher income-tax brackets, they become victims of what is referred to as "bracket creep." Employers then are encouraged to devise compensation plans that will help shelter employees from tax increases. Otherwise there is less incentive for employees to increase their incomes by working more hours or gaining promotions.

The Impact of Economic Conditions.   Economic conditions affect the need of an enterprise to hire or lay off employees. They affect also the firm's ability to provide employees with more pay and/or fringe benefits or to increase the size of the personnel budget. Typically, during periods of recession, the personnel budget is one of the first victims of an economy drive.

While economic recessions can force the curtailment of operations in the private sector, the opposite may be true in the public sector. Unemployment generated by a recession usually necessitates the expansion of agencies that provide welfare services. Expanding federal programs to combat a recession also may increase the need for more employees in these agencies to supervise these programs.

The Internal Environment

The environment that exists within an organization is its **internal environment**. As stated earlier, the internal environment consists also of physical, technological, social, political, and economic elements. These elements affect and are affected by the policies, procedures, and employment conditions that are involved in managing human resources. Therefore, the program developed for managing human resources must take into account the internal environment, as well as the external environment.

Physical Element.   Thy physical element of the internal environment includes the lighting, temperature, and humidity at the workplace. A part of it also are the dust, noise, radiation, toxic gases, and other hazards affecting employee health and safety. A favorable physical work environment can contribute to, but does not necessarily assure, higher employee morale and productivity. For example, the benefits of a favorable physical environment can be offset by poor management or interpersonal conflicts among personnel.

Technological Element.   The technological element of the internal environment interrelates closely with the physical one. It consists of the layout of the workplace; the process by which the work is performed; and the tools, equipment, and

machinery used in performing work. These factors, in turn, determine both the way work is to be processed and the requirements of the jobs to be performed.

The way in which work is organized affects interpersonal relations and interaction among employees within a work area. It influences the formation of informal work groups and the degree of cooperation or conflict created among employees. Technological systems increasingly are being integrated with the social systems within an organization, creating what is referred to as a **sociotechnical system**. Under this system, job design is based upon human as well as technological considerations.

Social Element.   The social element of the internal environment reflects the personalities and behaviors of employees, individually and in groups. It reflects also the interests, skills, abilities, and attitudes that employees have acquired through heredity, training, and experience. The social element also includes their interpersonal relations as determined by their job duties and by their personal preferences and prejudices with respect to one another.

Within every organization there exists a social climate created by the personalities of its members, particularly of its leaders. Chief executive officers tend to appoint subordinates who will support and emulate their attitudes and behavior. These subordinates are encouraged to do likewise on down the line. Critics maintain that this process generates conformity which can stifle initiative and independent thinking on the part of subordinates.

Political Element.   Politics is the art of compromise. Group participation is political in nature because it requires some members of the group to moderate their positions. Those in an organization who possess political power or influence are more likely to achieve their objectives by gaining favors in return for their concessions. In some organizations politics plays an important role in helping individuals to get ahead or to gain cooperation in carrying out their duties. Politics may be involved also in the power struggles between various individuals or factions. As long as these conditions exist in organizations, it is essential that members be aware of them and of the nature of the power structure if they are to be able to survive, let alone advance their careers.

Economic Element.   The economic element of an organization's internal environment reflects the organization's financial condition. The more favorable this condition, the more financial resources it will have to support its personnel program, including the compensation and benefits for employees. In the public sector a favorable economic environment internally is enhanced by having adequate tax revenues; in the private sector, by being able to generate profits.

CHANGES THAT CHALLENGE MANAGERS OF HUMAN RESOURCES

Changes occurring within society are being monitored more closely by human resources managers. They want to be able to anticipate these changes and adjust their personnel programs accordingly. The changes which command most of their attention are concerned with demographics, job trends, cultural factors, declining American productivity, and a growing exposure to the managerial philosophy and style of the Japanese.

Demographic Changes

Among the most significant challenges to human resources managers are the demographic changes occurring within the United States. They are significant because they affect the work force of an employer in terms of the socioeconomic status, ethnic mix, sex, age, and education of its employees. Figure 2–3 lists some of the implications these changes may have for human resources management.

Age Distribution of the Population.
The "baby boom" which occurred after World War II created a substantial increase in this nation's population. Those born during this boom now constitute a bulge in the age distribution of the population. As members of this group began to reach employment age during the early 1960s, they created a similar bulge in the labor force. That is, the size of this age group is considerably greater than the sizes of other age groups in the labor force.

This imbalance in the age distribution of our labor force has significant implications for employers. It means that those who comprise the population bulge are experiencing greater competition for advancement from others of approximately the same age. This situation challenges the ingenuity of managers to develop career patterns for members of this group and to motivate their performance. Providing pension and social security benefits for members of this group when they reach retirement age early in the next century also will create a very serious problem for employers and society. This is because of the drop in the birth rate following the "baby boom," which means that the labor force available to support the retirees will be smaller. The solution of these and other problems created by the imbalance in the age distribution of our labor force will require long-range planning on the part of both company and government leaders.

Women in the Work Force.
During the 1980s, as Figure 2–4 indicates, the proportion of women in the labor force will increase while the labor force itself will grow at a slightly lower rate. Women in the labor force have increased from 38 percent in 1960 to 43 percent in 1970 and to 52 percent in 1980.[3] This increase is partly due to the fact that the percentage of women without children is becoming greater. For example, among women in the 30–40 age group, 13 percent were childless in 1979 as compared with 8 percent in 1970.[4] Thus, it would appear that the number of women choosing a career over raising a family is increasing. Furthermore, more women with children are being forced by economic conditions to go to work to provide supplemental or sole support for the family.

The increasing number of women in the labor force is a trend that employers

---

3. U.S. Department of Commerce, Bureau of the Census, *Population Profile of the United States: 1980* (June, 1981), p. 4.
    4. *Ibid.*

Figure 2–3 **Attitudinal Implications of Work-Force Changes**

WORK FORCE CHANGES	IMPLICATIONS FOR		
	JOB INVOLVEMENT	WORK VALUES	JOB SATISFACTION
Sex			
More women	Work more important to many women, less to some men	More emphasis on career opportunities, self-fulfillment More concern with arrangements permitting homemaking and careers	Satisfaction with promotion prospects Dissatisfaction with "lock-step" jobs
Age			
Fewer under 30	Work more important to some, less to others	More emphasis on security, earnings, benefits	Less tendency to be dissatisfied, provided that material rewards are good and a person has developed leisure interests
More over 65		Less emphasis on self-fulfillment more concern about leisure time and retirement	
Education			
Higher average level		More emphasis on self-fulfillment	Greater overall satisfaction
More post-high school		More emphasis on work that uses abilities	More dissatisfaction with underutilization and lack of challenge
Socioeconomic status			
More middle-class urbanized	Work more important Second careers become more important	More emphasis on challenging and socially significant ("meaningful") activities More interest in leisure, less emphasis on subsistence Greater diversity	More dissatisfaction with socially irrelevant work Greater diversity of satisfaction—dissatisfaction
Ethnic mix			
More blacks	Work more important for those trying to "make it"	More emphasis on material aspects, security, and promotions	More dissatisfaction with low-paying, dead-end jobs

SOURCE: From Katzell in *Work in America: The Decade Ahead* edited by Clark Kerr and Jerome Rosow. Copyright © 1979 by Van Nostrand Reinhold Company. Reprinted by permission of the publisher.

Figure 2–4   **The Number of Women Workers Will Continue to Grow Faster than the Total Labor Force**

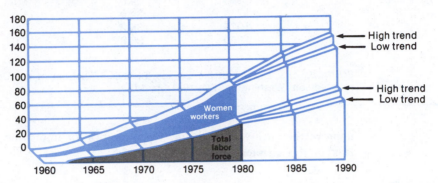

Percent increase from 1960

SOURCE: U.S. Department of Labor, Bureau of Labor Statistics, *Occupational Outlook Handbook*, 1982-83 Edition, Bulletin 2200, p. 15.

must recognize and accommodate. Employers will be under increasing pressure to provide equality for women with respect to employment, advancement opportunity, and compensation. They also will have to accommodate working mothers through part-time employment, flexible work schedules, and child-care assistance.

Rising Levels of Education.   One of the most significant demographic trends is the rising level of education among members of the work force. Table 2–1 reveals the increasing percentage of those in our population who are completing a high school and college education. Based upon the past growth rate of college graduates, it is projected that by 1985 about 20 percent of the population will possess a college degree. Unfortunately, except for graduates with degrees in engineering, science, technology, and other areas of high demand, a college degree no longer will be a passport to vertical social mobility. However, the *Occupational Outlook Handbook* does have a word of encouragement for those who seek or possess a college degree:

> Despite widespread publicity about the poor job market for college graduates, graduates still hold a relative advantage over other workers. They are more likely to hold the highest paying professional and managerial jobs. Persons interested in occupations that require college degrees should not be discouraged from pursuing careers that they believe match their interests and abilities, but they should be aware of job market conditions.[5]

To compensate their employees for the lack of job and advancement opportunities commensurate with their educational attainment, employers must try harder to

---

5. U.S. Department of Labor, Bureau of Labor Statistics, *Occupational Outlook Handbook*, 1980-81 edition, Bulletin 2075, p. 18.

Table 2–1 **Percentage of Population Completing High School and College**

YEAR	HIGH SCHOOL	COLLEGE
1960	24.6	7.7
1970	34.0	11.0
1975	36.2	13.9
1980	36.8	17.0

SOURCE: U.S. Bureau of the Census, *Statistical Abstract of the United States: 1981*, 102d edition (Washington, DC, 1981), p. 142.

improve the quality of work life. Opportunities for improving it will be discussed later in this chapter.

Job Trends

By the end of this decade, as Figure 2–5 indicates, the largest number of job openings will be for clerical workers and service workers, followed by those for operatives (except transport). The majority of these openings will be those created as a result of occupational transfers, deaths, and retirement. Since proportionately larger numbers of clerical and service jobs exist at the lower levels, special effort may be required to attract and retain employees in these jobs. Career ladders will be needed

Figure 2–5 **Replacement Needs Result from Occupational Transfers and Labor Force Separations**

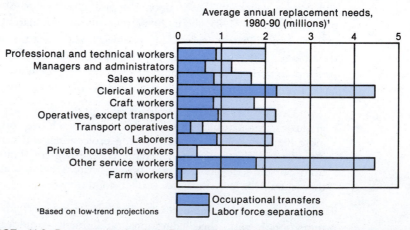

SOURCE: U.S. Department of Labor, Bureau of Labor Statistics, *Occupational Outlook Handbook*, 1982-83 Edition, Bulletin 2200, p. 19.

to enable the more capable ones to advance, and to provide greater psychological rewards for those unable to do so. On the other hand, for professional, technical, and managerial jobs employers will have to develop recruiting and selection programs that are appropriate for the type of applicants being sought. Effective human resources planning that involves career ladders and development programs will be essential to help employees gain these jobs through internal promotion.

Cultural Changes

The attitudes, beliefs, values, and customs of people in a society are an integral part of their culture. When brought to their jobs, their culture affects their behavior and the environment within the organization. Influenced are their reaction toward work assignments, leadership styles, and reward systems of their employer. Like the external and internal environments of which it is a part, culture is undergoing continual change. Personnel policies and procedures, therefore, must be adjusted to cope with this change.

The Psychology of Entitlement.

Since World War II, our society has enjoyed periods of unprecedented prosperity. American people have come to expect a continuing rise in their standard of living. Such expectations, in turn, increasingly are being perceived as entitlements, creating what some writers refer to as a **psychology of entitlement**. According to Louis Davis, there is a growing belief that the individual is not at fault if expectations are not met—rather it is the fault of the institution or society.[6] This belief represents a substantial shift from what traditionally was referred to as the **work ethic**. Under this ethic personal success was attributed to individual endeavors in meeting certain obligations. The work ethic held that "If I am not successful, something must be wrong with me!" With the decline of the work ethic, many individuals now believe that "Something is wrong but not necessarily wrong with me. It might have nothing to do with me but to the situation in which I find myself."[7] Thus, what were once considered privileges to be earned are now being regarded as entitlements, or rights. Included is the right to have an interesting, self-fulfilling, self-developing, individually centered job. Moreover, the cost of refusing to work or take an unacceptable job has been greatly reduced by our welfare system and unemployment insurance.[8] Research by Yankelovich, in an opinion poll, revealed that the proportion of those who believe that "hard work always pays off" declined from 58 percent in the mid-60s to 43 percent in the early 1970s. Among a poll of college students, the decline was even greater. However, a majority still believe that, if they are willing to work hard by the old rules, they can win the traditional rewards—but they question whether the old rules are worth the bother.[9]

6. Louis E. Davis, "Individuals and the Organization," *California Management Review*, Vol. XXII, No. 3 (Spring, 1980), p. 8.
7. *Ibid.*
8. *Ibid.*
9. Daniel Yankelovich, "New Rules in American Life: Searching for Self-fulfillment in a World Turned Upside Down," *Psychology Today*, Vol. 15, No. 4 (April, 1981), p. 76.

Changing Attitudes at Work. It is projected that certain cultural changes will be occurring in the future that will affect work and its role in society. Some of these projections are shown in Figure 2–6. Changing attitudes toward authority are becoming prevalent in today's labor force. Employees increasingly expect to exercise certain freedom from management control without jeopardizing their job security or chances for advancement. They are more demanding, more questioning, and less willing to accept the "I am the boss" approach.

Declining American Productivity

Of major concern to our society has been the slowdown in the growth rate of the nation's productivity. Among the various reasons cited for the slower growth rate is poorer employee performance. The changing attitudes toward work we have discussed undoubtedly have contributed to this drop in performance. As one supervisor lamented, "There's a work ethic that tells people they should go to work but it doesn't say they must do anything once they get there."[10] The adversary condition that exists in all too many management-union relationships also has reduced productivity. As one union officer admitted, "It's time our adversary system was changed. It's a system that is causing us to run second best."[11]

The large numbers of young and women workers entering the labor force probably have caused some decline in productivity. Efforts to achieve affirmative-action goals also have forced employers to devote more time to training, to the detriment of productivity. However, productivity has suffered also because of the

Figure 2–6   Projected Cultural Changes

The traditional economic significance of work will be supplemented by a rising concern with its psychological quality and social meaningfulness.

More workers at all levels will want a stronger voice in decisions affecting their jobs and to be less subject to hierarchical control.

A shrinking proportion of the work force will be content to have routine, unchallenging jobs.

More people will think in terms of long-range careers and even multiple careers, not just in terms of immediate jobs.

The importance of nonwork (family, community, retirement, leisure) will increasingly rival that of work.

The work force will exhibit a wider diversity of attitudes toward work, portending numerous departures from the foregoing.

SOURCE: From Katzell in *Work in America: The Decade Ahead* edited by Clark Kerr and Jerome Rosow. Copyright © 1979 by Van Nostrand Reinhold Company. Reprinted by permission of the publisher.

10. "Multiple Choice: Many Culprits Named in National Slowdown of Productivity Gains," *The Wall Street Journal*, October 21, 1980.

11. "Japan's Edge in Auto Costs," *Business Week* (September 14, 1981), p. 97.

failure of many managers to adjust to the cultural and attitudinal changes taking place within the work force. In managing human resources, leadership styles and motivational systems have not always kept abreast of these changes. Furthermore, many employers have neglected to improve their controls for monitoring employee performance and taking corrective action. On the other hand, management's ability to take disciplinary actions has been frustrated by the success of employees in having disciplinary actions reversed through grievance procedures and court litigation. Discouraged by these conditions, some managers have become more reluctant to initiate disciplinary actions even when justified.

The Japanese Management Style

Companies in Japan are becoming more successful in competing with those in the United States. In part at least, this success has been due to their ability to obtain high productivity and quality workmanship from their employees. Consequently, scholars and practitioners of management in the United States have begun studying Japanese companies to determine if any of their personnel practices might be utilized to improve the productivity of American workers.

The Japanese Philosophy on Worker Participation.
Cultural and sociological differences between the Japanese and the American workers may explain to some extent why workers in Japan are credited with being more productive and dedicated to their work. For example, the Japanese tradition of providing life-time employment and avoiding layoff, even at a financial sacrifice, has generated a sense of loyalty and commitment to employers among Japanese workers. Cole, in his research of Japanese management, concludes that Japanese workers tend to identify more with their employers and their employers' goals than American workers. However, he found them to be little different from American workers with respect to their dedication to the work ethic or to doing a decent job.[12]

Japanese culture and tradition, however, provide only a part of the reason why Japanese-managed companies are able to gain greater cooperation and productivity from their workers than American-managed companies. The Japanese philosophy on the management of employees is another contributing factor. This philosophy holds that the self-esteem and intelligence of the worker is deserving of respect. Some Japanese subsidiaries established in the United States have been able to apply this philosophy to the management of their American employees. The philosophy has been translated into action by encouraging their American workers to participate in decision making and to identify with company goals. Opportunities for participation are provided in different types of employee meetings.

The Quality Circle.
One form of worker participation that has received widespread publicity and now is being adopted by many American companies is the **quality circle (QC)**. Quality circles provide a forum through which employees meeting in small groups can offer suggestions for improving product quality. These

12. Robert Cole, *Work, Mobility and Participation: A Comparative Study of American and Japanese Industries* (Berkeley: University of California Press, 1979), pp. 251-253.

circles are an integral part of the Japanese concept of **total quality control (TQC)**. The TQC concept seeks to build quality into the product. It contrasts with the practice in Western countries of attempting to audit, through inspection, the quality that has (or has not) been built into the product.[13] The quality circle, however, is only a technique. Like other participative techniques, it requires a supportive climate within the organization.

Ironically enough, quality circles were imported from the United States by Japanese industries during the 1950s. Until recently these circles were not adopted widely in the United States because most employers did not embrace with enthusiasm the concept of employee participation. This lack of enthusiasm has caused employees and unions to perceive attempts to encourage participation as being divisive and manipulative. There has also been the fear that improved performance resulting from employee participation might lead to layoffs.[14]

An Example of Japanese Management in the United States.　The secret of human resources management in the more successful Japanese companies stems not so much from their use of quality circles, productivity circles, shop committees, or other participative techniques but from their genuine concern for the well-being of their employees. The Kyocera subsidiary in San Diego provides such an example. One of the practices this company brought from Japan is that of having a period of exercises followed by an inspirational message at the beginning of the workday. This practice, which evidently has gained the acceptance of its American employees, probably would never get off the ground in an American-managed company. However, according to one Kyocera employee (an American): "At the last company I used to work for, people meant nothing to them. As for the exercise period, at first I said, 'Hey! This is America, not Japan.' But the exercise period is a part of the Kyocera philosophy and now I kind of like it."[15]

The encouragement of employee participation in managerial decision making undoubtedly contributes to this company's unusually low turnover rate, but so does its emphasis on job security. Generally, even incompetency does not result in the loss of one's job; rather, it results in a "loss of face." During recessions, every effort is made to keep employees on the payroll, even if it means keeping them busy at maintenance work. As the manager of the Kyocera plant stated: "U.S. companies generate profits for shareholders first; but for Japanese firms, the employees come first. We would cut into retained earnings if the situation became critical."[16]

IMPROVING THE QUALITY OF WORK LIFE

Improving an organization's external environment is, to a large extent, beyond an employer's control. However, improving the organization's internal environment

---

13. Christopher S. Gray, "Total Quality Control in Japan—Less Inspection, Lower Cost," *Business Week* (December 14, 1981), p. 23.

14. "Will the Slide Kill Quality Circles?" *Business Week* (January 11, 1981), p. 108.

15. *The Sacramento Union*, September 8, 1981, p. A-8.

16. *Ibid.*

is definitely within the realm of an employer's influence. A major challenge confronting employers today is that of improving the **quality of work life (QWL)**. This challenge stems not only from the foreign competition, but also from the demographic and cultural changes that have just been discussed. Consequently, in many of our largest corporations, efforts are being directed toward making changes that will improve the well-being of employees. These efforts consist of making work more rewarding psychologically and of reducing anxieties and stresses of the work environment. They include job enrichment programs, the development of industrial democracy, and adjustments in traditional work schedules.

Job Enrichment

Job enrichment consists of any effort which makes work more meaningful or satisfying by adding variety or responsibility to an employee's job. Job enrichment may be accomplished horizontally or vertically. For example, lengthening the work cycle and adding tasks to a job is one way of accomplishing job enrichment horizontally.[17] Rotational assignments among jobs of the same level is another way to accomplish horizontal job enrichment.

Job enrichment may be accomplished vertically by increasing the autonomy and responsibility of employees. This allows them to assume a greater role in the decision-making process and become more involved in planning, directing, and controlling their own work. Vertical job enrichment can also be accomplished by organizing workers into teams and delegating to these teams greater authority for self-management.

Examples of Job Enrichment Programs.

Efforts to improve productivity and to reduce absenteeism and turnover among employees have generated different types of job enrichment programs here and abroad. Two programs that have gained recognition are those initiated by the Saab-Scania Company in Sweden and the Gaines Pet Food Company in the United States.

The Saab-Scania Experience. The Saab-Scania Company accomplishes assembly work on a group basis. In the engine assembly plant, for example, the unfinished engines are mounted on a wagon that runs along a mechanical track by the work areas. When a worker is ready to assemble a motor, the wagon is removed from the track and moved by hand around the assembly area. Each of the assemblers in the group push their motors around the same track. As one American woman discovered while working in the engine plant, each member must adapt to the group's pace. As she recalled from her experience,

> We begin work some distance from each other but the spacing doesn't last. If I work too slowly, the woman behind me will find herself on my back. If I work too fast, I will come up too close behind the woman in front of me. The ideal is for everyone to work at exactly the same pace, always evenly spaced out around the 'U'. But the ideal is

17. Research in German plants has revealed that worker dissatisfaction increases if the cycle time is less than 1-1/2 minutes—the minimum time dictated by many union contracts and legislation in that country.

impossible. Not only is one person always faster than another but each person has good days and bad days. Efficient work requires real teamwork. Members of the group have to do their best to assemble engines in tempo with each other. This may require helping someone who has run into a snarl, fitting two motors at once to keep from pushing up too close behind a slow beginner, or putting on a burst of speed if necessary to get out of someone's way.[18]

Although the employees working on engine assemblies have to meet a weekly quota established by management, they are granted considerable leeway in organizing their work. How well the group responds to this freedom depends upon how well the members of each group understand one another and get along.[19]

Reaction of Detroit Workers to the Saab-Scania Plan.
A group consisting of six American auto workers from Detroit, representing the United Auto Workers union, also worked a period of four weeks at the Saab-Scania plant. At the end of the period, they concluded that the physical conditions at the Swedish plant were superior to those in American plants. The male workers, however, objected to the pace and high degree of concentration demanded of group assemblers. Instead of performing work that allowed time for day-dreaming, as in the United States, assembly operations in Sweden required them to put every ounce of energy and thought into their jobs.[20] Some workers believed that the so-called enrichment efforts were too tightly organized and planned, leaving nothing to chance. Others noted that their negative reactions to their experiences at the Swedish plant were, to some extent, the result of the high expectations they had developed from literature they had read earlier.

The experiences of the Detroit workers tended to underscore the importance of planning and assessing changes in work design in the context of the total cultural environment.[21] Cultural differences between Sweden and the United States appeared to overshadow the differences in the way the workplaces are organized in the two countries. In Sweden, for example, American workers felt that their right to self-expression was inhibited. It appeared most important to them to be able to be their own persons, to object to what they did not like, and to press their needs without fear of the consequences. Less important was the matter of how their tasks were organized, what changes were being initiated to relieve boredom or create a better feeling at work, or whether or not they were represented on a council or committee.

The Gaines Pet Food Experience.
At the Gaines Pet Food plant the traditional assembly line was replaced by the team concept of production. The traditional hierarchy of job classifications also was eliminated, and personnel were given a more effective voice in the operation of the plant. The production teams are made responsible for their own quality control and for performing other functions such as industrial engineering, maintenance, and housekeeping. Each member of the

---

18. Kim Hayes, ''My Own Engine,'' *Sweden Now*, Vol. 10, No. 4 (April, 1976), pp. 24-27.
19. *Ibid.*
20. *A Work Experiment: Six Americans in a Swedish Plant* (New York, NY: The Ford Foundation, 1976), p. 42.
21. *Ibid.*, p. 40.

team is encouraged to learn and to perform as many jobs as possible and is rewarded accordingly. A unique feature of the program is the degree of responsibility delegated to each team. Not only is the team given the responsibility for dividing up its work and establishing policies and making the decisions relating to its performance, but also it is made responsible for interviewing and hiring new members of the team.[22]

As a result of this program, there was an increase initially of 40 percent in productivity and a reduction in quality rejects of 92 percent. Only 70 people were required to operate the plant in comparison with the 110 originally estimated by industrial engineers.[23] Although the short-term results of this program have been highly successful, these results may not continue to be achieved over the long run after the initial enthusiasm of the participants has had an opportunity to dissipate.

Limitations of Job Enrichment.   In spite of the benefits to be achieved through job enrichment, it must not be considered as a panacea for overcoming production problems and employee discontent. Job enrichment programs, for example, are more likely to achieve success in some jobs and work situations than in others. Job enrichment, as Sirota states:

> . . . is not *the* solution to the people problems of industry, but rather one of many that needs to be applied with thought and care. Even more important, there ought to be good evidence that the ailment under treatment is really one for which job enrichment is the appropriate medication.[24]

Thus, job enrichment is *not* the solution to such problems as dissatisfaction with pay, or with employee benefits, or with employment insecurity. Neither will it overcome such roadblocks to productivity as technical incompetence, poor tooling and materials, or inadequate clerical or administrative support.[25] Moreover, such factors as individual preferences, union resistance, and costs also constitute limitations of job enrichment programs.

Individual Preferences.   Not all employees object to the mechanical pacing of an assembly line. Some prefer it because it enables them to let their minds wander while performing their work. As the Detroit workers discovered at the Saab-Scania plant, being a member of a work team can entail considerable concentration as well as peer pressure. One member of the group commented, "If I've got to bust my (expletive) to be meaningful, forget it. I'd rather be monotonous."[26] Even some Swedish workers resist the idea of responsibility to a team and give up such assignments in order to return to a more routine type of work.

22. Richard W. Woodmand and John J. Sherwood, "A Comprehensive Look at Job Design," *Personnel Journal*, Vol. 56, No. 8 (August, 1977), p. 388.
23. *Ibid.*
24. David Sirota, "Is Job Enrichment Another Management Fad?" *The Conference Board Record*, Vol. X, No. 4 (April, 1973), p. 45.
25. *Ibid.*, p. 43.
26. "A Work Experiment," *op. cit.*, p. 31.

Union Resistance.   Job enrichment can conflict with the desires of some unions to maintain job control.[27] This control may be over the way work is to be performed, over production standards, or over the size of the work crews. The fact that many labor leaders are not enthusiastic about job enrichment should give management in unionized companies reason to proceed cautiously in the initiation of such programs.

The Cost Factor.   Finally, there is the cost factor to be considered. As Alber concludes from his research on job enrichment:

> Everyone talks about the benefits of job enrichment, but no one ever mentions the costs involved. If the issue of cost is referred to at all, it is in an offhand manner, yet the issue of cost is one of the paramount concerns a firm must face. A manager does not simply make a few adjustments in the way employees perform their work and then stand back while the organization is showered with benefits. The changes come hard. They are usually time-consuming—and they are often costly to make.[28]

Aside from the additional inventory, physical remodeling, training, and implementation costs of enrichment, there also may be the cost of added compensation.[29] Increases in responsibility and the difficulty level of jobs resulting from enrichment may subsequently cause employees to seek pay increases that are comparable with the increased demands placed upon them.

Industrial Democracy

Essential to the QWL is the development of **industrial democracy**. Basically industrial democracy requires bringing employees into the decision-making process and enabling them to participate in decisions relating to their work and employment conditions. It thereby creates a psychological partnership between management and employees.

Concepts and Applications.   The concept of industrial democracy is not a new one. The human relations movement helped to initiate efforts to make the work environment more democratic. This movement served to focus attention on methods for improving communication and for soliciting ideas and suggestions from employees. Unfortunately many early attempts to be democratic were largely cosmetic in nature. These attempts were long on methods and techniques and short on sincerity, largely because many managers were fearful of having their authority eroded. Even today the efforts of some companies to provide a more democratic environment are viewed with suspicion by their employees. In the words of one union leader, "For years and years the companies didn't have any concern for the

27. Bernard J. White, "Union Response to the Humanization of Work: An Explanatory Proposition," *Human Resource Management,* Vol. 14, No. 3 (Fall, 1975), pp. 2–9.

28. Antone F. Alber, "The Real Cost of Job Enrichment," *Business Horizons,* Vol. 21, No. 1 (February, 1979), p. 60.

29. *Ibid.*

human problems in their plants. All of a sudden when they are in trouble they ask for our help."[30]

Future Prospects.   In spite of management reluctance or employee suspicions concerning industrial democracy, it is the wave of the future. If only for reasons of survival, both sides must recognize that they have a mutual interest in working together to reduce costs and avoid becoming victims of foreign and domestic competition. Thus, there is a strong incentive to form joint union-management committees to probe ways of reducing costs and improving quality. General Motors, through its QWL program, is making substantial progress in providing avenues for employee input. Other companies in the automobile, steel, and other industries are following GM's example.

More enlightened business leaders recognize that basic changes in relations between employers and employees are essential. Many also are convinced that bringing workers into the decision-making process provides the most significant explanation for the success of Japanese companies which they seek to emulate. Industrial democracy, in the context of our culture and environment, is equally essential in the United States. Today's workers are better educated, more enlightened, and more demanding. Having become accustomed to privileges and freedoms in our democratic society, they are not about to park at their employer's doorstep what they perceive to be their constitutional rights.

Adjustments in Work Schedules

Some employers have departed from the traditional workday in their attempt to improve employee productivity and morale. The principal modifications of the traditional work schedules include the four-day workweek, flexible working hours, and job sharing.

The Four-Day Workweek.   Under the four-day workweek (or **compressed workweek**), the length of the workday is typically increased from eight to ten hours. In some instances, fewer than 40 hours per week are worked when some or all of the four workdays consist of less than ten hours a day. A reduction of the workweek also may be gained by having employees reduce the time for coffee breaks, lunch periods, and clean-up operations.

Reactions of Employers.   Some employers have found the four-day work-week to be an aid in recruiting applicants.[31] Those who have adopted this plan report improved morale and productivity, as well as reduced absenteeism. One employer even credits the four-day workweek as a factor in discouraging employees from voting for union representation. A majority of this company's employees believed that unionization would bring about an end to their four-day workweek.[32]

---

30. "Quality of Work Life: Catching On," *Business Week* (September 21, 1981), p. 76.
31. Ben A. Buisman, "4-day, 40-Hour Workweek: Its Effect upon Labor Management," *Personnel Journal*, Vol. 54, No. 11 (November, 1975), p. 566.
32. "4-Day Week," *The Wall Street Journal*, February 17, 1977, p. 19.

Not all compressed-workweek experiences, however, have proven to be satisfactory for employers. One reason cited is the employee fatigue which often begins about the seventh hour. When this occurs, in the words of one observer, "You have added two more inefficient hours to an eight-hour day." Other reasons for the failure of the four-day workweek include inadequate planning, poor management techniques, the inability to provide proper service to customers, and competition from organizations that operate on a five-day workweek.[33] Moreover, certain types of work cannot be adapted to a four-day operation. Add to this the fact that labor costs can be increased substantially when employers are required by union agreement or government legislation to pay overtime rates for hours worked in excess of eight hours a day.

Reactions of Employees. One of the principal advantages of the four-day workweek for employees is that it provides them with an extra day for personal matters or leisure activities. For married working couples, the extra day off a week provides an opportunity to do things together while their children are in school. Another advantage is the reduction of the time and expense of commuting to work by 20 percent each week. Particularly satisfied are employees who believe that "Once you are here, you may as well keep going an extra couple of hours and get a three-day weekend."[34]

On the other hand, some employees working a four-day week have complained that they are so fatigued by the end of the fourth day that it takes all of the fifth day to recuperate. A major source of complaint comes from working mothers for whom the long hours interfere with their child-rearing responsibilities.

Reactions of Unions. Some union leaders believe that the return to a ten-hour day represents a step backward in labor's long struggle to obtain an eight-hour day. Other leaders, however, view the four-day workweek of 40 hours as an opening wedge with which to gain eventually a four-day workweek of 32 hours—a long-time goal of labor.

Flexible Working Hours. Originating in Germany during the late 1960s, flexible working hours (or **flextime**) is now becoming popular in the United States. Under flextime, employees are given considerable latitude in scheduling their work and lunch periods, as Figure 2-7 indicates. However, there is a "core period" during the morning and afternoon when all employees are required to be on the job.

To insure that workers put in a 40-hour week, several electronic systems have been designed to keep track of workers on flextime. Generally, however, fears of cheating have proven unfounded. At the Metropolitan Life Insurance Company headquarters in Manhattan, for example, an office force of 11,000 employees has been working flextime schedules with only a simple sign-in and sign-out sheet to monitor their presence. According to the company, cheating has been negligible.[35] Although

---

33. "Why the 4-Day Week Hasn't Caught On," *U.S. News & World Report* (October 6, 1980), p. 82.

34. Buisman, *op. cit.,* p. 567.

35. Lee Smith, "Flexi-time: A New Work Style Catches On," *Dun's Review,* Vol. 109, No. 3 (March, 1977), p. 63.

Figure 2–7   The Flextime Schedule

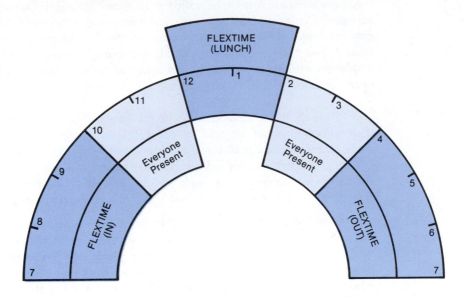

there will always be those who will take advantage of a system, most employees tend to respond favorably to the trust that management places in them under an honor-type system.

Advantages of Flextime.   By allowing employees greater flexibility in work scheduling, some of the traditional causes of tardiness and absenteeism can be reduced. Employees can adjust their work to accommodate their particular life-styles and, in doing so, gain greater job satisfaction.[36] Employees also can schedule their working hours when they are most productive. In addition, variations in arrival and departure times can help reduce traffic congestion at the peak hours. In some cases less time is required to commute, and the pressure and tension of meeting a fixed schedule is reduced.[37] Finally, employees can enjoy any extra hours they may have worked during the week by leaving early on Friday afternoon.

From the employers' standpoint, flextime can be most helpful as an aid in recruitment and retention of personnel. It has proven invaluable to hospitals, for example, in their efforts to cope with the shortage of nurses.[38]

36. Jason S. Johnson and Robert A. Zawacki, "Flexible Working Hours: Pros and Cons," *Colorado Business Review,* Vol. 49, No. 3 (March, 1976), p. 3.

37. Douglas L. Fleuter, *The WorkWeek Revolution* (Reading, MA: Addison-Wesley Publishing Co., 1975), p. 78.

38. Suzanne LaViolette, "Shortage Spurs Flurry of Flextime Experiments," *Modern Healthcare,* Vol. 11, No. 3 (March, 1981), p. 42.

Disadvantages of Flextime. There are, of course, several disadvantages of flextime. First, it is unsuited for some jobs. It is not feasible, for example, where specific work stations must be staffed at all times. Second, it can create problems for supervisors in communicating with and instructing employees. Flextime schedules may also force these supervisors to extend their workweek if they are to exercise control over their subordinates. Third, if the longer work period results in some employees working alone, safety problems can arise. Finally, keeping the premises open for a longer period will increase energy consumption.[39]

Job Sharing. The arrangement whereby two part-time employees perform a job that otherwise would be held by one full-time employee is called **job sharing**. Government agencies at all levels are demonstrating interest in job sharing. Both the League of California Cities and the National League of Cities have passed resolutions endorsing job sharing as a work option. Several states have passed legislation providing for job sharing plans, and more can be expected to follow.

Benefits of Job Sharing. Job sharing is suited to the needs of families where one or both spouses desire to work only on a part-time basis. It is suited also to the needs of older workers who want to phase into retirement by reducing the length of their workday. For the employer, the work of part-time employees can be scheduled to conform to peaks in the daily work load. Job sharing can also contribute to affirmative action by making it possible to employ women with families who could not work on a full-time basis.[40] A final benefit is that employees engaged in job sharing have time off during the week to accommodate personal needs; thus, they are likely to incur less absenteeism.

Problems with Job Sharing. Employers may not want to employ two people to do the work of one because the time required to orient and train a second employee constitutes an added burden. They also may want to avoid prorating the employee benefits between two part-time employees. This problem may be reduced, however, by permitting the employees to contribute the difference between the health insurance (or life insurance) premiums for a full-time employee and the pro rata amount that the employer would otherwise contribute for a part-time employee.

Opposition to Job Sharing. In spite of the favorable publicity and promotional efforts that job sharing has received, there is opposition to it. Some opponents who support women's rights argue that the part-time jobs generally pay low wages and offer little chance for advancement. Few men, they contend, take these jobs. They maintain that, to progress in the labor market, women should be encouraged to take full-time jobs.[41] Some unions complain that job sharing is an employer's device to keep labor costs down.[42]

---

39. Johnson and Zawacki, *loc. cit.*
40. Barney Olmstead, "Job Sharing—A New Way to Work," *Personnel Journal,* Vol. 56, No. 2 (February, 1977), pp. 78–81.
41. Ralph E. Smith, "The Effects of Hours Rigidity on the Labor Market Status of Women," *Urban and Social Change Review,* Vol. 11, Nos. 1 & 2, (1978), pp. 43–47.
42. Les Rich, "Job Sharing Another Way to Work," *Worklife,* Vol. 3, No. 5 (May, 1978), p. 5.

RÉSUMÉ

The internal and external environments of an organization can have a significant impact upon the productivity of its human resources and upon the management of them. For this reason human resources managers must be aware of the impact that these environments—and the changes occurring within them—may have upon their personnel programs. The failure of the management in many organizations to anticipate and to cope effectively with these changes has been one of the principal causes for the declining rate of productivity within the United States.

To improve the internal environment of organizations and thereby increase American productivity, greater efforts are being made by many organizations to enhance the quality of work life. These efforts include the establishment of job enrichment programs, a more democratic management style, and adjustments in the traditional work schedule. Job enrichment programs provide opportunities for employees to exercise more autonomy in performing their jobs, thus giving them greater job satisfaction. A more democratic management style enables employees to participate in managerial decision making, thereby creating a psychological partnership between management and employees. Changes in work schedules—which include the four-day workweek, flextime, and job sharing—permit employees to adjust their work periods to accommodate their particular life-styles. All these efforts reflect the increasing ability of employers to recognize and to cope effectively with the demands created by changes that affect the management of their human resources.

TERMS TO IDENTIFY

environment
external environment
environmental scanning
issue management
internal environment
sociotechnical system
psychology of entitlement
work ethic

quality circle (QC)
total quality control (TQC)
quality of work life (QWL)
job enrichment
industrial democracy
compressed workweek
flextime
job sharing

DISCUSSION QUESTIONS

1. What elements of the internal environment may affect the degree of industrial democracy achieved within an organization?
2. What are some of the problems employers may encounter with respect to the federal regulation of human resources management?
3. What impact will the growing proportion of women and the rising level of education within the work force have for employers?
4. How do you explain the successful use by Japanese companies of the quality circle? Will the adoption of QC by American companies prove successful?
5. What complaints did some of the Detroit workers make with respect to the Saab-Scania Company's job enrichment programs?

6. What have been some of the reactions of employees and unions to the four-day workweek?

7. On the basis of your work experience, what form of job enrichment would you prefer to receive within the limits that the employer can afford and/or is able to provide?

8. What is your opinion concerning the governmental regulation of human resources management? Do you consider the amount of regulation to be excessive, about right, insufficient? What would your viewpoint be if you were an employer? A union leader?

PROBLEM 2–1

WORK SATISFACTION IN AN ASSEMBLY PLANT

During a case-gathering interview, an industrial psychologist, Dr. Steele, was asked to indicate what he considered to be the basic causes for worker dissatisfaction in his company's assembly plants. Following are some of his observations on the subject:

In my opinion, the question of how to provide work satisfaction defies any simplistic answer. We have had more work stoppages and poor quality workmanship in some of our most modern plants than in some of our more antiquated ones. In some plants where we have the most problems the work force is relatively young, but in other plants where we have had fewer problems the workers are equally young. I believe that individual differences have a great deal to do with the satisfaction a particular worker derives from a job.

For example, in one of our small plants where truck cab and chassis units are assembled we experimented with four different assembly methods to determine which would be preferable from the standpoint of worker satisfaction and production efficiency. First, we used the traditional assembly line method. Next, we tried making subassemblies and putting these assemblies together. Then we tried having the workers follow the vehicle down the line, performing the various assembly operations in sequence. Finally, we organized work teams to build the entire vehicle in a work area. What we discovered from this experience was that each of the methods was preferred by some of the workers.

Individual differences appeared to be a major factor in determining a particular worker's preferences. Unfortunately, because of our tremendous volume of production, we are forced to use the assembly line method. We couldn't begin to meet the demand for our cars and trucks, for example, with the production methods used by Volvo. Consequently, I believe that by improving relations between people in our organization and by reducing adversary relationships between employees and management we can perhaps make the greatest contribution to improving worker satisfaction. In our organization, therefore, we are seeking to learn more about how people work together and how we can help them to work together better.

a. Should management be concerned about job satisfaction for its employees? Why or why not?

b. What is there in each of the four assembly methods that possibly made these methods preferable to some of the workers?

c. To what extent, if any, do the views of Dr. Steele correspond with the results of the Hawthorne Studies discussed in Chapter 1?

SUGGESTED READINGS

Brown, James K. *Guidelines for Managing Corporate Issues, Programs.* New York: The Conference Board, Inc., 1981.

_____. *This Business of Issues: Coping with the Company's Environments.* New York: The Conference Board, Inc., 1979.

Cherrington, David J. *The Work Ethic and Values That Work.* New York: American Management Associations, 1980.

Engleberger, Joseph F. *Robots in Practice: Management and Applications of Industrial Robots.* New York: American Management Associations, 1980.

Greenberg, Paul D., and Edward M. Glaser. *Some Issues In Joint Union Management Quality of Worklife Improvement Efforts.* Kalamazoo, MI: W.E. Upjohn Institute for Industrial Research, 1980.

Hogan, John D., and Anna M. Craig (eds.). *Dimensions of Productivity Research,* 2 Vols. Houston, TX: American Productivity Center, 1981.

Kendrick, John W. *Understanding Productivity: An Introduction to the Dynamics of Productivity Change.* Baltimore, MD: Johns Hopkins University Press, 1978.

Meier, Gretl S. *Job Sharing: A New Pattern for Quality of Work and Life.* Kalamazoo, MI: W.E. Upjohn Institute for Industrial Research, 1979.

Parnes, Steven. *Productivity and the Quality of Working Life: Highlights of the Literature.* Scarsdale, NY: Work in America Institute, Inc.

Simcha, Ronen. *Flexible Working Hours.* New York: McGraw-Hill Book Co., 1981.

Chapter Objectives:

- To understand how the organization operates as a system and how computers are contributing to this operation.
- To explain the role of authority and responsibility within an organization and the distinction between line authority and staff authority.
- To describe the characteristics of the two principal types of formal organization structure and the uses of a committee and a matrix structure.
- To recognize the impact of power structures and bureaucracy in the management of human resources.
- To describe the various roles of the human resources department and its relationship with other departments.
- To identify the principal elements of a personnel program and their importance in managing human resources.

3

Organizational Considerations in Managing Human Resources

In order to cope with the environmental changes and challenges discussed in the previous chapter, an enterprise must develop an effective organizational structure for managing its human resources. The organizational structure should reflect the particular needs of the enterprise as determined by the objectives it is seeking to achieve. This structure should provide the basis for grouping the activities to be performed into jobs and for determining the interpersonal relations that are to exist formally among the personnel performing these jobs. Human resources, therefore, can be managed effectively only if these resources are properly organized.

Organizational concepts, characteristics, and forms developed for managing human resources will be the subject of this chapter. Particular attention will be given to the role of the human resources department within an organization. We will emphasize also the relationship between this department and the other departments within an enterprise in performing the personnel functions and providing leadership for the personnel program.

THE ORGANIZATION AS A SYSTEM

A **system** is a network of interrelated components interacting within a particular environment. Every enterprise—public or private, profit or nonprofit—functions as a system. The interrelated and interacting components of an enterprise are the units (or departments) into which it has been organized, including the employees and the job activities within these units. The system through which the enterprise functions is commonly referred to as a **management system**.

The management system provides the framework for coordinating and directing employee performance toward the organization's objectives. Other components of the management system are the processes, methods, techniques, and tools used in managing the human resources of the organization. Linking these components together and functioning as the nervous system of the organization is the **management information system**.

Organizational Objectives

The formulation of organizational objectives, or goals, is the starting point for effective management. Objectives are the focus for managerial action. They provide a foundation for plans and strategies governing the management of each functional area, including the management of human resources.[1]

It is common practice for corporations in the private sector to state their objectives in terms of major groups with which they are involved. Typically these groups include stockholders, customers, and employees. For example, the objectives of the Varian Associates concerning these groups are:

---

1. Y. K. Shetty, "New Look at Corporate Goals," *California Management Review*, Vol. XXII, No. 2 (Winter, 1979), p. 71.

1. Our primary objective is to produce for our shareholders the maximum return on their investment in the company.
2. It is our objective to supply good, reliable products of high value to our customers.
3. It is our objective to provide our employees with a good environment, opportunity for personal growth, and satisfaction and respect for their views.[2]

If it is to succeed, every private enterprise must recognize its public obligation. One of the nation's outstanding business leaders once expressed this obligation as follows:

> The primary goal of any industry to be successful continuously must be to make a better and better product to be sold to more and more people at a lower and lower price. Profit, therefore, will and must be a by-product of services only.[3]

While profit is often described as being the primary objective of a business enterprise, it more accurately can be described as a motive for investing time, money, and other resources in the development of a private enterprise. Profits, therefore, constitute the rewards received in return for effectively serving the needs of the public. Whenever an enterprise fails to serve the public satisfactorily, it may be forced out of business by competition or by government regulations.

Management Processes

In order to manage human resources and other functional areas within an organization, certain management processes must be performed. These processes, which are interrelated and interacting, typically include planning, organizing, staffing, directing, and controlling. Every person in a management position engages in these processes. Briefly, these processes may be described as follows:

1. **Planning** is the process of determining the organization's objectives and making the provisions required for their achievement. Essentially it is a decision-making process. As such, it involves choosing a course of action from available alternatives.
2. **Organizing** entails dividing and grouping the activities to be performed into manageable units. This includes determining the activities to be accomplished; the jobs under which these activities are to be performed; and the duties, responsibilities, and interrelationship of these jobs.
3. **Staffing** includes the procurement, placement, and development of human resources that will perform the jobs within the organization. The staffing process is closely interrelated with the planning process, which seeks to anticipate the need for human resources.
4. **Directing** consists of overseeing and supervising the performance of employees. This process provides the guidance for translating organizational plans into action within the established framework. The subfunctions of this process are training, motivating, counseling, and disciplining of employees.
5. **Controlling** involves reviewing and measuring performance to determine how

2. Statement of Objectives and Policies of the Varian Associates.

3. James F. Lincoln, *Incentive Management* (Cleveland, OH: The Lincoln Electric Company, 1951), p. 14.

closely plans are being achieved. In managing human resources, controls can serve as a basis for evaluating employee performance, for correcting employee deficiencies, and for motivating employees to improve their performance.

Management Information Systems

Effective management requires a management information system (MIS) to provide current and accurate data for purposes of control and decision making. Joel Ross defines a management information system as:

> . . . a network of component parts developed to provide a flow of information to decision makers. It is composed of procedures, equipment, information, methods to compile and evaluate information, the people who use the information, and information management.[4]

The Role of Computers in the MIS.
Management information systems have been enhanced by advancements in computer technology, one of which is the self-contained minicomputer. The minicomputer enables a human resources department to develop data-processing systems that can be designed expressly for use in human resources management. Because the minicomputer is able to operate independently of a central computer center, it offers a great variety of applications, including word processing, with short lead time and low costs. A minicomputer can produce materials ranging from government-required reports to personalized letters. Operators of a minicomputer need not converse with it in a special language. Therefore, employees in a human resources department who have little or no background in computers can learn to operate the computerized MIS with a minimum of training.[5]

Contributions of MIS to Human Resources Management.
Management information systems can contribute to the more effective performance of each of the personnel management functions. For example, they can produce data for use in analyzing and evaluating job requirements, and for determining present and future human resources needs. In employee recruitment and selection, computers can match the candidate's qualifications with available openings, track them through the stages of the selection process, and validate the selection devices being used. They can produce letters to notify applicants of the decisions involving them and automatically create records of applicants processed—hired or rejected—according to race, sex, age, or some other basis. MIS can aid in evaluating performance, preparing career ladders, tracking individual progress on the basis of race, sex, or other factors. By means of these systems, salary structures may be constructed or evaluated and labor costs analyzed. Also compiled may be records of compensation and fringe benefit payments for internal control purposes. These records can be useful in collective bargaining, preparing government reports, and communicating with employees on the subject.

---

4. Joel E. Ross, *Management by Information System* (Englewood Cliffs, NJ: Prentice-Hall, Inc., 1970), p. 106.

5. Alfred J. Walker, "Arriving Soon: The Paperless Personnel Office," *Personnel Journal*, Vol. 59, No. 7 (July, 1980), p. 559.

RESPONSIBILITY AND AUTHORITY WITHIN THE ORGANIZATION

A major function of the organization structure is to establish the responsibility and authority of each employee. The structure establishes also the channels through which this responsibility is assigned downward to personnel at each successively lower level within the structure. To perform their respective jobs, employees must be delegated authority commensurate with their responsibility. Conversely, they must be held responsible for exercising this authority properly.

The Essence of Responsibility

Responsibility is the obligation of a subordinate to a superior to engage in certain activities or forms of behavior. The responsibility for managing an organization rests ultimately with its governing board. This responsibility is assigned by the board to the chief executive officer, who divides and reassigns it to his or her immediate subordinates. This division and reassignment of responsibility is repeated downward until employees at the lowest level are reached.

We should recognize, however, that the assignment of responsibilities by a superior to a subordinate does not relieve the superior's responsibility for results achieved by the subordinate. For example, if an employee at the lowest level produces poor work, that employee's supervisor must account for these poor results to his or her superior—and so on upward within the organization. Ultimately it is the governing board which must bear the responsibility for the actions of personnel at any level within the organization.

The Essence of Authority

In an organization, **authority** is the right to use discretion and to take action in directing, coordinating, and controlling the activities of subordinates. It is the coordinating power that binds together the activities of an organization toward the pursuit of its goals.

Formal authority originates with the governing board of an organization, but ultimately it rests with society, which grants the organization the right to exist. Through the process of **delegation**, formal authority is passed downward within the organization and divided among subordinate personnel. Individuals can rightfully exercise only that authority which has been delegated to them.

We might add that it is a waste of human resources if the capacities of employees are not fully utilized. One way to achieve full utilization is to give employees more autonomy and allow them to assume a greater role in decision making. By so doing, management can draw more on the knowledge, skills, and abilities of these employees for the benefit of the organization.

Delegation of Authority. Successful delegation of authority requires identifying those duties that subordinates are to perform. These duties should be those that subordinates have the ability and interest to perform. In addition, delegation of authority involves more than the mere mechanics of relinquishing authority to subordinates. It requires a willingness to allow them maximum independence and, unless there are reasons to the contrary, to accept their decisions. Through such actions managers can demonstrate confidence in their subordinates and respect for their capabilities. Most employees are perceptive enough to recognize whether or not these expressions of confidence in them by superiors are sincere. Effective delegation, therefore, must evolve from the heart as well as the head.

A part of the delegation process is establishing controls to determine how well subordinates are coping with their authority and responsibilities. Training and coaching subordinates to assume authority and responsibility are also a part of the delegation process. It is important that subordinates be allowed the opportunity to learn through making mistakes. This includes helping them to acquire self-confidence and motivating them to develop and utilize their potential.

Types of Authority.   Two basic types of authority are exercised within organizations: line authority and staff authority. **Line authority** is the right to give directions to subordinate personnel. Included with it is the right to initiate disciplinary action when these subordinates fail to carry out directions or to comply with established rules and regulations.

Staff authority, on the other hand, is the right to provide assistance, counsel, and service. It does not include the right to direct others or to initiate disciplinary action. Staff authority only serves to coordinate the activities involving the performance of a particular function. Established policies and procedures governing the performance of the function provide the framework for such coordination. These policies and procedures can lend powerful support to staff authority when they reflect the desires of top management and/or the requirements of law.

The authority of members of staff departments, such as the human resources department, is derived basically from their knowledge and expertise. In exercising this authority and getting others to follow their recommendations, staff members must rely primarily upon their powers of persuasion and their reputation.

ORGANIZATION STRUCTURES

An essential element of any formal organization is the structure through which its activities may be directed toward desired goals. This structure helps to determine the activities of each of the jobs comprising the organization. These activities become the duties of the employees assigned to each job. In most enterprises the formal structure is depicted by means of organization charts and/or manuals. Power and bureaucratic forces that may develop within an organization, however, can cause the enterprise to operate somewhat differently than these charts and manuals would indicate.

Characteristics of an Organization Structure

According to traditional theory, a formal organization structure establishes the channels through which authority is formally delegated and performance controlled.

It is through these channels that formal relations between superiors and their subordinates are intended to occur within the organization. The term used commonly to describe these channels is the **chain of command**. The managerial levels within the organization, from the chief executive to the worker level through which this chain passes, is called the **organizational hierarchy**.

The Chain-of-Command Concept. In theory, managers are expected to communicate through their subordinates in the chain of command. Conversely, subordinates are expected to report upward through the chain without bypassing any link within it. In practice, however, there is a tendency for some of the links to be bypassed.

As the size of the organization and the complexity of its operations increase, rigid adherence to formal channels of communication can impede efficiency. For this reason, employees are being given more freedom and are expected to do whatever is necessary to help an enterprise achieve its goals.[6] If bypassing a link in the chain of command by giving information directly to others will serve to speed up communication and contribute to greater efficiency, employees in many organizations are allowed or even encouraged to do so. However, because some individuals in the chain sometimes resent being bypassed, it may be advisable to inform them of the reasons for bypassing them.

Departures from rigid adherence to the chain-of-command concept coincide with current efforts to develop a more democratic work environment. Short-circuiting this chain at times can contribute to better and more rapid decision making by drawing directly upon the expertise of employees at the scene of action. The increasing use of the committee and the matrix organization, which will be discussed later in this chapter, represents a departure from the rigid chain-of-command concept.

Impact of the Organizational Hierarchy. How effectively the chain of command operates is determined in part by the number of management levels, or hierarchy, within the organization. Each additional level down the line serves to remove top management farther from the employee level and thus lengthens the lines of communication. An excessive number of management levels probably is one of the underlying reasons for the sluggishness of many American companies in coping with foreign competition. For example, Ford Motor Company has 12 layers of management compared with only 7 for Toyota in Japan.[7] Fewer levels thus enable management in Japan to be closer to the employee and to realize cost benefits from this relationship.

Types of Formal Organization Structures

The two basic types of formal organization structures are the line structure and the line-and-staff structure. Committees and matrix organizations may be formed to augment these basic structures and facilitate the achievement of their objectives.

---

6. David S. Brown, "How Breakable Is the Chain of Command?" *Supervisory Management* (January, 1981), p. 4.
7. "Japan's Edge in Auto Costs," *Business Week* (September 14, 1981), p. 97.

Line Organization Structure.   Also called the *scalar structure,* the **line organization structure** is the oldest and simplest type. As Figure 3–1 shows, it permits a clear line of authority to be maintained from the highest to the lowest level· within the structure. In this type of organization structure, each member of the organization is held directly responsible to only one superior.

The line organization structure is best suited to the needs of the small organization. In a small business enterprise this structure generally is divided into three departments headed by a sales manager, a production manager, and a controller. These managers have complete authority and responsibility over all the activities and personnel within their departments. Therefore, they must have broad and diversified qualifications in order to be able to cope with a variety of problems without relying upon staff assistance.

Line-and-Staff Organization Structure.   As the activities of the line departments grow in number and complexity, their managers become less able to remain knowledgeable and up to date with respect to some specialized activities of their departments. Eventually staff specialists must be employed to assist the managers in performing these activities, thereby creating a **line-and-staff organization structure.**

The line-and-staff organization structure provides for the exercise of both line authority and staff authority. The line departments are those that are concerned directly with the accomplishment of the organization's objectives. The staff departments provide assistance to line managers in specialized areas over which they have authority. This staff assistance enables line supervisors and managers to concentrate on the primary activities of their departments.

Figure 3–2 illustrates how a line-and-staff organization structure can be developed through the addition of a personnel department to the chart shown in Figure 3–1. The broken lines in Figure 3–2 represent the channels through which the

Figure 3–1   Line Organization Structure

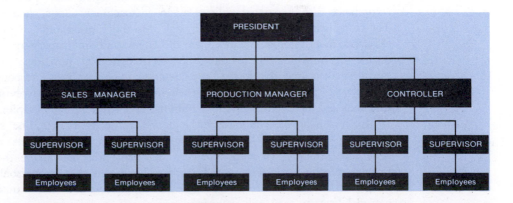

Figure 3–2 Line-and-Staff Structure

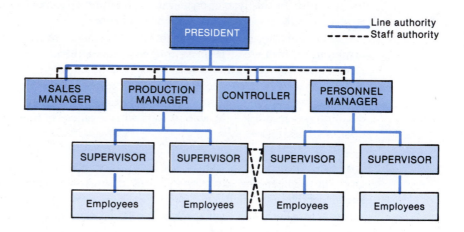

NOTE: For simplification, this line-and-staff structure is shown with only one staff department.

personnel manager and his or her subordinates exercise staff authority over line managers and their subordinates in other departments.

Unfortunately difficulties can arise from the nature of relationships between line positions and staff positions in a line-and-staff structure. These difficulties may arise from the failure of individuals to understand and conform to the role that their authority—whether line or staff—prescribes for them. Differences in their backgrounds can also contribute to these difficulties.

Misunderstanding the Role of Staff Positions. It is not uncommon for line managers and supervisors to perceive the efforts of staff specialists in gaining compliance with personnel policies as an encroachment upon their line authority. Therefore, with this fact in mind, staff personnel must offer their counsel and assistance in a diplomatic manner. On the other hand, line supervisors sometimes are unable or unwilling to assume fully their personnel functions. Personnel staff members then may be forced into assuming some of these responsibilities. For example, the personnel staff may be required to become more involved in such line functions as employee orientation, training, and handling of disciplinary problems. When this happens, the intended role and authority of the line supervisors in managing their subordinates are weakened. To help supervisors manage their subordinates more effectively, the personnel staff must encourage them to accept more training and coaching in these areas. This means that the personnel staff must gain the confidence and respect of these line supervisors and demonstrate to them the personal benefits they will gain from using staff assistance.

Background Differences. Typically line positions are held by managers with technical backgrounds who are primarily operations-oriented. Some of them have been able to rise through the ranks without a college education. With this background it is natural for some of them to be resentful toward staff specialists, particularly if they consider these specialists to be long on "book theory" and short on practical operating experience.

Since the line managers are in positions that contribute directly to the achievement of organizational objectives, their concerns are primarily with production deadlines, cost reduction, and quality control rather than with personnel policies and procedures. They may view personnel policies and procedures as "a lot of red tape" which deserves a lower priority of attention. Therefore, they may regard any paper work relating to job analysis, performance evaluation, or other personnel functions as an imposition on their operating responsibilities.

Staff specialists, on the other hand, may perceive the line supervisors as being closed-minded and unwilling to accept new ideas. In particular, they may lament the failure of many line supervisors to use staff assistance that ultimately would enable them to increase the productivity and reduce costs within their departments.

Committees. A **committee** is a group of employees within the organization who are formally assigned to meet for the purpose of discussing or solving some specific situation or activity. It may be of a permanent or a temporary nature. Current efforts of management to improve communications with employees and to involve them more in decision making are resulting in greater use of committees such as quality circles and shop committees.

Committees also may be used to appraise employee suggestions, to resolve grievances, to evaluate jobs and employee performance, to select candidates for promotion, and to administer recreation, safety, and benefit programs. The coordination of personnel policies, procedures, and practices can also be increased through the use of committees composed of those managers and supervisors who must administer the personnel program within their respective departments.

In order for a committee to make a maximum contribution, its purpose should be clearly set forth in the directive authorizing its formation. Most important, the members comprising the committee should possess the knowledge and information required for them to make a contribution to committee deliberation. An agenda also is desirable to enable committee members to prepare in advance for the meetings. Of critical importance is having a member who is able to organize, conduct, and chair the committee.

Potential Benefits of Committees. Committee membership provides employees with a means of contributing their knowledge and experience to the organization. It can have motivational value if they perceive it to be an expression of respect for their intelligence and abilities. By working as committee members, employees have the opportunity to express their viewpoints and to understand those of management and of fellow employees. In addition, they are made more familiar with the operating problems of the organization and gain experience in the problems and processes of making decisions.

Limitations of Committees. While committees can be very useful, they may not always represent the most productive approach to decision making. Therefore, the decision to use or not use a committee depends on whether a group decision is superior to one made by a capable individual. Committee consensus may require compromise and result in a weak decision. Furthermore, unless committee members have the necessary information and interest for deliberating on a problem, committee meetings may consume time that might better be utilized in performing regular job assignments.

One of the unfortunate trends in many organizations has been the formation of committees of questionable need which, once established, have continued to exist. Some organizations have attempted to reduce any unnecessary drain upon the time of committee members by providing certain controls over the formation and continuation of committees. The use of ad hoc committees can help to accomplish similar results. An **ad hoc committee** is established for a specific purpose which, when achieved, results in the dissolution of the committee.

The Matrix Organization.

As stated earlier, the **matrix organization** is a major departure from the traditional chain-of-command concept. This supplement to the basic organization structure preserves the traditional structure with its functional departments such as production and marketing. However, superimposed upon this traditional structure is an overlay of horizontal lines of authority to coordinate the work on a particular project or product through its various stages.[8] This matrix overlay creates a dual rather than a single chain of command. As a result, some individuals report to two bosses rather than to only one.[9]

Figure 3–3 is a schematic drawing of a matrix organization. Notice that Departments A, B, C, and D represent those that are responsible for functions traditionally performed within an organization. Projects I, II, III, and IV are those being undertaken through the functional departments A, B, C, and D. The managers of the functional departments and their subordinates are responsible for completing activities assigned to their departments in connection with each project. On the other hand, the project managers and their subordinates are responsible for insuring that each of the functional departments meets its schedule in completing its work on the projects. Due to this arrangement, a supervisor in Department A, for example, may be receiving directions from both the manager of Department A and the manager of Project I with respect to the completion of Project I.

Uses of the Matrix Organization. The matrix organization developed initially by aerospace companies has been adopted in modified forms by other industries. According to Davis and Lawrence, companies tend to utilize the matrix organization under the following conditions:

---

8. Kenneth Knight, ''Matrix Organization: A Review,'' *Journal of Management Studies,* Vol. 13, No. 2 (May, 1976), p. 113.

9. Stanley M. Davis and Paul R. Lawrence, ''Problems of Matrix Organizations,'' *Harvard Business Review,* Vol. 56, No. 3 (May-June, 1978), p. 134.

Figure 3–3   **A Matrix Structure**

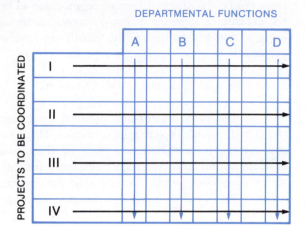

1. When it is absolutely essential that they be highly responsive to two sectors simultaneously, such as markets and technology.
2. When they face uncertainties that generate very high information-processing requirements.
3. When they must deal with strong constraints on financial and/or human resources.[10]

Davis and Lawrence conclude that the matrix organization can help to provide flexibility and balance decision making, but at the price of complexity.

Benefits and Pitfalls of the Matrix Organization.   Experience gained by the General Electric Company, the Equitable Life Insurance Company, and others using the matrix organization indicates that it can help to break down barriers created by the traditional vertical organizational hierarchy. The matrix serves to push decision making downward and within the organization, and puts a premium on teamwork. Users of the matrix organization hope to restore a measure of the small-company flexibility within large and complex organizations.

From the standpoint of human resources management, the matrix concept can help to foster decision making in a manner consistent with a cooperative problem-solving approach. In theory at least, the matrix form of organization has certain potential benefits. However, its success or failure, like any form of organization, depends upon the people involved and how effectively they are able and willing to work together. To insure success, particular care must be taken to clarify how authority is to be shared between those exercising vertical authority and those

---

10. *Ibid.*, p. 34.

exercising horizontal authority in the matrix. Precaution must be exercised to guard against power struggles which the matrix can encourage. Furthermore, the matrix must not be regarded as a form of organization to promote group decision making at the expense of achieving action. However, as managers acquire more experience in using a matrix organization, the pitfalls we have mentioned are more likely to be avoided.[11]

Forces That Affect the Operation of the Structure

Within every organization informal forces exist which do not appear in any charts and manuals depicting its operation. These forces can affect employee relations and organizational effectiveness. One of these forces is the power structure that develops within an organization based upon the influence certain employees are able to exercise over others. Another is the bureaucracy that evolves within an organization as various individuals utilize policies and procedures to protect their self-interests.

The Power Structure.   **Power** is the capacity to influence the behavior of others. The degree of power that managers possess is determined in part by the level they occupy in the formal organization structure, the number of subordinates they supervise, and the nature of the authority delegated to them. Power may be derived also from personal expertise and from informal leadership skills that enable managers to enlist the loyalty and support of others.

Tactics for Gaining Power.   Politics provides one of the means by which the power pie may be divided. **Organizational politics**, according to one definition, involves "intentional acts of influence to enhance or protect the self-interests of individuals or groups."[12] Virtually every organization has its share of politicians—from the shop floor up to mahogany row—who are eager for a slice of this pie. Among several tactics which are employed to gain political support in an organization are the following:

1. *Blaming or attacking others.* This tactic involves "scapegoating" and "trying to get off the hook." It may include disassociating one's self with an undesirable result or event, or blaming others for it.
2. *Using information.* Information can be used as a political tool by withholding it, distorting it, or overwhelming another with it. Information may be withheld when it is detrimental to one's own record or when it might benefit a rival's self-interest. (Staff members, for example, can derive considerable power from the information they possess.) Overwhelming another with information may be used to "bury" important details that might be harmful to one.
3. *Creating a favorable image.* Maintaining a particular style of dress or grooming consistent with the image a person wishes to convey is a well-known tactic.

11. *Ibid.,* pp. 132–141.

12. Robert W. Allen, Dan L. Madison, Lyman W. Porter, Patricia A. Renwick, and Bronston T. Mayes, "Organizational Politics: Tactics and Characteristics of Its Actors," *California Management Review,* Vol. XXII, No. 1 (Fall, 1979), p. 77.

Drawing attention to one's achievements and even distorting them, as well as taking credit for the ideas of others, also may be used in image-building efforts.

4. *Developing a base of support.* Political support may be achieved by getting others to understand one's ideas on a particular issue before a decision pertaining to this issue is made. Encouraging others to support these ideas and, if possible, gaining their commitment to do so can strengthen one's support base. Other forms of this tactic include developing allies, forming power coalitions, and associating with influential persons in official and social situations.

5. *"You scratch my back and I'll scratch yours" tactic.* This tactic involves the practice of providing services and favors to create obligations to return these favors.

6. *Ingratiating or fawning over the boss.* This tactic is also referred to as "apple polishing" and is sometimes described in more obscene terms.[13]

In one study conducted by Dale Tarnowieski, 82 percent of the respondents to a survey of nearly 3,000 U.S. businesspeople indicated that "pleasing the boss" is the critical factor in determining "promotability" in today's organization. An even larger proportion (88 percent) indicated that a dynamic personality and the ability to sell oneself and one's ideas are more the attributes to upward mobility than a reputation for honesty or an adherence to principles.[14]

Whether or not one may agree with the majority views expressed in the study, the fact remains that politics and power tactics are a part of life in all organizations—in government and elsewhere, as well as in business. Rather than ignore this fact, Auren Uris suggests that the power structure within an organization be analyzed by its members to find out what is going on inside. This analysis might seek to determine "Who are the 'big guns'? Who are the 'little guns'? Who's on top? And who will be on top tomorrow?"[15]

Implications of Power for the Human Resources Manager. Regardless of how political power in an organization is acquired, it is an important aid in managing human resources. It can provide a means of gaining the type of performance and behavior desired of employees in performing their jobs. The more power human resources managers are able to achieve within their organizations, the more successful they will be in getting other managers to cooperate in carrying out their own personnel responsibilities and in complying with established personnel policies and procedures[16]

The Bureaucratic Structure. For many people the term "bureaucracy" often is associated with rigidity, red tape, and inefficiency. As interpreted originally by Max Weber, however, **bureaucracy** was an administrative tool with which to facilitate the achievement of organizational goals. More recently, bureaucracy has been studied

---

13. *Ibid.,* pp. 70–80.
14. Peter Chew, "Backstabbing Inc.: Toadies Flourish, Talent Wilts Amid Office Politics," *The National Observer,* January 26, 1974.
15. *Ibid.*
16. John P. Kotter, "Power, Dependency and Effective Management," *Harvard Business Review,* Vol. 55, No. 4 (July-August, 1977), pp. 130-131.

as an instrument of power and influence that affects the formal and informal structures of an organization.

Characteristics of Bureaucracy. The growth of bureaucracy within an organization can have a definite impact upon the decision-making process as it relates to the management of human resources. Bureaucracy encourages personnel decisions to be made on a rational and consistent basis. In doing so, it seeks to avoid the influence of nepotism, personal judgment, prejudices, and the "cult of personality" or subjective influences that may affect an employee's welfare. According to Bennis, bureaucracy exhibits the following characteristics:

1. A division of labor based on functional specialization.
2. A well-defined hierarchy of authority.
3. A system of rules covering the rights and duties of employees.
4. A system of procedures for dealing with work situations.
5. Impersonality of interpersonal relations.
6. Promotion and selection based on technical competence.[17]

Criticisms of Bureaucracy. From a behavioral standpoint, one of the major criticisms of bureaucracy is that it treats employees impersonally on the basis of established policies, procedures, and rules. While it represents an improvement over the inconsistent and arbitrary treatment of earlier eras, bureaucracy is incompatible with the more humanistic approach of the present. The decline of bureaucracy therefore has been predicted on the basis of its inability to adapt to rapidly occurring changes within our environment.[18] Since bureaucracy is a very basic and mechanized instrument and well entrenched in most large organizations, any current forecasts of its impending demise may prove to be somewhat premature.

THE HUMAN RESOURCES DEPARTMENT IN AN ORGANIZATION

The human resources department is assuming a greater role in top-management planning and decision making within an organization. This trend reflects the contributions that human resources management can render to the success of the organization. As the president of one large corporation remarked, "We are a people business; the way our personnel function operates can make or break us."[19] A similar viewpoint has been expressed by the chief executive of one of the nation's airlines who stated:

The name of the game in business today is personnel. You can't hope to show a good financial or operating report unless your personnel relations are in order, and I

---

17. Warren G. Bennis, *Changing Organizations* (New York: McGraw-Hill Book Company, 1966), p. 5.
18. *Ibid.* See also Richard F. Shomper and Victor F. Phillips, Jr., *Management in Bureaucracy* (New York: AMACOM, 1973), pp. 6–10.
19. Robert F. Westcott, "Sliderule for the Personnel Manager," *Personnel Journal*, Vol. 54, No. 11 (November, 1975), p. 585.

don't care what kind of a company you are running. A chief executive is nothing without people.[20]

Legislated Role

Because of legislation and court litigation, the functions of the human resources department are becoming a matter of great concern to top management. In particular, this concern relates to personnel decisions that might involve possible discrimination in connection with hiring, promotion, compensation, retirement, or termination. Financial penalties involved for such discrimination can prove to be both embarrassing and financially damaging to an employer. For example, a few years ago the American Telephone and Telegraph Company settled two antidiscrimination suits at the cost of $25 million and $38 million, respectively.[21] Penalties such as these and the ones cited in Chapter 2 (see Figure 2–2 on page 26) have resulted in many preventive measures advocated by human resources departments to be taken by their top management.

Consulting Role

The primary role of the human resources department is to contribute in every way possible to the achievement of the organization's objectives. Although this department has an important responsibility in helping top management to avoid legal penalties, its primary role remains a positive one. This role includes helping the personnel program respond and contribute to the total needs of the organization.

A major contribution that the human resources staff can render is to serve as in-house human resources consultants to the managers and supervisors of other departments within the organization.[22] Alerting top management to contemporary issues and changes within society also is an important consulting responsibility. Closely related is the responsibility of monitoring new developments taking place in the personnel field and, when feasible, getting top management to adopt them.

Any consultation provided by the human resources staff must be based upon managerial and technical expertise. Furthermore, it should be concerned with the operating goals of the managers who are their consulting clients and should help these managers to make firm decisions.[23] These managers must be convinced that the human resources staff is there to assist them in increasing their productivity rather than to impose obstacles that interfere with its achievement. This requires not only being able to consider problems from the viewpoint of the line managers, but also communicating with them in language they can understand. While the use of "buzz words" and technical jargon may be appropriate when human resources specialists are

20. Herbert E. Meyer, "Personnel Directors Are the New Corporate Heroes," *Fortune,* Vol. XCIII, No. 2 (February, 1976), p. 88.

21. *Ibid.*

22. James W. Peters and Edward A. Mabry, "The Personnel Officer as Internal Consultant," *Personnel Administrator,* Vol. 26, No. 4 (April, 1981), p. 30.

23. Frank O. Hoffman, "Identity Crisis in the Personnel Function," *Personnel Journal,* Vol. 57, No. 3 (March, 1978), p. 162.

communicating with each other, such language may not be understood readily by the line managers.

Divisional Structure

As the size of the human resources department grows, divisions within it are established gradually to assist in the performance of personnel functions. The relative contribution of each function will help determine the need for new divisions, as well as the sequence in which they are established. In recent years, for example, changes in the legal environment have forced many companies to establish a division to oversee and coordinate EEO/AA efforts. The passage of the Employee Retirement Income Security Act (ERISA), together with employee pressure for expanded benefits, similarly has led companies to establish divisions to supervise these functions. Safety divisions likewise have been formed to insure compliance with the Occupational Safety and Health Act (OSHA). When a company becomes unionized, a separate division is likely to be established to oversee the labor relations function.

The importance which top management attaches to human resources management can serve to encourage or discourage departmental growth and specialization within the human resources department. Moreover, the ambition of the personnel staff in "empire building" also is a fact of life with respect to departmental growth and the direction it may take.

Figure 3–4 shows a chart containing those divisions into which a large human resources department may be organized. Depending upon factors we have already discussed, differences in the divisional structure of the human resources department will exist from one organization to another. In the final analysis, therefore, it is the specific needs of each organization and the conditions affecting its operation that will determine this structure.

Viewpoints on the Department's Role

As in the case of other departments within an organization, a variety of viewpoints exist concerning the functional role of the human resources department. According to Terrance S. Hitchcock, one extreme view is that "the use of the personnel department as a sort of dumping ground for maladjusted executives or for burned-out management personnel who need a little more time on the company's payroll so they will become eligible for a pension has lowered the standards of the personnel function."[24] The human resources department also has been criticized in some organizations for being assigned the "garbage functions." Such functions may include cafeteria services, vending machines, receptionists, office safety, guard force, fire brigade, typing pool, duplicating bureau, and credit unions. Frank Hoffman concludes that "the personnel function will continue to be the least valued of all staff services as long as it holds onto the idea that it must run any activity which, by any

---

24. Ernest L. Griffes, Terrance S. Hitchcock, and George E. Sherman, "The New Personnel Professional: Responsive to Change," *Personnel Journal*, Vol. 58, No. 1 (January, 1979), p. 18.

Figure 3–4   Organization of a Human Resources Department

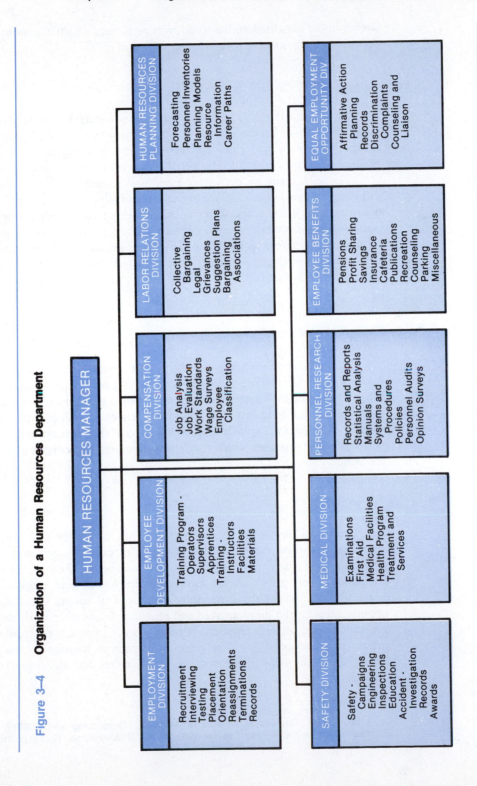

stretch of the imagination, has to do with employees which the more results-oriented departments are successful in foisting off upon it."[25]

Status of the Human Resources Manager

Although differences of opinion still exist concerning their status, the human resources manager increasingly is being accorded the rank of a vice-president who reports directly to the chief executive officer. In addition, more chief executive positions now are being filled by persons who once were human resources managers.

The movement of executives from line to staff positions also is occurring, including the assignment of line managers and supervisors to the human resources department for a few years. When these managers return to their line positions, they possess more knowledge and understanding about personnel programs. As they subsequently progress up the organizational ladder, they take with them the expertise they have gained in the personnel field, thereby helping top management to become more personnel-oriented.[26]

THE PERSONNEL PROGRAM

The personnel program constitutes the overall plan for managing human resources and for guiding managers and supervisors in decisions relating to their subordinates. It establishes the objectives, policies, procedures, and budget pertaining to the personnel functions that are to be performed. Within this program, more specific subprograms are developed to govern the performance of the various personnel functions over which the human resources department exercises functional control.

Personnel Objectives

Personnel objectives are determined by the objectives of the organization as a whole, as discussed earlier in this chapter. Increasingly, personnel objectives are reflecting more social responsibilities of organizations. These social responsibilities include not only those toward customers, employees, and stockholders but also responsibilities toward the community and the total society. Creating employment opportunities for the disadvantaged and providing a favorable work environment and greater financial security represent but a few ways in which companies can exercise greater social responsibility. The credo of Johnson & Johnson shown in Figure 3–5 covers a set of social objectives one organization has developed to govern its operations.

25. Hoffman, *loc. cit.*

26. Fred K. Foulkes and Henry M. Morgan, "Organizing and Staffing the Personnel Function," *Harvard Business Review*, Vol. 55, No. 3 (May-June, 1977), p. 152.

Figure 3–5 Social Objectives of Johnson & Johnson

Our Credo

We believe our first responsibility is to the doctors, nurses and patients,
to mothers and all others who use our products and services.
In meeting their needs everything we do must be of high quality.
We must constantly strive to reduce our costs
in order to maintain reasonable prices.
Customers' orders must be serviced promptly and accurately.
Our suppliers and distributors must have an opportunity
to make a fair profit.

We are responsible to our employees,
the men and women who work with us throughout the world.
Everyone must be considered as an individual.
We must respect their dignity and recognize their merit.
They must have a sense of security in their jobs.
Compensation must be fair and adequate,
and working conditions clean, orderly and safe.
Employees must feel free to make suggestions and complaints.
There must be equal opportunity for employment, development
and advancement for those qualified.
We must provide competent management,
and their actions must be just and ethical.

We are responsible to the communities in which we live and work
and to the world community as well.
We must be good citizens — support good works and charities
and bear our fair share of taxes.
We must encourage civic improvements and better health and education.
We must maintain in good order
the property we are privileged to use,
protecting the environment and natural resources.

Our final responsibility is to our stockholders.
Business must make a sound profit.
We must experiment with new ideas.
Research must be carried on, innovative programs developed
and mistakes paid for.
New equipment must be purchased, new facilities provided
and new products launched.
Reserves must be created to provide for adverse times.
When we operate according to these principles,
the stockholders should realize a fair return.

Johnson & Johnson

SOURCE: Johnson & Johnson. Reproduced by permission.

Personnel Policies

Closely related to personnel objectives are **personnel policies** which serve to guide the actions that are required to achieve these objectives. Policies thus provide the means for carrying out the management processes and as such are an aid to decision making. Like objectives, they may be idealistic or realistic; general or specific; flexible or inflexible; qualitative or quantitative; broad or narrow in scope. However, while objectives determine *what* is to be done, policies explain *how* it is to be done. They also differ from objectives in that they are effective when formulated and exist until they are revised or terminated. Objectives, on the other hand, are achievable at some period in the future rather than at the time when they are formulated.

Need for Personnel Policies.

Carefully developed personnel policies are vital because differences in the treatment of employees can become a source of dissatisfaction. When these policies are expressed in formal statements, they help not only to insure that employee treatment will be objective, but also to enable employees to know what to expect. Personnel policies enable personnel decisions to be made more rapidly. They also provide managers and supervisors with a more objective basis upon which to make and to defend their decisions.

Formulation of Personnel Policies.

The formulation of personnel policies for approval by top management should be a cooperative endeavor among managers, supervisors, and members of the personnel staff. Policy committees facilitate the pooling of experience and knowledge, including that from employees at the working level. Participation in policy formulation by operating managers is particularly essential because it is they who must live with the policies and whose cooperation is required for policy enforcement. On the other hand, the manager and staff of the human resources department have the responsibility for exercising leadership in formulating policies that are sound in terms of current research and organization needs. They also must make certain that these policies are compatible with current economic conditions, collective bargaining trends, and regulations at the federal, state, and local levels.

Written Personnel Policy Statements.

Personnel policies can be made more authoritative by putting them in writing. These statements, which may be compiled into a policy or operating manual, should provide the reasons for their existence in order to strengthen their effectiveness.[27] Written policy statements can serve as invaluable aids in orienting and training new personnel, administering disciplinary

---

27. See *How to Develop a Company Personnel Policy Manual* (Chicago: Dartnell), undated.

action, and resolving grievance issues with individuals and their unions. When distributed to employees, these policy statements can provide answers to many questions that might otherwise have to be referred to supervisors.

Administration of Personnel Policies. Policies should aid rather than hinder decision making. They must not be permitted to impair freedom of action or to discourage the use of initiative by managers in searching for better solutions. Furthermore, policies must never serve as an excuse for not taking action or for not approving a request. Instead they should serve as a guide for determining how to grant a request and how to satisfy employee desires. Personnel policies, like personnel objectives, must be dynamic in nature and change in accordance with the conditions affecting them. Periodic reviews of personnel policies, therefore, are essential in keeping them current and in eliminating those that have become obsolete.

Personnel Procedures

Personnel procedures serve to implement policies by prescribing the chronological sequence of steps to be followed in carrying out the policies. Procedures relating to employee selection, for example, might provide that individuals first be required to complete an application form, followed by an interview with a personnel office representative. Grievances, promotions, transfers, or wage adjustments likewise must be administered according to established procedures in order to prevent oversights from occurring. As an example, the failure to give written warning of a violation to the employee, as a step in the disciplinary procedure, might prevent the organization from discharging the employee for a second violation.

Personnel procedures, like personnel policies, must be treated as a means to an end, not an end in itself. As mentioned earlier, when organizations become more bureaucratic, complaints may be raised about excessive "red tape," inflexibility, and impersonality in making personnel decisions. Unfortunately, when procedures become too detailed or numerous, they can impair rather than contribute to the interests of the organization and its employees. In order to avoid this hazard, procedures must be reviewed periodically and modified to meet changes in conditions that may affect them.

The Personnel Budget

Statements relating to objectives, policies, procedures, or to a program as a whole can be meaningful only if they are supported financially through the budget. **A personnel budget** constitutes both a financial plan and a control for the expenditure of funds necessary to support the personnel program. As such, it provides one of the best indicators of management's real attitude toward the program.

Thus, while an organization's selection policy may be to hire only fully qualified applicants to fill vacancies, its ability to observe this policy will be contingent upon the expenditure of sufficient funds to permit applicants to be screened carefully. Similarly, a policy of paying a "fair wage" can be realized only if the organization is willing to establish a sound wage structure and provide funds that are necessary to support it. Securing adequate funds for the personnel budget, furthermore, requires that the personnel staff must be able to convince top management that the personnel program is cost effective and producing results. According to an ASPA-BNA survey, the cost of operating a human resources department at the beginning of this decade was approximately $410 per employee. This cost is increasing at a rate of about 8 to 9 percent per year.[28]

RÉSUMÉ

Every manager must to some extent engage in each of the basic processes of management. These processes are planning, organizing, staffing, directing, and controlling each of the jobs and the persons who perform them.

Effective management requires the development of a formal structure within which these processes of management may be performed. The most common type of organization structure is the line-and-staff. In this type of structure, the line departments are concerned with performing those activities contributing directly to the achievement of organizational objectives. The staff departments counsel, service, and give assistance in their area of expertise to managers and supervisors in the line departments. Exerting an influence upon the way in which an organization operates are the power structures and bureaucracy that develop informally within it. In managing human resources, therefore, this impact must not only be recognized but kept under control.

Government regulations covering EEO/AA have helped to increase the importance of the human resources department's role in most organizations. Consequently, the trend is for the functions of the personnel program to be coordinated more closely with those of other major programs within the organization. Nowhere is this coordination becoming more apparent than in connection with the planning process for the organization as a whole.

TERMS TO IDENTIFY

system
management system
management information system

planning
organizing
staffing

28. ASPA-BNA Survey No. 4, *Personnel Activities Budgets and Staffs: 1979–1980*, Bulletin to Management No. 1578 (Washington, DC: The Bureau of National Affairs, June 5, 1980).

directing
controlling
responsibility
authority
delegation
line authority
staff authority
chain of command
organizational hierarchy
line organization structure
line-and-staff organization structure

committee
ad hoc committee
matrix organization
power
organizational politics
bureaucracy
personnel objectives
personnel policies
personnel procedures
personnel budget

DISCUSSION QUESTIONS

1. Identify and define the basic processes of management.
2. In managing human resources, what are some of the benefits being derived from the use of minicomputers?
3. Distinguish between line authority and staff authority.
4. What is the chain of command? Is it being followed more or less rigidly today than formerly?
5. To what extent, if any, is bureaucracy beneficial and/or detrimental to effective human resources management?
6. What should be the role of the human resources department staff?
7. What is a personnel program and what are the elements comprising it?

8. Because of the presence of combustible materials, smoking is forbidden in the shipping department of a large company. Although notice of this rule is stated in the employee's handbook and is posted on signs throughout the department areas, it was not enforced until the company was required by fire insurance inspectors to do so. As a result of this development, notice was issued that any future violations would result in a three-day layoff without pay for the first offense and a discharge for a second offense.
   a. Comment on the reactions and problems this approach might create.
   b. What other approach, if any, might prove to be more desirable?

PROBLEM 3–1

PERSONNEL POLICY IN A DECENTRALIZED ORGANIZATION

One of the major reasons why General Motors has grown to its present size has been its ability to decentralize decision making within the corporation. The management of each of the operating divisions has been permitted to operate as autonomously as possible within a framework of corporate financial control.

However, divisional autonomy occasionally has caused personnel policy problems to arise. For instance, employees in the Chevrolet division still consider themselves basically to be General Motors employees and entitled to the same benefits as employees in other divisions such as Buick or Pontiac. This fact has created problems when certain policies governing personnel decisions have differed— even though only slightly—from one division to another.

To give an example, the granting of leaves of absence to employees holding an elective or an appointive office in government became a problem. In one Michigan county, membership on the county board of commissioners included employees from three different divisions of General Motors. One of these divisions had a policy of allowing employees to engage in public service activities if they did not draw pay for the periods they were absent. Another division permitted employees to be paid when absent for government service activities, provided they made up the time they were absent. Still another division allowed employees to receive pay for the period they were absent, without having to make up for the time spent on public service. In some instances they were also paid by the county for holding public office. It was natural for the employees serving on the county board of commissioners to compare notes on the differences between the policies of their respective divisions toward leaves of absence. Those receiving the least favorable treatment were obviously unhappy and made their feelings known to the company management.

Recognizing that the variations in division policy created a problem, the corporate personnel staff was given the task of working with a policy group. This group included representatives from the various divisions. Its job was to formulate a more uniform policy regarding leaves of absence for public service. In developing the policy, this group was asked to consider the effects a new policy might have upon: (1) the treatment of employees, (2) the corporation's image, and (3) the corporation's relations with government agencies. After several months of study which included consultations with the management of a number of assembly plants, a uniform policy was adopted by the corporation to serve as a guideline for all divisions.

a. What do you believe the corporate policy should be with respect to public service leaves?

b. What problems might arise if employees are paid by the corporation for spending time away from work to hold public office?

c. Should the corporation offer those employees serving in a public office any suggestions or other information concerning how they might vote on an issue in which the corporation might have some financial interest?

PROBLEM 3–2

CONSOLIDATION JITTERS

The Arbuckle Energy Corporation was the holding company for the Metropolitan and the Suburban Utility Companies which served adjoining areas in a western state. Although Metropolitan employed approximately 5,000 persons and Suburban only about 1,500, their organization structures were similar. As a result, certain functions being performed by each company were duplicated. Consequently, in an effort to reduce costs, the management of Arbuckle decided to consolidate the two companies into a single company. For nearly a year, planning for the consolidation proceeded secretly as members of top management with the assistance of outside consultants met to consider various organization structures, policies, and procedures governing the actual consolidation process. As it became necessary to broaden and implement the planning operation, task forces involving additional personnel were established.

As might be expected, news of the impending consolidation began to leak out and then spread rapidly through the grapevine. Suddenly the only conversation in the cafeterias or the lounges of the two companies was about the reorganization and how various individuals might be affected by it. Since the positions from executive vice-president to manager, and so on down the structure, existed in each company, everyone speculated as to which of the position holders in each of the companies would end up on top. Employees began to wonder whether their boss would stay or be replaced by one from the other company. Anxiety began to increase as managers in each company maneuvered to gain power, to impress the superior who might control their destinies, or to undercut the position of a rival. In the task force meetings, for example, hostilities between rivals often came to the surface and not infrequently were directed toward the subordinates of the rivals. During the planning period, employee morale and productivity suffered greatly.

Finally, the names of those who were to retain their existing positions and of those who were to be reassigned to other positions were announced. There was a reduction in rank and status for many of the management personnel. But in accordance with company policy communicated well in advance, none suffered either a loss of employment or a reduction in pay.

a. What is your reaction to the methods by which the consolidation was accomplished?

b. Would the fact that the companies were utilities rather than, say, aerospace companies, have had any effect upon the reaction of their management personnel to the consolidation?

c. Would it have been better to have made the consolidation gradually over a period of years, a division or function at a time?

SUGGESTED READINGS

Chruden, Herbert J., and Arthur W. Sherman, Jr. *Readings in Managing Human Resources*, 6th ed. Cincinnati: South-Western Publishing Co., 1984, Part 2.

Desatnick, Robert L. *The Expanding Role of the Human Resources Manager*. New York: American Management Associations, 1979.

Drucker, Peter F. *Management: Tasks, Responsibilities, and Practices*. New York: Harper and Row, 1974.

Gibson, James L., John Ivancevich, and James H. Donnelly, Jr. *Organization*, 4th ed. Plano, TX: Business Publications, Inc., 1984. Part 4.

Higginson, M. Vallant. *Management Policies 1: Their Development as Corporate Guides*. AMA Research Study 76. New York: American Management Associations, 1966.

Jacques, Eliot. *A General Theory of Bureaucracy*. New York: Halsted Press, 1976.

Mitchell, David. *Control Without Bureaucracy*. New York: McGraw-Hill Book Co., 1980.

Reeser, Clayton, and Marvin Loper. *Management: The Key to Organizational Effectiveness*. Glenview, IL: Scott, Foresman and Company, 1978.

Sisk, Henry L. and J. Clifton Williams. *Management and Organization*, 4th ed. Cincinnati: South-Western Publishing Co., 1981. Part 3.

Stewart, Rosemary. *The Reality of Organizations*. Garden City, NY: Doubleday & Company, Inc., 1972.

Tausky, Curt. *Work Organizations*. Itasca, IL: F. E. Peacock Publishers, Inc., 1970.

Wright, Robert Grandford. *The Nature of Organizations*. Encino and Belmont, CA: Dickenson Publishing Co., Inc., 1977.

Meeting Human Resources Requirements

part

2

- To understand the various considerations that must be taken in designing a job.
- To describe the system by which job analysis typically is accomplished.
- To recognize why job specifications must be based upon job-related requirements.
- To indicate why greater use is being made of functional job analysis.
- To understand the relationships of job requirements to the performance of personnel functions.

Job Requirements

In the previous chapter we discussed how the human resources of an enterprise may be organized to achieve its objectives. We pointed out that the organization structure of the enterprise formally groups the activities to be performed by its human resources into basic units. These basic units of the organization structure are referred to as jobs.

In this chapter we will discuss how jobs may be designed so as to best contribute to the objectives of the enterprise and at the same time satisfy the needs of the employees who are to perform them. The value of job analysis by defining clearly and precisely the requirements of each job will be stressed. We will emphasize that these job requirements provide the foundation for making objective and defendable decisions in managing human resources.

THE ROLE OF JOBS

A **job** is a unit of work consisting of those activities that have been grouped together formally so that they may be assigned to one or more individuals. When a job is assigned to one individual, the activities comprising that job become the duties and responsibilities of that person. If the volume of work in a job is greater than one individual can perform, then more than one position within that job must be created. The number of **positions** within each job must equal the number of employees required to perform it. On the other hand, if a job entails very little work, it may be combined with other jobs to comprise a position. Thus, each employee in an organization may be said to occupy a position and perform one or more jobs.

Jobs play a significant role from the standpoint of the organization, the employee, and society in general. As we will point out, the importance of the role of jobs within each of these segments is related to the design of jobs.

Role of Jobs in the Organization

Within the organization, each job established is designed to facilitate the achievement of the organization's objectives. If the design of a job does not facilitate the achievement of these objectives, that job either should be redesigned or eliminated. The delineation of jobs within the organization also facilitates the division of work. If the duties of each job are made clear and distinct from those of other jobs, it is less likely that any activity required to be performed within the organization will be neglected or duplicated.

Role of Jobs for Employees

Jobs provide employees with a primary source of income. Their jobs also determine their standard of living and establish the basis for possible upward social mobility, depending on the demands and titles of their jobs as well as their rates of pay. Because a job consumes a significant portion of an employee's life, the duties of the job and the conditions under which they are performed should satisfy the various personal needs that the employee seeks to fulfill.

As employees have gained greater protection from loss of employment through the enactment of several laws, they have come to regard a job more and more as a form of **property right.**[1] This is a right that cannot be expropriated without just cause or due process. Simply stated, it is the right of an employee to receive a fair hearing before being subjected to disciplinary action. It is also the right of an employee to appeal an employer's action to an arbitrator, an adjudication body, or a court of law. If the employer's action is not to be reversed through the appeal process, it must be supported by objective evidence. Such evidence invariably relates back to the job and the question of whether or not the job could be performed within human capabilities and limitations.

Role of Jobs in a Society

The creation of jobs contributes to the economic prosperity of a community, a region, or a nation as a whole. It is a rare community that does not seek to attract new enterprises which will provide jobs for its residents. The types of enterprises that a community particularly desires are those that will provide permanent employment in well-paying jobs, and whose presence will not damage the natural environment. In the private sector, existing jobs can be preserved and new ones created only if the enterprise is able to earn a profit over the long run. Its profitability, in turn, is determined by job performance which is contingent in part upon the design of jobs.

JOB DESIGN

The design of a job should reflect both technological and human considerations. It should facilitate the achievement of organizational objectives and the performance of the work the job was established to accomplish. At the same time, the design should recognize the capacities and needs of those who are to perform it. As Figure 4–1 reveals, contemporary job design embodies the contributions of industrial engineering and human engineering, as well as the emphasis currently being placed on improving the quality of work life. Quality-of-work-life considerations in designing or redesigning a job take the form of contemporary programs that were discussed in pages 36–44 of Chapter 2.

Industrial Engineering Considerations

The study of work is an important contribution of the scientific management movement. **Industrial engineering,** which evolved with this movement, is concerned with analyzing work methods and establishing time standards. Specifically, it involves analyzing the elements of the work cycles that comprise a particular job activity and determining the time required to complete each element.

---

1. Peter F. Drucker, ''The Job as a Property Right,'' *The Wall Street Journal,* March 4, 1980.

Figure 4–1   Basis for Job Design

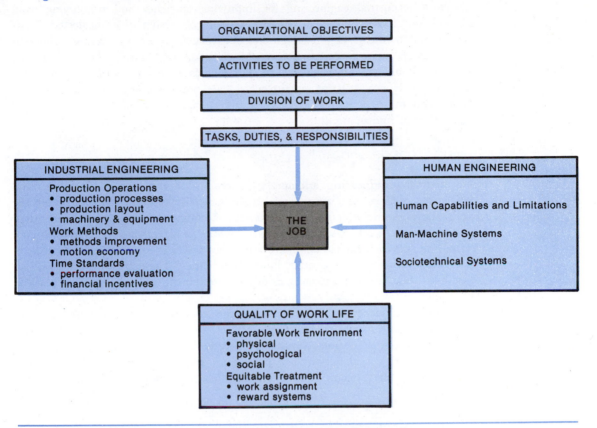

Development of Time Standards.   Identifying and timing the elements in a work cycle generally are the responsibilities of the industrial engineering staff. The work cycle is studied to determine which, if any, of its elements may be modified, combined, rearranged, or eliminated in order to reduce the time needed to complete the work cycle.

In establishing time standards, the time required to complete each element in the work cycle is measured by means of a stopwatch or work sampling techniques, and then recorded. When the times for each element are combined, the total time required for the work cycle is established. This time is subsequently adjusted to allow for the skill and effort demonstrated by the observed worker and for interruptions that may occur in performing the work. The adjusted time becomes the time standard for a particular work cycle. This time standard then provides an objective basis for evaluating and improving employee performance and for determining incentive pay.

Benefits and Limitations of Industrial Engineering.   Since jobs are created primarily for the purpose of enabling an enterprise to achieve its objectives, the efficiency goals of industrial engineering cannot be ignored. Industrial engineering does constitute a disciplined and objective approach to job design. Unfortunately the concern of industrial engineering for improving efficiency and simplifying work methods may cause the human considerations in job design to be neglected. What may be improvements in job design and efficiency from an engineering standpoint sometimes can prove to be psychologically unsound. For example, the assembly line with its simplified and repetitive tasks embodies sound principles of industrial engineering. However, these repetitive tasks are not rewarding psychologically for those who must perform them. Thus, job design must also provide for the satisfaction of human needs.

Human Engineering Considerations

Human engineering attempts to accommodate the human capabilities and deficiencies of those who are to perform the job. It is concerned with adapting the work, the work environment, and the machines, equipment, and processes to match human characteristics. Also referred to as *human factors engineering, ergonomics,* and *engineering psychology,* human engineering involves an effort to minimize the effects of carelessness, negligence, and other human fallibilities. These harmful effects otherwise may cause defective products, damage to equipment, or even injury or death to employees.

Human engineering recognizes that the equipment and processes used in performing a job operate as a system. This system is composed of interrelated and interacting parts that are intended to work together in achieving a common purpose. The people who operate, service, or monitor the equipment are an additional component of the system, thereby creating what is known as a **man-machine system.**[2]

People v. Machines.

In spite of technological advances, there will always be work that can be performed more economically or more effectively by people than by machines—even in this age of robotics. In some jobs it is possible to achieve greater flexibility by using people rather than machines. People can be reassigned or retrained to perform other work, whereas it may be too expensive or impossible to convert a machine to perform other jobs.

There are, however, those activities that machines can perform more effectively than people. Figure 4–2 lists the activities in which people and machines each excel. Therefore, in determining whether to use people or machines to perform certain jobs, the relative capabilities of each resource must be considered.

Human Engineering in Designing Machines and Jobs.

Machine design must facilitate the use of such human senses as vision, hearing, and touch. It must consider also the ability of operators to control these machines and to react to the information

---

2. To avoid the appearance of being sexist, we could use the term *person-machine system* instead of man-machine system. However, like the term *manpower,* the term *man-machine* is used to refer equally to women and men.

conveyed by means of these senses. Improvements in the visual or the auditory display of information through dials, instrument indicators, and the display of letters and numerals are examples of the contributions being rendered by human engineering. The design of equipment controls so that they are compatible with both the physical structure and reaction capacities of people who must operate them and

Figure 4–2   **Man** *v.* **Machine**

MAN EXCELS IN	MACHINES EXCEL IN
Detection of certain forms of very low energy levels	Monitoring (both men and machines)
Sensitivity to an extremely wide variety of stimuli	Performing routine, repetitive, or very precise operations
Perceiving patterns and making generalizations about them	Responding very quickly to control signals
Detecting signals in high noise levels	Exerting great force, smoothly and with precision
Ability to store large amounts of information for long periods—and recalling relevant facts at appropriate moments	Storing and recalling large amounts of information in short time periods
Ability to exercise judgment where events cannot be completely defined	Performing complex and rapid computation with high accuracy
Improvising and adopting flexible procedures	Sensitivity to stimuli beyond the range of human sensitivity (infrared, radio waves, etc.)
Ability to react to unexpected low-probability events	Doing many different things at one time
Applying originality in solving problems: i.e., alternate solutions	Deductive processes
Ability to profit from experience and alter course of action	Insensitivity to extraneous factors
Ability to perform fine manipulation, especially where misalignment appears unexpectedly	Ability to repeat operations very rapidly, continuously, and precisely the same way over a long period
Ability to continue to perform even when overloaded	Operating in environments which are hostile to man or beyond human tolerance
Ability to reason inductively	

SOURCE: Wesley E. Woodson and Donald W. Conover, *Human Engineering Guide for Equipment Designers* (2d ed.; Berkeley: University of California Press, 1964). Reproduced with permission of The Regents of the University of California.

the environment in which they work is another of its contributions.[3] Finally, human engineering also can aid in the design of jobs so as to take into account the limitations in the capacities of handicapped and elderly workers.

Job Design and the Problem of Overspecialization

Typically similar duties and tasks are combined into a job to facilitate the selection, training, and supervision of personnel who are to perform it. In doing so, organizations may create jobs that are monotonous to perform and do not provide employees with the breadth of experience necessary for them to qualify for advancement. The employees performing such jobs suffer from a condition that may be called **overspecialization.** This condition can impair flexibility in utilizing human resources. It also can lead to grievances over the duties employees are expected or not expected to perform in their job assignments.

Recognizing the problem created by overspecialization, some employers have initiated programs to consolidate the duties of several jobs under a single title. This process, referred to as **broadbanding,** is essentially one of job enlargement. For example, the city of New York broadbanded the jobs of Asphalt Worker, Laborer, Rammer, Flagger, Paver, and Cement Mason under the single title of Highway Repairer. Similarly, the 58 separate job titles in the clerical group were broadbanded into eight titles.[4]

This practice of job consolidation, however, can also create problems. Some employees either may be unable or unwilling to perform a broader range of duties. Furthermore, some employees and their unions perceive this practice as an attempt to increase the output of employees. Job consolidation also can affect the seniority of employees and their rights in connection with job assignments, layoffs, or other decisions affecting their employment. Thus, in a new job created by job consolidation, some employees may end up with less seniority than they possessed in their old jobs.[5]

JOB ANALYSIS

Job analysis is the process of compiling, maintaining, reviewing, and modifying information about jobs for the purpose of developing job descriptions and job specifications. A **job description** is a statement of the tasks, duties, and responsibilities of a job to be performed. A **job specification** states the knowledge, skills, and abilities required of the person who is to perform the job. The job specification may be prepared as a separate document or may be included as a part of the job description.

---

3. Alphonse Chapanis, "Engineering Psychology," *Handbook of Industrial and Organizational Psychology,* edited by Marvin D. Dunnette (Chicago: Rand-McNally College Publishing Co., 1976), pp. 701–706.

4. Peter Allan and Stephen Rosenberg, "Overcoming the Inefficiencies of an Overspecialized Title Structure," *Personnel Journal,* Vol. 58, No. 3 (March, 1979), pp. 166–167.

5. *Ibid.*

As contrasted to job design, which reflects subjective opinions about the *ideal* requirements of a job, job analysis is concerned with objective and verifiable information about the *actual* requirements of a job. The job descriptions and job specifications that are developed through job analysis should be as accurate as possible if they are to be of value to those who make personnel decisions. These decisions may involve any of the personnel functions—from recruitment to the termination of employees. The interrelationships between personnel functions and job requirements, as specified in job descriptions and job specifications, are discussed at the end of this chapter. Figure 4–3 illustrates the elements of the job analysis system.

The Job Analyst's Responsibilities

Conducting job analysis is usually the primary responsibility of the human resources department in an organization. If this department is large enough to have a division for compensation management, job analysis may be performed by members of this division. In any case, staff members of the human resources department who specialize in job analysis usually carry the title of **job analyst or personnel analyst**. Since the job carrying this title requires a high degree of analytical ability and writing skill, it sometimes serves as an entry-level job for graduates who choose a career in human resources management. The job description for a job analyst, shown in Figure 4–4, is taken from the *Dictionary of Occupational Titles* (DOT).

Although the job analysts are the ones primarily responsible for the job analysis program, they usually enlist the cooperation of the employees and supervisors in the departments where the jobs are being analyzed. It is these supervisors and employees who are the sources of much of the information about the jobs. If at all possible, these supervisors and employees may be asked to prepare the rough drafts of the needed job descriptions and job specifications.

Gathering Job Information. The job data from the sources of job information cited above may be obtained in several ways. One method is to conduct interviews

Figure 4–3 The Job Analysis System

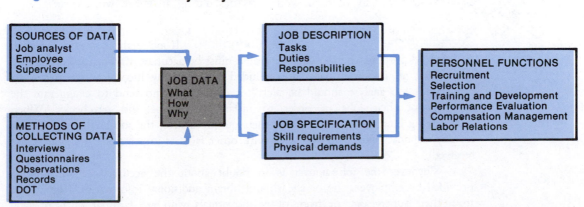

Figure 4—4   Job Description for a Job Analyst

166.267—018 JOB ANALYST (profess. & kin.) personnel analyst.
Collects, analyzes, and prepares occupational information to facilitate personnel, administration, and management functions of organization: Consults with management to determine type, scope, and purpose of study. Studies current organizational occupational data and compiles distribution reports, organization and flow charts, and other background information required for study. Observes jobs and interviews workers and supervisory personnel to determine job and worker requirements. Analyzes occupational data, such as physical, mental, and training requirements of jobs and workers and develops written summaries, such as job descriptions, job specifications, and lines of career movement. Utilizes developed occupational data to evaluate or improve methods and techniques for recruiting, selecting, promoting, evaluating, and training workers, and administration of related personnel programs. May specialize in classifying positions according to regulated guidelines to meet job classification requirements of civil service system and be known as POSITION CLASSIFIER (gov. ser.).

SOURCE: U.S. Department of Labor, Employment and Training Administration, *Dictionary of Occupational Titles*, 4th Edition (Washington, DC: U.S. Government Printing Office, 1977), pp. 99—100.

with the jobholders or supervisors, either on an individual basis or a group basis. Another method is to prepare carefully formulated questionnaires to be filled out by these sources. Observing the job being performed and recording the observations on standardized forms is still another method. Finally, the jobholders themselves may be asked to keep a diary of their work activities during an entire work cycle.

Controlling the Accuracy of Job Information.   If job analysis is to accomplish its intended purpose, the job data generated must be accurate. Care must be taken to insure that all important facts are included and that any incorrect statements are omitted. A job analyst should be alert for employees who tend to exaggerate the difficulty of their jobs in order to inflate their egos and paychecks. When interviewing employees or reviewing their questionnaires, the job analyst must look for any responses which do not agree with other facts or impressions the analyst has received.

Whenever the job analyst is in doubt about the accuracy of information provided by employees, he or she should obtain additional information from them, from their supervisors, or from other individuals who are familiar with or who perform the same job. It is common practice to have the descriptions for each job reviewed by the jobholder and his or her supervisor. The job description summaries contained in the DOT also can serve as a basis for the job analyst's review.

Writing Clearly and Specifically. When writing a job description, statements that are terse, direct, and simply worded are essential. Unnecessary words or phrases should be eliminated. Typically sentences that describe job duties begin with a verb in its present tense, with the implied subject of the sentence being the employee performing the job. The term "occasionally" is used to describe those duties that are performed "once in a while." The term "may" is used to describe those duties that are performed only by some workers on the job.

Even when set forth in writing, job descriptions and specifications can still be vague. Sometimes they may be made vague deliberately by those managers who still believe that subordinates should follow the job description to the letter. These managers usually conclude the list of duties in the job description with an "umbrella statement" such as "The employee shall perform *such other duties as may be assigned.*" To the consternation of many employers, however, today's legal environment has created what might be called an "Age of Specifics." Federal guidelines and court decisions now require that the specific performance requirements of a job be based on *valid* job-related criteria.[6] Personnel decisions that involve either job applicants or employees increasingly are being challenged successfully if these decisions are based on criteria that are vague or are not job-related.

Job Descriptions

Since there is no standard format for job descriptions, they tend to vary in appearance and content from one organization to another. However, most job descriptions will contain at least three parts: the job title, a job identification section, and a job duties section. If the job specifications are not prepared as a separate document, these specifications usually are stated at the concluding section of the job description. Figure 4–5 on pages 86–87 shows a job description for a Corporate Loan Assistant which, because it consists of only one position, carries the heading of "Position Description." You will note that the physical requirements for this position would restrict the employment of individuals with certain physical handicaps. However, these are restrictions which are job-related and for which physical accommodation is not possible.

The Job Title. Ideally the job title should be limited to three or fewer words.[7] If possible, the title should provide some indication of what the duties of the job entail. For example, such job titles as Meat Inspector, Engineer, Assembler, or Sweeper

---

6. These guidelines refer to the *Uniform Guidelines on Employee Selection Procedures* adopted by the Equal Employment Opportunity Commission, Civil Service Commission, Department of Labor, and the Department of Justice. They are reproduced in *The Federal Register*, Vol. 43, No. 166 (August 15, 1978), pp. 38290–38315.

7. *BNA Policy and Practice Series—Compensation* (Washington, DC: The Bureau of National Affairs, Inc., 1979), p. 317:334.

Figure 4–5   A Position Description for a Corporate Loan Assistant

POSITION DESCRIPTION

Exempt

FUNCTIONAL TITLE: Corporate Loan Assistant   DEPARTMENT: Corporate Banking
FUNCTION CODE: DIVISION:
INCUMBENT: LOCATION: Head Office
                                                    DATE: June, 19--

NOTE: Statements included in this description are intended to reflect in general the duties and
      responsibilities of this classification and are not to be interpreted as being all inclusive.

RELATIONSHIPS:

Reports to: Corporate Account Officer A or AA; or Sr.
                                     Corporate Account Officer B or BB

Subordinate Staff: None

Other internal contacts: Various levels of management within the Cor-
                                     porate Banking Department

External contacts: Major bank customers

SUMMARY STATEMENT:

Assist in the administration of commercial accounts, to ensure maintenance of profitable Bank
relationships.

Under the direction of a supervising loan officer: Analyze a customer company's history,
industry position, present condition, accounting procedures, and debt requirements. Review
credit reports, summarizing analysis and recommending course of action for potential
borrowers; review and summarize performance of existing borrowers. Prepare and follow up
on credit communications and reports and Loan Agreement Compliance sheets.

Help customers with banking problems and needs. Give out customer credit information to
valid inquirers. Analyze account profitability and compliance with balance arrangements;
distribute to customer. Direct the Corporate Loan Note Department in receiving and disbursing
funds and in booking loans. Correct internal errors.

Prepare credit reports, describing and analyzing customer relationship and loan commitments;
prepare for input into Information System. Monitor credit reports for accuracy.

Develop required loan documentation. Help customer complete loan documents. Review loan
documents immediately after a loan closing for completeness and accuracy.

Position Description   page 2

Build rapport with customers by becoming familiar with their products, facilities, and industry. Communicate with customers and other banks to obtain loan-related information and answer questions. Prepare reports on customer and prospect contacts, and follow up. Write memos on significant events affecting customers and prospects.

Assist assigned officers by preparing credit support information, summarizing customer relationship, and accompanying on calls or making independent calls. Monitor accounts and review and maintain credit files. Coordinate paper flow to banks participating in loans. Respond to customer questions or requests in absence of assigned officer.

Represent Bank at industry activities. Follow industry/area developments. Help Division Manager plan division approach and prospect for new business. Interview loan assistant applicants. Provide divisional back-up in absence of assigned officer.

Knowledges, Skills, and Abilities

Oral communication skills, including listening and questioning. Intermediate accounting skills. Writing skills. Researching/reading skills to understand legal financial documents. Organizational/analytical skills. Social skills to represent the Bank and strengthen its image. Sales skills. Knowledge of Bank credit policy and services. Skill to use Bank computer terminal. Knowledge of bank-related legal terminology. Independent work skills. Work efficiently under pressure. Courtesy and tactfulness. Interfacing skills. Knowledge of basic business (corporate) finance. Skill to interpret economic/political events.

Physical Requirements

See to read fine print and numbers. Hear speaker 20 feet away. Speak to address a group of five. Mobility to tour customer facilities (may include climbing stairs). Use of hands and fingers to write, operate a calculator.

Other Requirements

Driver's license. Willing to: work overtime and weekends occasionally; travel out of state every three months/locally weekly; attend activities after work hours; wear clean, neat business-like attire.

Typical Line of Promotion:

    From:

    To: Corporate Account Officer

Analyst	Incumbent	Date
	Superior	Date

SOURCE: Biddle & Associates, Inc., Sacramento, CA. Reproduced with permission.

obviously hint at the nature of the duties of these jobs. The job title also should indicate the relative level occupied by its holder in the organizational hierarchy. For example, the title of Junior Engineer implies that the job to which this title is attached occupies a lower level than that of a Senior Engineer. Other titles which indicate the relative level in the organizational hierarchy are Welder's Helper and Laboratory Assistant.

There are certain job titles that should be avoided by all means. For example, a series of identical titles with qualifiers, such as Inventory Clerk I, Inventory Clerk II, and so on, makes it difficult to distinguish one job from the other.[8] Job titles qualified by the terms "man" or "woman" are also being discarded to avoid the inference that the jobs can be performed only by members of one sex or the other. Thus, a Repair Man is now a *Repairer*; a Foreman or a Forelady, a *Supervisor*; and a Steward or a Stewardess, a *Flight Attendant*.

The Job Identification Section.

Included in the job identification section of a job description are such items as the departmental location of the job, the person to whom the jobholder reports, and the date the job description was last revised. This section usually follows the job title. Sometimes it also contains a payroll or code number, the number of employees performing the job, the number of employees in the department where the job is located, and the DOT code number. The "Statement of the Job" usually appears at the bottom of this section and serves to distinguish the job from other jobs—something the job title may fail to do.

The Job Duties Section.

The statements covering job duties typically are arranged in the order of their importance. These statements should indicate the weight, or value, of each duty. Usually but not always, the weight of a duty can be gauged by the percentage of time devoted to it. The responsibilities that all the duties entail and the results that they are to accomplish should be stressed. It is general practice also to indicate the tools and equipment used by the employee in performing the job.

Job Specifications

As stated earlier, the personal qualifications an individual must possess in order to perform the duties and responsibilities contained in a job description are compiled in the job specification. Typically the job specification covers two areas: (1) the skill required to perform the job, and (2) the physical demands that the job places upon the employee performing it.

Skills relevant to a job include education or experience, specialized training, personal traits or abilities, and manual dexterities. The physical demands of a job refer to how much walking, standing, reaching, lifting, or talking must be done on the job. The condition of the physical work environment and the hazards employees may encounter are also among the physical demands of a job.

---

8. *Ibid.*

The DOT and Job Analysis

Commonly referred to as the DOT, the *Dictionary of Occupational Titles* was first compiled by the United States Employment Service in 1939. Now in its fourth edition (1977), the DOT contains standardized and comprehensive descriptions for about 20,000 jobs. The purpose of the DOT is to "group occupations into systematic occupational classification structure based on interrelationships of job tasks and requirements." This grouping of occupational classifications is done under a coding system.[9]

The DOT Occupational Code.   Consisting of nine digits, the **DOT occupational code** is grouped into sets of three digits each. The first set of three digits represents occupational categories and subcategories. The first digit in this set indicates the *broad occupational group* in which the job is classified, such as a professional group or a clerical group. The second digit represents *a division within the broad occupational group,* such as an occupation in the sciences or an occupation in administrative specializations. The third digit represents an *occupational group within the division,* such as an occupation in purchasing management or an occupation in personnel administration. Thus, the first three digits—166—in the occupational code for a job analyst shown in Figure 4–4 on page 84 indicate that the occupation of job analyst is classified as a *professional* occupation in *administrative specializations,* specifically in *personnel administration.*

The middle set of three digits in the nine-digit code represents the worker function ratings of the tasks in a job with respect to data, people, and things, as illustrated in Figure 4–6. The less difficult the worker functions are, the higher the numbers assigned to these tasks. For example, the "coordinating" and "analyzing" tasks with respect to data are more complex than the "copying" task. Using the occupational code for the job analyst shown in Figure 4–4 on page 84 as an example, notice that the middle set of three digits are 267. Based upon the code, the worker functions of the job analyst are:

> 2—With respect to data, analyzing.
> 6—With respect to people, speaking-signaling.
> 7—With respect to things, handling.

The last set of three digits serves to differentiate, in alphabetical order of the titles, those occupations that have the same first six digits. If the first six digits apply to only one occupation, the last three digits are always 010.

Contributions of the DOT.   The DOT has helped to bring about a greater degree of uniformity in the job titles and descriptions used by employers in different sections of our country. This fact has facilitated the movement of workers from sections of the country that may be experiencing widespread unemployment to those sections where employment opportunities are greater. The DOT code numbers also facilitate

---

9. *Dictionary of Occupational Titles*, p. xiv.

Figure 4–6 **Difficulty Levels of Worker Functions**

DATA (4TH DIGIT)	PEOPLE (5TH DIGIT)	THINGS (6TH DIGIT)
0 Synthesizing	0 Monitoring	0 Setting-up
1 Coordinating	1 Negotiating	1 Precision Working
2 Analyzing	2 Instructing	2 Operating-Controlling
3 Compiling	3 Supervising	3 Driving-Operating
4 Computing	4 Diverting	4 Manipulating
5 Copying	5 Persuading	5 Tending
6 Comparing	6 Speaking-Signaling*	6 Feeding-Offbearing
	7 Serving	7 Handling
	8 Taking Instructions —Helping	

* Hyphenated factors are single factors.

SOURCE: U.S. Department of Labor, Employment and Training Administration, *Handbook for Analyzing Jobs* (Washington, DC: U.S. Government Printing Office, 1972), p. 5.

the exchange of statistical information about jobs. In addition, these code numbers are useful in reporting research in the personnel area, in vocational counseling, and in charting career paths through job transfers and/or advancements.

Functional Approaches to Job Analysis

In recent years employers have been forced to develop objective data concerning the requirements of the jobs they must staff. These data are needed to support personnel decisions with evidence that can be validated statistically. One of the more recent approaches to job analysis is called **functional job analysis** (FJA). This approach utilizes a compiled inventory of the various types of functions or work activities that can comprise any job. FJA thus assumes that each job involves performing certain of these functions, including those listed in Figure 4–6.

While still the subject of experimentation, FJA offers considerable promise.[10] One research study, for example, found FJA to be an effective technique for defining the work of the operating engineer. It provided information covering the knowledge, skills, and abilities required of this job that could be communicated easily to the courts and to the public. The information served as a basis for developing training objectives and for constructing work sample tests that could be used in evaluating the results of the apprenticeship training for operating engineers.[11] Among the more

10. Erich P. Prien, "The Function of Job Analysis in Content Validation," *Personnel Psychology,* Vol. 30, No. 2 (Summer, 1977), pp. 167–174.

11. Howard C. Olson, Sidney A. Fine, David C. Myers, and Margarette C. Jennings, "The Use of Functional Job Analysis in Establishing Performance Standards for Heavy Equipment Operators," *Personnel Psychology,* Vol. 34, No. 2 (Summer, 1981), p. 364.

widely recognized systems that use functional job analysis are the functional occupational classification (FOC) system and the Position Analysis Questionnaire (PAQ) system.

The Functional Occupational Classification System. As a result of several years of study and research, the United States Employment Service has developed and experimented with the **functional occupational classification** system. This system provides certain new types of information, as well as new methods of analyzing conventional information.[12] The five basic categories of information established under this system are:

1. *Worker functions.* The functions performed by workers on the job involve data, people, and things. A hierarchical scale has been established for each of these functions to indicate the level of difficulty at which it is being performed. The difficulty levels for each function, indicated by the numerical rating assigned to it, are those shown in Figure 4–6.
2. *Work fields.* The specific methods and/or techniques used in performing a job comprise this category. There are 99 subcategories in this group, among which are drafting, riveting, and sawing.
3. *Machines, tools, equipment, and work aids (MTEWA).* This category identifies the principal types of MTEWA that are used by employees.
4. *Materials, products, subject matter, and services (MPSMS).* A total of 508 subcategories are included in this group, some examples of which are lumber and wood products, business services, field crops, and meteorology.
5. *Worker traits.* This category is subdivided into training time, aptitudes, interests, temperaments, physical demands, and working conditions.[13]

As the preceding discussion would indicate, the functional occupational classification system is rather complicated and requires considerable experience and training to use. Once the technology of the system is learned, however, it can prove to be an invaluable tool. This system makes it possible for task banks to be developed for occupations in specific organizations. Task banks, in turn, can facilitate the reorganization of work flow, as well as the redesign of jobs and the development of career ladders. Through the use of various scales and inventories, quantifiable data can be developed that lend themselves more effectively to statistical validation than narrative information contained in traditional job descriptions and specifications.

The Position Analysis Questionnaire System. The **Position Analysis Questionnaire** was developed by McCormick, Jeanneret, and Mecham. This questionnaire, which is worker-oriented, covers 194 different tasks. By means of a five-point scale, this questionnaire seeks to determine the degree, if any, to which the different tasks,

12. Ernest J. McCormick, ''Job and Task Analysis,'' *Handbook of Industrial and Organizational Psychology,* edited by Marvin D. Dunnette (Chicago: Rand-McNally College Publishing Co., 1976), pp. 656–657.

13. U.S. Department of Labor, Employment and Training Administration, *Handbook for Analyzing Jobs* (Washington, DC: U.S. Government Printing Office, 1972), pp. 4–10.

or job elements, are involved in performing a particular job. The 194 different elements are grouped into the six divisions shown in Figure 4–7.[14]

A sample page from the PAQ covering 11 elements of the Information Input Division is shown in Figure 4–8. The person making an analysis with this questionnaire would rate each of the elements using the five-point scale shown in the upper right-hand corner of the sample page. The results obtained with the PAQ are quantitative in nature and can be subjected to statistical analysis. They also permit dimensions of behavior to be compared across a number of jobs or permit jobs to be grouped on the basis of common characteristics.

JOB REQUIREMENTS AND PERSONNEL FUNCTIONS

When work was less complicated and labor costs were much lower, the personnel function was largely one of "hiring good people" to perform their jobs. These jobs often involved "doing whatever needed to be done." However, because of the growing complexity of work and the need for greater productivity today, a job increasingly has involved performing specific duties to accomplish specific results. Consequently, employees must possess specific qualifications to perform a particular job.

Values of Written Job Requirements

Job requirements which are spelled out in job descriptions and job specifications are essential in order for members of the personnel staff to know what

---

Figure 4–7   Divisions and Number of Job Elements in the PAQ

DIVISION	NUMBER OF JOB ELEMENTS
Information Input (where and how does the worker get the information used in the job)	35
Mental Processes (what reasoning, decision making, planning, etc., are involved in the job)	14
Work Output (what physical activities do the workers perform, and what tools or devices do they use)	49
Relationships with Other Persons (what relationships with other people are required in the job)	36
Job Context (in what physical and social contexts is the work performed)	19
Other Job Characteristics	41

---

14. Ernest J. McCormick and Daniel R. Ilgen, *Industrial Psychology* (7th ed.; Englewood Cliffs, NJ: Prentice-Hall, Inc., 1980), p. 42.

Figure 4—8 **A Sample Page from the Position Analysis Questionnaire**

INFORMATION INPUT

1 INFORMATION INPUT

1.1 Sources of Job Information

Rate each of the following items in terms of the extent to which it is used by the worker as a source of information in performing his job.

	Extent of Use (U)
NA	Does not apply
1	Nominal/very infrequent
2	Occasional
3	Moderate
4	Considerable
5	Very substantial

1.1.1 Visual Sources of Job Information

1 U   Written materials (books, reports, office notes, articles, job instructions, signs, etc.)

2 U   Quantitative materials (materials which deal with quantities or amounts, such as graphs, accounts, specifications, tables of numbers, etc.)

3 U   Pictorial materials (pictures or picturelike materials used as *sources* of information, for example, drawings, blueprints, diagrams, maps, tracings, photographic films, x-ray films, TV pictures, etc.)

4 U   Patterns/related devices (templates, stencils, patterns, etc., used as *sources* of information when *observed* during use; do *not* include here materials described in item 3 above)

5 U   Visual displays (dials, gauges, signal lights, radarscopes, speedometers, clocks, etc.)

6 U   Measuring devices (rulers, calipers, tire pressure gauges, scales, thickness gauges, pipettes, thermometers, protractors, etc., used to obtain visual information about physical measurements; do *not* include here devices described in item 5 above)

7 U   Mechanical devices (tools, equipment, machinery, and other mechanical devices which are *sources* of information when *observed* during use or operation)

8 U   Materials in process (parts, materials, objects, etc., which are *sources* of information when being modified, worked on, or otherwise processed, such as bread dough being mixed, workpiece being turned in a lathe, fabric being cut, shoe being resoled, etc.)

9 U   Materials *not* in process (parts, materials, objects, etc., not in the process of being changed or modified, which are *sources* of information when being inspected, handled, packaged, distributed, or selected, etc., such as items or materials in inventory, storage, or distribution channels, items being inspected, etc.)

10 U   Features of nature (landscapes, fields, geological samples, vegetation, cloud formations, and other features of nature which are observed or inspected to provide information)

11 U   Man-made features of environment (structures, buildings, dams, highways, bridges, docks, railroads, and other "man-made" or altered aspects of the indoor or outdoor environment which are *observed or inspected* to provide job information; do not consider equipment, machines, etc., that an individual uses in his work, as covered by item 7)

SOURCE: From Position Analysis Questionnaire, Occupational Research Center, Department of Psychological Sciences, Purdue University. © Copyright, Purdue Research Foundation, West Lafayette, IN 47907. Reprinted by permission.

qualifications to look for in applicants when screening them for a particular job. Job descriptions, in particular, are of value to both the employee and the employer. From the employee's standpoint, job descriptions can be used to orient them to the duties of their jobs and to remind them of the results they are expected to accomplish. They also help to prevent employees from engaging in activities that are not a part of their job or in neglecting those that are. They thus establish employee authority and responsibility for performing these activities.

From the employer's standpoint, written job descriptions can serve as a basis for reducing or preventing any misunderstandings that occur between supervisors and their subordinates concerning the requirements of the latter's jobs. They also establish management's right to take corrective action when the duties covered by the job description are not performed as required.

Relationships of Job Requirements to Personnel Functions

Job requirements interrelate closely with each of the personnel functions that are performed in managing human resources. As Figure 4–9 reveals, these requirements help to determine both the objectives these functions seek to achieve and the processes by which they are achieved. When these objectives and processes are modified in any way, the necessary corresponding changes in job requirements must also be made.

Recruitment.   Because job specifications establish the qualifications required of applicants for a job opening, they serve an essential role in the recruiting function. These qualifications typically are contained in the notices of job openings. Whether posted on company bulletin boards or contained in help-wanted advertisements or employment agency listings, the job specifications provide a basis for attracting qualified applicants and discouraging the unqualified ones. When difficulties are encountered in recruiting applicants for certain jobs, the qualifications set forth in the specifications for these jobs may have to be lowered.

Selection.   In the past, job specifications used as a basis for selection sometimes bore little relationship to the duties to be performed under the job description. Examples of such non-job-related specifications abounded. Applicants for the job of laborer were required to possess a high school diploma. Firefighters were required to be at least six feet tall. And applicants for the job of truck driver were required to be male. These job specifications served to discriminate against members of certain groups, many of whom were excluded from these jobs.

In the landmark *Griggs v. Duke Power* Case, the U.S. Supreme Court ruled that a high school diploma requirement for a laborer's job served to discriminate against black applicants. This requirement was also held to violate the Civil Rights Act of 1964.[15] Subsequent court decisions, together with Federal Guidelines, support the

---

15. Students who desire to examine the Civil Rights Act of 1964 and the amendments to it should consult the *General Index to the United States Code Annotated.* In the practice of human resources management, one should be guided by the original act, all of the amendments and court interpretations of it, and any applicable state and local laws.

Figure 4–9   **Interrelationships of Job Requirements and Personnel Functions**

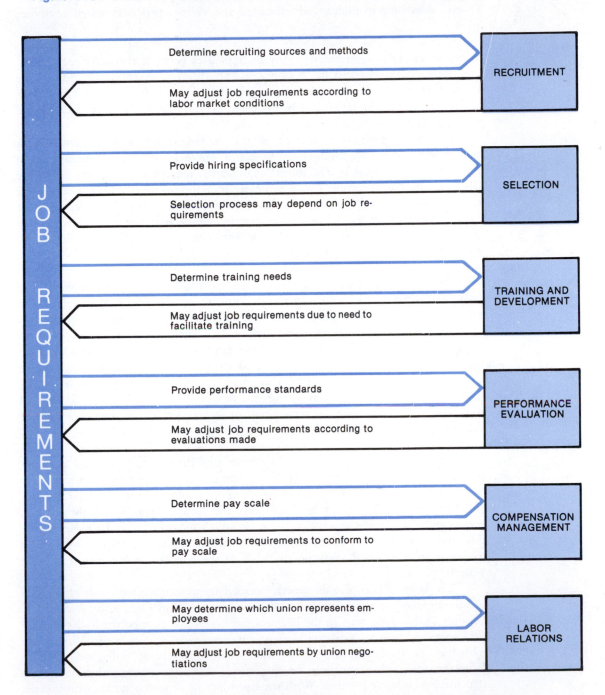

principle that the job specifications used in selecting employees for a particular job must relate specifically to the duties of that job. Job specifications also provide the criteria used in determining and validating the various personnel selection devices used.

Training and Development.

Any discrepancies between the knowledge, skills, and abilities demonstrated by a jobholder and the requirements contained in the description and specification of that job provide clues to training needs. Conversely, the results of training efforts can be evaluated on the basis of progress made toward meeting these job requirements.

Career development as a part of the training function is concerned with preparing employees for advancement to jobs where their capacities can be utilized to the fullest extent possible. The formal qualification requirements set forth in higher level jobs serve to determine how much more training and development is needed for employees to advance to those jobs. In some cases these training and development needs may result in the adjustment of certain requirements for those jobs. In any case, success in the career development of employees can contribute significantly to an employer's affirmative-action goals.

Performance Evaluation.

The requirements contained in the description of a job provide the criteria for evaluating the performance of the holder of that job. The results of performance evaluation may reveal, however, that certain requirements established for a job are not completely valid. Therefore, adjustments in these requirements may be necessary. As we have already stressed, these criteria must be specific and job-related. If the criteria used to evaluate employee performance are vague and not job-related, employees may accuse their employers of unfair discrimination. The person conducting the performance evaluation should bear in mind that the United States Supreme Court in several decisions has upheld employee charges of this nature.

Compensation Management.

In determining the rate to be paid for performing a job, the relative worth of the job is one of the most important factors. This worth is based upon what the job demands of an employee in terms of skill, effort, and responsibility, as well as the conditions and hazards under which the work is performed. The systems of job evaluation by which this worth may be measured are discussed in Chapter 17. In the absence of a formal system, the relative worth of a job must be determined solely on the basis of the opinions of those most familiar with it.

The issue of **comparable worth** pursued by women's groups will cause even greater attention to be focused upon job specifications. This issue, to be discussed in Chapter 17, is concerned with the different pay scales that exist between jobs that are predominantly held by women and those predominantly held by men. While these jobs may be dissimilar, they may require similar levels of skills and abilities. However, comparable worth can be determined only through an evaluation system that utilizes objective job data. With the development of such a system, adjustments in the requirements of certain jobs—whether held traditionally by women or by men—may be necessary to resolve this issue.

Labor Relations.   Long before it was required by law, consistent and equitable treatment of employees was required by union agreements. To avoid grievances and conflict with unions, employers often found it advantageous to prepare written job descriptions. These job descriptions served as a basis for determining which jobs in the organization were subject to union jurisdiction. This jurisdiction can be especially important if more than one union is contesting the right to perform certain work. For example, one union may claim that its members have the exclusive right to operate a particular piece of equipment, to turn off certain valves, or to perform repair work. If these activities are included in a particular job description, the union representing employees in that job generally can claim jurisdiction over those activities. On the other hand, the determination of the activities to be performed in a particular job may be reached through collective bargaining.

RÉSUMÉ

The job is the basic unit of an organization structure. Its design determines what activities are to comprise the job and how successfully employees are able to contribute to the organization's objectives. The job design affects also the quality of work life for employees.

Job information on the duties of the job and the qualifications employees must possess to perform it is contained in job descriptions and job specifications, respectively. Gathered through the process of job analysis, these data provide the criteria upon which employment and personnel decisions must be based.

It is the prevailing opinion of the courts that personnel decisions on employment, performance evaluation, and promotions must be based on specific criteria that are job-related. These criteria can be determined objectively only by analyzing the requirements of each job. By utilizing a functional approach to job analysis, researchers currently are developing data that may be used to validate statistically the various decisions involved in managing human resources. These data provide documentary evidence to support the fact that the employer's decisions indeed support equal employment opportunity. In providing this equal employment opportunity, each of the personnel functions relies upon the data contained in job descriptions and job specifications.

TERMS TO IDENTIFY

job
positions
property right
industrial engineering
human engineering
man-machine system
overspecialization
broadbanding
job analysis

job description
job specification
job analyst or personnel analyst
DOT occupational code
functional job analysis
functional occupational classification
Position Analysis Questionnaire
comparable worth

DISCUSSION QUESTIONS

1. What impact has industrial engineering had upon job design?
2. What does job analysis entail and who within an organization participates in the job analysis process?
3. Indicate some of the possible reasons why the job information provided by employees and/or their supervisors sometimes may not be completely accurate.
4. The DOT code for a personnel manager is 166.117-018.
   (a) What do the digits 117 tell you about the job?
   (b) What do the digits 018 tell you?
5. The courts have been fairly consistent in ruling that selection, performance evaluation, and similar decisions must be based upon job-related criteria. What are the implications of these rulings upon job analysis?
6. To what extent, if any, may the absence of formal job descriptions contribute to employee desires to unionize?
7. How do the more recent approaches to job analysis differ from the traditional approach?
8. As a project, prepare a job description describing a job at which you are currently working or have worked. Develop a specification listing the minimum qualifications required for the job. How do the qualifications required for the job compare with your own qualifications? Were you underemployed or overemployed?

PROBLEM 4–1

A PROBLEM OF JOB CLASSIFICATION

When his wife received an attractive promotion opportunity, Louie Wong concluded that it was too good for them to pass up. Therefore, he agreed to seek a comparable Federal Civil Service position as systems analyst in the metropolitan area where his wife's new position was located. After relocating, he discovered to his disappointment that, because of budget cuts, the best position he could obtain was that of a programmer in another federal agency. Even though the position was in a lower salary grade, he reluctantly accepted it. This position required him only "to interpret computer systems, programs and job flow specifications." His previous position had required him to "develop and formulate complex and extensive computer data processing procedures."

After a few weeks in his new position, Wong complained to his supervisor that his experience and capabilities were not being fully utilized. To better utilize his abilities, Wong was assigned most of the tasks normally performed by a systems analyst. These assignments, however, served only to reinforce his dissatisfaction with his job classification and pay grade.

Recognizing his talents and contributions to the organization, Wong's supervisor wrote a letter to the chief of the job classification section, requesting that Wong's position be reanalyzed and reclassified to that of systems analyst.

a. What are some of the arguments that might be advanced in favor and/or in opposition to this request?

b. What do you anticipate will be the response of the chief of the job classification section? Why?

_____ PROBLEM 4–2 _____

REALITY IN THE USE OF JOB DESCRIPTIONS

In the Tormaru Electronics Company's American subsidiary, the duties of each manager were not determined entirely by their job descriptions. The assignments they might perform from time to time depended also upon their particular abilities and by their past performance. Those who had performed well were likely to receive additional responsibilities, and those who had not were often relieved of certain responsibilities. The less effective managers consequently were likely to suffer the loss of responsibility and status rather than the loss of their jobs.

Because of this fact, the duties being performed by a particular executive might not coincide with those that their job title traditionally included. The manager of human resources, for example, admitted that she spent less than half her time with traditional personnel activities. A significant proportion of her work was spent working with the company's suppliers to help them overcome delivery schedule problems. Rigid adherence to formal job descriptions, thus, frequently did not determine the assignment which a particular manager might be given.

Quite obviously the management practices of this subsidiary of Tormaru Electronics Company differ from those of most American companies. Yet, in competing with American companies it has been quite successful. Furthermore, its workers had been sufficiently satisfied with their employment conditions to vote down union efforts to organize them.

a. What are the potential advantages and disadvantages of the company's practice not to limit a manager's assignment to the duties set forth in the description of that individual's job?

b. What possible contributions might the human resources manager make by working outside the company with a supplier?

_____ SUGGESTED READINGS _____

Berwitz, Clement J. *The Job Analysis Approach to Affirmative Action.* New York: John Wiley & Sons, 1975.

Davis, Louis E., and James C. Taylor (eds.). *Design of Jobs*, 2nd ed. Santa Monica, CA: Goodyear Publishing Company, Inc., 1979.

Gooding, Judson. *The Job Revolution.* New York: Walker & Company, 1972.

McCormick, Ernest J. *Job Analysis: Methods and Applications.* New York: American Management Associations, 1979.

Ulery, John D. *Job Descriptions in Manufacturing Industries.* New York: American Management Associations, 1981.

Chapter Objectives:

- To understand the importance of human resources planning and the two principal approaches by which it is accomplished.
- To recognize the advantages and disadvantages of staffing job vacancies with personnel from within the organization.
- To know the principal external sources from which applicants may be recruited and when these sources are likely to be utilized.
- To describe the barriers to job opportunities encountered by members of protected groups and the means by which these barriers are being overcome.
- To understand the impact that EEO/AA regulations are having upon employee recruitment.

5

Human Resources Planning and Recruitment

In earlier chapters we stressed that the effective organization of an enterprise and the design of the jobs within it are essential for the achievement of organizational objectives. These objectives, however, can be achieved only through the efforts of people. It is essential, therefore, that jobs within the organization be staffed with personnel who are qualified to perform them. Meeting these staffing needs requires effective planning for human resources.

Staffing requirements generally cannot be met by relying solely upon unsolicited applications. The staffing of many jobs requires positive recruiting efforts, particularly if applicants for them are in short supply. Positive recruiting efforts also are required to achieve the organization's equal employment opportunity/affirmative-action (EEO/AA) goals. The process of planning for human resources needs, the sources of applicants, and the methods of obtaining applicants will be discussed in this chapter.

HUMAN RESOURCES PLANNING

Human resources planning (HRP) is the process of anticipating and making provision for the movement of people into, within, and out of the organization. Its purpose is to optimize the utilization of these resources and to have available the required number of people with the needed qualifications to fill position openings *where* and *when* these openings occur.

Importance of Human Resources Planning

Planning, as we noted earlier in Chapter 3, is an essential process of management. Because management entails accomplishing results with and through people, the planning process must include the organization's human resources. HRP provides the foundation for an effective personnel program and for coordinating the personnel functions being performed within it.

Several intangible costs may result from inadequate HRP or lack of it. For example, inadequate HRP can result in vacancies remaining unstaffed. The resulting loss in efficiency can be costly, particularly when lead time is required to train replacements. Situations also may occur in which employees are being laid off in one department while applicants are being hired for similar jobs in another department. This may cause overhiring and result in the need to lay off those persons who were recently hired. Finally, lack of HRP makes it difficult for employees to make plans for effective career or personal development. As a result, some of the more competent and ambitious ones may seek other employment where their career opportunities can be more clearly identified.

HRP and Strategic Planning.

Human resources planning is but one part of the total planning process in which an organization must engage. **Strategic planning**, which is concerned with the steps to be taken in the achievement of organizational goals, relates closely to HRP because management strategies invariably involve the use of human resources. Conversely, the availability or lack of human resources must be considered when developing organizational strategies.

As discussed in Chapter 2, strategic planning should include environmental scanning and issue management. This is because any strategies developed must be consistent with those environmental trends and contemporary issues that may have an impact upon the organization. HRP in turn must anticipate the possible impact of these strategies upon human resources management.

Both the external and internal environments of an organization discussed in Chapter 2 are important considerations in HRP. The growing body of law governing EEO/AA attests to this fact. EEO/AA goals, therefore, must be closely integrated with the HRP goals and the functions performed within the personnel program. Another environmental influence—demographic changes in population—also must be monitored as a part of HRP. Such changes can affect the composition and performance of an organization's work force. These changes are important because EEO/AA goals must also take into account the demographic composition of the population in the area where the organization is located.

HRP and Management Development.   In theory, HRP requires a systems concept that integrates the performance of each personnel function into the planning process and recognizes the variables affecting employee performance. Unfortunately in many organizations HRP is confined to the management level. In fact, one research study reports that many HRP professionals who were contacted viewed human resources planning as synonymous with "management development." In such instances, the functions of promotion planning, replacement planning, career planning, and career development often were included as a part of management development.[1] Another study reached a similar conclusion that most of the organizations have better designed acquisition and development plans for managerial personnel than for clerical and blue-collar employees.[2]

Approaches to Human Resources Planning

There are two approaches to human resources planning: quantitative and qualitative. The **quantitative or top-down approach to HRP** is management-directed and involves the use of statistical and mathematical techniques. It is the approach used by theoreticians and professional planners. The quantitative approach views employees as numerical entities so that they are grouped according to race, sex, age, skills, tenure, job grade, pay level, or some other category. According to Mackey, the focus of this approach is on forecasting human resources shortages, surpluses, and career blockages; its aim is to reconcile the supply and demand for people in the light of the organization's objectives.[3]

1. Kendrith M. Rowland and Scott L. Summers, "Human Resource Planning: A Second Look," *Personnel Administrator*, Vol. 26, No. 12 (December, 1981), p. 78.

2. Guvenc G. Alpander, "Human Resource Planning in U.S. Corporations," *California Management Review*, Vol. XXII, No. 3 (Spring, 1980), p. 26.

3. Craig B. Mackey, "Human Resource Planning: A Four-Phased Approach," *Management Review*, Vol. 70, No. 5 (May, 1981), p. 19.

The **qualitative or bottom-up approach to HRP** is employee-directed and attempts to reconcile the interests, abilities, and aspirations of individual employees with the current and future needs of the organization. Human resources practitioners experienced in training, counseling, and management development techniques use this approach. The focus of the approach is on evaluations of employee performance and promotability, as well as management and career development.[4]

Ideally, human resources planning should include the use of both the quantitative and the qualitative approaches. In combination, the two approaches serve to complement each other and provide a more complete planning coverage. The contributions of both the theoreticians and the practitioners are brought together in the process.[5]

Requirements for Effective Human Resources Planning

There is evidence that HRP is becoming one of the fastest growing areas of human resources management.[6] Unfortunately such growth creates the risk that it might become a "personnel fad" which makes great promises and ends up as an equally great disappointment because of its failure to deliver on unrealistic expectations.[7] To prevent this from occurring, planning efforts must be in line with the size and financial resources of the organization. However, planning should not be neglected even in relatively small organizations.

Insuring Practical Application. Forecasting is a key component of HRP. When concentrating on resource needs, HRP is primarily quantitative in nature and is accomplished by highly trained specialists. This quantitative approach to HRP of which forecasting is a part can be highly sophisticated. However, the use of sophisticated analytical techniques in HRP has not been, without criticism. According to Mackey, "planners, especially those trained in the quantitative approach, may be tempted to create esoteric systems that are incompatible with the practical needs of line managers."[8] Craft adds that there has been little effort to deal with the problems of effectively implementing and enhancing the acceptability of HRP efforts among operating management personnel.[9] There also has been a tendency to pursue the quantitative approach to the neglect of the qualitative approach which would involve the operating managers more directly.

Bridging the Communication Gap. The communication gap that exists between the technicians who prepare the planning information and the action-oriented managers who use it is another source of criticism of HRP. Part of the cause for this gap is the technically oriented emphasis of the preparers and the managerial

4. *Ibid.*

5. James A. Craft, "A Critical Perspective on Human Resource Planning," *Human Resource Planning*, (1980), p. 43.

6. Alpander, *op. cit.*, p. 31.

7. Craft, *op. cit.*, p. 49.

8. Mackey, *loc. cit.*

9. Craft, *op. cit.*, p. 48.

orientation of the users.[10] Successful HRP therefore requires improvements in communication between technicians and managers. The preparers must become more concerned with developing the types of data that are understandable and useful to managers in making personnel decisions. On the other hand, the decision makers need to be better trained to recognize different types of data and understand how to use them in making valid decisions.

Balancing Supply and Demand Considerations.   HRP should strive for a proper balance not only between techniques and their application, but also between the emphases placed upon demand considerations as opposed to supply considerations. Demand considerations are based upon the forecast and projection of trends in business activity and their anticipated impact on the organization's activities and needs for resources. Projected customer demand for goods and/or services are converted into production schedules, performance standards, manning tables, job descriptions, and various other steps that contribute to the determination of human resources requirements. These requirements in turn are translated into the specific jobs and specific qualifications needed to perform them. In the process, however, upward adjustments must be made to allow for reduced efficiency created by personnel undergoing training or by employees being absent from work.

The supply considerations involve the determination of where and how candidates with the required qualifications are to be obtained to staff job vacancies. Due to the difficulty in obtaining applicants for the increasing number of jobs that require advanced training, this phase of planning is receiving greater attention. Greater planning effort also is needed in recruiting members of **protected groups**, such as women, minorities, the physically handicapped, and older persons, for managerial jobs and technical jobs that require advanced levels of education. Such planning may involve the development of programs that reach into colleges or even into high schools. These programs might encourage students with potential to take the preparatory courses and academic degrees needed for these jobs. The programs also may include both financial assistance to institutions that provide the education and scholarships for deserving recipients.

RECRUITING WITHIN THE ORGANIZATION

Recruiting is the process of attempting to locate and encourage potential applicants to apply for existing or anticipated job openings. During this process, efforts are made to inform the applicants fully about the qualifications required to perform the job and the career opportunities the organization can provide for them. Thus, potential applicants can be motivated to apply for the positions that are open. Whether or not a particular job vacancy will be filled by someone from within the organization or from outside will of course depend upon the organization's personnel policies and the requirements of the job to be staffed.

10. Stephen C. Wheelwright and Darrel G. Clarke, "Corporate Forecasting: Promise and Reality," *Harvard Business Review*, Vol. 54, No. 6 (November–December, 1976), pp. 47–48.

Advantages of Recruiting from Within

To the extent possible, most organizations try to follow a policy of filling job vacancies above the entry-level position through promotions and transfers. One study reveals that 76 percent of the responding participants filled more than half of their supervisory and managerial openings through internal promotion.[11] By filling vacancies through internal promotions and transfers, an organization can capitalize on the costs that it has invested in recruiting, selecting, and training its current employees.

Internal promotion serves to reward the employee receiving the promotion for his or her past performance and hopefully will result in continuing efforts by that individual. It also gives other employees reason to anticipate that similar efforts by them will lead to promotion, thus improving morale within the organization. This is particularly true for members of the protected groups who have encountered difficulties in gaining employment and have often faced even greater difficulty in achieving advancement within an organization. An internal promotion policy is an essential part of the EEO/AA programs that most organizations have adopted.

To have maximum motivation value, however, employees must be made aware of the organization's internal promotion policy. Such awareness can be facilitated through the preparation and dissemination of written statements covering this policy. The following is an example of a policy statement that a large hospital has prepared on the subject:

> "Promotion from within" is generally recognized as a cornerstone of good employment practice, and it is the policy of our hospital to promote from within whenever possible when filling a vacancy. The job vacancy will be posted for five calendar days to give all qualified full- and part-time personnel an equal opportunity to apply.[12]

While a transfer lacks the motivational value of a promotion, it sometimes can serve to protect an employee from layoff. Furthermore, the transferred employee's familiarity with the organization and its operations can eliminate certain orientation and training costs that recruitment from the outside would entail. Most important, management has knowledge of the employee's performance record. This knowledge is likely to be a more accurate predictor of the candidate's success than the data gained about outside applicants through the selection process.

Limitations of Recruiting from Within

Sometimes certain jobs at the middle and upper levels which require specialized training and experience that cannot be obtained within the organization must be filled from the outside. This situation is especially common in small organizations.

---

11. Herbert J. Sweeney and Kenneth S. Teel, "A New Look at Promotion from Within," *Personnel Journal*, Vol. 58, No. 8 (August, 1979), pp. 531–535.
12. *Ibid.*

Also, for certain openings it may be necessary to hire individuals from the outside who have gained from another employer the knowledge and expertise required for these jobs.

Even though personnel policy encourages job openings to be filled from within the organization, potential candidates from the outside should be considered occasionally to prevent the inbreeding of ideas. Applicants hired from the outside, particularly for certain management positions, can be a source of new ideas and may bring with them the latest knowledge acquired from their previous employers. Indeed, excessive reliance upon internal sources can create the risk of "executive cloning." Furthermore, in the competitive field of high technology, for example, it is not uncommon for firms to attempt to gain secrets from competitors by hiring away their employees.

Methods of Locating Qualified Job Candidates

The effective use of internal sources requires a system for locating qualified job candidates and for enabling those who consider themselves qualified to apply for the opening. Qualified job candidates within the organization can be located by computerized record systems, by job posting and bidding, and by recalling those who have been laid off.

Computerized Record Systems.
Computers have made possible the creation of **data banks** that contain the complete record of the qualifications of each employee. With these computerized records an organization can screen its entire work force in a matter of minutes to locate candidates who possess the qualifications required to fill an opening. These data also can be used to predict the career paths of employees and to anticipate when and where promotion opportunities for them may occur. Since the value of the data is contingent upon being current, the record system must include provisions for recording changes in employee qualifications and job placements as they occur.

Job Posting and Bidding.
Information concerning job openings may be communicated through a process referred to as **job posting**. Although this process once consisted largely of posting notices on a bulletin board, today it may involve the use of other communication media.

The system of **job bidding** functions most effectively when it is a part of a career development program in which employees are made more aware of the opportunities available to them within the organization. This system encourages employees to take the initiative in improving themselves and in seeking out positions which more closely match their interests and the qualifications they have developed.[13] Of course, the bidding system can accomplish its intended results only if the job openings are communicated successfully to the prospective bidders through job posting.

---

13. David R. Dahl and Patrick R. Pinto, "Job Posting: An Industry Survey," *Personnel Journal*, Vol. 56, No. 1 (January, 1977), pp. 40–41.

Recall from Layoff.   When economic conditions necessitate a reduction in force, the employees who are terminated are said to be laid off. Usually, when the economic outlook brightens again and job openings occur, former employees who were laid off while they were in good standing are recalled to their jobs.

In the case of unionized organizations, the criteria for determining an employee's eligibility for layoff generally are set forth in the union agreements. As a rule, seniority on the job receives significant weight in determining which employees are laid off first. Similar provisions in the union agreement provide for the right of employees to be recalled for jobs they are still qualified to perform. If the employees are not unionized, policies that establish the criteria for layoff and recall should be developed.

RECRUITING OUTSIDE THE ORGANIZATION

Unless there is to be a reduction in the work force, any vacancy occurring within the organization must eventually be filled with a replacement from the outside. Thus, when the president of an organization retires, a chain reaction of promotions may subsequently occur. This creates an opening for a messenger or a clerk at the bottom of the organization pyramid. The question to be resolved, therefore, is not one of determining whether or not to bring people into the organization, but rather one of determining the level at which they are to be brought in.

The recruitment function interrelates closely with the other personnel functions in the organization, as Figure 5–1 indicates. Changes in recruitment policies and practices can have an impact upon each of the other personnel functions. Conversely, anything that may affect one of the other functions may also have an impact on recruitment.

The Labor Market

The **labor market**, or the area from which applicants are to be recruited, will vary with the type of job to be filled and the amount of compensation to be paid for the job. Recruitment for executive or technical jobs requiring a high degree of knowledge and skill may be national or even international in scope. When staffing jobs that require relatively little skill, however, the labor market in which recruiting takes place may encompass only a relatively small geographic area. The unwillingness of people to move, however, may cause them to turn down offers of employment, thereby eliminating them from employment consideration beyond the local labor market. However, by offering an attractive level of compensation and by helping to defray moving costs, some applicants may be induced to move away from the locality where they have lived.

Impact of Commuting.   The ease with which employees are able to commute to work will also influence the boundaries of the labor market. The lack of suitable public transportation or extreme auto congestion on the streets and freeways can

Figure 5-1 Relationship of Recruitment to Other Personnel Functions

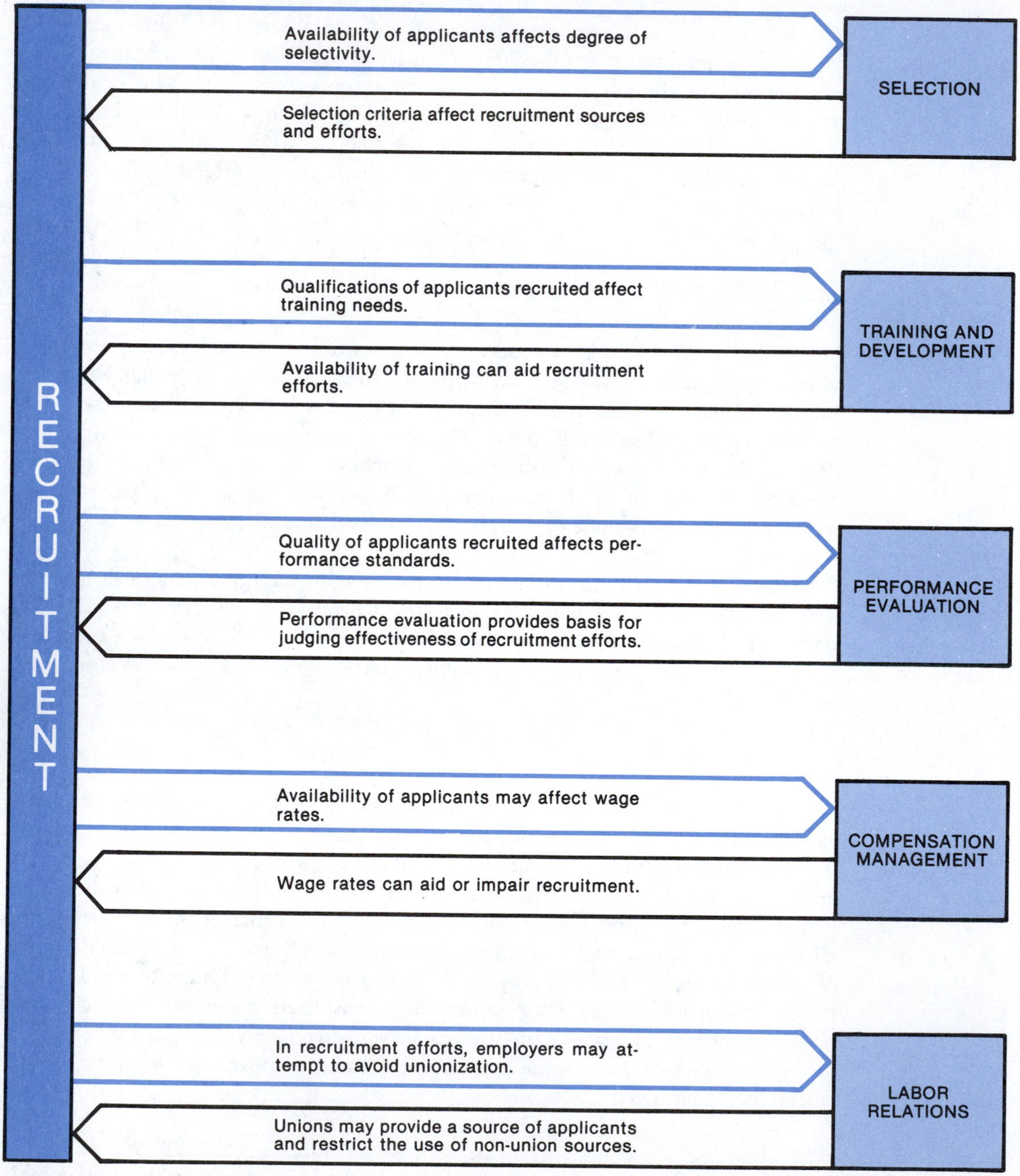

RECRUITMENT

Availability of applicants affects degree of selectivity.

Selection criteria affect recruitment sources and efforts.

SELECTION

Qualifications of applicants recruited affect training needs.

Availability of training can aid recruitment efforts.

TRAINING AND DEVELOPMENT

Quality of applicants recruited affects performance standards.

Performance evaluation provides basis for judging effectiveness of recruitment efforts.

PERFORMANCE EVALUATION

Availability of applicants may affect wage rates.

Wage rates can aid or impair recruitment.

COMPENSATION MANAGEMENT

In recruitment efforts, employers may attempt to avoid unionization.

Unions may provide a source of applicants and restrict the use of non-union sources.

LABOR RELATIONS

limit the distance employees are willing to travel to work, particularly to jobs of low pay. Population migration from the cities to the suburbs has had its effect upon the labor markets. If suitable employment can be obtained near where they live, many suburbanites are less apt to accept or retain jobs located in the central city. In spite of this fact, one government study reveals that one third of all workers commute to jobs outside the geographic area in which they live. Most of these commuters are suburban residents who are employed in the central cities.[14] Nevertheless, some employers, particularly those with white-collar employees, have moved to the suburbs where they believe qualified employees can be obtained more easily.

Problems of the Central City.   The movement of jobs and a large portion of the population of the suburbs has been disastrous for unemployed persons living in the central city. Unfortunately a significant percentage of those left behind are the minorities who, as a group, have the highest rate of unemployment. More than 60 percent of the nation's unemployed blacks, for example, live in the central cities. Those who might be able to qualify for jobs with employers in the suburbs become trapped in the core area of the city because of the absence of transportation and resources to commute to work outside the core area. Still, close to half of all black workers employed in the suburbs commute from the central city as compared with only 16 percent of the total (largely white) suburban workers. Ironically, improvements in public transportation systems to facilitate "reverse commuting" have not proven too successful. A major reason has been the low wages offered by suburban employers willing to hire central city residents.[15]

Outside Sources of Recruitment

The outside sources from which employees are to be recruited will vary with the type of job to be filled. A computer programmer, for example, is not likely to be recruited from the same sources as a machine operator in the plant. The condition of the labor market may also help to determine how productive a particular source will be. During periods of high unemployment, an adequate supply of qualified applicants may be obtained from among those who apply for work at the employment office. A tight labor market, on the other hand, may force the employer to advertise heavily and/or to seek assistance from local employment agencies. The extent to which an organization has been able to accomplish its affirmative-action goals may be still another factor in determining the sources from which applicants are recruited. Typically an employer at any given time will find it necessary to utilize several recruitment sources.

Advertisements.   One of the most common methods for contacting applicants is through advertisements. While newspapers and trade journals constitute the media used most commonly, radio, television, billboards, posters, and even sound trucks also

---

14. Diane N. Westcott, "Employment and Commuting Patterns: A Resident Analysis," *Monthly Labor Review*, Vol. 102, No. 7 (July, 1979), p. 3.
15. *Ibid.*, pp. 5—8.

have been utilized. Advertising has the advantage of reaching a large audience of possible applicants. Some degree of selectivity can be achieved by using newspapers and journals that are directed toward a particular group of readers. Professional journals, trade journals, and publications of unions and various fraternal or nonprofit organizations fall into this category.

According to one study, there appears to be a positive relationship between the accuracy and completeness of information being provided through advertisements and recruitment success.[16] Among the information increasingly being included in advertisements today is the fact that the vacancy is with an *Equal Opportunity Employer*.

The preparation of copy for advertisements and recruitment literature is not only time-consuming, but also requires specialized experience and talent. The high quality of recruiting materials being produced today, furthermore, requires the skills of media professionals. Based upon the responses of one group of professionals in the field, recruitment advertising will play an increasing role in meeting human resources needs of companies in the 1980s. It is predicted also that:

> . . . there will be greater use of corporate image advertising, more four-color advertising, very sophisticated and carefully planned recruitment ad programs, more recruitment ads in specialized business and professional magazines, and the development of recruitment advertising research programs.[17]

Advertising can place a severe burden on the employment office. Even though the specifications for the openings are described thoroughly in the advertisement, many applicants who know they do not meet the job requirements may still be attracted. They may apply in hopes that the employer will not be able to obtain applicants who meet the specifications.

Public Employment Agencies. Each of the 50 states maintains an employment agency that is responsible for administering its unemployment insurance program. Many of the state agencies bear such titles as Department of Employment or Department of Human Resources. They are subject to certain regulations and controls administered by the United States Employment Services (USES).

State agencies maintain local public employment offices in most communities of any size. Individuals who become unemployed must register at one of these offices and be available for "suitable employment" in order to receive their weekly unemployment checks. Consequently, public employment agencies are able to refer to employers with job openings those applicants with the required skills who are available for employment and, hopefully, are seeking it.

16. James A. Breaugh, "Relationships Between Recruiting Sources and Employee Performance, Absenteeism, and Work Attitudes," *Academy of Management Journal*, Vol. 24, No. 1 (March, 1981), pp. 142–147.

17. Margaret M. Nemec, "Recruitment Advertising—It's More Than Just Help Wanted," *Personnel Administrator*, Vol. 26, No. 2 (February, 1981), p. 60.

In addition to matching unemployed applicants with job openings, the public employment agencies may assist employers with employment testing, job analysis, evaluation programs, and community wage surveys. To those seeking employment, many public employment agencies also offer special assistance which includes vocational counseling, as well as training in how to apply and be interviewed for a job.

The USES has developed a nationwide computerized **job bank** to which all state employment offices eventually are to be connected. Most of these offices now have a local job bank that is published as a computer printout. The job bank makes it possible for employment interviewers in an agency to have a list of all job openings in the area for which applicants assigned to them may possibly qualify.

As a means of helping those seeking employment to become aware of openings in other regions, the USES distributes a monthly publication entitled *Occupations in Demand*. Looking to the future, the government is now experimenting with the use of satellites to provide instant information to employment offices throughout the country that can provide a means of matching applicants with jobs. Once the satellite system has been perfected, it may also be possible for an employer sitting before a television screen to conduct an interview with a prospective applicant sitting before a screen in some other part of the nation.

Private Employment Agencies. Because they charge a fee, private employment agencies are able to tailor their services to the specific needs of their clients. It is common for some agencies to specialize in serving a specific occupational area or professional field. Depending upon who is receiving the most service, the fee may be paid by either the employer or the job seeker or by both. Generally, however, it is the job seeker who pays the fee.

Private employment agencies differ in terms of services offered, professionalism, and the caliber of their counselors. If the counselors are paid on a commission basis, their desire to do a professional job may be offset by their desire to earn a commission. Thus, they may encourage job seekers to accept jobs for which they are not suited and from which they soon may be terminated. When seeking the services of an employment agency, therefore, one should exercise the same care and caution as would be used in the selection of legal, dental, medical, or other professional services. Most important, before signing an employment contract with an agency, a job seeker should study the contract carefully, particularly the fine print. Students and graduates of educational institutions would do well to utilize to the fullest extent possible the placement services offered by these institutions before turning to private employment agencies.

Executive Search Firms. In contrast to public and private employment agencies, the function of **executive search firms** is *not* to find positions for job seekers. These firms *do not* advertise in the public media for job candidates, *do not* accept a fee from the individual being placed, and *do not* accept assignments on a contingency basis. Their role is to seek out candidates with the qualifications that match the requirements of the positions that their client firm is seeking to fill.

The retainer fees charged by search firms may range from 25 to 35 percent of the annual salary for the position to be filled. This fee is paid whether or not the recruiting efforts result in an individual being hired. It is over this condition that search firms receive their greatest criticism. Still, according to one survey, about one out of every six chief executive officers was placed in that position through the services of an executive search firm.[18] Since high-caliber executives are in short supply, at least a significant number of the nation's largest corporations apparently believe that the use of search firms with proven track records is the best way to obtain such executives.

Educational Institutions.   The educational institutions typically are a source of young applicants with formal training but with relatively little full-time work experience. High schools usually are a source of employees for clerical and blue-collar jobs. Community colleges, with their various types of specialized training, can provide candidates for technical jobs. These institutions also can be a source of applicants for a variety of white-collar jobs including those in the sales and retail fields. Some management trainee jobs also are staffed from this source.

When filling technical and managerial positions, college and university graduates generally provide the primary source. Unfortunately for college graduates, the supply of applicants with bachelor and even advanced degrees increasingly is exceeding the available openings. Particular difficulty is experienced by graduates with degrees in the liberal arts, although some executives claim to prefer graduates with a broad background. The recruiters who represent these employers, however, tend to seek out people with specialized training who can make an immediate contribution in the jobs where they are placed. Recognizing their placement difficulties, many graduates in the liberal arts, according to some recruiters, have sharpened their job-seeking skills and are able to present their qualifications better than many graduates in business administration. Liberal arts majors also have made themselves more attractive to employers by gaining work experience through internship jobs or through part-time or temporary work assignments.[19]

Unfortunately some employers fail to take full advantage of college and university resources because of a poor recruitment program. Among other things, some visiting recruiters lack a firm grasp of the current mood of students on a campus. Consequently, their recruitment efforts fail to attract many potentially good applicants. Another common weakness is the failure to maintain a planned and continuing effort on a long-term basis. Furthermore, some recruiters sent to college campuses are not sufficiently well trained or prepared to discuss career opportunities or the requirements of specific openings with interested candidates. Attempts to visit too many campuses instead of concentrating on selected institutions and the inability to use the placement office effectively also are recruiting weaknesses. The misman- agement of applicant visits to the plant or company headquarters and the failure to

18. Richard J. Cronin, "Executive Recruiters: Are They Necessary?" *Personnel Admin- istrator*, Vol. 26, No. 2 (February, 1981), pp. 31–32.

19. Alva C. Cooper, "Putting the Liberal Arts Graduate to Work," *Personnel*, Vol. 53, No. 2 (March-April, 1976), pp. 61–65.

follow up on individual prospects or to obtain hiring commitments from higher management are among the other things that have caused well-qualified prospects to be lost to an employer.[20]

Employee Referrals. The recruitment efforts of an organization can be aided by **employee referrals**, or recommendations made by its current employees. According to one Univac executive, employee referrals often are "a better match" for the company than outside sources because "friends have briefed them."[21]

Unsolicited Applications. Many employers receive unsolicited applications by letter or in person from individuals who may or may not be good prospects for employment. Even though the percentage of acceptable applicants from this source may not be high, it is a source that cannot be ignored. In fact, Breaugh's study revealed that the performance of individuals who have been hired through their own initiated contact with the employer proved to be more successful than those recruited from college placement services or newspaper advertisements.[22]

Good public relations requires that any person contacting the organization for a job be treated with courtesy and respect. If there is no possiblity of employment in the organization for the present or future, the applicant should be tactfully and frankly informed of this fact. Telling applicants, "Fill out an application and we will keep it on file," when there is no hope for their employment is neither fair nor ethical.

Professional Organizations. Many professional organizations and societies offer a placement service as one of their benefits for members. Listings of members seeking employment may be advertised in their journals or publicized at the national meetings of these organizations. In fact, the job placement activities at some national meetings may attract more interest than the professional program that allegedly is the primary purpose for attending these meetings.

Labor Unions. Labor unions can be a principal source of applicants for blue-collar and for some professional jobs. Some unions, such as those in the maritime, printing, and construction industries, maintain hiring halls that can provide a supply of applicants, particularly for short-term needs. Furthermore, because of the power some unions can exercise over hiring practices, employers who desire to avoid a confrontation may find it prudent to use this union service.

EEO/AA IN RECRUITMENT

In meeting their legal obligations to provide equal employment opportunity, employers are expected to develop a formal EEO/AA program. An essential part of

20. Richard L. Brecker, "Ten Common Mistakes in College Recruitment—Or How to Try Without Really Succeeding," *Personnel*, Vol. 52, No. 2 (March-April, 1975), pp. 19–28.

21. *The Wall Street Journal*, July 14, 1981, p. 1.

22. *Breaugh*, op. cit., p. 145.

any EEO/AA program must be an affirmative effort to recruit members of protected groups. The steps that the Equal Employment Opportunity Commission (EEOC) recommends in developing this program are shown in Figure 5–2.

To increase hiring and advancement opportunities for protected groups, employers are encouraged to develop EEO/AA goals and demonstrate progress in achieving them. In order to achieve these goals, employers must locate not only candidates who are qualified, but also those who, with a reasonable amount of training or physical accommodation, can be made qualified for a job opening.

Recruitment of Women

The largest numbers among the protected groups are women. In 1977, they constituted more than two fifths of all workers.[23] It is projected that by 1990 they will make up about 45 percent of the labor force.[24] Unlike minorities, women do not have great difficulty in obtaining gainful employment. In fact, today employers often have difficulty in recruiting women for clerical, secretarial, and other jobs in which they traditionally have been employed. However, women are encountering barriers in gaining better paying jobs that have been traditionally performed by men and in rising to positions of managerial responsibility.

Essential to the EEO/AA efforts of employers is an understanding of the problems confronting women. Contrary to a common belief, many women do not go to work merely to get out of the house or to fulfill psychological needs. A majority

Figure 5–2   Basic Steps in Developing an Effective Affirmative-Action Program

A. Issue written Equal Employment Policy and Affirmative-Action Commitment.
B. Appoint a top official with responsibility and authority to direct and implement your program.
C. Publicize your policy and affirmative-action commitment.
D. Survey present minority and female employment by department and job classification.
E. Develop goals and timetables to improve utilization of minorities, males, and females in each area where utilization has been identified.
F. Develop and implement specific programs to achieve goals.
G. Establish an internal audit and reporting system to monitor and evaluate progress in each aspect of the program.
H. Develop supportive in-house and community programs.

SOURCE: *Affirmative Action and Equal Employment: A Guidebook for Employers*, Vol. 1 (Washington, DC: U.S. Equal Employment Opportunity Commission, 1974), pp. 16–17.

23. "Facts on Women Workers," U.S. Department of Labor, Office of the Secretary of the Women's Bureau, 1980, p. 1.
24. "Job Options for Women in the 80s," U.S. Department of Labor, Office of the Secretary of the Women's Bureau, Pamphlet 18, 1980, p. 5.

of women work because of economic necessity. Nearly two thirds of all women in the labor force in 1979 were single, widowed, divorced, separated, or had husbands whose earnings were less than $10,000 in 1978. Yet the average woman worker earns only about three fifths of what a man earns, even when both work full-time year round.

According to a study by the National Commission on Working Women (NCWW), "the average woman worker is a lonely person in a dead-end job, seething with frustration over her lot. Home and children only deepen her dissatisfaction because they raise problems of housework and child care." Of the women surveyed in this study, 40 percent felt that their jobs were boring and did not use their skills. Half of them said they had no chance to train for better jobs. Failure to advance is due often to educational deficiency which cannot be remedied because of the child-rearing responsibilities that they must shoulder in addition to full-time work.[25]

Employment Barriers Encountered by Women.   A major employment barrier encountered by women is the stereotyped thinking about them that persists within our society. Managers, who are mostly men, have been guilty of this stereotyped thinking. In some offices, managers still refer to women employees as "girls," and the younger ones as "chicks." Women's groups, however, are beginning to get the message across that such references to women are not appreciated—a fact that the manager in Figure 5–3 is learning belatedly!

Although often overlooked, a major barrier is that which exists in the minds of many women themselves. This barrier is created by the conflict between what some women consider to be the behavioral requisites for success on the job and the effects they perceive such behavior will have upon their self-image. Still another barrier concerns the lack of professional training and preparation for entrance or advancement into management positions. This situation, however, is changing rapidly with a significant increase in the enrollment of women in programs leading to degrees in management. Women are also discovering that volunteer work can help them sharpen old skills and acquire new ones. In the words of one volunteer, "it's become a useful route back."[26]

Providing employment opportunities for women in nontraditional jobs represents a significant step in overcoming these barriers. While efforts to desex job titles sometimes have gone to the extreme, the elimination of "men" or "man" from a job title helps to emphasize the fact that the job can be performed by women as well as by men. The elimination of qualifications pertaining to physical strength or physical size—where such job requirements have not been validated—also has helped to reduce employment barriers for women.

Women in the Trades.   The employment of women in production work is not new. Garment and food processing industries, as well as many of those in

---

25. "The Deep Discontent of the Working Woman," *Business Week* (February 5, 1979), pp. 28–29.

26. "How Volunteers Are Cracking the Job Market," *Business Week* (May 21, 1979), p. 159.

Figure 5–3   Stereotyped Thinking About Women

**"The employment agency sent over the
'young chick' you asked for."**

SOURCE: Used by courtesy of *New Woman* magazine. Copyright © 1976 by *New Woman.* All rights reserved throughout the world.

manufacturing, have long employed women to do blue-collar work. During World War II, women were employed extensively in defense factories and shipyards as riveters, welders, assemblers, and machine operators. Typically, however, women have been discouraged from entering or training for the skilled jobs that pay higher wages. In many of the skilled trades, few if any women were permitted until recently to enter apprenticeship programs leading to journeyman status.

Affirmative-action programs, however, are leading to changes in these conditions. Recruitment and Training Programs (R-T-P), Inc., through its 27 offices has placed some 685 women in apprentice trades. These trades have included carpentry, sheetmetal work, welding, tile setting, and the pipe trades. In Pascagoula, Mississippi, this organization was able to place 132 women in skilled trades within the shipbuilding industry in less than a year's time.[27]

27. Phyllis Lehmann, "Women Journey into the Skilled Trades," *Work Life,* Vol. 1, No. 8 (August, 1977), p. 28.

During the present decade, it is projected that the employment of women in blue-collar jobs will increase by 16.1 percent. The increase in women in the crafts is projected to be about 20 percent by 1990.[28]

Women in Industrial Sales.   While women have found opportunities for sales jobs in retailing, insurance, and real estate, they have found industrial selling a difficult field to enter. Ironically, sales is one field where women can readily demonstrate their abilities through the sales records they achieve. Yet some industrial customers have expressed reluctance to do business with a woman. In coping with such attitudes, one successful saleswoman states, "When a customer tells me he wants to do business with a man, I tell him I'm your man."[29]

Entrance of Men into Traditional Jobs for Women. EEO/AA requirements have also led to the recruitment of men for jobs that traditionally were held by women. Anyone traveling by air has become aware of the increasing presence of male flight attendants. Some airlines, however, believe that their predominantly male business passengers prefer to be served by young women—particularly if they are attractive. Ironically enough, some males are now being regarded as "sex objects" by women passengers. As one male attendant discovered, some women flirt brazenly. "One lady felt compelled to pat me on the rear, and she was traveling with her husband," he said.[30]

Men are increasingly performing jobs as secretaries, phone operators, and nurses. During a six-year period in the 1970s, the number of male nurses, for example, increased by 94 percent. While the entrance of males into jobs once exclusively held by women will deprive the latter of employment opportunities, it may benefit women in the long run. As one observer concludes, the willingness of men to assert themselves in jobs traditionally held by women will help make life easier for women in the process. "Guys get together and organize and are willing to fight for more. Once we get a 30 to 40 percent ratio of men in nursing, you'll see the whole status of the job improve.[31] However, if women begin to adopt the same attitudes, behavior, and tactics of men, they should be able to achieve similar results on their own.

Recruitment of Minorities

Since the passage of the Civil Rights Act of 1964, many members of minority groups have been able to realize a substantial improvement in their social and economic well-being. Increasing numbers of blacks and Hispanics are now in the upper-income tax brackets through their entrance into the professions, engineering,

---

28. "Job Options for Women in the 80s," *op. cit.*, p. 9.
29. "The Industrial Salesman Becomes a Salesperson," *Business Week* (February 19, 1979), p. 109.
30. "More Men Infiltrating Professions Historically Dominated by Women," *The Wall Street Journal*, February 25, 1981, p. 25.
31. *Ibid.*

and managerial positions. Unfortunately the proportion of minorities in these areas is still substantially below their proportionate numbers in the total population. As Table 5–1 indicates, unemployment among minorities, particularly the youth, is at a critically high level. Undoubtedly these rates were considerably higher during the recession of the early 1980s.

For those minorities who constitute what is referred to as the "hard-core," employment opportunities still remain exceedingly bleak because of educational and cultural disadvantages. Their opportunities are impaired also by the lack of employer understanding about their needs and by the realities of hard-core life that are described in Figure 5–4.

Difficulties in Reaching the Hard-Core.   Because the hard-core groups live in a different cultural environment, the traditional methods used in contacting applicants may prove to be ineffective in reaching them. In his study of the unemployed, Jacobs found that hard-core members relied heavily upon the grapevine in locating job openings. Even the public employment service was less effective because it existed outside their world.[32] Contact made through community action agencies, settlement houses, or church groups within their communities can provide a means of reaching hard-core members.[33]

Retention of Minority Employees.   Unless minorities can be retained within an organization, EEO/AA programs are likely to prove to be costly and of little lasting value. If the loss of minority employees is to be avoided, they must be made to feel welcome in their new jobs. Most important, they must be spared the feeling of failure in performing work that may be new and a source of anxiety and insecurity for them.

Table 5–1   **Distribution of Unemployment in 1979 Among Adults and Teenagers**

ADULTS	PERCENT	TEENAGERS	PERCENT
White men	3.6	White men	13.9
White women	5.0	White women	13.9
Hispanic men	5.7	Hispanic men	17.4
Hispanic women	8.9	Hispanic women	21.3
Black men	9.1	Black men	34.0
Black women	10.8	Black women	39.2

SOURCE: "20 Facts on Women Workers," U.S. Department of Labor, Office of the Secretary of the Women's Bureau, 1980.

32. Paul Jacobs, "Unemployment as a Way of Life," *Employment Policy and the Labor Market,* edited by Arthur M. Ross (Berkeley, CA: University of California Press, 1965), p. 396.
33. "Effectively Employing the Hard-Core," (New York: The National Association of Manufacturers, 1968), p. 4.

Figure 5-4   Realities of Hard-Core Life

The undereducated, unskilled, chronically unemployed poor persons tend to live in a different world from the one we inhabit. And the impact of their world colors all of their actions and reactions when they come into contact with the industrial world. This fact is stressed because any attempt to understand the behavior of disadvantaged persons coming into our plants is contingent upon the ability to step out of our own frame of reference and grasp the impact that living in poverty has on individuals.

Most of us find it difficult to appreciate the extent to which the minority group persons living in a white person's world suffer damage to their self-respect, dignity, and sense of manhood. Without spelling out how this damage comes about, it is important to bear in mind that the toughness, the surliness, the indifference of some disadvantaged persons is a mask that is worn for protection. Underneath that mask there is often hurt and anger.

SOURCE: "Effectively Employing the Hard-Core," (New York: The National Association of Manufacturers, 1968), p. 3. Reprinted with permission.

Recruitment programs for minorities should include provisions for encouraging present employees to cooperate in making these programs a success. Fears and anxieties toward the minorities entering the organization should be alleviated. The appointment of sponsors to assist them in adjusting to their new world can contribute to this end. Sponsors can serve as a communication link and bridge the gap between minorities, their supervisors, and other employees within the organization. Because many of them have had previous experiences with failure, minority group members are likely to look for evidences of failure in their new jobs. Employers, therefore, often must make a particular effort to reassure them about the progress they are making. Their mistakes must be corrected in a positive way that will not generate undue discouragement but rather will motivate continuing effort from them.

Recruitment of the Handicapped

According to figures cited at a Senate hearing, there are approximately 15 million disabled adults between the ages of 18 and 65 who are not institutionalized.[34] The handicapped—physically, mentally, or socially—often have been rejected for employment because of the mistaken belief that there were no jobs within the organization that they might be able to perform effectively. Fears that the handicapped might prove to have more accidents or that they might further aggravate existing disabilities also have deterred their employment. The lack of

---

34. Richard I. Lehr, "Employer Duties to Accommodate Handicapped Employees," *Labor Law Journal,* Vol. 31, No. 3 (March, 1980), p. 175.

special facilities to serve the needs of physically handicapped persons, particularly those in wheelchairs, also has been an employment restriction.

Physical handicaps that individuals may possess constitute limitations only with respect to specific job requirements. An employee in a wheelchair who might not be able to perform duties that involve certain physical activities can be quite capable of working at a bench or a desk. The United States Air Force, for example, estimates that the work of five blind inspectors of jet engine blades saves it several millions of dollars a year. Their keen sense of touch enables them to spot minor defects on blades which, if installed in a jet engine, might lead to mechanical failure and even the loss of life.

Advantages of Employing the Handicapped.

According to one survey, the use of handicapped employees versus the nonhandicapped offers several advantages. Among those cited most frequently were that the handicapped were more dependable, had superior attendance, were more loyal, had lower turnover, and were better employees.[35] In other studies, the handicapped were found to be more intelligent, better motivated, and better qualified than their nonhandicapped counterparts. As Freedman and Keller point out, however, the superior performance attributed to handicapped workers could also be the result of hidden biases toward them. These biases may cause employers to require that the handicapped be overqualified for an entry-level job and to avoid promoting them above it.[36]

The Reasonable Accommodation Concept.

By redesigning the physical layout of a workplace or by restructuring the duties of certain jobs, openings may be created where the abilities of handicapped employees can be fully utilized. In fact, federal regulations—particularly those set forth by the Office of Federal Contract Compliance Programs (OFCCP)—require such efforts. These requirements demand that contractors make **reasonable accommodation** to the physical and/or mental limitations of an employee or applicant.[37] However, exactly what constitutes reasonable accommodation has never been precisely defined by court litigation. Due to the diverse forms of handicaps, what is reasonable accommodation must be decided on an individual basis.

The Less-Publicized Handicaps.

In addition to the widely recognized forms of handicaps, there are others that can limit the hiring and advancement opportunities for those who possess them. One such handicap is ugliness, toward which employers can be biased even if only unconsciously. Ugly individuals are said to be those whose facial features are considered unattractive but who do not possess physical disfiguration that would put them in a physically handicapped category. Another less-publicized handicap in gaining and retaining employment is obesity. In extreme

---

35. Donald J. Petersen, "Paving the Way for Hiring the Handicapped," *Personnel,* Vol. 58, No. 2 (March-April, 1981), p. 51.

36. Sara M. Freedman and Robert T. Keller, "The Handicapped in the Work Force," *Academy of Management Review,* Vol. 6, No. 3 (July, 1981), p. 453.

37. Petersen, *op. cit.,* pp. 43—44.

cases, however, courts have held obesity to be a legitimate physical handicap. People with weight handicaps have formed the National Association to Aid Fat Americans (NAAFA) to represent their interests. Finally, there is the handicap of illiteracy. It is estimated that approximately 23 million Americans—or one out of every five adults— lack the reading and writing abilities needed to handle the minimal demands of daily living.[38] Even if these figures are somewhat exaggerated, employers are encountering increasing numbers of employees, including college graduates, whose deficiencies in reading and writing skills limit their performance on the job. In screening applicants, therefore, employers must not assume that the reading and writing skills of applicants are comparable to their level of education. If a job requires these skills, it may be advisable to test for them.

Recruitment of Older Persons

The Age Discrimination in Employment Act of 1967 (ADEA) protects individuals between 40 and 70 years of age. Unfortunately they have not received as much attention in many EEO/AA programs as that accorded to women, minorities, and the handicapped. Prejudice against older applicants deprives employers of many individuals who have much to offer and who will try harder to be dependable and productive employees than many younger applicants.

The Department of Labor reports that advertising violations account for the greatest number of complaints received concerning the act.[39] Employers therefore must exercise precaution not to indicate job restrictions based upon age in their job descriptions or in their recruitment advertisements and interviews. Furthermore, when terminating employees over 40 years of age, they also must be able to justify such action for reasons other than age.

RÉSUMÉ

Recruitment requires effective planning to determine both the specific human resources needs of the organization and the supply available to meet these needs. Also to be determined are the requirements of the jobs to be staffed which establish the qualifications of the applicants to be recruited and selected. Employers find it advantageous to fill as many openings as possible above the entry level by means of internal promotion. However some jobs above the entry level require reliance upon outside sources. These outside sources also are utilized to fill jobs requiring special qualifications to avoid excessive inbreeding and to obtain new ideas and technology. The specific outside sources and methods utilized in recruiting will depend upon the recruitment goals of the organization, the conditions of the labor market, and the specifications of the job to be filled.

The legal requirements governing EEO/AA make it mandatory that employers

---

38. "Ahead: A Nation of Illiterates," *U.S. News & World Report* (May 17, 1982), p. 53.
39. *BNA Policy and Practice Series—Personnel Management* (Washington, DC: The Bureau of National Affairs, Inc., 1978), pp. 201:701.

exert a positive effort to recruit and promote members of protected groups so that their representation at all levels within the organization will approximate their proportionate numbers in the labor market. These efforts include recruiting not only those members who are qualified, but also those who can be made qualified with reasonable training and assistance.

TERMS TO IDENTIFY

human resources planning (HRP)
strategic planning
quantitative or top-down approach to HRP
qualitative or bottom-up approach to HRP
protected groups
recruiting
data banks

job posting
job bidding
labor market
job bank
executive search firms
employee referrals
reasonable accommodation

DISCUSSION QUESTIONS

1. Distinguish between the quantitative and the qualitative approaches to human resources planning.
2. What are the comparative advantages and disadvantages of filling openings from internal sources?
3. Describe the relationships between the recruitment function and the functions of selection, performance evaluation, and compensation management.
4. In what ways do executive search firms differ from the traditional employment agencies?
5. Describe some of the barriers to the employment and advancement of women in organizations.
6. How can women benefit from the entrance of men into jobs traditionally performed by women?
7. Why are traditional methods often unsuccessful in recruiting members of the hard core? How may contact with them best be established?
8. An employment agency seeking to recruit sales people for an insurance company advertised for applicants in the local newspaper. The position was described as a "management trainee" job with an insurance company. The advertisement did not list the name of either the employment agency or the insurance company but gave only the telephone number of the agency. What are the possible reasons for this practice? What would be your reaction upon reading the ad? Upon learning all the facts about the job?

PROBLEM 5–1

PERSONAL RÉSUMÉ

JOHN M. ESPINO, JR.
135 Sutter Drive
Sacramento, CA 95815
Marital Status: Single
Height 6'1"

Telephone: 916-487-46XX
Age: 28
Weight: 160 pounds

Job Objective
To begin work in the technical department of a company dealing with electronics with the purpose of qualifying eventually for full management responsibilities. No geographic limitations.

Education
Graduated from the California State University, Sacramento, in June, 1979, with a B.S. degree. Major in Operations Management and Minor in Speech.

Honors
Dean's List, Beta Gamma Sigma National Honor Society in Business Administration, Blue Key National Honor Fraternity, Associated Students Service and Leadership Award, National Transportation Association Scholarship award.

Activities
Station Manager and Head Engineer of college radio station KERS-FM, member of the Society for the Advancement of Management, Vice-President of the Young Republicans.

Experience
United States Air Force, Electronics-Communications, 6–72 to 9–77. *Duties and responsibilities*: NCOIC Electronic Equipment Depot Overhaul and Fabrication Shop (supervised 8 persons in the overhaul and building of weather and ionospheric research equipment), Shift Chief Long-Haul Transmitter Site (supervised 3 persons in operation of 52 transmitters and 2 microwave systems), Team Chief Group Electronics Engineering Installation Agency (supervised 3 persons on installing weather and communications equipment), Tech-Writer (wrote detailed maintenance procedures for electronic equipment manuals), Instructor in Electronic Fundamentals (continuous 3-month classes of 10 persons each).

Special Qualifications : Federal Communications Commission First Class Radio Telephone License, Top Secret Clearance for Defense Work.

Summer and Part-Time: Manager, Campus Apartments; Disc Jockey for KXOA and KXRQ; Laboratory Assistant for Radio-TV Speech Department; Stage Technician.

Personal Background and Interests
Attended public elementary and high school in Crisfield, Maryland. Traveled while in Air Force through United States, Caribbean, Europe, Middle East, South Pacific, and Australia. Interested in water skiing, scuba diving, jazz, and building hi-fi equipment.

References
References available upon request at Placement Planning Center, California State University, Sacramento.

a. Comment on what you consider to be the strengths and weaknesses of this résumé in terms of organization and content.

b. If you were an employer, which of the data about Espino might impress you the most? the least?

c. Would you hire this man for a management trainee position?

_____ PROBLEM 5–2 _____

A RECRUITING AID

Like most companies in its field, the Orbit Energy Corporation had difficulty recruiting a sufficient number of college graduates with engineering and other technical degrees to meet its needs. For a number of years, the subsidiaries comprising the corporation had done their college recruiting independently of each other. The situation changed, however, with a corporation reorganization in which all subsidiaries were combined into a single structure. College recruitment then became the responsibility of the corporate personnel office. This change enabled corporate recruiters to offer applicants a choice of subsidiaries and the geographic regions in which they would like to work. Thus, applicants were afforded an opportunity to apply for openings in most of the 50 states, as well as in some foreign countries. By giving applicants a much greater choice of jobs and locations, the company was able to meet its recruitment goals without difficulty and without the need to offer any special financial inducement.

a. What possible negative features, if any, might the centralization of recruiting have had for some potential applicants?

b. What are some of the employment conditions that might serve to attract engineering and technical graduates?

_____ SUGGESTED READINGS _____

Appley, Lawrence A., and Keith L. Irons. *Manager Manpower Planning: A Professional Management System.* New York: American Management Associations, 1981.

Chruden, Herbert J., and Arthur W. Sherman, Jr. *Readings in Managing Human Resources*, 6th ed. Cincinnati: South-Western Publishing Co., 1984, Part 2.

Dickens, Floyd Jr., and Jacqueline B. Dickens. *The Black Manager: Making It in the Corporate World.* New York: American Management Associations, 1982.

Jaquish, Michael P. *Recruiting.* New York: John Wiley & Sons, Inc., 1968.

Johnson, Lawrence A. *Employing the Hard-Core Unemployed.* AMA Research Study, 98. New York: American Management Associations, 1969.

Kaumeyer, Richard A., Jr. *Planning and Using Skills Inventory Systems.* New York: Van Nostrand Reinhold Company, 1979.

Kreps, Juanita M. *Women and the American Economy: A Look to the 1980's* .Englewood Cliffs, NJ: Prentice-Hall, Inc., 1976.

Patten, Thomas H., Jr. *Manpower Planning and the Development of Human Resources.* New York: John Wiley & Sons, Inc., 1971.

Stanton, Erwin S. *Successful Personnel Recruiting and Selection.* New York: AMACOM, 1977.

Walker, James W. *Human Resource Planning.* New York: McGraw-Hill Book Co., 1980.

Analyzing the Qualifications of Job Candidates

6

The recruiting process typically yields a number of applicants whose qualifications must be assessed against the requirements for one or more jobs in the organization. This chapter will be primarily concerned with the information typically assembled on applicants and the methods used to obtain it. The ways in which the information is evaluated in the selection process will be covered in Chapter 7.

Today greater attention is being given to the selection process than ever before. Individuals who are thoroughly screened against carefully developed job specifications learn their job tasks readily, are productive, and generally adjust to their jobs with a minimum of difficulty. As a result, the individual, the organization, and society as a whole benefit from a careful selection process.

Where the job tenure of employees is protected by a union agreement or by civil service regulations, there is an additional incentive for management to have sound selection policies and procedures. It is typically more difficult to discharge unsatisfactory employees who have such protection.

The greatest impetus to improve the selection process has come from equal employment legislation and court decisions. What used to be the exclusive concern of the employment office may be carried into the courtroom. Throughout the discussion in this and the next chapters, the impact of equal employment laws, regulations, and court decisions upon the selection process will be very apparent.[1]

The selection program typically is the responsibility of the human resources department. However, managerial and supervisory personnel in all the departments of an organization also have an important role in the selection process. The final decision in hiring is usually theirs. It is important, therefore, that they understand the objectives and policies relating to selection. They also should be thoroughly trained in the most effective and acceptable approaches for evaluating applicants and should be motivated to use them.

MATCHING PEOPLE AND JOBS

Those individuals who are responsible for making selection decisions should have adequate information upon which to make them. Information about the jobs to be filled, the ratio of job openings to the number of applicants, and as much relevant information as possible about the applicants themselves is essential. However, care must be taken to insure that the information obtained does not result in unfair discrimination. The relationship between the information being solicited and job requirements must be clearly established.

Use of Job Specifications

In Chapter 4 the process of analyzing and developing specifications for jobs was discussed. Such requirements as skill, effort, responsibility, and job conditions provide

---

1. In this chapter "selection" refers primarily to the process of choosing from among applicants those individuals whose qualifications best fit the job requirements. The *Uniform Guidelines on Employee Selection Procedures* uses the term more broadly to cover selection for promotion, training, etc.

the basis for determining what types of information should be obtained from the applicant, from previous employers, or from other sources. The job specifications also form the basis for the administration of any applicable tests. Research has demonstrated that complete and unambiguous job information reduces the influence of racial and sex stereotypes and helps the interviewer to discriminate between qualified and unqualified applicants.

Ordinarily the managers and supervisors in an organization are well acquainted with the requirements pertaining to skill, physical demands, and other factors for jobs in their respective departments. Interviewers and other members of the personnel department who participate in selection should maintain a close liaison with the various departments in order that they may become thoroughly familiar with the jobs. Through a close liaison priorities can be established among the different qualifications that applicants should possess in order to fit the individuals to the position vacancies as closely as possible.

Recognizing the interrelationships between the selection function and the other human resources functions is also essential for effective management. The model in Figure 6-1 shows many of the variables that affect the selection function and the effect that it has on the other human resources functions. A careful study of the model will help to orient the reader for the discussion in this and the following chapter.

The Selection Process

In most organizations selection is a continuous process. An inevitable turnover occurs, with vacancies to be filled by current applicants from inside and outside the organization or by individuals whose qualifications have been assessed previously. It is common to have a waiting list of desirable applicants who can be called when there are permanent or temporary position openings.

The number of steps in the selection process and their sequence will vary, not only with the organization but also with the type and level of jobs to be filled. Each step should be evaluated in terms of its contribution. The steps that typically comprise the selection process are shown in Figure 6–2. Not all applicants will go through all of these steps. For example, some may be rejected after the preliminary interview, others after taking tests, etc.

Reliable and Valid Information About Applicants

As shown in Figure 6–2, several different methods are used to obtain information about applications. These include the use of application blanks, interviews, tests, physical examinations, and background investigations. Regardless of the methods used, it is essential that the information obtained be clearly job-related or predictive of success in that job. Furthermore, the seeking of information about an applicant that could be construed to discriminate unfairly is to be avoided. Above all, it is essential to obtain information that has proved to be sufficiently reliable and valid.

Figure 6–1   Relationship of Selection to Other Personnel Functions

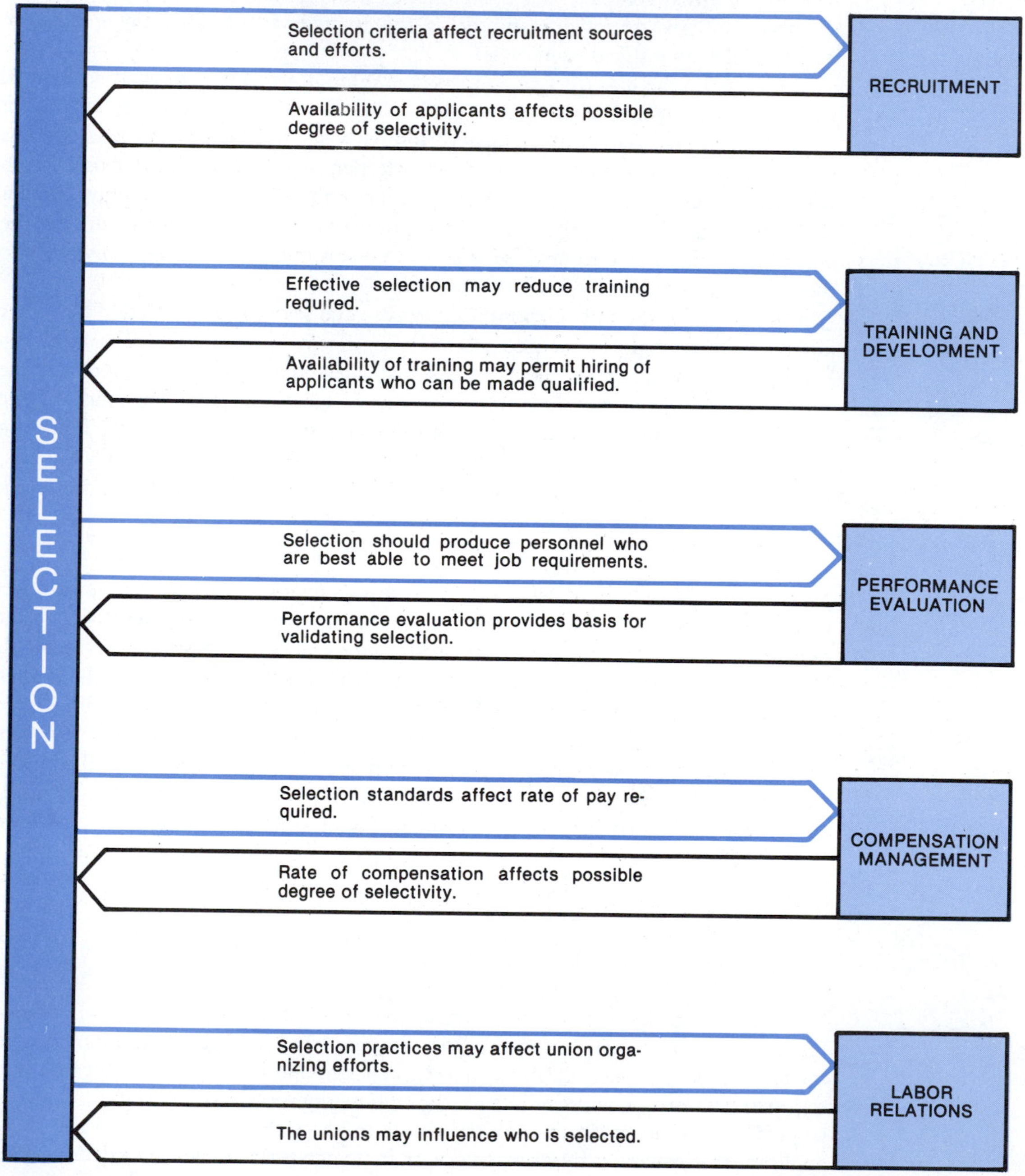

Selection criteria affect recruitment sources and efforts.

Availability of applicants affects possible degree of selectivity.

RECRUITMENT

Effective selection may reduce training required.

Availability of training may permit hiring of applicants who can be made qualified.

TRAINING AND DEVELOPMENT

Selection should produce personnel who are best able to meet job requirements.

Performance evaluation provides basis for validating selection.

PERFORMANCE EVALUATION

Selection standards affect rate of pay required.

Rate of compensation affects possible degree of selectivity.

COMPENSATION MANAGEMENT

Selection practices may affect union organizing efforts.

The unions may influence who is selected.

LABOR RELATIONS

SELECTION

Figure 6–2   **Steps in the Selection Process**

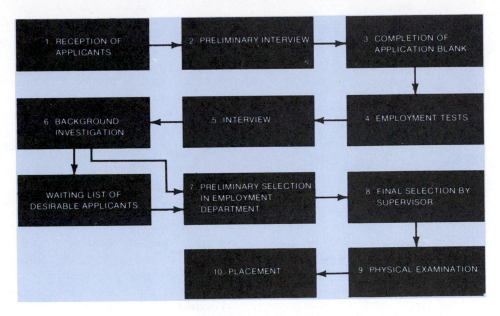

NOTE: An applicant may be rejected after any step in the process.

Reliability of Information.   The extent to which interviews, tests, and other selection tools yield comparable data over a period of time is referred to as **reliability**. That is, these tools are stable. Unless interviewers judge the capabilities of applicants to be the same today as they did yesterday, their judgments are unreliable. Likewise, a test that gives widely different scores when it is administered to an individual a few days apart is just as worthless as a scale in a supermarket that gives a different reading each time the same object is placed upon it. Both measures are unreliable, i.e., unstable.

Reliability also refers to the extent to which two or more methods (interviews, tests, etc.) yield similar results, or are consistent. **Interrater reliability**—a measure of agreement between two or more raters—is one example where consistency is important. Unless the data upon which selection decisions are to be based are reliable, both in terms of stability and consistency, they cannot be used as predictors.

Validity of Information.   In addition to having reliable information pertaining to a person's suitability for a job, it is also essential to have valid information. **Validity** refers to *what* a test or other selection device measures and *how well* it measures it. Essentially it is an indicator of how effectively a selection device does its job. Like a new medicine, a selection device must be carefully studied to determine its effectiveness as a predictor of the probable success of job applicants. The different approaches for assessing validity will be examined in the following chapter. Meanwhile, the reader should keep in mind the fact that the concept of validity is paramount in personnel selection.

SOURCES OF INFORMATION ABOUT JOB CANDIDATES

Many sources of information are used to provide a complete picture of an applicant's potential for success in the organization. Some of the methods used in obtaining this information provide for verification of the information supplied by the applicant. The employment interview plays such a unique role as a source of information that the next major section of this chapter will be exclusively devoted to it.

Application Forms

Most organizations require application forms to be completed because they provide a fairly quick and systematic means of obtaining a variety of information about the applicant. As with interviews, the EEOC and the courts have found that many questions asked on application forms disproportionately reject females and minorities and often are not job-related. Application forms, therefore, should be developed with great care and revised as necessary.

The information on application forms is generally used as a basis for further exploration of the applicant's background. This practice is supported by research that has shown that the application form is an essential and valuable component of the personnel selection process.[2] Application-form data are usually evaluated subjectively. There are procedures, however, for scoring the items on this form in much the same manner as tests are scored.

Even though applicants come armed with elaborate résumés, it is important that they complete an application form early in the process. Stanton warns that:

> . . . an applicant's résumé will tell us what the applicant wants us to know, not necessarily what we need to know. Some borderline and totally incompetent applicants engage the services of so-called employment consultants to help them design elaborate, attractive résumés that extol their alleged virtues and abilities. These résumés are little more than tributes to the writing skills of the people preparing them.[3]

As suggested in Figure 6–3, applicants may be motivated to exaggerate their qualifications, salary, and other information about themselves on résumés. They may also be untruthful in completing an application form.

---

2. David H. Tucker and Patricia M. Rowe, "Consulting the Application Form Prior to the Interview: An Essential Step in the Selection Process," *Journal of Applied Psychology*, Vol. 62, No. 3 (June, 1977), pp. 283-287.

3. Erwin S. Stanton, *Successful Personnel Recruiting and Selection* (New York: AMACOM, 1977), p. 80.

Figure 6–3. Exaggeration on Résumés

CATHY   **by Cathy Guisewite**

SOURCE: Copyright, 1978, Universal Press Syndicate.

Biographical Information Blanks

One of the oldest methods for predicting job success utilizes biographical information of job applicants. As early as 1917, the Life Insurance Agency Management Association constructed and validated a **biographical information blank (BIB)** for life insurance salespersons. It covers such items as hobbies, club memberships, sales experience, and investments. Certain responses to these items were found to be predictive of success on the job.

Both the BIB and the application form can be scored like tests. The development of a scoring system requires that the items that are valid predictors of job success be identified and that weights be established for different responses to these items. By totaling the scores for each item, it is possible to obtain a composite score on the blank as a whole for each applicant. Studies have shown that an objective scoring of BIB and application forms is one of the most potentially valid methods that can be used in predicting job success.[4] This method has been useful in predicting all types of behavior including employee theft.[5]

Background Investigations

If the interviewer is satisfied that the applicant potentially is qualified, previous employment and other information provided by the application form may be

4. Richard R. Reilly and Georgia T. Chao, "Validity and Fairness of Some Alternative Employee Selection Procedures," *Personnel Psychology*, Vol. 35, No. 1 (Spring, 1982), pp. 1–62.

5. Richard W. Rosenbaum, "Predictability of Employee Theft Using Weighted Application Blanks," *Journal of Applied Psychology*, Vol. 61, No. 1 (February, 1976), pp. 94–98.

investigated. Former employers, credit bureaus, and individuals named as references may be contacted for verification of pertinent information such as length of time on job, type of job, highest wage earned, etc. It is not safe to assume that the information furnished by the applicant is 100 percent true. The most common ruse, according to employers, involves an exaggeration of one's college background. "The pressure for higher education has pushed some people over the line," says Richard Bond, director of placement at the Adolph Coors Company. According to the National Credential Verification Service of Minneapolis, "It's very easy to get a college degree without ever going to college. The practice of falsification is rampant."[6]

Checking References.   In one study of over 122 public and private employers, 82 percent indicated that they verified *some* of the information on an application form while only 18 percent replied that they verified *all* of the information provided. A telephone call was the primary means of verification used by 12 percent of the respondents; a letter, by 11 percent; and a combination of the telephone call and letter, by 77 percent.[7]

When checking references, it is crucial to know who should be contacted in an organization. One recruiting firm executive was advised by the personnel director of a large trade association as follows:

> Rarely would I call another personnel department to check out someone (other than for routine information). You seldom get negative facts from personnel people; second, they don't know anything about the person's day-to-day activities. To get in-depth information about an executive or professional, you have to talk to his or her superior.[8]

Inadequate reference checking is one of the major causes of high turnover, employee theft, and white-collar crime. If sources in addition to former employers are used, one can obtain valuable information about an applicant's character and habits. For example, it is legal to use court records, litigation, bankruptcy, and workers' compensation records as long as the prospective employer is consistent in the use of information from these records. If an item on these records is grounds for denial of a job to one applicant, it should be grounds for denial also to any other applicant. Other points to remember are that the information should be job-related and that written documentation exists that the employment decision was based upon relevant information.[9]

---

6. "How Many Impostors Have You Hired?" *U.S. News & World Report* (July 13, 1981), pp. 71–72.

7. George Beason and John A. Belt, "Verifying Applicants' Backgrounds," *Personnel Journal*, Vol. 55, No. 7 (July, 1976), pp. 345–348.

8. Harry David, "The Art of Checking References," *Nation's Business*, Vol. 69, No. 6 (June, 1981), pp. 82–85.

9. Carole Sewell, "Pre-employment Investigations: The Key to Security in Hiring," *Personnel Journal*, Vol. 60, No. 5 (May, 1981), pp. 376–377.

Requiring Signed Requests for References. It is generally advisable to ask the applicant to fill out forms permitting information to be solicited from reference sources. Just as colleges require a signed request before they release a student's transcript, many companies refuse to supply information without a signed statement from a former employee. Even then, many organizations are reluctant to put into writing an evaluation of a former employee. One reason for this trend is that several firms have been sued by former employees who discovered that they had been given poor recommendations. Individuals have a legal right to examine letters of reference about them (unless they waive the right to do so) where protected by the Privacy Act of 1974 or state laws. While the Privacy Act applies only to the records maintained by the federal government agencies, it has influenced many employers to "clean up" personnel files and to open them up to review and challenge by the individual employees concerned. Furthermore, over half of the states have already passed privacy legislation and more may be expected to join the trend.[10]

Using Credit Reports. The use of consumer credit reports as a basis for establishing an applicant's eligibility for employment has become more restrictive for employers. Under the federal Fair Credit Reporting Act the employer must advise applicants if such reports will be requested. If the applicant is rejected on the basis of the report, the applicant must be advised of this fact and provided with the name and address of the reporting agency.

If an employer plans to use a more comprehensive type of consumer report, known as an investigative consumer report, for an employment purpose for which an individual has specifically applied, the applicant must be advised in writing. An **investigative consumer report** includes information based upon personal interviews with the applicant's friends, neighbors, or associates. The applicant must be told that, upon written request, additional disclosure concerning the complete nature and scope of the investigation will be provided.[11]

The Polygraph

Very few companies—4 percent of the total sample—surveyed by the Personnel Practices Forum require lie detector or polygraph tests of any prospective employee.[12] However, a survey of the nation's largest corporations showed a higher rate—20 percent of the responding firms—of polygraph use.[13]

The **polygraph** is a device that measures changes in breathing, blood pressure, and electrodermal response when a person is being questioned. It consists of a rubber

---

10. *Fair Employment Practices Bulletin,* No. 414 (Washington, DC: The Bureau of National Affairs, Inc., February 12, 1981), p. 4.
11. *BNA Policy and Practice Series—Personnel Management* (Washington, DC: The Bureau of National Affairs, 1982), p. 201:258.
12. "How Many Imposters Have You Hired?", *loc. cit.*
13. "Personal Business," *Business Week,* July 27, 1981, pp. 85–86.

tube around the chest, a cuff around the arm, and sensors attached to the fingers. These three sources record on a moving tape the physiological changes in the examinee as the examiner asks questions that call for an answer of "yes" or "no." Questions typically cover such items as whether or not a person uses drugs, has stolen from an employer, or has committed a serious undetected crime. Foremost-McKesson, a drug manufacturer, reports that about one quarter of its job applicants who undergo polygraph tests are screened out.[14]

The use of lie detectors by companies both to screen out "undesirable" job applicants and to curtail internal theft has met with strong resistance. The reliability of the polygraph device and the skill of the examiners are the central issues. A number of states have passed laws that stipulate licensing requirements for polygraph operators and/or limit the use of lie detectors in the areas of pre-employment and as a condition of employment.[15] In addition, some states have laws banning other lie-detection devices such as the **psychological stress evaluator** that is supposed to determine the truth or falsity of statements on the basis of vocal fluctuations or vocal stress.

The Physical Examination

The physical examination is one of the final steps in the selection process because it can be costly and because it should be given immediately prior to hiring. The use of the preemployment physical varies according to industry, but nearly three fourths of the companies surveyed by The Bureau of National Affairs give preemployment physicals to prospective employees.[16]

A physical examination is generally given to assure that the health of applicants is adequate to meet the job requirements. It also provides a base line against which subsequent physical examinations may be compared and interpreted. The last objective is particularly important in determinations of work-caused disabilities under workers' compensation laws. The preemployment physical is particularly valuable in the placement of handicapped persons, and it also provides an opportunity through laboratory analyses to detect those applicants who are on drugs.[17]

14. *Ibid.*

15. With some exceptions for jobs in law enforcement, government agencies, or drug-dispensing firms, the following states have banned compulsory or involuntary polygraphing in employment situations: Alaska, California, Connecticut, Delaware, the District of Columbia, Hawaii, Idaho, Maine, Maryland, Massachusetts, Michigan, Minnesota, Montana, Nebraska, New Jersey, New York, Oregon, Pennsylvania, Rhode Island, Utah, Washington, and Wisconsin. Virginia and New Mexico have certain restrictions. *BNA Policy and Practice Series—Personnel Management* (Washington, DC: The Bureau of National Affairs, Inc., 1982), p. 201:257.

16. *Selection Procedures and Personnel Records*, Personnel Policies Forum Survey No. 114 (Washington, DC: The Bureau of National Affairs, Inc., 1976), p. 6.

17. May R. Mayers, *Occupational Health* (Baltimore: The Williams and Wilkins Co., 1969), Chapter 37.

THE EMPLOYMENT INTERVIEW

Traditionally the employment interview has had an important role in the selection process. Various surveys that have been made over the past several decades have shown that it is considered to be the most important tool in selection. Many organizations that previously included employment tests in the selection process have discontinued their use and rely even more on the interview. Unfortunately many employers still use the **informal or unstructured interview.** This type of interview is characterized by little or no planning. It follows an uncharted course much as a conversation does. It is highly susceptible to distortion and bias. Finally, it is rarely totally job-related, is highly unreliable, and is lacking in validity. In order to obtain reliable and valid information from an interview, the methods that are used and the types of questions that are asked must be carefully selected.

Structured Interviewing Methods

Employment or selection interviews differ according to the methods that are used to obtain information and to elicit attitudes and feelings from an applicant. The most significant difference lies in the amount of structure, or control, that is exercised by the interviewer. In the highly **structured interview** the interviewer determines the course that the interview will follow as each question is asked. In the less structured interview the applicant plays a larger role in determining the way in which the discussion will go. An examination of the different types of interviews from the least structured to the most structured will reveal the differences.

Nondirective Interview.
In the **nondirective interview** the interviewer carefully refrains from influencing the applicant's remarks. The applicant is allowed the maximum amount of freedom in determining the course of the discussion. This is achieved by the interviewer asking broad, general questions, such as "Tell me more about your experiences on your last job," and by permitting the applicant to talk freely with a minimum of interruption. In general, the nondirective approach is characterized by such interviewer behavior as listening carefully and not arguing, interrupting, or changing the subject abruptly. It also involves using questions sparingly, phrasing responses briefly, and allowing pauses in the conversation. This latter technique is the most difficult for the beginning interviewer to master. The greater freedom afforded to the applicant in the nondirective interview is particularly valuable in bringing to the interviewer's attention any information, attitudes, or feelings that may often be concealed by more rapid questioning. This method is more likely to be used in interviewing candidates for higher level positions and as a counseling approach to be discussed in Chapter 13.

Depth Interview.
The **depth interview** goes beyond the nondirective interview by providing additional structure in the form of questions that cover different areas of the applicant's life which are related to employment. A form published by Martin M. Bruce provides 34 questions covering work, school achievement, and other areas to be responded to in depth by the applicant. Some of these questions are:

1. What do you consider are your most important skills?
2. What sort of supervision brings out the best in you?
3. What would you have liked to have learned at school that you were not taught?
4. Tell me about the people in your last job.
5. What do you hope to be doing ten years from now?
6. What responsibility did you have in your most recent job?[18]

Patterned Interview. The most highly structured type of interview is the **patterned interview** which adheres closely to a highly detailed set of questions on specially prepared forms. A portion of one of the commercially available patterned interview forms is shown in Figure 6–4. The questions in black ink are to be asked of the applicant during the course of the interview. The questions in color beneath the line are not asked of the applicant. They are provided to help the interviewer obtain complete information, interpret its significance, and become aware of inconsistencies. The interpretations are recorded later on a summary sheet that is completed on the basis of information obtained from the interview and from other sources. The training required for the patterned interview, as well as the fact that the procedure is standardized, probably have contributed to its moderate-to-highly-valid results.[19]

Figure 6–4   A Section of the McMurry Patterned Interview Form

How many times did you draw
unemployment compensation? _____ When? _____ Why? _____
Does applicant depend on self?

How many weeks have you
been unemployed in the past five years?_____ How did you spend this time? _____
Did conditions in applicant's occupation justify this time? Did applicant use time profitably?

What accidents have you
had in recent years? _____
Is applicant accident-prone? Any disabilities which will interfere with work?

SCHOOLING
How far did you go in school? Grade: 1 2 3 4 5 6 7 8 High School: 1 2 3 4 College: 1 2 3 4 Date of leaving school _____
Is applicant's schooling adequate for the job?

If you did not graduate from
high school or college, why not? _____
Are applicant's reasons for not finishing sound?

What special training have you taken? _____
Will this be helpful? Indications of perseverance? Industry?

Extracurricular activities (exclude military,
racial, religious, nationality groups)_____
Did applicant get along well with others?

What offices did you hold in these groups? _____
Indications of leadership?

SOURCE: Published by Dartnell, 4660 Ravenswood Avenue, Chicago, IL 60640. Reproduced with permission.

18. *Selection Interview Form (Revised)*, © 1977 by Benjamin Balinsky, Ph.D. Published by Martin M. Bruce, Ph.D., 50 Larchwood Road Larchmont, NY 10538. Reproduced with permission.

19. Roger M. Bellows and M. Frances Estep, *Employment Psychology: The Interview* (New York: Rinehart & Company, Inc., 1954); and Robert N. McMurry, *Tested Techniques of Personnel Selection* (rev. ed.; Chicago: Dartnell, undated).

Increasing Use of Highly Structured Interviews. More attention is being given to the highly structured type of interview as a result of AA/EEO requirements. For example, staff members of Weyerhauser Company's human resources department have developed a structured interviewing process with the following characteristics:

1. Is based exclusively on job duties and requirements that are critical to job performance.
2. Has four types of questions which may be used: situational questions, job-knowledge questions, job sample/simulation questions, and worker-requirements questions.
3. Has sample answers to each question determined in advance. Interviewee responses are rated on a five-point scale defined explicitly in advance.
4. Has an interview committee so that interviewee responses are evaluated by multiple raters.
5. Is consistently applied to each applicant. All procedures are consistently followed to insure that each applicant has exactly the same chance as every other applicant.
6. Is documented for future reference and in case of legal challenge.[20]

The use of a highly structured interview is more likely to provide the type of information that is needed for making sound decisions. It also helps to reduce the possibility of legal charges of unfair discrimination. One must be aware that the interview is highly vulnerable to legal attack and that more litigation in this area can be expected.[21]

Special Interviewing Methods

Most employment interviewers will follow only one of the methods that have just been discussed. However, there are other methods that are utilized for special purposes. One type of interview, commonly used by government agencies and the military services, involves a panel of interviewers who question and observe a single candidate. This is called a **board interview or panel interview.** Another type that was developed during World War II as a technique for selecting military espionage personnel places the candidate under considerable pressure and hence is known as the **stress interview.** It usually involves rapid firing of questions by several interviewers who verbally attack the character and the responses of the interviewee. Its use for most jobs is very questionable. One writer feels "that the onslaught of bad manners called stress interviewing must ensure a splendid crop of witless masochists in the companies that go for it."[22]

Types of Preemployment Questions to Ask

The entire subject of preemployment questioning is complex. There are differing and sometimes contradictory interpretations by the courts, the EEOC, and

20. Elliott D. Pursell, Michael A. Campion, and Sarah R. Gaylord, "Structured Interviewing: Avoiding Selection Problems," *Personnel Journal,* Vol. 59, No. 11 (November, 1980), pp. 907–912.

21. R. D. Arvey, "Unfair Discrimination in the Employment Interview: Legal and Psychological Aspects," *Psychological Bulletin,* Vol. 86, No. 4 (July, 1979), pp. 736–765.

22. R. B. Buzzard, "How Science Will Be Helping Men at Work," *Occupational Psychology,* Vol. 45, No. 3 (1971), pp. 183–191.

the Office of Federal Contract Compliance Programs about what is, in fact, lawful and unlawful. Under federal laws there are no questions that are expressly prohibited. However, the EEOC looks with disfavor on direct or indirect questions related to race, color, age, religion, sex, or national origin. Some of the questions that interviewers once felt free to ask can be potentially hazardous. In a series of precedent-setting cases over the past 15 years, federal courts have severely limited the area of questioning by a prying investigator. An interviewer, for example, can ask about physical handicaps if the job involves manual labor, but not otherwise.[23] Several states have fair-employment practice laws that are more restrictive than federal legislation.

Particular care has to be given to questions asked of female applicants about their family responsibilities. As illustrated by the cartoon in Figure 6–5, it is

Figure 6–5   Inappropriate Questions to Ask During Interviews

"Are you sure your duties as a father
won't conflict with your job?"

SOURCE: Used by courtesy of *New Woman* magazine. Copyright © 1977 by *New Woman*. All rights reserved throughout the world.

23. *Time* (March 3, 1980), p. 51.

inappropriate to ask applicants of either sex questions about matters that have no relevance to job performance.

Employers have found it advisable to provide those personnel conducting interviews with instructions on how to avoid potentially discriminating questions in their interviews. Some examples of appropriate and inappropriate questions shown in Figure 6–6 may serve as guidelines for application forms, as well as for preemployment interviews. Complete guidelines may be developed from current information available from district and regional EEOC offices and from state fair-employment practices offices.[24]

Once the individual is hired, the information needed but not asked in the interview may be obtained if there is a valid need for it and it does not lead to discrimination. In fact, in order for an employer to prepare the EEO-1 Report, it is necessary to obtain information from employees, such as that pertaining to race or national origin.

Guidelines for Employment Interviewers

Considerable caution should be exercised in the selection of employment interviewers. Qualities that are desirable are: humility; ability to think objectively; freedom from overtalkativeness, extreme opinions, and biases; maturity; and poise. Experience in associating with people who have a variety of backgrounds is also desirable.

A training program should be provided on a continuing basis for employment interviewers and, at least periodically, for managers and supervisors in other departments. Many books on employment interviewing are available as guides. For the personnel technician who desires to explore the topic in depth, a wealth of information is available in journals.

Since 1964, five separate reviews of research studies on the employment interview have been published.[25] Each of these reviews discusses and evaluates numerous studies concerned with such questions as "What traits can be assessed in the interview?" and "How do interviewers reach their decisions?" Figure 6–7 contains some of the major findings of these studies.[26] It shows that information that can be used to increase the validity of the data gained from interviews is available.

---

24. The states that have detailed guidelines on preemployment inquiries are: Arizona, California, Colorado, Delaware, Hawaii, Kansas, Maine, Michigan, Missouri, New Hampshire, New Jersey, New York, Ohio, Rhode Island, Utah, Washington, and West Virginia.

25. E. C. Mayfield, "The Selection Interview—A Reevaluation of Published Research," *Personnel Psychology,* Vol. 17, No. 3 (Autumn, 1964), pp. 239–260; Lynn Ulrich and Don Trumbo, "The Selection Interview Since 1949," *Psychological Bulletin,* Vol. 63, No. 2 (February, 1965), pp. 100–116; Orman R. Wright, Jr., "Summary of Research on the Selection Interview Since 1964," *Personnel Psychology,* Vol. 22, No. 4 (Winter, 1969), pp. 391–414; Neal Schmitt, "Social and Situational Determinants of Interview Decisions: Implication for the Employment Interview," *Personnel Psychology,* Vol. 29, No. 1 (Spring, 1976), pp. 79–101; and Richard D. Arvey and James E. Campion, "The Employment Interview: A Summary and Review of Recent Literature," Personnel Psychology, Vol. 35, No. 2 (Summer, 1982), pp. 281–322.

26. These are only a few of the findings from the many studies cited in the review articles listed in footnote 25.

Figure 6–6   **Some Inappropriate Questions and Recommended Substitute Questions**

INAPPROPRIATE QUESTIONS	MORE APPROPRIATE QUESTIONS
1. Do you have any physical defects?	1. Do you have any physical defects or impediments which might, in any way, hinder your ability to perform the job for which you have applied?
2. Have you had any recent or past illness or operations?	2. Have you had any recent or past illness or operations which might, in any way, hinder your ability to perform the job for which you have applied?
3. What was the date of your last physical exam?	3. Are you willing to take a physical exam at our expense if the nature of the job requires one?
4. Are you a U.S. Citizen?	4. Do you have the legal right to live and work in the U.S.?
5. Date of Birth?	5. Are you over 18 and less than 70?
6. Age?	6. Are you over 18 and less than 70?
7. Emergency Information: (Relationship)?	7. Emergency Information: Name, Address, Telephone No.
8. Do you possess a legal driver's license?	8. Only for applicants who desire a job driving a company vehicle: Do you possess a legal and current driver's license?
9. What are your hobbies? Interests?	9. Do you have any hobbies or interests which have a direct bearing on the job you are seeking?
10. Have you ever been convicted of a misdemeanor or felony?	10. Have you, since the age of 18, ever been convicted of a misdemeanor or felony? (Note: A conviction will not necessarily bar you from employment. Each conviction will be judged on its own merits with respect to time, circumstances and seriousness.)
11. Dates attended High School? Grammar School?	11. Did you complete grammar school? High School?
12. Date graduated or last attended High School? Grammar School?	12. Same as item 11.
13. In what extra-curricular activities did you participate? Clubs?	13. While in school, did you participate in any activities, or belong to any clubs, which have a direct bearing upon the job for which you are applying?
14. College subjects of interest?	14. While in college, did you take any courses that directly relate to the job for which you are applying?
15. What salary earnings do you expect?	15. If you are employed, are you willing to accept the prevailing wage for the job you are seeking?
16. Memberships (with or without EEO disclaimer)?	16. Have you ever belonged to a club, organization, society, or professional group which has a direct bearing upon your qualification for the job which you are seeking?

SOURCE: E.C. Miller, "An EEO Examination of Employment Applications." Reprinted from the March, 1980 issue of *Personnel Administrator,* copyright, 1980, The American Society for Personnel Administration, 30 Park Drive, Berea, OH 44017, $30 per year.

Figure 6–7 **Some Major Findings from Research Studies on the Interview**

1. Structured interviews are more reliable than unstructured interviews.

2. Interviewers are influenced more by unfavorable than by favorable information.

3. Interrater reliability is increased when there is a greater amount of information about the job to be filled.

4. A bias is established early in the interview and this tends to be followed either by a favorable or an unfavorable decision.

5. Intelligence is the trait most validly estimated by an interview, but the interview information adds nothing to test data.

6. Interviewers can explain why an applicant is likely to be an unsatisfactory employee but not why the applicant may be satisfactory.

7. Factual written data seem to be more important than physical appearance in determining judgments. This increases with interviewing experience.

8. An interviewee is given a more extreme evaluation when preceded by an interviewee of opposing value.

9. Interpersonal skills and motivation are probably best evaluated by the interview.

10. Allowing the applicant time to talk makes rapid first impressions less likely and provides a larger behavior sample.

11. An interviewer's race affects the behavior of the person being interviewed.

12. Experienced interviewers rank applicants in the same order although they differ in the proportion that they will accept. There is a tendency for experienced interviewers to be more selective than less experienced ones.

Conducting interviews under guidance should be included in a training program. Practice interviews may be recorded on videotape and evaluated later in a group training session. Some variation in technique is only natural. However, there are a few ground rules for employment interviews that are commonly accepted and supported by research findings. Their apparent simplicity should not lead one to underestimate their importance.

Establishing the Objectives and Scope of Each Interview. Even the most highly trained and experienced interviewer should prepare for an interview. The preparation typically includes examining the purposes of the interview and determining the areas and specific questions to be covered. A review of the application form, test scores, information from reference checks, etc., is desirable.

The interviewer should use the meeting for the purpose of obtaining and sharing information. He or she should not attempt to reach a decision during the interview. Rather, the interview time should be used to obtain as much relevant information as possible about the candidate for use later in arriving at a decision.

Establishing and Maintaining Rapport. The first step in an interview is to establish a cordial relationship with the interviewee. The interviewer achieves this condition, referred to as **rapport,** by greeting the applicant pleasantly, by displaying sincere interest in the applicant, and by listening carefully to what the applicant is trying to say, as well as to what the applicant is saying.

Listening. Employment interviewers must not only hear, but also listen to the language of the applicants. To listen means to understand, comprehend, and gain insight into what is only suggested or implied or may even be hidden—the words behind the words. It also necessitates a disciplined focus of attention upon the applicant. A good listener's mind is alert, and one's face and posture usually reflect this fact. Interest in the candidate may also be shown through questions and comments which encourage the candidate to talk further.

Observing Body Language. In addition to listening to what the applicant says, the interviewer should pay attention to facial expression, gestures, body position, and movements of hands, feet, and head—commonly referred to as **body language.** By watching the total body response, it is possible to detect inconsistencies that provide clues of a person's emotional state. For example, an interviewee may display a calm facial expression and a casual tone of voice yet betray anxiety by the twisting of hands.

Interviewers must also consider what they are communicating nonverbally. In general, the interviewer must strive to communicate positive attitudes toward the value of the interview itself, toward the interviewee, and toward the interviewee's cooperation. The aim is to obtain *maximal* information about the candidate with *optimal,* rather than maximal, interpersonal relations. Often the neophyte thinks that the interview was excellent because "rapport was perfect." However, the amount and clarity of relevant data obtained may be incomplete, superficial, and ambiguous.[27]

Giving Information. The interview affords an excellent opportunity to provide information to the applicant. Some years ago Bingham pointed out the following four duties of the employment interviewer that will never be delegated to a computer:

1. Answering fully and frankly the applicant's questions about the organization, the job, and the working conditions.
2. Convincing the applicant that it is a good organization to work for since it furnishes such and such opportunities for growth and advancement (if it does).
3. Steering the applicant toward a more suitable job.
4. Conveying a feeling of personal friendship.[28]

Using Questions Effectively. Public opinion pollers learned many years ago that the wording of questions greatly influences the type of response they receive. The

---

27. Raymond L. Gorden, *Interviewing: Strategy, Techniques, and Tactics* (rev. ed.; Homewood, IL: The Dorsey Press, 1975), p. 99.

28. Walter Van Dyke Bingham, "Today and Yesterday," *Personnel Psychology*, Vol. 2, No. 2 (Summer, 1949), pp. 272-274.

responses of job candidates also can be influenced by the wording of the questions. For example, the following questions can easily be reworded to make them more acceptable:

"You wouldn't care to work the swing shift, would you?"
"Were you a stenographer or a secretary on your last job?"
"You finished business school, I suppose."
"Are you one of those college boys (or girls)?"

In order to elicit a truthful answer, questions should be phrased as objectively as possible and with no indication of a desired response.

Separating Facts from Inferences.   On the basis of information and observations, the interviewer makes inferences, or interpretations, about the applicant's behavior. A useful form developed some years ago by Moyer of the New York Bell Telephone Company requires interviewers to record "findings" in one column and "interpretations" of these findings in another column. The interviewer might, for example, record the fact that an applicant "sings in the church choir." From this fact the interviewer might infer that the applicant's "conduct is wholesome." While this may be a reasonably sound inference, it is still an inference and not a fact.

Nervous behavior on the part of the applicant during the interview may be viewed by the interviewer as an indication of emotional maladjustment. Actually this reaction is very natural and may be an indication of the applicant's intense desire to obtain employment. Since employment interviewing involves making inferences, interviewers should be encouraged to compare their inferences with those of others.

Recognizing Biases and Stereotypes.   The opinions that interviewers have of applicants may be influenced by their biases which they may not recognize. One typical bias is for interviewers to consider strangers who have interests, experiences, and backgrounds similar to their own to be more acceptable. This type of bias is illustrated in exaggerated form in Figure 6–8.

Employment interviewers can be as prone as anyone to stereotype applicants. **Stereotyping** involves forming generalized opinions of how people of a given sex, religion, or race appear, think, feel, and act. Any type of stereotype keeps individuals from understanding one another. The influence of sex-role stereotyping is centrally important to sex discrimination in employment. Women have definitely felt it, and through controlled studies more is being learned about it. In one study professional personnel consultants rated a bogus applicant for selected masculine, feminine, and neuter jobs. Each résumé was identical with the exception of the systematic variation of the applicant's sex and the omission or inclusion of a photograph depicting the applicant as physically attractive or unattractive. The findings clearly substantiate the powerful influence of sexism and "beautyism" on personnel decisions regardless of the sex of these consultants.[29]

---

29. Thomas F. Cash, Barry Gillen, and D. Steven Burns, "Sexism and 'Beautyism' in Personnel Consultant Decision Making," *Journal of Applied Psychology*, Vol. 62, No. 3 (June, 1977), pp. 301-310.

Figure 6–8   An Exaggerated Form of Interviewer Bias

"We need more people
like you in our
organization!"

According to *Washington Post* columnist William Raspberry, discrimination against unattractive women is the most persistent and pervasive form of employment discrimination. Such discrimination, he insists, is all the more insidious because no one will admit that it exists. The problem is how to overcome it.[30]

Avoiding the Halo Error.   A common problem in interviewing is the **halo error.** This refers to the tendency to judge an individual favorably in many areas on the basis of one strong point on which the judge places high value. The interviewer who places a high value on personal neatness may judge applicants who are neat to have many other favorable qualities that they may or may not have. The halo error can also work in the opposite direction, for example, in causing an untidy individual to be judged unqualified.

Avoiding Questionable Approaches.   Although it may be unnecessary at this point to warn against using methods that have not been scientifically validated, one occasionally finds even trained and experienced personnel managers relying to some degree upon astrology, handwriting analyses (graphology), facial characteristics (physiognomy), and other approaches to assessment. Handwriting analysis, in

---

30. "Equality for Uglies," *Time* (February 21, 1972), p. 8.

particular, has been popular in European countries. It has become increasingly popular in the United States.[31] Like other selection methods its validity should be determined.

The use of physiognomy is a trap into which anyone can fall. From about 1915 to 1925 several professional physiognomists promoted it as a scientific approach to personnel selection. Dr. Katherine Blackford, a physician, wrote several books and articles in which she explained how to read faces. In 1953, *Fortune* published a serious and sympathetic account of a personnel selection system based on facial characteristics.[32] While most interviewers would be unlikely to use a system like Blackford's, they may well be influenced by the similarity of an applicant's facial characteristics to persons with whom they are familiar.

In a study conducted by Waterworth, trained interviewers who supposedly were aware of the fallacy of judging character and personality on the basis of facial features fell into the trap of making such judgments under experimental conditions.[33] One might assume, therefore, that interviewers and others engaged in personnel selection may, either consciously or unconsciously, be using methods that should be examined more closely.

EMPLOYMENT TESTS

Since the development of the *Army Alpha Test* of mental ability during World War I, tests have played an important part in the personnel programs of both the public and private sectors. In recent years, however, the percentage of business firms using tests in their selection programs has decreased substantially. Before the passage of the Civil Rights Act of 1964, over 90 percent of companies surveyed by The Bureau of National Affairs reported using tests. By 1976, only 42 percent were using tests.[34] Thus, one may safely infer that the rigid requirements of equal employment regulations are responsible for employers abandoning tests in favor of other methods of evaluation.[35] However, it should be recognized that tests in themselves, unlike most interviews, are objective and that their value should not be overlooked. Too

31. Jitendra M. Sharma and Harsh Vardhan, "Graphology: What Handwriting Can Tell About an Applicant," *Personnel*, Vol. 52, No. 2 (March-April, 1975), pp. 57–63.

32. Katherine Blackford and A. Newcomb, *The Job, the Man, the Boss* (Garden City, NY: Doubleday, 1919); P. Stryker, "Is There an Executive Face?" *Fortune*, Vol. 48, No. 5 (November, 1953), pp. 145–147, 162–168. For a critical analysis of the subject see: Anthony Brandt, "Face Reading—The Persistence of Physiognomy," *Psychology Today*, Vol. 14, No. 7 (December, 1980), pp. 90–96.

33. William H. Waterworth, "Analysis of Physiognomic Stereotypes Held by Professional Interviewers" (Master's thesis, California State University, Sacramento, 1960).

34. *Selection Procedures and Personnel Records*, Personnel Policies Forum Survey No. 114 (Washington, DC: The Bureau of National Affairs, Inc., 1976), p. 7.

35. R. L. Dipboye, R. D. Arvey, and D. E. Terpstra, "Equal Employment and the Interview," *Personnel Journal*, Vol. 55, No. 10 (October, 1976), pp. 520-522; and David E. Robertson, "Update on Testing and Equal Opportunity," *Personnel Journal*, Vol. 56, No. 3 (March, 1977), pp. 144–147.

often the interview is misused to measure or predict skills and abilities that can be measured or predicted more accurately by tests.[36]

Tests have played a more important part in government personnel programs where hiring on the basis of merit is required by law. Government agencies have experienced the same types of problems with their testing programs as have organizations in the private sector. However, their staffs have been forced to improve their testing programs rather than to abandon them.

Many organizations utilize professional test consultants to improve their testing programs and to meet the requirements of equal employment legislation. While the expertise of consultants is often needed, the personnel staff should be familiar with the various types of tests that are available and how they should be used in order to make an effective contribution to the personnel program.

The Nature of Employment Tests

An **employment test** is an objective and standardized measure of a sample of behavior that is used to measure a person's abilities, aptitudes, interests, and personality in relation to other individuals. The test can only sample the total aspect of behavior that it is designed to measure. The proper sampling of behavior—whether it be verbal, manipulative, or some other type of behavior—is the responsibility of the test author. It is also the responsibility of the test author to develop tests in such a manner that they meet accepted standards of reliability. In other words, they must measure the sample of behavior with a high degree of stability and consistency.[37]

Reliability is a function, in part, of the length of the test, as well as the adequacy of the sample of items included. Data concerning the reliability are ordinarily presented in the manual which accompanies the standardized test. While a test must be reliable in order to be of value, high reliability offers no assurance that the test is valid with respect to the purpose for which it is being used. It is the responsibility of the personnel staff, therefore, to determine the validity of any test before it is adopted for regular use. This aspect of a testing program will be covered in the next chapter.

While reliability and validity represent the fundamental requirements for personnel tests, other requirements should be considered. These are cost, time, ease of administration and scoring, and how relevant the test appears to the individuals being tested, commonly referred to as **face validity**.

Classification of Employment Tests

Employment tests may be classified in different ways. Most of them are **group tests**, in contrast to **individual tests** which usually require one examiner for each

---

36. Robert M. Guion and Andrew S. Imada, "Eyeball Measurement of Dexterity: Tests As Alternatives to Interviews," *Personnel Psychology,* Vol. 34, No. 1 (Spring, 1981), pp. 31–36.

37. Standards that psychological tests and testing programs should meet are described in *Standards for Educational and Psychological Tests* (Washington, DC: American Psychological Association, Inc., 1974).

person being tested. Another classification relates to the manner in which the individual responds to the test items. For example, **paper-and-pencil tests** require the examinee to respond by writing or marking answers on a booklet or answer sheets. On the other hand, **performance tests or instrumental tests** require the examinee to manipulate objects or equipment. The *Stromberg Dexterity Test* shown in Figure 6–9 is an example of a performance test. Paper-and-pencil tests are the most commonly used since they can be administered easily to groups, as well as to individuals, with minimum cost. In Figure 6–10, sample items from a paper-and-pencil test are shown. It is interesting to note that this type of test was originally a performance test that employed blocks to be inserted in a board.

Human resources managers may obtain **specimen sets** of paper-and-pencil tests for examination. These sets include a test manual, a copy of the test, an answer sheet, and a scoring key. A **test manual** provides the essential information about the construction of the test, its recommended use, and instructions for administering, scoring, and interpreting the test. The manual also reports the nature of the subjects upon which norms, reliability, and validity were established.

Commercially Available Tests. In addition to the classifications mentioned above, there is a more fundamental breakdown of tests according to the characteristics that are measured. In Figure 6–11 the types of tests that are available from commercial sources are shown, along with what they are designed to measure and some of the jobs for which they are used. The publishers of tests in these various categories provide descriptions in their catalogs that are useful in making an initial selection of tests.

Figure 6–9 Stromberg Dexterity Test

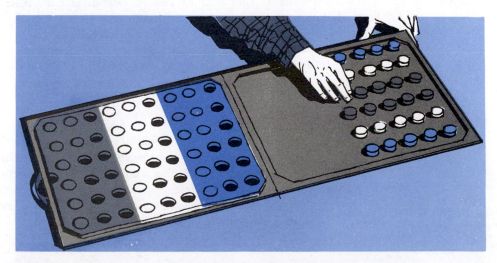

SOURCE: Reproduced with permission of The Psychological Corporation.

Figure 6–10 Sample Items from the Revised Minnesota Paper Form Board

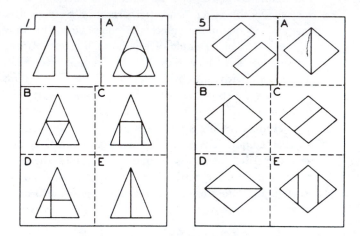

For each item, the examinee is to choose the figure that would result if the pieces in the top left section were assembled.

SOURCE: Reproduced from The Revised Minnesota Paper Form Board Test by permission. Copyright 1949, renewed 1969 by The Psychological Corporation, New York, NY. All rights reserved.

Sophisticated test users do not rely entirely on the material furnished by the test author and publisher. They refer to *Tests in Print II* and the *Mental Measurements Yearbook*—major sources of consumer information about tests.[38] The former is primarily a listing of tests with information about whom the test is designed for, the forms available, and other details. The latter contains descriptive information plus critical reviews by experts in the various areas of testing. The reviews are useful in evaluating a particular test for use. Both books contain the names and addresses of test publishers.

Custom-Made Tests. Some large organizations do not rely upon outside sources for tests. For various reasons they develop their own tests. Probably test security is a major reason. Another good reason is that a tailor-made test is usually a better fit to the jobs and to the organization. Most organizations, however, do not construct their own mental ability, aptitude, and personality tests. If they do build tests, the tests are more likely to be job knowledge and job sample tests.

---

38. See listings of Buros's publications in the Suggested Readings at the end of the chapter.

Job knowledge tests. Government agencies and licensing boards usually develop **job knowledge tests**, a type of achievement test designed to measure a person's level of understanding about a particular job. Most civil service examinations, for example, are used to determine whether an applicant possesses the

Figure 6–11 **Types of Standardized Tests Commercially Available for Use in Personnel Testing**

TYPE OF TEST	WHAT IS MEASURED	EXAMPLES OF JOBS FOR WHICH USED
General mental ability	Academic intelligence or scholastic aptitude.	Managerial or executive jobs. Technical and clerical jobs.
Multiaptitude	Several different aptitude areas such as verbal, numerical, spatial, mechanical comprehension.	Wide variety of jobs from executive to unskilled.
Dexterity	Finger dexterity. Tweezer dexterity. Assembly.	Watch and instrument assembly. Radio and electric parts assembly.
Clerical aptitude	Verbal aptitude, numerical aptitude, perceptual speed.	Clerical jobs, inspectors, checkers, packers.
Mechanical aptitude	Mechanical comprehension. Spatial relationships.	Variety of engineering and mechanical jobs.
Personality	Range of personality characteristics including emotional adjustment, self-confidence, perseverance, etc.	Salespersons. Managers and supervisors.
Supervisory and managerial abilities	Attitudes and perceptions. Administrative skills. Decision-making abilities.	Managerial and supervisory jobs.
Interest inventories	Major interest areas such as scientific, literary, investigative, computational, etc.	Career planning.

information and understanding that will permit placement on the job without further training.[39] Job knowledge tests also have had a major role in the enlisted personnel programs of the United States Army, Navy, and Air Force. They should be considered as useful tools for business organizations.

A large number of tests is required to cover all jobs, but the number can be reduced by isolating job elements (see page 91 in Chapter 4) and by building tests to cover the job elements. For example, if the element "operating bookkeeping equipment" appears in several jobs, one test to measure that element could be used for all of these jobs.

Job sample tests.   The **job sample tests or work sample tests** require the examinee to perform tasks that are actually a part of the work to be performed on the job. They are commonly used to measure such skills as typing, shorthand, driving, and machine stitching. They also have been devised for many different jobs: a map-reading test for traffic control officers, a lathe test for machine operators, a complex coordination test for pilots, an in-basket test for managers, a group discussion test for supervisors, a judgment and decision-making test for administrators, etc.[40] The job sample test is one of the best predictors of job success, as well as success in a training program. One reason may be that the face validity of work sample tests may serve to motivate the examinees to perform better on them than on intelligence or other types of tests that lack the appearance of job-relatedness.[41]

The practicality of job sample tests has an appeal that should not be overlooked. The developer of an equipment mechanic test for use by the Civil Service Commission of the City of Des Moines reported that the shop supervisor remarked: "It screened the competent applicants from the incompetent applicants like a hot knife going through butter." The work sample procedure seemed to raise the morale of the equipment mechanics already in the garage. It was judged to be a highly effective and practical procedure.[42]

The city of Miami Beach has used job sample tests for jobs as diverse as plumber, planner, and assistant chief accountant. The city likewise reports that this type of test is cost effective, reliable, valid, fair, and acceptable to applicants.[43] The

---

39. It is interesting to note that the origins of the system go back to 2200 B.C. when the Chinese emperor examined officials every three years to determine their fitness for continuing in office. In 1115 B.C. candidates for government posts were examined for their proficiency in music, archery, horsemanship, writing, arithmetic, and the rites and ceremonies of public and private life. (See Philip H. DuBois in Suggested Readings at the end of the chapter.)

40. James J. Asher and James A. Sciarrino, "Realistic Work Sample Tests: A Review," *Personnel Psychology*, Vol. 27, No. 4 (Winter, 1974), pp. 519–533.

41. Michael E. Gordon and Laurence S. Kleiman, "The Prediction of Trainability Using a Work Sample Test and an Aptitude Test: A Direct Comparison," *Personnel Psychology*, Vol. 29, No. 2 (Summer, 1976), pp. 243–253.

42. Paul M. Muchinsky, "Utility of Work Samples," *Personnel Journal*, Vol. 54, No. 4 (April, 1975), pp. 218–220.

43. Wayne F. Cascio and Niel F. Phillips, "Performance Testing: A Rose Among Thorns?" *Personnel Psychology*, Vol. 32, No. 4 (Winter, 1979), pp. 751–766.

job sample test may also be used to select employees for promotion. For example, International Harvester Company has developed clerical qualification tests for about 30 jobs for use in promoting employees.[44]

RÉSUMÉ

The selection process should provide as much information as possible about applicants in order that their qualifications may be carefully matched with job specifications. The information that is obtained should be clearly job-related or predictive of success on the job and free from potential discrimination.

Interviews and tests are customarily used in conjunction with application forms, background investigations, physical examinations, and other sources of information about job applicants. The interview is quite an important source of information about job applicants. Those who conduct interviews should receive special training and be evaluated on their performance. The training should acquaint them with the various interviewing methods and AA/EEO considerations. It should also provide an opportunity for them to become more aware of the major findings from research studies on the interview and to apply these findings.

While the popularity of tests in employment has declined, their value should not be overlooked. Tests are more objective than the interview and can provide a broader sampling of behavior. In addition to using tests that are commercially available, organizations may develop their own job knowledge or job sample tests.

TERMS TO IDENTIFY

reliability
interrater reliability
validity
biographical information blank (BIB)
investigative consumer report
polygraph
psychological stress evaluator
informal or unstructured interview
structured interview
nondirective interview
depth interview
patterned interview
board interview or panel interview
stress interview

rapport
body language
stereotyping
halo error
employment test
face validity
group tests
individual tests
paper-and-pencil tests
performance tests or instrumental tests
specimen sets
test manual
job knowledge tests
job sample tests or work sample tests

---

44. Robert M. Guion, *Personnel Testing* (New York: McGraw-Hill Book Company, 1965), pp. 406–409.

DISCUSSION QUESTIONS

1. It once was fairly common for employers to ask female applicants about the number and ages of their children under 18 years and the arrangements being made for their care. Are such questions discriminatory? Explain.

2. What are some of the problems that arise in checking references furnished by job applicants? Are there any solutions to them?

3. Compare briefly the major types of employment interviews described in this chapter. Which type would you prefer to conduct? Why?

4. What characteristics do job knowledge tests and job sample tests have that often make them more acceptable to the examinees than other types of tests?

5. The term "intelligence" is not commonly used in personnel work, and the concept of IQ (intelligence quotient) is never used. Can you suggest any reasons for this practice?

6. Personality tests, like other tests used in employee selection, have been under attack for several decades. What are some of the reasons why applicants find personality tests objectionable? On what basis could their use for selection purposes be justified?

7. Recall some of the situations in which you were a member of a group being administered psychological tests. What do you recall about the administrators and their skill in giving the tests? What were your own feelings during the testing period? How can you utilize these experiences if you are called upon to administer tests or supervise test administrators?

8. The Supreme Court of the United States has consistently interpreted Title VII of the Civil Rights Act of 1964 as prohibiting not only intentional discrimination but also neutral practices which have a discriminatory effect. Thus, practices that are discriminatory in intent *and* effect are prohibited by Title VII. What are some employment practices that are discriminatory in effect, even if not in intent? What should be done with respect to these practices?

PROBLEM 6–1

AVOIDING DISCRIMINATION IN THE SELECTION INTERVIEW

In this chapter we have observed that the interview is used widely as a method for learning as much as possible about job applicants. While conducting an interview, one must be very careful not to ask questions that are or could be interpreted to be discriminatory under equal and/or fair-employment laws.

Study the following questions that employment interviewers might ask in the course of a preemployment interview. Evaluate each question in relation to equal and/or fair-employment laws. Is it acceptable or not? Rephrase those questions that you believe can be made generally acceptable under federal and/or state laws relating to discrimination in employment.

1. Do you have any hobbies?
2. From the ring on your finger I assume that you are married. Am I correct?
3. What type of work does your husband do?
4. I notice on your application form that you are a college graduate. Did you take any courses that are related to the job that you are seeking?
5. Do you have any physical handicaps?

6. Do you own your own home or do you rent?
7. Would you be willing to take a physical examination at our expense?
8. You stated that you are a veteran. Did you have any experience in the military service that relates to the job that we are discussing?
9. Have you ever been arrested?

a. What are the general rules concerning what may be asked of applicants in a preemployment interview?

b. How can an interviewer avoid asking questions that are or may be construed to be discriminatory?

PROBLEM 6–2

INTERPRETING BEHAVIORAL FACTS

The importance of separating facts from inferences or interpretations in the employment interview was discussed in this chapter. We encouraged comparing or checking one's inferences with others, preferably with a member of the human resources department.

Listed below are some facts that could apply to a large number of individuals. Respond to each factual statement with your interpretation of it in terms of its implications for success on a job. Compare your responses with those of others.

FACT	INFERENCE
1. Browses in the library frequently	
2. Had a paper route as a child	
3. Attends adult night school	
4. Grows vegetables organically	
5. Is well groomed	
6. Reads *Playboy* regularly	
7. Plays golf every Saturday	
8. Has had 3 different jobs in the last 12 months	
9. Speaks slowly and distinctly	

a. Why do different interviewers make different inferences from the same facts?

b. In evaluating a job applicant, how much weight should be given to a single fact? How does one know how predictive of success a particular fact is?

SUGGESTED READINGS

Adkins, Dorothy C. *Test Construction*, 2d ed. Columbus, OH: Charles E. Merrill Books, Inc., 1974.

Anastasi, Anne. *Psychological Testing*, 5th ed. New York: The Macmillan Company, 1982.

Buros, O. K. *Eighth Mental Measurements Yearbook*. Lincoln: University of Nebraska, Buros Institute of Mental Measurements, 1978.

_____. *Tests in Print, II*. Lincoln: University of Nebraska, Buros Institute of Mental Measurements, 1974.

Chruden, Herbert J., and Arthur W. Sherman, Jr. *Readings in Managing Human Resources*, 6th ed. Cincinnati: South-Western Publishing Co., 1984, Part 2.

DuBois, Philip H. *A History of Psychological Testing*. Boston: Allyn and Bacon, Inc., 1970. Chapter 1.

Meyer, John J., and Melvin W. Donaho. *Getting the Right Person for the Job: Managing Interviews and Selecting Employees*. Englewood Cliffs, NJ: Prentice-Hall, Inc., 1979.

Schneider, Benjamin. *Staffing Organizations*. Pacific Palisades, CA: Goodyear Publishing Company, Inc., 1976.

- To describe the four types of validity used in the selection process.
- To understand how validity coefficients and expectancy charts are used.
- To describe the factors to be considered and the strategies used in reaching hiring decisions.
- To cite the major federal laws affecting selection policies.
- To explain the concept of adverse impact.
- To identify the groups for whom special selection considerations are often required.

Making Selection Decisions

7

In the preceding chapter we discussed the sources from which information about applicants may be obtained. Once this information is assembled, a decision must be reached about each job applicant. Some of them will be accepted for employment; others, rejected. Some will be placed in jobs for which they applied. Others will be placed in jobs where their talents can be utilized more effectively.

What happens in the selection process is important to the individual applicants and to the organization whose success is dependent upon the quality of its human resources. Both benefit from decisions that are made on the basis of reliable and valid information and an objective weighing of all of the facts.

VALIDATION AND THE SELECTION PROCESS

Hugo Münsterberg was among the first to write about the validation of personnel selection tools, especially tests.[1] From Münsterberg's time until the mid-1960s, personnel managers were constantly exhorted to validate their tests and other selection tools. Some took the advice seriously, many ignored it. Since the enactment of several laws relating to discrimination in employment during the 1960s and 1970s, validation has been a topic of growing concern for human resources managers.

Four Types of Validity

We emphasized in the last chapter that validity refers to *what* a test or other selection tool measures and *how well* the test or tool measures it. Essentially validity is an indicator of how effectively a selection device does its job. The process of validation is sometimes referred to as "testing the test." Therefore, the validity of tests and other selection tools should be established *before,* not after, they are used operationally.

There are four types of validity: content validity, construct validity, criterion-related validity, and synthetic validity. Everyone who is engaged in personnel selection should be familiar with these types in order to be able to perform in a professional manner and to comply with affirmative-action and equal employment opportunity (AA/EEO) requirements.

Content Validity.   The degree to which a test, interview, or other selection tool measures the skill, knowledge, or ability that is required for successful performance on the job is called **content validity.** The closer the content of the selection tool is to actual work samples or behaviors, the greater the content validity. For example, a civil service examination for accountants has content validity when it requires the solution of accounting problems representative of those found on the job. Similarly, asking an applicant to lift a 60-pound bag is a selection procedure that has content

---

1. Hugo Münsterberg, *Psychology and Industrial Efficiency* (Boston: Houghton Mifflin Company, 1913), Chapter 8, "Experiments in the Interest of Electric Railway Service."

validity if the job description indicates that employees be able to meet this requirement.

Content validity is the most direct and least complicated type of validity to assess. It is used primarily to evaluate job-knowledge and skill tests and is generally not appropriate for evaluating tests that measure the ability to learn new skills. While many experts are of the opinion that content validity should not be used as a substitute for other types of validity, it has been gaining greater reception in recent years.[2]

Construct Validity.   The extent to which a selection tool measures a theoretical construct, or trait, is known as **construct validity.** Typical constructs are intelligence, mechanical comprehension, anxiety, etc. They are in effect broad, generalized categories of human functions that are based upon the measurement of many discrete behaviors. For example, a mechanical comprehension test consists of a wide variety of tasks that are assumed to measure the construct of mechanical comprehension.

Measuring construct validity requires showing that the psychological trait is related to satisfactory job performance and that the test accurately measures the psychological trait. Construct validation is a relatively new procedure in the employment field, and there is a lack of literature covering this concept as it relates to employment practices.

Criterion-Related Validity.   The extent to which a selection tool is predictive of or significantly correlated with important elements of work behavior is indicated by **criterion-related validity.** Performance on a test, for example, is related to actual job performance, commonly referred to as the **criterion.** The criterion may be production records, supervisory ratings, training outcomes, and other measures of success that are appropriate to each type of job. In a sales job, for example, it is common to use dollar sales figures. In production jobs quantity and quality of output may provide the best criteria of job success.

There are two types of criterion-related validity: concurrent and predictive. **Concurrent validity** involves obtaining criterion data at about the same time as test scores (or other predictor information) are obtained from *present employees.* **Predictive validity**, on the other hand, involves testing *applicants* and obtaining criterion data *after* they have been on the job for an indefinite period.

Use of Correlational Methods.   Correlational methods are generally used to determine the relationship between test scores and criterion data. The correlation scatterplots in Figure 7–1 illustrate the difference between a selection test of zero validity (A) and one of high validity (B). Each dot represents a person. Note that in Scatterplot A there is no relationship between test scores and success on the job; in other words, the validity is zero. In Scatterplot B those individuals who score low on the test tend to have low success on the job, whereas those who score high on the test tend to have high success on the job, indicating high validity. In actual practice

2. Robert M. Guion, " 'Content Validity' in Moderation," *Personnel Psychology*, Vol. 31, No. 2 (Summer, 1978), pp. 205-213.

Figure 7–1 **Correlation Scatterplots**

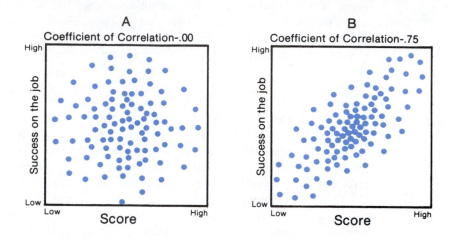

we would apply a statistical formula to the data to obtain a coefficient of correlation which is referred to as a **validity coefficient.**

A thorough survey of the literature shows that the averages of the maximum validity coefficients are .45 where tests are validated against *training* criteria and .35 where tests are validated against *proficiency* criteria. These figures represent the predictive power of single tests.[3] A higher validity may be obtained by combining two or more tests or other predictors (interview, biographical data, etc.) using the appropriate statistical formulas. The higher the overall validity, the greater the chances for hiring individuals who will be the better producers.

Use of Expectancy Charts. Validity is often communicated better through the use of an **expectancy chart** which provides a method for interpreting test scores in terms of predicted job performance standards. Data in the organization's files are used as a basis for interpreting scores made by applicants. Figure 7–2 shows an expectancy chart for one test—the *Minnesota Paper Form Board*—where job success is defined as the rated success of junior drafters in a steel company.

The expectancy chart graphically portrays the fact that individuals with the higher test scores are more likely to be rated above average in job performance. The scores of applicants are thus interpreted in the light of job performance of former applicants who became employees.

Synthetic Validity. A measure of how well a test battery predicts performance on the components, or elements, of a job rather than overall proficiency on a specific job

3. Edwin E. Ghiselli, "The Validity of Aptitude Tests in Personnel Selection," *Personnel Psychology*, Vol. 26, No. 4 (Winter, 1973), pp. 461–477.

Figure 7–2   **An Expectancy Chart**

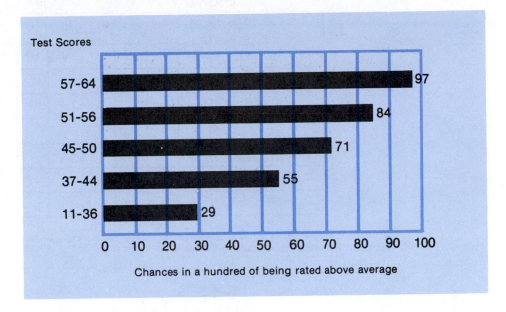

SOURCE: Ernest J. McCormick, Daniel R. Ilgen, *INDUSTRIAL PSYCHOLOGY*, 7th ed., ©1980, p. 122. Reprinted by permission of Prentice-Hall, Inc., Englewood Cliffs, NJ.

is called **synthetic validity or job component validity.** It involves inferring the validity of a battery of tests from predetermined validities of individual tests in the battery for specific components of the total job. The principle is illustrated in Figure 7-3. The X's in each column represent the two best predictors out of six for each of seven different job elements. The appropriate test battery for any job consists of those tests that are valid for each element involved in the job in question. If one is considering employees for a job consisting of Elements I and IV, for example, a battery consisting of Tests A, B, and D would be used. If the opening were for a job consisting of Elements IV and V, the battery would consist of Tests A,B, and F.[4]

Synthetic validity was first used in small businesses. However, trends toward job enrichment, technical employment, and service occupations and away from large numbers of workers performing identical functions make the need for synthetic validity greater.

4. For a detailed discussion of synthetic validity, see Robert M. Guion, *Personnel Testing* (New York: McGraw-Hill Book Company, 1965), pp. 169-172 and C. W. Lawshe and Michael J. Balma, *Principles of Personnel Testing* (2d ed.; New York: McGraw-Hill Book Company, 1966), pp. 250-261.

Figure 7–3   Model of Test Criterion Validity Matrix for Use in Synthetic Validity

Predictor	Job Element						
	I	II	III	IV	V	VI	VII
A	X			X	X		
B		X		X			
C		X				X	
D	X						X
E			X			X	
F			X		X		X

SOURCE: Robert M. Guion, *Personnel Testing* (New York: McGraw-Hill Book Company, 1965), p. 170. Reproduced with permission.

The Selection Ratio

While a validity coefficient should be as high as possible, there is a related factor that contributes to selecting the best qualified persons. It is selectivity through having an adequate number of applicants or candidates from which to make a selection. Selectivity is typically expressed in terms of a **selection ratio** which is the ratio of the number of applicants to be selected to the total number of applicants. A ratio of .10, for example, means that 10 percent of the applicants will be selected. A ratio of .90 means that 90 percent will be selected. If the selection ratio is low, only the most promising applicants would normally be hired. When the ratio is high, very little selectivity will be possible since even those applicants of mediocre ability will have to be hired if the vacancies are to be filled. A low selection ratio is desirable because it can compensate somewhat for low validity. However, it should not be used as a substitute for higher validity.[5]

REACHING A SELECTION DECISION

While all of the steps in the selection process are important, the most critical one is the decision to accept or reject applicants. Because of the cost of placing new employees on the payroll, the short probationary period in many organizations, and

5. Robert M. Guion, *Ibid.*, p. 153.

AA/EEO considerations, the final decision must be as sound as possible. This requires systematic consideration of all of the relevant information about applicants.

Summary of Information About Applicants

In the preceding chapter the importance of using job specifications as a basis for obtaining information was emphasized. These specifications provide a sound basis for collecting and assembling all of the relevant information needed for making employment decisions. It is common to use summary forms and checklists to insure that all of the pertinent information has been included in the evaluation of the applicant.

"Can Do" and "Will Do" Factors.   Fundamentally, an employer is interested in what an applicant *can do* and *will do.* An evaluation of candidates on the basis of assembled information should focus on these two factors shown in Figure 7-4.[6] The **can do factors** include knowledge and skills, as well as the aptitude or potential for acquiring new knowledge and skills. The **will do factors** include motivation, interests, and other personality characteristics. Both factors are essential to successful performance on the job. The individual who has the ability *(can do)* but is not motivated to use it *(will not do)* is little better than the employee who lacks the necessary ability.

It is much easier to measure what individuals *can do* than what they *will do.* The *can do* factors are readily evident from test scores and verified information. What the individual *will do* can only be inferred. Responses to interview questions may be used as a basis for obtaining information for making inferences about what an individual *will do.*

Mutual Expectations.   It is desirable to examine in depth the expectations that both the applicant and management have about the nature of the work, what is

Figure 7-4   **Employers Should Consider "Can Do" and "Will Do" Factors in Selecting Personnel**

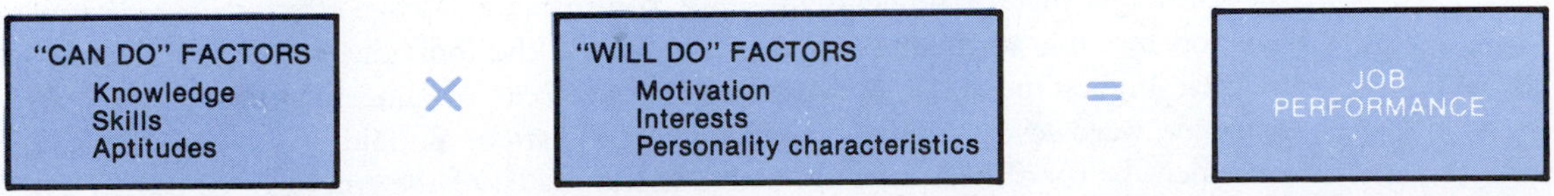

```
┌──────────────────────┐        ┌──────────────────────────────┐        ┌──────────────────┐
│ "CAN DO" FACTORS     │        │ "WILL DO" FACTORS            │        │   JOB            │
│   Knowledge          │   X    │   Motivation                 │   =    │   PERFORMANCE    │
│   Skills             │        │   Interests                  │        │                  │
│   Aptitudes          │        │   Personality characteristics│        │                  │
└──────────────────────┘        └──────────────────────────────┘        └──────────────────┘
```

6. These two factors are emphasized in a system developed by Robert N. McMurry, *Tested Techniques of Personnel Selection* (rev. ed.; Chicago: Dartnell, undated). His system includes a summary sheet for rating the applicant on "can do" and "will do" factors and for summarizing the ratings.

required for success, and what penalties and rewards are likely. For example, a job opening might entail the following:

> ...plying the nomadic, often lonely craft of the sales representative, as well as dealing with and getting along with people who frequently aren't particularly pleasant, interesting, or friendly. A person who wants an easy life—that is, a mere order taker—cannot do the job. What is required is a person who is able to set high personal and business goals and has the persistence to achieve them.[7]

Applicants who are considered for the position described above should have been asked many questions that relate to such job conditions. Some of these questions are: "How do you imagine you would spend an average day in a job as a sales representative in a territory?" "What is the best way to work with unfriendly people?" Recorded answers to such questions serve as further evidence of what an applicant can do and will do.

Value Systems.　Most managers can adequately assess the prospective employee's education, skills, and experience. However, they may not do as well when it comes to understanding the dimensions of the applicant's "values" relative to the job for which he or she is being considered. Applicants whose value systems are compatible with the work and the work environment make better employees and are more likely to stay with the organization.

According to one system, work values may be classified as security-oriented, self-oriented, systems-oriented, success-oriented, society-oriented, and meaning-oriented. Developers of this system advise that "applicants should not be chosen on the basis of how well they mirror the values of those who select them. They should be chosen in accordance with how well their value systems match their work and work environments." For example, systems-oriented persons enjoy work that follows a structure and involves processes which they repeat over extended periods of time. An accounting position is stereotypical of these requirements.[8]

Decision Strategy

There are many other factors to be considered in hiring decisions. The strategy used for one category of jobs may differ from that used for another category. Some of the questions that personnel staffs must consider are: What effect will a decision have on meeting affirmative-action goals? Should the individuals be hired according to their highest potential or according to the needs of the organization? At what grade or wage level should the individual be started? Should initial selection and placement be concerned primarily with an ideal match of the employee to the present job or should the strategy be to select and place applicants who have the highest

7. Thomas A. Petit and Terry W. Mullins, "Decisions, Decisions: How To Make Good Ones on Employee Selection," *Personnel*, Vol. 58, No. 2 (March-April, 1981), pp. 71–77.

8. Debra L. Heflich, "Matching People and Jobs: Value Systems and Employee Selection," *Personnel Administrator*, Vol. 26, No. 3 (March, 1981), pp. 77–85.

overall potential for growth and advancement within the organization? Should individuals who are overqualified for a job be hired?[9]

In addition to these types of factors, consideration must also be given to the approach that will be used in making decisions. There are two basic approaches to decision making: clinical and statistical.

Clinical Approach. In the **clinical approach to decision making**, those making the selection decision review all of the data on applicants. Then, on the basis of their understanding of the job and the individuals who have been successful in that job, they make a decision. Different individuals may arrive at different decisions about an applicant when they use this approach.

Statistical Approach. In contrast to the clinical approach, the **statistical approach to decision making** is entirely objective. It involves identifying the most valid predictors and weighting them through sophisticated statistical methods. A comparison of the clinical approach with the statistical approach in a wide variety of situations has shown that the statistical approach is superior to the clinical approach.[10] Although this superiority has been known for many years, the clinical approach continues to be the one most commonly used. This is a surprising circumstance in the light of the widespread utilization of technology in production, finance, and marketing.[11]

There are two major types of statistical methods used in decision making. These are the multiple cutoff method and the multiple regression method.

Multiple Cutoff Method. The **multiple cutoff method**, sometimes referred to as the **successive hurdles method**, requires the applicant to clear in succession several hurdles (tests, interviews, etc.) in the selection process. At each hurdle the applicant is permitted to go on to the next hurdle or is rejected, depending upon whether or not he or she qualified at that hurdle. The hurdles are arranged in the order of their effectiveness in predicting the success or failure of an applicant in a particular job. Under this method only those applicants who successfully meet the established requirements at each of the hurdles are hired.

Multiple Regression Method. The **multiple regression method**, like the multiple cutoff method, is based on analyses of the manner in which the information obtained (i.e., test scores, interview ratings, and application-blank items) is related to success on the job.[12] The major difference between this method and the multiple

9. Frank J. Landy and Don A. Trumbo, *Psychology of Work Behavior* (rev. ed.; Homewood, IL: The Dorsey Press, 1980), pp. 186–196.

10. P. E. Meehl, *Clinical v. Statistical Prediction* (Minneapolis: University of Minnesota Press, 1954); and J. Sawyer, "Measurement *and* Prediction, Clinical *and* Statistical," *Psychological Bulletin*, Vol. 66, No. 3 (September, 1966), pp. 178–200.

11. Charles F. Schanie and William L. Holley, "An Interpretative Review of the Federal Uniform Guidelines on Employee Selection Procedures," *Personnel Administrator*, Vol. 25, No. 6 (June, 1980), pp. 44–48.

12. Standard computer programs are readily available for computing multiple regressions and other formulas that are used in personnel selection programs.

cutoff method is that the multiple regression method requires the applicant to go through the entire selection process in order to obtain complete data. These data, which are usually reduced to scores, are then combined. If the combined score is above the level needed to qualify, the applicant is hired; otherwise that person is rejected. Unlike the multiple cutoff method, this method is based on the assumption that strength in one ability may compensate for inadequacy in another.[13]

Cutoff Scores.   The use of a statistical approach requires that a decision be made about that point in the distribution of scores above which a person should be considered and below which the person should be rejected. The score that the applicant must achieve is the **cutoff score**. Depending upon the labor supply, it may be necessary to lower or raise the cutoff score.

The effects of raising and lowering the cutoff score are illustrated in Figure 7–5. Each dot in the center of the figure represents the relationship between the test score (or a weighted combination of test scores) and the criterion of success for one individual. In this instance, the test has a fairly high validity as represented by the

Figure 7–5   A Scatterplot Showing the Relationship Between Test Scores and the Criterion with Hypothetical Cutoffs Indicated

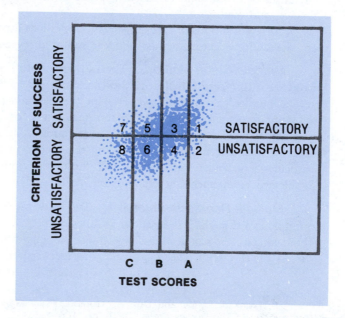

13. Regardless of the method that is used, cross-validation is essential. Cross-validation is a process in which a test or test battery is administered to a different sample (drawn from the same population) for the purpose of verifying the results obtained from the original validation study.

elliptical pattern of dots. Note that the high-scoring individuals are concentrated in the satsifactory category on job success, whereas the low-scoring individuals are concentrated in the unsatisfactory category.

If the cutoff score is set at A, only the individuals represented by areas 1 and 2 will be accepted. Nearly all of them will be successful. If more employees are needed (i.e., increasing the selection ratio), the cutoff score may be lowered to point B. In this case a larger number of potential failures will be accepted. Even when the cutoff score is lowered to C, the total number of satisfactory individuals selected (represented by the dots in areas 1, 3, and 5) is in excess of the total number selected who are unsatisfactory (areas 2, 4, and 6). Thus the test serves to maximize the selection of probable successes and to minimize the selection of probable failures. This is all that we can hope for in predicting job success: the probability of selecting a greater proportion of individuals who will be successful rather than unsuccessful.

Sometimes a test is valid for several groups. However, using the same cutoff score for a particular group may not be justified. This is illustrated by a test in which the test scores of blacks in the 50-60 range are predictive of criterion scores of 75, while the same level of job performance is predicted for whites with test scores of 70-80. This use of differential cutoffs for the same level of criterion performance is known as **differential validity**. The use of different cutoffs does not favor any group as long as an equivalent level of job performance is predicted.

The Final Decision

After a preliminary selection has been made in the employment department, those applicants who appear to be most promising are then referred to departments having vacancies. There they are interviewed by the managers or supervisors of these departments who usually make the final decision and communicate it to the employment department.

Notifying applicants of the decision and making job offers is generally the responsibility of the human resources department. This department should confirm the details of the job, working arrangements, wages, etc., and specify a time limit in which the applicant must reach a decision.

In government agencies the selection of individuals to fill position vacancies is made from lists or registers of eligible candidates. Ordinarily three or more names of individuals at the top of the register are submitted to the requisitioning official. This arrangement provides some latitude in making a selection and, at the same time, preserves the merit system.

LEGAL REQUIREMENTS THAT SHAPE SELECTION POLICIES

Each function in a program of human resources management should be performed according to established policies that reflect the philosophy of the organization. Prior to the passage of the Civil Rights Act of 1964, employers were essentially free to establish their own hiring policies.[14] Since 1964, employers have been compelled to develop selection policies that incorporate the body of laws, executive orders, regulations, and court decisions (case law) designed to end job discrimination. This section of the chapter will emphasize the role of these legal requirements in shaping selection policies.

It should be emphasized that intentional or overt discrimination in employment has been unlawful since the passage of the Civil Rights Act of 1866 and 1871. The Civil Rights Act of 1964, however, not only reaffirmed the unlawfulness of overt discrimination but also made it unlawful for an employer to use personnel practices that, while unintentional, nevertheless limit the employment and advancement opportunities of applicants and employees.

While only federal requirements will be discussed, the reader should always keep in mind the fact that an organization will also be responsible for complying with state and local laws governing employment. Fair employment practice statutes are found in nearly every state and are often more comprehensive than the federal laws. For example, state laws may cover very small firms normally excluded under federal law, or expand protection to include certain groups such as homosexuals or ex-convicts. They may also prohibit certain practices such as the use of lie detector tests in personnel decisions.[15]

Major Federal Laws

As early as the nineteenth century the public was aware of discriminatory employment practices in the United States. However, little was done about it until the 1960s. In 1963, the Equal Pay Act was passed. In the same year, President Kennedy formally proposed civil rights legislation that contained provisions outlawing employment discrimination, which became law in 1964. Subsequent laws (see Figure 7–6) have strengthened the provisions of the Civil Rights Act of 1964.

Equal Pay Act of 1963. The Equal Pay Act is designed to outlaw discrimination in pay based upon the sex of the worker. It covers employees engaged in interstate commerce and most employees of federal, state, and local governments. This law will be examined in the discussion of compensation management in Chapter 17.

Civil Rights Act of 1964. Title VII of the Civil Rights Act of 1964 expressly prohibits discrimination in employment on the basis of race, color, religion, sex, or national origin. It also created an Equal Employment Opportunity Commission (EEOC) to assist in implementing its provisions. An amendment to the act, known as the Tower Amendment to Title VII, expressly permitted the use of professionally

---

14. There were some restrictions by federal executive order in the case of government contracts beginning with the New Deal legislation in the 1930s. State fair employment practices committees also made recommendations, but no enforcement power was provided.

15. Terry L. Leap, William H. Holley, Jr., and Hubert S. Field, "Equal Employment Opportunity and Its Implications for Personnel Practices in the 1980s," *Labor Law Journal*, Vol. 31, No. 11 (November, 1980), pp. 669–782.

Figure 7–6 Major Laws Affecting Selection Policies

Equal Pay Act of 1963	Requires all employers covered by the Fair Labor Standards Act and others to provide equal pay for equal work, regardless of sex.
Title VII of Civil Rights Act of 1964	Prohibits discrimination in employment on the basis of race, color, religion, sex, or national origin. Created the Equal Employment Opportunity Commission to enforce the provisions of Title VII.
Age Discrimination in Employment Act of 1967	Prohibits private and public employers from discriminating against a person 40 to 70 years of age in any area of employment because of age. Exceptions are permitted where age is a bona fide occupational qualification.
Equal Employment Opportunity Act of 1972	Amended Title VII of Civil Rights Act of 1964. Strengthens EEOC's enforcement powers and extends coverage of Title VII to government employees, faculty in higher education, and other employers and employees.
Pregnancy Discrimination Act of 1978	Broadens the definition of sex discrimination to include pregnancy, childbirth, or related medical conditions. Prohibits employers from discriminating against pregnant women in employment benefits if they are capable of performing their job duties.

developed ability tests. However, there were numerous questions concerning the appropriateness of specific testing procedures for personnel decisions. Public policy was shaped by the guidelines covering the use of tests and other selection devices that were drawn up by the Office of Federal Contract Compliance Programs (OFCCP) and the Equal Employment Opportunity Commission (EEOC). The Supreme Court ruling in the case of *Griggs v. Duke Power Company* is particularly important because of the ruling that selection tests and other types of information used in selection must be job-related.

Age Discrimination in Employment Act of 1967. The Age Discrimination in Employment Act (ADEA) prohibits certain employers from discriminating against a person 40 to 70 years old in any area of employment, including selection, because of age. These employers are those with 20 or more employees, unions with 25 or more members, employment agencies, and the federal, state, and local governments. Exceptions are permitted, however, where age is a **bona fide occupational qualification (BFOQ)**. For example, an older person could legitimately be excluded from consideration for employment as a model for teenager designer jeans. The ADEA, however, does provide a comprehensive framework to protect elderly employees.

Equal Employment Opportunity Act of 1972. In 1972 the Civil Rights Act was amended by the Equal Employment Opportunity Act. This amendment changed Title VII to cover all private employers of 15 or more persons, all public and private educational institutions, state and local governments, public and private employment agencies, labor unions, and joint labor-management committees for apprenticeship and training. The Equal Employment Opportunity Act also strengthened the enforcement powers of the EEOC by allowing it to go directly to court to enforce the law. Regional litigation centers were established with substantial legal staffs to provide more rapid and effective court action.

Pregnancy Discrimination Act of 1978. Prior to the passage of the Pregnancy Discrimination Act, pregnant women could be forced to resign or take a leave of absence because of pregnancy. In addition, employers did not have to provide disability or medical coverage for pregnancy. The Pregnancy Discrimination Act amends the Civil Rights Act of 1964 by stating that pregnancy is a disability and that pregnant employees must receive the same benefits as individuals with any other disability.

Other Federal Laws and Executive Orders

Since the major laws affecting equal employment do not cover *agencies* of the federal government and since state laws do not apply to federal employees, it has been necessary for the President to issue executive orders to protect federal employees. Executive orders are also used to provide equal employment opportunity to individuals who are employed by government contractors. The federal laws and executive orders that are applicable to government agencies and government contractors are shown in Figure 7–7. Since many companies have contracts and subcontracts with the federal government, managers must comply with the provisions of the listed executive orders as well as the laws.

Judicial Interpretations

The responsibility for interpreting equal employment opportunity laws rests with the courts. While the lower courts play an important role in the legal process, the Supreme Court of the United States is the predominant influence in interpreting Title VII, other antidiscrimination laws, regulations, and the *Uniform Guidelines*. The human resources manager must constantly be alert to new court decisions and be prepared to implement the rulings. In the limited space available in this text, it is possible to cite only the more important or landmark decisions of the United States Supreme Court. These are listed in Figure 7–8. On the job, the human resources manager should be in regular communication with the legal counsel and/or sources of information that are available on a subscription basis from The Bureau of National Affairs, Inc., Commerce Clearing House, and Prentice-Hall, Inc.

Figure 7–7   **Equal Employment Opportunity Laws and Executive Orders Applicable to Agencies of and Contractors with the Federal Government**

Vocational Rehabilitation Act of 1973	Provides for federal funding of rehabilitation services for handicapped persons and requires affirmative action in their employment by covered federal government contractors.
Vietnam Era Veterans Readjustment Assistance Act of 1974	Requires firms holding federal contracts or subcontracts of $50,000 or more to take affirmative action to hire and advance Vietnam-era veterans.
Executive Order 11141 (1964)	Prohibits discrimination in employment on the basis of age.
Executive Order 11246 (1965) as amended by Executive Order 11375 (1966)	Prohibits discrimination on the basis of race, color, religion, sex, or national origin. Establishes Office of Federal Contract Compliance Programs (OFCCP).
Executive Order 11478 (1969)	Prohibits discrimination in government agencies and the Postal Service on the basis of race, color, religion, sex, national origin, handicap, or age.

Uniform Guidelines on Employee Selection Procedures

In the past, employers frequently have been uncertain about the appropriateness of specific selection procedures, especially those relating to testing. Although some guidelines were available in the mid-1960s, it was not until 1970 that a comprehensive statement was issued. The current *Uniform Guidelines on Employee Selection Procedures* (1978) has become a very important procedural manual for managers of human resources.[16] It is designed to assist employers, labor organizations, employment agencies, and licensing and certification boards to comply with the requirements of federal laws prohibiting discriminatory practices.

Essentially the *Uniform Guidelines* require that an employer be able to demonstrate that the selection procedures used are valid in predicting or measuring performance in a particular job. The guidelines also define discrimination as follows:

---

16. Equal Employment Opportunity Commission, Civil Service Commission, Department of Labor, and Department of Justice, *Adoption by Four Agencies of Uniform Guidelines on Employee Selection Procedures* (1978), as reproduced in the *Federal Register*, Vol. 43, No. 166 (August 25, 1978), pp. 38290–38315. Discussion relating to the adoption of the *Uniform Guidelines* by the four agencies comprises several pages. The *Uniform Guidelines* are published on pages 38295–38309. Further clarification and expansion on the *Guidelines* may be found in the *Federal Register*, Vol. 44, No. 43 (March 2, 1979), pp. 11996–12009.

Figure 7–8   A Sample of Landmark Cases Relating to AA/EEO in Selection Procedures

Griggs *v.* Duke Power Company (1971)	Job requirements must be related to success on the job. The burden of proof is on the employer to show that a hiring standard is job-related. Under Title VII good intent or absence of intent to discriminate is not sufficient defense.
McDonnell Douglas Corporation *v.* Green (1973)	An employee can establish a prima facie case of intentional discrimination by initially showing (1) that he or she was a member of a racial minority; (2) that he or she applied and was qualified in an opening for which the employer sought applicants; (3) that despite qualifications he or she was rejected; and (4) that after rejection the position remained open and the employer continued to seek applicants. In this case blacks were treated differently (disparate treatment).
Albemarle Paper Company *v.* Moody (1975)	EEOC Guidelines are entitled to great deference as an administrative interpretation of Title VII. More stringent requirements are placed on employers to demonstrate job-relatedness of tests. Employers would be financially penalized for Title VII violations even if they acted in good faith.
Regents of the U. of California *v.* Bakke (1978)	Most famous of the reverse discrimination cases. Involves medical school admission rather than employment. The decision was approving of affirmative-action programs where prior discrimination has been established. Allows race to be considered in selection decisions.
United Steelworkers of America *v.* Weber, *et al* (1979)	Nothing contained in Title VII shall be interpreted to require any employer to grant preferential treatment to any group or race to correct racial imbalances in the work force. However, Kaiser-USWA Plan is consistent with Title VII which permits voluntary efforts to correct racial imbalances.
Fullilove *v.* Klutznick (1980)	Racial quotas are constitutional if they are imposed directly by Congress to remedy past discrimination and are kept flexible and temporary.
Burdine *v.* Texas Department of Community Affairs (1981)	Clarified the burden of proof in individual Title VII cases. Employer need only articulate, not prove, it had a legitimate reason for an employment decision that appears to result in disparate treatment. Employer need not prove one applicant's qualifications were superior to another in order to justify an employment decision.

The use of any selection procedure which has an adverse impact on the hiring, promotion, or other employment or membership opportunities of members of any race, sex, or ethnic group will be considered to be discriminatory and inconsistent with these guidelines, unless the procedure has been validated in accordance with these guidelines (or, certain other provisions are satisfied.)[17]

Adverse Impact. For an applicant or employee to pursue a discrimination case successfully, it must be established that the employer's selection procedures result in an adverse impact on a protected group. **Adverse impact** refers to a significantly higher percentage of a protected group in the population under consideration which is being rejected for employment, placement, or promotion.[18]

There are three ways that adverse impact can be shown:

1. *Disparate rejection rates.* According to the *Uniform Guidelines*, a selection program has an adverse impact when the selection rate for any racial, ethnic, or sex group is less than four-fifths (or 80 percent) of the rate of the group with the highest selection rate. Thus, if 100 out of 500 white applicants are selected (20 percent), at least 16 percent of minority applicants (80 percent of 20 percent) should be selected.

2. *Restricted policy.* Any evidence that an employer has a selection procedure that excludes members of a protected group, whether intentional or not, constitutes adverse impact.

3. *Population comparisons.* This involves comparing the percentage of protected-group employees in an organization with the percentage of that group in the general population of the surrounding community.

While the *Uniform Guidelines* do not require an employer to conduct validity studies of selection procedures where no adverse impact exists, they do encourage employers to use selection procedures which are valid. Organizations that have validated their selection procedures on a regular basis and have used interviews, tests, and other procedures in such a manner as to avoid adverse impact will generally be in compliance with the principles of equal employment legislation. Affirmative-action programs also reflect on employer intent. The motivation for using valid selection procedures, however, should be the desire to achieve effective management of human resources rather than the fear of legal pressure.

Handling Charges of Adverse Impact. The plaintiff has the burden of showing that adverse impact exists. Once the court has established the presence of adverse impact, the burden shifts to the employer (defendant) who has to prove that the selection procedure is significantly job-related. As the term implies, *job-related* refers to the requirement that the employer must show that its selection procedures are related to success on the job. Documented evidence that shows findings from validity studies, or documented evidence showing why a validity study cannot or need not be performed and why continued use of the procedure is consistent with federal law, is required.

---

17. *Uniform Guidelines*, Sec. 3A.
18. *Ibid.*, Sec. 4D. Adverse impact need not be considered for groups which constitute less than 2 percent of the relevant labor force.

Bottom-Line Concept. The 1978 revision of the *Uniform Guidelines* introduced the **bottom-line concept**, which specifies that an employer is not required to evaluate each component of the selection process individually. However, the end result of the selection process must be predictive of future job performance if adverse impact is present. The *Guidelines* also require that employers consider alternative selection devices if adverse impact is present and maintain detailed records from which adverse impact can be detected.

Legal Defenses Against Discriminatory Charges. In some instances an employer may legitimately use the defenses of (1) business necessity, or (2) bona fide occupational qualification (BFOQ) in response to allegations of discriminatory practices. **Business necessity** has been interpreted by the court as a practice that is necessary to the safe and efficient operation of the business. A bona fide occupational qualification is a suitable defense only in those instances where religion, sex, age, or national origin is a BFOQ. Religion for example, is a BFOQ in religious organizations that require employees to share a particular religion.

Affirmative-Action Programs and Reverse Discrimination.

In Chapter 5 the steps in developing an affirmative-action program were outlined. As noted in Figure 7–7, affirmative-action programs are required by the Office of Federal Contract Compliance Programs (OFCCP) of employers who have federal contracts greater than $50,000. The OFCCP has the power to terminate lucrative government contracts and thus can usually obtain broader and more immediate results than the EEOC. Since there are over 29,000 employers who contract with the federal government, the OFCCP is a major force in AA/EEO compliance.[19]

These programs may also be required by a federal court where an employer has been found guilty of past discrimination. Many employers wisely develop their own affirmative-action programs to insure that women and members of minority groups receive fair treatment in all aspects of employment.

In pursuing affirmative-action efforts, employers may be accused of **reverse discrimination** which refers to giving preference to members of protected groups to the extent that unprotected groups believe that they are suffering from discrimination. Two lawsuits that went to the Supreme Court of the United States introduced the question of reverse discrimination. The first case involved medical school admission rather than employment. Allan Bakke, a white male, was denied admission to medical school even though he scored higher on admission criteria than some minority members who were accepted. The court ruled in Bakke's favor. At the same time it reaffirmed that race could be considered in selection decisions.[20]

A later case involved Brian Weber, a white, male employee of Kaiser Aluminum and Chemical Company, who sued after he was allegedly denied a place in an on-the-job training program exclusively because of his race. The lower courts

19. E. Richard Larson, *Sue Your Boss—Rights and Remedies for Employment Discrimination* (New York: Farrar, Straus, Giroux, 1981), p. xxi.

20. 438 US 265 (1978).

ruled that Kaiser's actions were illegal because they fostered reverse discrimination. The Supreme Court reversed its decisions and ruled that the Kaiser-USWA plan is consistent with Title VII which permits voluntary efforts to correct racial imbalances.[21] These decisions appear to support affirmative-action programs.

Testing and Discrimination

There have been many charges that employment tests may have been used, inadvertently or deliberately, as instruments of discrimination. The now famous Motorola case in which a black applicant was awarded compensation in connection with failure to pass an employment test has served to focus attention on the whole topic of employment testing, especially where disadvantaged persons are concerned.[22] As Figure 7–8 on page 170 shows, the enforcement activities of the EEOC and OFCCP, the publication of the *Uniform Guidelines on Employee Selection Procedures,* the *Griggs v. Duke Power Company* case ruling, and a whole array of subsequent court decisions have all had profound effects on employment testing.[23]

The number of hours devoted to understanding and complying with federal requirements for testing programs is astronomical. Personnel directors, test specialists, attorneys, government officials, and representatives of a number of professional organizations, such as the American Psychological Association, the International Personnel Management Association, and others, have found this issue to require a significant portion of their time. The legal requirements for testing are probably the primary cause for decline in the use of tests.[24]

Tests and testing programs present special problems for personnel administrators. In the first place, many individuals have negative feelings about tests as a result of previous experiences with them, especially in schools. If they are then required to take tests that appear to be unrelated to the job, or that contain questions that are unnecessarily vague or complicated, their response is predictable. Claims that they are being discriminated against are to be expected.

There are many factors that may contribute to a test being discriminatory or being viewed that way. It should be recognized that disadvantaged persons, as a group, score lower on many aptitude tests as a result of cultural deprivation. Disadvantaged persons may score poorly on tests partly because of anxiety resulting from their lack of familiarity with the testing situation, as well as the fact that tests are administered by persons representing more advantaged backgrounds. Poor testing conditions in terms of space, lighting, and freedom from noise can contribute to anxiety and should be avoided.

---

21. 443 US 193 (1979).
22. Myart *v.* Motorola, FEP Commission, State of Illinois, 1964.
23. Another document designed to provide professional guidance for testing programs that has received increasing recognition by the courts is *Principles for the Validation and Use of Personnel Selection Procedures* (2d ed.; Berkeley, CA: American Psychological Association, Division of Industrial-Organizational Psychology, 1980). This publication may be obtained from the APA, 1200 Seventeenth Street, Washington, DC 20036.
24. Mary L. Tenopyr, "The Realities of Employment Testing," *American Psychologist*, Vol. 36, No. 10 (October, 1981), pp. 1120–1127.

In addition, test administration should not be delegated to someone who views it as an unwanted and annoying interruption. Such an individual can contribute to the unreliability of the test and possibly even cause legal action to be taken by examinees.

Finally, many paper-and-pencil tests emphasize material to which disadvantaged persons may never have been exposed. If paper-and-pencil tests are used, the vocabulary requirement should be appropriate for the job. The use of shorter sentences, the elimination of unnecessary verbiage in the tests, and the development of more simplified instructions are recommended.

The Future of EEO in the Courts

For two decades the courts have become involved in almost every aspect of the selection process. Some trends are now emerging that deserve our attention. Arvey offers a few predictions of possible court activity in the future. These predictions can serve to guide human resources specialists in their activities.

1. The courts are likely to give more interpretative "weight" to the 1978 *Uniform Guidelines on Employee Selection Procedures*. These latest guidelines present a more representative point of view than the 1970 version.
2. The courts are likely to deal with more litigation involving employment discrimination against the handicapped and elderly.
3. The courts will exhibit an increased statistical knowledge and sophistication. The use of statistics in establishing a case of adverse impact has received considerable attention.
4. Content validity will be used more frequently.
5. The impact of "reverse discrimination" suits is likely to have a significant effect on selection procedures. More pressure will be placed on organizations to ensure the validity of selection procedures.[25]

OTHER CONSIDERATIONS THAT SHAPE SELECTION POLICIES

In addition to having policy statements that are consistent with AA/EEO requirements, it is desirable to have statements covering other important aspects of selection. In recent years greater attention has been given to the impact of recruiting and selection policies upon society.

Ethical Considerations

The selection process involves procedures that should be examined from an ethical, as well as a legal, standpoint. Application blanks, for example, frequently ask for information that may be construed as an invasion of privacy. The same is true of certain tests, particularly personality inventories.

Questions pertaining to personal habits, attitudes about sex, etc., are considered

25. Richard D. Arvey, *Fairness in Selecting Employees* (Reading, MA: Addison-Wesley Publishing Co., 1979), pp. 225–228.

to be an unwarranted invasion of the applicant's rights to privacy. During Congressional hearings concerning the use of tests in government agencies, however, it was argued that individual rights were not being violated because an applicant or employee consented to take the tests. Even so, the validity of this argument was questioned on the basis that individuals can hardly be said to consent voluntarily when they know they will probably not be hired if they do not submit to testing. Furthermore, consent is meaningless unless the examinees understand what consent entails. The same reasoning could be applied to personality testing for nongovernmental jobs.[26]

In view of the special knowledge and understanding required to use personality tests, it is recommended that they be used only upon the advice of a professional test consultant and that the fundamental question be asked: "How is performance on the test related to job success?"[27]

Other sources of information used in selection, such as that gained by means of the polygraph (lie detector), the voice analyzer, peepholes, see-through mirrors, hidden cameras, and recorders have come under severe attack because they tend to invade the applicant's privacy. The use of these devices is not only considered unethical, but also is restricted or outlawed in several states. Finally, the ethical handling of personnel matters requires that confidentiality be demanded of all individuals who have access to private information and that the security of personnel files be strictly enforced.[28]

Consideration for the Physically Handicapped

As a result of the success that has been experienced in the employment of handicapped persons, the slogan "Hire the handicapped—it's good business" has become a standard policy for many organizations. This slogan does not suggest that handicapped persons can be placed in any job without giving careful consideration to their disabilities, but rather that it is good business to hire qualified persons who can work safely and productively. Members of the personnel staff should be trained in the assessment of individual types and degrees of limitations and be aware of how these restrictions are related to different jobs in the organization. In many cases, as noted in Chapter 4, the restructuring of jobs or the use of special equipment permits handicapped persons to qualify for employment.

Consideration for Other Groups

In an effort to assume a greater responsibility for alleviating some of society's problems, many organizations have established policies relating to the employment of individuals with special needs such as those who have been released from

---

26. John H. Kirkwood, "Selection Techniques and the Law: To Test or Not to Test," *Personnel*, Vol. 44, No. 6 (November-December, 1967), pp. 18–26.
27. Christopher Orpen, "The 'Correct' Use of Personality Tests: A View from Industrial Psychology," *Public Personnel Management*, Vol. 3, No. 3 (May-June, 1974), pp. 228–229.
28. For detailed instructions on security of personnel offices, see Ed San Luis, *Office Building Security* (New York: Security World Publishing Company, 1973).

confinement in prison. These individuals typically need assistance of many types, but probably none is more important to them than help in getting a job. Policies concerning the hiring of individuals with such backgrounds can be established and administered effectively.[29]

Cost-Benefit Considerations

The costs of a selection program often constitute a major portion of the human resources department's budget. The achievement of the program is dependent upon trained and experienced professionals, as well as upon a staff of clerical and administrative personnel whose salaries constitute a major part of its cost. As with other functions, there will be overhead costs plus shared costs for such requirements as legal assistance and computer time. However, the benefits to be derived from a well-organized and efficiently managed selection program far exceed the costs. Applicants who are carefully screened against job requirements and organizational needs are generally found to be easier to train, more productive, and better able to assume responsible roles in the organization. A strong, competent work force will minimize the costs that are associated with inefficiency, waste, turnover, accidents, and similar problems. The best way to achieve it is through an effective selection program.

RÉSUMÉ

For decades employers have been urged to validate their tests. In the past two decades, however, validation has become a requirement, especially where adverse impact has been found to exist. Each of the different types of validity has its place in the selection process. Increasing selectivity by adjusting the selection ratio was shown as a way of maximizing the effects of obtained validity.

In the process of making selection decisions, all *can do* and *will do* factors should be assembled and weighted systematically in order that the final decision may be based upon a composite of the most reliable and valid information. While the clinical approach to decision making is used more than the statistical approach, it lacks the accuracy of the latter approach. Whichever approach is used, the best that can be hoped for is the probability of selecting a greater proportion of individuals who will be successful rather than unsuccessful on the job.

Since 1964, selection policies have been influenced more and more by equal and fair employment laws and court decisions. Employers are responsible for creating personnel policies and procedures that will be consistent with the various antidiscriminatory requirements. Avoiding adverse impact is possible through a program of validation and affirmative action for those groups who have in the past been treated unfairly.

---

29. Richard A. Schaffer, "Erasing the Past—Effort Grows to Assist Job Hunters Haunted by Criminal Records," *The Wall Street Journal*, November 13, 1973. *See also* George H. Ebbs and Bert C. Shlensky, "Want to Cut Crime Costs? Hire the Ex-Offender," *The Personnel Administrator*, Vol. 19, No. 2 (March–April, 1974), pp. 15–19.

TERMS TO IDENTIFY

content validity
construct validity
criterion-related validity
criterion
concurrent validity
predictive validity
validity coefficient
expectancy chart
synthetic validity or job component validity
selection ratio
"can do" factors
"will do" factors

clinical approach to decision making
statistical approach to decision making
multiple cutoff method
successive hurdles method
multiple regression method
cutoff score
differential validity
bona fide occupational qualification (BFOQ)
adverse impact
bottom-line concept
business necessity
reverse discrimination

DISCUSSION QUESTIONS

1. What is meant by the term "criterion" as it is used in personnel selection? Give some examples of criteria used for jobs with which you are familiar.
2. What type of information is provided by expectancy charts? What cautions should be observed in using the data that they provide?
3. Explain the basic difference between the two major types of statistical methods used in decision-making. Could both methods be used in selecting individuals for a job?
4. Cite some of the major laws and court decisions that have affected the personnel selection process.
5. What is meant by adverse impact? How is it revealed?
6. The burden of proof is placed on employers to show their selection procedures have not resulted in unlawful discrimination against a particular group.
   a. What steps should an employer take to avoid such charges?
   b. What types of records should be kept to refute such charges?
7. A battery of tests was administered to a group of employees who had been told that the tests were for experimental purposes only. At a later date, after the tests had been proved to be valid, the personnel manager ordered that the scores be entered on the employees' records. What is your opinion of the personnel manager's decision?
8. It was mentioned in this chapter that disadvantaged persons often obtain low scores on employment tests.
   a. What is meant by a disadvantaged person?
   b. What causes many of them to obtain low scores on tests?
   c. Are there any characteristics of a paper-and-pencil test that may discriminate unfairly against a disadvantaged person?
   d. What can be done to overcome this problem immediately? In the future?

PROBLEM 7–1

TESTING THE TESTERS

Every year thousands of individuals are rejected for jobs on the basis of scores made on aptitude and ability tests of the paper-and-pencil, multiple-choice type. Many of these individuals sincerely believe that they could perform the tasks on the job in spite of their unsatisfactory test scores. As one union shop steward stated, "These tests don't give a guy a chance. So many people just get cut off from jobs right at the start. I know guys who freeze up on tests, but up in the plant with the hard tools they're brilliant."

After ten of its members failed to get acceptable scores on tests to qualify for better skilled jobs with Detroit Edison, the Utility Workers of America decided to take their case to the National Labor Relations Board. Union leaders argued that: "All we want is to police these tests. We can police everything else. If they tell us a guy's been absent too often, they've got to show us. But if they tell us a guy failed the psychological tests, right now we've got no choice but to believe them." The National Labor Relations Board voted to order Detroit Edison to give the union copies of its tests and scores so that the union could determine the extent to which questions were asked that called for knowledge beyond the job requirements. The NLRB ordered the union officials not to release copies of the tests to past or future test-takers.

The decision was challenged by Detroit Edison, and the case went to the 6th United States Court of Appeals that upheld the NLRB decision. The 6th Circuit Court decision was then appealed to the United States Supreme Court. In an *amicus* brief, the American Psychological Association and the United States Chamber of Commerce suggested that the entire future of psychological testing would hang on the outcome of the case. They asserted that disclosure of tests to persons with no professional obligation to protect their security will destroy the validity of the tests. They also feared that private companies would stop spending the money necessary to develop new tests if unions can readily obtain copies of them.

In a 5–4 decision, the Supreme Court ruled in March, 1979, that the union's insistence that it needs information to process an employee's grievance "does not automatically oblige the employer to supply all the information in the manner requested." The majority also found that "the union's guarantee that the tests and score results would be kept confidential and not reproduced" does not adequately protect the security of the tests. They also agreed that the union "should not be permitted to invade the individual employees' interest in the confidentiality of test results without their consent."

a. How valid is the union's argument that it should have access to the tests used for promotion to higher-level jobs?

b. How far should the company go in protecting information, including test scores, concerning individual employees?

c. Is it likely that the security of tests would be jeopardized if the union has access to them? How could the security objection of the psychologists be handled?

d. Do you believe that the issues raised have been completely resolved by the court's decision?

SUGGESTED READINGS

Anastasi, Anne. *Psychological Testing*, 5th ed. New York: The Macmillan Company, 1982.

Chruden, Herbert J., and Arthur W. Sherman, Jr. *Readings in Managing Human Resources*, 6th ed. Cincinnati: South-Western Publishing Co., 1984. Part 2.

Cronbach, Lee J. *Essentials of Psychological Testing*, 3d ed. New York: Harper and Row, 1970.

Lemke, Elmer, and William Wiersma. *Principles of Psychological Measurement*. Chicago: Rand McNally College Publishing Co., 1976.

Siegel, Jerome. *Personnel Testing Under EEO*. New York: AMACOM, 1980.

Developing Effectiveness in Human Resources

part 3

Chapter Objectives:

- To cite some of the characteristics of an effective orientation program.
- To understand the scope of organizational training programs.
- To identify and describe the three phases of the systems approach to training.
- To identify the types of training methods used primarily with nonmanagerial personnel, as well as the most effective use of each method.
- To know the different types of training methods for developing managers.
- To identify the preconditions for and the basic principles of learning.

8

Training Employees

The functions of recruiting and selecting human resources are only the initial stages in building an effective work force. Managers, supervisors, and employees also require training and continual development if their potential is to be utilized effectively. The training of human resources, in fact, should be viewed as beginning with their orientation and continuing throughout their employment with the organization.

Human resources training has become increasingly vital to the success of modern organizations. Rapidly changing technology requires that employees possess the knowledge and skills necessary to cope with new processes and production techniques. The growth of organizations into large, complex operations whose structures are continually changing makes it necessary for managers, as well as employees, to be prepared for new and more demanding assignments.

There has been a definite trend in recent years for organizations to take a broader view of human resources by creating career development programs. Such programs involve attempts to develop the employee's career in a way that will benefit both the organization and the individual. Special attention will be given to those programs in the next chapter.

In this chapter the emphasis will be on such functions as the orientation of employees, the design and evaluation of training programs, training methods, and the application of learning theory. To understand the interrelationship between training programs and other human resources functions, the reader should study the model in Figure 8–1.

ORIENTATION

The first step in the training process is to get new personnel off to a good start. This is generally accomplished through a formal orientation program. The orientation or induction program should provide new employees with an understanding of how job performance contributes to the success of the organization and how the services or products of the organization can contribute to society.

The type and amount of information that employees will need will vary with the job. However, it is customary to initially provide information about matters of immediate concern to them, such as working hours, pay, and parking facilities. New employees should have a clear understanding of safety rules, security requirements, and any other important matters. Later on, attention may be devoted to informing them about those areas that have a lower priority and/or that require more time for presentation and comprehension. Regardless of the type of orientation program, an effective one should be characterized by: a continuous process, a cooperative endeavor, careful planning, and a follow-up and evaluation.

Continuous Process

Since an organization is faced with ever-changing conditions, its plans, policies, and procedures must change with these conditions. Unless present employees are kept up to date on these changes, they may embarrassingly find themselves unaware

Figure 8–1   **Relationship of Training and Development to Other Personnel Functions**

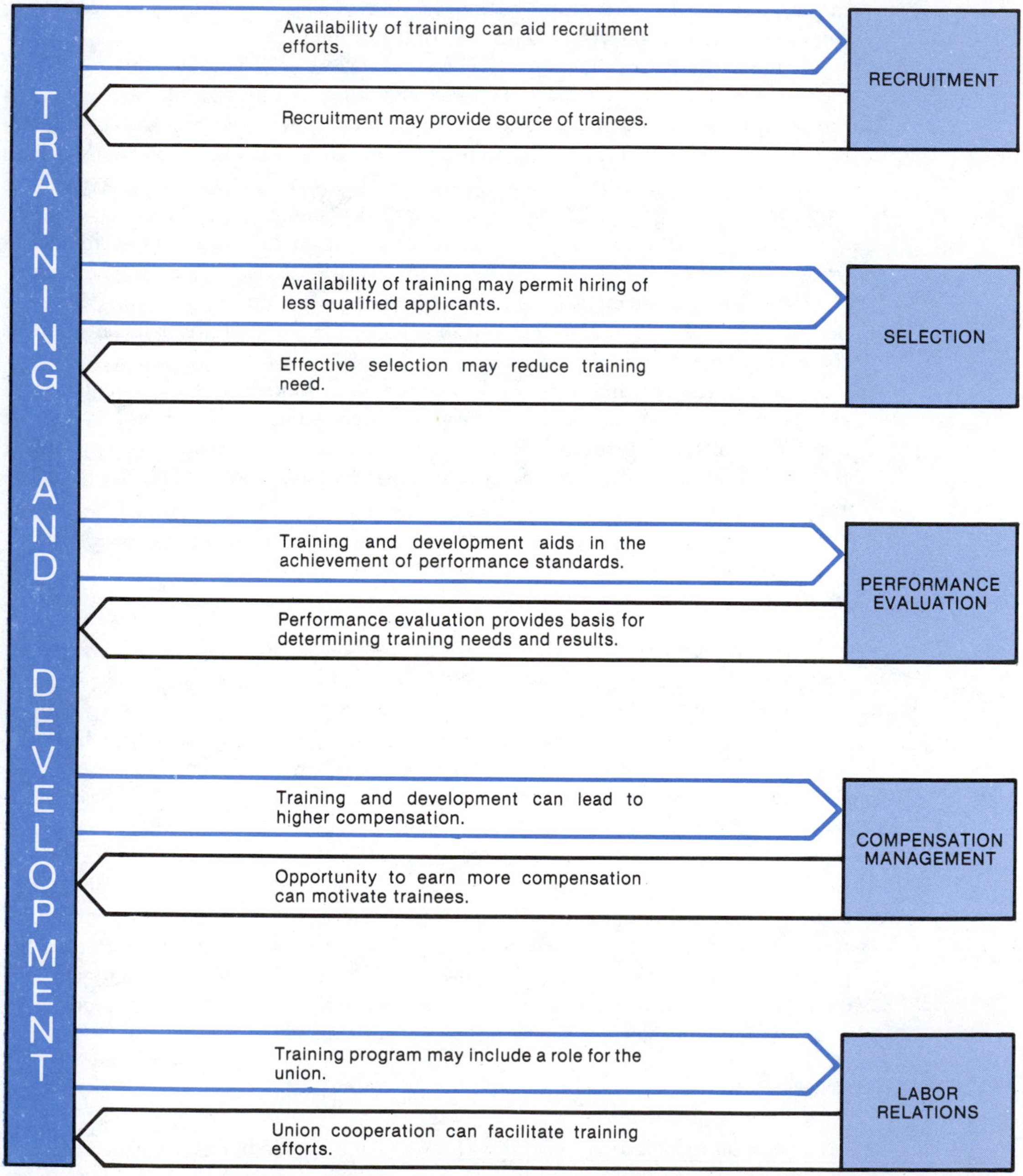

TRAINING AND DEVELOPMENT

Availability of training can aid recruitment efforts.

Recruitment may provide source of trainees.

RECRUITMENT

Availability of training may permit hiring of less qualified applicants.

Effective selection may reduce training need.

SELECTION

Training and development aids in the achievement of performance standards.

Performance evaluation provides basis for determining training needs and results.

PERFORMANCE EVALUATION

Training and development can lead to higher compensation.

Opportunity to earn more compensation can motivate trainees.

COMPENSATION MANAGEMENT

Training program may include a role for the union.

Union cooperation can facilitate training efforts.

LABOR RELATIONS

of activities about which new employees are currently being advised. While the discussion that follows focuses primarily upon the needs of new employees, it is important that *all* employees be continually reoriented to changing conditions.

Cooperative Endeavor

For a well-integrated orientation program, cooperation between line and staff is essential. The human resources department ordinarily is responsible for coordinating orientation activities and for providing new employees with information concerning conditions of employment, pay, benefits, and other areas that are not directly under the supervisor's direction. However, supervisors have the most important role in the orientation program. The new employee is primarily interested in what the boss says and does and what the co-workers are like. Prior to the arrival of the new person, it is desirable for the supervisor to inform the work group that a new employee is coming.

The importance of an employee's first day on the job is well expressed by Meyer as follows:

> Whether it be an assembly line worker, a secretary, or a manager, the first day will always leave a lasting impression. It can be good or bad. For the company, it is a day that presents a unique opportunity to make that impression a good one. It begins with one distinct advantage. A recruit almost always starts a new job with a reserve of goodwill towards the new employer. But that should not lead to complacency. That reservoir can easily be tapped dry within the first few days if the induction program fails to satisfy the needs of the individual.
>
> Confusion and enthusiasm are the two dominant emotions during the new employee's first day at work. A good induction program attempts to diminish the former and foster the latter.[1]

Careful Planning

An orientation program can make an immediate and lasting impression which may mean the difference between an employee's success or failure on the job. Thus, careful planning with emphasis upon program goals, topics to be covered, and methods of organizing and presenting them is essential. Successful programs emphasize the individual's needs for information, understanding, and a feeling of belonging.

Use a Checklist.   To avoid overlooking items that are important to employees, many organizations devise checklists for use by those responsible for conducting some phase of orientation. The use of a checklist in the initial orientation of new employees compels a supervisor to pay more attention to each new employee at a time when personal attentiveness is critical to building a long-term relationship.

---

1. Mary Coeli Meyer, "Six Stages of Demotivation," *International Management*, Vol. 32, No. 4 (April, 1977), pp. 14–17.

Focus on What's Important.   Those who plan orientation programs frequently expect the new employee to assimilate readily all types of detailed and assorted facts about the organization. While there are many things that the new employee should know, most of them can be learned over a period of time and in a series of meetings. Don't greet the person with a canned program about how great the organization is. Instead, the initial emphasis should be on the one-to-one relationships necessary to give a person a sense of belonging. Later on is time enough for the "dog and pony show" about the company, benefits, and other corporate topics.[2]

Develop an Orientation Packet.   Orientation sessions should be supplemented with a packet of materials that new employees can read at their leisure. Some materials that a packet might include are shown in Figure 8–2. Instructions to the employee on how to use the packet are recommended.

Reduce Employee Anxiety.   The planning of an orientation program should take into account findings from a classic study conducted at Texas Instruments. This study showed that for most new employees (1) the first few days on the job are anxious and uncertain ones, (2) "new employee initiation practices" by peers

Figure 8–2   Items for an Orientation Packet

- □ A company organization chart
- □ A projected company organization chart
- □ Map of the facility
- □ Key terms unique to the industry, company and/or job
- □ Copy of policy handbook
- □ Copy of union contract
- □ Copy of specific job goals and descriptions
- □ List of company holidays
- □ List of fringe benefits
- □ Copies of performance evaluation forms, dates, and procedures
- □ Copies of other required forms (e.g., supply requisition and expense reimbursement)
- □ List of on-the-job training opportunities
- □ Sources of information
- □ Detailed outline of emergency and accident-prevention procedures
- □ Sample copy of each important company publication
- □ Telephone numbers and locations of key personnel and operations
- □ Copies of insurance plans

SOURCE: "The Complete Employee Orientation Program," by Walter D. St. John, copyright May 1980. Reprinted with the permission of *Personnel Journal*, Costa Mesa, CA; all rights reserved.

2. Daniel N. Kanouse and Philomena I. Warihay, "A New Look at Employee Orientation," *Training and Development Journal,* Vol. 34, No. 7 (July, 1980), pp. 34–38.

intensify anxiety, and (3) such anxiety interferes with the orientation and training process. To overcome these problems, an experimental group of new employees had no contact with their peer work group but had unlimited opportunities to talk with each other and with company personnel who made informal orientation presentations. It was considered a one-day, anxiety-reduced session. Compared with a control group that did not receive this session, training time, training costs, absenteeism and tardiness, and waste and rejects were lowered remarkably, saving $35,000. Improvement in job performance of the experimental group as compared with the control group represented an additional savings of over $50,000.[3] It would appear that some time spent at the beginning of an orientation period to reduce the anxiety level of the new employees will result in greater productivity and reduced personnel costs.

Another danger of letting employees be oriented by their peers is that unwritten codes of conduct that do not conform to the organization's policies are perpetuated. These informal, unwritten codes of conduct that develop can undermine the organization's formal operating procedures.[4]

Follow-Up and Evaluation

The supervisor should consult with the new employee after the first day and again after the first week on the job. When all of the items on the orientation checklist for the employee have been completed, both the supervisor and the employee should sign it. This record should then be placed in the employee's personnel file. After the employee has been on the job for a month and again at the end of a year, a personnel staff member should follow up to determine the current effectiveness of the orientation. Evaluations can then be conducted through in-depth interviews, unsigned questionnaires and surveys, and discussion groups.[5]

TRAINING PROGRAMS

Many new employees come equipped with most of the knowledge and skills needed to start work. Others may require extensive training before they are ready to make much of a contribution to the organization. A majority, however, at one time or another will require some type of training in order to maintain an effective level of job performance. While training may be accomplished on an informal basis, better results are usually attained through a well-organized, formal training program.

Training may be defined as any procedure initiated by the organization to foster learning among organizational members. The primary purpose of a training program is to help achieve the overall organizational objectives. At the same time, an

---

3. Earl R. Gomersall and M. Scott Myers, "Breakthrough in On-the-Job Training," *Harvard Business Review,* Vol. 44, No. 4 (July-August, 1966), pp. 62–72. Note that the savings reported are in 1966 dollars.

4. George F. Truell, "Tracking Down the 'Aroundhereisms'—or, How To Foil Negative Orientation," *Personnel,* Vol. 58, No. 4 (July-August, 1981), pp. 23–31.

5. Diana Reed-Mendenhall and C. W. Millard, "Orientation: A Training and Development Tool," *Personnel Administrator,* Vol. 25, No. 8 (August, 1980), pp. 40–44.

effective training program must demonstrably contribute to the satisfaction of the trainee's personal goals.[6]

Scope of Training Programs

The primary purpose of training at the beginning of an individual's employment is to bring the knowledge and skills required for effective performance up to a satisfactory level. As the individual continues on the job, training provides opportunities to acquire new knowledge and skills. As a result of the training, the individual may then be more effective on the job and may qualify for jobs at a higher level.

Automation has had a major impact on training programs. Training is now even more important for the reasons that (1) some jobs will be enlarged, thereby requiring additional skills and knowledge, (2) others will require a narrower range of skills, and (3) many jobs will be replaced entirely by newly created jobs. *Business Week* forecasts the following great changes ahead:

> . . . U.S. industry is beginning to automate at a pace that will soon change the face of American factories and offices. Within reach are computer-controlled systems of robots and other sophisticated machines that will replace most humans on plant floors and produce unprecedented gains in productivity. Automated equipment is moving into offices, too, and both trends portend a radical restructuring of work, with jobs becoming more technical and more complex than ever. Altogether these changes will affect more than 45 million jobs, many of them during the next 20 years.[7]

Training Beyond Job Requirements. Within any one organization there are likely to be hundreds of jobs each of which involves many different skills and knowledges. Thus, training programs may cover a wide range of content reflecting the particular demands of the jobs. In addition to providing training for specific jobs, many employers provide training opportunities that go beyond specific job requirements. Economics, psychology, communications, statistics, computer science, speed-reading, and personal growth and development are among the subject areas that may also be included in training programs. Many other subject areas will also be found in the training programs of larger organizations. Some companies also have an educational assistance program that covers the tuition for courses that are of specific and direct benefit to an individual's present job performance.

Managerial and Supervisory Training. Formal training opportunities to equip employees to advance to supervisory and managerial jobs are provided in most of the larger organizations. These programs focus on human relations, communication, time management, work measurement, performance evaluation, labor-management rela-

---

6. John R. Hinrichs, ''Personnel Training,'' *Handbook of Industrial and Organizational Psychology,* edited by Marvin D. Dunnette (Chicago: Rand McNally College Publishing Company, 1976), pp. 832–833.

7. ''The Speedup in Automation,'' *Business Week,* (August 3, 1981), pp. 58–67.

tions, and grievance handling. Even the owners of small businesses are able to provide some of these training programs.[8]

A Systems Approach to Training

Since the goal of training is to contribute to the organization's overall goals, as well as to the employee's personal goals, training programs should be developed systematically. Too often one method or gadget becomes the main focus of a program. Or, the objectives may be hazy. Evaluation is rare. Hinrichs describes the current personnel training scene as not being too different, except in content and emphasis, from that of the 1950s or 1940s. He notes that:

> The major emphasis in most organizations tends to be on the "training program." The premium and organizational reward in real life most often is on doing something— anything seen as being responsive to organizational needs. In the rush to "do something," the practitioners all too often lose sight of the problem.
> There is little or no concern today with using theory in the design of programs, much less with building new theory. The good program is one that is attention getting, dramatic, contemporary, or fun. Whether or not it changes behavior becomes secondary.[9]

A recommended solution to the problem of the haphazard approach to training is the **systems approach to training** which emphasizes:

1. Formulating instructional objectives.
2. Developing learning experiences to achieve these objectives.
3. Having performance criteria to be met.
4. Obtaining evaluative information.

This approach also emphasizes the complex interaction among the components of the system. A model of an instructional system that is useful to designers of training programs is presented in Figure 8–3. Notice that the model consists of three phases: assessment, training and development, and evaluation.[10]

Assessment Phase. Managers and personnel staff members should be alert for indicators of training needs. The failure of employees to achieve production standards, for example, may indicate needed training. Similarly, an excessive number of rejects or a waste of material may imply inadequate training. Excessive turnover in a unit may reflect a need for supervisory training in human relations. All of these deficiencies suggest that training could possibly be useful. However, in order to approach training needs more systematically, three different analyses are recommended for the assessment phase: organizational analysis, task analysis, and person analysis.[11]

---

8. D. L. Howell and W. Randy Boxx, "Supervisory Training in Small Business Organizations," *Personnel Journal*, Vol. 57, No. 2 (February, 1978), pp. 91–92.

9. Hinrichs, *op. cit.,* p. 830.

10. Irwin L. Goldstein, *Training: Program Development and Evaluation* (Monterey, CA: Brooks/Cole Publishing Company, 1974), pp. 17–18.

11. *Ibid.,* pp. 20–21.

Figure 8–3   An Instruction System Model

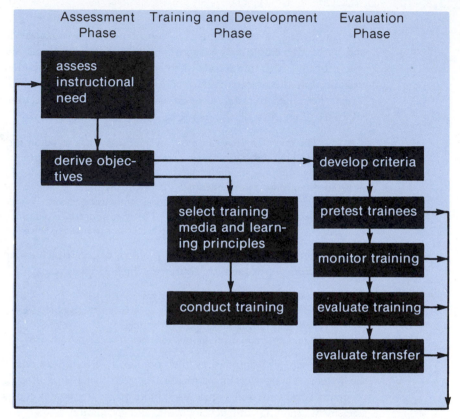

SOURCE: *Training: Program Development and Evaluation,* by I. L. Goldstein. Copyright © 1974 by Wadsworth, Inc. Reprinted by permission of the publisher, Brooks/Cole Publishing Company. Monterey, CA.

Organizational Analysis. An examination of the goals, resources, and environment of the organization to determine where training emphasis should be placed is called **organizational analysis.** The resources that are available to meet objectives, such as equipment, financial resources, and human resources also must be considered.

Personnel policies and organizational climate have an impact on the goals of the training program. Similarly, external factors, such as public policy as reflected in laws, regulations, and court decisions, have important implications for training programs in determining where the emphasis will be placed.[12]

12. *Ibid.,* pp. 30–31.

Organizations typically collect information that may be used in the analysis process such as direct and indirect labor costs, quality of goods or services, absenteeism, turnover, and accidents. Availability of potential replacements and the time required for training them are still important factors in analyzing organizational needs.

Task Analysis.   Designing a specific training program requires a review of the job description in which the activities performed on the job and the conditions under which they are performed are indicated. This review is followed by a **task analysis,** which involves determining what the content of the training program should be based upon the study of the tasks or duties involved in the job.

The first step in the task analysis is to list all the tasks or duties that are included in the job. The second step is to list the steps involved in each of the tasks on the list in terms of what the person does when performing the step, rather than in terms of what must be known. Figure 8–4 illustrates the task-detailing procedure for taking an X ray of the chest. This task is only one of the tasks performed by radiological technicians. Separate task analyses would also be made for such other tasks as "processing X-ray film," "maintaining files and records," etc. In addition to the steps in performing the task, the type of performance and the learning difficulty are indicated. With the type of performance identified, the selection of content and training method is facilitated.[13]

Person Analysis.   Once the organizational and task analyses are made, it is necessary to perform **person analysis,** which determines what skills, knowledge, and attitudes are required of people on the job. Person analysis involves both determining whether task performance is acceptable or substandard and studying the characteristics of individuals and groups who will be placed in the training environment. It is important to determine what prospective trainees can and cannot do in order that the training program may be designed to yield maximum results at minimum cost.[14]

Behavioral Objectives.   After all the analyses have been made, a picture of the training needs emerges. The desired outcomes of training programs should then be stated formally in what are referred to as *behavioral objectives.* Generally these objectives involve the acquisition of skills or knowledge or the changing of attitudes.

One type of behavioral objective, the performance-centered objective, is utilized widely because it lends itself best to an unbiased evaluation of results. For example, the stated objective for one training program might be that "the trainee will be able to operate a keypunch at the rate of 40 WPM with less than 1 percent error for a period of 10 minutes." Performance-centered objectives typically include precise terms such as to calculate, to repair, to adjust, to construct, to assemble, to classify, etc.[15]

13. Robert F. Mager and Kenneth M. Beach, Jr., *Developing Vocational Instruction* (Belmont, CA: Fearon Publishers/Lear Siegler, Inc., 1967), pp. 44–51.
14. Goldstein, *op. cit.,* pp. 38–44.
15. Mager and Beach, *op. cit.,* Chapter 5.

Figure 8–4   Task-Detailing Sheet

TASK: TAKE AN X RAY OF THE CHEST

No.	Steps in Performing the Task	Type of Performance	Learning Difficulty
1.	Patient is asked to prepare for the X ray by removing excess clothing.	Speech	Easy
2.	Correctly position the patient, giving special instructions.	Manipulation, speech	Moderately difficult
3.	Position and check the proper distance of the tube with respect to the patient.	Discrimination	Moderately difficult
4.	Turn on the X-ray equipment and adjust machine.	Recall	Easy
5.	Insert the X-ray film and identification marker into the proper holder.	Manipulation	Easy
6.	Expose film and release patient from exposing room.	Manipulation	Moderately difficult
7.	Process film.	Manipulation	Difficult
8.	Check film for specified positioning or developing errors.	Discrimination	Very difficult
9.	Release patient if film is acceptable to the radiologist.	Recall	
10.	Clean examining table and film areas.	Manipulation	

SOURCE: Robert F. Mager and Kenneth M. Beach, Jr., *Developing Vocational Instruction* (Belmont, CA: Fearon Publishers/Lear Siegler, Inc., 1967), p. 22. Reproduced with permission.

Training and Development Phase. Once the needs for training have been determined and the behavioral objectives specified, the next step is to develop the type of environment necessary for achieving these objectives. A major consideration in creating a training environment is that of choosing a method or media that will enable the trainee to learn most effectively. The methods that are commonly used in training personnel at all levels—managerial, supervisory, and nonmanagerial—will be discussed later in this chapter.

Evaluation Phase. Training, like any other personnel function, should be evaluated to determine its effectiveness. Unfortunately, information concerning the achievement of objectives and the most effective methods to reach them are obtained in only a few instances, and then by research methods that are often inadequate.

According to Goldstein, while efforts at evaluation are evolving, too many decisions about training effectiveness are based upon anecdotal trainee and trainer reactions.[16]

Not only should trainees be tested before and after receiving training, but also the same tests or evaluations should be made of individuals in a control group which has not received the training and whose members are matched with the trainees on the basis of relevant variables such as experience and level of job.

Some of the criteria that are used in evaluating the effectiveness of training are: increased productivity, greater total sales, decreased costs and waste, and similar evidence of improved performance. If a course is designed to change the behavior of supervisors, the evaluation should be in terms of supervisory behavior, not knowledge.

An evaluation should be undertaken in order to provide data for a specific decision. Whether or not a course should be adopted or continued is one type of decision to be made. The second type of decision concerns modification of the course. For example, do changes in the job require changes in course content? Planning the evaluation around specific questions or decisions increases the likelihood that findings will produce concrete actions.[17]

Training directors have handicapped themselves by not being able to prove their effectiveness objectively. Quite often the training director's clout with the organization has depended upon the goodwill of top management rather than the benefits of training to the organization and the costs of obtaining them.

Cost-Benefit Considerations

Hundreds of millions of dollars are spent annually in the development and training of employees at all levels. Much of this cost is for professional trainers and for the time that managers and supervisors devote to developing their subordinates. Many of the larger organizations also have generous budgets for enrolling their personnel in special training courses that cover a wide range of topics. Provision is also made for covering some or all of the costs of employees who attend meetings of professional and technical societies.

The ability to measure the benefits derived from training varies according to the type of job. Where employees are performing relatively simple tasks, the effects of training may show up quite dramatically. For more complex jobs, such as those at the managerial and professional levels, the benefits are more obscure. It is generally found, however, that the benefits will far exceed the costs where the objectives to be met by a training program are clearly defined, where the most suitable instructional techniques are used, and where trainee motivation is high.

The benefits that are experienced by an organization are similar to those found through a carefully developed selection program. Increased productivity and ability of the trainees to assume more responsible roles in the organization are the major

16. Irwin L. Goldstein, "Training in Work Organizations," *Annual Review of Psychology* (Palo Alto, CA: Annual Reviews, Inc., 1980), pp. 229—272.

17. Martin E. Smith, "Evaluating Training Operations and Programs," *Training and Development Journal.* Vol. 34, No. 10 (October, 1980), pp. 70—78.

benefits. Reduction of waste, accidents, and similar problems are also important contributions of a training program.

TRAINING NONMANAGERIAL EMPLOYEES

A wide variety of methods are available for training personnel at all levels. Some of the methods have a long history of usage. Newer methods have developed over the years out of a greater understanding of human behavior, particularly in the areas of learning, motivation, and interpersonal relationships. More recently, technological advances, especially in electronics, have resulted in training devices that in many instances are more effective and economical than more traditional training methods. In the process of selecting training methods, however, one should avoid fads and gimmicks in favor of those methods that have been proved to be generally effective.

On-the-Job Training

On-the-job training is the most commonly used method in the training of nonmanagerial employees. It is conducted by the supervisor or by a senior employee who is responsible for instructing employees. It has the advantage of providing "hands on" experience under normal working conditions and an opportunity for the trainer to build good relationships with new employees.

Off-the-Job Training

In addition to on-the-job training, it is usually necessary to provide employees with training in settings away from their usual workplace. Various methods are available for use within the organization's facilities. Others involve having the employee travel to locations outside of the organization.

Conference or Discussion Method.
A method of individualized instruction frequently used where the training involves primarily the communication of ideas, procedures, and standards is the *conference or discussion method*. This method allows for considerable flexibility in the amount of employee participation that is encouraged or permitted.

Classroom Training Method.
The maximum number of trainees may be handled by a minimum number of instructors in *classroom training*. This method lends itself particularly to instruction in areas where information and instructions can be imparted by lectures, demonstrations, films, videotapes, and other types of audiovisual media. In the larger organizations it is common to find several classrooms fully equipped with all types of training devices. Many public school teachers would envy the facilities that are often utilized in industrial training.

A special type of classroom facility is used in **vestibule training**. Trainees are given instruction in the operation of equipment like that found in operating departments. The emphasis is on instruction rather than production. In a survey of 124 companies participating in programs for the disadvantaged, vestibule training is reported as being the most successful of the training methods used in terms of overall on-the-job performance.[18]

Programmed Instruction Method.   Since the late 1950s, organizations have been making increasing use of *programmed instruction.* While some of the programmed materials use a book or manual format, teaching machines offer a more dramatic means of presenting programmed subject matter. A program represents an attempt to break down subject matter content into highly organized, logical sequences which demand continuous responses on the part of the trainee. After being presented a small segment of information, the trainee is required to answer a question either by writing an answer in a response frame or by pushing a button on a machine. If the response is correct, the trainee is advised of that fact and is presented with the next step (frame) in the material. If the response is incorrect, further explanatory information is given and the trainee is then told to "try again."

A critical analysis of 32 evaluation studies of the programmed instruction method concludes that (1) this method reduces training time by a significant amount, the average time saved being one third; (2) such materials do not usually improve performance on measures of immediate learning and retention; and (3) the application of programmed methods in industry has had slightly more positive results than when applied in academic settings.[19]

Computer-Assisted Instruction Method.   Programmed instruction has evolved into the more sophisticated *Computer-Assisted Instruction* (CAI). The memory and storage capabilities of computers make it possible to provide drill and practice, problem solving, simulation, gaming forms of instruction, and certain very sophisticated forms of individualized tutorial instruction. CAI has been used by the United States Navy for a variety of tasks including remedial math, oscilloscope simulation, and for teaching interpersonal skills.[20]

Simulation Method.   For some jobs it is either impractical or unwise to train the worker on the equipment that is used on the job. An obvious example is found in the training of personnel to operate aircraft and space equipment. The design of *simulators* emphasizes realism in equipment and its operation at minimal cost and maximum safety. American Airlines found that the use of simulators saved more than 11.5 million gallons of jet fuel in one year.[21]

18. William H. Holley, Jr., "Evaluation of Programs to Facilitate Effective Performance of the Disadvantaged Worker," *Training and Development Journal,* Vol. 27, No. 2 (February, 1973), pp. 18—21.

19. Allan N. Nash, Jan P. Muczyk, and Frank L. Vettori, "The Relative Practical Effectiveness of Programmed Instruction," *Personnel Psychology,* Vol. 24, No. 3 (Autumn, 1971), pp. 397—418.

20. Goldstein, "Training in Work Organizations," *op. cit.,* p. 261.

21. "Training at American Airlines: A Total Commitment," *Training and Development Journal,* Vol. 31, No. 12 (December, 1977), pp. 18—21.

Use of Other Training Devices. In teaching skills and procedures in production jobs, certain training devices may be used. For example, devices that look like a portable TV set use slides or videotape to illustrate the steps in the manufacture and assembly of electronic and other components.

Closed-circuit television and videotape recording equipment have become popular as training devices. Closed-circuit television allows an instructional program to be transmitted to many locations simultaneously. The use of video cassettes permits on-the-spot recording and immediate playback which are valuable for any type of instructional program. Video cassettes may also be used to conduct training in diverse locations. For example, the Holiday Inn chain has a self-paced video training program called VIDNET. More than 25 different training cassettes on subjects from deep-fat frying to guest empathy are distributed to inns throughout this chain.[22]

Apprenticeship Training

A system of training in which the young worker entering industry is given thorough instruction and experience, both on and off the job, in the practical and theoretical aspects of the work in a skilled trade is known as **apprenticeship training**. Apprenticeship programs are based on voluntary cooperation between management and labor, industry and government, the company and the school system. Although apprenticeship wages are less than those of fully qualified workers, this method does provide training with pay for individuals who are interested in qualifying for jobs such as machinists, appliance repairers, laboratory technicians, patternmakers, and others. Since 1978, United States Department of Labor regulations require apprenticeship program operators to take affirmative action in recruiting and hiring women and to establish goals and timetables for doing so.

Cooperative and Supplementary Training

Training programs which combine practical on-the-job experience with formal classes are called **cooperative training**. The term cooperative training is also used in connection with high school and college-level programs which incorporate part-time work experiences.

Supplementary training provided by high schools, colleges, and universities has become increasingly popular. With the explosive growth of new knowledge making its influence felt at nearly every level of the work force, an ever-increasing number of organizations are using tuition-aid plans to encourage more of their employees to enroll in courses that will improve their performance. Many employers encourage colleges and universities to offer courses where people work. At Disney World, for example, courses in management, business law, landscaping, automotives,

---

22. "Holiday Inn University: 'More Than a Training Facility,'" *Training and Development Journal*, Vol. 28, No. 9 (September, 1974), pp. 36–37.

etc., are offered by instructors from a nearby college and university who make weekly visits to the grounds.[23]

TRAINING MANAGERS AND SUPERVISORS

Some of the methods discussed in the preceding section may also be used in training managers and supervisors. However, because of the broader knowledge and skills required of managerial and supervisory personnel, other methods, such as those discussed below, are used.

On-the-Job Experiences

Management skills and abilities cannot be acquired just by listening and observing or by reading about them. They must be acquired through actual practice and experience in which a person has an opportunity to perform under pressure and to learn by mistakes. On-the-job experiences are used most commonly by organizations to develop executive personnel. Such experiences should be well planned and supervised and should be meaningful and challenging to the participant. Several different methods of providing on-the-job experiences are:

1. *Coaching*—involves a continuing flow of instructions, comments, and suggestions from the superior to the subordinate.
2. *Understudy assignment*—grooms the individual to take over the superior's job by gaining experience in handling important functions of the job.
3. *Job rotation*—provides, through a variety of work experiences, a broadened knowledge and understanding required to manage more effectively.
4. *Lateral promotion*—involves horizontal movement through different departments along with upward movement in the organization.
5. *Project and committee assignments*—provide an opportunity for the individual to become involved in the study of current organizational problems and in planning and decision-making activities.
6. *Staff meetings*—enable participants to become more familiar with problems and events that are occurring outside of their immediate area by exposing them to the ideas and thinking of other managers.

Although the abovementioned methods are used most frequently in developing managers for higher-level positions in the organization, they provide valuable experiences for individuals who are being developed for other types of positions, too.

Off-the-Job Experiences

While on-the-job experiences constitute the core of management development, certain methods of development away from the job can be used to supplement work

---

23. M. H. Cook, "What Can I Do For You?" *Training and Development Journal*, Vol. 28, No. 9 (September, 1974), pp. 30–34.

experiences. These experiences may be provided on either an individual or a group basis and may be conducted during or after normal working hours.

Case Study Method.

Particularly useful in classroom learning situations are *case studies*. These studies, which may have been developed from actual experiences within their organizations, can help managers learn how to obtain and interpret facts, to become conscious of the many variables upon which a management decision may be based and, in general, to improve their decision-making skills.

Incident Method.

A variation of the case method is the **incident method** in which the participants are given only a brief statement of a problem or incident. Any details or facts that may be pertinent to the problem must be drawn from the discussion leader through questioning. Whether or not the group can gain sufficient information will depend upon its ability to determine what information is relevant and to elicit it from the leader.

In-Basket Training Method.

Another method that can be used to simulate a problem situation is the **in-basket technique**. In this technique the participants are given several documents, each describing some problem or situation, the solution of which requires an immediate decision. They are thus forced to make decisions under the pressure of time and also to determine the priority with which each problem should be considered.

Management Game Method.

Training experiences have been brought to life and made more interesting through development of *management games*. Participants who play the game are faced with the task of making a continuing series of decisions affecting the enterprise. The simulated effects that each decision has upon each functional area within the enterprise can be determined by means of an electronic computer which has been programmed for the game. A major advantage of this technique is the high degree of participation that it requires.

The game approach does not always require a computer, however. It has, for example, been used in teaching the basic principles of EEO. Some years ago, Motorola developed a game, "EEO: It's Your Job." It was originally devised to fill its own affirmative-action needs but is now commercially available for use in training programs.[24] A game kit accommodates up to 24 players at a single session, divided into teams of four. The players, as shown in Figure 8–5, get caught up in the competitive spirit of a game and absorb and remember government regulations. They also become aware of the way in which their own daily decisions commit the employer to compliance or noncompliance with such regulations. The game is reinforced with a slide presentation.

Role Playing Method.

Role playing consists of assuming the attitudes and behavior of and acting out the roles of individuals, usually a supervisor and a

---

24. Corporate Affirmative Action and Compliance Department, Motorola, Inc., 1303 E. Algonquin Road, Schaumburg, IL 60196.

Figure 8–5 **Supervisors Learn EEO Principles with Motorola's Game: EEO: It's Your Job**

SOURCE: Motorola, Inc. Reproduced with permission.

subordinate who are involved in a personnel problem. Role playing can help participants to improve their ability to understand and to cope with the problems of the other person. It should also help them to learn how to counsel others.

Sensitivity Training Method. One of the training methods that has grown rapidly in popularity is **sensitivity training**. This method, pioneered by the National Training Laboratories, is used with small groups—referred to as "T" (training) groups—whose members work together for a number of days. As the term would indicate, sensitivity training has as its primary goal the development of greater sensitivity on the part of its participants, including self-insight and an awareness of group processes. It provides also the opportunity to participate constructively in group activities.[25]

25. Henry Clay Smith, *Sensitivity Training* (New York: McGraw-Hill Book Company, 1973), p. 30.

In recent years sensitivity training programs have tended to be modified to produce more organization- and job-oriented discussion, with less probing into personal feelings and behavior. The trend generally is away from creating a situation which Odiorne describes as:

> . . . a great psychological nudist camp in which he (the participant) bares his pale, sensitive soul to the hard-nosed autocratic ruffians in his T-Group and gets roundly clobbered. He goes away with his sense of inferiority indelibly reinforced.[26]

Even for a less threatening type of environment, the question is often asked if sensitivity training has psychologically disturbing consequences for the participants. Based on a review of several studies, Cooper concludes that there is some evidence indicating that sensitivity training may be less stressful than university examinations. It may, in fact, enable participants to cope better with aggressive stimuli and stressful periods in their lives. He recommends, however, that a systematic screening procedure be used to weed out potential participants who may be risks.[27]

Behavior Modeling Method. Training programs designed simply to change supervisors' attitudes are no longer as necessary as in the past. Supervisors now must be shown how to put their attitudes to work. One approach is **behavior modeling or interaction management**. This approach emphasizes the involvement of the supervisory trainees in handling real-life employee problems and receiving immediate feedback on their performance.[28] The main purpose of behavior modeling is to achieve behavioral change.

There are four basic steps in behavior modeling:

1. Supervisory trainees view films or videotapes in which a model supervisor is portrayed dealing with an employee in an effort to improve or maintain the employee's performance. The model shows specifically how to deal with the situation.
2. Trainees participate in extensive practice and rehearsal of the behaviors demonstrated by the models. The greatest percentage of training time is spent in these skill-practice sessions.
3. As the trainee's behavior increasingly resembles that of the model, the trainer and other trainees provide such social reinforcers as praise, approval, encouragement, and attention. Videotaping such behavior rehearsals adds feedback and reinforcement.
4. The principles of transferring the training to the job are emphasized throughout the training period.[29]

26. As quoted by Spencer Klaw, ''Inside a T-Group,'' *Think Magazine*, 1965.

27. Cary L. Cooper, ''How Psychologically Dangerous Are T-Groups and Encounter Groups?'' *Human Relations*, Vol. 28, No. 3 (April, 1975), pp. 249–260.

28. Bernard L. Rosenbaum, ''A New Approach to Changing Supervisory Behavior,'' *Personnel*, Vol. 52, No. 2 (March-April, 1975), pp. 37–44.

29. Richard Kritzer, ''The Use of Videotape in Behavioral Change,'' *Public Personnel Management*, Vol. 3, No. 4 (July-August, 1974) pp. 325–331.

Several controlled studies have demonstrated behavior change on the part of supervisors, as well as measurable increases in worker productivity.[30]

Other Methods. Many large organizations maintain extensive business and technical libraries for their personnel. Professional readers are sometimes employed to digest the information from the more significant articles that appear in professional and trade publications. The digested information is made available to management personnel by means of tape recordings or printed abstracts.

Organizations also may rely upon the assistance of educational institutions and professional consultants. The educational training conducted by these media frequently proves to be more effective and more economical than that conducted by the organization itself. Many colleges and universities now offer advanced and middle-management programs to meet the growing demands of organizations for management development assistance.

PSYCHOLOGICAL PRINCIPLES OF LEARNING

The success of a job training program depends upon more than the identification of training needs and the preparation of the program. If the trainee has not learned, it is probably because some important principle of learning has been overlooked. Because the success or failure of a training program is frequently related to this simple fact, those who are concerned with developing instructional programs should recognize that attention must be given to the basic psychological principles of learning.

The different methods or techniques used in training personnel vary in the extent to which they utilize the principles of learning. Figure 8–6 from Bass and Vaughn presents this information in summary form.

Preconditions for Learning

There are two preconditions for learning that will increase the success of those who are to receive training: trainee readiness and motivation. The condition known as **trainee readiness** refers to both maturational and experiential factors in the background of the trainee. Prospective trainees should be screened to determine that they have the background knowledge or the skills necessary for learning what will be presented to them. Recognition of individual differences in readiness is as important in organizational training as it is in any other learning situation. It is often desirable to group individuals according to their capacity to learn, as determined by scores from tests, or to provide a different or extended type of instruction for those who need it.

The other precondition for learning is that the trainee be properly motivated. That is, for optimum learning the trainee must recognize the need for acquiring new information or for having new skills; and a desire to learn as training progresses must be maintained. While people at work are motivated by certain common needs, they differ from one another in the relative importance of these needs at any given

---

30. Rosenbaum, *op. cit.*, pp. 40–42. *See also* Stephen Wehrenberg and Robert Kuhnle, "How Training Through Behavior Modeling Works," *Personnel Journal*, Vol. 59, No. 7 (July, 1980), pp. 576–580.

time. Under laboratory conditions, Bryan and Locke found that having specifically designated goals results in better performance than having general or nonspecific goals.[31] These findings suggest that clearly defined objectives will produce increased motivation in the organizational training process.

Figure 8-6 Extent to Which Training Techniques Utilize Certain Principles of Learning

	Motivation: Active Participation of Learner	Reinforcement: Feedback of Knowledge of Results	Stimulus: Meaningful Organization of Materials	Responses: Practice and Repetition	Stimulus-Response Conditions Most Favorable for Transfer
On-the-Job Techniques:					
Job-instruction training	Yes	Sometimes	Yes	Yes	Yes
Apprentice training	Yes	Sometimes	?	Sometimes	Yes
Internships and assistantships	Yes	Sometimes	?	Sometimes	Yes
Job rotation	Yes	No	?	Sometimes	Yes
Junior board	Yes	Sometimes	Sometimes	Sometimes	Yes
Coaching	Yes	Yes	Sometimes	Sometimes	Yes
Off-the-Job Techniques:					
Vestibule	Yes	Sometimes	Yes	Yes	Sometimes
Lecture	No	No	Yes	No	No
Special study	Yes	No	Yes	?	No
Films	No	No	Yes	No	No
Television	No	No	Yes	No	No
Conference or discussion	Yes	Sometimes	Sometimes	Sometimes	No
Case study	Yes	Sometimes	Sometimes	Sometimes	Sometimes
Role playing	Yes	Sometimes	No	Sometimes	Sometimes
Simulation	Yes	Sometimes	Sometimes	Sometimes	Sometimes
Programmed instruction	Yes	Yes	Yes	Yes	No
Laboratory training	Yes	Yes	No	Yes	Sometimes
Programmed group exercises	Yes	Yes	Yes	Sometimes	Sometimes

SOURCE: Bernard M. Bass and James A. Vaughn, *Training in Industry: The Management of Learning.* © 1966 by Wadsworth Publishing Company, Inc., Belmont, CA 94002. Reprinted by permission of the publisher, Brooks/Cole Publishing Company.

31. Judith F. Bryan and Edwin A. Locke, "Goal Setting as a Means of Increasing Motivation," *Journal of Applied Psychology*, Vol. 51, No. 3 (June, 1967), pp. 274–277.

Basic Principles of Learning for Trainers to Understand

After the trainees are placed in the learning situation, their readiness and motivation should be assessed further. In addition, trainers should understand certain basic principles of learning which are discussed below.

Meaningfulness of Materials. One principle of learning is that the material to be learned should be organized in as meaningful a manner as possible. The material should be arranged so that each successive experience builds upon preceding ones and that the trainee is able to integrate the experiences into a usable pattern of knowledge and skills.

Reinforcement. Anything which strengthens the trainee's response is called **reinforcement**. It may be in the form of approval from the trainer or the feeling of accomplishment that follows the performance; or it may simply be confirmation by a teaching machine that the trainee's response was correct. It is generally most effective if it occurs immediately after a task has been performed.

In recent years some industrial organizations have utilized **behavior modification**, a technique that operates on the principle that behavior that is rewarded—positively reinforced—will be exhibited more frequently in the future, whereas behavior that is penalized or unrewarded will decrease in frequency. Emery Air Freight Corporation has used the behavior modification principles set forth by B. F. Skinner in scientific and popular publications throughout its organization. The executives report improved profits, as well as greater contentment, on the part of the employees.[32]

Transfer of Training. Unless what is learned in the training situation is applicable to what is required on the job, the training effort will have been of little value. The ultimate effectiveness of learning, therefore, is to be found in the answer to the question, "To what extent does what is learned *transfer* to the job?" **Transfer of training** to the job can be facilitated by having conditions in the training program as close as possible to those on the job. Another approach is to teach trainees the principles for applying to the job the behaviors they have learned.

Other Principles of Learning

Other principles of learning also have been developed over the past several decades primarily as a result of laboratory studies. The principles apply in varying degrees to different types of materials to be learned. They have been found to have application in many job training programs.

Knowledge of Progress. As an employee's training progresses, motivation may be maintained and even increased by providing *knowledge of progress*. Progress, as determined by tests and other records, may be plotted on a chart, commonly referred

---

32. "New Tool: Reinforcement for Good Work," *Psychology Today*, Vol. 5, No. 11 (April, 1972), pp. 68–69.

to as a **learning curve**. Figure 8–7 is an example of a learning curve that is common in the acquisition of many job skills.

In many learning situations there are times when progress does not occur. Such periods of no return show up on the curve as a fairly straight horizontal line, which is called a *plateau*. A plateau may be the result of ineffective methods of work, or it may come because of reduced motivation. Proper guidance by the instructor may reveal the cause of a plateau and may enable the instructor to assist the trainee by such means as suggestions for new work procedures or aid in establishing new incentives.

Distributed Learning.   Another factor that determines the effectiveness of training is the amount of time given to practice in one session. Should trainees be given training in 5 two-hour periods or in 10 one-hour periods? It has been found in most cases that spacing out the training will result in more rapid learning and more permanent retention. This is the principle of **distributed learning**. Since the most efficient distribution will vary according to the type and complexity of the task to be learned, it is desirable to make reference to the rapidly growing body of research in this area when an answer is required for a specific training situation.[33]

Whole v. Part Learning.   Most jobs and tasks can be broken down into parts that lend themselves to further analysis. The analysis of the most effective manner for completing each part then provides a basis for giving specific instruction. Typing, for example, is made up of several skills that are part of the total process. The typist starts by learning the proper use of each finger; eventually, with practice, the

Figure 8–7   A Typical Learning Curve

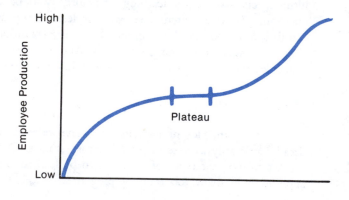

33. *The Journal of Applied Psychology* is an excellent source of research studies of this type. Its articles are indexed in *Psychological Abstracts*.

individual finger movements become integrated into a total pattern. Practice by moving individual fingers is an example of part learning. In evaluating *whole v. part learning*, it is necessary to consider the nature of the task to be learned. If the task can be broken down successfully for part learning, it probably should be broken down in order to facilitate learning; otherwise, it probably should be taught as a unit.

Practice and Repetition.   It is those things we do daily that become a part of our repertoire of skills. Trainees should be given frequent opportunity to practice their job tasks in the manner that they will ultimately be expected to perform them. The individual who is being taught to operate a machine should have an opportunity to practice on it. Similarly, the supervisor who is being taught "how to train" should have supervised practice in training.

Training the Trainers

The success of any training program will depend in large part upon the teaching skills of those persons who are responsible for conducting the various classes and other types of training sessions, including on-the-job training. Trainers should be carefully selected and provided with the necessary training in instructional methods. When instructors are given training, the trainees will show much greater progress than when the instructors are not given such training. Making certain that the trainers are equipped to do their job is thus a very important part of any training endeavor.

RÉSUMÉ

Because of rapid changes in technology and the growth of organizations into large, complex operations, training and development programs are vital to an organization's success. In recent years such programs have broadened their scope to include the career development of personnel at all levels. A development program begins with the important process of orientation.

In designing training programs, a systems approach should be followed. This involves three phases: the assessment phase, the training and development phase, and the evaluation phase. From the wide variety of methods available for training both managerial and nonmanagerial personnel, those methods should be selected that best meet the fulfillment of the training objectives and that utilize as many of the principles of learning as possible. While new methods must always be explored, the focus should be on the objectives to be attained through training. In planning and conducting training programs, trainers should give special attention to the psychological principles of learning.

_____ TERMS TO IDENTIFY _____

training
systems approach to training

organizational analysis
task analysis

person analysis
on-the-job training
vestibule training
apprenticeship training
cooperative training
supplementary training
incident method
in-basket technique
sensitivity training

behavior modeling or interaction
   management
trainee readiness
reinforcement
behavior modification
transfer of training
learning curve
distributed learning

DISCUSSION QUESTIONS

1. How is training and development related to recruitment, selection, performance evaluation, labor relations, and compensation management?
2. The new employee is likely to be anxious the first few days on the job.
   a. What are some possible causes of such anxiety?
   b. How may the anxiety be reduced?
3. What analyses should be made to determine the training needs of an organization? After the needs are determined, what is the next step?
4. Indicate what training methods you would use for each of the following jobs. Give reasons for your choices.
   a. file clerk
   b. keypunch operator
   c. automobile service station attendant
   d. pizza maker
5. Compare programmed instruction to the lecture in regard to the way they use the different psychological principles of learning.
6. Suppose that you are the manager of an accounts receivable unit in a large company. You are switching to a new system of billing and record keeping and need to train your 3 supervisors and 28 employees in the new procedures. What training method(s) would you use? Why?
7. Participants in a training course are often asked to evaluate the course by means of a questionnaire. What are the pros and cons of this approach? Are there better ways of evaluating a course?
8. If you were assigned the task of developing an orientation program for host personnel at one of the theme parks such as Disneyland or Great America, what would you include in the program? Keep in mind the employees' responsibilities for patron enjoyment and safety.

PROBLEM 8–1

HOW MUCH STRUCTURE IN MANAGEMENT DEVELOPMENT COURSES?

Diversified Products, Inc., with operating divisions in North America and abroad, recognized a need to provide its managers with a refresher course in personnel management. It was believed that these managers needed to be made more aware of government regulations affecting their relations with employees and be better able to document decisions affected by these regulations. Also, improvements in their leadership and motivation skills were considered to be necessary in order for them to cope better with the changes in attitudes and behavior their younger employees reflect.

The company decided to develop a course to be conducted by company personnel, making use of some guest instructors from the outside. Sessions lasting 8 days each were held at a resort hotel for groups of 15 to 20 managers drawn from a variety of positions and locations in the corporation. Since these managers worked under highly structured conditions, it was believed that an unstructured course would be a beneficial change for them. Accordingly, at the first session of each course, participants were given a list of possible topics to discuss. They were told that it would be up to them to decide how the course was to be conducted. The participants were to decide on the nature of the topics, whether or not the class would be divided into discussion groups, and who would be invited as outside resource people.

Experience gained over a period of time with a number of groups revealed that it took about three to four days for participants to begin to make progress. By this time their reactions to the unstructured nature of the course were about evenly divided. About one half of them were highly enthusiastic about the course, whereas the remainder hated it. Some disliked it so much that they abandoned the sessions and returned to work.

It proved to be almost impossible to determine, in advance of the course, which managers would react unfavorably to the unstructured format of the sessions. This determination could not be reached until several sessions had elapsed. In spite of the negative reactions, top management and the personnel staff considered the unstructured course format to be sufficiently worthwhile to justify its continuance.

a. How do you account for the sharp difference in the reactions of participants to the course?

b. What is to be gained by having the course unstructured?

c. Do you agree with the company's decision to continue the course with an unstructured format?

SUGGESTED READINGS

Chruden, Herbert J., and Arthur W. Sherman, Jr. *Readings in Managing Human Resources,* 6th ed. Cincinnati: South-Western Publishing Co., 1984. Part 3.

Connellan, Thomas K. *How to Improve Human Performance: Behaviorism in Business and Industry.* New York: Harper & Row, 1978.

Craig, Robert L. (ed.). *Training and Development Handbook: A Guide to Human Resource Development,* 2d ed. American Society for Training and Development. New York: McGraw-Hill Book Company, 1976.

Hinrichs, John R. *Handbook of Industrial and Organizational Psychology,* edited by Marvin D. Dunnette. Chicago: Rand McNally College Publishing Company, 1976. Chapter 19, "Personnel Training."

McGehee, William. *Training and Development,* edited by Dale Yoder and Herbert G. Heneman. ASPA Handbook of Personnel and Industrial Relations Series. Washington: The Bureau of National Affairs, Inc., 1977. Chapter 5–1, "Training and Development Theory, Policies, and Strategies."

Nadler, Leonard. *Developing Human Resources,* 2nd ed. Austin, TX: Learning Concepts, 1979.

Stockard, James G. *Career Development and Job Training: A Manager's Handbook.* New York: AMACOM, 1977.

- To identify the phases of career development.
- To describe the favorable climate that helps make career development programs successful.
- To understand how job opportunities may be inventoried.
- To describe the ways in which career development for women and minorities can be planned.
- To understand how career decisions are made in various stages of one's life.
- To describe the factors that should be considered in choosing an appropriate career.

9

Career Development

The functions of human resources management that we have discussed so far have a fairly long history. Typically they have been carried out with organizational needs as the primary concern. Since the mid-1970s, increasing attention has been given to the needs that employees have for careers rather than merely for jobs. Career development programs have been established in many organizations to enable employees to match their needs for personal growth and development with the needs of the organization. Career planning is important to management as a means of increasing productivity, improving employee attitudes toward work, and developing greater worker satisfaction.

Many forces have converged to induce employers to organize career development programs. Concern about the quality of work life—with emphasis on self-actualization or doing work that is self-fulfilling—is one of the major forces. Equal employment legislation, affirmative-action pressures, white-collar unionization, and the desire of employees to advance in their organizations have also been major forces. There is also a growing awareness that the processes by which individuals choose careers and organizations leave much to be desired. As we examine career development programs, it will become apparent that they are the integration of many of the personnel functions with a focus on better utilization of personnel.

PHASES OF A CAREER DEVELOPMENT PROGRAM

Traditionally organizations have engaged in human resources planning and development. This activity involves charting the moves of large numbers of employees through various positions in the organization and identifying future staffing needs. Career development programs with greater emphasis on the individual introduce a personalized aspect to the process. Such programs typically involve several specific activities including career counseling, career pathing, training, computerized inventorying of backgrounds and skills, and job posting.

Matching Individual and Organizational Needs

In an ideal system for human resources planning and development, individuals would seek to match a particular organization's human resources needs with their own needs for personal career growth and development. According to Schein, the basic system can be depicted as involving both individual and organizational planning and a series of matching activities which are designed to facilitate mutual need satisfaction. It is also assumed that both individual and organizational needs change over time, as shown in Figure 9–1.

In the right-hand column of Figure 9–1, the basic stages of the individual's career throughout the life cycle are shown. While not everyone will go through these stages in the manner depicted, there is growing evidence that, for organizational careers in particular, these stages typify the movement of people through their adult lives. The left-hand column of the diagram shows the organizational planning activities which must occur if human resources are to be managed in an optimal

Figure 9–1   A Developmental Model of Human Resources Planning and Development

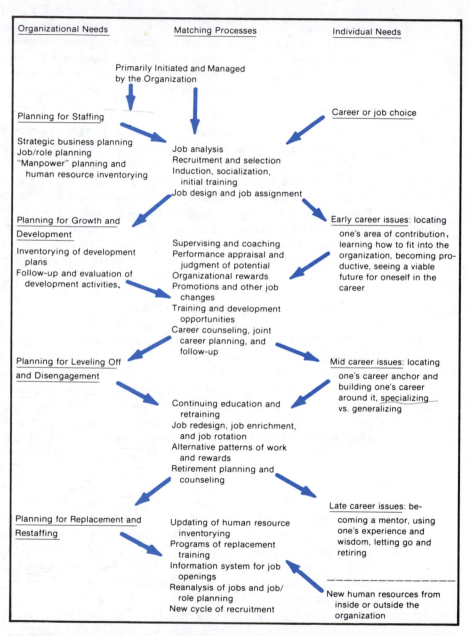

Organizational Needs   Matching Processes   Individual Needs

Primarily Initiated and Managed
by the Organization

Career or job choice

Planning for Staffing

Strategic business planning
Job/role planning
"Manpower" planning and
   human resource inventorying

Job analysis
Recruitment and selection
Induction, socialization,
   initial training
Job design and job assignment

Planning for Growth and
Development

Inventorying of development
   plans
Follow-up and evaluation of
   development activities.

Supervising and coaching
Performance appraisal and
   judgment of potential
Organizational rewards
Promotions and other job
   changes
Training and development
   opportunities
Career counseling, joint
   career planning, and
   follow-up

Early career issues: locating
   one's area of contribution,
   learning how to fit into the
   organization, becoming productive, seeing a viable
   future for oneself in the
   career

Planning for Leveling Off
and Disengagement

Mid career issues: locating
   one's career anchor and
   building one's career
   around it, specializing
   vs. generalizing

Continuing education and
   retraining
Job redesign, job enrichment,
   and job rotation
Alternative patterns of work
   and rewards
Retirement planning and
   counseling

Late career issues: be-
   coming a mentor, using
   one's experience and
   wisdom, letting go and
   retiring

Planning for Replacement and
Restaffing

Updating of human resource
   inventorying
Programs of replacement
   training
Information system for job
   openings
Reanalysis of jobs and job/
   role planning
New cycle of recruitment

New human resources from
   inside or outside the
   organization

SOURCE: Edgar H. Schein, "Increasing Organizational Effectiveness Through Better Human Resource Planning and Development," *Sloan Management Review,* Fall 1977, pp. 1–20. Illustration used by permission.

manner and if changing job requirements are to be assessed and monitored properly. The middle column shows the various matching activities that have to occur at various career stages. A careful examination of the diagram will reveal a comprehensive approach to the growth and development of the individual in the organization. Many of the listed activities require the help of specialists, but line supervisors and top management must be held responsible for carrying them out. "It is they who control the opportunities and the rewards," says Schein.[1]

Creating Favorable Conditions

While a career development program requires many special processes and techniques, to be described later, some basic conditions must be present if it is to be successful. These conditions, which are discussed below, create a favorable climate for the program.

Management Support. If career development is to succeed, it must receive the complete support of top management. Ideally, senior line managers and human resources department managers should work together to design and implement a career development system.[2] Managerial personnel at all levels will then need to have training in the fundamentals of job design, performance appraisal, counseling, and career planning. With such training as a background, managers and supervisors are prepared to become career developers.

Goal Setting. Before individuals can engage in meaningful career planning, they must have a clear understanding of the organization's goals. When this is not the case, they may plan for personal change and growth but not know if or how their own goals fit those of the organization. If individuals are to plan their futures, the organization must also have a human resources strategy. For example, if the technology of a business is changing and new skills are needed, should the company retrain to meet this need or hire new talent? Is there growth, stability, or decline in the number of employees needed? How will turnover affect this need? A definite plan is essential to support individual career planning.[3]

Changes in Personnel Policies. In order for a career development program to be effective, it may be necessary to alter personnel policies. For example, a policy of lifelong job rotation can counteract obsolescence and maintain employee flexibility. Another policy that can aid development involves lateral and downward job transfers. **Lateral transfers** to jobs at the same level in the organization can be used to develop new skills without promoting the individual. Such transfers are good for the

---

1. Edgar H. Schein, "Increasing Organizational Effectiveness Through Better Human Resource Planning and Development," *Sloan Management Review,* Vol. 19, No. 1 (Fall, 1977), pp. 1–20.

2. Milan Moravec, "A Cost Effective Career Planning Program Requires a Strategy," *Personnel Administrator*, Vol. 27, No. 1 (January, 1982), pp. 28–32.

3. Donald B. Miller, "Career Planning and Management in Organizations," *SAM Advanced Management Journal*, Vol. 43, No. 2 (Spring, 1978), pp.33–43.

individual and for the organization when an organization is growing very slowly or not at all. **Downward transfers or demotions** can provide developmental opportunities but are ordinarily considered undesirable, especially to the individuals demoted. **Promotions**—changing to a job that provides an increase in pay and status and demands more in terms of skill and/or responsibility—typically involve certain risks for the individual. Risks may be reduced by making the new job a temporary assignment or the promotion an acting or temporary one which becomes permanent only if the individual succeeds and/or if the job is not eliminated.[4]

Many organizations now provide an **outplacement service** to help employees terminate and get a job somewhere else. This service can be used to enhance a productive employee's career, as well as to terminate an employee who is unproductive. If an organization cannot meet its career development responsibilities, personnel policy should provide assistance to the individuals in obtaining more suitable career opportunities. For the unproductive employees, it is a way of "terminating them that preserves their dignity, recognizes their past contributions, and enables them to find a new job quickly and relatively painlessly."[5] Professional outplacement counseling as an organized profession is of fairly recent origin. It is being added to many employee benefit packages as another form of employee assistance.[6]

Announcement of the Program. The career development program should be announced widely throughout the organization. Notices on bulletin boards, articles in company publications, distribution of pamphlets, and other available channels can be used. These announcements should discuss the general purpose and philosophy of the program, its goals, and the activities involved. Employees should be encouraged to consider their own concepts of career planning and to assess the degree to which they believe that the program is suitable for them.[7]

Inventorying Job Opportunities

While career development usually involves many different types of training experiences discussed in the preceding chapter, the most important influences occur on the job. It is there that the individual is exposed to a wide variety of experiences and where contributions are made to the organization.

Job Competencies. It is important that the jobs in an organization be studied carefully to identify and assign weights to the knowledges and skills that are

4. Douglas T. Hall and Marilyn A. Morgan, "Career Development and Planning," *Contemporary Problems in Personnel,* edited by W. Clay Hammer and Frank L. Schmidt (rev. ed.; Chicago: St. Clair Press, 1977), pp. 205—226.
   5. Eric Berg, "Outplacement Helps Take the Sting Out of Firings," *Chicago Tribune,* July 9, 1980.
   6. Thomas M. Camden, "Use Outplacement as a Career Development Tool," *Personnel Administrator,* Vol. 27, No. 1 (January, 1982), pp. 35—37.
   7. Philip G. Benson and George C. Thornton, III, "A Model Career Planning Program," *Personnel,* Vol. 55, No. 2 (March-April, 1978), pp. 30—39.

required. This can be achieved by using job analysis and evaluation systems such as those used in compensation programs. The Hay System, used at Sears, measures three basic competencies for each job: *know-how, problem solving,* and *accountability.* Know-how is broken down into three types of job knowledge: technical, managerial, and human relations. Problem solving and accountability also have several dimensions. Scores for each of these three major competencies are assigned to each job, and a total value for each job is computed. For any planned job transfer, the amount of increase (or decrease) the next job represents in each of the skill areas, as well as in the total point values, can be computed. This information is then used to make certain that a transfer to a different job is a growth-demanding assignment. Sears designs career development paths to provide the following experiences: (1) an increase in at least one skill area on each new assignment; (2) an increase of at least 10 percent in total points on each new assignment; and (3) assignments in several different functional areas.[8]

Job Progressions. Once the skill demands of jobs are identified and weighted according to their importance, it is then possible to plan *job progressions.* A new employee with no experience is typically assigned to a "starting job." After a period of time in that job, the employee can be promoted to one that requires more knowledge and/or skills. While most organizations have concentrated on developing job progressions for managerial, professional, and technical jobs, progressions can be developed in all categories of jobs. These job progressions then can serve as a basis for developing the *career paths* for individuals.

Many organizations have prepared interesting and attractive brochures to describe the career paths that are available to employees with each type of training and experience. In its brochure on career opportunities in technical management, Kaiser Aluminum & Chemical Corporation shows the career path for maintenance management (see Figure 9–2). This career path provides for development in both management and technical areas. The career path shown in the illustration will be varied according to the experience level of the person entering the program, the needs of the company, and individual preferences. General Motors has prepared a *Career Development Guide* that groups jobs by fields of work such as engineering, manufacturing, communications, data processing, financial, personnel, scientific, and others. These groupings enable an employee to obtain a better understanding of the career possibilities in the various fields of work.

Training Needs. There are likely to be points in an individual's career path where training beyond that received on the job is essential. Such points should be identified and appropriate training made available to prevent progress from being impaired by a lack of knowledge or skills. Differences in the training needs of individuals concerning their jobs require that these needs be monitored closely.

8. Harry L. Wellbank, Douglas T. Hall, Marilyn A. Morgan, and W. Clay Hammer, "Planning Job Progression for Effective Career Development and Human Resources Management," *Personnel,* Vol. 55, No. 2 (March-April, 1978), pp. 54–64.

Figure 9–2 Career Path at Kaiser Aluminum & Chemical Corporation

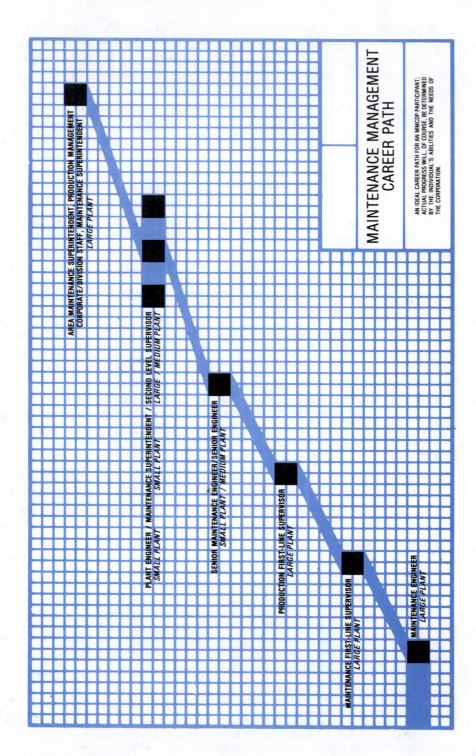

MAINTENANCE MANAGEMENT
CAREER PATH

AN IDEAL CAREER PATH FOR AN MMCDP PARTICIPANT;
ACTUAL PROGRESS WILL, OF COURSE, BE DETERMINED
BY THE INDIVIDUAL'S ABILITIES AND THE NEEDS OF
THE CORPORATION.

AREA MAINTENANCE SUPERINTENDENT, PRODUCTION MANAGEMENT
CORPORATE/DIVISION STAFF, MAINTENANCE SUPERINTENDENT
LARGE PLANT

PLANT ENGINEER / MAINTENANCE SUPERINTENDENT / SECOND LEVEL SUPERVISOR
SMALL PLANT   *SMALL PLANT*   *LARGE / MEDIUM PLANT*

SENIOR MAINTENANCE ENGINEER/SENIOR ENGINEER
SMALL PLANT / MEDIUM PLANT

PRODUCTION FIRST-LINE SUPERVISOR
LARGE PLANT

MAINTENANCE FIRST-LINE SUPERVISOR
LARGE PLANT

MAINTENANCE ENGINEER
LARGE PLANT

SOURCE: Reproduced by permission of Kaiser Aluminum & Chemical Corporation.

Determining Employee Potential

Probably the most important phase of any career development program is that of determining the potential of employees for success in one or more career paths. These objectives may be achieved in various ways. All of them, however, involve the participation of the employees concerned. According to an American Management Associations survey, informal counseling by personnel staff and by supervisors is used widely. In many companies, communications on educational assistance, AA/EEO programs and policies, salary administration, and job requirements are also basic practices. Career planning workbooks and workshops also are popular as means of helping employees identify their potential.[9]

Career Planning Workbooks. Several organizations use workbooks to guide individual employees through systematic self-assessment of values, interests, abilities, goals, and personal development plans. General Motors' *Career Development Guide* contains a section on "What do you want your future to be?" in which the individual makes a personal evaluation. General Electric has developed an extensive set of manuals for its career development program, including two workbooks for employee exploration of life issues that affect career decisions. Syntex's workbook, *How To Work for a Living and Like It*, may be used by an individual or in a group workshop.

Some companies prefer to use workbooks prepared for the general public. Popular ones include *What Color Is Your Parachute?* by Richard N. Bolles and *Career Strategies: Planning for Personal Growth* by Andrew H. Souerwine. These materials have considerable appeal because they require initiative and an investment of the employee's time. Workbooks provide the stimulus to thinking about one's job and career objectives, strengths and limitations, and development needs.

Career Planning Workshops. Workshops provide experiences similar to those available in workbooks. They have the advantage, however, of fostering discussion and providing for a comparison of attitudes, concerns, and plans. Some focus on current job performance and development plans. Others deal with broader life and career plans and values.

Career Counseling. The AMA survey of company practices found that counseling is used widely in career development. Career counseling involves discussing with employees their current job activities and performance, their personal job and career interests and goals, their personal skills, and suitable career development objectives. Such counseling is usually voluntary for employees, although it may be included as part of an annual performance review. Counseling may be provided by the personnel staff, superiors, specialized staff counselors, or by outside professionals.[10]

---

9. James W. Walker and Thomas G. Gutteridge, *Career Planning Practices*, An AMA Survey Report (New York: AMACOM, 1979), pp. 1−2.
10. *Ibid.*, p. 11.

CAREER DEVELOPMENT PROGRAMS FOR SPECIAL GROUPS

Many organizations introduce career development programs to meet specifically identified needs. Surveys show that special programs are more common than "across the board" career programs. Specific programs for management trainees and fast-track management candidates were found in two thirds of the companies in the AMA survey. Over one third had developed specific programs for women employees and minority employees. Programs for mid-career employees, the handicapped, and older workers are relatively rare.[11] Hopefully, in the future more employers will design programs for these individuals.

Management Development Programs

Contemporary organizations must have competent managers to cope with the growing complexity of the problems affecting their operations. A formal development program helps to insure that developmental experiences both on and off the job are coordinated and in line with the needs of the individual and the organization.

Inventorying Management Requirements and Talent.
An important part of the program is the maintenance of an inventory of managerial positions. The inventory serves to direct attention to the developmental needs of employees in terms of their present jobs and managerial jobs into which they may be promoted. Identifying employees who may be groomed to replace managers as they are reassigned, retire, or otherwise vacate a position is an equally important part of a management development program.

Responsibility of Managers to Identify Talent.   Identifying individuals for managerial positions is a responsibility which all managers should share. As they conduct formal appraisals, they should be concerned with their subordinates' potential for managerial jobs and encourage their growth in that direction. In addition to recommendations of the immediate superior, there should be others in the organization who have the power to evaluate, nominate, and sponsor individuals with promise. Companies that emphasize developing human assets as well as producing profits typically have the talent they need and some to spare.[12] Some companies—IT&T, IBM, Xerox, General Electric, and General Motors, to name a few—have become "academy" companies for other organizations that lack good management development programs.

Identification of Talent Through Assessment Centers.   Pioneered in the mid-1950s by Dr. Douglas Bray and his associates at AT&T, corporate-operated assessment centers have proliferated from just over 100 companies in 1973 to over 2,000 today. An **assessment center** is a process in which individuals are evaluated as they participate in a series of situations which resemble what they might be called

---

11. *Ibid.*, p. 21.
12. Eugene E. Jennings, "How To Develop Your Management Talent Internally," *Personnel Administrator*, Vol. 26, No. 7 (July, 1981), pp. 20—24.

upon to do on the job. The popularity of the assessment center can be attributed to its capacity for increasing a company's ability to select employees who will perform successfully in management positions.[13]

The assessee is observed in a wide variety of settings: management games, leaderless group discussions, case analyses, in-basket exercises, and interviews conducted over a two- or three-day period. At the end of the period, the observations of the assessors are combined in an attempt to get an overall assessment of the participants' qualifications for promotion. A report is usually submitted to top management and feedback is given to the participants. Figure 9–3 shows an example of skills measured for each participant in one assessment center program.

Increasing attention is being given to the validity of assessment-center procedures. Before the assessment center is run, the characteristics or dimensions to be studied should be determined through job analyses. The exercises used in the center should reflect the job for which the person is being evaluated, i.e., the exercises should have content validity.[14] While the assessment-center methodology lends itself readily to content validation, predictive validity has also been observed in many instances. A strong positive relationship is found between ratings and future performance on the job.[15]

Determining Individual Development Needs.   Because the requirements of each management position and the qualifications of those performing it are different, no two managers will have identical developmental needs. For one individual, self-development may consist of developing the ability to write reports, give talks, or lead conferences. For another, it may require learning to communicate and relate more effectively with others in the organization. Periodic evaluations of performance can provide a basis for determining each manager's progress. Conferences covering these evaluations are an essential part of self-improvement efforts.

Career Development for Women

Earlier in Chapter 5 we discussed some of the current trends relating to employment of women in jobs that until recently were held predominately by men. Included among these jobs are management-level jobs. Organizations currently are under considerable pressure, as a result of AA/EEO requirements, to increase the proportion of women who are employed at this level.

Recognizing and Eliminating Barriers to Advancement.   Women in management have been handicapped by the fact that they generally have not been part of the **old boys' network.** This network of informal, interpersonal relationships provides a means of passing on to the junior members news of possible advancement

13. Leland C. Nichols and Joseph Hudson, "Dual Role Assessment Center: Selection and Development," *Personnel Journal*, Vol. 60, No. 5 (May, 1981), pp. 380–386.

14. William C. Byham, "Starting an Assessment Center," *Personnel Administrator*, Vol. 25, No. 2 (February, 1980), pp. 27–32.

15. Cabot L. Jaffee and Joseph T. Sefcik, Jr., "What Is An Assessment Center?" *Personnel Administrator*, Vol. 25, No. 2 (February, 1980), pp. 40–43.

Figure 9–3   Assessment Center Profile

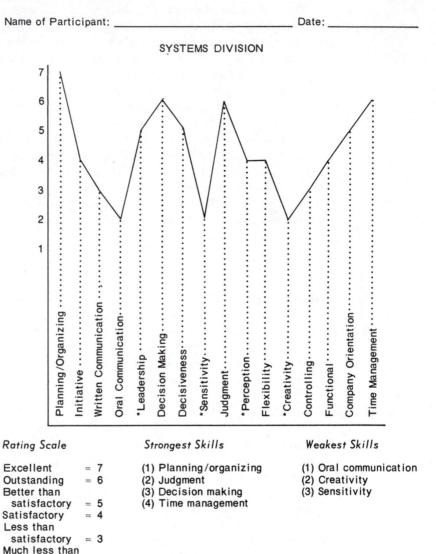

Name of Participant: _____ Date: _____

SYSTEMS DIVISION

Rating Scale

Excellent	= 7
Outstanding	= 6
Better than satisfactory	= 5
Satisfactory	= 4
Less than satisfactory	= 3
Much less than satisfactory	= 2
Weak	= 1

Strongest Skills

(1) Planning/organizing
(2) Judgment
(3) Decision making
(4) Time management

Weakest Skills

(1) Oral communication
(2) Creativity
(3) Sensitivity

(Each assessment center will give a full definition of the skills measured.)

*Skills essential to the successful operation of the division.

SOURCE: Reprinted, by permission of the publisher, from *PERSONNEL,* May-June 1980, © 1980 by AMACOM, a division of American Management Associations. All rights reserved.

opportunities and behind-the-scenes assistance from senior members of the network. Neither have women had the guidance and assistance from someone higher up in the organization serving in the role of mentor. In contrast, it has not been uncommon for men to be aided in their upward struggle by someone who counsels and guides them in the intricacies of organizational politics. However, since not many women as yet have reached the upper levels of management, in most organizations there have been very few female mentors who can give a helping hand to other women struggling upward.[16]

Formation of Women's Networks.   To combat their problem in advancing to management positions, women in several organizations have developed their own **women's networks.** A women's network at Ralston Purina in St. Louis that any female employee may join serves as a system for encouraging and fostering career development and for sharing information, experiences, and insights. At regularly scheduled meetings, corporate officers are invited to discuss such matters as planning, development, and company performance. Its members view these sessions as an opportunity to let corporate officers know that there are women who are interested in and capable of furthering their careers. Other corporations where women's networks have been established include Hoffman-LaRoche, Metropolitan Life Insurance, General Electric, Atlantic Richfield, Scholastic Magazines, and CBS.[17] What started to be a female network at Equitable Life Assurance Society now includes males as approximately 10 percent of its membership. Its organizer noted that "Men need career planning, too. Many of the men never had their own networks."[18]

Elimination of Sex-Role Myths.   The status of women in management is complicated and blurred by a series of sex-role stereotypes that have shaped the destiny of women and working women in particular. Some of the more prominent myths were discussed in Chapter 5. Fortunately, there is substantial evidence that the attitudes of women with regard to these stereotypes are changing.[19] Hopefully, as women pursue career goals assertively and the attitudes of men are changed, the status of women in management will be more favorable. The attitude of younger male managers toward women in management positions tends to be more receptive than that of older male managers. As the younger male managers move up into positions of greater responsibility and power, organizations will be more receptive to the advancement of women in management. According to Linda Keller Brown, "What is needed is a twofold push: the pressure of organized women and the empathy and support of powerful men."[20]

16. Harold W. Fox and Stanley R. Renas, "Stereotypes of Women in the Media and Their Impact upon Women's Careers," *Human Resource Management,* Vol. 16, No. 1 (Spring, 1977), p. 29.

17. "How Networks Work for Women," *Management Review,* Vol. 70, No. 8 (August, 1981), pp. 43—45.

18. Margaret M. Nemec, "Networking: Here's How at Equitable," *Personnel Administrator,* Vol. 25, No. 4 (April, 1980), pp. 63—64.

19. Ellyn Mirides and Andre Cote, "Women in Management: Strategies for Removing the Barriers," *Personnel Administrator,* Vol. 25, No. 4 (April, 1980), pp. 25—28.

20. Linda Keller Brown, "How Management Myths Hurt Women," *Working Woman,* Vol. 5, No. 12 (December, 1980), pp. 75—78.

Preparing Women for Management.   Although progress has been slow, the opportunity for women to obtain positions in management is definitely improving. In addition to breaking down the barriers to advancement, the development of women managers requires a better understanding of women's needs and the requirements of the management world.

Special Training Needs.   According to one group of authors, a program for developing women for management positions must take into account the special needs of women, among which are the following:

1. Women need to raise their self-esteem as managers. Programs for bringing women into management must stress that achievement needs are as appropriate for women as for men. Women may need help in learning how to cope with the conflict that they may encounter when seeking to achieve in a male-dominated world.

2. Women need to learn new behaviors for managing interpersonal conflict. Development programs for women may need to place more emphasis upon helping them to develop skills for handling interpersonal conflicts and negative feelings constructively. Traditionally women have tended to cope with this barrier by suppressing their negative feelings or by avoiding conflicts.

3. Women need to develop leadership and team-building skills. Women often have played only supportive roles in the business world. Cultural conditioning has, in the past, caused many women to inhibit leadership behavior but develop effective interpersonal skills. Development programs should help them to capitalize on these skills.

4. Training for women only is desirable initially. A training group consisting of women can often provide a good climate for examining some of the barriers in pursuing a management career. In a mixed group, women may feel defensive and be reluctant to assume a leadership role or to express their feelings with complete candor.[21]

Formal Training Opportunities.   In the past few years the proportion of women enrolled in college and university degree programs in management has increased significantly. The percentage of women attending four-year colleges (now 42 percent) is increasing faster than that of men. While only 25 percent of the colleges of business offer a course or program dealing exclusively or partially with the special needs of women in management, almost 25 percent more plan to include a course of this type in their management curriculum. Hopefully, as more women are trained in management, they will become members of business school faculties in departments other than secretarial and basic business skills. Robert J. Master, II of Purdue University urges that "Every organization must change any antiquated male-dominated programs and examine its attitudes toward the development of women as professionals if the optimization of human potential and resources is to be achieved in our changing society."[22]

21. Paraphrased from J. Stephen Heinen, Dorothy McGlauchlin, Constance Legeros, and Jean Freeman, "Developing the Woman Manager," *Personnel Journal*, Vol. 54, No. 5 (May, 1975), p. 238.

22. Rose K. Reha, "Preparing Women for Management Roles," *Business Horizons*, Vol. 22, No. 2 (April, 1979), pp. 68–71.

Many employers now provide special training opportunities for women who are in a management career path. They may use members of their own staff or outside firms. According to *Business Week,* career development for women is "a mushrooming mini-industry of seminars and workshops, offering instruction in everything from assertiveness training to corporate politics and varying in scope from $5 lunchtime career counseling sessions to $500 weekend management programs."[23]

Perspectives Through Reading.   In addition to formal training opportunities, today's women are provided with a wealth of information and guidance through books and magazines. Special sections in bookstores are stocked with hundreds of books written especially for women who want to have a better understanding of themselves, their roles, and the society in which they live. Many books are devoted to the pursuit of a career in many areas of endeavor.[24] One of the more candid and humorous books is *Think Like a Man, Act Like a Lady, Work Like a Dog* by Derek A. Newton—a practical guide for women who want to get ahead in their business careers. Excerpts from this book are presented in Figure 9–4.

Popular magazines that contain many articles about women and jobs include *Working Woman, New Woman, Ms, Savvy, The Executive Female,* and *Enterprising Women.* These magazines are also recommended reading for men who desire to have a better understanding of the problems that women face in the world of work. Through understanding and action, men can help to make that a better world.

Career Development for Minorities

Over a third of the companies reported in the AMA survey of career planning practices have specific career planning programs for minority employees. Such programs are often mandated as part of a company's affirmative-action commitments. These programs are intended to equip employees with career planning skills and development opportunities that will help them compete effectively for advancement.

We observed in Chapter 5 that many employers make a special effort to recruit minorities. Once individuals from minority groups are on the job, it is important for employers to provide a supportive environment that will enable them to move ahead in the organization as they develop the necessary competencies.

Assigning Minorities to Management Positions.   The area of employment for minorities that has been the slowest to respond to affirmative-action appeals is the assignment of blacks to middle- and top-management positions.

Our country's 11 percent black population is only beginning to enter middle management in significant numbers and is represented at higher levels chiefly by an occasional vice-president. Personnel and public relations jobs make up a disproportionately high 25 percent of positions held by black executives. One black bank executive observes, "By and large, companies remain unwilling to put blacks in

---

23. "Corporate Woman—Teaching Women How To Manage Their Careers," *Business Week*, May 28, 1979, pp. 148–150.

24. A few of these books are listed in the Suggested Readings section at the end of this chapter.

sensitive positions where they haven't been tested, where they can affect the bottom line. . . . Better to put them in personnel or urban affairs where the worst they can do is give out too many tickets to the baseball game." Black executives argue that companies could overcome obstacles to the development of black managers by putting talented people on a "fast track" which gives them wide experience in a shortened time. They also say that the same could be done to move promising blacks up in the corporate ranks faster.[25]

Figure 9–4   **Some Suggestions for Women Who Aspire to Responsible Managerial Positions**

THINK LIKE A MAN

Getting Ahead	Successful people get ahead because of their intellect, energy, determination, character, interpersonal skill, charisma, and luck. None of these characteristics is a sex-linked phenomenon.
Mythology	Business is riddled with uncritically held beliefs. Avoid them. Some of the most prevalent mythologies are: "We've always done it this way." "It won't work." "Men will . . ." "Women can't . . ."

ACT LIKE A LADY

Femininity	Find your personal line between being feminine and being seductive, and don't cross it. You should be and have every right in business to be the former; you should not be and have no right in business to be the latter.
Warmth	The management of personal warmth is perhaps the most difficult aspect of being a woman in business. It is potentially your biggest plus and your biggest minus. Too little warmth and you won't be liked. Too much warmth and you won't be taken seriously.

WORK LIKE A DOG

Business problems	Never go to your boss with problems. Bosses have enough of their own. Go to them with solutions. Good managers love to talk about solutions. Say, "Here's the situation I'm in. Here are some options I've come up with. Could you help me think them through?"
Repairmen	Don't feel guilty if you have to take a couple of hours off to let the plumber in to repair your sink. Your boss takes time off for this kind of thing, too. Don't overdo it, however. It's easier to get a new sink than a new job.

SOURCE: Excerpts from *Think Like a Man, Act Like a Lady, Work Like a Dog* by Derek A. Newton. Copyright © 1979 by Derek A. Newton. Reprinted by permission of Doubleday & Company, Inc.

25. Jonathan Kaufman, "Rights Frontier—Black Executives Say Prejudice Still Impedes Their Path to the Top," *Wall Street Journal*, July 9, 1980, pp. 1 and 23.

Providing More Training in Math and Science Courses. Companies that want to hire black college graduates to develop their own executives are complaining of a shortage of black engineering and MBA graduates. This problem is being faced by some organizations that are specifically designed to encourage bright minority students who choose to study in these areas. Inroads, Inc., offers the minority college student a package of tutoring, counseling, and summer internships with a local corporation. The basic aim of Inroads is to help talented minority students overcome both the lack of business-oriented role models in their home environment and the fact that they usually did not have experience in math and science courses.[26]

Training opportunities for black managers also are offered by such organizations as the American Management Associations. Their course titled "Self-Development Strategies for Black Managers" is conducted in several cities throughout the country. Major topics include black realities in corporate life, race-related stresses, effective interpersonal relationships, situational leadership, handling racial discrimination, and personal self-assessment.

PERSONAL CAREER DEVELOPMENT

Up to this point the discussion of career development has emphasized what the employer can do to integrate the needs of the organization with those of the individual employee to the mutual satisfaction of both parties. To be effective as a human resources specialist, one should have some understanding of the forces that are involved in making individual career choices and in choosing an organization.

Making Career Decisions

It should be emphasized that in the lifetime of an individual many decisions related to a career will have to be made. While the decisions to be made early in life often appear to be difficult, those to be made later in life are often more difficult.

The Early Years. From early childhood individuals begin to imagine or fantasize themselves as being in various jobs. As they mature, the self-concept begins to emerge, interest patterns are more clearly defined, and needs are recognized. All of these developments occur and are influenced by the successes and failures that the individual experiences in a myriad of activities both in and out of school. Gradually, as strengths and weaknesses in ability are recognized, the individual begins to explore occupations with a view toward finding those that appear to be realistic as far as abilities and personality are concerned. In this process of exploration, one is aided or restricted by social and economic conditions. The opportunities that exist for the individual will be a major factor in influencing a career choice. Once a choice has been made, it may last throughout a person's working life or it may change. For many individuals, especially those with advanced education, the "floundering" process can last into the thirties.

26. "Ghetto to Management—a Tough Training Plan," *Business Week*, June 2, 1980, pp. 54–61.

The Middle Years.   As individuals mature into their forties, they usually become engaged in a realistic reconsideration of what they are doing and what it means to them. This has come to be known as the "mid-life crisis."[27] At this point they may feel a need for a change of job and/or employer. Whether or not they can make such a change will depend upon many factors that they will need to explore in an extremely realistic manner. Assistance from professional persons such as career counselors may be helpful.

The Later Years.   Upon reaching retirement, some individuals may still need or desire to have some type of employment. More and more of these individuals find it desirable to have a job that will satisfy their ego and social needs as well as their financial needs. It is not uncommon to find individuals who retire after a lifetime with one organization and start with another or become self-employed. This practice has been referred to as **repotting.** Many retired persons with experience in various aspects of business serve as consultants on a fee basis or as participants in volunteer programs such as Service Corps of Retired Executives (SCORE) sponsored by the Small Business Administration.

Choosing an Appropriate Career

When asked about career choice, Peter Drucker said, "The probability that the first job choice you make is the right one for you is roughly one in a million. If you decide your first choice is the right one, chances are that you are just plain lazy."[28] The implications of this statement are that one must often do a lot of searching and changing to find a career path that is psychologically and financially satisfying.

Use of Available Resources.   In the process of finding a satisfying career, one may find it advisable to use the various resources that are available. Counselors in colleges and universities, as well as those in private practice, are equipped to assist individuals in evaluating their aptitudes, abilities, interests, and values as they relate to career selection. A sample of business schools accredited by the American Assembly of Collegiate Schools of Business (AACSB) reveals that only 22 percent have a formal program for career planning. There is, however, a broad interest among the business schools in a formal instructional program on career planning and development. The survey shows that other units in the institutions, such as placement offices and continuing education centers, offer some type of assistance in 90 percent of them.[29]

Accuracy of Self-Evaluation.   Successful career development depends in part on the ability of the individual to conduct an accurate self-evaluation. In making a self-

---

27. Douglas T. Hall, *Careers in Organizations* (Santa Monica, CA: Goodyear Publishing Company, Inc., 1976), p. 24.

28. Mary Harrington Hall, "A Conversation with Peter Drucker," *Psychology Today,* Vol. 1, No. 10 (March, 1968), p. 22.

29. Thomas G. Gutteridge and Raymond E. Hill, "Career Planning and Development—A Survey of Business School Instructional Practices," *Collegiate News and Views,* Vol. 35, No. 2 (Winter, 1981—82), pp. 5—9.

evaluation one needs to consider the factors that are significant to her or him in a personal sense. Stair has devised what she calls an "open model for career decision making." It is shown in Figure 9–5. The model includes the most important factors to be considered in career decisions. It is "open" in that it provides spaces to include additional factors. Note that it is divided into internal and external factors. On a scale of 0 to 5, the individual is to give a personal weighting to indicate the relative

Figure 9–5   Career Decision-Making Model

INTERNAL FACTORS

Aptitudes and attributes

_____ Academic aptitudes and achievement
_____ Occupational aptitudes and skills
_____ Social skills
_____ Communication skills
_____ Leadership abilities
_____ _____
_____ _____
_____ _____
_____ _____

Interests

_____ Amount of supervision
_____ Amount of pressure
_____ Amount of variety
_____ Amount of work with data
_____ Amount of work with people
_____ _____
_____ _____
_____ _____
_____ _____

Values

_____ Salary
_____ Status/prestige
_____ Advancement opportunity
_____ Growth on the job
_____ _____
_____ _____
_____ _____
_____ _____

EXTERNAL FACTORS

Family influence

_____ Family values and expectations
_____ Socioeconomic level
_____ _____
_____ _____
_____ _____
_____ _____
_____ _____
_____ _____

Economic influence

_____ Overall economic conditions
_____ Employment trends
_____ Job market information
_____ _____
_____ _____
_____ _____
_____ _____
_____ _____

Societal influence

_____ Perceived effect of race, sex, or ethnic background on success
_____ Perceived effect of physical or psychological handicaps on success
_____ _____
_____ _____
_____ _____
_____ _____

SOURCE: Lila B. Stair, *Careers in Business: Selecting and Planning Your Career Path* (Homewood, IL: Richard D. Irwin, Inc., 1980), p. 8. © 1980 by Richard D. Irwin, Inc. Reproduced with permission.

importance of each factor to career decisions. There are nine chapters in her book devoted to careers in various areas of business. At the end of each chapter, the individual is to evaluate the suitability of each career area against the original self-evaluation.[30] Models such as Stair's help to insure that the individual does not overlook factors that may be critical in the decision-making process.

Significance of Interest Inventories.

Psychologists who specialize in career counseling typically administer a battery of tests such as those mentioned in Chapter 6. The *Strong Vocational Interest Blank (SVIB)* developed by the late E. K. Strong, Jr., during the 1920s was among the first of the interest tests.[31] Somewhat later, G. Frederic Kuder developed inventories that measure the degree of interest in mechanical, clerical, scientific, and persuasive activities, among others. Both the Strong and the Kuder interest inventories have been used widely in vocational counseling.

Strong found that there are substantial differences in interests which vary from occupation to occupation and that a person's interest pattern, especially after age 21, tends to become quite stable. By administering his test, now known as the *Strong-Campbell Interest Inventory (SCII)*, it is possible to tell the client the degree to which his or her interests correspond with those of successful people in a wide range of occupations. The results which are profiled on the basis of computer scoring also reveal one's personality type, using Holland's categories.

According to Holland, most persons can be categorized into the following types: realistic, investigative, artistic, social, enterprising, or conventional. These categories characterize not only a type of person, but also the type of working environment that a person would find most congenial. In the actual application of Holland's theory, combinations of the six types are examined. For example, a person may be classified as Realistic-Investigative-Enterprising (RIE). Jobs in the RIE category include mechanical engineer, watch repairman, lineman, air traffic controller, and many others.[32]

Evaluation of Long-Term Employment Opportunities.

In making a career choice, one should attempt to determine the probable long-term opportunities in the occupational fields that one is considering. While even the experts can err in their predictions, one should at least give attention to what opinions are available. A source of information that has proven valuable over the years is the *Occupational Outlook Handbook* published by the United States Department of Labor. Most libraries have this book. Many libraries also have extensive holdings of other publications which provide details about jobs and career fields.

---

30. Lila B. Stair, *Careers in Business—Selecting and Planning Your Career Path* (Homewood, IL: Richard D. Irwin, Inc., 1980), pp. 2–14.

31. E. K. Strong, Jr., of Stanford University, was active in the measurement of interests from the early 1920s to the time of his death in 1963. Since his death, his work has been carried on by the staff of the Measurement Research Center, University of Minnesota.

32. John I. Holland, *Making Vocational Choices: A Theory of Careers* (Englewood Cliffs, NJ: Prentice-Hall, Inc., 1973), Chapters 2 and 3 and Appendix B.

Choosing an Employer

Once an individual has made a career choice, even if only on a tentative basis, the next major decision to be made involves deciding where to work. The choice of employer may be based primarily upon location, immediate availability, starting salary, and other basic considerations. The college graduate, however, who has prepared for a professional or managerial career is likely to have more sophisticated concerns. Hall proposes that people frequently choose an organization on the basis of its climate and how it appears to fit their needs. According to Hall:

> People with high needs for achievement may choose aggressive, achievement-oriented organizations. Power-oriented people may choose influential, prestigious, power-oriented organizations. Affiliative people may choose warm, friendly, supportive organizations. We know that people whose needs fit with the climate of an organization are rewarded more and are more satisfied than those who fit in less well, so it is natural to reason that fit would also be a factor in one's choice of an organization.[33]

Hall suggests that, because the relevant theory and measurement technology are available, the prediction of organizational choice is a promising, untapped area for researchers.

Keeping a Career in Perspective

Work, for most people, is a primary factor in determining the overall quality of their lives. It provides a setting for satisfying practically the whole range of human needs and thus is of considerable value to the individual. Nevertheless, it is advisable to keep one's career in perspective in order that other important areas of life are not neglected.

Off-the-Job Interests.   Satisfaction with one's life is a product of many forces. Some of the more important ingredients are physical health, emotional well-being, harmonious interpersonal relationships with significant persons, freedom from too much stress, and achievement of one's goals. While one's career can provide some of the satisfaction that one would like to have, it is generally necessary to turn to interests and activities outside of one's career. Off-the-job activities not only provide a respite from daily work, but also offer satisfactions that are independent of one's career.

Marital and/or Family Life.   The career development planning of an individual as well as of an organization must take into account the needs of spouses and children, if there are any. The one event that often causes the greatest threat to family needs is relocation. Conflicts over the desire to have increased income and status that are inherent in a promotion with a strong reluctance to move often border on the disastrous. Many employers now provide complete assistance in this area, including

---

33. Douglas T. Hall, *Careers in Organizations, op. cit.,* p. 36.

relocation counseling, in an effort to reduce the severity of the pain that can accompany relocations.

The person who is "married" to the job to the extent that he or she fails to provide the attention and caring that are essential to marriage and family relations is lacking in an understanding of what life is all about. One should always be aware that "to be a success in the business world takes hard work, long hours, persistent effort, and constant attention. To be a success in marriage takes hard work, long hours, persistent effort, and constant attention .... The problem is giving each its due and not shortchanging the other."[34]

Two-Career Couples.   There are many situations in which both husband and wife pursue careers more or less continually and also share a family life together. A significant number of corporations are concerned with the problems facing two-career couples and are beginning to offer assistance to them. The main problem that these couples face is relocation. It is reported that two thirds of 374 major companies surveyed have experienced resistance to relocation, primarily because a proposed transfer would interfere with a spouse's career. A large percentage of the wives who were surveyed said that, unless they could maintain their current career levels or unless the net gain from the move was "irresistible," they would be unlikely to relocate again to advance their husbands' careers. Other problems that two-career couples face are child care, allocation of time, and emotional stress. Money is reported to be the single greatest advantage, but it is also a problem.[35]

Many of the major companies now offer some kind of job-finding assistance for spouses of employees who are relocated. This includes paying fees charged by employment agencies, job counseling firms, and executive-search firms. The vice-president of an executive recruiting firm calls the two-career couple "a time bomb confronting American industry in the 1980's." The employee's growing reluctance to relocate at the dictate of the company will mean all kinds of compromises for business organizations.[36]

More and more companies are also bending old rules against hiring husband and wife. Most of these companies, however, do not place husband and wife in the same department or have them reporting to each other.

RÉSUMÉ

Concern for the quality of work life, equal employment opportunities, and other demands have resulted in the growth of career development programs. To be successful, such programs are dependent upon management support, well-defined goals, effective communication, and compatible personnel policies. It is essential that

34. Richard W. Ogden, *How to Succeed in Business and Marriage* (New York: AMACOM, 1978), p. 2.

35. *BNA Fair Employment Practices Bulletin*, No. 427 (Washington: The Bureau of National Affairs, Inc., August 13, 1981), pp. 5–6.

36. "Firms Increasingly Help Spouses of Transferred Employes Find Jobs," *Wall Street Journal*, January 21, 1982, p. 25.

a career development program include a comprehensive inventory of job opportunities with carefully organized progressions from one job to the next. The process of choosing a career path should involve maximum participation of the individual concerned.

Many organizations have special career development programs for women and minorities. Such programs are designed to overcome the barriers to advancement that women and minorities have traditionally encountered.

The human resources specialist should understand the process by which individuals typically make career choices and be aware of some of the more scientific approaches to career selection that are available In making a choice, one should use the best sources of information that are available.

TERMS TO IDENTIFY

lateral transfers
downward transfers or demotions
promotions
outplacement service

assessment center
old boys' network
women's networks
repotting

DISCUSSION QUESTIONS

1. What are the reasons for the trend toward increased emphasis upon career development programs?
2. Bank of America maintains a special suite of offices in its world headquarters in San Francisco for its retired executives. Two of the bank's former chief executives use their offices regularly.
   a. Of what value is this arrangement to the corporation? to the individuals?
   b. Should a maximum age limit be set for eligibility for having an office?
3. Why is it that some of the companies with the best developmental programs experience the greatest loss of young management personnel?
4. One recruiter has said that "Next to talent, the second most important factor in career success is taking the time and effort to develop visibility." What are some ways of developing visibility?
5. Over 50 percent of all MBA's leave their first employer within five years. While the change may represent career growth for the individuals, it represents a loss to the employers. What are some of the probable reasons for their leaving?

6. A group of managers from different companies were discussing management development in a conference. One executive expressed the opinion that those executives who had the potential talent in her firm would find ways of developing themselves. Another one stated that his firm had several promising young persons who were qualified for promotions but who could not be advanced because all positions at the higher level were filled. He stated that his company would be wasting money in training persons either for positions that they had already outgrown or for positions that would not be open for several years. What is your reaction to the statements of each of these two executives?
7. What are some of the barriers that have limited advancement opportunities for women in many organizations?
8. There is a rapidly developing trend for companies to hire couples when both parties are interested in pursuing careers. What changes would probably have to be made in existing personnel policies to make this possible?

PROBLEM 9–1

THE AMBITIOUS TELEPHONE OPERATOR

Sue Ann Scott was a telephone operator at the headquarters of a large corporation. A high school graduate, she had no particular skills other than a pleasing voice and personality. Nevertheless, Ms. Scott was highly desirous of improving her economic position. Recognizing her educational limitations, she began taking accounting courses on a random basis in an evening adult education program. Unfortunately she did not have any particular plan for career development.

Ms. Scott also took advantage of the corporation's job bidding system by applying for openings that were posted, even though in many instances she did not meet the specifications listed for them. After being rejected several times, she became discouraged. Her depressed spirits were observed by Mrs. Burroughs, one of the senior executives in the corporation. Mrs. Burroughs invited Ms. Scott to come to her office for a talk about Scott's problems. Ms. Scott took full advantage of the opportunity to express her frustrations and disappointments. As she unburdened herself it became apparent that, besides lacking any special skills or career objectives, during interviews she tended to apologize for having "only a high school education." This made it difficult for the interviewers to select her over other candidates who were putting their best foot forward. Mrs. Burroughs suggested that perhaps Ms. Scott might try taking a more positive approach during her interviews. For example, Ms. Scott could stress her self-improvement efforts at night school and the fact that she was a dependable and cooperative person who was willing to work hard to succeed in the job for which she was applying.

Following Mrs. Burroughs' advice, Ms. Scott selected a job for which she felt she could qualify. She made a very forceful and positive presentation during her interview, stressing those favorable qualities that she possessed. As a result of this approach, she was selected for the job of invoice clerk. While this job did not pay much more than that of telephone operator, it did offer an avenue for advancement into the accounting field where the accounting courses she was taking would be of value. After a few months in her clerical position, she was able to move up into a regular accounting position.

a. What are some of the possible reasons why Ms. Scott did not seek or receive assistance or advice from her immediate supervisor?

b. What can the corporation do to avoid future situations such as that experienced by Ms. Scott?

c. This problem occurred in the early 1970s. Since then, greater emphasis has been placed upon equal employment opportunity and affirmative action. What changes has management probably made by this time?

SUGGESTED READINGS

Hennig, Margaret, and Anne Jardim. *The Managerial Woman.* Garden City, NY: Anchor Press/Doubleday, 1977.

Higginson, Margaret V., and Thomas L. Quick. *The Ambitious Woman's Guide to a Successful Career.* New York: AMACOM, 1975.

Jelinek, Mariann. *Career Management for the Individual and the Organization.* Chicago: St. Clair Press, 1979.

Lynch, E. M. *Decades: Personal Fulfillment and Career Success.* New York: AMACOM, 1980.

Morgan, Marilyn A. (ed.). *Managing Career Development.* New York: Van Nostrand Reinhold Company, 1980.

Stockard, James G. *Career Development and Job Training: A Manager's Handbook.* New York: AMACOM, 1977.

Taylor, B., and G. L. Lippitt (eds.). *Management Development and Training Handbook.* New York: McGraw-Hill Book Company, 1975.

Thornton, George C. III, and William C. Byham. *Assessment Centers and Managerial Performance.* New York: Academic Press, Inc., 1982.

Chapter Objectives:

- To cite the various objectives of performance evaluation programs.
- To identify the basic considerations in selecting criteria for evaluation.
- To cite the factors brought out in major court decisions involving performance evaluation procedures.
- To describe the types of errors that are commonly found in rating approaches to evaluation.
- To describe the process for developing behaviorally anchored rating scales (BARS).
- To understand the relationship between different approaches to measuring performance and the objectives of performance evaluation.
- To identify the different approaches to performance evaluation interviewing.

10

Evaluating and Improving Performance

In the preceding chapters the programs for procuring and developing a productive work force were discussed. In this chapter we turn to performance evaluation programs, which must also be developed in order to maintain this productivity. Performance evaluation occurs whether or not there is a formal evaluation program. Superiors are constantly observing the manner in which subordinates are carrying out their assignments and forming impressions as to their relative worth to the organization. Most large and many small organizations do have a formal program to facilitate and to standardize the evaluation of employees. Such programs exist under a variety of labels. The traditional term "merit rating" has generally been superseded by such terms as "performance appraisal" and "performance evaluation."

The success or failure of performance evaluation is dependent upon the philosophy underlying it and the attitudes and skills of management and supervisory personnel responsible for its administration. Many different methods are available for gathering information about the performance of subordinates. However, this is only the first step in the evaluation process. The information must be evaluated in the context of organizational needs and communicated to the individuals in a manner that will result in the attainment of high levels of performance.

PERFORMANCE EVALUATION PROGRAMS

Evaluation programs are a major function of human resources management in most organizations. A study conducted by The Bureau of National Affairs indicates that, among survey respondents, 84 percent have regular procedures for evaluating office personnel and 54 percent have procedures for evaluating production employees. Performance evaluations are conducted annually for 74 percent of office employees and 58 percent of production groups. Semiannual reviews are made in 25 percent of the office group and 30 percent of the production group. Performance evaluations are made more frequently during the probationary period or during the first year on a job.[1]

A performance evaluation program benefits both the organization and the subordinates whose performance is being appraised. For the organization, performance evaluation is a management information system that provides input into all aspects of human resources management. For the individual, it provides feedback about performance.

Well-designed and properly used appraisal systems are essential to the effective functioning of most organizations. New demands for performance accountability, brought about by "belt-tightening" campaigns, have caused greater attention to be focused on performance evaluation.[2] Furthermore, AA/EEO decisions have made it

---

1. *Employee Performance: Evaluation and Control*, Personnel Policies Forum Survey No. 108 (Washington, DC: The Bureau of National Affairs, Inc., February, 1975), pp. 1–3.
2. William H. Holley, Hubert S. Field, and Nona J. Barnett, "Analyzing Performance Appraisal Systems: An Empirical Study," *Personnel Journal*, Vol. 55, No. 9 (September, 1976), pp. 457–459, 463.

essential for employers to have accurate, objective records of employee performance in order to defend themselves against possible charges of discrimination in connection with such personnel actions as discharges, promotions, and/or salary increases.[3] The interrelationships between the performance evaluation function and the other major personnel functions are shown in Figure 10–1. You may wish to study it now before reading further about the development of an evaluation program.

Development of an Evaluation Program

As we noted in Chapter 3, the human resources department ordinarily has the primary responsibility for overseeing and coordinating the evaluation program. However, managers from the operating departments also should be actively involved in it, particularly in helping to establish the objectives for the program.

Objectives of an Evaluation Program.
Some of the more important objectives are the following:

1. To provide employees with adequate feedback concerning their performance.
2. To serve as a basis for modifying or changing behavior toward more effective working habits.
3. To provide managers with data which they may use to judge future job assignments and compensation.[4]

A study of over 200 organizations by Locher and Teel indicates that performance appraisals are used most widely as the basis for making compensation decisions and planning individual performance improvement programs. It was also found that small organizations (less than 500 employees) make significantly greater use of appraisals in compensation and promotion decisions than do large organizations (more than 500 employees). Large organizations, on the other hand, make greater use of appraisals for performance improvement and feedback.[5]

Qualifications of Evaluators.
Managers and supervisors traditionally have served as evaluators of their subordinates. In most instances they are in the best position to perform this function but not necessarily qualified to do so. In order to be qualified, there are certain criteria that they should meet. These are:

1. *Opportunity to observe.* The appraiser must be in a position to collect relevant information about the person being evaluated . . . through personal observation, reviewing records, or talking with others who have direct knowledge of the person.

---

3. Alan H. Locher and Kenneth S. Teel, "Performance Appraisal—A Survey of Current Practices," *Personnel Journal*, Vol. 56, No. 5 (May, 1977), pp. 245–247, 254.
4. Harry Levinson, "Appraisal of *What* Performance?" *Harvard Business Review*, Vol. 54, No. 4 (July-August, 1976), pp. 30–46.
5. Locher and Teel, *loc. cit.*

Figure 10–1 Relationship of Performance Evaluation to Other Personnel Functions

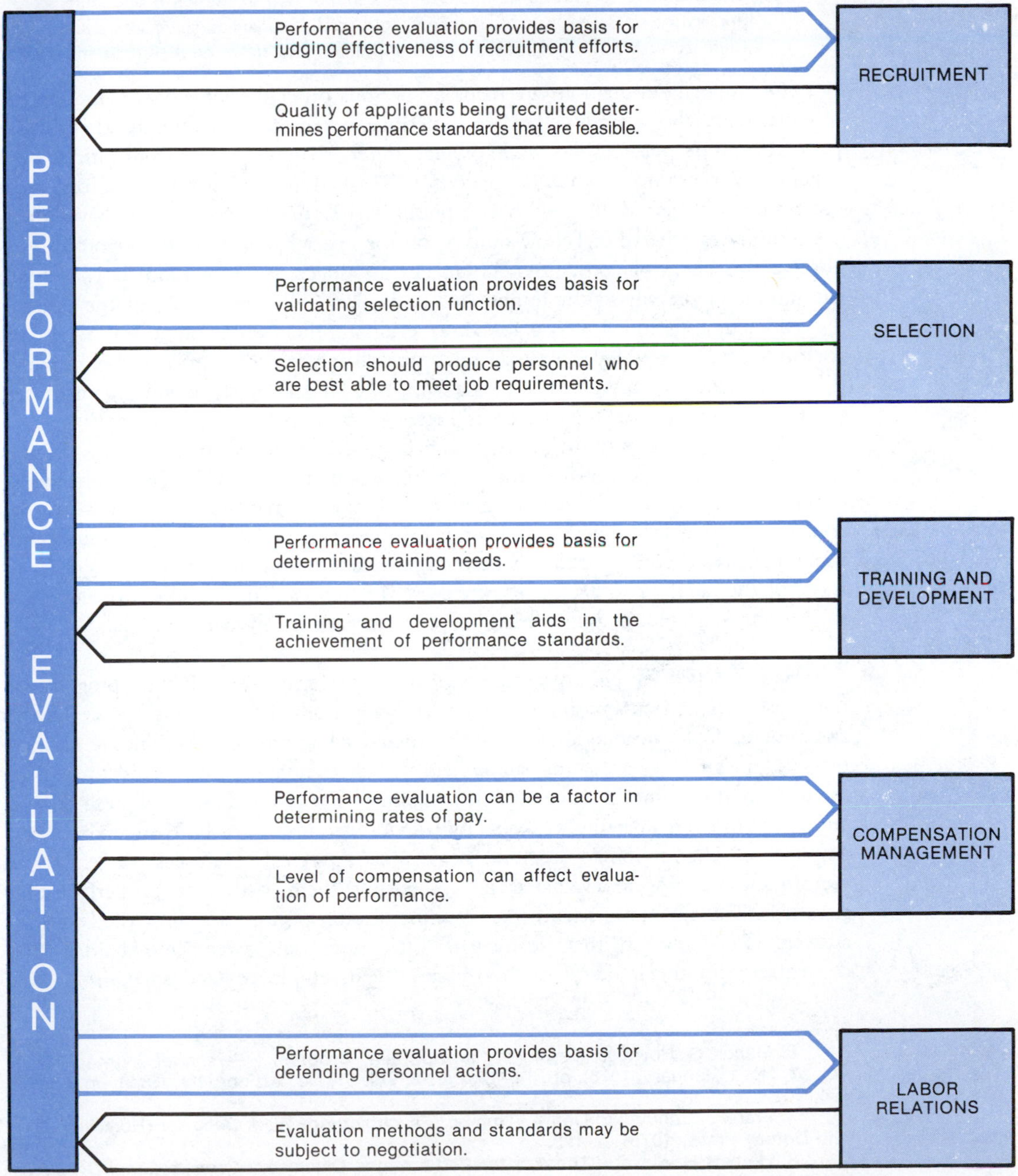

P E R F O R M A N C E   E V A L U A T I O N

Performance evaluation provides basis for judging effectiveness of recruitment efforts.

Quality of applicants being recruited determines performance standards that are feasible.

RECRUITMENT

Performance evaluation provides basis for validating selection function.

Selection should produce personnel who are best able to meet job requirements.

SELECTION

Performance evaluation provides basis for determining training needs.

Training and development aids in the achievement of performance standards.

TRAINING AND DEVELOPMENT

Performance evaluation can be a factor in determining rates of pay.

Level of compensation can affect evaluation of performance.

COMPENSATION MANAGEMENT

Performance evaluation provides basis for defending personnel actions.

Evaluation methods and standards may be subject to negotiation.

LABOR RELATIONS

2. *Understanding of job requirements.* A clear understanding of job requirements and standards of satisfactory performance is required.

3. *Having an appropriate point of view.* One's point of view influences which observed performance is considered desirable or undesirable. For example, in one study of the appraisal of salesmen by sales managers and credit managers, there was a significant difference between the sales manager's appraisals and those of the credit manager.[6]

Occasionally evaluations are made by persons other than a superior. Individuals of equal rank who work together are sometimes asked to evaluate each other. These **peer appraisals** provide information which differs to some degree from ratings by a superior. For example, when a supervisor is asked to rate a patrol officer on a dimension such as "dealing with the public," the supervisor may not have much opportunity to observe it. Fellow officers, on the other hand, have the opportunity to observe this behavior constantly. As far as this aspect of performance is concerned, the ratings of the supervisor might tend to be less valid than those of the peers.[7]

Sometimes employees are asked to evaluate themselves on a **self-appraisal form.** According to Meyer, when a self-appraisal is completed prior to performance discussion, the appraisal tends to be modest. Under most other circumstances, individuals tend to see themselves as better performers.[8]

Appraisal by subordinates has been used in some instances to provide superiors with feedback on how their subordinates view them. Gulf Oil conducted an experiment in which 21 senior members of the human resources staff in the corporation anonymously evaluated the performance of their senior vice-president. In some instances the vice-president's perception of his performance was quite similar to those of the raters; in other cases there were differences. The vice-president accepted the summarized report as the basis for a performance improvement plan.[9]

Training of Evaluators.

A weakness of many performance evaluation programs is that managers and supervisors are not adequately trained for the task as evaluators and provide little meaningful feedback of their evaluations to subordinates. Lacking precise standards for evaluating subordinates, their evaluations often tend to become inflated to the point of having little meaning. The United States Forest Service attempted to overcome this weakness by providing training for both supervisors and employees. The training program began with typical examples of employee performance that were evaluated by comparing them with sets of performance standards. The appraisers scored their training session responses against the "correct" answers. In doing so they learned if their appraisals were "too hard," "too concentrated in the middle," or "too easy." Next, employees and supervisors were

---

6. Marion G. Haynes, "Developing an Appraisal Program," *Personnel Journal,* Part 1: Vol. 57, No. 1 (January, 1978), pp. 14–19; Part 2: Vol. 57, No. 2 (February, 1978), pp. 66–67, 104, 107.

7. Frank J. Landy and Don A. Trumbo, *Psychology of Work Behavior* (Homewood, IL: The Dorsey Press, 1976), p. 123.

8. Herbert H. Meyer, "The Pay for Performance Dilemma," *Organizational Dynamics,* Vol. 3, No. 3 (Winter, 1975), pp. 39–50.

9. Gerald W. Bush and John W. Stinson, "A Different Use of Performance Appraisal: Evaluating the Boss," *Management Review.* Vol. 69, No. 10 (October, 1980), pp. 14–17.

shown how to conduct effective appraisal discussions. Finally, both groups were exposed to the feedback and monitoring system. Through the feedback system supervisors learned how their ratings compared with those of other supervisors.[10]

Evaluators should be made aware of various factors that may influence their evaluations. Studies indicate that a supervisor's evaluations are influenced by the proportion of workers in the unit who are considered as having "poor attitudes." It was found that the greater the proportion of subordinates manifesting poor attitudes, the more favorable the performance ratings for those subordinates with good attitudes.[11]

Training should also stress the development of interviewing skills. Role playing can simulate the actual conditions that might be encountered in the work situation. Videotaping the role playing permits managers and supervisors to view and critique their own performance and progress and to experiment with different interview techniques.[12]

Finally, a training program for evaluators should cover ethical considerations in employee appraisal.[13] To assist managers in recognizing ethical issues in appraisals, Kellogg has prepared the checklist shown in Figure 10–2.

Figure 10–2 **Manager's Checklist on Employee Appraisal Ethics**

1. Know the reason for appraisal.
2. Appraise on the basis of *representative* information.
3. Appraise on the basis of *sufficient* information.
4. Appraise on the basis of *relevant* information.
5. Make an honest appraisal.
6. Keep written and oral appraisals consistent.
7. Present appraisal as opinion.
8. Give appraisal information only to those who have a good reason to know it.
9. Don't imply the existence of an appraisal that hasn't been made.
10. Don't accept another's appraisal without knowing the basis for it.
11. Decide on a retention policy for appraisals and adhere to it.
12. Convey appraisal data to a third party only if you've given it to the person.
13. Make written appraisals available to employees.
14. Provide a right of appeal to employees.
15. Open appraisals to employee input.

SOURCE: Reprinted by permission of the publisher, from *What To Do About Performance Appraisal*, Marion S. Kellogg, © 1975 by AMACOM, a division of American Management Associations. All rights reserved.

10. Richard L. Prather, "Extending the Life of Performance Appraisal Systems," *Personnel Journal*, Vol. 53, No. 10 (October, 1974), pp. 739–743.

11. Ronald J. Grey and David Kipnis, "Untangling the Performance Appraisal Dilemma: The Influence of Perceived Organizational Context on Evaluative Processes," *Journal of Applied Psychology*, Vol. 61, No. 3 (June, 1976), pp. 329–335.

12. Thomas W. Zimmerer and Thomas F. Stroh, "Preparing Managers for Performance Appraisal," *SAM Advanced Management Journal*, Vol. 39, No. 3 (July, 1974), pp. 36–42.

13. Marion S. Kellogg, *What To Do About Performance Appraisal* (rev. ed.; New York: AMACOM, 1975), pp. 10–11.

Selection of Performance Criteria

Before any evaluation occurs, the criteria against which employees are to be evaluated should be clearly defined. These criteria, or standards, must be based on job requirements. Although the specific criteria vary from one job to another, in general they are based upon the concepts of quantity and quality of performance.

In selecting performance criteria there are three basic considerations:

1. *Relevance.* This refers to the extent to which criteria relate to the objectives of the job.
2. *Freedom from contamination.* A comparison of performance among production workers, for example, should not be contaminated by the fact that some have newer machines than others. Similarly, a comparison of the performance of traveling salespersons should not be contaminated by the fact that territories differ in sales potential.
3. *Reliability.* The reliability of a criterion refers to its stability or consistency. It refers to the extent to which individuals tend to maintain a certain level of performance over time. In ratings, it may be measured by correlating two sets of ratings made by a single rater or by two different raters.[14]

In addition to these basic considerations, there is also the requirement that the criteria be acceptable to management.

Equal Employment Opportunity Considerations

The importance of having carefully defined and measurable criteria has been emphasized in recent years by the courts. In one landmark case involving test validation, Albermarle Paper Company *v.* Moody, the United States Supreme Court found that employees had been ranked against a vague standard, open to each supervisor's own interpretation. The court stated that "there is no way of knowing precisely what criteria of job performance the supervisors were considering, whether each supervisor was considering the same criteria, or whether indeed, any of the supervisors actually applied a focused and stable body of criteria of any kind."[15]

In an earlier case—Brito *v.* Zia Company—the Tenth Circuit Court of Appeals ruled that Zia Company had violated Title VII of the Civil Rights Act of 1964 when it laid off several Spanish-surnamed employees on the basis of poor performance ratings. The court concluded that the practice was illegal because the performance appraisals were based upon subjective supervisory observations, caused a disproportionate reduction in the number of Spanish-surnamed employees, and were not administered in a controlled and standardized fashion. Furthermore, two of the three supervisors did not have daily contact with the employees being evaluated. The court concluded that the evaluations were based upon the "best judgments and opinions" of the evaluators, but not on any identifiable objective criteria supported by some

14. Ernest J. McCormick and Daniel R. Ilgen, *Industrial Psychology* (7th ed.; Englewood Cliffs, NJ: Prentice-Hall, Inc., 1980), pp. 52–55.
15. 95 S. Ct. 2362 (1975).

type of record. As a result, the court determined that Zia Company had failed to produce evidence of validity for its performance appraisal system.[16]

While the acceptable method for measuring the validity of a performance appraisal procedure has not been clearly established, the emphasis on such validation has had some effect. It has resulted in the elimination of vague descriptions of behavior such as attitude, cooperation, dependability, initiative, and leadership. Generally, the elimination of these vague performance traits or characteristics will improve the appraisal process.[17]

Another case, involving promotions and transfers, that bears on performance appraisal is Rowe *v.* General Motors.[18] In this case the Fifth Circuit Court of Appeals concluded that the selection of blacks for promotion or transfer resulted from the recommendations of supervisors, all of whom were white. The court also concluded that the supervisors' recommendations were based upon subjective and vague standards.

Why Performance Evaluation Programs Fail

In actual practice, formal performance evaluation programs may yield disappointing results. A number of reasons have been advanced for this fact. Lazer states that the primary culprits are multiple uses of the program, lack of top-management support, lack of job-relatedness, rater bias, and too many evaluation forms to complete on each individual.[19]

If an evaluation program is used to provide a written evaluation for salary action and at the same time to motivate subordinates to improve their work, the two purposes may be in conflict. As a result, the evaluation interview essentially becomes a salary discussion in which the superior seeks to justify the action taken. Consequently, the discussion has little influence upon future job performance.

As in all personnel functions, if the support of top management is lacking, the evaluation program will not be successful. The best conceived evaluation program cannot function effectively in an environment where managers are not encouraged by their superiors to take the program seriously. Furthermore, their effectiveness in evaluating subordinates should be a factor upon which managers are evaluated.

Other possible reasons for the failure of performance evaluation programs to yield the desired results are that:

1. Managers perceive that little or no benefit will be derived from the time and energy spent in the process.
2. Managers dislike the face-to-face confrontation.
3. Most managers are not sufficiently skilled in conducting evaluation interviews.
4. The judgmental process required for evaluation is in conflict with the helping role of developing employees.

16. 478 F. 2d 1200 (1973).

17. Harvey Kahalas, "The Environmental Context of Performance Evaluation and Its Effect on Current Practices," *Human Resource Management*, Vol. 19, No. 3 (Fall, 1980), pp. 32–40.

18. 457 F. 2d 348 (1972).

19. Robert I. Lazer, "Performance Appraisal: What Does the Future Hold?" *Personnel Administrator*, Vol. 25, No. 7 (July, 1980), pp. 69–73.

Performance appraisal is sometimes considered to be a once-a-year activity in which the evaluation interview often resembles a legal case. The superior seeks to document the case instead of conducting a developmental discussion.[20] Meyer reminds us that "Performance feedback and coaching must be a day-to-day activity. Effective coaching must be associated immediately and directly with the performance at issue."[21]

Cost-Benefit Considerations

The cost of establishing and maintaining a performance evaluation program is related to its scope and complexity. The time spent in preparing reports and in conducting interviews will constitute the bulk of the costs. The salaries or fees of professional persons who develop the program, analyze the reports, and prepare various summaries for use by management are also chargeable to the program. The salaries of personnel who maintain the files of evaluation reports must also be considered.

Having a sound basis for improving performance is one of the major benefits of an evaluation program. Performance evaluation data may also be used to assess the effectiveness of other aspects of the personnel program and thus provide information that may reveal the need for improvements. Performance evaluation reports have been found to be valuable as measures of employee success that may be used in validating the tests used in selection and in determining the relative worth of jobs under a job evaluation program. Such reports may be used to substantiate personnel actions that may result in the filing of a grievance or a charge of discrimination. Finally, it is important to recognize that the success of the entire personnel program depends upon knowing how the performance of employees compares to the goals established for them. This knowledge can best be obtained from a carefully planned and administered personnel evaluation program.

PERFORMANCE EVALUATION METHODS

Methods for evaluating personnel that are in use today have evolved from a procedure developed by Walter Dill Scott for rating salespersons. This procedure was originally termed *man-to-man rating scale.* It involved comparing the performance of salespersons against named individuals whose performance represented standards at different levels. The scale was adapted to meet the needs of the United States Army in World War I. It has been replaced with other methods that represent technical improvements and are more consistent with the purposes of evaluation. In the

---

20. Ronald J. Burke, "Why Performance Appraisal Systems Fail," *Personnel Administration,* Vol. 35, No. 3 (June, 1972), pp. 32–40; James C. Conant, "The Performance Appraisal: A Critique and an Alternative," *Business Horizons,* Vol. 16, No. 3 (June, 1973), pp. 73–78.

21. Herbert H. Meyer, "The Annual Performance Review Discussion—Making It constructive," *Personnel Journal,* Vol. 56, No. 10 (October, 1977), pp. 508–511.

discussion that follows, those methods that have widespread usage will be examined in detail. Those methods that are used less frequently will be mentioned briefly.

In the Locher and Teel study, 216 organizations reported on a checklist the primary appraisal technique they each used. Over half (56 percent) reported that they used the rating scale as the primary technique; 25 percent, essay; 13 percent, MBO; and 5 percent, "all other techniques."[22]

Rating Scale Method

In the **rating scale method** each trait or characteristic to be rated is represented by a line or scale on which the rater indicates the degree to which the individual possesses the trait or characteristic. An example of this type of scale is shown in Figure 10–3. There are many variations of this type of scale. The differences are to be found in (1) the characteristics or dimensions on which individuals are to be rated, (2) the degree to which the performance dimension is defined for the rater, and (3) the degree to which the points on the scale are clearly defined. In Figure 10–3 the dimensions are defined briefly and some attempt is made to define the points on the scale.

Global Ratings. While a rating scale with several relevant dimensions is preferable, many organizations simply ask for a single rating of overall job performance. Such a rating, commonly referred to as a **global rating,** is useful for making various personnel decisions. It is, however, of little value in communicating performance evaluations to subordinates and is likely to be viewed as discriminatory. It should, therefore, be used only in addition to ratings on specific characteristics.

Rating Errors. With any rating device there are certain types of errors that can arise and should be considered. The halo error discussed in Chapter 6 also is common with respect to rating scales, especially those that do not have carefully developed statements of employee behavior. The provision for rater remarks on the rating form, as shown in Figure 10–3, tends to reduce halo error.

It is common for some raters to give unusually high ratings. This gives rise to the **leniency error.** One way to reduce the leniency error is to clearly define the characteristics or dimensions and to provide meaningful descriptions of behavior, known as **anchors,** on the scale. Another approach is to require raters to conform to some pattern. For example, it may be required that 10 percent of their ratings be poor (or excellent). This is similar to the requirement in some educational institutions that instructors grade on a "curve."

Raters who are reluctant to assign either extremely high or extremely low ratings commit the **error of central tendency.** To such individuals it is a good idea to explain that, among large numbers of employees, one may expect to find differences in behaviors, production, and other characteristics.

---

22. Locher and Teel, *loc. cit.* Another more recent article states that MBO has been used by nearly half of the *Fortune* 500 firms. See Raymond J. Pack and William M. Vicars, "MBO—Today and Tomorrow," *Personnel*, Vol. 56, No. 3 (May-June, 1979), pp. 68–77.

Behaviorally Anchored Rating Scales (BARS). We mentioned earlier that one way to improve a rating scale is to have descriptions of behavior along the scale, or continuum. These descriptions permit the rater to identify readily the point where a particular individual fits on the scale. An evaluation procedure has been developed that attempts to identify many dimensions of performance in behavior-specific terms. It utilizes a device referred to as the **behaviorally anchored rating scale** (BARS).

The BARS consist of a series of five to ten vertical scales—one for each important dimension of job performance anchored by the incidents judged to be critical. A *critical incident* occurs when employee behavior results in unusual success

Figure 10–3   Rating Scale with Provision for Rater Comments

Appraise employee's performance in PRESENT ASSIGNMENT. Check (√) most appropriate square.
Appraisers are *urged to use freely* the "REMARKS" sections for significant comments descriptive of the individual.

1. KNOWLEDGE OF WORK: Understanding of all phases of his work and related matters.	Needs instruction or guidance.	Has required knowledge of own and related work. ✓✓	Has exceptional knowledge of own and related work.
	Remarks: *Is particularly good on gas engines*		
2. INITIATIVE: Ability to originate or develop ideas and to get things started.	Lacks imagination. ✓✓	Meets necessary requirements.	Unusually resourceful.
	Remarks: *Has good ideas when asked for an opinion, but otherwise will not offer them. Somewhat lacking in self-confidence.*		
3. APPLICATION: Attention and application to his work.	Wastes time. Needs close supervision	Steady and willing worker. ✓✓	Exceptionally industrious.
	Remarks:		
4. QUALITY OF WORK: Throughness, neatness, and accuracy of work	Needs improvement.	Regularly meets recognized standards.	Consistently maintains highest ✓✓ quality.
	Remarks: *The work he turns out is always of the highest possible quality.*		
5. VOLUME OF WORK: Quantity of acceptable work.	Should be increased.	Regularly meets recognized ✓✓ standards.	Unusually high output.
	Remarks *Would be higher if he did not spend so much time checking and rechecking his work.*		

or unusual failure on some part of the job.[23] The critical incidents are located along the scale and are assigned points according to the opinions of experts. One of the BARS for the job of patrol officer is shown in Figure 10–4. Note that this particular scale is for the dimension described as "Awareness of procedures, laws, court rulings, and changes in them."

BARS are typically developed by committees which include both raters and ratees. The committee's task is to identify all of the relevant job characteristics or dimensions for the job. Behavioral anchors in the form of statements are then established for each of the job dimensions. The anchors are given to several participants who are asked to indicate which job dimension each anchor illustrates. Only those anchors which at least 70 percent of the group agree belong with a particular dimension are retained. Finally, anchors are attached to their job dimensions and placed on the appropriate scales according to values that the group assigns to them.[24]

At the present time there is no strong evidence that BARS reduce the rating errors mentioned previously. However, some studies have shown that scales of this type can yield better ratings.[25] The major advantage of BARS is that personnel outside of the human resources department participate in the development of the BARS. Their participation is conducive to better acceptance of the scales. The procedures followed in developing BARS also result in scales that have a high degree of content validity. The main disadvantage of BARS is that they require considerable time and effort to develop.

Essay Method

Unlike the rating scales that provide a high degree of structure for evaluations, the **essay method** requires the evaluator to compose a statement that best describes the individual being evaluated. The evaluator usually receives instructions to describe the individual's strengths and weaknesses and to make recommendations for his or her development.

The essay method provides an excellent opportunity to point out the unique characteristics of an employee. A major limitation of this method is that an essay that covers all the essential characteristics of an employee is a very time-consuming composition task. This method, however, is usually combined with other evaluation methods so that the evaluator is not required or expected to compose a lengthy statement.

23. John C. Flanagan, "The Critical Incident Technique," *Psychological Bulletin,* Vol. 51, No. 4 (July, 1954), pp. 327–358.

24. Craig Eric Schneier and Richard W. Beatty, "Developing Behaviorally-Anchored Rating Scales (BARS)," *Personnel Administrator,* Vol. 24, No. 8 (August, 1979), pp. 59–68.

25. J. Campbell, M. Dunnette, R. Arvey, and L. Hellervik, "The Development and Evaluation of Behaviorally Based Rating Scales," *Journal of Applied Psychology,* Vol. 57, No. 1 (February, 1973), pp. 15–22.

Figure 10—4 A Behaviorally Anchored Scale for Patrol Officer

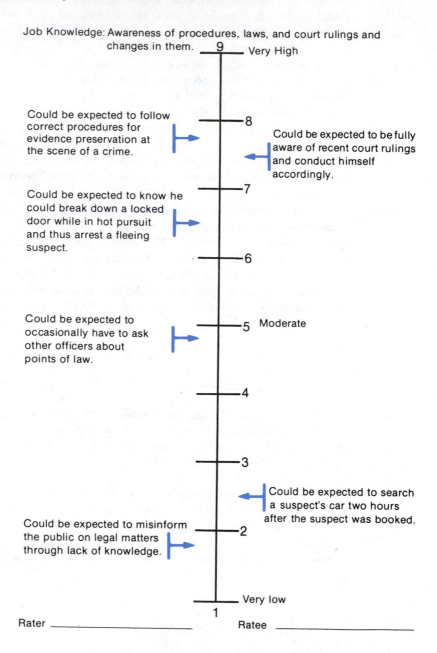

Job Knowledge: Awareness of procedures, laws, and court rulings and changes in them.

9 — Very High

Could be expected to follow correct procedures for evidence preservation at the scene of a crime.

8

Could be expected to be fully aware of recent court rulings and conduct himself accordingly.

7

Could be expected to know he could break down a locked door while in hot pursuit and thus arrest a fleeing suspect.

6

Could be expected to occasionally have to ask other officers about points of law.

5 — Moderate

4

3

Could be expected to search a suspect's car two hours after the suspect was booked.

Could be expected to misinform the public on legal matters through lack of knowledge.

2

Very low

1

Rater _____   Ratee _____

SOURCE: Frank J. Landy and Don A. Trumbo, *Psychology of Work Behavior* (rev. ed.; Homewood, IL: The Dorsey Press, 1980), p. 128. © 1980 by the Dorsey Press.

Management By Objectives Method

Management by objectives (MBO) is a philosophy of management first proposed by Peter F. Drucker in 1954.[26] It seeks to judge the performance of managers on the basis of their success in achieving the objectives they have established through consultation with their superiors. Performance-improvement efforts under MBO are focused upon the *goals* to be achieved by managers rather than upon the activities performed or the traits exhibited by them in connection with their assigned duties.

Management by objectives is a system involving a cycle (see Figure 10–5) that begins with a study of the organization's common goals and returns to that point. A significant feature of the cycle is the establishment of goals by individuals (Step 3) using a broad statement of responsibilities prepared by their superiors. The goals or targets are accompanied by a detailed account of the actions they propose to take in order to reach them. This document is then discussed with the superior and modified until both are satisfied with it (Step 4). Progress that the subordinate is making toward the goal is then assessed as objective data are made available (Step 5). At the conclusion of a period of time (usually six months), the subordinates make their own appraisals of what they have accomplished relative to the targets they had set earlier, substantiating their self-appraisal with factual data wherever possible. The "interview" is an examination of the subordinate's self-appraisal by the superior and subordinate together (Step 6).

Requirements for Successful MBO.

Management by objectives requires that individual executive responsibilities be defined in terms of the objectives of the total organization. The expected results must be consistent with the controllable areas of responsibility for the individual manager; e.g., profit, cost of product made, cost per unit of service delivered, etc. Odiorne states that the success of MBO depends heavily upon three points of emphasis:

1. MBO is a system of managing, not an addition to the manager's job.
2. The managers who adopt MBO as a system of managing must plan to drop some of their more time-consuming vocational hobbies, i.e., they must delegate.
3. The system of MBO entails a behavioral change on the part of both superior and subordinate.[27]

Advantages of MBO.

The MBO system enables managers to plan and measure their own performance, as well as that of their subordinates, in terms of concrete results. It shifts the emphasis from rater appraisal to self-analysis, and from focus on the past to focus on the future. In addition, subordinates are helped in relating their career planning to the needs and realities of the organization through consultation with their superiors.

---

26. Peter F. Drucker, *The Practice of Management* (New York: Harper and Brothers, 1954).

27. George S. Odiorne, *Management by Objectives* (New York: Pitman Publishing Corporation, 1965), pp. 77–79.

A major advantage of MBO is that it is possible for individuals to gain a greater sense of accomplishment, growth, and progress when they are being measured against their own objectives rather than against those of their peers. Other appraisal systems in which individuals are compared to each other may enable only a few to have feelings of improvement.[28]

Figure 10–5 The Management by Objectives Cycle

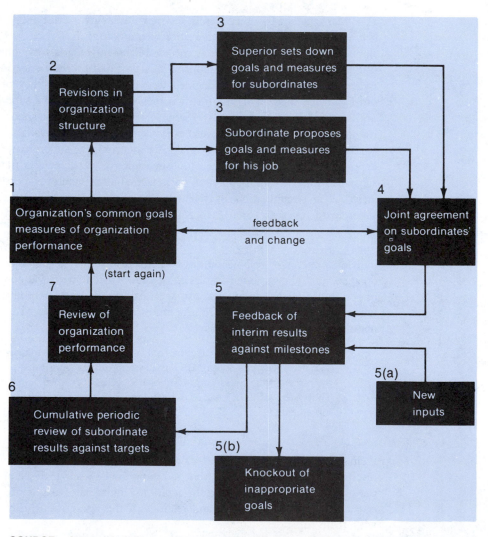

SOURCE: George S. Odiorne, *Management by Objectives* (New York: Pitman Publishing Corporation, 1965). Copyright, © 1965 by Pitman Publishing Corporation.

28. Paul H. Thompson and Gene W. Dalton, "Performance Appraisal: Managers Beware," *Harvard Business Review*, Vol. 48, No. 1 (January-February, 1970), pp. 149–157.

Criticisms of MBO. The MBO system is not without its critics. One critic contends that "the track record of MBO, based strictly on performance against promised rewards of profitability or organizational effectiveness, is indeed mediocre." This critic admits, however, that part of the problem stems from the great expectation held for MBO; namely, that it will provide some automatic control over the organization that will prevent it from going astray. There is nothing in the MBO approach that will insure that the proper objectives are set or that the need for sound decision making or other required abilities of a competent manager is eliminated.[29] Furthermore, one cannot be certain that all of the parts of the MBO system are used in a given organization by all of the managers. Lack of consistency has made it difficult to evaluate the effectiveness of MBO.[30]

There are other criticisms of MBO. One is that the performance data used in the appraisals are designed to measure end results on a short-term rather than a long-term basis. Thus, line supervisors, for example, may let their machines suffer to reduce maintenance costs. Furthermore, according to Levinson, we need to measure both activities and results. In fact, in any job where there are interactions with others, it is not enough to meet certain production or sales objectives. There must also be concern for human relationships.[31] Thus, to be realistic, the results and the method by which one achieves them should be considered. Kearney recommends incorporating the BARS method with MBO to provide subordinates with data that will help them in improving ineffective job behavior.[32]

Other Methods of Performance Evaluation

Other methods of performance evaluation are used to a lesser degree than those methods just described. One of these, which has become increasingly popular in recent years, is the assessment center. As noted in Chapter 9, the assessment center provides a broadband approach to evaluation by persons other than the immediate superior. At the present time this method is used almost exclusively for managerial personnel.

One of the oldest methods is the **checklist method.** It consists in having the rater check those statements on a list that are judged to be characteristic of the employee's performance or behavior. One such checklist developed for salespersons includes a large number of statements. A few of them are:

_____ Somewhat in a rut on some of the brand talks.

_____ Tends to keep comfortably ahead of the work schedule.

_____ Is a good steady worker.

29. William C. Giegold, "MBO After All These Years," *The Conference Board Record*, Vol. 12, No. 7 (July, 1975), pp. 50–52.

30. Jack N. Kondrasuk, "Studies in MBO Effectiveness," *Academy of Management Review*, Vol. 6, No. 3 (1981), pp. 419–430.

31. Harry Levinson, *loc. cit.*

32. William J. Kearney, "Behaviorally Anchored Rating Scales—MBO's Missing Ingredient," *Personnel Journal*, Vol. 58, No. 1 (January, 1979), pp. 20–25.

A more sophisticated form of the checklist employs the **forced-choice method.**[33] The evaluator is forced to choose from statements, often in pairs, that appear equally favorable or equally unfavorable.

Many organizations set work standards to determine what is a realistic output. Where the **work-standards method** is used, it provides an objective basis for evaluating employee performance. This approach is usually applied to nonmanagerial jobs.

Among other methods that at one time enjoyed some degree of popularity is the **ranking method.** This method requires each evaluator to arrange subordinates in rank order from the best to the poorest. Since employees are usually compared only in terms of overall suitability, this method may result in a legal challenge. (See Albermarle Paper Company *v.* Moody discussed earlier on page 236.)

The **critical-incident method** described earlier in connection with BARS has been used also as a method of evaluation. Unless both favorable and unfavorable incidents are discussed, subordinates may have negative feelings about this method. Some employees have been known to refer to it as the "little black book" approach. Perhaps its greatest contribution is in developing job specifications and in constructing other types of evaluation procedures such as BARS.

The reader who is interested in examining these and other methods of evaluation more thoroughly may wish to consult one of the books on performance evaluation listed at the end of this chapter.

Which Performance Evaluation Method to Use?

The choice of method(s) to be used should be based largely on the purpose of the appraisal. Figure 10–6 shows six approaches to performance appraisal that were evaluated by Steers. Note that the easiest and least expensive techniques are also the least accurate. They are also the least useful for purposes of personnel decisions and employee development. The more sophisticated and more time-consuming methods offer more useful information. Managers must make cost-benefit decisions about which methods to use.[34]

Review of an Evaluator's Appraisal

The assessment center automatically provides for a review of a superior's evaluation of subordinates. Where supervisors evaluate employees independently, as is usually the case, provision is made for a review of their evaluations by the evaluator's superior. In some organizations a review system which requires supervisors to substantiate their evaluations before a committee comprised of peer supervisors also is used. Having appraisals reviewed by an evaluator's superior reduces the chance of superficial or biased evaluations. Reviews by superiors generally

33. D. E. Sisson, "Forced-Choice: The New Army Rating," *Personnel Psychology*, Vol. 1, No. 3 (Autumn, 1948), pp. 365–381.

34. Richard M. Steers, *Introduction to Organizational Behavior* (Santa Monica, CA: Goodyear Publishing Company, Inc., 1981), pp. 412–413.

Figure 10–6 **Major Strengths and Weaknesses of Various Appraisal Techniques**

	Ratings	Rankings	Critical Incidents	BARS	MBO	Assessment Centers
Meaningful dimensions	Sometimes	Seldom	Sometimes	Usually	Usually	Usually
Amount of time required	Low	Low	Medium	High	High	High
Developmental costs	Low	Low	Low	High	Medium	High
Potential for rating errors	High	High	Medium	Low	Low	Low
Acceptability to subordinates	Low	Low	Medium	High	High	High
Acceptability to superiors	Low	Low	Medium	High	High	High
Usefulness for allocating rewards	Poor	Poor	Fair	Good	Good	Fair
Usefulness for employee counseling	Poor	Poor	Fair	Good	Good	Good
Usefulness for identifying promotion potential	Poor	Poor	Fair	Fair	Fair	Good

SOURCE: From *Introduction to Organizational Behavior* by Richard·M. Steers. Copyright © 1981 Scott, Foresman and Company. Reprinted by permission.

are more objective and provide a broader perspective of employee performance than do evaluations by immediate supervisors.

The reviewer who is typically required to make comments that will be meaningful to both the evaluator and the person being evaluated has a more difficult role than the supervisor. It involves communicating with two individuals rather than one.[35] In the process reviewers should, moreover, be aware of the types of errors discussed earlier in the chapter and of the biases that can enter the process.

FEEDBACK OF EVALUATIONS

The success of a performance evaluation program is ultimately dependent upon the effective utilization of the information that results from the appraisal process.

35. Peter J. McGuire, "Why Performance Appraisals Fail," *Personnel Journal*, Vol. 59, No. 9 (September, 1980), pp. 744–746, 762.

Such information may be used as the basis for various types of personnel actions to be discussed later. The information should also be communicated to the individual employee by the person who has made the evaluation.

Evaluation Interviews

The evaluation interview provides the superior an opportunity to discuss the subordinate's performance record and to explore areas of possible improvement and growth. It also provides an opportunity to identify the subordinate's attitudes and feelings more thoroughly, and thus improve communication between the parties that may lead to a feeling of harmony and cooperation.

The format for the evaluation interview will be determined in large part by the purpose of the evaluation. Most interviews, however, provide for feedback to employees on how well they are performing their jobs and for making plans for future development. Interviews should be scheduled sufficiently in advance in order that the subordinate as well as the superior can prepare for the discussion. Usually ten days to two weeks is about the right amount of lead time. It is also desirable for employees to have a guide to follow in planning for the interview.

Areas of Emphasis.
Since a major purpose of the evaluation interview is to make plans for improvement, it is important to focus the subordinate's attention upon the future rather than the past. The interviewer should:

1. Emphasize strengths on which the individual can build rather than stress weaknesses to be overcome.
2. Avoid suggestions involving the changing of traits but rather suggest more acceptable ways of acting.
3. Concentrate on opportunities for growth that exist within the framework of the individual's present position.
4. Limit plans for growth to a few important items that can be accomplished within a reasonable period of time.

Procedural Guidelines.
Many of the principles of effective interviewing discussed in Chapter 6 apply to performance evaluation interviews. Other guidelines that should also be considered are given below.

Listen More than You Talk. The ratio of a subordinate's input to the total has been measured by recording the interview, transcribing it, and counting the words. Johnson reports that in the more effective interviews the superior contributes only about 10 percent of the total words in the interview. As the proportion of words spoken by the interviewer increases, the effectiveness of the interview is correspondingly reduced.[36]

Vary the Questions. Questions are asked to get the subordinate to thinking and talking. Minimize the number of questions that call for a "yes" or "no" answer.

---

36. Robert G. Johnson, *The Appraisal Interview Guide* (New York: AMACOM, 1979), p. 72.

Use a variety of types of questions. Straight open-ended questions such as "What could we do to reduce costs?" can be used in combination with other types of questions. A useful variation to this type of questioning might be that of posing a real problem to be solved.

Avoid the "Sandwich Technique." Studies indicate that many supervisors use the "sandwich technique" in which praise serves to cushion criticisms. That is, positive statements are followed by negative ones which are then followed by positive statements. According to Kay, Meyer, and French, this approach is not effective because praise alerts the individual that criticisms will be forthcoming. Positive comments following the criticism then indicate to the individual that no more negative comments will come for awhile. They also found that an individual can absorb only a certain amount of criticism before defensive tendencies begin to appear. For those individuals with a low level of occupational self-esteem, criticism was found to have a distinctly dampening effect. They suggest that more frequent sessions be held with the individual so that the absolute number of negative comments in any one session is reduced.[37]

Reflect Feelings. The skillful interviewer makes use of a technique used by clinicians. It is one of recognizing the feelings that are being expressed and reflecting them back to the person. For example:

> Subordinate: The worst part of my job is having to take a lot of guff from angry customers.
> Superior: You find some customers almost too much.
> Subordinate: Yes, I sure do. But there are only a few.

Note that the feeling expressed is reflected back to the subordinate in the form of a restatement. This method, which will be described in greater detail in Chapter 13, lets the subordinate know that his or her feelings are important and that the superior is listening carefully and with understanding.

Three Types of Evaluation Interviews. Probably the individual who has studied different approaches to performance evaluation interviews most thoroughly is Norman R. F. Maier. In his classic book, *The Appraisal Interview,* he analyzes the cause-and-effect relations in three types of evaluation interviews: tell-and-sell, tell-and-listen, and problem-solving.

Tell-and-Sell Method. The skills required in the **tell-and-sell method** include the ability to persuade the person to change in the prescribed manner. This may require the development of new needs in the person, as well as a knowledge of how to make use of the kinds of incentives that motivate each particular individual.

Tell-and-Listen Method. In the **tell-and-listen method** the skills required include the ability to communicate the strong and weak points of a subordinate's job performance during the first part of the interview. During the second part of the

---

37. E. Kay, H. H. Meyer, and J. R. P. French, Jr. "Effects of Threat in a Performance Appraisal Interview," *Journal of Applied Psychology,* Vol. 49, No. 5 (October, 1965), pp. 311–317.

interview, the subordinate's feelings about the evaluation are thoroughly explored. The superior is still in the role of a judge, but the method requires listening to disagreement and coping with defensive behavior without attempting to refute any statements. It is assumed that the opportunity to release frustrated feelings through catharsis will help to reduce or remove unpleasant ones.

Problem-Solving Method. The skills associated with the **problem-solving method** are consistent with the nondirective procedures of the tell-and-listen method in that listening, accepting, and responding to feelings are essential. However, the objective of the problem-solving interview is to go beyond an interest in the subordinate's feelings. It thus seeks to stimulate growth and development in the subordinate by discussing the problems, needs, innovations, satisfactions, and dissatisfactions encountered in the performance of the job since the last evaluation interview. Maier recommends this method since the objective of evaluation normally should be to stimulate growth and development in the employee.[38]

Employee Reactions to Performance Evaluation

As part of its personnel audit procedures, each organization should obtain employee opinions of its performance evaluation system. Detailed questions about all aspects of the appraisal system should provide information that can be used to improve it.

One of the main concerns of employees is the fairness and accuracy of the system since the process is central to many personnel decisions. Two studies by a group of Pennsylvania State University researchers were designed to identify elements that might account for an individual's perception of the fairness and accuracy of performance evaluation. Data on 950 employees were gathered in the production division of a large manufacturing organization. This organization had instituted an MBO system several years prior to the data collection. The researchers found that the following factors were significantly related to perceptions of fairness and accuracy of performance evaluation:

1. Frequency of evaluation.
2. Identification of goals to eliminate weaknesses.
3. Supervisory knowledge of a subordinate's level of performance and job duties.[39]

IMPROVING PERFORMANCE

In many instances the evaluation interview with the subordinate will provide the basis for noting deficiencies in employee performance and for making plans for

---

38. Norman R. F. Maier, *The Appraisal Interview* (New York: John Wiley & Sons, Inc. 1958) and *The Appraisal Interview—Three Basic Approaches* (San Diego, CA: University Associates, 1976).

39. Frank J. Landy, Janet L. Barnes, and Kevin R. Murphy, "Correlates of Perceived Fairness and Accuracy of Performance Evaluation," *Journal of Applied Psychology,* Vol. 63, No. 6 (December, 1978), pp. 751–754. *See also* Frank J. Landy, Janet Barnes-Farrell, and Jeannette N. Cleveland, "Perceived Fairness and Accuracy of Performance Evaluation: A Follow-Up," *Journal of Applied Psychology,* Vol. 65, No. 3 (June, 1980), pp. 355–356.

improvement. As a result, corrective action can then be initiated normally by the employee's superior. Unless these deficiencies are brought to the subordinate's attention, they are likely to continue until they become quite serious. Sometimes underperformers, unless they are so informed, may not understand exactly what is expected of them. However, once their responsibilities are clarified, they are in a better position to take the corrective action needed to improve their performance.

Sources of Ineffective Performance

There are many possible reasons why a subordinate's performance may not meet the expected standards. First, each individual has a unique pattern of strengths and weaknesses that must be considered. In addition, other factors—such as the work environment, the external environment including home and community, and the personnel operations—have an impact upon job performance. To have a better understanding of possible sources of ineffective performance related to these environments, Miner has devised a comprehensive list shown in Figure 10–7.

Managing Ineffective Performance

The first step in managing ineffective performance is to determine its source. Once the source is known, a course of action may be planned. In some instances the solution may lie in providing training in areas that would increase the knowledge and/or skills needed for effective performance. A transfer to another job or department may provide an opportunity for an individual to become a more effective member of the organization. In other instances greater attention may have to be focused upon the ways of motivating the individual.

There will always be some individuals who require assistance with emotional problems, family-related problems, and physical problems. Techniques for helping subordinates with these and other problems will be discussed in detail in Chapters 13 and 20.

Where ineffective performance persists, it may be necessary to demote an employee or to take disciplinary action with possible discharge from the organization. Whatever action is taken to cope with ineffective performance should be done with objectivity, fairness, and a recognition of the feelings of the individuals who are involved.

RÉSUMÉ

The success of an organization is largely dependent upon the performance of its personnel. To determine the contributions of each individual, it is necessary to have a formal evaluation program with clearly stated objectives. Carefully defined criteria that are relevant and reliable are essential foundations for evaluation.

If evaluation interviews and any corrective actions are to be based upon valid information, managers and supervisors should be thoroughly trained in the particular methods that they will use in evaluating their subordinates. Participation in developing scales, such as BARS, automatically provides such training. Whatever methods are used should meet the objectives of evaluation.

Figure 10–7 **Sources of Ineffective Performance**

PROBLEMS ORIGINATING IN COMPANY POLICIES AND HIGHER-LEVEL DECISIONS

- insufficient organizational action
- placement error
- organizational overpermissiveness
- excessive spans of control
- inappropriate organizational standards and criteria

MOTIVATIONAL PROBLEMS

- strong motives frustrated at work (pleasure in success, fear of failure, avoidance, dominance, desire to be popular, social motivation, need for attention, and so on)
- unintegrated means used to satisfy strong motives
- excessively low personal work standards
- generalized low work motivation

EMOTIONAL PROBLEMS

- frequent disruptive emotion (anxiety, depression, anger, excitement, shame, guilt, jealousy)
- neurosis (with anxiety, depression, anger, and so on predominating)
- psychosis (with anxiety, depression, anger, and so on predominating)
- alcohol and drug problems

PROBLEMS CAUSED IN THE WORK GROUP

- negative consequences associated with group cohesion
- ineffective management
- inappropriate managerial-standards of criteria

PROBLEMS GROWING OUT OF THE WORK CONTEXT AND THE WORK ITSELF

- negative consequences of economic forces
- negative consequences of geographic location
- detrimental conditions in the work setting
- excessive danger
- problems in the work itself

PROBLEMS OF INTELLIGENCE AND JOB KNOWLEDGE

- insufficient verbal ability
- insufficient special ability
- insufficient job knowledge
- defects of judgment or memory

FAMILY-RELATED PROBLEMS

- family crises (divorce, death, severe illness, and the like)
- separation from family and isolation
- predominance of family considerations over work demands

PROBLEMS STEMMING FROM SOCIETY AND ITS VALUES

- application of legal sanctions
- enforcement of societal values by means other than the law (including the use of inappropriate value-based criteria)
- conflict between job demands and cultural values (equity, freedom, moral and religious values, and so on)

PHYSICAL PROBLEMS

- physical illness or handicap, including brain disorders
- physical disorders of emotional origin
- inappropriate physical characteristics
- insufficient muscular or sensory ability or skill

SOURCE: Adapted from *The Challenge of Managing* by John B. Miner. Copyright 1975 by the W. B. Saunders Company. Reprinted with permission of John B. Miner.

The degree to which the performance evaluation program benefits the organization and its members is directly related to the quality of the interviews that superiors conduct with their subordinates. The development of interviewing skills is best learned through instruction and supervised practice. In the interview, deficiencies in employee performance can be discussed and plans for improvement can be made.

TERMS TO IDENTIFY

peer appraisals
self-appraisal form
appraisal by subordinates
rating scale method
global rating
leniency error
anchors
error of central tendency
behaviorally anchored rating scale
essay method

management by objectives (MBO)
checklist method
forced-choice method
work-standards method
ranking method
critical-incident method
tell-and-sell method
tell-and-listen method
problem-solving method

DISCUSSION QUESTIONS

1. What are the major purposes of performance evaluation and in what ways may they be contradictory?

2. Describe the relationship between performance evaluation and recruitment, selection, compensation management, training and development, and labor relations.

3. Describe the characteristics of the ideal appraiser.

4. What criteria could be used to evaluate the performance of people working in the following jobs?
   a. tile setter
   b. TV repairer
   c. director of nursing in a hospital
   d. personnel manager
   e. air traffic controller

5. How have the various court decisions affected the manner in which performance evaluation programs are now conducted?

6. In many organizations evaluators submit ratings to their immediate superiors for review before discussing them with the individual employees they have rated. What advantages may result from this procedure?

7. Three types of appraisal interviews are described in this chapter.
   a. What different skills are required for each of the three types of appraisal interviews? What reactions can one expect from using these different skills?
   b. How can one develop the skills needed for the problem-solving type of interview?
   c. Which method do you feel is the least desirable? Why?

8. What are the major sources of ineffective performance that may be identified in the performance evaluation process?

PROBLEM 10–1

JUST HOW GOOD AM I, DOCTOR?

Ms. Carlisle, a middle-aged woman with several university degrees, was employed by the federal government in a public health position prior to coming to Mentor County General Hospital. At Mentor she served as the County Mental Health Educator under Dr. Haller, Chief of the Mental Health Services Division. Ms. Carlisle's job involved giving lectures to schools, business firms, and clubs upon request and conducting training classes on mental health education for new teachers, social workers, and nurses. She was proud of her performance record which contained mainly superior ratings and nothing below excellent. She liked her boss, too, not only because he had given her an opportunity to use her talents, but also because he was always kind and considerate.

Performance evaluations at Mentor were made every six months, and the customary procedure was for the reports to be prepared and placed in each employee's mailbox. Employees could discuss them with their supervisors if they wished to do so, but they were expected to sign them. One day Ms. Carlisle found her evaluation in her mailbox and became very upset over it. Instead of superior and excellent ratings on the scale, she found excellent and good ratings. There was no explanation given for the drop in ratings, only the statement that "Ms. Carlisle continues to do good work as in the past." Ms. Carlisle asked to see Dr. Haller immediately.

The interview between Ms. Carlisle and Dr. Haller took place that afternoon. Ms. Carlisle was quite blunt and wanted to know what was wrong with her work. Dr. Haller explained that her work was fine and he could not understand why she was upset. She pointed out the difference in this last rating compared with others he had given her in the past and asked him to explain the difference. Dr. Haller said that he thought it was a good evaluation and explained that he had changed his methods of evaluation. He refused to explain further, but assured Ms. Carlisle that her work was good and encouraged her to maintain this high standing. Ms. Carlisle did not want to sign the evaluation but later conceded, inserting "signed under protest" under her name. She then made plans for appealing the rating to the County Employees Association and the Civil Service Commission.

a. How do you account for Dr. Haller's change in methods? Could he have been influenced in some way to change his methods? Or is he using this as an excuse for giving her lower ratings?

b. What effect is Ms. Carlisle's appeal likely to have on her ratings? On Dr. Haller's evaluations in the future?

SUGGESTED READINGS

Baird, Lloyd S., Richard W. Beatty, and Craig Eric Schneier. *The Performance Appraisal Sourcebook.* Amherst, MA: Human Resource Development Press, 1982.

Carroll, Stephen J., and Craig E. Schneier. *Performance Appraisal and Review Systems.* Glenview, IL: Scott, Foresman and Company, 1982.

Chruden, Herbert J., and Arthur W. Sherman, Jr. *Readings in Managing Human Resources,* 6th ed. Cincinnati: South-Western Publishing Co., 1984. Part 3.

Henderson, Richard. *Performance Appraisal: Theory to Practice.* Reston, VA: Reston Publishing Company, Inc., 1980.

Kellogg, Marion. *What to Do About Performance Appraisal,* rev. ed. New York: AMACOM, 1975.

Latham, Gary P., and Kenneth N. Wexley. *Increasing Productivity Through Performance Appraisal.* Reading, MA: Addison-Wesley Publishing Company, 1981.

Creating a Productive Work Environment

part 4

- To indicate why it is difficult to understand the motivational forces operating in a given situation.
- To explain the three components of motivation.
- To cite the unique contributions of each of the theories of motivation.
- To describe the symptoms of frustration and conflict.
- To explain what management can do to reduce frustration and conflicts that impair productivity.
- To describe the relationship between job satisfaction and job performance, turnover, and absenteeism.

11

Motivating Employees to Work

In Part 3 we observed how the training and development function and the performance evaluation function contribute to achieving a competent work force. In Part 4 we will be concerned with how to create a productive work environment to attain organizational and personal goals. The three chapters in this part will cover the subjects of motivating employees, developing cooperation, and the techniques for supervising employees.

We noted in the discussion of personnel selection that management is concerned not only with what an employee *can do* but also with what an employee *will do.* Insofar as possible, predictions about what an individual *will do* are made during the selection process. However, once individuals are hired and trained, it is not enough to assume that they will make full use of their abilities. What they *will do* is dependent to a large degree on the forces in the work environment that motivate them to release their energy toward maximizing their performance on the job. Job performance is thus the result of the application of energy to one's abilities.

MOTIVATION: THE KEY TO PERFORMANCE

The study of motivation involves trying to find the answers to such questions as: Why does one person strive harder than another? Why do some employees seek higher levels of responsibility and some do not? Why do wage incentives stimulate some employees and not others? These and similar questions are continually being raised by those who are responsible for the management of human resources. Because of the complex nature of the motivational process, it is not possible for the answers to such questions to be clear-cut. There are many variables that must be identified and considered in order to understand the motivational process.

The Motivational Process

The term **motivation** originally was derived from the Latin word *movere* which means "to move." While a number of definitions of it are to be found in the current literature, there is no one definition that describes motivation adequately. An analysis of major definitions indicates that motivation is primarily concerned with three factors: what energizes behavior, what directs or channels such behavior, and how this behavior is maintained or sustained. According to Steers and Porter, each of these three components of motivation is important to our understanding of human behavior at work.

The first component of motivation points to energetic forces within individuals that "drive" them to certain types of behavior. Environmental forces often trigger these drives. The second component refers to goal orientation, with behavior being directed toward something. The third component is concerned with forces within the individual and within their environment that reinforce the intensity of their drives and the direction of their energy.[1]

---

1. Richard M. Steers and Lyman W. Porter, *Motivation and Work Behavior* (3d ed.; New York: McGraw-Hill Book Company, 1983), pp. 3–4.

Difficulties in Understanding Motivational Forces.   Because motivation is a complex process, it can be difficult to understand the motivational forces operating within an individual. In the first place, motives cannot be seen. They can only be inferred from behavior. Therefore, the attempt to identify and label motives is difficult. Money, for example, may be an incentive (goal) for different underlying motives such as satisfying the desire for status, providing a greater sense of economic security, or furnishing a symbol of power.

Secondly, a particular motive rarely exists by itself. An individual may experience a wide range of inner desires or anticipations at the same time. Some of these may conflict with each other. A desire to live a carefree life, for example, may be in direct conflict with the desire to become financially independent.

In the third place, individuals may respond to the same incentives differently. Not only do they differ in what they seek from their jobs, but they differ in the ease with which their needs may be satisfied. One person, striving to achieve status, may appear to be rather easily satisfied after a single promotion. Another person, also motivated by status needs, may continue to strive for advancement after receiving a promotion.

Finally, we know that some motives, such as hunger, thirst, and sex, are temporarily diminished after being gratified. However, those motives which have their basis in the anticipation of enjoyment—e.g., need for achievement or the need for esteem—are often actually strengthened by goal attainment. Thus, the attainment of the goal serves simply to whet the appetite for still more of the same.[2]

When studying motivation in the work situation, we need to give consideration to three important sets of variables: the characteristics of the individual employee, the behavioral implications of the required job tasks (autonomy, variety, etc.), and the characteristics of the work environment (supervision, rewards, etc.).[3] The first set of variables—characteristics of the individual—will be emphasized in the discussion that follows. How characteristics of the job and work environment affect the motivational process will be examined later in the context of the various theories of motivation.

Variables in Employee Individuality.   In earlier chapters we observed how employees differ from each other in abilities and aptitudes. We also recognized the fact that, without the requisite abilities or aptitudes, an employee is not going to be able to perform satisfactorily. Before we can apply the principles of motivation, there are other dimensions of human personality that we should understand. How does the employee perceive the job and the work environment? What are the employee's attitudes and values, interests, and feelings? How would we describe the individual's personality characteristics? An understanding of the uniqueness of each person will enable us to apply the principles of motivation more effectively.

2. Marvin D. Dunnette and Wayne K. Kirchner, *Psychology Applied to Industry* (New York: Appleton-Century-Crofts, 1965,) pp. 126–129.
3. Steers and Porter, *op. cit.,* pp. 18–20.

Perception. Each person sees the world from an individual viewpoint. The individual's **perception** of the world is determined by personal experiences that create a filter through which the world is viewed. Therefore, the supervisor should attempt to learn how each subordinate is likely to respond to the different events that occur at work. Each subordinate will perceive management instructions, actions, and communications in a somewhat different way.

An important part of perception is how people perceive themselves. Their self-perception, or **self-concept**, is a primary determiner of how they will act in a particular situation. Because of the central role of the self-concept in the human personality, it is the key to understanding the individual.

Attitudes and Values. As one interacts with others, their attitudes and values become apparent. An **attitude** may be defined as a relatively stable predisposition to evaluate an object (person, organization, process, issue) in a favorable or unfavorable manner. For example, we all have attitudes toward unions, toward supervisors, toward democracy. Such attitudes involve strong beliefs and feelings.

What an employee values is a strong determinant of behavior. **A value** is any object, activity, or orientation that an individual considers to be very important to his or her life. Values have been shown to be related to decision making, motivation, selection, communication, and managerial success.[4]

Values are influenced largely by the culture in which we live and work. For most of this century, and in particular during the period from 1945–1970, the value system of most Americans centered around those of the middle class. According to Yankelovich, these values gave people a sense of self-esteem, a clear identity, well-defined goals, and a conviction that one's private goals and behavior contributed to the well-being of others. Because people defined their identity through their work role, they had a sense of loyalty to their employers. If women could afford to stay at home and not work at a paid job, they did so. The incentive system—mainly money and status rewards—was successful in motivating most employees.

Yankelovich also points out that our values with regard to work have changed. Three of the more striking manifestations of the current work-related values are: the increasing importance of leisure, the symbolic significance of the paid job, and the insistence that jobs become less depersonalized.[5]

Today our attention goes beyond values that are work-related. Broad issues such as one's orientation toward other people, the environment, and how one's time and energy should be used are a matter of concern. The type of life-style that one adopts is a reflection of a broad spectrum of values that have strong implications for employee motivation.

4. Barry Z. Posner and J. Michael Munson, "The Importance of Values in Understanding Organizational Behavior," *Human Resource Management*, Vol. 18, No. 3 (Fall, 1979), pp. 9–14.

5. Daniel Yankelovich, "The New Psychological Contracts at Work," *Psychology Today*, Vol. 11, No. 2 (May, 1978), pp. 46–50.

Interests. An employee's interests play an important role in motivation. For example, the employee who is highly interested in the tasks involved in a job is likely to derive a reward from the satisfaction that comes from performing them. Thus, intrinsic rewards may be valued more than any extrinsic reward, such as higher pay, that may be available in a different job for which the employee qualifies. Giving consideration to the employee's interests in assigning tasks and in interpersonal contacts will benefit both the organization and the individual.

Feelings. We like to think that we always approach life in a rational and objective manner. However, it is apparent that much of what we do is influenced by our feelings. Not too long ago, feelings were viewed as something to be suppressed at the workplace. Employees generally recognized the wisdom of not expressing their feelings, especially those that might appear to be negative to management. With the advent of the human relations movement, feelings began to be recognized as a legitimate concern of management. We now know that the extent to which an employee's feelings are recognized and respected will have a strong influence on his/her motivation. Some of the techniques recommended for handling feelings will be discussed in the context of supervision in Chapter 13.

Personal Traits. One of the most apparent differences among individuals is in their personal traits, or what we commonly call "personality." Personal traits are enduring behavioral characteristics that give each individual the uniqueness that we identify with that person. Thousands of words are used to describe personal characteristics such as assertive, self-reliant, responsible, dogmatic, or defensive. Our understanding of an individual's characteristic modes of behavior helps us to interact more effectively with that person. With such an understanding of people on the job, we can create motivating conditions that will enable them to make maximum use of their abilities.

Theories of Motivation

Since the days of the early Greek philosophers, attempts have been made to understand what motivates human behavior. The early philosophers emphasized the **principle of hedonism,** which states that people tend to seek pleasure and avoid pain. When psychology emerged as a science in the late 1800s, other forces, such as instincts and drives, were popular explanations. In contemporary behavioral science several different types of theories are receiving the attention of theorists and researchers. An examination of these theories will help to explain the complex nature of the motivational process and offer some guidance for those who manage others. The applications of these theories will be mentioned in the discussion of them.

Need-Hierarchy Theory. One theory that has had considerable impact on thinking concerned with motivation in organizations comes from the late A. H. Maslow. His theory is known as the **need-hierarchy theory** because human needs are arranged according to a priority. This theory groups needs into five categories:

1. *The physiological needs.* Included in this group are the needs for food, water, air, rest, etc., that are required for maintaining the body in a state of equilibrium.
2. *The safety needs.* These include the need for safety and security, both in a physical and psychological sense.
3. *The belongingness and love needs.* The need for attention and social activity are the major needs in this category. An individual desires affectionate relationships with people in general and desires to have a respected place in the group.
4. *The esteem needs.* These include the desire for self-respect, for strength, for achievement, and for independence and freedom. Also included in this group is the desire for reputation or prestige or respect and esteem from other people.
5. *The need for self-actualization (realization).* This refers to a person's desire for self-fulfillment; namely, to the tendency to become actualized in what he or she is potentially. "What one *can* be, one *must* be." This tendency might be phrased as the desire to realize one's potential.[6]

According to Maslow's theory, human needs are arranged according to the priority shown in Figure 11–1. The physiological needs are the most fundamental; they must be satisfied before other needs. Once the physiological needs are satisfied, the safety needs become predominant. When both the physiological and the safety needs are fairly well satisfied, the belongingness and love needs (the next step) will emerge as dominant in a person's need structure. As the lower needs are satisfied, the needs for esteem and self-actualization become dominant. As people experience growth and self-actualization, they want more. This is particularly evident among managerial personnel.[7]

Figure 11–1 Priority of Human Needs

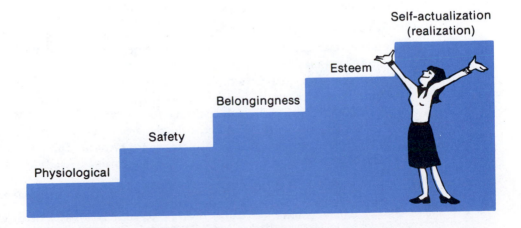

6. Paraphrased and adapted from A. H. Maslow, *Motivation and Personality* (2d ed.; New York: Harper & Brothers, 1970).

7. Edward E. Lawler, III, *Motivation in Work Organizations* (Monterey, CA: Brooks/Cole Publishing Company, 1973), p. 25.

Maslow's need hierarchy has proved to be very useful in guiding managerial personnel who otherwise would probably overlook important individual needs. In addition to expecting financial rewards, employees expect their needs for affiliation, esteem, and self-actualization to be considered important by management.

While Maslow's hierarchy has been very useful for managers, Maslow himself warned of its restrictions.[8] Employee needs, for example, are not static but constantly changing. Furthermore, more than one level of need may be operating simultaneously. Experimental studies also have indicated that needs may only be at two levels instead of five.[9] However, research has confirmed Maslow's theory in general, i.e., that the higher-level needs will appear only when the lower-level ones are satisfied.[10]

ERG Theory.   A newer motivation theory, Alderfer's **ERG theory**, is also based on needs.[11] This theory proposes the following three need categories:

1. Existence (E) needs—those needs required to sustain human existence (including Maslow's physiological and safety needs).
2. Relatedness (R) needs—those needs involving relationships with others at work (corresponding to Maslow's safety, social, and certain ego-esteem needs).
3. Growth (G) needs—those needs relating to creative or personal growth on the job (corresponding to Maslow's self-esteem and self-actualization needs).

Alderfer's ERG theory differs from Maslow's in other respects. First, it allows more than one need to operate at the same time. Secondly, in addition to individuals progressing up the hierarchy as a result of the satisfaction of lower-order needs, the ERG theory includes a frustration-regression process. When an individual is continually frustrated in attempts to satisfy growth needs, relatedness needs will reemerge as a primary motivating force. For example, the talented individual who strives but is unable to progress to a managerial job may redirect energies toward establishing close relationships with other employees.

Achievement Motivation Theory.   Another theory that has been used in the study of managerial behavior is the **achievement motivation theory**. This theory states that a major portion of one's performance can be explained by the intensity of that individual's need for achievement. The theory grew out of the work of H.A. Murray who developed a system for classifying individuals according to the strengths of various needs which have the potential for motivating behavior. Murray lists more than 20 psychogenic or social needs. In the area of human resources management, most of the interest has been in the need for achievement. This need is defined as the need to excel in relation to competitive or internalized standards.[12]

8. Abraham H. Maslow, *Eupsychian Management: A Journal* (Homewood, IL: Richard D. Irwin, Inc., and The Dorsey Press, 1965), p. 3.

9. L. K. Waters and Darrell Roach, "A Factor Analysis of Need-Fulfillment Items Designed to Measure Maslow Need Categories," *Personnel Psychology*, Vol. 26, No. 2 (Summer, 1973), pp. 185–190.

10. Lawler, *op. cit.,* p. 40.

11. Clayton P. Alderfer, *Existence, Relatedness, and Growth* (New York: Free Press, 1972).

12. D. C. McClelland, J. W. Atkinson, R. A. Clark, and E. L. Lowell, *The Achievement Motive* (New York: Appleton, 1953), pp. 78–81.

The achievement motive is prominent among successful executives. These individuals generally perceive themselves to be hard-working and achieving persons who must accomplish in order to be satisfied. Executive positions typically provide incentive opportunities through which they may satisfy their needs. According to McClelland, who has studied the achievement motive in various groups of individuals, business executives like situations in which they take personal responsibility for finding solutions to problems, have a tendency to set moderate achievement goals and to take "calculated risks," and want concrete feedback as to how well they are doing.[13] More recently, the need for power (control and influence over others) and the need for affiliation (warm, friendly relationships) have been considered important needs because of their relationship to success in business and government organizations.

Motivator-Hygiene Theory. One of the early theories of job motivation is the **motivator-hygiene theory.** This theory emphasizes the roles of motivator factors and hygiene factors. Herzberg calls those factors that produce job satisfaction **motivator factors** because they satisfy the employee's need for self-actualization. The major motivator factors are achievement, recognition, the work itself, responsibility, and advancement. According to the theory, **hygiene factors**—company policy and practices, supervision, and working conditions—are important, but they are not motivators. When hygiene factors deteriorate to a level below that which the employee considers acceptable, then job dissatisfaction ensues. While both motivator and hygiene factors meet the needs of the employee, it is primarily the motivator factors that bring about the kind of improvement in performance that industry seeks from its work force.[14]

Like any well-formulated theory, the motivator-hygiene theory has stimulated a considerable amount of research, as well as controversy.[15] In spite of the controversy, the theory and the research stimulated by it have contributed to a better understanding of employee motivation. A major impact of the theory is the redesign of jobs to maximize the motivator factors. Through the concept of job enrichment, the motivator-hygiene theory has had considerable impact on the world of work. All of the proposals for enriching jobs that were discussed in Chapter 4 have the goal of increasing personal growth and advancement, enhancing the sense of achievement and responsibility, and providing recognition. In other words, they all facilitate the satisfaction of the motivator needs.

13. David C. McClelland, "Business Drive and National Achievement," *Harvard Business Review,* Vol. 40, No. 4 (July-August, 1962), pp. 99–112.

14. Frederick Herzberg, Bernard Mausner, and Barbara B. Snyderman, *The Motivation to Work* (2d ed.; New York: John Wiley & Sons, Inc., 1959), pp. 113–114. *See also* Frederick Herzberg, *Work and the Nature of Man* (Cleveland: The World Publishing Company, 1960).

15. Robert J. House and Lawrence A. Wigdor, "Herzberg's Dual-Factor Theory of Job Satisfaction and Motivation: A Review of the Evidence and a Criticism," *Personnel Psychology,* Vol. 20, No. 4 (Winter, 1967), pp. 369–389; and N. King, "Clarification and Evaluation of the Two-Factor Theory of Job Satisfaction," *Psychological Bulletin,* Vol. 74 (1970), pp. 18–31.

Equity Theory.   Another model of work motivation is found in **equity theory**. This theory states that the presence of feelings of inequity will motivate an individual to reduce that inequity. It is fairly common for employees to feel that, compared to other employees, they are putting more effort and talent into the job than they are receiving in satisfaction, pay, and fringe benefits. According to equity theory, the strength of the motivation is proportional to the magnitude of the perceived inequity.

Several different ways by which an individual may reduce feelings of inequity are presented by Adams:

1. Altering one's inputs—increase or reduce production.
2. Altering one's outcomes—seeking more pay or other rewards.
3. Distorting one's inputs and outcomes cognitively—rearranging one's thoughts so as to reduce perceived discrepancies.
4. Leaving the field—quitting a job, obtaining a transfer, engaging in absenteeism.
5. Acting on other persons—including getting others to lower their inputs.
6. Changing the basis of comparison.

In the resolution of a particular perceived injustice, Adams suggests that the person will choose whichever method is easiest.[16]

Adams' equity theory has been tested largely under laboratory settings. There appears, however, to be an increase in the number of studies using field simulations. Research has focused on the effects of wage inequity and how equity may affect the attractiveness of rewards. The majority of the studies generally support equity theory predictions about underpayment. Studies involving overpayment, however, have not supported the theory.

Equity theory provides the following practical guidelines for managers to consider:

1. The emphasis is upon equitable rewards for employees.
2. The decision concerning equity or inequity involves comparison with other workers both within and outside of the organization.
3. The reaction to inequity can take many different forms.[17]

Applications of this theory to compensation management will be discussed in Chapter 17.

Expectancy Theory.   The **expectancy theory** has developed out of the work of those psychologists who consider human beings as thinking, reasoning persons who have beliefs and anticipations concerning future events in their lives. This theory argues that motivational force to perform (effort) is a function of the expectancies that individuals have concerning future outcomes times the value they place on these outcomes. Vroom defines an expectancy as a "momentary belief concerning the

16. J. S. Adams, "Inequity in Social Exchange." *Advances in Experimental Social Psychology*, edited by L. Berkowitz (New York: Academic Press, 1965), pp. 276–299.

17. Andrew D. Szilagyi, Jr. and Marc J. Wallace, Jr., *Organizational Behavior and Performance* (2d ed.; Santa Monica, CA: Goodyear Publishing Company, Inc., 1980), p. 122.

likelihood that a particular act will be followed by a particular outcome."[18] Thus, a belief that "hard work leads to quick promotions" or "coming in early will win the boss's favor" are expectancies. Expectancies thus serve as guidelines by which an individual can go about planning to fulfill personal needs.

Interest in the expectancy theory has grown significantly since Vroom's book was published in 1964. Others have expanded on the theory and have conducted many empirical studies. Because of the complexity of the theoretical model, it is difficult to test fully. However, there is substantial support for its general principles. "It can provide the manager with a framework for explaining the direction of behavior of employees and for highlighting certain organizational influences that may have an effect on their motivated behavior."[19]

Reinforcement Theory. The importance of reinforcement in the learning situation was discussed in Chapter 8. The same principle is found in a theory of motivation. **Reinforcement theory** states that behavior is contingent upon reinforcement. In other words, when rewards follow performance, performance improves. When rewards do not depend upon performance, performance deteriorates. Thus, the kind of outcome involved reinforces a person's response either positively (leading to a greater frequency) or negatively (leading to less frequency). The process of influencing behavior through reinforcement is known as **operant conditioning**.

In an organizational context, positive reinforcement can be used in behavior modification to increase the frequency of desired responses among subordinates. It basically involves the use of praise and recognition when employees perform in a desired manner. Emery Air Freight Corporation was the first to use the behavior modification principles set forth by B. F. Skinner.[20] It is reported to have cut costs by $2 million a year. More than a hundred organizations have since used these techniques, some with even greater success. The 3M Company reports savings of $3.5 million in 1977 alone. Other companies include Frito-Lay, Addressograph-Multigraph, B. F. Goodrich, Weyerhaeuser, and Warner-Lambert. Some managers who are now using the techniques are reluctant to call their programs behavior modification, opting for such terms as "performance improvement" or "contingency management."[21] In Figure 11–2, the procedures for implementing behavior modification techniques in an organization are presented. It should be emphasized that relating rewards to performance is a powerful approach to motivating employees.

Goal-Setting Theory. The setting of work goals can have a significant impact on the motivation and performance of employees. Goal setting, in fact, is incorporated in some manner in all of the theories that have been discussed. The **goal-setting**

---

18. Victor H. Vroom, *Work and Motivation* (New York: John Wiley and Sons, 1964), p. 170.
19. Szilagyi and Wallace, *op. cit.,* p. 120.
20. "New Tool: Reinforcement for Good Work," *Psychology Today,* Vol. 5, No. 11 (April, 1972), pp. 68–69.
21. "Productivity Gains from a Pat on the Back," *Business Week,* No. 2518 (January 23, 1978), pp. 56–62.

Figure 11–2   How to Implement Behavior Modification Techniques

1. Create a consistent work environment.
2. Determine the desired behaviors of subordinates.
3. Determine the types of rewards to use.
4. Communicate desired behaviors and rewards clearly to subordinates.
5. Provide rewards for desired behaviors immediately.
6. Provide rewards on a variable-ratio schedule. It has been found to be superior to a fixed-ratio schedule.
7. Minimize the use of punishment.

SOURCE: Reprinted, by permission of the publisher, from *Supervisory Management*, February 1976, pp. 22–28, © 1976 by AMACOM, a division of American Management Associations, New York. All rights reserved.

theory is generally associated with Locke, who has demonstrated the effect of goal setting on individual performance. His major proposition, which has been supported experimentally, is that those employees who set or accept harder goals perform at levels higher than those who set or accept easier goals. Locke states that individuals will set goals for themselves whether instructed to or not.[22] In order that management's goals may be attained, supervisors should play an active role in goal setting for subordinates. The MBO programs which were discussed in Chapter 10 provide for superior-subordinate participation in goal setting.

Further Application of Motivation Theories

We have attempted to show that each one of the motivation theories discussed provides a point of view that is helpful in understanding the complex process of motivation. Throughout the discussion, examples of the application of each theory to the job were provided. Until one theory is found to be the only valid one, it is practical to select the theory that appears most pertinent to the specific problem under consideration. Each of the theories has stimulated thinking and research and thus has contributed to the understanding of the motivational process as summarized in Figure 11–3.

As we have seen, motivation is not simply a force that resides inside individuals. It is affected by the internal environment of the organization. The size, the organizational structure's shape (i.e., tall or flat), the organizational climate, job requirements, the actions of supervisors and other managers, and the work group are the major factors influencing the motivational process. Because of the nature of the

22. E. A. Locke, "Toward a Theory of Task Motivation and Incentives," *Organizational Behavior and Human Performance*, Vol. 3, No. 2 (May, 1968), pp. 157–189. *See also* Gary Latham and Gary Yukl, "A Review of the Research on the Application of Goal Setting in Organizations," *Academy of Management Journal*, Vol. 18, No. 4 (December, 1975), pp. 824–845.

Figure 11–3 Major Contributions of Theories of Motivation

THEORY	EMPHASIS AND CONTRIBUTIONS
Need-hierarchy	Individuals have needs and act in a manner to satisfy them. There is a priority in needs.
ERG	More than one need may be operating at a given time. Lack of satisfaction of the higher-level needs will make the lower-level needs more desired.
Achievement motivation	A major portion of an employee's performance can be explained by the intensity of the need for achievement. The need for achievement is prominent among successful executives.
Motivator-hygiene	Needs are prime motivators. Certain factors (motivators) motivate employees, other factors (hygiene factors) do not.
Equity	Individuals compare their inputs and outcomes with those of other individuals.
Expectancy	Individuals place certain values on work-related rewards. They also make conscious estimates of effort-performance-reward relationships.
Reinforcement	Desired behavior can be increased and undesirable behavior decreased by proper application of rewards and punishments.
Goal setting	Having specific goals increases performance. Difficult goals result in higher performance than easy goals.

supervisory role, employee motivation is a major responsibility of supervisors. Some guidelines for supervisors that are consistent with the theoretical ideas presented may be found in Figure 11–4. These guidelines can be used selectively to strengthen the level of motivation.

FRUSTRATION AND CONFLICT

An examination of the events in the daily life of an employee confirms the fact that not all needs are satisfied fully. The employee may be prevented from reaching a particular goal or incentive, or there may be conflicting goals. Either condition may keep one in a state of dissatisfaction and tension that may interfere with job performance and ability to work harmoniously with fellow employees. Managers and supervisors should understand the forces that make for dissatisfaction and tension in their subordinates so that they may create a work environment that will be as free as possible of these conditions.

Figure 11—4 Motivation Guidelines for Supervisors

1. *Clarify the task role.* The easiest way to test the understanding of employees is to ask, "What do you believe is expected of you in this job—in terms of results?"
2. *Provide positive feedback.* Verbal acknowledgment costs nothing, and yet it provides assurances to the employees that they are doing the right thing and that their contribution is valued.
3. *Personalize the causes of performance.* Supervisors should help subordinates to realize the ways in which personal efforts affect performance.
4. *Make apparent the personal gains.* If system-administered benefits (job assignments, promotions, etc.) are to serve as incentives, they need to be specified in advance. Let subordinates know what they stand to gain by performing at a certain level.
5. *Personalize pride in accomplishment.* To stimulate a higher level of task motivation, make sure that the employees are enjoying the feeling of success.
6. *Encourage personal goal clarification.* Work with the individual to help define personal goals that are to some degree organizationally aligned.
7. *Match the job with personal motives.* Enable employees to engage in tasks where the required behavior is compatible with their underlying need and will provide internalized satisfaction.
8. *Remove supervisory roadblocks.* Do not permit unnecessary hassles and obstacles to occur. Be observant of changes in employee expectations or behavior.
9. *Remove organizational roadblocks.* Superior performance cannot be expected if resources are not provided or if obstacles surround the employees.

SOURCE: Adapted from Curtis W. Cook, "Guidelines for Managing Motivation," *Business Horizons,* Vol. 23, No. 2 (April, 1980), pp. 61—69. Reproduced with permission.

Frustration on the Job

The presence of a barrier to goal attainment and need satisfaction creates a frustrating condition with the result that the individual's inner state of disequilibrium persists or becomes stronger. One who is blocked from achieving a goal by some barrier—either external or internal—is said to be experiencing frustration. Some typical external barriers that block employees are discriminatory practices, hostile supervisors, monotonous jobs, unpleasant working conditions, economic insecurity, and similar conditions. Some of the possible internal barriers are poor working habits, undesirable personality traits, or lack of aptitude or interest for a particular job. A perceived inadequacy is just as real to the person as an external barrier.

Common Reactions to Frustration. A frustrated person may respond by selecting an acceptable substitute goal that is attainable or by engaging in behavior that is maladaptive.

Selecting a Substitute Goal.   Striving to reach a substitute goal generally is considered to be more adaptive because it leads to need satisfaction. An example may be found in the employee who has a strong need to lead others and aspires to be a manager but, because of some barrier which prohibits attainment of a managerial position, satisfies leadership needs by becoming an officer in the union (a substitute goal). Unattainable goals often have alternatives that can be equally satisfying and thus should not be overlooked.

Engaging in Maladaptive Behavior.   In the absence of a substitute goal, an employee's responses sooner or later are likely to become maladaptive in nature. A common maladaptive response to frustration is aggression or hostility. Aggression typically involves verbal or physical attacks against the person or persons perceived to be the cause of the frustration. Frequently, however, where it is too dangerous or too painful to attack the frustrator directly, attacks may be made against other persons or objects. It should be observed, however, that frustration does not always lead to aggression. Some employees withdraw, others seek assistance.

Reducing Frustration.   Managers and supervisors have a responsibility to be sensitive to the needs of their subordinates and to create a work environment in which these needs may be satisfied and frustration minimized. Causes of frustration may include changing technology and conditions of work, economic insecurity of the job, insignificance of the job and the work group, and unfulfilled expectations. Not all of the sources of frustration are under the direct control of management. However, an awareness of potential areas of employee frustrations and sincere efforts to handle them effectively through better organization, planning, and communication can help to ameliorate many of the conditions that give rise to frustration. In the next chapter some recommendations will be made for creating the type of environment that meets the need requirements of employees.

Conflict on the Job

Having two or more strong motivational patterns that cannot be satisfied together is a conflict. A conflict typically involves a choice or decision-making situation in which the needs, goals, or methods for attaining the goals are incompatible. A conflict involving needs is seen in the employee who has an urge to ask the boss for a promotion and yet is afraid to do so. The urge to ask because of the chances for promotion and the fear of being judged as not qualified represent forces tugging at each other. A conflict involving goals is illustrated by the individual who desires to be an executive and, at the same time, to have freedom from responsibility. A conflict in methods arises when the approach to attaining the goal involves incompatible means. For example, in handling a business transaction one cannot be honest and dishonest at the same time.

An organization frequently creates conflicts within and among its members that can be harmful to both employees and the organization. One common type of conflict involves the desire that employees have for independence, on the one hand, and for dependence and support on the other. Much anxiety is created over these opposing needs. Organizations promote this type of conflict by creating conditions that foster dependency while stressing the need for members to demonstrate initiative and independence. Therefore, conditions that create conflict should be identified and eliminated.

Symptoms of Frustration and Conflict

Typically the employee who experiences frustration or conflict feels tense and uncomfortable—a condition that is commonly referred to as anxiety. This condition is often accompanied by unconscious defense mechanisms.

Anxiety.   When individuals sense that they are in danger, they may experience a feeling of anxiety. In contrast to fear, anxiety results when the source of danger cannot be clearly identified. However, one is aware of physical symptoms similar to those that one associates with fear such as trembling, nausea, a pounding heart, and dryness in the throat. Prolonged anxiety is a form of stress that is emotionally and physically harmful to the employee as well as to job performance. It is, however, not the only form of stress. There are other sources of work-related stress that will be discussed in the context of employee health in Chapter 20.

Anxiety may account for various employee behaviors that are often misunderstood or misinterpreted. For example, resistance to change is fundamentally caused by the anxiety that arises from a proposed change in job, work methods, or merely the relocation of a desk. Employees who resist changes, therefore, are not going out of their way to be "difficult" but, rather, feel threatened or frightened at the prospects of a change. Similarly, anxiety may cause supervisors to distrust employees who exhibit ambition or initiative.

Defense Mechanisms.   Another symptom of frustration and conflict is the defense mechanism. A defense mechanism serves to protect one's self-concept. The choice of which defense mechanism is used will depend primarily upon one's personality and characteristic modes of response. Aside from the aggressive reactions to frustrations that were discussed earlier, there are other defense mechanisms that we all use to protect our self-concepts. Among the more common defense mechanisms observed in work situations are:

1. Exaggerated behavior, such as using big words.
2. Bossiness, or compensation.
3. Making excuses for our behavior, or rationalization.
4. Resisting the suggestion of others, or negativism.
5. Blaming others, or projection.

JOB SATISFACTION

The satisfaction that individuals receive from their employment is largely dependent upon the extent to which the job and everything associated with it meets their needs and wants. *Wants* are the conscious desires for things or conditions that an individual believes will provide satisfaction. Most attempts to measure job satisfaction involve studying wants through questionnaires and interviews. The manner in which an individual responds to the specific questions is dependent not only upon the conditions themselves but also upon how the individual perceives them. Perceptions are influenced by occupational level, educational level, age, sex, health, family relationships, personality, and many other factors. In addition to questionnaires and interviews which will be examined in Chapter 21, job satisfaction is reflected in employee behavior.

Factors Affecting Job Satisfaction

As we have just observed, there are many personal characteristics that affect how an employee perceives a particular job. Supervisors must consider these personal factors in assessing the satisfaction of their subordinates. It is equally important to examine the characteristics of the work environment. A comprehensive review of empirical studies of job satisfaction by Locke reveals that there are seven working conditions that lead to job satisfaction for most people. These conditions, listed in Figure 11–5, are under the control of managerial personnel and human resources managers.

Job Satisfaction and Employee Behavior

At one time it was assumed that, if management could provide satisfactory working conditions for its employees, all types of desirable ends would be achieved. It now appears, however, that the relationship between job satisfaction and employee turnover, absenteeism, and performance is not as simple as once believed.

Turnover and Absenteeism. Job satisfaction has been shown to be closely related to turnover and absenteeism. The higher an employee's satisfaction, the less

Figure 11–5 Working Conditions Conducive to Job Satisfaction

1. Mentally challenging work with which the individual can cope successfully.
2. Personal interest in the work itself.
3. Rewards for performance in line with personal aspirations that are just and understood.
4. Work which is not too tiring physically.
5. Working conditions which are compatible with the individual's physical needs and work goals.
6. High self-esteem on the part of the employee.
7. Help in attaining interesting work, pay, and promotions and in minimizing role conflict and ambiguity.

SOURCE: Edwin A. Locke, "The Nature and Causes of Job Satisfaction," *Handbook of Industrial and Organizational Psychology*, edited by Marvin D. Dunnette (Chicago: Rand McNally College Publishing Company, 1976), p. 1328. Reproduced with permission.

likely resignation will occur. In view of the high cost of turnover, the importance of this finding should be apparent to managerial personnel. The relationship between job satisfaction and absenteeism is similar but not as strong as for turnover. However, when unexcused absences from the job and frequency of absences are considered, a strong relationship has been found. The employee with high job satisfaction is less likely to be absent frequently, particularly for unexcused reasons.[23]

Job Performance.   There is no simple relationship between job satisfaction and job performance. In an analysis of 20 correlational studies using both supervisory ratings and objective performance measures, no positive relationship was found between satisfaction and performance.[24] This finding is consistent with that of other research. Thus, satisfaction does not necessarily lead to better job performance.

Lawler and Porter have suggested that it is the other way around, i.e., job performance leads to job satisfaction, as shown in Figure 11–6. Employees may derive rewards from their performance that are a source of satisfaction. The rewards may be of an intrinsic nature, such as the feeling of having done something worthwhile; or of an extrinsic nature, such as increased pay, a promotion, etc. Lawler and Porter conclude that managers can affect job satisfaction through appropriately structuring the rewards and the ways that these rewards will be viewed by the employee. The extent to which the employee perceives the reward to be equitable

Figure 11–6 Performance Leads to Satisfaction

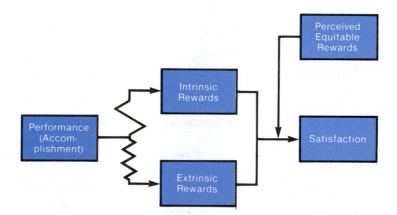

SOURCE: Edward D. Lawler, III, and Lyman W. Porter, "The Effect of Performance on Job Satisfaction," *Industrial Relations*, Vol. 7, No. 5 (October, 1967), pp. 20–28. Reprinted with permission.

23. Lyman W. Porter and Richard M. Steers, "Organizational, Work, and Personal Factors in Employee Turnover and Absenteeism," *Psychological Bulletin*, Vol. 80, No. 2 (August, 1973), pp. 151–176.

24. V. H. Vroom, *op. cit.,* Chapter 6.

has been found to be important. If the reward is perceived as not being consistent with the rewards that others are receiving, dissatisfaction will result.[25] While there is yet much to be discovered about job satisfaction and its relationship to productivity, the application of what is known can contribute to the individual and the organization.

RÉSUMÉ

Effective management of human resources depends upon an understanding of the characteristics that interact within the human organism. Since job performance is largely dependent upon those factors in the work environment that will release the potential of employees, the role of the motivational process deserves special consideration. Human needs—especially those at the higher levels—and the various ways in which they may be satisfied, should be understood.

While there are various theories of motivation with different emphases, each has practical implications for management to use in releasing human potential. Positive steps should be taken to create a work environment that will reduce the causes of frustration and minimize the conflict situations that invariably develop in an organization. Recognizing the wants of employees and understanding how they perceive their working conditions can contribute to a higher level of job satisfaction.

TERMS TO IDENTIFY

motivation
perception
self-concept
attitude
value
principle of hedonism
need-hierarchy theory
ERG theory
achievement motivation theory

motivator-hygiene theory
motivator factors
hygiene factors
equity theory
expectancy theory
reinforcement theory
operant conditioning
goal-setting theory

DISCUSSION QUESTIONS

1. In what ways are an employee's values likely to affect job performance and behavior at work?

2. What is motivation? How is it related to employee performance?

3. What are the reasons for the different theories of motivation? Does the fact that there are different theories mean that none of them is valid?

25. Edward E. Lawler, III, and Lyman W. Porter, "The Effect of Performance on Job Satisfaction," *Industrial Relations*, Vol. 7, No. 5 (October, 1967), pp. 20—28.

4. Which of the theories of motivation discussed in the chapter do you feel would be the most useful in the management of personnel? Why does it appeal to you?

5. What can management do to reduce employee frustration and minimize conflicts?

6. What are some of the barriers that women and minority groups are likely to encounter at work? Identify the needs that are frustrated under such conditions.

7. Negativism was listed in the chapter as being a common defense mechanism. What examples of negativism have you observed in people at work? What effect did it have on others? What steps can a supervisor take to cope with negativism in subordinates?

8. What factors help determine the degree of satisfaction an employee may derive from his or her job? How much control does management have over these factors?

PROBLEM 11-1

HANDLING FRUSTRATION

The following statements describe frustrations that individuals have experienced at work. Read them and then answer the questions at the end.

1. An employee is unable to perform satisfactorily on the job because of a lack of ability to do the mathematical computations that the job requires.

2. An employee tries to please the supervisor but is constantly rebuffed by sarcastic personal and performance-related remarks about this employee.

3. A supervisor is eager to have the work group make a good showing but job insecurity prevents this person from taking disciplinary action at times when it is appropriate.

4. A career executive who is highly regarded for competency and valued by superiors does not feel sufficiently educated to move up to higher-level positions in this organization.

a. For each of the above situations, indicate whether the barrier is internal or external.

b. What can each individual do to overcome the cause of the frustration, assuming that the individual recognizes the cause?

PROBLEM 11-2

THE PAJAMA FACTORY*

Many years ago an experiment was conducted at the Harwood Manufacturing Company. The plant had about 500 women and 100 men engaged in manufacturing pajamas. The average age of the employees was 23 years, and the average education was 8 years of grammar school. Most of the employees were from the rural, mountainous areas surrounding the town and had no prior industrial experience. Because of its policies, the company had enjoyed good labor relations since the day that it commenced operations.

*Adapted from an experiment by L. Coch and J. R. P. French, Jr., "Overcoming Resistance to Change," *Human Relations*, Vol. 1 (1948) pp. 512–532.

The experiment was designed to determine why employees often resist changes that are made in various aspects of their jobs. Management had determined that it was necessary to change work methods in order to reduce production costs and used this opportunity to study employee resistance to change.

One group of employees—the control group—went through the usual factory routine when their jobs were changed. The production department modified the job, and a new piece rate was set. A group meeting was then held in which the control group was told that the change was necessary because of competitive conditions and that a new piece rate had been set. The new piece rate was thoroughly explained by the time-study man, and questions were answered.

The experimental group was handled quite differently. In a group meeting that was held with all the employees to be affected by the change, the need for the change was presented as dramatically as possible by showing two identical garments produced in the factory; one was produced in 1946 and had sold for twice as much as the other one produced in 1947. The group was asked to identify the cheaper one and could not do it. The demonstration effectively showed the need for cost reduction. A general agreement was reached that a savings could be effected by removing the "frills" and "fancy" work from the garment without affecting the folders' opportunity to achieve a high efficiency rating. Management then presented a plan to set the new job and piece rate, as follows:

1. Make a check study of the job as it was being done.
2. Eliminate all unnecessary work.
3. Train several operators in the correct methods.
4. Set the piece rate by time studies on these specially trained operators.
5. Explain the new job and rate to all the operators.
6. Train all operators in the new method so they can reach a high rate of production within a short time.

The group approved this plan and chose the operators to be specially trained. A submeeting with the chosen operators was held immediately following the meeting with the entire group. They displayed a cooperative and interested attitude and immediately presented many good suggestions. This attitude carried over into the working out of the details of the new job. When the new job and piece rates were set, the "special" operators referred to "our job," "our rate," etc. The "special" operators served to train the other operators on the new job.

The results for the two groups that worked under the same supervisor were quite different. The control group improved little beyond their earlier performance. Resistance developed almost immediately after the change occurred. Marked expressions of aggression against management occurred such as conflict with the methods engineer, expression of hostility against the supervisor, deliberate restriction of production, and lack of cooperation with the supervisor. There were 17 percent "quits" in the first 40 days. The experimental group, on the other hand, showed an unusually good relearning curve. At the end of 14 days, their group averaged 61 units per hour. During the 14 days, their attitude was cooperative and permissive. They worked well with the methods engineer, the training staff, and the supervisor. There were no "quits" in this group in the first 40 days.

a. What employee needs were purposely ignored in management's handling of the control group?

b. Would the fact that employees are members of groups have any effect on their performance as individuals?

c. If you were a supervisor, how much resistance to change may you expect from your subordinates? What can you do to help prevent resistance from occurring?

SUGGESTED READINGS

Cherrington, David J. *The Work Ethic—Working Values and Values That Work.* New York: AMACOM, 1980.

Chruden, Herbert J., and Arthur W. Sherman, Jr. *Readings in Managing Human Resources,* 6th ed. Cincinnati: South-Western Publishing Co., 1984, Part 4.

Hampton, David R. *Behavioral Concepts in Management,* 3d ed. Belmont, CA: Wadsworth Publishing Company, Inc., 1978.

Rosenbaum, Bernard L. *How To Motivate Today's Workers: Motivational Models for Managers and Supervisors.* Highstown, NJ: McGraw-Hill Book Company, 1982.

Rychlak, Joseph F. *Personality and Life-Style of Young Male Managers.* New York: Academic Press, 1982.

Sanzotta, Donald. *Motivational Theories and Applications for Managers.* New York: AMACOM, 1977.

Yankelovich, Daniel. *New Rules—Searching for Fulfillment in a World Turned Upside Down.* New York: AMACOM, 1981.

Chapter Objectives:

- To describe the role and importance of the informal organization.
- To identify the major characteristics of work groups.
- To cite the requisites for effective communication.
- To describe the different types of formal communication.
- To identify the barriers to communication.
- To understand the contribution of transactional analysis to organizational communication.

Developing Employee Cooperation

12

In Chapter 11 we discussed the major forces which influence the productivity, behavior, and satisfaction of employees at work. The focus was primarily upon how we can utilize what is known about motivation to foster the attainment of organizational and personal goals. Attaining these goals also requires cooperation between managers, supervisors, and subordinates. Since these subordinates are typically members of a work group, their attitudes and behavior are influenced by their co-workers. By understanding the characteristics of work groups and how groups function, we will be in a better position to elicit their cooperation in the achievement of the desired goals. Attaining cooperation from employees as individuals and as members of groups is dependent upon effective communication within an organization. This chapter will emphasize the importance of effective communication.

LEADERSHIP AND WORK GROUPS

In the study of people at work, one must be aware of the groups into which employees are organized. A group is composed of individuals who have a unique pattern of abilities, aptitudes, and other characteristics. Just as individuals differ from each other, each group has its own unique pattern of characteristics that distinguishes it from other groups.

Work groups are groups that have been formally organized for the accomplishment of the organization's objectives. Within and between work groups are found subgroups that have emerged on an informal basis. In examining the groups within an organization, attention should be given to both formal and informal groups. Research on group behavior has yielded some valuable information that has provided managerial personnel with new concepts to guide them.

In every organization there will be interaction between the various groups that exist within it. How to establish conditions between groups that will enhance the productivity of each and result in favorable human relations is a problem with which management is continually confronted. One of the major problems between groups is that of handling competition. Competition sometimes may cause one group to regard a competing group as the enemy while it views itself as faultless. As a result, hostility toward the other group is likely to increase while interaction with it decreases. It is natural for supervisors to be interested primarily in their own groups. However, supervisors should be trained to recognize the importance of cooperation between their groups and other groups in the organization.

The Role of Leaders

Organizational structures provide many positions of leadership, ranging from that of the chief executive to that of the first-line supervisor. Each of these positions requires the person occupying it to exercise leadership responsibilities by performing two types of activities: (1) those that are directed toward task accomplishment, and (2) those that maintain stability in the work group and enhance the personal need satisfaction of group members. An organization's success is influenced by the ability of its managers to handle both types of activities simultaneously.[1]

Specific responsibilities that will vary according to the leader's position will be considered in Chapter 13. In this chapter the discussion will focus on the leadership role of first-line supervisors and those individuals within a work group who function in an informal leadership role. The roles that formal and informal leaders exercise in a group will determine, in part, the manner in which the group is to function.

Formal Leadership.   The supervisor is the formal leader of the group by virtue of the authority of his or her position. Supervisory success, however, is dependent upon more than this source of authority. It is dependent upon many skills that will be discussed in Chapter 13. In connection with work groups, the greater the supervisor's skill in developing cooperation among the members of the group, the greater the productivity and satisfaction of the work group is likely to be. Under such circumstances employees have been found to cooperate more with each other and to have better team spirit and better interpersonal relationships. By encouraging the members of the group to be tolerant of the attitudes and behavior of one another, the supervisor can develop a climate that "brings out the best" in each member. Such a climate encourages the individual members to subordinate their personal interests for the good of the group.[2]

Informal Leadership.   Although the supervisor is the formal leader of the group, there may be one or more informal leaders in a work group to whom its members also give their support. This support may result from the recognition of an unofficial leader's technical skill or knowledge, seniority, the type of work performed, or, more frequently, the leader's ability to communicate with others and to satisfy their personal needs. The supervisor who is able to recognize the status of informal leaders within the group can often use their influence to the advantage of the organization.

Coping with the Informal Organization

Research in the behavioral sciences has done much to make practitioners aware of the important role played by the informal organization. The term **informal organization** was first used by the Mayo group during the well-known Hawthorne Studies at the Western Electric Company (see Chapter 1). It refers to the network of personal and social relations not established or required by formal authority but arising spontaneously as employees associate with one another.

The Influence of Informal Groups.   Most employees are members of one or more informal groups. Generally, they meet for companionship and to share mutual concerns which may or may not be job-related. Informal groups tend to develop

---

1. Richard M. Steers, *Organizational Effectiveness—a Behavioral View* (Santa Monica, CA: Goodyear Publishing Company, Inc., 1977), p. 155.
2. Rensis Likert, *New Patterns of Management* (New York: McGraw-Hill Book Company, 1961), pp. 171-172.

certain sentiments, values, and folkways to which its members are under pressure to conform if they are to remain in good standing with the group. An informal group may also develop norms (standards of conduct or performance) that its members are expected to observe, to either the benefit or detriment of management's expectations. It is not uncommon for a group to adopt informal limits of output, or "bogeys," to protect the slower worker and to insure a constant backlog of work which is sufficient to guarantee the continued employment of its members.

Informal communication takes place between employees whose relationships to one another may be independent of their authority and/or job functions. It occurs as the result of their desires to socialize and to share information. While these contacts follow patterns that are independent of the formal organizational structure, they nevertheless provide an important channel of communication. This channel of communication is frequently referred to as the **grapevine** because it fans out through the organization without regard to the formal channels of communication. In most instances the grapevine provides for a rapid transmission of information *and* misinformation; therefore, it presents a challenge to formal communication. Keeping the channels of communication open and presenting positive and truthful facts about all topics help to build faith in the credibility of management communication. Formal communication will be discussed later in this chapter.

Making Use of the Informal Organization.   The informal organization provides an opportunity for employees with potential leadership abilities to use these talents. An informal leader may serve in the roles of disciplinarian, spokesperson, arbitrator, or counselor for group members. More than one leader can emerge within an informal group. The use of informal leaders in some instances can permit management to gauge the opinion of group members or to gain the support of the group for management goals. Informal leaders also may be possible candidates who can be trained for supervisory positions.

Informal group activities can serve to relieve the monotony of certain routine production jobs by facilitating social interaction and encouraging cooperation. One type of informal group activity that is commonly observed is **schmoozing**. It refers to employees engaging in such activities as telling jokes, lingering at the water fountain, and wandering around the office or lab for the purpose of socializing to relieve boredom. According to Robert Schrank, "most factory work, and much office work as well, is repetitious and dull." White-collar workers have the freedom to schmooze whereas blue-collar workers have to punch a time clock and get permission to leave their work sites. He recommends that making the production line more "congenial and humane" would in no way detract from the level of production.[3]

CHARACTERISTICS OF WORK GROUPS

The characteristics of work groups have been studied intensively for only about 50 years. Kurt Lewin, a German psychologist who later came to the United States,

---

3. *Bulletin to Management* No. 1482 (Washington, DC: The Bureau of National Affairs, Inc., July 20, 1978), p. 2.

initiated and conducted extensive research in group behavior. In keeping with his overall theory of human behavior, he viewed the group as an organism that functioned as a holistic entity rather than as an aggregate of individuals. Lewin introduced the type of leadership training that today is referred to as sensitivity training. It is through the work of Lewin and those who followed him that we have a better understanding of the characteristics of work groups. Many factors have been identified and studied, but only those that relate to the structure for group activity will be discussed here. These characteristics include role, status, cohesiveness, and conformity *v.* innovation.[4] An understanding of these factors will enable us to perform the functions of human resources management more effectively.

Role

In examining the behavior of groups, one should not lose sight of the fact that the group is comprised of individuals, each of whom has a different role. A role is the pattern of action or behavior that is expected of individuals by virtue of their membership in a particular group. Because they are usually members of several groups on and off the job, most individuals exercise several roles.

Formal Roles. At work the formal role of an employee is determined by the duties and responsibilities of the job being performed. In the role of supervisor, for example, an individual must direct and assist others in the performance of their jobs. A supervisor must also make personnel decisions, such as those relating to transfers, promotions, or disciplinary actions, that will affect the lives of subordinates. Subordinates, on the other hand, are expected to accept and comply with directions and instructions from the supervisor and to cooperate and get along with others within the work group.

Informal Roles. In addition to their formal roles, employees also may exercise various informal roles within their work group. One employee, for example, may perform the role of informal leader, another may be the shop clown, and still another may serve as the "official" griever for the group. Other members may assume the role of being followers and do their work without making any waves. Employees who hold union offices may exercise still another role in the group.

Members of the group are often assigned a role by their peers on the basis of who dominates whom. Through assertion and intimidation an accepted order of privilege, authority, and dominance may be established among the members of the group. This "pecking order" establishes a pattern that indicates the relative status of the members of the group.

Role Perception. An employee's role in an organization is affected by **role perception,** which means how the employee perceives the role he or she is expected

---

4. For a thorough analysis of intragroup behavior see Andrew D. Szilagyi, Jr. and Marc J. Wallace, Jr., *Organizational Behavior and Performance* (2d ed.; Santa Monica, CA: Goodyear Publishing Company, Inc., 1980). Chapter 7.

to perform. Often supervisors do not perceive the performance of subordinates as their subordinates do. Many of the grievances that arise in connection with performance evaluation or disciplinary action could be avoided if there were a better understanding between the employee and the supervisor concerning the employee's role. How supervisors perceive their roles will largely determine their effectiveness in leading the work group. One common fault of supervisors is their failure to perceive the nature of their role as a manager and to act accordingly.

Role Conflict.   The demands placed upon employees within an organization frequently create role conflicts. A **role conflict** results from varying expectations as to how an employee is expected to behave in a given role. Management, for example, expects supervisors to carry out management policies and procedures and generally concern themselves with the organization's goals. Subordinates, on the other hand, expect supervisors to look after their interests and to protect them from management abuse. For supervisors, trying to fill both roles leads to conflict. Other go-between roles subject to conflict include quality control inspectors who are often caught between the demands for quality and quantity.[5]

Status

The roles that an individual performs, along with pay, job title, and other factors, provide a source of status. Status refers to the relative rank a person possesses with respect to others. The abilities that jobs require of individuals, as well as the duties, the working conditions, and pay, all help to determine their status on the job. Status in turn contributes significantly to the individual's feelings of self-esteem.

Tangible and visible expressions which are commonly referred to as **status symbols** can serve to call the attention of others to one's status. The location of an individual's desk or workplace, the tools and equipment that are used, and the clothes that are worn may symbolize status. At the executive level, office location and furnishings, reserved parking space, and the like are typical status symbols that may provide executives a source of ego satisfaction.

Improving Employee Status.   Many organizations are making an effort to improve the status of their blue-collar employees and to provide them with a sense of equality with their white-collar counterparts. For example, even companies that still compute the pay of some personnel on an hourly basis have eliminated the use of the time clock. As a representative for one such company stated, "Taking out the time clocks was a sign we wanted to treat our employees like adults, not control them like children or mechanical devices."[6]

Avoiding Status Inconsistency.   Since an employee's status is determined by many different factors, it is quite possible for some of these factors to be inconsistent

---

5. H. Joseph Reitz, *Behavior in Organizations* (rev. ed.; Homewood, IL: Richard D. Irwin, Inc., 1981), p. 286.

6. James MacGregor, "The Honor System," *The Wall Street Journal*, May 22, 1970, p. 1.

with others. This situation is referred to as **status inconsistency** and may cause frustration and anxiety on the part of those who are the subject of the inconsistency. Employees, for example, are quick to resent the fact that someone in a job on a lower level within the structure may be receiving higher pay or more privileges than they. Similarly, those individuals who have more status by virtue of their seniority, age, qualifications, or other factors may expect to receive preference with regard to work assignments and conditions of employment over the other employees with less status. If these expected "privileges of rank" are ignored when personnel decisions are made, individuals who possess greater status may become resentful of this fact and become a problem. Consistency with respect to the factors by which status is determined can help to improve employee security and personal adjustment. Inconsistency, on the other hand, can contribute to **status anxiety** in which individuals experience feelings of discomfort as the result of not knowing how they rank with respect to their colleagues.

Cohesiveness

Another characteristic of work groups is their **cohesiveness,** or the extent of employees' loyalty toward their group and each other. Cohesive groups are those in which the members act toward a common goal. Groups that are low in cohesion are characterized by an inability to achieve the degree of unification which makes group action possible.

Several factors influence cohesiveness. One of these is the degree of the individual's dependency on a group for need satisfaction. Another factor is size, with cohesiveness being reduced as the number of persons in the group increases. Stability of the group membership also contributes to cohesiveness. If a group competes with other groups, its cohesiveness generally increases. However, excessive competition among the members of a group can reduce this cohesiveness.

Cohesiveness is the most important factor in morale—the condition of well-being among members of a group. Other factors determining morale are: the existence of goals which members of the group strive to achieve, observable progress toward reaching the goals, and a sense of participation among the individuals of the group in working toward the goals.

Conformity v. Innovation

There is a constant struggle in organizations between the pressures for conformity and those for innovation. If an organization is to survive, it must require some degree of conformity. However, if it is to progress, it must also encourage innovation. The development and implementation of new and better solutions to problems can be encouraged by the presence of an organizational climate and a positive program that will maximize the creation of new ideas.[7]

7. John F. Patrick, "Organization Climate and the Creative Individual," *Public Personnel Review,* Vol. 31, No. 1 (January, 1970), pp. 31-35.

It should be recognized, however, that innovation and conformity are also under the control of the informal groups in an organization. These groups typically have their own beliefs and attitudes toward the work, supervision, and other important matters that their members are expected to assume. Such **attitude conformity** may serve the interests of management—e.g., a group has a tradition of adhering carefully to company rules and exerts group pressure on an individual who has fallen into the habit of breaking certain rules. Or, attitude conformity may sometimes be contrary to management's interests. For example, an employee is punished by the group for producing significantly more than the amount upon which the group has informally agreed.

THE VITAL ROLE OF COMMUNICATION

As one observes the behavior of people in organizations, the importance of communication becomes apparent. Communication is often referred to as the network that binds together all of the members and activities within an organization. Through the transmission of information, ideas, and attitudes, the personnel and their activities may be coordinated in the pursuit of organizational and individual goals.

In the past, management has measured the effectiveness of communication primarily in terms of how well it was telling its story. However, management is becoming more aware of the importance and value of obtaining feedback from employees. A climate with open, two-way communication improves the opportunity for high productivity and job satisfaction.

Functions of Organizational Communication

Organizational communication has many facets. In the modern world it is essential that management maintain effective communication with the employees, union, community, government agencies, stockholders, retirees, educational institutions, and the general public. The nature and quality of communication with individuals and groups outside of the organization affect its human resources management program as well as other organizational programs.

In this chapter we are primarily concerned with communication within the organization as it relates to human resources management. According to Deutsch, there are four different, though interrelated, functions in which communication is important. One of these is staffing. Another involves motivation, morale, and productivity. The need to acclimate employees and prepare them for various kinds of job-related change is a third function. Finally, human resources communications are used to express or reach some special goals related to employment such as affirmative action.[8]

8. Arnold R. Deutsch, *The Human Resources Revolution—Communicate or Litigate* (New York: McGraw-Hill, Inc., 1979), p. 102.

A study conducted by the International Association of Business Communicators (IABC) and a consulting firm—Towers, Perrin, Forster, and Crosby—reveals some interesting findings. They surveyed over 45,000 employees in 40 organizations to determine the subjects about which employees wanted management to communicate. The subjects that employees wanted to know more about, in the order of importance, are listed in Figure 12–1.

The Communication Process

In any communication there are steps through which an idea or concept passes from its inception by one person (the sender) until it is acted upon by another person (the receiver). Through an understanding of these steps and of some of the possible barriers that may occur, more effective communication may be achieved.

Steps in the Communication Process.   As shown in Figure 12–2, the first step is **ideation** by the sender. This is the intended content of the message the sender wants to transmit. In the next step, **encoding**, the ideas are organized into a series of

Figure 12–1 Subjects That Employees Want Communicated

RANK	SUBJECT	COMBINED VERY INTERESTED/INTERESTED RESPONSES
1	Organizational plans for the future	95.3%
2	Productivity improvement	90.3%
3	Personnel policies and practices	89.8%
4	Job-related information	89.2%
5	Job advancement opportunities	87.9%
6	Effect of external events on my job	87.8%
7	How my job fits into the organization	85.4%
8	Operations outside of my department or division	85.1%
9	How we're doing v. the competition	83.0%
10	Personnel changes and promotions	81.4%
11	Organizational community involvement	81.3%
12	Organizational stand on current issues	79.5%
13	How the organization uses its profits	78.4%
14	Advertising/promotional plans	77.2%
15	Financial results	76.4%
16	Human interest stories about other employees	70.4%
17	Personal news (birthdays, anniversaries, etc.)	57.0%

SOURCE: From 1982 Survey co-sponsored by IABC and TPF&C. Reproduced with permission.

symbols designed to communicate to the intended receiver(s). Suitable words or phrases that can be understood by the receiver(s) and the appropriate media to be used—memorandum, conference, etc.—are selected. The third step is **transmission** of the message as encoded through selected channels in the organizational structure. The fourth step is **receiving** by tuning in to receive the message. If it is an oral message, failure to listen or to concentrate results in the message being lost. The fifth step is **decoding**, as, for example, changing words into ideas. At this step the decoding may not agree with the idea that the sender originally encoded because of the difference in perceptions between the receiver and the sender as to the meaning of words, or semantics. Finally, the receiver takes **action**, or responds, by filing the information, asking for more information, or taking some other action. There can be no assurance, however, that communication has taken place unless there is some type of **feedback** to the sender in the form of an acknowledgment that the message was received.

Nonverbal Communication.   While the preceding analysis has been in terms of the communication of verbal symbols, it should be recognized that nonverbal communication is occurring simultaneously. In face-to-face communication the parties are also responding to facial expressions, gestures, bodily positions, and other nonverbal stimuli that are just as important to the communication process as the words that are being spoken. These expressions, gestures, and bodily positions together constitute our body language, as it is commonly called, and it conveys to others our attitudes and feelings.[9] Often the body language confirms the words being

Figure 12–2   The Communication Process

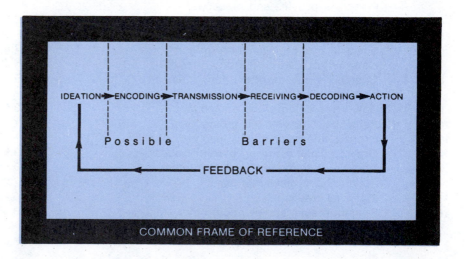

9. Julius Fast, *Body Language* (New York: M. Evans and Company, Inc., 1970).

spoken. However, when it contradicts verbal communication, it tends to reduce the credibility of what is said.

Similarly, problems are created when there is a discrepancy between verbal communication and overt behavior. For example, the boss who says, "My door is always open" but is invariably busy when employees request a conference is guilty of transmitting conflicting messages. Whenever the meaning of a nonverbal message conflicts with that of the verbal, the receiver is likely to find the nonverbal more believable.

Barriers to Communication

The mere existence of various avenues and media for communication does not insure that communication will occur. The grouping of people into a complex organization imposes additional conditions and factors affecting human relationships which may constitute potential barriers to communication. In order for communication to be effective, it is essential for the manager or supervisor to recognize these potential barriers and to plan communication so that these barriers may be overcome or at least minimized.

Differences Among Individuals.
A major barrier in communicating with a large number of individuals in an organization lies in the simple fact that no two individuals are alike. Individuals are born with different potentialities. They have had different experiences during their childhood and youth. As adults they have had employers and supervisors who have exerted a variety of influences upon them.

Differences in Perception. One result of prior experiences is that each employee brings to the job a unique way of looking at things, or, in other words, a personal frame of reference. This frame of reference determines the way in which whatever is seen or heard will be interpreted. If, for example, the supervisor is perceived as a "parent figure," the employee may accept or reject everything the supervisor says, depending upon personal experiences. Similarly, employees who have been "let down" by previous supervisors are likely to view a new supervisor as someone not to be trusted.

Some older persons often find it difficult to "tune in" on the same wavelength or frame of reference of youth and thus have problems in communicating with them. Managers and supervisors should learn enough about each individual to know what meaning will be applied to their messages and what emotional overtones will be inferred. Feedback is the key to open communication.

Differences in Listening Ability. We can learn more about how the world looks to others or what motivational and emotional states they may be experiencing by *listening.* In addition, Carl Rogers suggests going one step further. Instead of following our natural tendency to judge, to evaluate, to approve (or disapprove) the statement of the other person, we should practice **nonevaluative listening.**[10] This

---

10. Carl R. Rogers and F. J. Roethlisberger, "Barriers and Gateways to Communication," *Harvard Business Review*, Vol. 30, No. 4 (July-August, 1952), pp. 46—52.

means that we should try to understand the other person's frame of reference or point of view. Once this is achieved, we have overcome a major barrier to communication, and mutual understanding is possible. Nonevaluative listening fosters understanding by encouraging the other person not only to listen more carefully, but also to present more information. When the other person experiences the openness and freedom of a nonthreatening environment, that person may also have a clearer perception of what he or she is saying.

Differences in Interpretation (Semantics).   Words, like gestures, can be interpreted in various ways, thus creating a barrier to communication. Since there is not necessarily a connection between the symbol (the word) and what is being symbolized (the meaning), the communication may be received quite differently than it was intended. For example, to the executive the word "profit" may represent a measure of success and a return deserved by the company. To the employee, "profit" may represent some of the funds that should have gone into higher wages. Thus, in selecting words the communicator should consider the audience and its likely interpretation of the words being used.

Differences in Status.   The position of the individual in the organizational structure will also influence the quality of communication that takes place. Persons of equal status, such as two supervisors, will probably find it easier to share information and feelings than a supervisor and a subordinate. In the latter instance, the differences in rank in the organizational hierarchy can create barriers.

In downward communication every effort must be made by management personnel to reduce the amount of unnecessary **dilution** of information in order that subordinates may have as much information as possible. They should also recognize that subordinates will often give them only partial information and will color events in such a manner as to conceal news that the boss may find unpleasant. This conscious manipulation of the "facts" to color events is called **filtering**. It is motivated primarily by the subordinate's desire to appear competent in the eyes of the boss.

Bias.   In Chapter 6, the problem of bias in relation to employment interviewing was discussed. Bias may be a barrier in other types of face-to-face communication, as well as in written communication. In one study, for example, the same article was read by several persons. For some of the readers, the article was accompanied by a picture of an attractive female designated as its author. For other readers the article was accompanied by a picture of an unattractive female. The article written by the attractive female author was evaluated by both male and female readers as being higher in quality than that written by the unattractive author.[11] If this influence on the evaluation of the quality of the article is present in written material, one might safely infer that this type of bias is present in all types of communication situations.

---

11. Beverly Sherman, "Evaluation of Articles Based on the Physical Attractiveness and Biographical Descriptions of Female Authors" (Master's thesis, California State University, Sacramento, CA, 1978), pp. 35—36.

The Psychological Climate. One organization may encourage individuals to express themselves and to participate in important activities. Another organization may be autocratic and discourage participation and freedom of expression. Members of top and middle management can have a considerable influence on communication. Their perceptions of their own roles and their attitudes and sensitivity toward subordinates are important factors in their own ability to communicate.

Steps Toward More Effective Communication

Communication even between friends often can be difficult and at times almost impossible. It may be expected, therefore, that where hierarchical relationships exist, as in an organization, the communication process will require even more attention and effort if it is to yield the level of understanding necessary for efficient operations. In spite of the complexity of the process, there are some fundamentals which, if heeded, can make communications more effective.

Sincerity. In planning communications with subordinates, managers should recognize that their sincerity or insincerity soon will become apparent. If management has a record of fair and honest dealings with employees, its communication is more likely to be accepted.

Feedback and Listening. In any communication there must be feedback from the receiver to the sender. Furthermore, the recipient must be made to feel free to respond fully. Unfortunately feedback procedures too often are established but are not utilized because managers may send out nonverbal signals of indifference or tend to listen very ineffectively to what their subordinates are trying to communicate to them. Listening has often been referred to as probably the most important, and yet the most neglected, dimension of communication. In Figure 12–3 some tips to improve listening are presented.

Understanding Needs. There is a close relationship between motivation and communication that must always be considered. It is human nature to listen to someone who has something to say about those things in which we are interested. Therefore, management's attention to employees' needs, interests, and attitudes can go a long way toward facilitating employee receptivity.

Proper Timing. The importance of the proper timing of a communication should not be overlooked. An announcement made at one time may be received enthusiastically by the employees. The same announcement made at another time may create havoc. For example, the premature announcement of the merger of two companies, both of which are considerably overstaffed, is likely to create many problems. On the other hand, if the announcement is made after new contracts have been received or after arrangements have been worked out for placing excess personnel in other related jobs, it may be received and accepted more readily.

Announcing a bonus plan, an extended stock option plan, and a new incentive plan for top executives on the same day that a labor contract calling for deep cuts in

Figure 12–3 Tips for Better Listening

1. Listen actively. Sit up and look directly at the speaker.
2. Concentrate on what the speaker is saying. Resist distractions.
3. Listen objectively. Do not tune out the speaker whose ideas and biases differ from your own.
4. Listen not only for what is expressed verbally. Pay attention to what is being expressed nonverbally.
5. Listen with empathy and understanding.
6. Forget personal characteristics of the speaker that may cause you to reject what is being said.
7. Listen for the main ideas and supporting facts.
8. Ask questions at the appropriate time if something is not clear.
9. Restate the content and feelings of the speaker to show understanding and acceptance.
10. Make notes when it is appropriate and will not interfere with the communication process.

wages and fringe benefits was signed had unfortunate consequences for one automobile manufacturer. While executive incentives and reductions in total labor costs were considered to be essential, the corporation chairman admitted, "It was the timing that was wrong."[12]

Appropriate Channels and Media. For maximum effectiveness in communication, the channels and media to be used should be appropriate. A wide variety of written media and oral/visual media are available. Generally it is desirable to use several media.

While written media are still used, closed-circuit television and video cassettes are now used widely for in-house communications. Xerox, Equitable Life Assurance Society of the U.S., Standard Oil Company of California, and Bank of America are among the pioneers in this type of communication.

There has been an increased use of company advertising designed to communicate with employees as well as potential customers. Advertisements promising that their employees will "be friendly" or "try harder" indicate to employees how they are expected to perform.[13] Greater attention is also being given to employees in the annual reports. Through an award program sponsored by the American Society for Personnel Administration, companies are encouraged to emphasize in their annual reports the contribution of employees and corporate advances in human resources management.[14]

12. Amanda Bennett, "GM's Bonus Flap: 'The Timing Was Wrong,' " *The Wall Street Journal*, April 30, 1982, p. 26.

13. Franklin Acito and Jeffrey D. Ford, "How Advertising Affects Employees," *Business Horizons*, Vol. 23, No. 1 (February, 1980), pp. 53–59.

14. Scott Dever, "Annual Reports and the Human Approach," *Personnel Administrator*, Vol. 25, No. 7 (July, 1980), pp. 63–67.

Transactional Analysis

An approach that has been used to improve the quality of organizational communication is **transactional analysis,** commonly referred to as "TA." This technique was developed originally by Eric Berne as a simplified approach to psychotherapy.[15] According to Berne, three primary "ego states"—Parent, Adult, and Child—exist in all of us. In each social situation or *transaction,* one of the ego states predominates. The one that is predominant depends upon many factors including early life experiences, the circumstances under which the transaction takes place, and the other person's ego state. To know which ego state is predominant in a given transaction, one needs to analyze posture and facial expressions (body language), as well as verbal expressions and vocal tone. The behavioral characteristics for the three ego states are given in Figure 12–4. A study of them will reveal that the labels—Parent, Adult, and Child—reflect the type of behavior one thinks of as being characteristic of parents, adults, and children. TA's fundamental strength "is that it is essentially a language that translates past psychological ideas into easily understood concepts that even lay people can handle."[16]

Uses of TA.   There are many specific applications of TA to various activities within organizations—e.g., supervising personnel, developing better relations with customers,

Figure 12–4 **Ego/State Contributions to Behavior**

WHAT THE PARENT DOES	WHAT THE ADULT DOES	WHAT THE CHILD DOES
Nurtures	Processes information	Invents
Criticizes	Takes objective action	Expresses curiosity
Restricts	Thinks, then acts	Acts on impulse
Judges	Organizes	Acts selfishly
Blames	Plans	Loves
Encourages	Solves problems	Imagines/brainstorms
Supports	Estimates risks	Acts belligerently
	Ferrets out assumptions	Complains
Source—the relationship between you and your parents.	*Source*—the emergence of independent thinking in early life and its subsequent development.	*Source*—the best and worst of your young self.

SOURCE: Charles Albana, "Transactional Analysis on the Job," *Supervisory Management,* Vol. 19, No. 1 (January, 1974), pp. 2–12. Reproduced with permission.

15. Eric Berne, *Transactional Analysis in Psychotherapy* (New York: Grove Press, 1961).
16. Dr. Donald Bower as quoted in "Business Tries Out 'Transactional Analysis'," *Business Week* (January 12, 1974), pp. 74–75.

counseling employees—but in all of them the major contribution of TA is the improvement of interpersonal communication and feelings. In TA workshops managers, supervisors, and employees learn how to understand themselves and others through a study of TA principles and practices in analyzing various interpersonal transactions.

At the beginning the participants are asked to identify reactions to common situations by indicating whether they are Parent, Adult, or Child reactions such as the following:

> *A clerk loses an important letter.*[17]   (circle one)
>   1. "Why can't you keep track of anything you're
>   responsible for?"   P A C
>   2. "Check each person who may have used it in the
>   last two days and try to trace it. Perhaps
>   Mrs. Smith can help you."   P A C
>   3. "I can't solve your problems. I didn't take your
>   old letter."   P A C

With an understanding of P-A-C reactions, participants then go to analyze such basic transactions as:

1. Complementary transactions, in which people are on the same wavelength and there is good communication.
2. Crossed transactions, in which individuals attempting to communicate with each other are shut off by what one or both say.
3. Ulterior transactions, in which individuals say one thing but mean another.

Broader Implications of TA.   Although TA originally started as a treatment approach and is now widely used by professional therapists for that purpose, it is equally popular for use in developing individuals for more effective functioning in organizations. As Harris, author of *I'm O.K., You're O.K.*, has stated: "It is a teaching and learning device rather than a confessional or an archaeological exploration of the psychic cellars."[18] TA is also valuable in laying bare the psyche of corporations, as well as of individual executives, by revealing the patterns or "scripts" by which organizations are managed. Jongeward states that corporations that play the parent role "may be locked into this autocratic pattern, spending their energies maintaining the old script rather than keeping up with the times." The script can be altered by

17. The answers are as follows: (1) P, (2) A, (3) C. This example is from Dorothy Jongeward and Muriel James, *Winning with People—Group Exercises in Transactional Analysis* (Reading, MA: Addison-Wesley Publishing Company, 1973), p. 38. For a detailed discussion of TA as applied to organizations, see Dorothy Jongeward, *Everybody Wins: Transactional Analysis Applied to Organizations* (Reading, MA: Addison-Wesley Publishing Company, 1973). *See also* Charles Albana, "Transactional Analysis on the Job," *Supervisory Management*, Vol. 19, No. 1 (January, 1974), pp. 2–12; No. 2 (February, 1974), pp. 12–27; No. 3 (March, 1974) pp. 14–20; and No. 4 (April, 1974), pp. 22–36.

18. Thomas A. Harris, *I'm O.K.—You're O.K: A Practical Guide to Transactional Analysis* (New York: Harper & Row, 1969), p. xvii.

making people think about their relationships with others and giving them some kind of framework to evaluate and improve them.[19]

TYPES OF FORMAL COMMUNICATION

Unlike informal communication, formal communication is under the control of management. Formal communication takes place among personnel through lines of authority that are established by management. Job instructions, procedures and practices, evaluations of employee performance, and indoctrination in organizational goals are transmitted through specified channels in *downward* communication from higher management to subordinate personnel.[20] Management also establishes the formal channels for *upward* communication through which subordinates can express their ideas, attitudes, and feelings about themselves, their jobs, organizational policies and practices, and similar matters of concern to them.

It is also important that management seek to create the appropriate social environment that will be conducive to *lateral* communication among personnel within approximately the same level in the organization. Lateral communication among personnel is essential in the performance of their job responsibilities.

Written Communication from Managers

Managers at all levels spend a good portion of their time in reading and preparing written communications. Staff managers, including the human resources manager, are responsible for all types of written communications. Written communications include job descriptions, policy and procedure manuals, bulletins, employee handbooks, letters to employees' homes, paycheck stuffers, and organization newspapers and magazines.

In preparing written communications special attention should be given to clarity. Both the spoken and the written word may be misunderstood if the communicator uses words of many syllables or uses long, complex sentences. "Gobbledygook," as it is called, should be eliminated through training and experience in plain talking and writing.

The publications editor of the Industrial Division of the Caterpillar Tractor Company offers these easy rules to better writing:

1. Keep words simple—avoid "ten dollar" words.
2. Don't sacrifice communication for rules of composition.
3. Write concisely. Express your thoughts, opinions, and ideas in the fewest number of words consistent with completeness and smoothness.
4. Be specific.[21]

Many organizations have improved their communication by enrolling their managers and others whose jobs require them to write reports, letters, etc., in writing

19. "Business Tries out 'Transactional Analysis'," *loc. cit.*
20. Daniel Katz and Robert L. Kahn, *The Social Psychology of Organizations* (2d ed.; New York: John Wiley & Sons, Inc., 1978), pp. 440–443.
21. Robert F. DeGise, "Writing: Don't Let the Mechanics Obscure the Message," *Supervisory Management*, Vol. 21, No. 4 (April, 1976), pp. 24–28.

courses.[22] Many such courses are based on the early work of Rudolf Flesch, who has developed methods for improving the readability of written material.[23]

Written Communication from Employees

Most of the communication from employees to management will take place through face-to-face communication. It is important, however, that procedures be established whereby an employee is able to communicate to higher management on matters of personal concern. In addition to correspondence and grievance procedures, other methods are usually available to employees.

Suggestion Programs. The **suggestion program** is a type of upward communication that is widely used to stimulate participation by rewarding employees for suggestions. The suggestions may cover such areas as work methods and procedures, equipment design, safety devices, and other matters related to the effectiveness of the organization. In order for the program to be successful, the support of managers and supervisors is essential.

Attitude Surveys. The **employee attitude survey** is another communication method designed for employees to communicate with management. The survey is accomplished through the use of questionnaires. When completed anonymously, the questionnaires provide information that can be used to help the organization become more successful in satisfying employee wants. Survey techniques and suggestions for utilizing their findings are discussed in Chapter 21.

Oral Communication

Modern organizations make extensive use of oral communication because it is quick, easy, and provides immediate feedback. Where it is necessary to have a record of the communication, a tape recorder may be used.

Face-to-Face Communication. The face-to-face communication that occurs between superiors and subordinates is probably the most important because of its effect on the subordinate's attitudes and behavior. This type of communication can be used to:

1. Advise subordinates what is to be done.
2. Increase goal aspirations and hence motivation.
3. Communicate the consequences of their performance to employees.
4. Provide for employee feedback to management.[24]

22. William E. Blundell, "Confused, Overstuffed Corporate Writing Often Costs Firms Much Time—and Money," *The Wall Street Journal*, August 28, 1980, p. 19.

23. *The Art of Plain Talk* (1946), *The Art of Readable Writing* (1949), *How To Test Readability* (1951), and *How to Make Sense* (1954)—all published by Harper & Brothers, New York. A more recent book is his *Say What You Mean* (New York: Harper and Row, 1972).

24. L. L. Cummings and Donald P. Schwab, *Performance in Organizations—Determinants and Appraisal* (Glenview, IL: Scott, Foresman and Company, 1973), pp. 51—52.

It can also be used to advise subordinates on matters that are of interest and concern to them and to counsel them on problem situations.

Your career success will depend in part on the type of communication that you have with the manager to whom you are assigned. Figure 12–5 shows the guidelines in Hewlett-Packard's communication workshop which provide valuable suggestions that you can follow when communicating with your manager.

Telephone Communication. Most of us take the telephone for granted and rarely think about its efficiency as a medium for communication. We also do not

Figure 12–5 Guidelines for Communicating with Your Manager

WHAT TO COMMUNICATE TO YOUR MANAGER

Your plans and your progress.
Your ideas and suggestions (as well as your achievements and success).
Problems that you might not be able to solve yourself.
Problems, complaints, or requests for your people.

WHEN TO COMMUNICATE WITH YOUR MANAGER

When your manager may properly be held accountable by others.
When disagreement or controversy may arise.
When your manager's advice or coordination is required.
When recommendations for change, or variances from established policy, are involved.
When good sense tells you information must be shared by your manager and the group to be effective in their jobs.

HOW TO COMMUNICATE WITH YOUR MANAGER

Be open and honest with your manager. You're asking for problems if your manager learns to distrust your communication.
Communicate honestly and directly what you feel you need to get a job done. Telling only what you think your manager wants to hear can hurt the organization.
When you are given an assignment that will cause difficulty with your people, explain what you think may happen. Maybe you and the manager can work out a better plan together.
Take your irritations and work complaints to your manager so you can work them out. You can't be a considerate, pleasant manager if you are upset and angry. Remember, your manager doesn't want you to be unhappy any more than you want your people to be unhappy.

SOURCE: Management Development Program—Communication Workshop, Hewlett-Packard Co., 1977. Reproduced with permission.

stop to analyze telephone behavior except perhaps for clarity and courtesy. Studies have shown that sometimes we operate more effectively on the telephone than we do face to face. Apparently there are fewer distracting and misleading signals to sort out. An analysis of telephone conversations suggests that people disagree more over the phone than in face-to-face talks. Other studies have shown that people can solve complex problems and process information just as efficiently on the telephone as in person. Also, interviewers may find it easier to detect deception on the phone than in person.[25]

Video Communication.   Some companies are now using equipment that includes the advantages of the telephone and face-to-face communication. Picturephone® Meeting Service (PMS) available from AT&T enables a group in one city to communicate face to face with a group in another city, as shown in Figure 12–6. This medium facilitates the timely exchange of information and avoids the

Figure 12–6 A Picturephone® Meeting

SOURCE: AT&T. Reproduced with permission.

25. Howard Muson, "Getting the Phone's Number," *Psychology Today,* Vol. 16. No. 4 (April, 1982), pp. 42–49.

inconvenience and expense associated with travel. The use of films, video casettes, and closed-circuit television has already been discussed in Chapter 8 in connection with training. These video devices are being used increasingly for in-house communication.

Committees and Conferences. Communication may be facilitated through the use of committees and conferences. In conducting a committee, as well as other types of meetings, the individual who has the chairperson's role should use a leadership style that fits the purpose of the meeting or a given portion of the meeting. Figure 12–7 illustrates various styles of communication that are possible between a leader and the members of the group. Decision-making groups (3 and 4 in the illustration) are examined in detail in the next chapter.

Personnel managers typically utilize committees and conferences in an effort to

Figure 12–7 **Different Meetings Require Different Leadership Styles**

Your leadership style should fit the purpose of the meeting

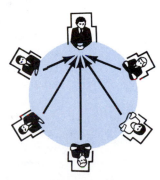

1. Information giving

2. Information collecting

3. Decision making

4. Decision making

5. Problem solving

SOURCE: Reprinted with special permission of *Factory* (April, 1960). Copyright Morgan-Grampian, Inc., 1960.

involve as many individuals as possible in resolving important issues. For several decades Pitney-Bowes has had a personnel council—a monthly forum where representatives of management and employees sit down to discuss mutual problems and opportunities. This is done on the sectional, departmental, and divisional levels with the main council serving as the top tribunal.[26]

Brainstorming. A special type of committee interaction used to obtain new ideas is **brainstorming.** It was first suggested by a marketing executive.[27] Participants are instructed to "let themselves go" and state their ideas. No attempt is made to evaluate the ideas until the participants have exhausted all possibilities. As a result, the participants are not quite as inhibited as they would ordinarily be in a meeting. However, there is considerable evidence that individual brainstorming is more effective. This can be done easily by having individuals dictate ideas onto an audiotape in private and under time limitations.[28]

RÉSUMÉ

By studying the social groupings of employees within an organization, we can help to create conditions that will elicit cooperation and thus maximize the attainment of organizational and personal goals. We have observed that both formal and informal employee groups influence the attitudes and behavior of their members. An understanding of the characteristics of groups—such as role, status, cohesiveness, and conformity *v.* innovation—enhances our ability to interact effectively with and plan for individual employees as well as groups.

The study of groups reveals the importance of communication in binding together the members and activities of an organization. Overcoming barriers is essential for effective communication. Also, management should give special attention to sincerity, understanding needs, feedback, proper timing, and using appropriate channels and media for effective communication. While originally a simplified approach to psychotherapy, transactional analysis has been used quite extensively among organizations to improve interpersonal communication and feelings. Many different types of formal written and oral communication are available to both managers and employees.

TERMS TO IDENTIFY

informal organization	status inconsistency
grapevine	status anxiety
schmoozing	cohesiveness
role perception	attitude conformity
role conflict	ideation
status symbols	encoding

26. Fred T. Allen, "Ways to Improve Employee Communications," *Nation's Business*, Vol. 63, No. 9 (September, 1975), pp. 54–56.

27. A. F. Osborn, *Applied Imagination* (New York: Scribner's, 1953).

28. Barbara K. Maginn and Richard J. Harris, "Effects of Anticipated Evaluation in Individual Brainstorming Performance," *Journal of Applied Psychology*, Vol. 65, No. 2 (April, 1980), pp. 219–225.

transmission
receiving
decoding
action
feedback
nonevaluative listening

dilution
filtering
transactional analysis
suggestion program
employee attitude survey
brainstorming

DISCUSSION QUESTIONS

1. What determines the cohesiveness of a group and what effect does it have on group behavior?
2. Discuss the advantages and disadvantages of "schmoozing" to the organization. What is your position on this subject?
3. Some managers feel that effective leadership is primarily dependent upon the quality of the relationships established between the leader and the individuals in the group and that too much emphasis is given to "group relationships."
   a. What is your opinion?
   b. Can you think of jobs where the supervisor must give close attention to group relationships, as well as to individuals?
4. Why do some individuals who have established themselves as the informal leaders of their groups fail to become effective formal leaders when assigned to supervisory positions?
5. Many people are not good listeners.

   a. How do you account for this fact?
   b. What effect may this deficiency have on an individual's progress in a job and in other areas of life?
   c. How can listening ability be improved?
6. What problems have you experienced in your attempts to communicate with individuals who are younger or older than you? Have you been able to make any improvements in such communication? What approaches have you used?
7. Role perception in organizational relationships was emphasized in this chapter.
   a. What is role perception?
   b. Why should managers and supervisors give special attention to it in their relationships with subordinates and other activities?
8. How is the internal communication of a company related to its communication with customers and the community?

PROBLEM 12-1

FACTS AND INFERENCES*

Read the following story and take for granted that everything it says is true. Read carefully because, in spots, the story is deliberately vague. Don't try to memorize it since you can look back at it at any stage.

Then read the numbered statements about the story and decide whether you consider each one true, false, or questionable. Circling the "T" means that you feel sure the statement is definitely true. Circling the "F" means you are sure it is definitely false. Circling the "?" means you cannot tell whether it is true or false. If you feel doubtful about any part of a statement, circle the question mark.

Take the statements in turn, and do not go back later to change any of your answers. Do not reread any of the statements after you have answered them. Such altering or rereading will distort the test.

*From the "Uncritical Inference Test" by William V. Haney. Copyright 1961. Reproduced with permission of William V. Haney.

The Story

John Phillips, the research director of a midwestern food products firm, ordered a crash program of development on a new process. He gave three of his executives authority to spend up to $50,000 each without consulting him. He sent one of his best men, Harris, to the firm's West Coast plant with orders to work on the new process independently. Within one week Harris produced a highly promising approach to the problem.

Statements About the Story

1. Phillips sent one of his best men to the West Coast plant . . . . .T   F   ?
2. Phillips overestimated Harris's competence . . . . .T   F   ?
3. Harris failed to produce anything new . . . . .T   F   ?
4. Harris lacked authority to spend money without consulting Phillips . . . . .T   F   ?
5. Only three of Phillips' executives had authority to spend money without consulting him . . . . .T   F   ?
6. The research director sent one of his best men to the firm's West Coast plant . . . . .T   F   ?
7. Three men were given authority to spend up to $50,000 each without consulting Phillips . . . . .T   F   ?
8. Phillips had a high opinion of Harris. . . . . .T   F   ?
9. Only four people are referred to in the story . . . . .T   F   ?
10. Phillips was research director of a food products firm . . . . .T   F   ?
11. While Phillips gave authority to three of his best men to spend up to $50,000 each, the story does not make clear whether Harris was one of these men. . . . . .T   F   ?

a. Why is it important to distinguish between facts and inferences?

b. In what ways can managers use their knowledge about facts and inferences in communications with subordinates?

SUGGESTED READINGS

Chruden, Herbert J., and Arthur W. Sherman, Jr. *Readings in Managing Human Resources,* 6th ed. Cincinnati: South-Western Publishing Co., 1984. Part 4.

Hackman, J. Richard, Edward E. Lawler, III, and Lyman W. Porter (eds.). *Perspectives on Behavior in Organizations,* 2d ed. New York: McGraw-Hill Book Company, 1983.

Hayakawa, S. I. *Language in Thought and Action,* 2d ed. New York: Harcourt Brace, and World, 1964.

Mohr, Lawrence. *Explaining Organizational Behavior.* San Francisco: Jossey-Bass, Inc., 1982.

Naylor, James C., Robert D. Pritchard, and Daniel R. Ilgen. *A Theory of Behavior in Organizations.* New York: Academic Press, Inc., 1980.

Wallace, Mark J., Jr., and Andrew D. Szilagyi, Jr. *Managing Behavior in Organizations.* Glenview, IL: Scott, Foresman and Co., 1982.

- To describe the attitudes and abilities that are important in managing employees.
- To understand the differences among the three major approaches to the study of leadership
- To know the major findings of leadership studies in work organizations.
- To explain how supervisors may use a participative approach.
- To list the benefits to be derived from employee participation in decision making.
- To describe the types of assistance that supervisors can provide to subordinates.

Supervising Personnel

13

In the two previous chapters the responsibilities of managers and supervisors in attaining organizational and personal goals have been mentioned. Now it is time to take a closer look at what is involved in the day-to-day process of supervising personnel. Success in performing supervisory functions depends not only upon assigned authority but also upon the manager's skills in working effectively with and through subordinates.

In this chapter the focus will be upon the leadership processes used by managerial personnel to influence their subordinates to achieve organizational and personal goals. Special attention will be given to the role of first-line supervisors who play a major part in the human resources management program.

MANAGERIAL AND SUPERVISORY LEADERSHIP

We observed earlier that the management processes typically include planning, organizing, staffing, directing, and controlling. At all levels within an organization, managerial personnel engage in these processes. Their contribution to the organization is determined by how well they accomplish each one of these functions.

Abilities Required of Managers

The performance of management functions is dependent in large part upon the abilities that managerial personnel possess. Three different types of abilities have been identified: technical, conceptual, and human relations.

Technical Ability.   Knowledge and/or skills used in any type of process or technique are referred to as **technical ability**. The skills learned by computer programmers, word processors, accountants, engineers, and medical technicians are examples of technical abilities.

Conceptual Ability.   Abstract thinking in terms of broad interrelationships among various elements of a situation is called **conceptual ability**. In order to do long-range planning for an organization, this type of ability is required. As managers advance upward from the supervisory level, their jobs require less use of their technical ability and greater use of their conceptual ability.

Human Relations Ability.   The ability to work effectively with others as individuals or as members of a group is known as **human relations ability**. As shown in Figure 13–1, the ability to relate effectively to others is an equally important qualification for managers at all levels. Effective human relations is based upon the nature of the attitudes and beliefs that one has about others.

Attitudes and Behaviors of Managers

The methods that managers and supervisors use to direct and control the activities of their subordinates have received considerable attention. The importance

Figure 13–1 Abilities Required at Different Managerial Levels

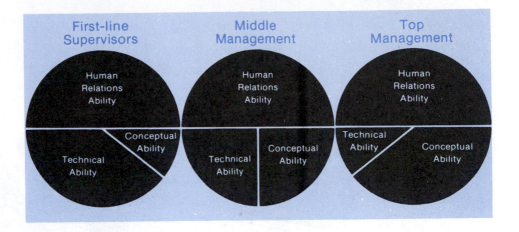

of these methods as determiners of productivity over the long run and the degree of satisfaction that employees receive from the performance of their jobs is well recognized. McGregor was among the first to analyze the attitudes and behavior of managerial personnel and to propose a theory of leadership that has had a major impact upon practitioners.

McGregor's Theory X. McGregor (1960) assumed that the behavior of managers is strongly influenced by their beliefs. According to **McGregor's Theory X**, most managers believe that the average employee has an inherent dislike of work, prefers to be directed, wishes to avoid responsibility, has relatively little ambition, and wants security above all.[1] Managers who hold this view typically use an authoritarian, or autocratic, approach like the boss in Figure 13–2. The employees definitely know who is boss and know that they are expected to do what they are told. The motivation of employees is imparted typically through fear rather than through positive rewards.

McGregor's Theory Y. According to McGregor, the Theory X approach to leadership is invalid. If managers want to improve employee performance and productivity, they should adopt principles that are consistent with a participative approach. These principles, which comprise **McGregor's Theory Y**, are listed in Figure 13–3.

Theory Y, in contrast to Theory X, emphasizes managerial leadership through motivation by objectives and by permitting subordinates to experience personal

---

1. Douglas M. McGregor, *The Human Side of Enterprise* (New York: McGraw-Hill Book Company, 1960), pp. 33–35.

Figure 13–2

"Quit saying, 'You're the boss!' I know I'm the boss!"

SOURCE: Drawing by Dana Fradon; © 1975. *The New Yorker Magazine, Inc.*

satisfaction as they contribute to the achievement of objectives. While McGregor has received some impressive tributes, according to Allen there are no data to support McGregor's view that most managers in business organizations were Theory X types of leaders at the time Theory Y was proposed.[2]

Theory Z. In recent years several writers have proposed Theory Z, a new theory of leadership which concurs with Theory Y assumptions. However, **Theory Z** further contends that the responsibilities sought by employees and over which they are capable of self-control are "culture related." As a result of changing societal needs and goals, yesterday's motivators may not be effective today. Therefore, new strategies in motivating subordinates are required. No longer are productivity and rewards the only goals of employers. Improving the quality of working life also is essential.[3]

2. Louis A. Allen, "M for Management: Theory Y Updated," *Personnel Journal*, Vol. 52, No. 12 (December, 1973), pp. 1061–1067.

3. Robert J. Thierauf, Robert C. Klekamp, and Daniel W. Geeding, *Management Principles and Practices* (New York: John Wiley & Sons, 1977), pp. 108–112.

Figure 13–3 Principles of Theory Y

1. The expenditure of physical and mental effort in work is as natural as play or rest. Depending upon controllable conditions, work may be a source of satisfaction (and will be voluntarily performed) or a source of punishment (and will be avoided if possible).
2. External control and the threat of punishment are not the only means for bringing about effort toward organizational objectives. Individuals will exercise self-direction and self-control in the service of objectives to which they are committed.
3. Commitment to objectives is a function of the rewards associated with their achievement. The most significant of such rewards, e.g., the satisfaction of ego and self-actualization needs, can be direct products of effort directed toward organizational objectives.
4. The average human being learns, under proper conditions, not only to accept but also to seek responsibility.
5. The capacity to exercise a relatively high degree of imagination, ingenuity, and creativity in the solution of organizational problems is widely, not narrowly, distributed in the population.
6. Under the conditions of modern industrial life, the intellectual potentialities of the average human being are only partially utilized.

SOURCE: Douglas M. McGregor, *The Human Side of Enterprise* (New York: McGraw-Hill Book Company, 1960), pp. 33–35. Reproduced with permission.

We observed in Chapter 2 that American firms are becoming increasingly concerned with the quality of working life. Some of this concern has grown out of the observations of the success that Japanese companies have attained. In his book, *Theory Z: How American Business Can Meet the Challenge*, William Ouchi emphasizes the importance of lifetime employment, security, career development, participation by employees in decision making, teamwork, and management concern for the self-esteem of employees.[4]

CONTRIBUTIONS OF LEADERSHIP STUDIES

For many decades leadership has been studied in a wide variety of work and nonwork situations. As with motivation theory, there is no one theory of leadership that is universally accepted. The early theories—from the 1920s to the 1950s—emphasized the role of personal characteristics such as intelligence, alertness, dominance, etc. Hence, they are known as **trait theories**. In the 1950s, behavioral theories of leadership began to emerge. **Behavioral theories** propose that leaders are effective by virtue of what they do such as communicating and giving directions.

4. William Ouchi, *Theory Z: How American Business Can Meet the Challenge* (Reading, MA: Addison-Wesley Publishing Company, 1981).

Since the 1950s, increasing attention has also been given to the situation in which leaders function. According to **situation theories**, the characteristics of subordinates and the situation also must be considered in addition to leadership characteristics and style.

Emphasis upon Traits

In spite of the fact that the study of traits has been overshadowed by the behavior and situational approaches, there is still considerable interest in searching for traits that differentiate leaders from nonleaders.

Early Studies. The early trait approach tended to treat personality variables in an atomistic fashion, suggesting that each trait acted singly to determine leadership effects. From 1904 to 1947, hundreds of studies were conducted in which leaders were compared with nonleaders on such variables as age, height, weight, appearance, fluency of speech, intelligence, scholarship, dominance, emotional control, and social skills. While studies showed that leaders as a group often exceeded nonleaders in many of these traits, there was very little consistency in the findings.[5]

Later Studies. A review by Stogdill of trait studies conducted between 1948 and 1970 shows greater promise for the validity of trait theories. He found that there are some general characteristics that seem to be present in the most effective leaders in most situations. Vigor and persistence in the pursuit of goals, self-confidence, ability to influence others, and ability to tolerate frustration are among those that he found. These characteristics hold little predictive or diagnostic significance when considered singly. In combination, however, they interact to generate a "leadership personality." The conclusion that personality is a factor in leadership does not, however, represent a return to the trait approach.[6]

Emphasis upon Leader Behavior

Dissatisfaction with the trait approach led behavioral scientists to study the behavior of leaders of work groups. Rather than focusing on the traits of successful managers, the emphasis was on behavior that facilitated the effective interaction of work group members.

Employee-Centered and Production-Centered Leadership. In the late 1940s, the Survey Research Center of the University of Michigan embarked upon a program to determine how the behavior of leaders affected work group performance and employee satisfaction. One of the major findings of the studies was that the **production-centered supervisors**, who are concerned primarily with production, are less effective in terms of actual productivity records than the **employee-centered supervisors**, who give their attention to the people who do the work and also have

5. Bernard M. Bass, *Stogdill's Handbook of Leadership—a Survey of Theory and Research* (rev. and expanded ed.; New York: The Free Press, 1981), pp. 65–68.
6. *Ibid.*, pp. 81–82.

high performance goals and enthusiasm for achieving them. The studies revealed that the employees who work for the employee-centered supervisors felt that the supervisors were personally interested in them, found the supervisors available for discussion, and viewed them as nonthreatening individuals.[7]

Structure and Consideration.   At about the same time that the University of Michigan researchers were studying leadership behaviors, a group at Ohio State University was engaged in identifying behavioral characteristics of supervisors. In one of their studies, two major dimensions of supervisory behavior—consideration and structure—were identified. These two characteristics, which were found to be independent of each other, are described as follows:

1. **Consideration** includes behavior indicating mutual trust, respect, and a certain warmth and rapport between the supervisor and the group. This does not mean that this dimension reflects a superficial "pat-on-the-back," "first-name calling" kind of human relations behavior. This dimension appears to emphasize a deeper concern for group members' needs and includes such behavior as allowing subordinates more participation in decision making and encouraging more two-way communication.

2. **Structure** includes behavior in which supervisors organize and define group activities and their relations to the group. Thus, they define the role they expect each member to assume, assign tasks, plan ahead, establish ways of getting things done, and push for production. This dimension seems to emphasize overt attempts to achieve organizational goals.[8]

These dimensions of supervisory behavior, which have been subjected to a vast amount of research, may be measured by inventories developed by Fleishman. The *Leadership Opinion Questionnaire* is designed for administration to supervisors.[9] The *Supervisory Behavior Description* is for administration to subordinates.[10] The results of these inventories are quite useful in stimulating discussion of consideration and structure in managerial and supervisory development programs.

A device known as the *Managerial Grid* has been popular as a basis for training managers and supervisors.[11]   The Grid expresses the relationship between the Concern for People (Consideration) and Concern for Production (Structure). By referring to the Grid and identifying their behavior on the two dimensions or areas of concern, namely for production and for people, managers or supervisors are better able to understand the approach that they use with their subordinates. The Grid itself, however, only provides the conceptual framework. It must be implemented

---

7. Rensis Likert, *New Patterns of Management* (New York: McGraw-Hill Book Company, 1961).

8. Edwin A. Fleishman and Edwin F. Harris, "Patterns of Leadership Behavior Related to Employee Grievances and Turnover," *Personnel Psychology,* Vol. 15, No. 1 (Spring, 1962), pp. 43–46.

9. Published by Science Research Associates, 155 North Wacker Drive, Chicago, IL 60606.

10. Published by Management Research Institute, Suite 900, 4330 East-West Highway, Washington, DC 20014.

11. Robert R. Blake and Jane S. Mouton, *The Versatile Manager* (Homewood IL: Richard D. Irwin, Inc., 1981). Earlier books about the Grid by these authors were published in 1964 and 1978.

through participation in seminars if it is to be effective. In the Grid seminars managerial and supervisory personnel learn to identify needed personal and organizational changes and to become more effective in their interpersonal relationships and in their work groups.

Emphasis upon the Situation

As research on leadership dimensions progressed, it became increasingly apparent that the trait theories and behavioral theories were inadequate. An awareness of the importance of situational variables—such as the nature of the task, the characteristics and expectancies of the subordinates, and the organizational climate—led to the formulation of situational theories. Situational theories recognize that the type of leadership behavior required in one situation will not be appropriate in a different situation.

Fiedler's Contingency Leadership Model.

Fred Fiedler and his associates were among the first to develop a situational theory of leadership. It is known as the **Contingency Model of Leader Effectiveness**. It states that the performance of a group is contingent upon both the motivational system of the leader (task oriented *v.* relationship oriented) and the degree to which the leader has control and influence in a particular situation. The nature of the leadership situation is assessed by examining three factors: leader-member relations, the degree to which the task is structured, and position power.[12]   According to Fiedler, the factor that is most important in determining one's leadership influence is **leader-member relations**, which refers to the degree to which the group members trust and like the leader and are willing to follow the leader's guidance.

Over the years, Fiedler and others have conducted research on a contingency model with industrial, military, and educational leaders. The general findings from analyzing these relationships are:

1. Task-oriented leaders perform best in situations in which the leader has position power, good relations with the work group, and a relatively well-structured task. The group is ready to be directed and expects to be told what to do. In a very unfavorable leadership situation, a task-oriented leader is also more effective than a relationship-oriented leader.
2. Relationship-oriented leaders perform best in situations that are moderately favorable or moderately unfavorable for the leader, such as when an accepted leader faces an ambiguous task, or when the task is structured but the leader is not well accepted.[13]

Fiedler recommends a program of "organizational engineering" in which the nature of the situation is changed to match the style of a particular leader.[14]

12. Fred E. Fiedler and Marvin M. Chemers, *Leadership and Effective Management* (Glenview, IL: Scott, Foresman and Company, 1974), p. 73.

13. *Ibid.*, pp. 78–91.

14. *Ibid.*, pp. 150–152.

Despite significant criticisms, Fiedler's model has proved to be a major addition to the study of leadership in organizations. It emphasizes that a manager's style may be effective in one situation but not in another.

Path-Goal Theory. The path-goal theory of leadership is based on the expectancy theory of motivation described in Chapter 11. In the **path-goal theory** two classes of situational variables are considered to be contingency factors. These are: characteristics of the subordinates, including ability, locus of control, and needs and motives; and characteristics of the work environment, including subordinates' tasks, primary work group, and the formal authority system.

In spite of the fact that the path-goal theory is relatively new, it has stimulated a considerable amount of research interest. Some of the findings from various studies support the following generalizations:

1. When the task or work situation is ambiguous, a directive style of leadership is desirable. When task demands are clear, directiveness is a hindrance.
2. Supportive leadership has its most positive effect on satisfaction for subordinates who work on stressful, frustrating or dissatisfying tasks.
3. In nonrepetitive ego-involving tasks, employees are more satisfied under a participative style of leadership than a nonparticipative style.[15]

In all likelihood the path-goal theory will assume a more prominent position in the study of leadership. However, more research is needed to refine and further validate the theory.

Perspective on Leadership Studies

Three major approaches to the study of leadership—trait, behavioral, and situational—have just been presented above. The fact that three different approaches are still being discussed indicates that there is no universally accepted approach to the study and practice of leadership in work organizations.

Studies relating to trait theories have shown that there are some personal characteristics which distinguish effective leaders from ineffective leaders. Research on managerial behavior leads us to the conclusion that there are two distinct dimensions of leadership. These are variously described as (1) employee-centered, relationship-oriented, or consideration, and (2) production-centered, task-oriented, or structure. These findings coincide with McGregor's theory and are accepted by most researchers.

Finally, we have observed that the personal characteristics and behavior of the leader do not in themselves determine leadership effectiveness. The perceptions of the subordinates, the nature of the tasks, the work group, and the organization must all be considered. Thus, there is considerable support for the situational theories of leadership.

---

15. Robert J. House and Terence R. Mitchell, "Path-Goal Theory of Leadership," *Journal of Contemporary Business*, Vol. 3, No. 4 (Autumn, 1974), pp. 81–98.

In their discussion of leadership theories, Szilagyi and Wallace conclude that:

> Perhaps the most significant issue for practicing managers is the development of the skill and ability to diagnose and evaluate the many factors that impact on the leadership process. It is only through this ability to diagnose and evaluate that a manager can alter his or her behavior for maximum effectiveness.[16]

The fact that managerial behavior can be altered provides the basis for improvement of the quality of supervision.

THE SUPERVISOR'S ROLE IN THE ORGANIZATION

While all of the managerial personnel in an organization perform leadership functions, we are especially interested in the role of first-line supervisors. It is estimated that there are over one million first-line supervisors in the United States alone.[17] Their responsibility for direct supervision of the largest portion of an organization's human resources places them in a critical position. The success of a human resources management program is dependent in large part upon their effectiveness as leaders. It is also dependent upon the degree of rapport that exists between first-line supervisors and the personnel department.

The first-line supervisor, who is the lowest ranking member of the management hierarchy, has direct responsibility for supervising nonmanagerial employees. Since the passage of the Taft-Hartley Act in 1947, the supervisor has been legally considered to be a member of management. A supervisor is defined as:

> . . . any individual having authority, in the interest of the employer, to hire, transfer, suspend, lay off, recall, promote, discharge, assign, reward or discipline other employees, or the responsibility to direct them, or to adjust their grievances, or effectively to recommend such action, if in connection with the foregoing the exercise of such authority is not of a merely routine or clerical nature, but requires the use of independent judgment.[18]

Another law which specifies that supervisors are a part of management is the Fair Labor Standards Act of 1938.[19] This law states that supervisors can spend no more than 20 percent of their time doing the same kind of work as their subordinates. It also stipulates that supervisors be paid a salary regardless of how many hours they work. They are exempt from the overtime provisions of the act and thus are referred to as **exempt employees**. Most employers, however, compensate them for overtime work. Although supervisors are considered under law to be a part of management, they must identify themselves closely enough with their subordinates to be successful in their leadership role.

---

16. Andrew D. Szilagyi, Jr. and Marc J. Wallace, Jr., *Organizational Behavior and Performance* (2d ed.; Santa Monica, CA: Goodyear Publishing Company, Inc., 1980), p. 309.

17. Lester R. Bittel, *What Every Supervisor Should Know* (4th ed.; New York: Gregg Division, McGraw-Hill Book Company, 1980), p. 2.

18. National Labor-Management Relations Act (Taft-Hartley), 1947, as amended. Section 101, Subsection 2 (11).

19. U. S. Code 1976, Title 29, par. 201, et seq., June 25, 1938, c. 676, 52 STAT 1060.

Serves as a "Linking Pin"

The supervisor has been described as a **linking pin** who belongs to two groups within the organization, as illustrated in Figure 13–4. The supervisor is the superior in one group and a subordinate in the other. As shown by the arrows, the supervisor is a link between these two groups.

In order to function effectively, however, a supervisor must have sufficient influence with his or her superior. About 40 years ago, F. J. Roethlisberger wrote a classic article, "The Foreman: Master and Victim of Double-Talk."[20] In this article he emphasized the dilemma of supervisors and documented the conflicting expectations that management had of them. The condition not only still exists but has become worse. The supervisors of today are being held responsible for functions over which they no longer have any real authority because of staff control. Each staff group—quality control, personnel, engineering, etc.—wants to assert itself to establish a power base and to protect its own area of expertise. In unionized plants, unions have deprived supervisors of much of their remaining authority.[21]

Many organizations have unnecessary layers of middle management, with the result that the supervisor's responsibilities and accountabilities are not clearly defined. Unless higher management and staff departments, such as personnel, help to

Figure 13–4   The Linking Pin

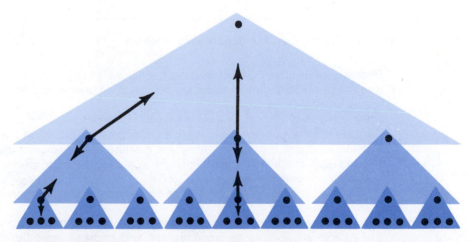

SOURCE: Rensis Likert, *New Patterns in Management* (New York: McGraw-Hill Book Company, 1961), p. 113. Reproduced with permission.

20. F.J. Roethlisberger, "The Foreman: Master and Victim of Double-Talk," *Harvard Business Review*, Vol. 23, No. 2 (Spring, 1945), pp. 283-298. This article has been designated as one of the HBR Classics.

21. W. Earl Sasser, Jr. and Frank S. Leonard, "Let First-Level Supervisors Do Their Job," *Harvard Business Review*, Vol. 58, No. 2 (March-April, 1980), pp. 113-121.

strengthen the influence the supervisors have, the ability of supervisors to carry out their functions that are critical to the success of the organization will suffer. In Figure 13–5 some steps that managers above first-level supervisors can take to strengthen the position of supervisors are presented.

Motivates and Controls Employee Performance

Probably the most important functions performed by the supervisor are those of motivating and controlling employee performance. It is the supervisor's responsibility not only to structure the work but to provide incentives that will motivate employees to achieve the objectives established for their jobs and for the department. The supervisor must then determine the extent to which the goals are being achieved, whether or not prescribed quality standards are being maintained, and whether or not employees are conforming to organizational policies, procedures, and regulations.

Good Human Relations.
Today's supervisor is expected to build good human relations with employees, both as individuals and as members of a work group, while at the same time meeting production goals. Building effective human relations is frequently one of the more difficult aspects of supervision since effective human relationships depend upon attitudes, as well as skills.

A critical factor in supervisor-subordinate relationships is employee perception of the supervisor's honesty and impartiality.[22] While it is desirable for supervisors to develop their human relations skills, these are no substitute for sincerity. According

Figure 13–5 How to Strengthen the Supervisor's Position

Become aware of the actual working conditions of supervisors.
Keep supervisors informed about the corporate perspective as it relates to their operation.
Keep them aware of upper-level managers' priorities.
Educate them about new technological developments that might affect their job.
Provide feedback on how well they are meeting management's expectations.
Provide supervisors an opportunity on company time to work together on specific problems affecting their job.
Assist them in keeping the work force up to date on any information that may affect their jobs.
Provide training to enable them to improve their skills in dealing with people.
Encourage supervisors to stand up for and express their beliefs to upper management.

SOURCE: Adapted from W. Earl Sasser, Jr. and Frank S. Leonard, "Let First-Level Supervisors Do Their Job," *Harvard Business Review,* Vol. 58, No. 2 (March-April, 1980), pp. 113–121. Reproduced with permission.

22. D. K. Lindo, "How Do You Rate as a Supervisor?" *Supervision,* Vol. 43, No. 8 (August, 1981), pp. 9–11.

to Sartain and Baker, the most fundamental factor in effective supervision is *trust and confidence* on the part of both parties—supervisor and subordinate—in each other.[23]

Effective human relations also depends upon a concern for ethical values. Supervisors should be encouraged through examples by top management to give careful attention to these ethical values in the performance of their duties. One way to emphasize the importance of ethical values is to have a formal code of ethics like the one shown in Figure 13–6.

Employee Productivity. The supervisor has a responsibility to see that subordinates contribute their full potential. When the duties, responsibilities, and formal relationships are properly planned, organized, and controlled, employees are better able to direct their energies into productive and satisfying activities. Thus, frustrations are minimized.

It is also desirable to plan for employees to have as much opportunity as possible for self-direction. In order to encourage individual initiative, the supervisor must have a clear understanding of the subordinates' abilities and self-understanding. As illustrated in Figure 13-7, ambivalence about how much authority can be delegated can readily create conflicts for subordinates.

The supervisor's responsibility for maintaining high levels of efficiency requires that corrective action be taken as needed. Subordinates who do not possess the abilities for the job, who are insufficiently motivated, or who engage in behavior that impairs their performance or that of fellow employees require special attention. Some of the types of problems that supervisors encounter will be discussed later in this chapter.

Figure 13–6 A Code of Ethics for Supervisors

1. Set a high standard by your own example.
2. Emphasize the future rather than the past.
3. Look for and treat causes rather than symptoms.
4. Admit your mistakes and learn from them.
5. Accept responsibility; don't pass the buck.
6. Consider long-run as well as short-run results.
7. Seek solutions which benefit everyone involved.
8. Use legal and ethical means to achieve legal and ethical ends.
9. Respect the dignity of every individual.
10. Try to understand others and make yourself understood by them.

SOURCE: Industrial Relations Center, California Institute of Technology, revised 1978. Reproduced with permission.

23. Aaron Q. Sartain and Alton W. Baker, *The Supervisor and the Job* (3d ed.; New York: McGraw-Hill Book Company, 1978), p. 123.

Figure 13–7.

"I want you to think and act on your own initiative—but check with me first."

SOURCE: Reprinted by permission of *Supervision* magazine, © 1977 by The National Research Bureau Inc., 424 North Third St., Burlington, IA 52601.

Develops Employee Participation

For the past several decades much has been written about the desirability of involving employees in decisions relating to their work. Supervisors who are employee-centered recognize the importance of allowing subordinates more participation in decision making and encourage more two-way communication. While an autocratic approach is not necessarily bad, employees have come to expect to share in the making of decisions. In Western Europe, decision making by employees goes even further with the concept of codetermination or joint management. More and more European workers are dividing their time between taking orders on the shop floor and participating in corporate policy.[24]

24. "Co-determination: When Workers Help Manage," *Business Week*, No. 2389 (July 14, 1975), pp. 133–134.

Degree of Employee Participation.

Participation in decision making is typically conducted on a work group basis. Supervisors should be selective as to which decisions they submit to the group and the type of participation they desire from the group.

The changing of work methods, the scheduling of coffee breaks and vacations, and the handling of excessive use of sick leave are a few of the problems that supervisors have successfully passed on to the work group. As supervisors and groups obtain experience in such participative efforts, supervisors are usually willing to let the subordinates participate in decisions about more important matters.[25] Only those problems or decisions that fall within a supervisor's jurisdiction may be submitted to the group for participation. The type or degree of participation may vary from one topic to another.

Figure 13–8 shows a continuum of power, described by Tannenbaum and Schmidt, which is to be shared in varying degrees by managers and nonmanagers.[26] The points on the continuum designate the types of manager and nonmanager behavior that become possible when a particular amount of freedom (shown by the space below the diagonal broken line) is available to subordinates.[27] The arrows indicate the continual flow of interdependent influence between systems and people.

Each situation or problem calling for a decision requires a different approach. The choice should be made on the basis of an evaluation of forces within the supervisor, within the subordinates, and in the situation. These forces which are to be considered are shown in Figure 13–9. According to Tannenbaum and Schmidt, the most effective managers are those who recognize the major forces that are involved in the leadership of a group and who are flexible in the approach that they use in carrying out their leadership responsibilities.

Benefits of Participation.

Research conducted with various groups has revealed that maximum participation (represented by the right side of the continuum) has several values. One of its major values lies in the acceptance of decisions by the members of the group. People are more likely to accept the decisions that they feel responsible for, as a result of having participated in making them. Furthermore, experience has shown that the quality of decisions made by groups has generally been high. For example, groups that participate in setting goals often place higher demands upon themselves than the supervisors and methods engineers would have made upon them.[28]

Using a science-based management development system, Likert and his

---

25. Norman R. F. Maier and Gertrude Casselman Verser, *Psychology in Industrial Organizations* (5th ed.; Boston: Houghton Mifflin Company, 1982), pp. 162–188.

26. Robert Tannenbaum and Warren H. Schmidt, "How to Choose a Leadership Pattern," *Harvard Business Review*, Vol. 36, No. 2 (March-April, 1958), pp. 95–101.

27. Figure 13–8 represents an updated version of the continuum of leadership behavior that appeared in the article cited in footnote 26. According to the authors, "The new continuum is both more complex and more dynamic than the 1958 version, reflecting the organizational and societal realities of the 1970s." The 1973 version appears in *Harvard Business Review*, Vol. 51, No. 3 (May-June, 1973), pp. 162–170. This article has been designated as one of the HBR Classics.

28. Maier and Verser, *op. cit.*, pp. 168–174.

Figure 13–8 Continuum of Manager-Nonmanager Behavior

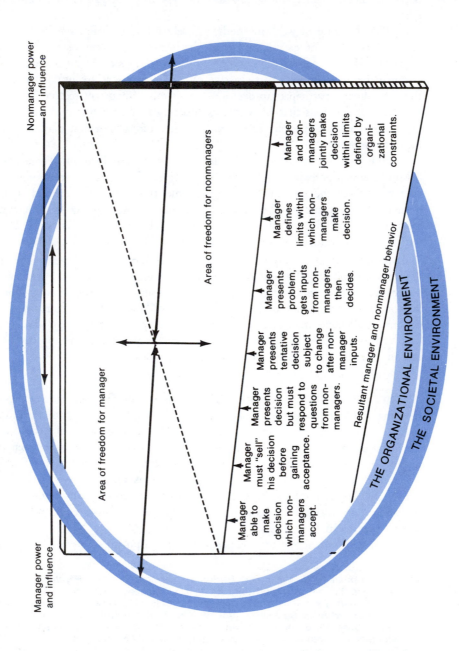

Manager power and influence

Nonmanager power and influence

Area of freedom for manager

Area of freedom for nonmanagers

Manager able to make decision which nonmanagers accept.

Manager must "sell" his decision before gaining acceptance.

Manager presents decision but must respond to questions from nonmanagers.

Manager presents tentative decision subject to change after nonmanager inputs.

Manager presents problem, gets inputs from nonmanagers, then decides.

Manager defines limits within which nonmanagers make decision.

Manager and nonmanagers jointly make decision within limits defined by organizational constraints.

Resultant manager and nonmanager behavior

THE ORGANIZATIONAL ENVIRONMENT

THE SOCIETAL ENVIRONMENT

SOURCE: Reprinted by permission of the *Harvard Business Review*. An exhibit from "How to Choose a Leadership Pattern" by Robert Tannenbaum and Warren H. Schmidt (May/June 1973). Copyright © 1973 by the President and Fellows of Harvard College; all rights reserved.

Figure 13–9 **Forces in Decision Making**

FORCES WITHIN THE SUPERVISOR	FORCES WITHIN THE SUBORDINATES	FORCES IN THE SITUATION
Value system Leadership inclinations Feelings of security in an unknown situation	Interest in the problem Understanding and identification with the goals of the organization Effectiveness as a group Knowledge and readiness to share in decision making Degree of tolerance for ambiguity Expectancy to share in decision making	Type of organization Organizational environment Size and location of working units The problem itself Pressure of time

SOURCE: Robert Tannenbaum and Warren H. Schmidt, "How to Choose a Leadership Pattern," *Harvard Business Review* (May/June 1973). Adapted with permission.

associates found that **System 4**, a supportive and participative approach, generally produces better results in terms of productivity, costs, absenteeism, and turnover. System 4 also produces a better organizational climate characterized by excellent communication, high peer-group loyalty, high confidence and trust, and favorable attitudes toward the superiors.[29]

The general findings have shown that, although employees want their organizations to use participative methods, they are confronted with autocratic or consultative methods.[30] An empirical study of the use of participative management approaches concludes that "contrary to many claims, there does not seem to be much reason to believe that participative management is very widely employed in the United States today." The conclusion is based in part on findings that interest in participation was more than twice as great as the level of current practices.[31]

Quality Circles.   The productivity of Japanese firms has stimulated American managers to examine more closely the Japanese managerial approaches. As noted in Chapter 2, one form of group participation that is being adopted by many American companies is the Quality Circle. Quality Circles (QC) are small groups of employees

29. Rensis Likert, *The Human Organization* (New York: McGraw-Hill Book Company, 1967).

30. D. Anthony Butterfield and George F. Farris, "The Likert Organizational Profile: Methodological Analysis and Test of System 4 Theory in Brazil," *Journal of Applied Psychology,* Vol. 59, No. 1 (February, 1974), pp. 15–23.

31. William E. Halal and Bob S. Brown, "Participative Management: Myth and Reality," *California Management Review,* Vol. 23, No. 4 (Summer, 1981), pp. 20–38.

doing similar or related work who meet together regularly to identify, analyze, and suggest solutions to problems of product quality and on-the-job production. The process, as shown in Figure 13–10, begins with QC members brainstorming and gathering data. Then management considers the recommendations made by the QC members before decisions are made. The process ends with an important feature—recognizing and rewarding QC members.

The membership of a QC is about ten persons. Circles generally meet for about an hour three or four times a month. Supervisors commonly serve as leaders of the groups, but workers may also serve as leaders. In principle, participation is voluntary; however, in many companies both peer pressure and management pressure push the participation rates of blue-collar workers to 90 percent and above.[32]

Figure 13–10 **The Quality Circle Process**

SOURCE: Pacific Coast Research Institute, 5516 Waverly Avenue, La Jolla, CA 92037. Reproduced with permission.

32. Robert E. Cole, "Made in Japan—Quality-Control Circles," *Across the Board*, Vol. 16, No. 11 (November, 1979), pp. 72–78.

An estimated 750 corporations and government organizations in the United States are now using QCs, and the number is growing daily. While the aerospace industry was among the first to organize QCs, companies as diverse as General Motors, Polaroid, Dana, Herman Miller, TRW, and Procter and Gamble use Quality Circles.[33]

Those companies that have a history of employee participation have found QCs to be a natural extension of their philosophy. The climate in such companies is supportive, and the supervisors are likely to have the skills that are needed. A QC program, however, requires the management of a unionized company to work closely with the unions representing its work force. Management also must give consideration to the extent to which financial incentives will be included in the QC program, and specify the role and responsibilities of each of the circles.[34]

Disciplines Problem Employees

The supervisor's responsibility for maintaining high levels of productivity in the work group requires that appropriate corrective action be taken with individuals who engage in behaviors that impair their performance or that of fellow employees. Behaviors that are problems for supervisors are listed in Figure 13–11. A few of them warrant special attention.

Absenteeism. It has been estimated that absenteeism costs over $10 billion a year. Over one third of our nation's work force has tendencies to be chronically absent from work.[35] In fact, it is a way of life for many individuals. When many workers believe that "the time is coming to us" and management does not have controls that discourage absenteeism, it is not unusual to expect employees to use sick leave when they are not sick.

Many absences are involuntary—such as illness and accidents—and thus are excusable. However, those that are not involuntary require the supervisor's attention. To handle the problem of absenteeism, Steers and Rhodes recommend analyzing the problem systematically, increasing pressure to attend, and taking steps to encourage employees to maintain physical health. Sponsoring day-care centers and providing transportation for employees in outlying areas are also recommended.[36]

Supervisors cannot be expected to control absenteeism in an environment where management has failed to define expected and accepted standards of behavior. Management's commitment to attendance goals and its views toward absenteeism have an important impact on attendance. In most organizations the various functions of human resources management can be utilized more fully in reducing absences. For

---

33. Charles G. Burck, "What Happens When Workers Manage Themselves?" *Fortune*, Vol. 104, No. 2 (July 27, 1981), pp. 62–65, 68–69.

34. Gerald D. Klein, "Implementing Quality Circles: A Hard Look at Some of the Realities," *Personnel*, Vol. 58, No. 6 (November–December, 1981), pp. 11–20.

35. Joseph W. R. Lawson, II, *How To Reduce Absenteeism, Cure Tardiness, and Build Employee Morale* (Chicago: The Dartnell Corporation, 1980), p. i.

36. Richard M. Steers and Susan R. Rhodes, "A New Look at Absenteeism," *Personnel*, Vol. 57, No. 6 (November-December,1980), pp. 60–65.

Figure 13–11 Common Disciplinary Problems

ATTENDANCE PROBLEMS

Unexcused absence
Chronic absenteeism
Unexcused/excessive tardiness
Leaving without permission

DISHONESTY AND RELATED PROBLEMS

Theft
Falsifying employment
  application
Willful damage to company
  property
Punching another employee's
  time card
Falsifying work records

ON-THE-JOB BEHAVIOR PROBLEMS

Intoxication at work
Insubordination
Horseplay
Smoking in unauthorized places
Fighting
Gambling
Failure to use safety devices
Failure to report injuries
Carelessness
Sleeping on the job
Abusive or threatening language
  to supervisors
Possession of narcotics or alcohol
Possession of firearms or other
  weapons
Sexual harassment

example, employers can ask for information about attendance in reference requests, can emphasize attendance during orientation, and can use attendance as a factor in performance appraisal.[37]

Several studies have implicated the supervisor as a factor in absenteeism. In a study of over one-quarter million employees, one of the conclusions was that there was a definite connection between an employee's absence record and how he or she felt about the immediate supervisor. Feeling free to discuss job problems and finding the supervisor available for discussion were important factors.[38]

Alcoholism. Alcoholism is essentially a personal problem. But when a personal problem spills over into the workplace and affects job performance, it also becomes a management problem. Most organizations have established policies and procedures for handling such problems. These will be examined more fully in Chapter 20. At this point it should be noted that the immediate supervisor is the key to early detection and proper handling of alcoholism. The typical approach is to have the supervisor keep a record of attendance, production, and any undesirable behavior. The record is then discussed with the individuals, and assistance is offered. Usually individuals are referred to company physicians or outside agencies.

37. Robert F. Allen and Michael Higgins, "The Absenteeism Culture: Becoming Attendance Oriented," *Personnel*, Vol. 56, No. 1 (January-February, 1979), pp. 30–39.
38. Joseph W. R. Lawson, II., *op. cit.*, pp. 35–36.

Drug Abuse.   Detecting a drug addict is a more difficult task than spotting an alcoholic. For legal reasons caution must be used in accusing an employee of addiction or in examining a personal locker. However, supervisors should look out for such symptoms as absenteeism, tardiness, unexplained absences from the work area, frequent telephone calls, and frequent and lengthy visits to the washroom. Frequent changes in mood during the day, unsteady gait, and trembling of hands or mouth are a few of the behavioral signs of drug abuse of which supervisors should be aware.[39] Managers should instruct supervisors in what the organization is going to do about the drug problem and what management expects supervisors to do.[40] Some of the recommended courses of action are discussed in Chapter 20.

Sexual Harassment.   One of the problems that supervisors often ignored in the past—sexual harassment—now demands their attention and action. Sexual harassment is a violation of Section 703 of Title VII of the Civil Rights Act of 1964. Effective November 10, 1980, the EEOC *Guidelines* state that unwelcome sexual advances, requests for sexual favors, and other verbal or physical conduct of a sexual nature constitute sexual harassment when these behaviors are made a condition of employment, are used as the basis for employment decisions, or create an intimidating or offensive working environment.[41]

The *Guidelines* further state that, unless immediate and appropriate corrective action is taken, an employer is responsible for acts of sexual harassment in the workplace where the employer or supervisory personnel know or should have known of such conduct. Special training programs for the elimination of sexual harassment are a logical first step in meeting the requirements of the new *Guidelines.*[42]

One study of federal employees revealed that 42 percent of the female employees and 15 percent of the male employees claimed sexual harassment in some form in a two-year period. Most women were harassed by older men of the same race or ethnic background. In 71 percent of the incidents, the harasser was a fellow employee; in 40 percent, the harasser was an immediate or higher-level supervisor.[43] Since supervisors are often involved in such incidents, a personnel representative should be available to assist employees with harassment problems. Documentation of such assistance is essential to prove that the organization was responsive.

Provides Assistance to Subordinates

Employees can have problems of a personal nature that demand the supervisor's attention. These problems may or may not be job-related. Employees may ask to talk

39. Other symptoms are listed in *BNA Policy and Practice Series—Personnel Management* (Washington, DC: The Bureau of National Affairs, Inc., 1978), pp. 245:141–146.

40. Carl D. Chambers and Richard D. Heckman, *Employee Drug Abuse: A Manager's Guide for Action* (Boston: Cahners Publishing Co., Inc., 1972).

41. *Final Amendment to Guidelines in Discrimination Because of Sex* (EEOC), *Federal Register,* Vol. 45, No. 219, November 10, 1980, pp. 74676–74677.

42. Michele Hoyman and Ronda Robinson, "Interpreting the New Sexual Harassment Guidelines," *Personnel Journal,* Vol. 59, No. 12 (December, 1980), pp. 996–1000.

43. *BNA Fair Employment Practices,* No. 406 (Washington, DC: The Bureau of National Affairs, Inc., October 9, 1980).

with the supervisor about their problems. At times, the fact that an employee needs some type of assistance is manifested in departures from his or her typical behavior.

The supervisor should recognize changes in behavior, such as excessive absenteeism, tardiness, hostility, moodiness, withdrawal, and decline in job perform- ance, as indicators that the individual requires understanding and assistance. Similarly, the worrier, the crank, the bully, the chronic complainer, and the other types of "problem employees" that frequently demand the supervisor's attention are people who are having difficulties in adjusting to the world about them. In most instances these individuals are also problems to themselves and feel uncomfortable about their own behavior.

Since supervisors interact with their subordinates frequently, they are usually in the best position to observe changes in their subordinates' behavior and to assist in identifying and resolving their problems. The supervisors should know how to make referrals and should be ready to assume responsibility for providing help where it is needed.[44]

Counseling Methods.   In attempting to help an employee who has a problem, the supervisor may use a variety of counseling methods. All of these methods, however, depend upon active listening. According to the message in Figure 13-12, listening is not easy for everyone. Sometimes the mere furnishing of information may prove to be the solution to what at first appeared to be a knotty problem. More frequently, however, the problem cannot be solved as easily as this because of frustrations or conflicts that are accompanied by strong feelings such as fear, confusion, or hostility. In such cases the supervisor may be inclined to furnish advice to the employee, and in many instances advice-giving falls short of what is required in the situation.

The Nondirective Approach.   The maximum degree of assistance can often be realized by the use of the nondirective approach in which the employee being counseled is permitted to have maximum freedom in determining the course of the interview. The importance of nonevaluative listening as a communication skill was described in Chapter 12. Nonevaluative listening is also a primary technique used in nondirective counseling. Fundamentally the approach is to listen, with understanding and without criticism or appraisal, to the problem as it appears to the troubled person. The counselee is encouraged, through the counselor's attitude and reaction to what is said or not said, to express feelings without fear of shame, embarrassment, or reprisal. As the interview progresses, the counselor should strive to reflect the feelings of the employee by restating them. For example, if the employee has discussed several situations which indicate feelings of being treated unfairly, the counselor at the conclusion of this particular statement would probably say, "You feel that you have been treated unfairly." While questions may be used at appropriate places in the interview, the interviewer should use general questions that

44. For a comprehensive analysis of the helping relationship see Lawrence M. Brammer, *The Helping Relationship—Process and Skills* (2d ed.; Englewood Cliffs, NJ: Prentice-Hall, Inc., 1979). This excellent book should be read by everyone, not just supervisors.

Figure 13–12   **Listening Is Not Easy**

SOURCE: ©1965 United Feature Syndicate, Inc.

stimulate the employee to pursue an examination of those areas which are troublesome. Questions that call for "yes" or "no" answers on the part of the employee should be avoided.[45]

Values of Nondirective Counseling. The free expression that is encouraged in the nondirective approach tends to reduce tensions and frustrations. The employee who has had an opportunity to release pent-up feelings through catharsis is usually in a better position to view the problem more objectively and with a problem-solving attitude. The permissive atmosphere allows the individual to try to "work through" the entanglements of the problem and to see it in a clearer perspective, often to reach a more desirable solution. The supervisor should not feel, however, that a nondirective approach must always be used. There are times when a

45. For a detailed discussion of nondirective techniques, see Carl R. Rogers, *Counseling and Psychotherapy* (Boston: Houghton Mifflin Company, 1942), and his *Client-Centered Therapy* (Boston: Houghton Mifflin Company, 1951). Specific applications of this method to business are discussed in Maier and Verser, *op. cit.*, Chapter 18; and in William A. Ruch, "The Why and How of Nondirective Counseling," *Supervisory Management,* Vol. 18, No. 1 (January, 1973), pp. 13–19.

directive approach will be more suitable, such as when employees ask for specific information or when it is essential that supervisors express their opinions or inform subordinates of rules that may have been violated.

Use of Professional Counselors.   Since the supervisor may not have the skill or time in which to handle the more complex personal problems of employees, there should be an established system for making referrals to trained counselors. Such referrals should be made on the basis of the severity and complexity of the problem. Likewise, if the problem area is one over which the supervisor has little or no influence, as for example the employee's family relationships, it may be advisable for the supervisor to refer the employee to specialists that are available or may be contacted. Needless to say, the act of referring an employee for professional assistance requires the exercise of considerable skill and tact.

RÉSUMÉ

The talents and enthusiasm of the members of an organization are of little value unless their superiors have the requisite abilities and attitudes that enable them to utilize these human resources effectively. Studies of managers and supervisors have revealed that their personal traits are important. However, their behavior and the work situation have a greater impact upon their success in achieving results through their subordinates. Being aware of all of the forces that affect their performance as leaders is essential to their success.

We have observed that first-line supervisors have one of the most important leadership roles. They have many responsibilities, but of primary importance is the part they play in developing productive employees. The manner in which supervisors motivate and control employee behavior may vary, but the effective supervisor is one who is flexible in relationships with individuals and the work group. The supervisor's ability to provide for group participation was cited as one of the leadership skills that could be developed. Supervisors must also be prepared to discipline problem employees and to provide assistance where it is needed.

TERMS TO IDENTIFY

technical ability
conceptual ability
human relations ability
McGregor's Theory X
McGregor's Theory Y
Theory Z
trait theories
behavioral theories
situation theories
production-centered supervisors

employee-centered supervisors
consideration
structure
Contingency Model of Leader Effectiveness
leader-member relations
path-goal theory
exempt employees
linking pin
System 4

DISCUSSION QUESTIONS

1. Describe the differences in the manager's perception of subordinates under Theories X, Y, and Z. Why have managers moved toward the approaches of Theories Y and Z?
2. Why should a supervisor be flexible in leadership style? Of what value is the continuum of leadership behavior illustrated in Figure 13–8 on page 316?
3. What are the forces that a supervisor should consider in the process of determining how much the work group should participate in the making of a decision on a particular matter? What are some of the personal concerns that the supervisor may have in a specific situation?
4. One of the important skills in using the group decision approach is the ability to state a problem to a group in such a manner that the members of the group will not feel threatened and become defensive. How would you state the problems in the following situations that concern you as a supervisor?
   a. Employees have taken sick leave far in excess of what they had taken at the same time a year ago.
   b. Some members of the group are not producing as much as they are able to produce, and other members of the group are having to make up for their deficiencies.
   c. Employees are failing to heed safety rules and are taking dangerous shortcuts.
5. What can managers do to strengthen the role of their first-line supervisors? What can the human resources department do?
6. How prevalent is sexual harassment in work organizations? To what extent do you believe that the EEOC *Guidelines* will help reduce this problem?
7. What are the major advantages and disadvantages of the supervisor serving as a counselor to subordinates with problems not directly related to the job?
8. Why is it necessary to provide special training for managers and supervisors in human resources management?

PROBLEM 13–1

TOUCHY TEACHER*

Wayne Koven, a trainer in the operation of radio equipment, was accused of sexual harassment by six female employees who were assigned to him for instruction. According to the women, Koven had "deliberately allowed his hands to fall upon their bodies and had fondled them in an offensive manner." Management investigated the harassment reports and suspended Koven for five days for "immoral and indecent conduct."

Protesting the suspension, Koven denied that he had touched any of the six women. He further pointed out that he had an "unblemished work record of 28 years with the company and that there were no witnesses to the misconduct with which he was charged." He also claimed that his due process rights had been violated because management's investigation of the alleged incidents "was not as thorough as it should have been."

* Adapted by permission from *BNA Bulletin to Management*, No. 1670, March 25, 1982. Copyright © 1982 by The Bureau of National Affairs, Inc., Washington, DC.

In the arbitration hearings, management maintained that it had conducted a thorough and sifting investigation and that Koven had been given all due process. The investigator's findings supported the claims of the six female trainees, and no collaboration was found among them. Observing that its work rules provided for the removal of employees guilty of "major misconduct," the employer contended that the five-day suspension was "appropriate" discipline for a worker "who otherwise had a spotless record."

a. In your opinion, should the employee have received a five-day suspension? Why or why not?

b. What might have been the result of management's failure to take disciplinary action?

c. What effect is the suspension likely to have on Koven? On other male employees? On female employees?

d. How would you describe Koven's attitude toward female employees? Is it prevalent among male managerial and supervisory personnel?

SUGGESTED READINGS

Argyris, Chris. *Increasing Leadership Effectiveness.* New York: Wiley-Interscience, 1976.

Backhouse, Constance, and Leah Cohen. *Sexual Harassment on the Job.* Englewood Cliffs, NJ: Prentice-Hall, Inc., 1981.

Chruden, Herbert J., and Arthur W. Sherman, Jr. *Readings in Managing Human Resources* 6th ed. Cincinnati: South-Western Publishing Co., 1984. Parts 3 and 4.

Evered, James F. *Shirt-Sleeves Management.* New York: AMACOM, 1981.

Haimann, Theo, and Raymond L. Hilgert. *Supervision: Concepts and Practices of Management,* 3d ed. Cincinnati: South-Western Publishing Co., 1982.

Kossen, Stan. *Supervision—a Practical Guide to First-Line Management.* New York: Harper and Row, 1981.

Neugarten, Gail Ann, and Jay M. Shafritz. *Sexuality in Organizations: Romantic and Coercive Behaviors at Work.* Oak Park, IL: Moore Publishing Company, Inc., 1980.

Labor
Relations

part

5

Chapter Objectives:

- To recognize the reasons why employees join unions.
- To describe the process by which unions organize the employees and gain recognition as their bargaining agent.
- To describe the composition of organized labor and the functions labor unions perform at the national and local levels.
- To know the principal federal laws which provide the framework for labor relations.
- To cite some of the effects that changing conditions are having upon labor unions and how the unions are coping with the changes.

14

The Dynamics of Labor Relations

In preceding chapters the discussion focused upon human resources management as it involves relations with employees on an individual basis. This and the next two chapters will discuss the impact on human resources management that employee membership in a labor organization can have. Specifically, this chapter will be concerned with the role of labor organizations, the structure and leadership of labor unions, government regulation of labor relations, and contemporary challenges to labor organizations.

Unions and other labor organizations can affect significantly the ability of managers to direct and control the performance of employees who are members. Therefore, it is essential that managers understand how unions operate and be skillful in their relations with them. Managers also must be knowledgeable with respect to the growing body of law governing labor relations to avoid additional difficulties with unions. Labor relations thus is a highly specialized function of human resources management to which employers must give appropriate consideration.

THE ROLE OF LABOR ORGANIZATIONS

Individually, employees are able to exercise relatively little power in their relations with employers. The treatment and benefits they receive are thus dependent in a large part upon the value their employers believe them to be worth and whether or not the employers recognize the benefits they gain by managing employees in a consistent and equitable manner. If employees believe they are not being treated fairly, they, of course, have the option of quitting. However, they have another option of seeking to correct the situation by organizing and bargaining with the employer collectively. In doing so, they can exercise monopolistic control over the services they provide in much the same manner as farmers control the marketing of their products through an agricultural cooperative.

Types of Labor Organizations

The predominant type of organization through which employees exert their power collectively is the labor union. Traditionally, unions that represent skilled craft workers, such as carpenters or machinists, have been referred to as **craft unions**. Those that represent unskilled and semiskilled workers employed primarily in the mass-production industries have been referred to as **industrial unions**. While this distinction still exists, technological change and competition among unions for members have helped to reduce it. Today the skilled and unskilled workers, white-collar and blue-collar workers, and professional groups are being represented by both types of unions.

Besides unions, there also are **employee associations** representing various groups of professional and white-collar employees. In competing with unions, these associations, for all purposes, may function as unions and become just as militant as unions in representing members.

Why Employees Join Unions

Most employees join a union for one of two reasons. They join either because of external pressure or compulsion or because they believe it is in their self-interest to do so. In industries and geographic regions which are highly unionized, employees who do not view unions as a protective necessity join them anyway as a result of peer pressure. Others may join because of the union-shop provisions of the labor agreement. In states where it is permitted, a **union shop** is a provision of the labor agreement with the union which requires employees to join the union as a condition of employment. Even when compelled to join, however, many employees accept the concept of unionism once they become involved in the union as a member.

Employees whose needs for status and recognition are being frustrated by their employers join unions as a means of satisfying these needs.[1] Through their union, they have an opportunity to become better acquainted and to fraternize with other employees who have similar desires, interests, problems and gripes. Joining the union also enables them to put latent leadership talents to use. Because their union offers protection against management retaliation, employees can disagree more openly with supervisors and challenge what they may consider to be unfair treatment. Collectively, therefore, employees have far greater strength than they would have otherwise as individuals.

Whether or not a union is able to organize and become the bargaining agent for a group of employees will be influenced by the employees' degree of dissatisfaction, if any, with their employment conditions. It will depend also upon whether or not they perceive the union to be a useful instrument for improving these conditions. Dissatisfaction with wages, benefits, and working conditions on the job appear to provide the strongest inducements to join a union. These are the traditional "bread and butter issues" upon which unions are built. The failure of employers to allow employees an opportunity to participate in exercising some influence over their work environment also may encourage union membership among employees who believe it to be their right. In the final analysis, however, the extent to which the perceived benefits of joining a union outweigh the costs associated with membership is likely to be the deciding factor.[2]

Employees who do not have a strong desire to do so may be spared the need to belong to a union if management will minimize the employees' dissatisfactions with their employment conditions. Effective two-way communication helps to alert management to discontent when it occurs and permits management to take corrective action. It also can enable management to become aware of any outside efforts to unionize employees.

To avoid unionization, some employers hire the services of labor consultants. These consultants help employers correct weaknesses in their personnel and

1. Ross Stagner and Hjalmar Rosen, *Psychology of Union Management Relations* (Belmont, CA: Wadsworth Publishing Company, Inc., 1965), p. 40.

2. Thomas A. Kochan, "How American Workers View Labor Unions," *Monthly Labor Review*, Vol. 102, No. 4 (April, 1979), pp. 23–27.

communication programs that aid a union's organizing efforts.[3]   However, because their services are directed toward frustrating a union's organizing efforts, these consultants sometimes are referred to by labor leaders as "union busters."

Organizing Campaigns

An organizing campaign may be initiated by either a union seeking to represent a group of employees or by employees acting in their own behalf. Since organizing campaigns can be expensive, union leaders must evaluate carefully their chances of success and the possible benefits to be gained from their efforts. Important in this evaluation is the targeted employer's vulnerability to unionization. Union leaders should also consider the effect that allowing an employer to remain nonunion may have upon the strength of their union within the area. A nonunion employer can impair a union's efforts to standardize employment conditions within an industry or geographic area, as well as weaken the union's bargaining power with employers it has unionized.

Union Tactics.   One of the union's first steps in a campaign is to form an organizing committee composed of employees who can provide leadership to the campaign. The committee's role is to interest employees in joining the union and in supporting its campaign. Typically the union's campaign focuses upon the employer's shortcomings and the employees' need for a union as a means of forcing the management to resolve problems and issues relating to their employment.[4]

It is essential for the union to maintain momentum in its organizing campaign. It may do so by holding rallies for campaign workers and prospective members to emphasize the issues around which the campaign is centered. In addition, handouts like that illustrated in Figure 14–1 may be distributed at employee entrances to reinforce the idea among employees that they really need union protection.

Employer Tactics.   In counteracting a union campaign, employers must not threaten employees with the loss of their jobs or with other dire consequences if they vote to unionize. However, within the limits permitted by the Taft-Hartley Act, employers can express their views about the disadvantages of being represented by a union. When possible, employers will stress the favorable relationship they have experienced in the past with employees without a union. Employers may emphasize any advantages in wages, benefits, or working conditions the employees may enjoy in comparison with those provided by companies with which the organizing union has a labor agreement. "While you have a right to join a union," the employers may remind their employees, "you also have a right not to join one and deal directly with the company free from outside interference."

Employers may also emphasize any unfavorable publicity the organizing union has received with respect to corruption or the abuse of members' rights by its leaders.

3. Richard J. Anthony, "When There's A Union at the Gate," *Personnel*, Vol. 53, No. 6 (November-December, 1976), pp. 47–52.

4. William E. Fulmer, "Step by Step Through a Union Campaign," *Harvard Business Review*, Vol. 59, No. 4 (July-August, 1981), p. 98.

If the union has engaged in a number of strikes, this fact may be stressed to exploit employee fear of disruption and loss of income. The cost to employees of union dues and special assessments, along with any false promises raised by the union in the

---

Figure 14–1 Example of an Organizing Campaign "Handout"

"THE PROGRESSIVE LOCAL UNION"

Paternalism

It's a
BIG WORD...but
What does it mean?

You hear that word 'paternalism' around the plant a lot these days. And for good reason. 'Paternalism' is what the employer believes in and practices.

The word's getting around about what 'paternalism' really means. 'Paternalism' means "DADDY (the boss) knows best."

It means DADDY will give you all sorts of presents (like picnics and smoking privileges) so long as you forget you are adults and let him fire you whenever he pleases, promote just his pets and pay you whatever he decides.

PATERNALISM IS A TRICK TO TRY TO KEEP THE UNION OUT. That's pretty obvious when you stop and think about it. The employer knows that when the employees form a union, he won't have things all his own way. The employer knows that a union contract will guarantee promotions on a fair basis; he knows that under a union contract he won't be able to fire somebody just because he doesn't like the way his hair curls.

The employer knows that a union means COLLECTIVE BARGAINING for higher wages, better working conditions and increased benefits for the employees.

The real objective of 'paternalism' is to fool the employees into thinking all good things come from the generous nature of the employer. The real aim of 'paternalism' is to keep the union out. Spoon-feeding is great for babies; but it's not for adults.

Let the employer know that you're big enough to make some of your own decisions—and you CAN MAKE THEM THROUGH YOUR UNION.

SIGN YOUR AUTHORIZATION CARDS!
MAIL IT TODAY!

course of its campaign, are not likely to be ignored.[5]   Employers also may initiate legal action should union members and/or their leaders engage in any unfair labor practices or criminal acts.

How Employees Become Unionized

The employees toward whom a union's organizing efforts are directed comprise the bargaining unit to be covered by the labor agreement. Prasow defines a **bargaining unit** as a group of employees recognized by an employer, or designated by an agency, as appropriate for representation by an employee organization for purposes of bargaining.[6]   Appropriate bargaining units are determined by the National Labor Relations Board (NLRB) based upon a community of interest among employees within the unit. Where the NLRB lacks the jurisdiction to do so, the appropriate state agency makes this determination.

The employees comprising the bargaining unit or units can be very important to occupational groups within an organization. For example, if a single bargaining unit is established within a plant, both the skilled as well as the semiskilled production line employees must be represented by the same union. If more than one bargaining unit is established, however, it may be possible for certain groups of skilled employees to have a separate bargaining unit in which their particular occupational interests may be represented more effectively. Or, employees within a bargaining unit may choose not to have any union represent them.

Employer Recognition.   Once a union is able to demonstrate that at least 30 percent of the employees within a bargaining unit want it to represent them, the union may request recognition by the employer. Typically this evidence is produced in the form of authorization cards signed by employees. If no other union is competing to represent the employees, the employer at this point can simply agree to recognize the union and negotiate an agreement with it. However, if the employer believes that a majority of employees do not want to belong to a union or if more than one union is attempting to gain recognition, the employer can insist that a representation election be held. This election will determine which union, if any, the employees prefer to have represent them.

Union representation elections are conducted by the NLRB or by a state labor agency if the election is subject to the state's jurisdiction. The petition to hold representation elections usually is initiated by the union although employers, under certain conditions, have the right to petition for one.

Types of Representation Elections.   If the petition to hold a representation election is not contested, the election is conducted by secret ballot without holding a pre-election hearing. An election conducted under these conditions is known as a

---

5. *Ibid.,* pp. 96–98.
6. Paul Prasow, *Unit Determination in Public Employment—Concepts and Problems,* Institute of Industrial Relations, Reprint No. 198 (Los Angeles: University of California, 1969), p. 60.

consent election. Should the request for representation be contested by the employer or should more than one union be seeking recognition, then pre-election hearings must be held to determine voting choices to appear on the ballot, followed by a **formal election**. The ballot provides for the choice of "no union" and the names of any unions that are seeking recognition. If none of the available choices receives a majority of the votes, a **runoff election** must be conducted between the two choices receiving the largest number of votes. Unless the majority votes "no union," the union that receives a majority of the votes in the initial or the runoff election is the one certified by the NLRB as the bargaining agent for a period of at least a year, or for the duration of the labor agreement.

Impact upon Human Resources Management

The unionization of employees can affect the management of human resources in several ways. Perhaps most significant is the effect that it can have upon the previously exercised prerogatives by management in making decisions involving employees. Furthermore, unionization restricts the freedom of management to formulate personnel policy unilaterally and also can cause the authority of supervisors to be challenged.

Challenges to Management Prerogatives.
Unions typically attempt to achieve greater participation in management decisions that affect their members. Specifically, these decisions may involve such issues as the subcontracting of work, the introduction of laborsaving devices, work schedules, work loads, production standards, and job content. Employers quite naturally seek to claim many of these decisions as their exclusive **management prerogatives**, that is, decisions over which management claims exclusive jurisdiction. However, these prerogatives increasingly are being subject to challenge and erosion by the union. They may be challenged at the bargaining table, through the grievance procedure, and through strikes.

Bilateral Formulation of Personnel Policies.
Some personnel policies, such as those that cover wages, work hours, work rules, and fringe benefits, must be consistent with the terms of the labor agreement. However, to gain the union's acceptance of these policies and their cooperation in administering them, management should consult with the union when formulating the policies. Because unions are alert for inconsistencies in the treatment of employees, a more centralized coordination in the enforcement of personnel policies may be required. Of necessity, such coordination provides a greater role for the personnel staff.

Possible Dilution of Supervisory Authority.
The focal point of the union's impact is at the operating level where supervisors administer the terms of the labor agreement. These terms can determine what corrective action is to be taken in directing and in disciplining subordinates. When disciplining employees, supervisors must be certain they have just cause for their actions because these actions can be challenged by the union through the grievance procedure. If challenged, the supervisor may occupy the role of defendant during a grievance hearing. Furthermore,

the reversal of a supervisor's disciplinary actions can cause that person to lose status. This may reduce his or her effectiveness in coping with subsequent disciplinary problems.

COMPOSITION, FUNCTIONS, AND LEADERSHIP OF LABOR UNIONS

Craft unions have existed at the local level in this country since colonial times. It was not until about the Civil War, however, that local craft unions were able to unite to form national unions. These national unions ultimately became affiliated in a federation.

Formation of the AFL-CIO

In 1886, under the leadership of Samuel Gompers, the American Federation of Labor (AFL) was established. As the term federation implies, the AFL was a loosely knit group of autonomous national unions which constituted the real power within the organization. This situation remains the same today. Although its membership by 1900 totaled only about 548,000, the AFL was able to survive to the present, overcoming the adversities of economic depressions and employer opposition.

Initially most of the craft unions within the AFL were opposed to the admission of industrial workers into their ranks. This opposition was based upon a fear among craft members that their status and control would be weakened by taking in large numbers of lesser skilled workers from the mass-production industries. It was not until the Congress of Industrial Organizations (CIO) began vigorously to organize industrial workers that the AFL started to organize them.[7]

The CIO was formed by several unions whose efforts to organize the mass-production industries caused their expulsion from the AFL. In an organizing drive spearheaded by John L. Lewis and his United Mine Workers, the CIO unions embarked upon a vigorous organizing campaign to recruit industrial workers. The AFL unions then embarked upon a similar course of action. Competition between the AFL and the CIO unions led to bitter rivalries and jurisdictional disputes. After two decades of conflicts—some of which were violent—the national unions comprising the two groups agreed in 1955 to unite into a single AFL-CIO organization.

A diagram showing the structure and composition of the AFL-CIO is contained in Figure 14–2. Membership in this organization, as Table 14–1 reveals, totals about 17 million.[8] The chief advantage of belonging to the AFL-CIO is that it affords protection to member unions against "raiding" by other unions within the federation. A violation of this "no raiding" provision can lead to expulsion from the federation.[9]

---

7. The letters CIO initially stood for Committee of Industrial Organizations which subsequently became the Congress of Industrial Organizations.

8. U.S. Department of Labor, Bureau of Labor Statistics, *Directory of National Unions and Employee Associations* (Washington, DC: U.S. Government Printing Office, 1979), p. 57.

9. Arthur A. Sloane and Fred Witney, *Labor Relations* (3d ed.; Englewood Cliffs, NJ: Prentice-Hall, Inc., 1977), p. 146.

Membership in Unaffiliated Unions

Although the majority of the national and international labor unions belong to the AFL-CIO, a number of them representing about 4.7 million members are unaffiliated (see Table 14–1). Among the more important of the unaffiliated unions

Figure 14–2 **Structure of the AFL-CIO**

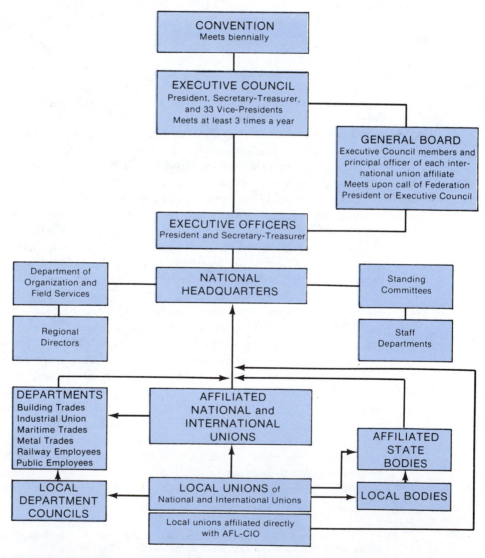

SOURCE: *Directory of National Unions and Employee Associations*, Bureau of Labor Statistics, 1977.

Table 14–1   Membership of Unions and Employee Associations

ORGANIZATIONS		MEMBERSHIP
Unions		21,784,000
AFL-CIO Affiliates	17,024,000	
Unaffiliated Unions	4,760,000	
Associations		2,635,000
Total Unions and Associations		24,419,000

SOURCE: *Directory of National Unions and Employee Associations*, Bureau of Labor Statistics, 1979, p. 57.

are the United Mine Workers, United Transportation Workers, United Auto Workers, and Teamsters. In addition, there are approximately 2.6 million employees who are members of associations representing their professional fields (refer to Table 14–1). During the past decade, as we mentioned earlier, most of these associations have become increasingly militant and union-like in their relations with their employers.

Functions of National Unions

The largest of the national unions are shown in Table 14–2. A **national union**, through its constitution, establishes the rules and conditions under which the local

Table 14–2   Membership of the Largest National Labor Unions

NATIONAL UNION	MEMBERSHIP
Teamsters	1,891,000
Automobile Workers	1,357,000
Steel Workers	1,238,000
Food and Commercial	1,300,000
Electrical Workers (IBEW)	1,041,000
State, County	1,098,000
Machinists	754,000
Communication Workers	551,000
Teachers	551,000
Clothing and Textile	455,000

SOURCE: *News: Department of Labor*, September 18, 1981, p. 2.

unions may be chartered. Most national unions have regulations governing dues, initiation fees, and the internal administration of the locals. National unions also may require that certain standard provisions be included in labor agreements with employers. In return for these controls, they provide professional and financial assistance during organizing drives and strikes and help in the negotiation and administration of labor contracts.

The task of organizing a nonunion employer usually is assumed by the national union. This task may include conducting a public relations campaign to gain community support for the organizing campaign. The national union might also generate a boycott of the products of the employer it is seeking to organize. This tactic was used in the United Farm Workers' campaign against the grape and lettuce growers. Attempts by employees to unionize the Farah Manufacturing Company or the J. P. Stevens Company would have been unsuccessful had it not been for the financial contributions and boycotts sponsored by the national organizations of the Amalgamated Clothing Workers and the United Textile Workers, respectively.

Structure and Functions of Local Unions

The officers of a local union usually have the responsibility for negotiating the local labor agreement and for insuring that management decisions involving their members are equitable and in compliance with the agreement. Most important, they assist in preventing the members of the local union from being treated by their employers in a manner that is not in accord with established personnel policies and practices.

The officers of a local union typically include the president, vice-president, secretary-treasurer, business representative, and various committee chairpersons. Depending upon the size of the union, one or more of these officers, in addition to the business representative, may be paid by the union to serve on a full-time basis. The remaining officers are members who have regular jobs and who serve the union without remuneration except perhaps for token gratuities and expense allowances. In many locals, the business representative is the dominant power. In some locals, however, the dominant power is the secretary-treasurer or the president.

Role of the Business Representative.

Negotiating and administering the labor agreement and working to resolve problems arising in connection with it are major responsibilities of the **business representative**. In performing these duties, business representatives must be all things to all persons within their unions. They frequently are required to assume the role of counselor in helping the members with both personal and job-related problems. They also are expected to dispose satisfactorily of the members' grievances that cannot be settled by the stewards.

Administering the daily affairs of the local organization is another significant part of the business representative's job. This task may include maintaining headquarters facilities, supervising an administrative staff, collecting dues, and recruiting new members. The handling of internal and external publicity for the local, coordinating social activities, and arranging for business and committee meetings also are generally a part of the business representative's duties.

Role of the Union Steward.

The **union steward** represents the interests of members in their relations with their immediate supervisors and other members of management. In some industries, such as the auto industry, the union steward has the title of **district committeeman**.[10] The district committeeman, whose salary is paid by the company, devotes full time to reconciling disputes involving union members in connection with the interpretation and administration of the labor agreement.

In describing the role of a district committeeman named Charlie Bragg in an assembly plant of the Ford Motor Company, one author expressed these observations:

> He might be called, in fact, "the fixer"—the man to whom workers can turn in times of trouble . . . Unofficially, Mr. Bragg is the union to his people and often the only union representative they deal with. . . .
>
> "The main function of a committeeman is to settle problems right on the floor," Mr. Bragg says. "I'm a mediator, a foot-soldier out there. Without the committeeman, Ford couldn't run this plant."
>
> Ford might dispute this assertion, but there is no denying that Mr. Bragg's meanderings uncover problems—or that he is the man on the spot. It is Charlie Bragg and the men like him who are fighting disciplinary actions, getting supply racks fixed, arranging days off, getting bathrooms cleaned and drinking fountains unclogged. (On the average day, Mr. Bragg handles about 20 individual problems.)
>
> In the course of attacking such problems, Mr. Bragg avoids threats and confrontations. His prime goal, he says, is keeping his constituents happy. But he also must remain on working terms with their supervisors, who, he feels, must regard him as tough, but flexible. Indeed, he uses his ultimate weapon—the formal, written grievance— sparingly; and he says he tries hardest to avert, rather than win, disciplinary cases.[11]

It is evident from the preceding quotation that stewards and committeemen, if they perform their positions effectively, serve as a very important link between union members and their employer. Their attitudes and actions can have an important bearing upon union-management cooperation and upon the efficiency and morale of the employees they represent.

Union Leadership

To be able to interpret effectively the behavior of union leaders, one must understand the nature of their backgrounds and ambitions and recognize the political nature of the offices they occupy. The leaders of many national unions have been able to develop political machines that enable them to suppress opposition and to perpetuate themselves in office. Tenure in office for the leaders in a local union, however, is less secure. In the local union, officers periodically must run for

---

10. Since the titles of steward and committeeman make reference to the sex of the position holder, it is quite probable that these titles in the future will be changed in many unions to conform to the trend of eliminating sex designation in job titles.

11. Walter S. Mossberg, "On the Line: As Union Man at Ford, Charlie Bragg Deals in Problems, Gripes," *The Wall Street Journal,* July 26, 1973, p. 1. Reprinted with permission of *The Wall Street Journal,* © Dow Jones & Company, Inc. (1973). All Rights Reserved.

reelection. If they are to remain in office, they must be able to convince a majority of the membership that they are serving them effectively.

Sources of Union Leaders.

Most labor leaders have worked their way up within the labor organization. They may have been motivated to do so by a desire for status and recognition within the union, as well as a dedication to the labor movement. The opportunity to gain freedom from tight supervisory control can be another reason.

Lately, however, unions have begun to recognize that the practice of obtaining leaders from within the ranks may not be beneficial for their organizations. Therefore, they are seeking to induce college-trained persons to become union officers rather than just staff specialists—the role that college graduates traditionally have assumed.

The placement of college graduates in leadership positions may be aided by the fact that there will not be sufficient professional and other white-collar job opportunities for all of them. As more college graduates are forced to accept blue-collar employment, some undoubtedly will aspire to become union officers where their education can be utilized more effectively. Professional and white-collar unions, on the other hand, have a relatively high proportion of college graduates as members from which leadership talent may be drawn.

Leadership Approaches.

Employers, as well as members of the general public, are prone to equate a union leader's authority with that of an executive in a public or private enterprise. Consequently, they may exaggerate the power and influence that these leaders may be able to exercise over union actions. As Bok and Dunlop point out, many employers assume that their failure to achieve harmonious employee relations within their organization is the result of some opportunistic union leader leading their employees astray.[12] Although some blame for strikes and other forms of labor strife may be attributed to their leaders, Bok and Dunlop suggest that the rank-and-file members can and often do exercise a very strong influence over these leaders, particularly with respect to the negotiation and administration of the labor agreement. The leader who ignores the demands of these members may risk (1) being voted out of office, (2) having them vote the union out as their bargaining agent, (3) having them refuse to ratify the union agreement, or (4) having them engage in wildcat strikes or work slowdowns.[13]

According to another study, however, union leaders play an administrative role that, as far as their relations with subordinates are concerned, is similar to that of administrators in other types of organizations. Union leaders, for example, tend to view themselves as being more capable and dependable than their followers. Because they may have reservations about the capacities of the members for sound judgment, they actually may be fearful of the consequences of member participation. However, since union leaders recognize the value of participation in building the loyalty and morale of members, they may resort to participative techniques in the belief that it

12. Derek C. Bok and John T. Dunlop, "How Trade Union Policy Is Made," *Monthly Labor Review*, Vol. 93, No. 2 (February, 1970), p. 17.

13. *Ibid.*, p. 18.

will produce better support for their decisions, but not necessarily better decisions. This attitude of union officers toward participation, in the study cited, was found to be more apparent in industrial than in craft unions.[14]

The success of union leaders in gaining participation will be influenced by whether or not members perceive their participation to be effective in contributing to their self-interest. Members who perceive their participation to be effective, according to Anderson, are more likely to involve themselves in union activities. On the other hand, those who do not perceive the union to be effective would still like to influence and participate in union affairs provided that they did not consider such effort to be a waste of time.[15] Thus, in order for union leaders to get members to participate, the leaders must be able to demonstrate that the union is rendering a contribution in behalf of its members.

GOVERNMENT REGULATION OF LABOR RELATIONS

Employers who are vulnerable to organizing efforts of labor unions or whose employees are already unionized must be concerned with the growing body of state and federal law on labor relations. This body of law has evolved out of common law and civil law, as well as court interpretations of these laws. Keeping abreast of current legislation and court interpretations of it requires specialized expertise in the field of labor law.

The first federal law pertaining to labor relations involved the railroad industry. In the 1930s, it was expanded to cover employers in other industries. The principal laws that affect labor relations in the private sector today are the Wagner Act, the Taft-Hartley Act, and the Landrum-Griffin Act. For labor relations with federal employees, various Executive Orders and the Civil Service Reform Act of 1978 apply.

Wagner Act

The Wagner Act of 1935 (National Labor Relations Act) has had by far the most significant impact on union-management relations. It placed the protective power of the federal government firmly behind employee efforts to organize and bargain collectively through representatives of their choice. Although this act was amended by the Taft-Hartley Act, most of its major provisions that protected employee bargaining rights were retained. Section 7 of the Wagner Act guaranteed these rights as follows:

> Employees shall have the right to self-organization, to form, join, or assist labor organizations, to bargain collectively through representatives of their own choosing, and to engage in concerted activities, for the purpose of collective bargaining or other mutual aid or protection....

---

14. Raymond E. Miles and J.B. Ritchie, "Leadership Attitudes Among Union Officials," *Industrial Relations*, Vol. 8, No. 1 (October, 1968), p. 115.

15. John C. Anderson, "Local Union Participation: A Re-examination," *Industrial Relations*, Vol. 18, No. 1 (Winter, 1979), pp. 30-31.

Other provisions of the Wagner Act that were retained include those of defining certain unfair labor relations practices of employers. These practices are defined as follows:

1. To interfere with, restrain, or coerce employees in the exercise of their rights guaranteed in Section 7.
2. To dominate or interfere with the formation or administration of any labor organization, or to contribute financial or other support to it.
3. To discriminate in regard to hiring or tenure of employment or any term or condition of employment so as to encourage or discourage membership in any labor organization.
4. To discharge or otherwise discriminate against an employee because he has filed charges or given testimony under this act.
5. To refuse to bargain collectively with the duly chosen representatives of his employees.

As a result of the protection that the Wagner Act afforded them, unions were able to recruit nearly 10 million new members in the decade that followed the passage of the Wagner Act.

Taft-Hartley Act

Because the bargaining power of unions increased significantly following the passage of the Wagner Act, certain restraints on union labor relations practices were considered to be necessary. The Taft-Hartley Act of 1947 (also known as the Labor-Management Relations Act) defined the following activities as unfair union practices:

1. Restraint or coercion of employees in the exercise of their Wagner Act rights.
2. Restraint or coercion of employers in the selection of the parties to bargain in their behalf.
3. Persuasion of employers to discriminate against any of their employees.
4. Refusal to bargain collectively with an employer.
5. Participation in secondary boycotts and jurisdictional disputes.
6. Attempt to force recognition from an employer when another union is already the certified representative.
7. Charge of excessive initiation fees.
8. "Featherbedding" practices requiring the payment of wages for services not performed.

Enforcement of the Taft-Hartley Act.

The agency responsible for administering and enforcing the Taft-Hartley Act is the National Labor Relations Board (NLRB). Its responsibilities are the following:

1. To determine what the bargaining unit or units within an organization shall be. (A unit contains those employees who are to be represented by a particular union and are covered by the agreement with it.)
2. To conduct representation elections by secret ballot for the purpose of determining which, if any, union shall represent the employees within a unit.
3. To investigate unfair labor practices charges filed by unions or employers and to prosecute any violations revealed by such investigations.

Results of the Taft-Hartley Act.   One of the major results of the Taft-Hartley Act was to relax the restrictions that the Wagner Act had placed upon an employer's freedom of speech. The Taft-Hartley Act gave employers the opportunity to express their views regarding unions and unionizing efforts—provided that no attempt was made to threaten, coerce, or bribe employees concerning their membership in a union or their decision to join or not to join one.

The Taft-Hartley Act also denied supervisors legal protection in forming their own unions. The act attempted, without too much success, to reduce jurisdictional disputes and the mishandling of union welfare funds. The right of employers to sue a union for damages arising from the union's violation of the labor agreement or from unfair labor practices committed by it was clarified.

The Taft-Hartley Act enlarged the conditions under which court injunctions might be issued in labor disputes. It allowed the NLRB to initiate action against certain illegal strikes and other unfair labor practices by the unions. The act also provided that the President of the United States, through the Attorney General, may seek an injunction against strikes or lockouts affecting the nation's health and welfare for a period of 80 days. If the dispute has not been settled after the injunction has been in effect for 60 days, the NLRB is required to take a secret vote among the employees involved in the dispute to determine if they are willing to accept the employer's "final offer."

Landrum-Griffin Act

As provisions of the Taft-Hartley Act were put into practice and tested in the courts, the need for changes became evident. Congressional investigations into corrupt practices occurring within the field of union-management relations revealed that the existing statutes were inadequate to protect the rights of individual union members. Neither did they protect the equities of members in union welfare funds, nor prevent racketeering or unscrupulous practices from being committed by certain employers and union officers. As a result, Congress passed the Landrum-Griffin Act of 1959 (also known as the Labor-Management Reporting and Disclosure Act).

Bill of Rights of Union Members.   One of the most important provisions of the Landrum-Griffin Act is the Bill of Rights of Union Members, which requires that every union member must be given the right to: (1) nominate candidates for union office, (2) vote in union elections or referendums, (3) attend union meetings, and (4) participate in union meetings and vote on union business. Members who are deprived of this right are permitted to seek appropriate relief in a federal court. The court's action may include obtaining an appropriate injunction. Union members are also granted the right to examine union accounts and records in order to verify information contained in union reports and to bring suit against union officers to protect union funds.

Control of Trusteeships.   The Landrum-Griffin Act establishes certain ground rules governing the use of trusteeships by labor organizations in order to protect the rights of members within the trusteed locals. A **trusteeship** is established when the national union takes away the authority to administer a local union from its officers and places it in the hands of a trustee appointed by the national organization. At times in the past, local unions had been subjected to the abuses of national unions. Members can now bring civil action against the officers of their national unions.

Reporting and Bonding Provisions. Under the Landrum-Griffin Act unions are required to submit a financial report annually to the Secretary of Labor. Union officers are required to be bonded for an amount not less than 10 percent of the union funds that they handle.

Employers must report any expenditures that are made in attempting to persuade employees to exercise their bargaining rights. Labor consultants, similarly, must report agreements with employers involving efforts to persuade employees to exercise their bargaining rights or to supply information about union activities during a labor dispute.

Executive Orders

Regulations that govern labor relations with federal employees have been modeled after those developed for the private sector. However, the rights granted to labor associations under these regulations are less than those accorded by the Taft-Hartley Act.

Issued in 1962 by President Kennedy, Executive Order 10988 contained provisions similar to those in Section 7 of the Taft-Hartley Act. These provisions stated that federal employees have the right to:

> . . . freely and without fear of penalty or reprisal to form, join, or assist any labor organization or to refrain from such activity.[16]

Included in this executive order are provisions for establishing bargaining units within government agencies. Labor organizations also are permitted to bargain collectively with the government in reaching a labor agreement for members.

Issued in 1971 by President Nixon, Executive Order 11491 defined the bargaining rights of federal employees more precisely and provided procedures for safeguarding these rights. This Executive Order created the Federal Labor Relations Council to hear appeals relating to unfair practices and bargaining issues. A Federal Service Impasses Panel also was established to deal with collective bargaining deadlocks.[17]

Civil Service Reform Act of 1978

The Civil Service Reform Act of 1978 made the regulation of labor relations in the federal government even more consistent with those contained in the Taft-Hartley Act for the private sector. A Federal Labor Relations Board (FLRB) similar

---

16. 3 CFR (Code of Federal Regulations) 1959-1963, Compilation p. 521.
17. Charles J. Coleman, "The Civil Service Reform Act of 1978: Its Meaning and Its Roots," *Labor Law Journal*, Vol. 31, No. 4 (April, 1980), pp. 201–202.

to the NLRB was created to decide unfair practice and representation cases and to enforce the provisions of the act. An Office of General Counsel, similar to that provided by the Taft-Hartley Act, also was created. Its function is to investigate and decide which unfair labor practices and complaints are to be prosecuted.[18]

Even with the Civil Service Reform Act, labor organizations representing federal employees do not have rights equal to those provided by the Taft-Hartley Act. Most important, they lack the legal right to strike to enforce their bargaining demands—as the Professional Air Traffic Controllers Organization (PATCO) discovered, to its misfortune, in 1981.[19] Furthermore, management rights in the federal government are accorded greater protection than those of employers in the private sector. Rules, procedures, and area restrictions that govern bargaining further reduce the influence that labor organizations can exercise over employment conditions in federal agencies.[20]

CONTEMPORARY CHALLENGES TO LABOR ORGANIZATIONS

Changes that are occurring within our society are having an effect upon labor organizations as well as upon employers. Among the changes that constitute contemporary challenges to labor organizations today are the changing characteristics of union members, economic adversities, a decline in labor's public image, and the slow rate of growth of union membership.

Changing Characteristics of Union Members

Just as the people in our society today differ from those of a generation ago, so do the members in labor unions. Currently a larger proportion of union members are better educated. They are also less willing to accept arbitrary decisions and follow autocratic leaders or to be subjected to discrimination. Furthermore, most of them now belong to the predominant middle class.

Divergence of Interests. The so-called generation gap is creating its share of problems for organized labor. Control of the national unions still is, to a large extent, in the hands of the older members. The majority of members, on the other hand, are under 40 years of age. Naturally there is a divergence of interests between members of the two groups. The younger militants are demanding better treatment on the job. They are equally angry about what they regard as authoritarian bosses in the plants and unresponsive bureaucrats in their unions. While the older members are concerned with bread-and-butter issues, the young members are demanding union

---

18. Henry B. Frazier, III, "Labor-Management Relations in the Federal Government," *Labor Law Journal*, Vol. 30, No. 3 (March, 1979), p. 132.

19. Suzanne Garment, "PATCO's Strike: Trying to Find Out the Reasons," *The Wall Street Journal*, Friday, Aug. 14, 1981, Editorial Page. *See also*, "How Safe Are Our Airways," *U.S. News & World Report* (August 24, 1981), pp. 14–18.

20. Coleman. *op. cit.*, pp. 205–207.

action on health and safety, production speedups, and other nonfinancial issues.[21] One of the big problems confronting the leaders of the union is that of reconciling the interests of the two groups.

Frustrations of Minority and Female Union Members.

The civil rights and the women's rights movements have given rise to some very significant problems for unions. Blacks and other members of disadvantaged groups have become frustrated because they believe that they have not been accorded fair and equal opportunity to participate in the gains being realized by organized labor as a whole. In particular, many minority groups complain that because of racial prejudices they have been denied their share of membership opportunities in the craft and other unions representing the higher-paying jobs. As a result, membership opportunities for them have been restricted primarily to unions representing jobs of lower skill and pay. Minorities also resent the fact that they have had a very limited chance to become officers, even in those unions that have large minority group representations.

In recent years some unions have been making a more aggressive effort to recruit women members. As a result of such recruiting efforts, women now comprise at least half of the members in 26 unions. Their membership in U.S. unions totals about 5.2 million (another 1.6 million are members of employee associations). In spite of the growth in their union membership, female representation on union governing boards still lags. Even though women constitute 24.2 percent of the union membership, only 7.2 percent of union board members are women.[22] Because of this situation women members from at least 58 international unions have organized the Coalition of Labor Union Women (CLUW) to push more aggressively for a larger role in labor affairs, higher wages, and improved working conditions for female workers.[23]

Coping with Economic Adversities

Economic adversities in the form of inflation, deflation, and foreign competition can create problems that are as serious for unions as they are for employers. These adversities affect union leaders in their relations with both union members and employers.

Problems of Inflation.

A major impact of inflation is the pressure from members to gain pay increases to offset their ever-increasing costs of living. Union leaders at the same time must seek increases in dues from these members to offset rises in operating costs. This task can prove to be extremely difficult and can force reductions in the size of union staffs and expenditures. Some unions, to their advantage, have been able to remove the structure of union dues from the political arena by tying it to a formula based upon the pay raises of their members. A formula developed by the Oil, Chemical and Atomic Workers International, for example, provides that union

21. "New Stress on Old Solidarity," *Business Week* (May 30, 1977).
22. *Directory of National Unions and Employee Associations, op. cit.*, p. 66.
23. "Women Push for Union Power," *Business Week* (March 10, 1974), p. 102.

dues increase one penny per month each time the pay of its members increases by one penny per hour.[24]

Problems of Deflation.   Efforts to control excessive inflation inevitably produce the seeds of deflation and recession which, in turn, lead to layoffs and the loss of union membership. Particularly hard hit during the recession of the early 1980s were the unions representing workers in the auto, rubber, steel, and other manufacturing industries. The loss of revenue from union dues resulting from a decline in membership forced these unions to curb their activism. It also weakened severely their economic power to bargain aggressively with employers.

Competition from Foreign Labor.   Since the mid-1960s, there has been an increase in the importation of steel, consumer electronics, autos, wearing apparel, textiles, and shoes, with a corresponding loss of jobs in the United States for workers who produce these products.[25] Foreign subsidiaries of American corporations producing some of these goods have been accused by labor unions of "exporting the jobs of American workers." Unfortunately workers in the labor-intensive industries, which have been the hardest hit by foreign competition, often have been middle-aged and either women or minorities, or both. These individuals cannot be easily retrained, reshuffled, and reslotted.[26] As a result of these unfavorable conditions, unions are demanding more government protection against foreign imports. Such protection, however, is likely to create higher prices for the American consumer who is having enough difficulty trying to "make ends meet" and therefore is not likely to be very receptive to these union demands.

Declining Public Image of Labor

In addition to economic problems, organized labor also has suffered a decline in its public image. During inflationary periods, labor critics cite large wage increases gained by labor unions as a major factor contributing to inflation. They claim that these increases help to drive American products out of the foreign and domestic markets. The opinion also exists that some unions have become too powerful with respect to their political influence. Furthermore, resentment toward strikes by public employee unions has affected the image of all labor unions. The failure of those unions representing higher-paid jobs to recruit women and minorities into their ranks has weakened the support for organized labor from these groups. Publicized instances of corruption and racketeering of which some labor leaders have been found guilty also have generated unfavorable public reaction toward labor as a whole.

Recognizing their unfavorable rating in opinion polls, the AFL-CIO and some unaffiliated national unions have begun a counteroffensive to improve it. Part of this offensive has been directed toward the news media—particularly television. Charges

---

24. "Union Managers Feel Inflation's Pinch, Too," *Business Week* (July 30, 1970). pp. 28–29.
25. Irwin Ross, "Labor's Big Push for Protection," *Fortune* (March, 1973), p. 94.
26. *Ibid*.

have been made that news about union members and their activities is often presented in a negative vein. One union official, for example, complained that "The blue-collar worker is always a guy who can't pronounce his words right, and his wife is always 75 to 80 pounds overweight with curlers in her hair."[27] The offensive against television also has included monitoring prime-time shows for what are considered to be glaring inequities. Such inequities include portraying the American business leader as the "pillar of the community" and the blue-collar worker as a "selfish, bigoted, almost illiterate person."[28]

Unfortunately for labor, the threat of advertising their boycotts and letters of complaint to the Federal Communication Commission in protest of television coverage sometimes can prove to be counterproductive. An approach more likely to produce positive results is one taken by the International Ladies' Garment Workers' Union and several other unions. This approach involves purchasing advertising time on television to get the union's message across. The message stresses that union members are people just like those viewing the program—people who are trying to earn a living and raise a family and with whom the viewers can identify.

Overcoming Slow Rate of Growth

A major challenge confronting organized labor has been that of maintaining a satisfactory growth rate. The magnitude of the problem is shown in Figures 14–3 and 14–4, which illustrate how the growth rate of union membership has leveled off in terms of total numbers and percentage of the total labor force. This trend reflects, in part, the failure of unions to draw membership from among the white-collar ranks where the labor force is growing most rapidly.

Efforts to Unionize White-Collar Employees.

Traditionally white-collar employees tended to identify themselves with owners or managers and to perform similar work activities in proximity with them. As a group they enjoyed certain privileges (such as not being required to punch a time clock) and socioeconomic status which blue-collar workers did not possess. Those improvements for which union members in the shop have had to make sacrifices generally have been extended to the white-collar group. The high turnover rate of employees in clerical jobs also increased the difficulty of organizing them. For these reasons and the fact that any union drives to organize white-collar employees were not attuned psychologically to the latter's needs and thinking, white-collar employees have been slow to unionize. However, in recent years, growth in the size of private enterprises has tended to impersonalize the work of white-collar groups and to isolate them from management. The lack of white-collar job security during layoffs, together with growing difficulties in attempting to resolve grievances, have helped to push them toward unionization.

Unions at the same time are attempting to increase their appeal to white-collar workers. Some industrial unions have established special departments for white-collar

---

27. "How Unions Try to Clean Up Their Image," *U.S. News & World Report* (October 22, 1979), p. 69.

28. *Ibid.*, p. 70.

Figure 14–3 **Membership of National Unions, 1930–1978**

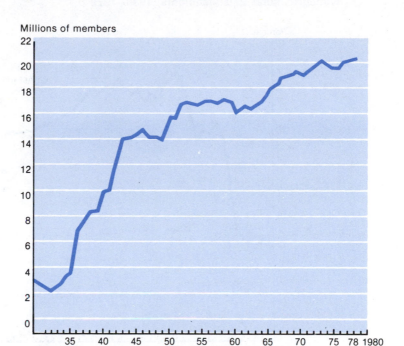

Millions of members

Excludes Canadian membership but includes members in other areas outside the United States. Members of AFL-CIO directly affiliated local unions are also included. Members of single-firm and local unaffiliated unions are excluded. For the years 1948-52, midpoints of membership estimates, which were expressed as ranges, were used.

SOURCE: *Directory of National Unions and Employee Associations,* Bureau of Labor Statistics, 1979, p. 58.

workers and are hiring college graduates as organizers. Industrial unions, such as the United Auto Workers and United Steel Workers, are redoubling their efforts to organize employees in the offices of those companies where they already represent blue-collar workers.[29] The mass layoff of white-collar employees in the auto industry has made this group much more receptive to unionization. In fact, requests have been made to the United Auto Workers by some of these employees for assistance in organizing.[30] These and other events have served to increase union optimism regarding the possibility of expanding their white-collar membership.

29. "Unions Woo Office Workers in Earnest," *U.S. News & World Report* (April 13, 1981), p. 74.
30. Amanda Bennett, "Salaried Staff at G.M. Flirts with Unions," *The Wall Street Journal,* May 17, 1982, p. 29.

Figure 14–4 **Union Membership as a Percent of Total Labor Force and of Employees in Nonagricultural Establishments, 1930–1978**

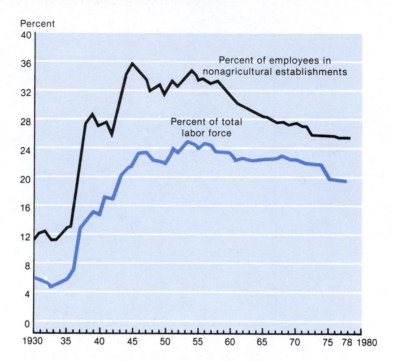

Excludes Canadian membership. Total labor force includes employed and unemployed workers, self-employed, members of the Armed Forces, etc. Employment in nonagricultural establishments excludes the Armed Forces, self-employed, as well as the unemployed, agricultural workers, proprietors, unpaid family workers, and domestic servants.

SOURCE: *Directory of National Unions and Employee Associations*, Bureau of Labor Statistics, 1979, p. 62.

Efforts to Unionize Professional Employees. The professional employees have been receiving greater attention as the result of strikes being conducted by teachers, engineers, nurses, and other professional groups. Unionization and strikes by those groups traditionally have been regarded as being incompatible with their professional status. Professionalism has been associated with such prestigious occupations as law and medicine, whereas unionism has been associated with manual occupations. However, the fact that members of professional groups increasingly are becoming employees rather than being self-employed makes it necessary for them to bargain with employers over the conditions of their employment.[31] Their lack of success in

31. Archie Kleingartner, "Professionalism and Engineering Unionism," *Industrial Relations*, Vol. 8, No. 3 (May, 1969), pp. 225–226. *See also* Dennis Chamot, "Professional Employees Turn to Unions," *Harvard Business Review*, Vol. 54, No. 3 (May–June, 1976), pp. 119–126.

bargaining individually often has forced them to seek collective action either by unionizing or by encouraging their professional societies to become their bargaining agents. As a result of these developments, unions and professional societies often find themselves competing with each other for members.

RÉSUMÉ

In our society the right of employees to organize and bargain collectively over conditions of employment is well established. While some employees may join because they are required to do so, most belong to unions because they are convinced it helps them to satisfy various economic and psychological needs.

In order to gain recognition and serve as the bargaining agent for an employer's personnel, unions often must recruit aggressively. This effort may encounter strong resistance from employers whose position is likely to be stronger if they have been treating their employees in a consistent and equitable manner.

Most local unions with whom members have direct contact operate under a charter granted by the national organization. The majority of these national organizations in turn are affiliated with the AFL-CIO. While the bargaining strength of a particular union is affected considerably by the size of its membership and treasury resources, it also is affected by the caliber of its leaders. Good management and leadership is as important to a union as it is to a business organization. Therefore, union leaders must be skillful in administration, leadership, and politics if they are to remain in their elected offices.

Much of the current power of unions has been gained as the result of the Wagner Act, which has helped to protect and encourage union organizing and bargaining activities. In more recent years the passage of the Taft-Hartley and the Landrum-Griffin Acts has served to establish certain controls over the internal affairs of unions and their relations with employers.

Union leaders today are confronted with numerous problems. Many of their unions are suffering from a decline in membership. To rectify this situation union leaders are trying to recruit members in white-collar, professional, and government employment. The changing nature of the membership, furthermore, has created demands by women, minorities, and younger members to have their particular interests served more effectively. Such demands require that these groups be given a greater role in union administration. Also required are leadership practices that are more attuned to the current environment.

TERMS TO IDENTIFY

craft unions
industrial unions
employee associations
union shop
bargaining unit
consent election
formal election

runoff election
management prerogatives
national union
business representative
union steward
district committeeman
trusteeship

Discussion Questions

1. How is the management of its human resources likely to be affected by the unionization of an organization's employees?
2. Contrast the arguments concerning union membership that are likely to be presented by the union with those presented by the employer.
3. What are the functions of the national union and of the local union?
4. Under the provisions of the Taft-Hartley Act, which unfair practices apply to both unions and employers?
5. What are some of the actions being taken by unions to cope with some of the contemporary challenges confronting them?
6. Describe the possible effects of inflation and deflation upon the operation of a union.
7. Why have attitudes toward organized labor on the part of certain segments of our society tended to become less favorable than they were in the past?

PROBLEM 14–1

GETTING TOGETHER

The Apollo Corporation is a large diversified manufacturing company producing a variety of industrial and consumer products. It has a national agreement with the Brotherhood of Metalworkers, which is augmented by agreements with the local unions representing the employees in its various assembly plants. In some of its plants, relations with the local unions are fairly good; in others, it has taken more than a year for an agreement with the local union to be worked out after an agreement with the national union has been reached. In an effort to improve union-management relations at its assembly plants, the corporate industrial relations department embarked upon a program to encourage plant managements to meet with local union officers and seek ways to reduce any adversary conditions that might exist between the union and management. In some of the plants, the informal meetings that were held periodically between union and management representatives did much to reduce hostilities and to develop better understanding between the two groups.

The leaders of the local union at the Continental Division assembly plant agreed that such meetings might prove to be mutually beneficial and asked the plant management to proceed with arrangements for the first meeting. The plant manager suggested that the first meeting be held on neutral grounds at one of the large motels and be accompanied by an informal luncheon and a social hour at the end of the meeting. However, the union leaders objected on the grounds that some union members might view these arrangements unfavorably since the union officers would be getting together with management in rather luxurious surroundings. Some of their more militant members might even accuse these officers of being "bought off" by management. The union leaders offered a counterproposal that the meetings be conducted at the plant. Management objected on the grounds that there were no adequate facilities available there. Furthermore, management felt that phone calls and plant noise might interfere with the conduct of the meeting.

The management then proposed that the meetings take place at the union hall where there were adequate facilities. Some of the union officers objected on the grounds that it might not look good to some members for the union to be playing host to management at the union headquarters. After being unable for the third time to agree on a site for the meeting, interest in having the meeting appeared to lag. As a result, it was never held.

a. How do you explain the inability of the two parties to agree upon a place to hold a meeting designed to reduce the adversary relationship between them? Is the choice of a meeting place such a big problem?

b. What should the management of the Continental Division plant attempt to do in complying with the request from corporate headquarters to improve union-management relations in their plant?

SUGGESTED READINGS

Chruden, Herbert J., and Arthur W. Sherman, Jr. *Readings in Managing Human Resources* , 6th ed. Cincinnati: South-Western Publishing Co., 1984. Part 5.

Foulkes, Fred K. *Personnel Policies in Large Non-Union Companies* . Englewood Cliffs, NJ: Prentice-Hall, Inc., 1980.

Gregory, Charles O., and Harold A. Katz. *Labor and the Law* , 3d ed. New York: W. W. Norton & Company, 1979.

Kilgour, John G. *Preventative Labor Relations* . New York: American Management Associations, 1981.

Serrin, William. *The Company and the Union* . New York: Alfred A. Knopf, 1973.

Sloane, Arthur A., and Fred Witney. *Labor Relations*, 3d ed. Englewood Cliffs, NJ: Prentice-Hall, Inc., 1977.

Stanley, David T. *Managing Local Government under Union Pressure*. Washington, DC: The Brookings Institution, 1972.

Stieber, Jack. *Public Employee Unionism: Structure, Growth, Policy*. Washington, DC: The Brookings Institution, 1973.

U.S. Department of Labor, Bureau of Labor Statistics. *A Brief History of the American Labor Movement*, Bulletin 1000. Washington, DC: Superintendent of Documents, 1976.

Chapter Objectives:

- To understand the bargaining process and the bargaining goals and strategies of the union and the employer.
- To describe the forms of bargaining power that the union and the employer may utilize to enforce their bargaining demands.
- To cite the principal methods by which bargaining deadlocks may be resolved.
- To give examples of the current collective bargaining trends occurring within industry and the reasons for these trends.
- To recognize the principal differences that exist between collective bargaining in the private sector and in the public sector.
- To identify the typical provisions of a labor agreement and the forms of security it may provide for the union.

15

Collective Bargaining and the Labor Agreement

A major function of labor organizations is to bargain collectively for union members over conditions of employment. This bargaining process involves reconciling the inevitable differences between the union and the employer concerning these conditions. The labor agreement that ultimately is negotiated establishes the wages, hours, employee benefits, job security, and other conditions under which union members agree to work.

This chapter is concerned with the process by which an agreement is reached between labor and management. It is concerned also with the changes that are occurring in the bargaining relationship as it has evolved from an adversary to a more cooperative one. Even under cooperative conditions, however, collective bargaining requires negotiators to possess special skills and knowledge if they are to represent their parties successfully.

Negotiators for the union must be able to produce a labor agreement for members that is acceptable to them. The employer's negotiators, on the other hand, must come up with an agreement that will allow the company to remain competitive. It also must be an agreement that can be administered with a minimum of conflict and that can facilitate the management of human resources.

THE BARGAINING PROCESS

Once a union has been recognized as the representative for employees within a bargaining unit, the employer is obligated to negotiate in good faith with the union's representative over conditions of employment. Good faith requires the employer's representatives to meet with their union counterparts at a reasonable time and place to discuss these conditions. It requires also that the proposals submitted by each party be realistic in nature. In discussing the other party's proposals, each side must offer reasonable counterproposals for those it is unwilling to accept. Finally, both parties must sign the written document containing the agreement reached through negotiations.

As Barbash points out, however, negotiation is only a part of the **collective bargaining** process.[1] Collective bargaining also may include the use of economic pressures in the form of strikes and boycotts by the union. Lockouts, plant closures, and the replacement of strikers constitute similar pressures by the employer. In addition, either or both parties may seek support from the general public or from the courts as a means of pressuring the opposing side.

Preparing for Negotiations

Preparing for negotiations includes planning the strategy and assembling data to support bargaining proposals. This will permit collective bargaining to be conducted on a more orderly, factual, and positive basis with a greater likelihood of achieving desired goals. Assuming that the labor agreement is not the first to be

---

1. Jack Barbash, "Collective Bargaining and the Theory of Conflict," *Industrial Relations*, Vol. 34, No. 4 (1979), p. 647.

negotiated by the parties, preparation for negotiations ideally should start soon after the previous agreement has been signed. Such practice will allow negotiators to review and diagnose mistakes and weaknesses evidenced during the preceding negotiations while the experience is still current in their minds.

Sources to Consult.

Internal data relating to grievances, disciplinary actions, transfers and promotions, layoffs, overtime, individual performance, and wage payments are useful in formulating and supporting the employer's bargaining position. The supervisors and executives who must live with and administer the labor agreement can be very important sources of ideas and suggestions concerning changes that are needed in the agreement. Their contact with union members and representatives provides them with a firsthand knowledge of the changes in the agreement that union negotiators are likely to propose. Data on general economic conditions, cost of living trends, and the profit outlook can help to support the employer's position during negotiation.

Bargaining Patterns.

When unions negotiate provisions covering wages and other benefits, they generally seek to achieve increases at least equal to those provided in other agreements existing within the industry or region. Employers quite naturally try to minimize these increases by citing other employers who are paying lower wages and benefits. Other negotiated labor agreements can establish a pattern which one side or the other may seek to follow if it is advantageous to do so in support of their bargaining position. This practice is known as **pattern bargaining**. In preparing for negotiations, therefore, it is essential for both the union and the employer to be fully aware of established bargaining patterns within the area or the industry that may be introduced to support a bargaining position.

Bargaining Strategies.

Negotiators for the employer should develop a plan covering their bargaining strategy. This plan should consider the proposals that the union is likely to submit, based on the most recent agreements with other employers and the demands that remain unsatisfied from previous negotiations. The plan should also consider the goals that the union is striving to achieve and the extent to which it may be willing to make concessions or to resort to strike action in order to achieve these goals.

The employer's negotiators will be better able to adhere to their planned course of action if their positions are carefully prepared as a written document. In some bargaining situations the union and the employer will exchange such documents in advance of actual negotiation. Even when this is not the case, the process of reducing proposals to written form can help an employer's negotiating team to identify the relative importance of each proposal and the chances of realizing each of them.[2]

Certain elements of strategy are common to both the employer and the union. Generally, the initial demands presented by each side are greater than those that it

---

2. Frank P. Doyle, "When It's Your First Time to Negotiate with Labor," *Administrative Management*, Vol. 34, No. 2 (February, 1973), pp. 20–22, 90.

actually may hope to achieve so as to provide room for concessions. Each party, furthermore, usually will avoid giving up the maximum that it is capable of conceding in order to allow for further concessions, should this become necessary in order to break a bargaining deadlock.

Union strategy sometimes may include making **bridgehead proposals.** These proposals are aimed at gaining *new* concessions from the employer by establishing a precedent upon which the union can expand in future agreements. A bridgehead proposal might also constitute a major breakthrough in a labor agreement that establishes a precedent for other employers to grant. The labor agreement granting the United Auto Workers (UAW) the right to have a member on the board of the Chrysler Corporation, for example, represents such a breakthrough. This may well establish a precedent that the UAW will seek to extend to other companies in the auto industry.

Conducting the Negotiations

The conditions under which negotiations take place, the experience and personalities of the participants on each side, the goals they are seeking to achieve, and the strength of their relative positions are among the factors that tend to make each bargaining situation unique. Some labor agreements can be negotiated informally within a matter of a few hours, particularly if the terms are based upon the pattern that has been established by the industry. Other agreements, however, may require months of negotiation before a final settlement can be reached.

Many negotiators, over a period of time, acquire the ability "to read their opponents' minds" and to anticipate their actions and reactions. Inexperienced negotiators bargaining together for the first time, on the other hand, may misinterpret actions and statements of their opponents. As a result, they may precipitate a deadlock unintentionally. Furthermore, those who lack experience may be unaware of the rules, rituals, and steps to be followed to keep negotiations moving toward their intended objectives.

Opening the Negotiations.

The initial meeting of the bargaining teams is a particularly important one because it may establish the climate that will prevail during the ensuing negotiations. A cordial attitude with perhaps the injection of a little humor can contribute much to a relaxation of tensions and help the negotiations to begin smoothly. The first meeting usually is devoted to establishing the bargaining authority possessed by the representatives of each side and to determining the rules and procedures to be used during negotiations. If the parties have not submitted their proposals in advance, these may be exchanged and clarified at this time.

It is particularly advisable for the employer's negotiators to request their union counterparts to explain fully each proposal and their reasons for seeking it. The union's responses may help to reveal both the amount of thought devoted to each proposal and the importance attached to it, thereby enabling the employer's negotiators to deal with them accordingly.

Analyzing the Proposals.   The negotiation of a labor agreement can have certain of the characteristics of a poker game in which each side attempts to determine its opponent's position while not revealing its own. Each party normally will try to avoid disclosing the relative importance that it attaches to a proposal in order that it will not be forced to pay a higher price than is necessary to have the proposal accepted. Thus, as in the case of sellers who will try to get a higher price for their products if they think the prospective buyer strongly desires them, negotiators will try to get greater concessions in return for granting those their opponents want most.

The proposals that each side submits generally may be divided into those that it feels it must achieve, those that it would like to achieve but on which it will compromise, and those that it is submitting primarily for trading purposes. Proposals that are submitted for trading purposes, however, must be realistic in terms of the opponent's ability and willingness to concede them. Unrealistic proposals may serve only to antagonize the opponent and can precipitate a deadlock. Unrealistic demands, as one author emphasizes, "can have a nasty way of becoming real issues."[3]

The proposals may be discussed in the order of their appearance in the agreement or in some other sequence. The sequence in which the proposals are to be discussed can in itself become a subject for collective bargaining since it can affect bargaining results for either or both sides. If the discussion of the more important proposals can be deferred until the last, these proposals may serve as leverage for gaining agreement on proposals of lesser importance which precede them. Since union members are more willing to strike over major issues than over minor ones, the union is likely to want issues of major importance to it placed near the end of the bargaining agenda.

Resolving the Proposals.   The proposals submitted, regardless of the degree of importance that is attached to them, must be disposed of if an agreement is to be consummated. These proposals may be withdrawn, or they may be accepted by the other side in their entirety or in some compromise form.

In order for each bargaining issue to be resolved satisfactorily, the point at which agreement is reached must be within limits that the union and the employer are willing to concede. Stagner and Rosen call the area within these two limits the **bargaining zone.** In some bargaining situations, such as the one illustrated in Figure 5–1, the solution desired by one party may exceed the tolerance limit of the other party. Thus, that solution is outside of the bargaining zone. If that party refuses to modify its demands sufficiently to bring them within the bargaining zone or if the opposing party refuses to extend its tolerance limit to accommodate the demands of the other party, a bargaining deadlock will result.[4]

The Union's Power in Collective Bargaining

During negotiations, it is necessary for each party to retreat sufficiently from its original position to permit an agreement to be achieved. If this does not occur, the

---

3. *Ibid.*, p. 22.
4. Ross Stagner and Hjalmar Rosen, *Psychology of Union-Management Relations* (Belmont, CA: Wadsworth Publishing Company, Inc., 1965), pp. 95–97.

Figure 15–1 Tolerance Limits That Determine the Bargaining Zone

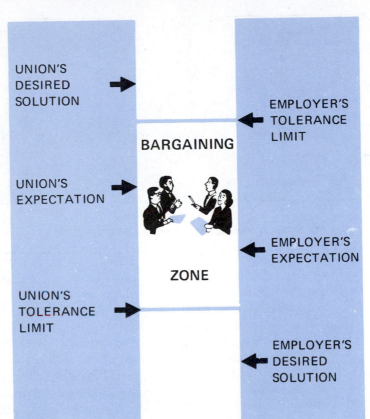

SOURCE: Ross Stagner and Hjalmar Rosen, *Psychology of Union-Management Relations* (Belmont, CA: Wadsworth Publishing Company, Inc., 1965), p. 96. Reproduced with permission.

negotiations will become deadlocked. This situation may force the union to resort to the use of economic power to achieve its demands. Otherwise its only alternative will be to have members continue working without a labor agreement once the old one has expired. The economic power of the union may be exercised by striking, picketing, or boycotting the employer's products and encouraging others to do likewise. The ability to engage or even threaten to engage in such activities also can serve as a form of pressure.

Striking the Employer. A **strike** is the refusal of a group of employees to perform their jobs. Figure 15–2 shows the prevalence of strikes in the United States as indicated by the number of work stoppages that occurred each month between

Figure 15–2 **Number of Work Stoppages by Month, 1976-1980**

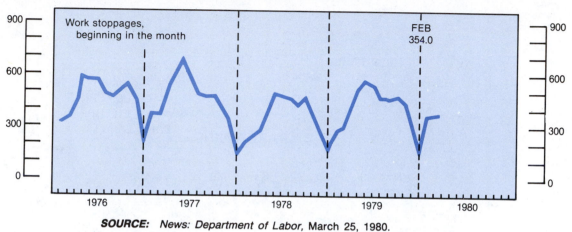

SOURCE: *News: Department of Labor,* March 25, 1980.

1976 and 1980. Notice from this figure that work stoppages tend to peak during the summer. This is a time when strikers are most likely to find other temporary employment or "go fishing." On the other hand, these stoppages reach their low during the holiday season when both the physical and psychological climates cause union members to be less inclined to want to "hit the bricks."

Since a strike can have serious effects upon the union and its members, the prospects for its success must be analyzed carefully by the union. It is most important for the union to estimate the members' willingness to endure the personal hardships resulting from a strike, particularly if it proves to be a long one. Also of critical importance is the extent, if any, to which the employer will be able to continue operating through the use of supervisory and nonstriking personnel and employees hired to replace the strikers. The greater the ability of the employer to continue operating, the less will be the union's chances for gaining the demands it is attempting to enforce through the strike. Failure to achieve such a desired settlement can result in the employees voting either the union officers out of office or the union out of the organization. Other factors the union must consider are the effects that losing a strike may have upon future relations with the employer. The degree of support the union may expect from the public and the likelihood of government intervention also must be considered by the union.

Unions usually will seek strike authorization from their members to use as a bargaining ploy to gain concessions that will make a strike unnecessary. A strike vote by the members does not mean they actually want or expect to go out on strike. Rather, it is intended as a vote of confidence to strengthen the position of their leaders at the bargaining table.

Picketing the Employer.   When a union goes on strike, it will **picket** the employer by placing persons at plant entrances to advertise the dispute and to discourage persons from entering or leaving the premises. Even when the strikers represent only a small proportion of the employees within the plant, they can cause the shutdown of an entire plant if a sufficient number of the plant's employees refuse to cross their picket line. Also, a picket line may serve to prevent trucks and railcars from entering the plant to deliver and pick up goods.

Picketing carried on by nonemployees is called **stranger picketing**, and it is sometimes used by unions in an effort to unionize an employer. Because peaceful picketing has traditionally been regarded as a form of free speech, the courts have been reluctant to curb it even when it has been used unfairly. If a strike fails to stop an employer's operations, the picket line may serve as more than a passive weapon. Employees who attempt to cross the line may be subjected to verbal insults and even physical violence. **Mass picketing** in which large groups of pickets try to block the path of people attempting to enter a plant may also be used. However, the use of picket lines to exert physical pressure and to incite violence may harm more than help the union cause.

Boycotting the Employer.   Another economic weapon of unions is the **boycott**, which is a refusal to patronize the employer. This action can hurt an employer if conducted by a large enough segment of organized labor. In contrast to a strike, a boycott may not end completely with the end of the dispute. Many former customers may have developed either a bias against the employer's products or a change in buying habits during the boycott that are not easily reversed. Most unions levy heavy fines against members if they are discovered patronizing an employer who is the subject of a union boycott. The refusal of a union to allow its members to patronize a business enterprise where there is a labor dispute is a **primary boycott**. This type of boycott under most circumstances is legal. A union may go a step further, however, and attempt to induce third parties, primarily suppliers and customers, to refrain from business dealings with the employer with whom it has a dispute. A boycott of this type is called a **secondary boycott** and generally is illegal under the Taft-Hartley Act.

Since the United Farm Workers are not covered by the Taft-Hartley Act, they have been able, with varying degrees of success, to utilize the secondary boycott by restricting the sale of lettuce, grapes, or wines produced by growers from whom the union is attempting to gain recognition. In one court decision it was ruled that the use of pickets at a store to discourage the purchase of a particular product (in this instance Washington State apples) did not constitute a secondary boycott. The court held that the union was merely urging customers to refrain from purchasing apples rather than from patronizing the store.[5]

The Employer's Power in Collective Bargaining

A major source of employer power lies in the freedom to determine the use of capital within the enterprise. This freedom enables an employer to close a plant or

---

5. *NLRB v. Fruit and Vegetable Packers, Local 760*, Supreme Court of the United States, 1964, 377 U.S. 58, 84, S.Ct. 1063, 12L Ed. 2d 129.

certain operations within it. The employer also can transfer these operations to other locations or to subcontract them to other employers through what is being called **outsourcing**. In exercising their economic freedom, however, employers must be careful that their actions are not interpreted by the NLRB to be an attempt to avoid bargaining with the union—which is an unfair labor practice.

Operating During Strikes. When negotiations become deadlocked, typically it is the union that initiates action and the employer that reacts. In reacting, employers must weigh the cost of taking a strike against the long- and short-term costs of acceding to union demands. They also must consider the effects that either course of action may have on union demands in negotiating future agreements. The extent to which employers will be forced to close operations and the length of time that they and the unions will be able to endure a strike also must be considered. An employer who chooses to accept a strike must then decide whether or not to continue operating if it is possible to do so. According to a study by Hutchinson, some of the advantages of continuing to operate were found to be the following:

1. Unions were taught a lesson and the prestige of their leaders was lowered.
2. Managers learned things about their operations that they had not known before the strike.
3. Terms more favorable to the company were gained as a result of the strike.
4. Cost reduction and efficiency improvement initiated during the strike continued after it ended.
5. Vital services were continued during the strike.

Hutchinson reported that the disadvantages of operating during the strike are:

1. Loss of orders and revenues during (or before or after) the strike.
2. Bitterness between nonstrikers and strikers resulting during and after the strike.
3. Public relations image suffered.
4. Strike created long-term bitterness that might affect future negotiations.
5. Property damage and/or personal injuries were caused by the strike.[6]

Using the Lockout. A **lockout** occurs when the employer takes the initiative by ceasing to operate. The lockout generally is initiated when one or more members of an employer association have been struck by the union. It is invoked on the premise that "a strike against one is a strike against all." Lockouts also may be used by employers to combat union slowdowns, damage to their property, or violence within their plant that may occur in connection with a labor dispute even though a strike may not be in progress. Employers, however, are reluctant to resort to a lockout because of the loss of revenue during the shutdown and because of their fear that such action might generate unfavorable public opinion. Depending upon the circumstances, the NLRB may also rule that the lockout constitutes the unfair labor practice of refusing to bargain.

---

6. John G. Hutchinson, *Management Under Strike Conditions* (New York: Holt, Rinehart, and Winston, Inc., 1966), pp. 29, 34.

Resolving Bargaining Deadlocks

When a strike or a lockout occurs, both parties soon are affected by it. The employer will suffer a loss of profits and customers, and possibly public goodwill. The union members will suffer a loss of income that is likely to be only partially offset by strike benefits or outside income. The union's leaders risk the possibility of losing members, of being voted out of office, and of losing public goodwill. They also risk the possibility of having the members vote to decertify the union as their bargaining agent. As the losses to each side mount, the participants usually become more anxious to achieve a settlement.

Mediation and Arbitration.   When the two parties are unable to resolve a deadlock, a third party serving in the capacity of either a mediator or an arbitrator may be called upon to provide assistance. A **mediator** establishes a channel of communication between them. Typically, the mediator meets with one party and then the other in order to suggest compromise solutions or to exact concessions from each side that will lead to an agreement without causing either to suffer loss of face. An **arbitrator**, on the other hand, assumes the role of a judge or umpire and determines what the settlement between the two parties should be. Generally one or both parties are reluctant to give a third party the power to make the settlement for them. Consequently, a mediator typically is used to break a deadlock and assist the parties in reaching an agreement. An arbitrator generally is called upon to resolve disputes arising in connection with the administration of the agreement.

Government Intervention.   In some situations deadlocks may have to be resolved directly or indirectly as the result of government intervention, particularly if the work stoppage is a threat to the national security or to the public welfare. Government intervention may include plant seizure or the threat of seizure, the issuance of injunctions, or the cancellation of government contracts. Government pressure also may be exerted through the appointment of a **fact-finding board** to investigate a bargaining deadlock. Although these boards do not have power to force the parties to reach a settlement, they do provide additional information that can serve to fix the responsibility for the deadlock. The influence of this information upon public opinion can place one or both parties under considerable pressure to make the concessions necessary to reach an agreement.

TRENDS IN COLLECTIVE BARGAINING

Inflation, deflation, and recession have all had their impact upon labor-management relations. These economic conditions have affected the attitudes and objectives of both employers and unions in collective bargaining. These conditions also have influenced the climate in which the bargaining must occur and the bargaining power each is able to exercise.

Changes in Collective Bargaining Relationships

Traditionally the collective bargaining relationship between the employer and the union has been an adversary one. The union has held the position that, while the employer has the responsibility for managing the enterprise, the union has the right to challenge certain actions of management. Unions also have taken the position that the employer has an obligation to operate the enterprise in a manner that will provide adquate compensation to employees. Furthermore, unions maintain that their members should not be expected to subsidize poor management by accepting less than their full entitlement.

Most unions have been sufficiently enlightened to recognize the danger of making bargaining demands that will bankrupt the employer. However, this fact has not stopped them from bargaining for what they consider to be a fair slice of the "profit pie." By pursuing the precedent established by Samuel Gompers, the founder of the AFL, the goal of organized labor has been to bargain for "more." However, mass layoffs caused by recessions and foreign competition can force both sides to change past bargaining goals and tactics.

Greater Union-Management Cooperation. "This was a tough union town," stated the president of a company in Jamestown, New York. "When I first came here, their definition of labor-management cooperation was that the president of the union and the president of the company could talk to each other without insulting each other's mothers."[7] The preceding statement rather typifies the concept of cooperation that until recently prevailed in all too many union-management relationships. Letting unions have "more say" were fighting words to managers seeking to preserve their prerogatives.

The extent to which the attitudes of some managers are changing is reflected in a Harris Poll. Of those responding, a large proportion of the executives in heavily unionized companies expressed a preference for a cooperative rather than an adversary relationship. Recognizing that they are not going to get rid of the unions, these managers apparently have concluded that they might as well try to work with them. However, among executives in companies with fewer union members, a smaller proportion was opposed to maintaining an adversary relationship with the union. The majority of these executives were more willing to force concessions from the union, even to the point of eliminating the union.[8]

Improving union-management cooperation generally requires a restructuring of attitudes by both management and unions and, most important, by the union members. The crisis of survival has forced unions, their members, and management to make concessions at the bargaining table and to collaborate in solving problems on which survival is contingent. However, if cooperation is to continue after the crisis has passed, a more solid foundation for it must exist. This foundation requires an effective program for managing human resources. Figure 15–3 illustrates some of

---

7. Terry Kirkpatrick, "Management and Labor Join Same Team, Win," *The Sacramento Union,* October 5, 1980, p. 6.

8. "Management Split Over Labor Relations," *Business Week* (June 14, 1982), p. 19.

Figure 15–3 Relationship of Labor Relations to Other Personnel Functions

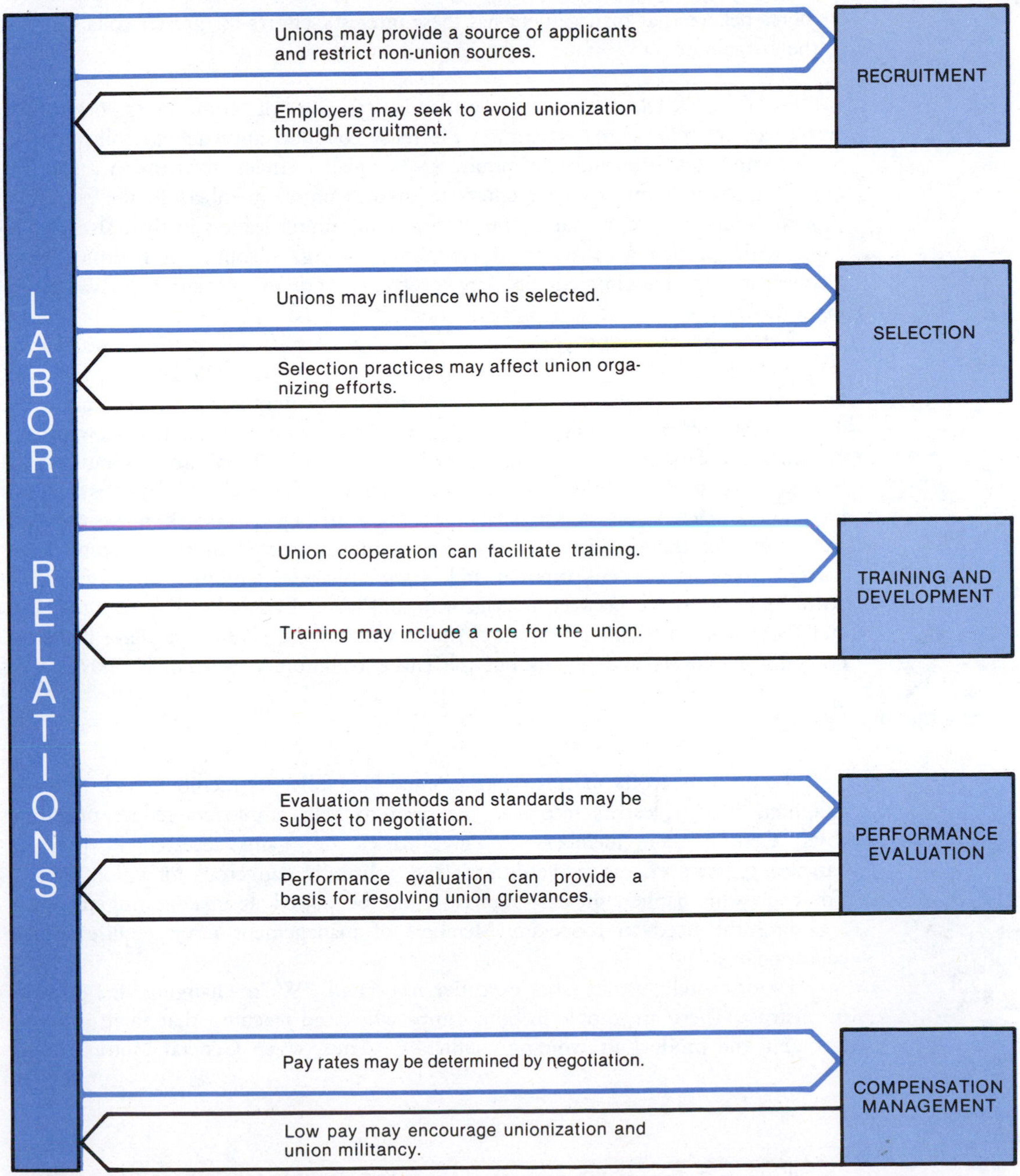

LABOR RELATIONS

Unions may provide a source of applicants and restrict non-union sources.

Employers may seek to avoid unionization through recruitment.

RECRUITMENT

Unions may influence who is selected.

Selection practices may affect union organizing efforts.

SELECTION

Union cooperation can facilitate training.

Training may include a role for the union.

TRAINING AND DEVELOPMENT

Evaluation methods and standards may be subject to negotiation.

Performance evaluation can provide a basis for resolving union grievances.

PERFORMANCE EVALUATION

Pay rates may be determined by negotiation.

Low pay may encourage unionization and union militancy.

COMPENSATION MANAGEMENT

the interrelationships that exist between labor relations and other personnel functions.

A foundation for cooperation requires also that union members be convinced that management is sincerely interested in their personal well-being. Unless union members believe that management has these interests, efforts for greater collaboration at the bargaining table stand to be rejected by them.

Forms of Collaboration.

Management's creation of committees on which employees are represented constitutes the most common approach to collaboration. Shop committees, department committees, and quality circles, to mention a few, are examples of union-management efforts to involve union members in the personnel program. Furthermore, managements are involving union leaders in their attempts to cope with problems such as absenteeism, loafing, alcohol, and drug abuse. Cooperation in handling disciplinary problems and in resolving grievances as expeditiously as possible can prove mutually beneficial.

Labor-management committees, which flourished for patriotic reasons to spur production during World War II, also are being revived. The Federal Mediation and Conciliation Service has assisted in establishing a number of these committees. The director of the National Association of Area Labor-Management Committees describes the function of such committees as follows: "They aren't some wooly-headed social scientist's model for a new industrial society. They're put together by hard-nosed, practical business and labor leaders, and they only work where there's a real reason for them to exist."[9] Reason enough has existed in those communities where strikes have been common and where misunderstandings and unfavorable attitudes have existed between management and labor. Evansville, IN, Scranton, PA, and Portsmouth, OH are examples of towns where these committees have benefited not only employers and unions but the entire community as well.[10]

Concessionary Bargaining

To prevent layoffs and plant closures and hopefully put members back to work, enlightened labor leaders recognize the need to help employers reduce operating costs. Getting their members to "give back" any gains received in previous bargaining, however, can prove difficult and politically dangerous for union officers. To reduce this danger, greater emphasis must be placed upon educating members regarding the need to cooperate. Members of management often require similar education.

Unfortunately, as one labor executive has stated, "We're changing after 30 years of mistrust. There are people in both camps who need teaching that there is a very favorable end product in avoiding conflict."[11]   Thus, when General Motors sought

---

9. Urban C. Lehner, "Committees of Labor and Management Enjoying Resurgence in Communities," *The Wall Street Journal,* August 8, 1979, p. 6.

10. *Ibid.*

11. "Detroit Gets a Break from UAW," *Business Week* (November 30, 1981), p. 94.

concessions from its workers in 1981, it had greater success in those plants where managers had been able to develop good labor relations. At the Ford Motor Company, management efforts to explain the concession package to plant employees rather than relying upon union leaders to do so has accounted for the surprisingly high percentage of local unions accepting the package.[12]

Concessions Sought by Employers.

Companies in the auto, steel, and other depressed industries have been seeking concessions before their agreements have expired. This represents a departure from traditional bargaining. Concessions sought by them usually are directed toward (1) putting a cap on rises in compensation and (2) increasing employee productivity.

To gain wage concessions, employers are offering **gains-sharing plans** which link compensation to productivity or sales. Profit sharing and stock ownership are other plans being offered to motivate employees and reward improvements in performance. Unfortunately for employers, job and income guarantees can in the long run increase costs, reduce flexibility, and divert funds from equipment to improve productivity.

The wage concessions granted by unions generally have involved the temporary freezing of **cost of living adjustments (COLA).** UAW locals representing General Motors workers, for example, agreed to the freezing of COLA increases for 18 months and to the elimination of personal holidays. Teamsters, to cite another example, agreed to the diversion of a portion of their COLA increases to help fund health benefit costs which were rising by 12 to 15 percent per year.[13] Union members, however, are likely to resist strongly any permanent elimination of COLA which they fought to acquire over the years.

Work rules are becoming particularly troublesome to companies because, in this age of technology, these rules soon can become obsolete and detrimental to productivity. Changes in these rules represent another area in which unions have been willing to make concessions. In a plant that produces engines, for example, the UAW agreed to let millwrights do the work of welders by combining these two job classifications. This concession cut $15 off the cost of each engine.

In some companies, such as those in the machine tool industries, machine-time allowances have become much too liberal. For example, in one company the workers needed to work only one-half day to meet production quotas. With half its member workers laid off, the union agreed to the tightening standards. "It got out of hand," admitted the union's negotiator.[14]

Reciprocal Concessions Sought by Unions.

In return for concessions they are granting to employers, unions are demanding provisions for greater job security. Provisions for such security will be a major union goal in future agreements to be negotiated by such unions as the Teamsters, Oil Workers, Rubber Workers, and Auto Workers. General Motors has agreed to a lifetime employment experiment covering 80 percent of its work force at four plants. It has agreed also to what is

---

12. *Ibid.,* p. 81.

13. "Labor Seeks Less," *Business Week* (December 12, 1981), p. 85.

14. "Can GM Change Its Work Rules?" *Business Week* (June 14, 1982), p. 69.

termed a "guaranteed income stream" to protect high-seniority workers threatened by layoff.

Unions also are likely to demand provisions in their agreements restricting the transfer of work, outsourcing (subcontracting), and plant closures by employers. Providing advance notice of shutdowns, as well as severance pay and transfer rights for displaced employees, will be high on the "want lists" of union negotiators. Unions also are likely to gain the right to be consulted on more decisions affecting the welfare of members. Increased participation of employees on advisory committees and greater emphasis upon QWL programs will become more common.

Decline in Pattern Bargaining

Unions are willing to grant concessions only when convinced of the necessity to do so. By recognizing the differences in the ability of each employer within an industry to provide the same employee benefits, unions are in effect abandoning their traditional reliance upon pattern bargaining. The pace-setting company within the industry or geographic area is less likely to provide the basis for a union's demand for similar concessions from other companies. Instead, the company's ability to pay and its need to improve productivity, is replacing the issues of wage comparability and cost of living for members when the union bargains over compensation.[15]

Growth of Collective Bargaining in the Public Sector

During the past two decades, unions and employee associations in the public sector have been actively recruiting new members. Their growth in size and political power has prompted them to demand the right of public employees to bargain and to strike over conditions of employment. As yet, however, collective bargaining at the federal level is restricted to certain issues. In those states listed in Figure 15–4, public employees are allowed to bargain collectively with certain restrictions. In other states, public employees may have the right only to "meet and confer" with representatives of management for the purpose of developing "memoranda of understanding."[16] Employees complain that this right grants them only the right to "meet and beg."

Political Foundation of Labor Relations in Government. Government employees are not able to negotiate with their employers on the same basis as their counterparts in private enterprise. Because of inherent differences that exist between the public and private sectors, it is doubtful that they will ever be able to do so. One of the significant differences is that labor relations in the private sector has an economic foundation, whereas in government its foundation is political. Since employers in the private sector must stay in business in order to sell their goods or services, their employees are not likely to make demands that could bankrupt the

---

15. "Moderation's Chance to Survive," *Business Week* (April 19, 1982), p. 123.

16. David T. Stanley, *Managing Local Goverment Under Union Pressure* (Washington, DC: The Brookings Institution, 1971), pp. 11–12.

Figure 15-4 States Permitting Public Employees to Bargain Collectively

Alabama	Idaho	Michigan	New York
Alaska	Illinois	Minnesota	North Dakota
Arizona	Indiana	Missouri	Oregon
California	Iowa	Montana	Pennsylvania
Colorado	Kansas	Nebraska	Rhode Island
Connecticut	Louisiana	Nevada	South Dakota
Delaware	Maine	New Hampshire	Vermont
Florida	Maryland	New Jersey	Washington
Hawaii	Massachusetts	New Mexico	Wisconsin

SOURCE: Reprinted by permission from *BNA Policy and Practice Series*, copyright 1982 by The Bureau of National Affairs, Inc., Washington, DC, pp. 87: 19-87: 20.

enterprise. When a strike occurs, it is a test of economic staying power in which the customer may have alternative sources of supply.

Governments, on the other hand, must stay in business because alternative services usually are not available. However, unions representing government employees are not reluctant to press for financial gains that will be paid by the public. Public employees exert influence not only as union members, but also as pressure groups and voting citizens.[17]

Problems Relating to Managerial Authority. Another difference between the public and private sectors is the source of management authority. In a private enterprise the authority flows downward from the board of directors and ultimately from the stockholders who elect them. Company management can resist union demands for greater participation in management on the grounds that it requires flexibility to achieve profit goals and to meet obligations to the board of directors and to the stockholders.

In the public sector, however, authority flows upward from the public at large to their elected representatives and to the appointed or elected managers. While the chief executive in a private enterprise commits the company to the labor agreement that has been negotiated, the chief executive of a government agency cannot do so. New revenues or changes in existing statutes are likely to be required to meet the new terms of the labor agreement. Such changes require legislative approval and, in some cases, ratification by the voters. Decisions by these managers are subject to public scrutiny and debate. Their performance is judged in part by their ability to stay within the budget, to prevent taxes from rising, and, if possible, to locate new sources of revenue that the majority of voters will not have to bear. Both the public and legislative bodies, furthermore, become involved in evaluating a public manager's performance. This can make the job of a public manager very difficult, particularly

17. "The Growing Threat of Public Employee Strikes," *Nation's Business,* Vol. 64, No. 9 (September, 1976), p. 68.

when the ability to resist union encroachment upon management decisions affecting public services may constitute a major criterion upon which the manager's performance is to be judged.[18]

Strikes in the Public Sector.   Strikes by government employees create a problem for lawmakers and for the general public. Because of the essential nature of the services that government employees provide, public policy is opposed to strikes by them. Most state legislatures have not granted them the right to strike. With few exceptions, court decisions relating to this issue have held that public employees have no right to strike in the absence of permissive legislation.[19] This position goes back to the concept of government sovereignty and "the right of kings" which holds that "government employees have only those rights given to them by their sovereign."[20] Public employee unions contend, however, that by denying them the same right to strike as that accorded employees in the private sector, their members are relegated to the role of second-class citizens.[21]

Despite the absence of any legal right to do so, public employees in practice do strike, and often with impunity. These strikes occur both in jurisdictions that permit collective bargaining and in those that do not. As a result, various possibilities are being explored for resolving collective bargaining deadlocks. One is **compulsory binding arbitration** for employees, such as police officers and firefighters, and similar jobs where strikes cannot be tolerated. A plan proposed in connection with such arbitration is the **final offer arbitration** in which the arbitrator has no power to compromise but must select one or other of the final offers submitted by the two parties.[22] This plan can serve to discourage one or both parties from avoiding concessions in hopes that they will come out ahead should the arbitrator make a settlement by "splitting the difference" between the two deadlocked positions. Instead, the arbitrator's award is more likely to go to the party that has moved the closest toward a reasonable position for a settlement.[23]

THE LABOR AGREEMENT

After an agreement has been reached through collective bargaining, it must be reduced to writing and signed by the representatives of both parties. This written

18. Archie Kleingartner, "Collective Bargaining Between Salaried Professionals and Public Sector Management," *Public Administration Review,* Vol. 33, No. 2 (March-April, 1973), p. 169.

19. Kenneth McClennan and Michael H. Moskow, "Public Education," *Emerging Sectors of Collective Bargaining,* edited by Seymour L. Wolbein (Morristown, NJ: General Learning Corporation, 1970), p. 252.

20. David T. Stanley and Carole L. Cooper, *Managing Local Government Under Union Pressure* (Washington, DC: The Brookings Institution, 1971), p. 17.

21. Robert Booth Fowler, "Normative Aspects of Public Employee Strikes," *Public Personnel Management,* Vol. 3, No. 2 (March-April, 1974), pp. 134–135.

22. Charles M. Rehmus, "Labor Relations in the Public Sector in the United States," *International Labour Review,* Vol. 109, No. 3 (March, 1974), p. 213.

23. Peter Feuille, "Final Offer Arbitration and the Chilling Effect," *Industrial Relations,* Vol. 14, No. 3 (October, 1975), pp. 304–305.

document, which typically tends to expand with each succeeding agreement, may vary from a few typewritten pages to a printed document well in excess of 100 pages, depending upon the size of the employer and the union that it covers. Figure 15–5 shows some of the subjects typically covered by a labor agreement.

Wording of the Agreement

The wording of the labor agreement can be very important in preventing difficulties from arising over its interpretation. The fact that the language of an agreement may be subject to different interpretations makes it essential that each provision be discussed thoroughly to insure that both parties agree upon its precise meaning. Prasow and Peters cite the following contract provision as an example of one that inevitably will be subject to differences in interpretation: "An employee who does not work the day before the holiday or the day after the holiday will not be paid for the holiday."[24] Depending upon the voice intonation patterns of the persons reciting this statement, some listeners will interpret it to mean that the employee need work only one day, either before or after the holiday, in order to qualify for holiday pay. Others will interpret the statement to mean that the

Figure 15–5 Articles of a Labor Agreement

ARTICLES

I. Union recognition	XVI. Posting
II. Union security	XVII. Notification and publicity
III. Working conditions	XVIII. Financial support
IV. Discrimination and coercion	XIX. Information
V. Working hours: straight time—overtime	XX. Traveling time and expenses
VI. Wage rates	XXI. Local understandings
VII. Holidays	XXII. Income extension aid
VIII. Continuity of service—service credits	XXIII. Military pay differential
IX. Vacations	XXIV. Retraining program
X. Transfers	XXV. Jury duty
XI. Reduction or increase in forces	XXVI. Absence for death in family
XII. Union and local representatives and stewards	XXVII. Sick and personal pay
XIII. Grievance procedure	XXVIII. Upgrading and job posting
XIV. Strikes and lockouts	XXIX. Responsibility of the parties
XV. Arbitration	XXX. Issues of general application
	XXXI. Duration of agreement
	XXXII. Modification and termination
	XXXIII. Notices

SOURCE: Agreement between the General Electric Company and Electrical Workers (IUE).

24. Paul Prasow and Edward Peters," "The Semantic Aspects of Collective Bargaining," *ETC: A Review of General Semantics*, Vol. 25, No. 3 (September, 1968), pp. 292–293.

employee must work both the day before and the day after the holiday in order to qualify for holiday pay. As a means of eliminating the ambiguity existing in the statement, therefore, it should read: "An employee who does not work *either* the day before the holiday or the day after the holiday, etc." or "An employee who does not work *both* the day before the holiday *and* the day after the holiday, etc."

When differences of opinion arise over the interpretation of a provision in the agreement, a solution may be achieved by going back and reviewing the minutes of the bargaining sessions pertaining to it to determine what the intent of the parties may have been when the provision was agreed upon. If the differences in the interpretation of a provision cannot be resolved, however, they may be submitted to an arbitrator whose interpretation becomes the binding one.

The Issue of Management Rights

Management rights pertain to those decisions governing conditions of employment over which management is able to exercise exclusive jurisdiction. Since virtually every management right can and has been challenged successfully by unions, the ultimate determination of these rights will depend upon the relative bargaining power of the two parties. Furthermore, in order to achieve union cooperation or concessions, employers have had to relinquish some of these time-honored rights. Allowing employees, through their committee assignments, the opportunity to participate in the decision-making process reduces the area in which management determination is exclusive. Giving unions the right to be consulted on changes affecting their members also correspondingly reduces management's rights in this area.

Reserved Rights.   In the labor agreement, management rights may be treated as reserved rights or as defined rights. The **reserved rights concept** holds that:

> . . . management's authority is supreme in all matters except those it has expressly conceded in the collective agreement, or in those areas where its authority is restricted by law. Put another way, management does not look to the collective agreement to ascertain its rights; it looks to the agreement to find out which and how much of its rights and powers it has conceded outright or agreed to share with the union.[25]

Employers subscribing to the reserved rights concept consider it preferable not to mention management rights in the labor agreement on the grounds that they possess such rights already. To mention them might create an issue with the union.

Defined Rights.   The **defined rights concept**, on the other hand, is intended to reinforce and clarify what rights are exclusively those of management. It serves to reduce confusion and misunderstanding and remind union officers, union stewards, and employees that management never relinquishes its status quo. In one survey all but two out of 400 labor agreements contained provisions covering management

25. Paul Prasow and Edward Peters, "New Perspectives on Management Rights," *Labor Law Journal* (January, 1967), pp. 5—6.

rights.[26] The following is an example of a general statement defining management rights in one labor agreement:

> It is agreed that the company possesses all of the rights, powers, privileges, and authority it had prior to the execution of this agreement; and nothing in this agreement shall be construed to limit the company in any way in the exercise of the regular and customary functions of management and the operation of its business, except as it may be specifically relinquished or modified herein by an express provision of this agreement.[27]

Forms of Union Security

Nearly 84 percent of the labor agreements included in a BNA survey provide for one of the following forms of union security: closed shop, union shop, modified union ship, agency shop, maintenance-of-membership shop, simple recognition shop, and dues checkoff.[28]

Closed Shop.   The **closed shop** requires that an employer hire only those individuals who are union members. Although the closed shop is forbidden by the Taft-Hartley Act, it exists for all practical purposes in certain industries, such as the maritime and construction fields, where employers obtain their personnel through union hiring halls.

Union Shop.   The union shop provides that any person who is hired, if not a union member at the time, must join the union within a prescribed period—usually 30 days—or be terminated. In the survey mentioned above, 62 percent of the agreements provided for the union shop. There are a total of 20 states that forbid the union shop through their **right-to-work laws**. These states are listed in Figure 15–6.

Modified Union Shop.   In the **modified union shop** certain employees are permitted to be exempt from joining the union. For example, those who are employed before a certain date, those who are Christmas workers, students in work study programs, or those who object to union membership on religious grounds can be exempted. The modified union shop is much less common than the union shop. It appeared in only about 12 percent of the agreements surveyed.

Maintenance-of-Membership Shop.   The **maintenance-of-membership shop** requires that employees who voluntarily join a union must remain members in good standing during the life of the agreement. It also may provide an escape period during which those who wish to do so may drop their membership before it becomes

---

26. *Collective Bargaining: Negotiations and Contracts.* Vol. 2 (Washington, DC: The Bureau of National Affairs, Inc., 1979), p. 65:1.
27. Wabash Fibre Box Company and Paperworkers.
28. *Collective Bargaining: Negotiations and Contracts,* Vol. 2, *op. cit.,* pp. 87:1, 87:2, and 87:3.

Figure 15–6 States with Right-to-Work Laws

Alabama	Nevada
Arizona	North Carolina
Arkansas	North Dakota
Florida	South Carolina
Georgia	South Dakota
Iowa	Tennessee
Kansas	Texas
Louisiana	Utah
Mississippi	Virginia
Nebraska	Wyoming

SOURCE: Reprinted by permission from *BNA Policy and Practice Series*, copyright 1982 by The Bureau of National Affairs, Inc., Washington, DC, pp. 87:19–87:20.

effective. This form of union security appeared in only about 7 percent of the labor agreements surveyed.

Agency Shop. While the **agency shop** does not require employees in the bargaining unit to join the union, it does require that they pay dues to the union which serves as their bargaining agent within the organization. The agency shop was at one time ruled to be illegal by the NLRB. However, it now has limited adoption primarily in those states that have right-to-work laws. Only 12 percent of the agreements surveyed provided for the agency shop.

Simple Recognition Shop. Unions that fail to achieve one of the forms of security mentioned above may operate through a simple recognition shop. Under the **simple recognition shop** the employer recognizes a union as the exclusive bargaining agent for all employees within the bargaining unit.

Dues Checkoff. Under the **dues checkoff** provision the employer withholds the union dues from the paycheck of each union member who signs an affidavit agreeing to such a deduction. This provision requires the employer to perform an accounting function for the union. At the same time it eliminates the need for union officers to come on the employer's premises to collect from delinquent members. It also eliminates the possibility that the employer be forced to discharge a capable employee who has been expelled from the union for nonpayment of dues. Of the agreements surveyed, 86 percent of them provide for a dues checkoff.[29]

29. *BNA Policy and Practices Series—Labor Relations* (Washington, DC: The Bureau of National Affairs, Inc., 1982), pp. 87:1–87:3.

Threats to Union Security

Unions today, especially in the construction industry, are being threatened by the growth of the **open shop** in which no union is recognized. There is also a trend in this industry for contractors to go "double-breasted" by establishing nonunion subsidiaries.[30] This situation is forcing a reversal in the upward trend of wages for construction workers which a decade ago were outpacing wage increases for workers in manufacturing. To counteract this trend, some local unions in the building trades have agreed to accept either wage cuts or a moratorium on increases. Some also have agreed to eliminate restrictive work rules and allow the introduction of laborsaving devices.

Union security and power also are being threatened in the courts. There have been several court rulings in which it has been held that a union may not use the agency shop or union shop dues for political or ideological purposes. One court ruling has gone so far as to forbid the use of agency shop fees for organizing efforts, publishing newspapers, and holding conventions. This ruling also forbids the paying of per capita dues to the AFL-CIO. If upheld in the higher courts, labor leaders predict that this ruling may bring an end to the union shop.

RÉSUMÉ

The rights of employees to unionize, to bargain collectively with an employer over their conditions of employment, and to exert economic pressures to enforce these demands have become firmly accepted by American society. A growing body of law, furthermore, has been developed to protect these rights, to facilitate collective bargaining, to minimize conflicts, and to prevent abuse by either side in the maintenance of a bargaining relationship. While some employers may resent sharing with a union the authority to make various decisions relating to the operation of their organizations, the existence of unions and their participation in these areas have become an established fact. Therefore, it is to the best interests of every employer who must deal with a union to develop the ability to bargain effectively and to maintain a satisfactory relationship with union leaders.

Collective bargaining includes not only the actual negotiations that occur in attempting to achieve a labor agreement, but also the power tactics used to support negotiating demands. When negotiations become deadlocked, bargaining becomes a power struggle to force from either or both parties the concessions needed to break the deadlock. The need for companies to survive and continue to provide jobs has placed both unions and employers under pressure to make the concessions required to reach an agreement. Concessions made by unions are helping to reduce operating costs, and concessions made by employers are providing union members with greater employment security.

In the public sector, labor organizations are attempting to achieve bargaining rights and power equal to that existing in the private sector. The fact that economic

30. "Building Trades Lose Ground," *Business Week* (November 9, 1981), p. 103.

bargaining pressures are incompatible with the public's need for certain government services, however, prevents labor organizations in government from achieving bargaining parity with those in the private sector.

TERMS TO IDENTIFY

collective bargaining
pattern bargaining
bridgehead proposals
bargaining zone
strike
picket
stranger picketing
mass picketing
boycott
primary boycott
secondary boycott
outsourcing
lockout
mediator
arbitrator
fact-finding board

labor-management committees
gains-sharing plans
cost of living adjustments (COLA)
compulsory binding arbitration
final offer arbitration
reserved rights concept
defined rights concept
closed shop
right-to-work laws
modified union shop
maintenance-of-membership shop
agency shop
simple recognition shop
dues checkoff
open shop

DISCUSSION QUESTIONS

1. Is collective bargaining the same as negotiating? Explain.
2. Of what significance is the "bargaining zone" in the conduct of negotiations, and what determines the limits of this zone?
3. What are some of the possible reasons why an employer may take a strike that may result in a loss of customers and profits?
4. How does mediation differ from arbitration, and in what situations are each of these processes most likely to be used?
5. What are some of the bargaining concessions being sought by employers and by the unions in return for the concessions they may grant?
6. In the public sector, what are some of the problems encountered by unions attempting to bargain collectively that are not encountered in the private sector?

7. What are some of the developments that are posing a threat to union security?
8. At an election conducted among the 20 employees of the Exclusive Jewelry Store, all but two of them voted in favor of the Jewelry Workers Union, which subsequently was certified as their bargaining agent. In negotiating its first agreement, the union demanded that it be granted a union shop. The two employees voting against the union, however, informed the management that they would quit rather than join the union. Unfortunately for the store, the two employees were skilled gem cutters who were the most valuable of its employees and would be difficult to replace. What position should the store take with regard to the union shop demand?

WORKING TOGETHER

In a number of its plants, the Futura Products Corporation has been able to establish fairly good rapport with the officers of the local union representing its employees. Increasingly, the plant management recognizes that the union is equally anxious to "straighten out" problem employees (those with problems relating to drug and alcohol abuse, as well as financial and domestic difficulties). The union feels that employees who are problems to the corporation are likely to be problems to the union also. As a result of this union-management cooperation, the company frequently resolves its difficulties with a problem employee without resorting to disciplinary action. If disciplinary action becomes necessary, usually it is taken only after the union has been given an opportunity to assist in resolving the problem.

Because of this cooperative relationship with the union, the corporation has been able to develop a rather unique supervisory training program. This program, which originally was intended to help supervisors understand human behavior better and to cope more effectively with employee relations problems, is also made available to the union stewards. Through this program the corporation is able to help both supervisors and stewards become more knowledgeable about personnel problems and about how they might work together more effectively in resolving such problems. The joint training sessions also enable a supervisor and a steward to understand better each other's responsibilities in performing their respective roles.

a. Why might some unions object to the type of supervisor-steward training sessions being conducted by this company?

b. What is your opinion of these sessions?

A QUESTION OF AMNESTY

In response to a new state law granting teachers collective bargaining rights, negotiations between the North Bay Teachers Association and the Bayshore Unified School District began early in January. It was not until the middle of October that a tentative agreement was reached with the help of a state mediator. This agreement, however, was rejected at a mass meeting of Association members. A 15-day strike was called to which a majority of the Association members and members of a rival teachers' union responded. Among the several issues the striking teachers demanded to be resolved was the issue of amnesty for their involvement in the strike. On October 31, after considerable negotiation, the District agreed to insert the following "no reprisal clause" into the Agreement:

> The District covenants not to sue in any court of law, before the Labor Board, or before any other judicial body, any District employee, student, the Association, Association employees, or Association officer(s) for any conduct arising from concerted actions which preceded agreement on this contract.

The District further covenants not to take any punitive action or reprisal against any District employee, student, the Association, Association employee, or Association officer(s) for any conduct arising from the concerted action which preceded agreement on this contract.

However, several issues still remained unresolved. On November 3, as the negotiations stalled, about 200 teachers decided to pressure the District negotiators by occupying the District administration building. Police were summoned and the strikers were ordered to leave the building. These orders were obeyed by all of the teachers except six who were members of the rival union. After having been instructed individually to leave the building by police officers, the six teachers were placed under citizen's arrest by the District superintendent and booked at the local police station. Since the County Attorney was on an extended trip, the charges against the six teachers were not formally signed until the County Attorney's return on November 15. Meanwhile, agreement was finally reached between the Association and the District and ratified by the Board of Education on November 8. Because the District, after ratifying the Agreement, refused to drop the charges against the teachers who had been arrested, the Association charged that the District was violating the "no reprisal" section of the Agreement. Accordingly, on November 28, Sarah Cheng, president of the Association, filed a formal grievance charging the District with a violation of the Agreement.

a. By refusing to drop the charges against the six teachers, did the District violate the "no reprisal" section of the Agreement?
b. What do you anticipate would be the verdict of the municipal court with respect to the charges brought against the six teachers?

SUGGESTED READINGS

Beal, Edwin F., Edward D. Wickersham, and Philip K. Kienast. *The Practice of Collective Bargaining,* 5th ed. Homewood, IL: Richard D. Irwin, Inc., 1976.

Cohen, Sanford. *Labor in the United States,* 4th ed. Columbus, OH: Charles E. Merrill Publishing Co., 1975.

Davey, Harold W. *Contemporary Collective Bargaining,* 3d ed. Englewood Cliffs, NJ: Prentice-Hall, 1972.

Holley, William H., and Kenneth M. Jennings. *The Labor Relations Process.* New York: The Dryden Press, Holt, Rinehart and Winston, 1980.

Prasow, Paul, and Edward Peters. *Arbitration and Collective Bargaining.* New York: McGraw-Hill, 1970.

Richardson, Reed C. *Collective Bargaining by Objectives.* Englewood Cliffs, NJ: Prentice-Hall, 1977.

Schmidt, Emerson P. *Union Power and the Public Interest.* Los Angeles: Nash Publishing Co., 1973.

Sloane, Arthur A., and Fred Witney. *Labor Relations,* 3d ed. Englewood Cliffs, NJ: Prentice-Hall, 1977. Part 3.

Chapter Objectives:

- To understand the purpose and characteristics of progressive discipline.
- To know how to proceed with the investigation of a disciplinary problem.
- To cite some of the legal barriers to employee terminations.
- To describe the steps comprising a typical grievance procedure.
- To recognize the distinction between expressions and causes of grievances.
- To describe the arbitration process and the basis upon which arbitration awards are determined.

Disciplinary Actions and Appeal Procedures

16

We have emphasized that in the negoti-ation of the labor agreement the union normally exercises the initiative to which the employer reacts. Once the agreement is in effect, however, the employer exercises the initiative in administering its provisions. Any management decisions that are considered to be in violation of the agreement are in turn subject to challenge by the union through the grievance procedure. Many of these challenges involve the treatment of individual employees by the employer. This treatment frequently concerns disciplinary action.

Because disciplinary actions are subject to challenge and possible reversal through the grievance procedure, management should make a positive effort to prevent the need for such actions. When disciplinary action becomes impossible to avoid, however, it should be taken in accordance with the provision of the labor agreement and carefully developed personnel policies and procedures. In this chapter we will focus on the policies and procedures which should govern disciplinary actions, the procedures for handling grievances, and the arbitration of grievances.

THE RIGHT TO TAKE CORRECTIVE ACTION

In the private sector, management must be able to take such corrective action involving its employees as may be necessary to maintain efficiency and insure the survival of the enterprise. Similar actions are required in the public sector if public services are to be provided at a reasonable cost. In both sectors, however, these actions affect the duties and working conditions of employees and their continued employment.

Management traditionally has had the right to take corrective action. This right, however, carries with it an obligation to act in a manner that is consistent and equitable for employees who are affected. Since employees have the freedom to come and go at will, the rationale under the common law "at will" **doctrine** is that employers should have equal freedom to employ them at will. This freedom includes the right of management to unilaterally determine the conditions of employment and to make personnel decisions. It also includes the right to terminate employees *at will*. Court decisions and legislation, however, are serving to curb employers' rights under the common law doctrine. Nevertheless, as Coulson points out, "the termination 'at will' doctrine still lives."[1]

When employees are organized, the employer's right to take corrective action is determined by the labor agreement. As we noted in the previous chapter, this right may be detailed in the agreement or may be implied to exist if it is not specifically restricted by the agreement. Generally a labor agreement requires that management's right to take corrective action be based on **just cause**. This means that the corrective action must be for clear, compelling, and justifiable reasons. The most common grounds for a labor organization to challenge a disciplinary action is that management did not have just cause for the action. Thus, many of the disputes

1. Robert Coulson, *The Termination Handbook* (New York: The Free Press, 1981), p. 114.

between labor and management are not over the right of management to take disciplinary action, but over whether or not management has just cause to do so.

The primary purpose of corrective action is to eliminate the cause of ineffective performance rather than to punish the employee. Hopefully such action can be of a positive nature that will prevent the need for any punitive action.

The Positive Approach

Through the use of incentives and leadership, the positive approach seeks to motivate employees to perform their jobs effectively. Thus, the positive approach utilizes the "carrot" rather than the "stick." This approach also places emphasis on preventing the development of problems that might necessitate disciplinary action. If performed effectively, each of the processes of the personnel management program that has been described in this book thus far can reduce the need for corrective disciplinary action. Grievances and disciplinary actions can be reduced, for example, by:

1. Preparing accurate job descriptions and specifications.
2. Staffing each job with a person who understands and has the qualifications to match the job requirements.
3. Selecting individuals whose personal qualifications or emotional makeup are suited for the organization.
4. Developing effective orientation, training, communication, and performance evaluation programs.

The Use of Progressive Discipline

If positive measures fail to correct unsatisfactory performance or behavior, then disciplinary action becomes the only alternative. When disciplinary action is taken, generally it is imposed in a progressive manner, as Figure 16–1 illustrates. From a verbal warning that subsequent unsatisfactory behavior or performance will not be tolerated, the action may progress to a written warning, to a suspension without pay, and to a discharge. Thus, the focus of discipline is upon doing everything possible to

Figure 16–1 Progressive Discipline

DISCHARGE
↑
SUSPENSION
↑
WRITTEN WARNING
↑
ORAL WARNING
↑
INSTRUCTING - COACHING - EVALUATING

Figure 16–2 Factors Determining the Severity of a Disciplinary Action

1. Degree of severity of the offense.
2. Employee's length of service with the company.
3. Provocation, if any, that may have led to the offense.
4. The number of previous offenses.
5. The nature of the previous offenses.
6. Previous warnings or other disciplinary action for previous offenses.
7. Company rules: Are they clear? Are they reasonable? Have they been communicated to the employee?
8. Have company rules and regulations been consistently applied?
9. Past disciplinary actions for similar offenses by other companies.
10. Employee's pattern of conduct.
11. Supervisory practices.
12. Is the penalty reasonable and appropriate to the offense?

SOURCE: Maurice S. Trotta, *Arbitration of Labor Management Disputes* (New York: AMACOM, American Management Associations, 1974), pp. 236–237.

retain employees by encouraging and helping them to correct their deficiencies. The "capital punishment"' of discharge is utilized only as a last resort.

Since each situation is unique, a number of factors must be considered when determining the severity of a disciplinary action. Some of the factors suggested by Trotta are listed in Figure 16–2. These are also the factors usually considered by an arbitrator or an adjudication body in deciding whether or not to uphold a disciplinary action, should the employee appeal it.[2]

DISCIPLINARY POLICIES AND PROCEDURES

If disciplinary action is to be objective and consistent, there must be effective policies and procedures to govern its use. These provisions serve to assist those responsible for taking such action and to help insure that employees will receive fair and constructive treatment. Equally important, these guidelines help to prevent disciplinary action from being avoided or from being reversed through the appeal system.

A major responsibility of the human resources department is the development for approval by top management of the policies and procedures governing disciplinary action. Such development, however, must involve the participation of the supervisors and managers who must conform to these policies and procedures in their relations with subordinates. Their practical experience can contribute to more effective coordination and consistency in the use of disciplinary action throughout the

---

2. Maurice S. Trotta, *Arbitration of Labor-Management Disputes* (New York: AMACOM, American Management Associations, 1974), pp. 236–237.

organization. It is the responsibility of the department also to insure that disciplinary policies, as well as any disciplinary action taken against employees, are consistent with the labor agreement (if one exists) and in conformity with current law.

The primary responsibility for preventing or correcting disciplinary problems rests with the employee's immediate supervisor. The supervisor is best able to observe evidence of unsatisfactory behavior or performance and to discuss the matter with the employee. Such discussions frequently may be sufficient to correct the problem so that taking disciplinary action becomes unnecessary. However, when disciplinary action becomes necessary, the supervisor should attempt to use a problem-solving approach. The causes underlying the problem are as important as the problematic behavior itself, and any attempt to prevent further recurrence will require an understanding of these causes. Admittedly, it is often difficult for supervisors to maintain an objective attitude toward infractions of employees. If supervisors can approach such infractions with a problem-solving attitude, however, they are more likely to come up with a diagnosis that is nearer the truth than would be possible were they to use the approach of a trial lawyer.

In attempting to uncover reasons for unsatisfactory behavior, the supervisor must keep in mind the fact that employees may not be aware of certain work rules. Before initiating any disciplinary action, therefore, it is essential that supervisors consider whether or not they have given their employees careful and thorough indoctrination in the rules and regulations relating to their jobs.

Investigating the Disciplinary Problem

There is a natural temptation for supervisors to tolerate employee behavior that should be subject to disciplinary action. Some supervisors may fear that taking disciplinary action may cause an unpleasant situation to become even more unpleasant. Consequently, they may wait until an employee's behavior becomes intolerable. Then, with their courage reinforced by anger, they seek to terminate the employee only to have such action reversed through the appeal system. If that employee remains under the supervisor, cooperation in the future may become even more difficult to obtain.

The Investigative Interview. Before any disciplinary action is initiated, employees should be made fully aware in an investigative interview of their deficiencies or violations. The interview is necessary because the supervisor's perceptions of a particular employee's behavior may not be entirely accurate. Any investigative interview or counseling session should be conducted according to the suggestions pertaining to performance evaluation interviews discussed in Chapter 10.

The investigative interview should concentrate upon the requirements of the job and/or upon the performance and behavior expected of the employee. The discussion should avoid getting into "personalities" or areas unrelated to job performance. Most important, the employee must be given a full opportunity to explain his or her side of the issue so that any deficiencies for which the organization may be responsible are revealed. In short, the purpose of the interview is to make the employee aware of perceived deficiencies and to correct them. The purpose is not to impugn the employee's self-esteem or to provide a therapeutic release for the supervisor.

Since the interview may turn out to be the first of several more progressive steps in taking disciplinary action, it is advisable for supervisors not to say anything that might jeopardize management's position. A flippant remark or a careless statement, for example, could prove detrimental if cited out of context during the appeal hearing to indicate prejudice and/or discrimination on the part of the supervisor. It is good practice, following a disciplinary interview, for a supervisor to prepare a memorandum for the record in case a future need for it arises. The memorandum should indicate the time and place of the meeting, the deficiencies discussed, and the corrective action agreed upon by the employee. This record can be used to refute any subsequent claims by the employee of not having been informed of performance deficiencies or improper conduct. It can also help to verify the fact that the session was conducted in a constructive and objective manner.

Employee Representation at Investigative Hearings. If an investigative hearing concerns an offense that could result in discharge, it is only logical for the employee to want a union representative or legal counsel to be present during the hearing. Employers often have opposed the presence of such representatives on the grounds that it is a management prerogative to question employees on matters relating to activities within the enterprise. They also have held that, in the absence of any charges or punitive action, the employee has no basis for requesting representation. However, a growing number of NLRB and court cases are refuting this employer position.[3]

In the *J. Weingarten, Inc.* case, to cite one example, the United States Supreme Court upheld the NLRB ruling in favor of the employee's right to representation.[4] The court decided that, since the employee had reason to believe the interview might result in action jeopardizing her job security, she had the right to representation. It ruled also that the NLRB's review of the case was justified on the basis of new and significant developments of industrial life. These developments include the use of such security measures as closed-circuit TV, undercover agents, and lie detectors.[5] The decisions in this and other cases thus introduce additional precautions to be observed by those conducting disciplinary interviews.

Compiling a Disciplinary Record

An oral warning may fail to attain improvement on the part of an employee. The next step in administering progressive discipline, as Figure 16–1 on page 381 indicates, is to issue a written warning to the employee. A copy of this is usually placed in the individual's personnel file. After an established period—frequently six

---

3. John S. Gannon, "How to Handle Discipline Within the New National Labor Board Requirements," *Personnel Administrator*, Vol. 26, No. 3 (March, 1981), pp. 43–47, 88.

4. *NLRB v. Weingarten, Inc.*, 95 S. Ct. 959 (1975) 402 U.S. 251, 43 L Ed 2nd 171.

5. Paul N. Erickson, Jr., and Clifford E. Smith, "The Right of Union Representation During Investigative Interviews," *Arbitration Journal*, Vol. 33, No. 1 (March, 1978), pp. 31–32.

months—this warning is usually removed, provided that it has served its purpose. Otherwise the warning remains in the file to serve as evidence should a more severe penalty become necessary later.

The employee's personnel file provides a complete work history of the employee. It serves as a basis for determining and supporting disciplinary action and for evaluating the company's disciplinary policies and procedures. Maintenance of proper records also provides management with valuable information about the soundness of its rules and regulations. Those rules that are violated most frequently should receive particular attention. The need for them may no longer exist, or some alteration might be made to facilitate their enforcement. If the rule has little or no value, it should be revised or rescinded. Otherwise employees are likely to feel that they are being restricted unnecessarily.

Initiating Disciplinary Action

Regardless of the level at which disciplinary action is to occur, it should be taken as soon as possible after the need for it arises. Such action is in accordance with the psychological principle of reinforcement discussed in Chapter 11. It is also consistent with the **hot stove approach** explained below. If no action is taken, or if action is taken very much later, additional problems may result.

The Hot Stove Approach. A hot stove with its radiating heat gives warning that it should not be touched. Those who ignore the warning and touch it, like employees who violate a rule, are assured of being burnt. The punishment (in this case the burn) is immediate and directly associated with the rule for not touching a hot stove. Like the hot stove which will immediately burn anyone who touches it, an established rule for employees to follow should be enforced consistently and should apply to *all* employees. While discipline should not be administered in the rigid and impersonal manner of a hot stove, it should have similar reinforcement and preventative value.

The Results of Inaction. Failure to take disciplinary action only helps to aggravate a problem which eventually must be resolved. Such failure implies that the performance of the employee concerned has been satisfactory. If the disciplinary action is taken eventually, the delay will make it more difficult to justify the action if appealed. In defending against such an appeal, the employer is likely to be asked why the employee was kept on the payroll if he or she had not been performing or behaving satisfactorily. Or, an even more damaging question might be asked of the employer, such as, "Why did that employee receive satisfactory performance ratings (or perhaps even merit raises)?" Such contradictions in personnel practice can only aid employees in successfully challenging management's corrective actions. Unfortunately there are supervisors who try to build a case to justify their corrective actions only *after* they have decided that a particular employee should be discharged. In attempting to accomplish their objectives by merely going through the motions of progressive discipline, their efforts are likely to backfire under the scrutiny of an appeal system.

Terminating Employees

Following the verbal and written warnings and suspension (usually without pay), the ultimate action in progressive discipline is the discharge. Of course, if the grounds for it are sufficient, the discharge may be accomplished without taking any preceding steps.

Informing the Employee.

Regardless of the reasons for a discharge, it should be accomplished with personal consideration for the individual affected. Every effort should be made to ease the trauma a discharge creates. Therefore, the employee must be informed honestly, yet tactfully, as to the exact reasons for the termination. Such candor can help the employee face the problem and adjust to it psychologically in a constructive manner.

Although the employee may not regard the discharge as a favor at the time, later it may prove to be a blessing if the employee realizes that he or she was unsuited for the position. Instead of following the line of least resistance and remaining in a job where there is no future opportunity, the discharged employee is forced to seek new employment where hopefully the future will be brighter. Discharge also has been known to help shock some individuals into correcting undesirable behavioral traits that were a factor in causing their discharge.

Utilizing Outside Assistance.

Some employers utilize employment agencies or outside consultants to assist in locating other employment for employees who are being terminated. This assistance is more likely to be provided for employees, particularly executives, who are being terminated for economic reasons or because they don't fit the current corporate mold. Rather than being called a discharge, a termination under such conditions may be referred to as **disemployment, outplacement, or dehiring.** An increasing number of employers are also utilizing the services of **outplacement consultants** to assist the employee being terminated. In addition to helping reduce the anger and grief of the terminated individual, outplacement consultants can help this individual regain self-confidence and begin seriously the search for a new job. Some consultants performing this function prefer to be called **career continuation specialists.** They believe the term outplacement, particularly in the case of executives, emphasizes the negative aspect of the release and serves to diminish the person's status. Career continuation, in their opinion, represents the more positive approach that the executives are "in" but are actively looking for a new job or even a new career.

Since many terminated employees have been out of the job market for some time, they may lack current knowledge and skill in how to look for a job. The outplacement specialists can coach them in how to develop contacts, how to probe for job openings through systematic letter writing and telephone campaigns, and how to handle employment interviews and salary negotiations.

Many companies apparently believe that this service is worthwhile. For example, one executive's reaction to the use of consultants was: "Not only do they advise you not to be overly generous in severance pay, but they get the person thinking about a new job so he doesn't vent his venom and inflict turmoil on the company."[6] Some executives, however, do not look with favor on the use of outplacement consultants. One of them had this comment to make: "This business of having a consultant come in after the man has been fired is terribly cold and calculating. Why, it's like calling in an undertaker to pick up the body."[7] Still other executives believe that capable individuals, particularly executives, should have enough contacts and talent to find a new job independently. They maintain also that a corporate human resources department should have personnel who are sufficiently qualified to handle problems relating to employee terminations without requiring assistance from the outside.

Observing Legal Restrictions on Discharge

In addition to restrictions created by appeal systems, there are also certain curbs imposed by federal and state laws that limit the employer's freedom to discharge employees. The Taft-Hartley Act, it will be recalled from Chapter 14, makes it an unfair practice for an employer to discharge or otherwise discriminate against an employee because of his or her union activities. If the employee to be discharged is a union leader or activist, the case against that individual must be particularly strong to withstand the charges of union discrimination that are likely to be raised by the union.

State fair-employment practice laws, the federal Civil Rights Act of 1964, and other statutes prohibit discrimination in personnel decisions on the basis of race, religion, color, sex, and age. Also prohibited are reprisals against employees who exercise their rights under Title VII of the Civil Rights Act. All these antidiscrimination laws make it essential that managements review their discharge decisions carefully to insure that there is no evidence of bias or prejudice being exercised on the part of supervisors who have initiated the decisions.

Wrongful Discharge Suits. Some employees have brought suits against their former employers for "wrongful or retaliatory discharge."[8] These suits have been filed by employees who were discharged for refusing to obey such employer requests as to commit perjury, to falsify reports, or to violate consumer codes. They sometimes are referred to as "whistle blowers" because of their disclosures of illegal action or incompetency on the part of their superiors. In their lawsuits these employees have sought to establish exceptions to the "at will" doctrine mentioned earlier as well as to obtain awards for damages suffered. The basis for the exceptions to the doctrine is that discharge for such reasons is not in the best interest of the economic system or the public good.[9]

---

6. "How Consultants Make Firing Easier," *Business Week* (July 20, 1974), pp. 67–68.

7. *Ibid.*

8. Lipman G. Feld, "Protection from Unfair Dismissal: It's Up to the Judge," *Administrative Management,* Vol. 38, No. 1 (April, 1977), pp 59–61.

9. Theodore A. Olsen, "Wrongful Discharge Claims Raised by At Will Employees: A New Legal Concern for Employers," *Labor Law Journal,* Vol. 32, No. 5 (May, 1981), pp. 279–281.

"At Will" Terminations.   At the present time the confusion and conflict between the traditional right of employers to terminate at will and the right of employees to be protected against discharge for public policy reasons is far from resolved. Furthermore, damage suits against employers can prove to be costly, with no guarantee of success. Unfortunately for those employees whose rights are not protected by a labor agreement or legal statute, their protection against wrongful discharge is minimal at best. However, if the trend in recent years continues, it is likely that the "at will" termination doctrine will be subject to further exceptions and erosion. Furthermore, sometime in the future, laws similar to those in some European countries are likely to be enacted to offer employees greater protection against wrongful discharge.

APPEALING MANAGEMENT ACTIONS

Since the legal recourse against management actions is both costly and time consuming, employees generally utilize it only as a last resort. In organizations that are unionized, provisions for appeal or for airing grievances virtually always are contained in the labor agreement. As we mentioned earlier, the desire for a formal grievance system can serve to encourage employees to unionize.

Increasingly, companies are taking positive steps to protect employees against arbitrary and inequitable treatment by their superiors. Undoubtedly the desire to avoid unionization may be a reason in some instances. These steps include improving communication with employees. Particular emphasis is being placed upon creating a climate in which employees are assured that they can voice their dissatisfaction with their superiors without fear of retaliatory action. Included also in the communication programs of some companies are formal procedures for resolving grievances.

Negotiated Grievance Procedures

The **grievance procedure** is considered by some authorities to be the heart of the bargaining agreement or the safety valve that gives vital flexibility to the whole system of collective bargaining.[10] As negotiated, it typically provides for the union to represent the interests of its members (and nonmembers as well) in processing a grievance.

Grievance procedures determine how the grievance is to be initiated, the number of steps that are to comprise the procedure, and the identity of representatives from each side who are to be involved in the hearings at each step. They also usually set forth any methods and limitations as to the number of working days within which an unresolved grievance must be taken to the next step in the hearing procedure. When a grievance cannot be resolved at one of these steps by the parties involved, most agreements provide for the grievance to be submitted to a third party—usually an arbitrator—whose decision is final. It is not the function of an

---

10. Frank Elkouri and Edna Asher Elkouri, *How Arbitration Works* (3d ed.; Washington, DC: The Bureau of National Affairs, Inc., 1973), pp. 106–107.

arbitrator to help the two parties reach a compromise solution. Rather, it is the arbitrator's job to adjudicate their differences by rendering an award that mandates how the grievance is to be resolved.

Initiating the Formal Grievance. In order for a grievance to be considered formally, it must be expressed orally and/or in writing. If good communication exists, the logical person to whom the grievance should be presented and discussed initially would be the employee's immediate supervisor. Should the employee be unable to communicate effectively with the supervisor, the grievance may be taken to the union steward, who will discuss it with the supervisor. Since grievances are often the result of an oversight, or a misunderstanding, many of them can be resolved at this point. Figure 16–3 illustrates, for example, the high proportion of grievances that are resolved at the first step in the General Motors Corporation, just as they are in most other organizations.

Whether or not it is possible to resolve a grievance at the initial step will depend upon the ability and willingness of the supervisor to discuss the problem

Figure 16–3 Disposition of Written Grievances

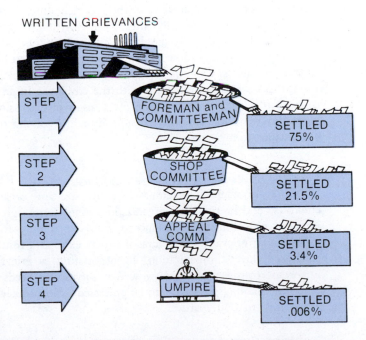

WRITTEN GRIEVANCES

STEP 1 → FOREMAN and COMMITTEEMAN → SETTLED 75%

STEP 2 → SHOP COMMITTEE → SETTLED 21.5%

STEP 3 → APPEAL COMM → SETTLED 3.4%

STEP 4 → UMPIRE → SETTLED .006%

An unsettled grievance will not necessarily be carried to the final step, hence the small unaccounted-for difference at this point in the handling of written grievances.

SOURCE: Disposition of written grievances during 1980 under the General Motors-United Auto Workers National Agreement. Reproduced with permission of the Industrial Relations Staff, General Motors Corporation.

with the employee and the steward. Supervisors should be trained formally in how to resolve grievances. This training should include familiarization with the terms of the labor agreement and the development of counseling skills to facilitate a problem-solving approach.

Preparing the Grievance Statement.

In some instances a satisfactory solution may not be possible at the first step because of honest differences of opinion between the employee and the supervisor. It may also not be possible because the supervisor does not have the authority to take the action required to satisfy the grievant. Furthermore, personality conflicts, prejudices, emotionalism, ordinary stubbornness, or other factors may be barriers to a satisfactory solution.

Most labor agreements require that grievances carried beyond the initial step must be stated in writing, usually on a multicopy form similar to the type shown in Figure 16–4. Requiring a written statement reduces the chance for various versions of the grievance to appear because of lapses in memory. It also forces the employees to be more rational and to think more carefully about their grievances. Thus, grievances which stem from trivial complaints or feelings of hostility are less likely to be pursued beyond the first step.

In preparing the written statement of a grievance, the employee usually obtains assistance from the union steward who represents members in the work area. Because of the union steward's familiarity with the union agreement and experience in evaluating the validity of complaints, this person can provide a valuable service. If the complaint appears to be a valid one, the steward can help the employee write the grievance statement on the official form. If the complaint does not appear to be valid, the steward can discuss it with the employee in an attempt to get at the real cause of the latter's dissatisfaction. As a result of discussions with the employee, the steward may be able to assist the supervisor in resolving the problem without taking any further formal steps.

Number of Steps in the Grievance Procedure.

The number of steps in the grievance procedure is determined by the size and organizational structure of the enterprise and by the labor organization. Many labor agreements provide for a time limit for processing the grievance at each step. Figure 16–5 illustrates some of the variations in grievance procedures that may exist as a result of differences in the size of an employer's organization. In negotiating a grievance procedure, the most important consideration is how well it serves the needs of the employer and the union in enabling grievances to be processed expeditiously and resolved in a manner satisfactory to both parties.

Resolving Grievances.

If a grievance is to be resolved successfully, representatives of both management and the union must be able to discuss the problem in a rational and objective manner. A grievance should not be viewed as something to be won or lost. Rather, both sides must view the situation as an attempt to solve a human relations problem. Furthermore, neither side should expect to have all the grievances decided in its favor.

If a grievance cannot be resolved through established grievance procedures, several alternatives are available. One of the parties may back down from the position it has been holding. Or, the grievance can be submitted to arbitration by outside parties if the agreement so provides. If the agreement does not provide for arbitration and the deadlock cannot be broken, then the union will either have to drop the grievance or resort to some form of economic pressure such as a strike or a slowdown.

Figure 16-4 Grievance Statement

GRIEVANCE STATEMENT

EMPLOYEE: Roland Smith   CLOCK NO: 65891   SHIFT: Swing

JOB CLASSIFICATION: Bench Mach.   PLANT: 2   DEPT.: 616

DEPT. FOREMAN: R. M. Lancaster

STATEMENT OF GRIEVANCE: I received only a 47-cent wage increase on my eighth-month review. Everyone else in my department has received an increase to the top of the rate in the past. A man who was hired later than I received the top of the rate. I am doing the same type, quality, and quantity of work as others in this classification who have received the top of the rate. When I hired in, the supervisor told me that I would receive the top of my rate on the eighth-month review. This was not the case. I feel that I have been discriminated against and should receive back pay to my eighth-month review for top rate of Bench Machinist.

EMPLOYEE: *Roland Smith*
Signature

DEPT. STEWARD: *Oscar Black*
Signature

RECEIVED BY: *L. M. Lancaster*
Supervisor or Foreman

TIME: 9:30 a.m.   DATE: 1/16/--

Prepare in quadruplicate for distribution

1. Original and one copy (Labor Relations)
2. Department
3. Chief Steward

UNION FILE NO. _____

LABOR RELATIONS NO. 1-84-32

Figure 16–5 **Grievance Procedures in Organizations of Different Sizes**

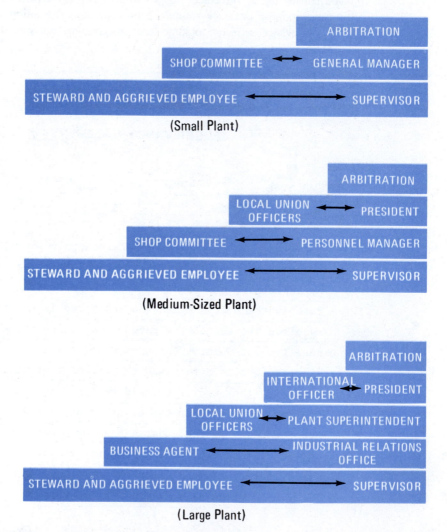

(Small Plant)

(Medium-Sized Plant)

(Large Plant)

SOURCE: C. Wilson Randle, *Collective Bargaining* (4th ed.; Boston: Houghton Mifflin Company, 1966), p. 235. Reproduced with permission.

Grievance Procedures in Nonunion Enterprises

Even though formal grievance procedures are confined largely to unionized companies, such procedures also can and should be developed in nonunion enterprises. Unfortunately the majority of these enterprises have not established a formal grievance procedure that will accomplish the results comparable to those achieved by unionized companies. Although there has been no extensive study of the subject, an informal study by Trotta revealed that there is a trend for nonunion companies to establish some type of grievance procedure for their employees. In some instances this trend involves only the so-called open door policy, or a policy statement allowing employees to present their complaints to higher levels of management. However, of the 34 nonunion companies surveyed, Trotta found that 18 had formal grievance procedures involving the general manager at the final step, and 4 had formal procedures ending in binding third-party arbitration.[11]

The Open-Door Mechanism *v.* a Formal Procedure.

In a BNA survey, 54 percent of the respondents reported having an open-door mechanism for handling employee complaints. A formal grievance procedure was provided by 44 percent of them. Interestingly, the open-door mechanism was more prevalent and the formal grievance procedure was less prevalent in manufacturing companies than in nonmanufacturing companies.[12]

In a negotiated grievance procedure, employees have a union representative to serve as an advocate in processing their grievances through to arbitration if necessary. Most nonunion grievance procedures, on the other hand, suffer from the lack of such advocacy. They often suffer also from the lack of supervisor enthusiasm and support. Supervisors who may be the cause of some grievances can hardly be expected to support a procedure that may reflect unfavorably upon their competency. A formal grievance procedure in a nonunion organization also may serve to raise employees' expectations and draw their attention to perceived dissatisfactions. If the procedure does this without providing the desired relief, it may actually prove to be more detrimental than beneficial. As Swann emphasizes, the sole purpose of a nonunion grievance procedure is to promote and encourage better communication with employees and to demonstrate a desire to treat them fairly.[13] However, if this purpose can be achieved without it, employees may be less likely to feel the need for a formal grievance system.

Role of the Ombudsman.

The use of an **ombudsman** to resolve grievances also is receiving increasing acceptance.[14] While ombudsmen have been used more commonly to protect individuals from abuses by government agencies, they also are being used more in governmental, educational, and other nonprofit organizations to assist employees in resolving their problems. Ombudsmen are found in some corporations, too. Xerox and General Electric are examples of two corporations that have had considerable success with them. To function successfully, ombudsmen must be able to operate within an atmosphere of confidentiality that does not threaten the

---

11. Trotta, *op. cit.,* p. 218.

12. *BNA Policy and Practice Series—Personnel Management* (Washington, DC: The Bureau of National Affairs, Inc., 1980), p. 263:131.

13. James P. Swann, Jr., "Formal Grievance Procedures in Nonunion Plants," *Personnel Administrator,* Vol. 26, No. 8 (August, 1981), p. 70.

14. *Webster's New World Dictionary of the English Language,* 2d ed., defines an ombudsman as a "public official appointed to investigate citizens' complaints against local or national government agencies that may be infringing on the rights of individuals."

security of the managers or subordinates who are involved in a complaint. While ombudsmen do not have power to overrule the decision made by an employee's supervisor, they should be able to appeal the decision up the line if they believe an employee is not being treated fairly. Aside from helping to achieve equity for employees, ombudsmen can help to provide management with a check on itself.[15]

Grievance Procedures in Government Organizations

Civil service systems in most government jurisdictions provide procedures by which employees may appeal management decisions affecting them. Those procedures established by the governing body are referred to as statutory procedures. Employee input in determining the procedures usually is limited to what political influence they can bring to bear upon the governing body. Employee appeals terminate with an adjudication decision by an appeals body such as a civil service commission or by an adjudicator appointed by it.

Where government employees are permitted to unionize, the grievance procedure is subject to negotiation. A study by Hayford and Pegnetter concludes that a negotiated procedure is superior to a statutory one for the following reasons:

1. The scope of issues to be submitted generally is broader.
2. Greater assurance is provided for employee representation at adjudication hearings.
3. The selection of the adjudicator is by mutual employee-employer consent.
4. Employee perception as to the neutrality and expertise of the adjudicator is greater.
5. The finality of the initial adjudication is enhanced.[16]

Hayford and Pegnetter therefore recommend that statutory procedures be modeled after the negotiated ones.

Reducing Grievances

The most effective approach in reducing grievances is to encourage them to be "brought out into the open." Once expressed, they should be resolved quickly in the most mutually satisfactory manner possible.

Some employees may have little difficulty or hesitancy in revealing their grievances, but others may not be so inclined. They may be unable either to recognize the true nature of their grievances or to describe them accurately. The personnel department may uncover evidence of dissatisfaction through the analysis of statistical data that it compiles or through its direct communication with employees. However, immediate supervisors who are in continual contact with employees are better able to draw out and listen to any grievances. For this reason it is important for supervisors to create the type of climate and rapport that will encourage subordinates to speak up and discuss anything that may be bothering them without

15. "Where Ombudsmen Work Out," *Business Week* (May 3, 1976), pp. 114–116.

16. Stephen L. Hayford and Richard Pegnetter, "Grievance Adjudication for Public Employees: A Comparison of Rights Arbitration and Civil Service Appeals Procedures," *The Arbitration Journal*, Vol. 35, No. 3 (September, 1980), pp. 22–27.

fear of provoking resentment. Since some individuals may have difficulty in expressing themselves or in identifying accurately the exact cause of their dissatisfaction, the supervisor should learn to become skillful in helping them to express their feelings. In doing so, employees may be able to uncover the true nature of their grievances.

Symptoms of Grievances.   Usually the grievances that are the most difficult for supervisors to resolve are those that employees are unable or unwilling to express. These grievances may be evidenced by such symptoms as sullenness, moodiness, tardiness, indifferent attitudes, insubordination, or a decline in quality and quantity of work. The supervisor who can avoid interpreting symptoms incorrectly, such as viewing them as a personal attack, will have better results in resolving grievances. Such results can be achieved with an approach aimed at diagnosing the causes underlying the symptoms. In many grievances, the symptoms represent only the exposed "tip of the iceberg."

Causes of Grievances.   The fact that grievances may result from one or more causes can make them difficult to diagnose. Some of the causes of grievances include those relating to the labor agreement, to the employee's job, and to problems of a personal nature.

Causes Relating to the Labor Agreement.   Many grievances related to the labor agreement result from omissions or ambiguities in its provisions. The grievances may result also from union attempts to gain changes in the agreement that it was unable to achieve at the bargaining table. At times, union representatives may solicit grievances simply to demonstrate to employees what the union can do for them or to divert the attention of members from union weaknesses or leadership deficiencies. Court decisions, as we have noted, also have made union officers more prone to process grievances which formerly might have been dropped.

Causes Relating to the Job.   Job-related grievances may stem from the failure of employees either to meet the demands of their jobs or to gain satisfaction from performing them. Employees who are placed in the wrong job or who lack adequate orientation, training, or supervision are more likely to perform unsatisfactorily. This can cause them to become dissatisfied with their employment and be a problem to their supervisors. Work-related grievances, therefore, often are a result of how well individuals are suited to and able to meet the demands of their jobs. The supervisor's attitude and behavior toward individual workers and the union may also be a cause for job-related grievances. Supervisors who play favorites, who fail to live up to promises, or who are too demanding are likely to encounter many grievances from workers.

Causes Relating to Personal Problems.   Poor health, family illness, marital discord, or financial difficulties are typical of personal problems that employees bring with them to the job. The frustration resulting from these problems may cause employees to find fault with their jobs or with others around them. Their expressed complaints thus may not accurately represent the real cause of their dissatisfactions.

Grievances stemming from personal problems frequently cannot be resolved by changing jobs or employment conditions. Since the cause of these problems is not job-related, corrective action requires the individual to make the necessary adjustments. Therefore, an important part of every supervisor's job is to counsel troubled subordinates and to help them to recognize and to work out solutions to their personal problems. This can be done through the counseling process, which was discussed in Chapter 13.

ARBITRATING GRIEVANCES

The function of **arbitration** is to provide the solution to a grievance that the union and the employer have been unable to resolve by themselves. Arbitration is performed by a neutral third party, known by such titles as arbitrator, **adjudicator, or impartial umpire.** This third party's decision dictates how the grievance is to be settled. Both disputing parties are obligated by the agreement to comply with the decision.

It is possible for a grievance to be resolved through mediation. The role of the mediator is to help the two parties resolve the grievance through compromise as if it were a bargaining deadlock.[17] Whether the third party being brought in is to function as an arbitrator or as a mediator should be established before the grievance is submitted to that person. Individuals who are appointed to arbitrate a grievance may encounter severe criticism if they attempt to assume the role of mediator. The reason for this is that the disputing parties have brought in the arbitrator to resolve the grievance by determining which one of them is right and which one is wrong.

Sources of Arbitrators

The arbitrator must be an individual who is acceptable to both parties. An arbitrator who is retained on a permanent basis to resolve all grievances arising under the agreement has the advantage of being familiar with the agreement and the labor-management relationship. Most grievances, however, are resolved by arbitrators who are appointed on an *ad hoc* basis. If both parties are satisfied with the arbitrator's performance, that person may be called upon to resolve subsequent grievances.

The mechanics of selecting an *ad hoc* arbitrator frequently involves choosing one whose name appears on a list of acceptable arbitrators submitted by each party. If this method fails to produce an arbitrator, the two parties may seek recommendations from such organizations as the American Arbitration Association, the Federal Mediation Service, or the appropriate state agency. Typically arbitrators are professionals such as professors, industrial engineers, members of the clergy, or retired government labor mediators. Because of their professional backgrounds, they tend to be identified with neither labor nor management and therefore are able to occupy a position of neutrality.

---

17. Mollie H. Bowers, "Grievance Mediation: Another Route to Resolution," *Personnel Journal,* Vol. 59, No. 2 (February, 1980), pp. 132–136.

The Decision to Arbitrate

If a grievance cannot be resolved through the grievance procedure, each disputing party must decide whether or not to allow it to go to arbitration. The alternatives would be for the union to withdraw the grievance or for the employer to concede to it. In deciding whether or not to go to arbitration, each party must weigh both the costs involved against the importance of the case and the prospects of gaining a favorable award. It would seem logical that neither party would allow a weak case to go to arbitration if there were little possibility of gaining a favorable award. Logic, however, does not always prevail. For example, it is not unusual for the union to take a weak case to arbitration in order to demonstrate to the members that the union is willing to exhaust every remedy in looking out for their interests. Union officers also are not likely to refuse to take to arbitration the grievances of members who are popular or politically powerful in the union, even though their cases are weak. Moreover, under the **fair representation doctrine** unions have a legal obligation to provide assistance to members who are pursuing grievances. Because members can bring suit against their unions for failing to process their grievances adequately, many union officers are reluctant to refuse taking even weak grievances to arbitration.

Management, on the other hand, may allow a weak case to go to arbitration to demonstrate to the union officers that management "cannot be pushed around." Also, managers at lower levels may be reluctant to risk the displeasure of top management by stating that a certain personnel policy is unworkable or unsound. Instead, they simply let a policy-related grievance go to an arbitrator whose award will emphasize the unsoundness of the policy. Plain stubbornness and mutual antagonism also may force many grievances into arbitration because neither party is willing to make concessions to achieve agreement, even when it may recognize that it is in the wrong.

The Arbitration Process

The issues to be resolved through arbitration may be described formally in a document known as a **submission agreement.** However, these issues are frequently presented orally to the arbitrator by the two parties at the beginning of the hearing. If they have been prepared, minutes and memoranda covering the meetings held at earlier stages of the grievance procedure are sometimes submitted prior to the formal hearing to inform the arbitrator of the issues to be resolved by arbitration.[18]

In arbitrating a dispute it is the responsibility of arbitrators to insure that each side receives a fair hearing during which it may present all of the facts it considers pertinent to the case. The procedures for conducting arbitration hearings and the restrictions governing the evidence that may be introduced during these hearings are more flexible than those permitted in a court of law. Hearsay evidence, for example,

---

18. Harold W. Davey, "What's Right and What's Wrong with Grievance Arbitration: The Practitioners Air Their Views," *The Arbitration Journal,* Vol. 28, No. 4 (December, 1973), pp. 219–220.

may be introduced provided that it is considered as such when evaluated with the other evidence presented during the hearing. The primary purpose of the hearing is to assist the arbitrator in obtaining the facts necessary to resolve a human relations problem rather than a legal one. The arbitrator, therefore, has a right to question witnesses or to request additional facts from either party in the course of the hearing.

Depending upon the importance of the case, the hearings may be conducted in either an informal or a very formal manner not unlike that of a court trial. If desired by either or both parties, or by the arbitrator, a court reporter may be present during the hearing to prepare a transcript of the proceedings. After conducting the hearing and receiving posthearing briefs (should the parties choose to submit them), the arbitrator customarily has 30 days in which to consider the evidence and to prepare a decision.

The Arbitration Award

The **arbitration award** should include not only the arbitrator's decision but also the rationale for it. The reasoning behind the decision can help provide guidance concerning the interpretation of the labor agreement and the resolution of future disputes arising from its administration. In pointing out the merits of each party's position, the reasoning that underlies the award can help ameliorate the disappointment and protect the self-esteem of those representing the unsuccessful party. In short, tact and objective reasoning can help to reduce disappointment and hard feelings.

Basis for the Award.

The foundation for the arbitrator's decision is the labor agreement and the rights it establishes for each party. In many instances the decision may hinge upon whether or not management's actions were justified under the terms of this agreement. Sometimes it may hinge upon the arbitrator's interpretation of the wording of a particular provision. Established personnel policies and past practices also can provide the basis for determining the award.

In many grievances, such as those involving performance or behavior on the job, the arbitrator must determine whether or not the evidence supports the employer's action against the grievant. The evidence must also indicate whether or not the employee was accorded the right of **due process,** which means the employee's right to be informed of unsatisfactory performance and to have an opportunity to defend against these charges. Under most labor agreements, as we noted earlier, the employer is required to have *just cause* for the action taken which should be confirmed by the evidence presented.

If the arbitration hearing indicates that the employee was accorded due process and the punitive action was for just cause, the severity of the penalty must then be assessed. The penalty may be judged on the basis of those factors listed in Figure 16–2 on page 382 which provide guidelines in assessing a penalty. However, it is within the arbitrator's power, unless denied by the submission agreement, to reduce the penalty. It is not uncommon, for example, for an arbitrator to reduce a discharge to a suspension without pay for the period the grievant has been off the payroll.

Concern for Precedents.   Unlike decisions in a court of law, awards—at least in theory—are supposed to be reached on the basis of the facts of the case rather than on the basis of precedents established by previous cases. The reason for this is that no two cases are exactly alike. Therefore, each case should be decided upon individual merits. In practice, however, precedents do have some influence at times upon the decision of an arbitrator who may seek guidance from decisions of other arbitrators in somewhat similar cases. These decisions are compiled and published by the American Arbitration Association and by such labor services as The Bureau of National Affairs, Commerce Clearing House, and Prentice-Hall. They can help an arbitrator to stay in line with contemporary standards of industrial jurisprudence.

Status of the Award.   Although both parties agree in advance to abide by the arbitrator's award, the one receiving an unfavorable award may seek to have it overturned by the courts. Historically the courts have been reluctant to do so even when the decision was a poor one. More recently, however, some arbitration awards have been overturned because they were based upon the arbitrator's concept of industrial jurisprudence rather than upon a strict interpretation of the labor agreement. With the successful challenges of arbitration awards in the courts,, the "golden age" of arbitration, according to Hogler, appears to be drawing to an end.[19]

Arbitration of Discrimination Grievances

Grievances pertaining to discrimination of the type forbidden by the Civil Rights Act of 1964 may well create a problem for arbitrators. Rather than resorting to legal actions permitted by the Act, individuals who believe themselves to be victims of discrimination in employment may seek to resolve their grievances through the established grievance procedure. This course of action can save costly litigation for both the grievant and the employer. However, whether or not the union *can* and *will* represent the grievant effectively in such cases, particularly if it has been a contributing party to the discrimination, may be open to question. Furthermore, should some civil rights group intervene in behalf of the grievant at one of the steps in the grievance procedure, a legal question conceivably may arise with respect to the union's contractual role of being the exclusive agent for its members. Finally, discrimination grievances create a new set of issues which many arbitrators may not be too well equipped to handle. This is because the standards they have acquired in resolving the typical union-management disputes and the body of industrial jurisprudence upon which they must rely for decisions frequently are not applicable.[20]

---

19. Raymond L. Hogler, "Industrial Due Process and Judicial Review of Arbitration Awards," *Labor Law Journal*, Vol. 31, No. 9 (September, 1980), pp. 570–571.

20. Richard I. Block, "Arbitrating Discrimination Grievances—A New Approach," *Michigan Business Review*, Vol. 22, No. 5 (November, 1970), pp. 16–32.

Criticisms of Grievance Arbitration

One of the major problems relating to arbitration, according to some critics, is that "most grievance arbitration has acquired characteristics which contradict the objectives and needs of the parties and thereby threaten its future."[21] Specifically, arbitration is criticized for taking too much time, becoming too expensive, and often creating frustration for the aggrieved employee and/or the supervisor in the dispute. Busy schedules on the part of the arbitrator, the union, and management officials, as well as a backlog of cases, frequently result in unnecessarily long delays in resolving relatively simple disputes. Extravagant amounts of time devoted by the arbitrator to a case as a result of reading lengthy transcripts or briefs, or of attempting to write an impressive opinion, also contribute to the added expense and delay in resolving grievances.

Excessive Costs. The cost and time required in the preparation of briefs by each party or of a transcript of the hearings often are excessive and unnecessary. In an endeavor to expedite cases and reduce costs, a new streamlined process, which grievants have the option of using, has been used experimentally in the steel industry. Under this process, panels have been created from which arbitrators are designated to handle cases on a rotating basis. Arbitration hearings must be held within 10 days of the appeal, and the award must be made within 48 hours after the hearing. No briefs or transcripts are utilized, and the cases for each party are presented by local plant and local union representatives rather than the usual labor "pros" who are attorneys or labor relations specialists. So far, the new expedited process appears to be succeeding in producing decisions more rapidly and at less cost.[22]

Creeping Legalism. Arbitration also has been criticized for its "creeping legalism" with its increasing use of attorneys and legal procedures in labor arbitration. In the opinion of its critics, the trend portends a movement away from the original purposes of labor arbitration.[23] Increasing legalism has been fostered, in part, by laws governing equal opportunity with their overlapping jurisdictions. This growth of government authority often has been at the expense of the collective bargaining process. It has forced the arbitrator to become an interpreter of law rather than an adjudicator of human relations problems. Ignoring the law relevant to a case, however, may trigger a lawsuit by the unsuccessful party. If the arbitrator addresses the law directly, he or she may be accused of acting beyond the scope of the arbitral function.[24]

21. Ben Fischer, "Arbitration: The Steel Industry Experiment," *Monthly Labor Review*, Vol. 95, No. 11 (November, 1972), p. 7.

22. *Ibid.*

23. "Structural Change in the Labor Arbitration Profession," *Personnel Journal*, Vol. 55, No. 11 (December, 1976), pp. 616–620.

24. J.S. Raffael, "Labor Arbitration and the Law: A Non-Lawyer Point of View," *Labor Law Journal*, Vol. 29, No. 1 (January, 1978), pp. 27–28.

RÉSUMÉ

Traditionally it has been the right of management to take those personnel actions considered necessary to achieve efficient operations. Increasingly, however, these rights are being restricted through collective bargaining, legislation, and court decisions. The restrictions provide employees with an opportunity to challenge those decisions affecting their welfare. Grievance procedures and legal actions are the principal means of challenge.

Restrictions limiting management's authority have forced it into exercising greater precaution and a more positive approach when taking disciplinary actions. Greater emphasis also has been given to the concept of progressive discipline. The focus is upon coping with the unsatisfactory performance and dissatisfactions of employees before they become major problems. In taking personnel actions, management should be aware of the basis upon which its actions may be reversed by an arbitrator or a court of law. Any action it takes, therefore, must be in accordance with industrial and legal jurisprudence, as well as sound principles of human relations.

TERMS TO IDENTIFY

"at will" doctrine
just cause
hot stove approach
disemployment, outplacement, or dehiring
outplacement consultants
career continuation specialists
grievance procedure
ombudsman

arbitration
adjudicator or impartial umpire
fair representation doctrine
submission agreement
arbitration award
due process

DISCUSSION QUESTIONS

1. What should be the purpose of an investigative interview and the approach to be observed in conducting it?
2. Why are some employers making use of outplacement consultants to assist them with employee terminations?
3. What are some of the criticisms raised with respect to the resolving of grievances in nonunion organizations?
4. What are some of the reasons why the union or the employer may allow a weak grievance to go to arbitration?
5. What are some of the criticisms being raised against the current arbitration proce-

dures and what is being done to improve these procedures?
6. If you were the arbitrator of a discharge case, what facts would you analyze carefully in deciding whether to uphold or reverse the employer's actions?
7. Some advocates believe that legislation should be passed regulating an employer's right to terminate employees. This legislation might include provisions for a labor court similar to those existing in some European countries to which employees might appeal their termination. Would you favor such legislation? Why or why not?

PROBLEM 16–1

JUDGING THE ARBITRATOR

The labor agreement between the Peerless Delivery Service and the Drivers' Union provided that "employees may be discharged for *just cause.*" Specifically listed in the agreement as *just cause* was the failure of a driver to settle within 24 hours any bills or funds collected for the company.

In a grievance taken to arbitration, the driver had been discharged for retaining a check from a consignee for a period of one week. At the end of this period, the driver had exchanged it with the consignee for cash which was then used to settle the account. At the arbitration hearing the representative for the employer maintained that under the agreement there had been *just cause* for the discharge. The arbitrator's award, after hearing the case, was that the employee be reinstated without back pay. This award was based upon the finding that the employer had not used progressive discipline. Rather than carry out the award, the employer appealed it to the court on the grounds that the arbitrator had acted improperly.

a. Based solely upon the grievant's violation, was there *just cause* for the discharge?

b. If you were a member of the appeals court to which this case eventually was submitted, what would your decision be?

SUGGESTED READINGS

Baer, Walter E. *Discipline and Discharge Under the Labor Agreement.* New York: AMACOM, American Management Associations, 1972.

Coulson, Robert. *The Termination Handbook.* New York: The Free Press, 1981.

Elkouri, Frank, and Edna Asher Elkouri. *How Arbitration Works*, 3d ed. Washington, DC: The Bureau of National Affairs, Inc., 1973.

Kilgour, John G. *Preventive Labor Relations.* New York: AMACOM, American Management Associations, 1981.

Morin, William J., and Lyle Yorks. *Outplacement Techniques: A Positive Approach to Terminating Employees.* New York: AMACOM, American Management Associations, 1982.

Prasow, Paul, and Edward Peters. *Arbitration and Collective Bargaining.* New York: McGraw-Hill Book Company, 1970.

Trotta, Maurice S. *Arbitration of Labor Management Disputes.* New York: AMACOM, American Management Associations, 1974.

Compensation and Security

part

6

- To identify the various factors that comprise the wage mix.
- To understand the mechanics of each of the major job evaluation systems.
- To develop a wage curve and know the effect that the degree of its slope can have upon wage rates and labor costs.
- To construct a wage structure with ranges for each job class.
- To explain the major provisions of the federal laws affecting compensation.
- To understand the current issues concerning equal pay for comparable work.

17

Managing Employee Compensation

In Chapter 2 we emphasized that employees entering the work force during recent years are more concerned than their predecessors with the quality of their work life and with the psychological rewards to be derived from their employment. It is doubtful, however, whether many of them would continue working were it not for the money they derive from it. Pay, therefore, is still a major consideration in human resources management because it provides employees with a tangible reward for their services, as well as a source of recognition and livelihood.

For the employer, the payroll constitutes a sizable operating cost. A sound compensation program, therefore, is essential in order that pay may serve to motivate employee production sufficiently to keep labor costs at an acceptable level. This chapter will be concerned with the management of the compensation program and the job evaluation systems and pay structure for determining the wage payments. Included will be a discussion of federal regulations that affect wage rates. The current controversial issues involving pay rate determination will be discussed also.

THE COMPENSATION PROGRAM

As Figure 17–1 indicates, significant interaction occurs between compensation management and the other functions of the personnel program. Because of its importance in managing human resources, a formal program should be developed to govern employee compensation. This program establishes both the objectives it is intended to achieve and the policies for determining and disbursing compensation payments. Included as a part of the program should be the communication of pay information to employees.

Compensation Objectives and Policies

The objectives of a compensation program, like those pertaining to other personnel functions, should facilitate the effective utilization and management of an organization's human resources. Compensation objectives also should contribute to the overall objectives of the organization. The compensation program, therefore, must be tailored to the needs of the organization and of its employees. Some of the typical objectives of a compensation program are listed in Figure 17–2.

To achieve the objectives stated in Figure 17–2, policies must be established to guide management in making decisions. Compensation policies typically include the following:

1. The rate of pay within the organization and whether it is to be above, below, or at the prevailing community rate.
2. The extent to which individual bargaining should permit deviations from the established rates and pay structure.
3. The pay level at which new employees may be recruited and the pay differential which should be maintained between new and more senior employees.
4. The intervals at which pay raises are to be granted and the extent to which merit and/or seniority are to influence the raises.

Figure 17–1 **Relationship of Compensation Management to Other Personnel Functions**

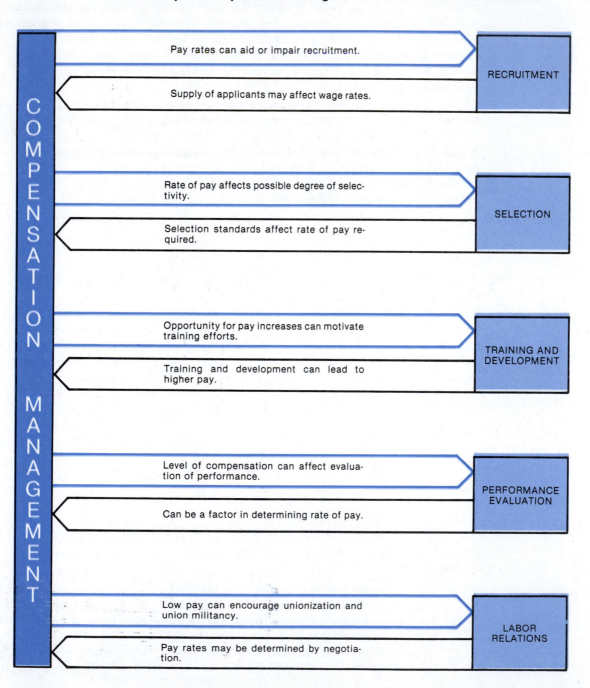

Figure 17–2 Common Objectives of a Compensation Program

1. The program should help to attract the number and kinds of employees needed to operate the organization.
2. In profit-making organizations it should help to facilitate the achievement of a competitive position in marketing the products or services.
3. The nature of the program and the time and cost of it must be reasonable and proportionate to the resources of the organization and priority demands of other personnel functions.
4. The program must gain employee acceptance.
5. The program must play a positive role in motivating employees to perform to the best of their abilities.
6. In the private sector the program must gain the acceptance of its publics, including stockholders, customers, the government, and the general public.
7. The program must provide employees with the opportunity to achieve reasonable aspirations within the framework of impartiality and equity.
8. It should provide employees with an incentive to improve their skills and abilities.

SOURCE: Reprinted, by permission of the publisher, from COMPENSATION, by Robert E. Sibson, © 1974 by AMACOM, a division of American Management Associations, pp. 8, 9. All rights reserved.

The Motivating Value of Compensation

Pay constitutes a quantitative measure of an employee's relative worth. For most employees, pay has a direct bearing not only upon their standard of living but also upon the status and recognition they may be able to experience both on and off the job. Since an employee's pay represents a reward received in exchange for his or her contributions, it is essential, according to the equity theory discussed in Chapter 11, that the pay be equitable in terms of these contributions. It is essential also that an employee's pay be equitable in terms of what other employees are receiving for their contributions. The relative amount an employee is paid in contrast to what others receive for their contributions can have an important bearing upon that individual's performance and job satisfaction.

Employee Perception of Compensation. Pay must not only be equitable but be so perceived by employees. Employee perception of the relationship between the contribution they make and the rewards they expect to receive in return is important. The expectancy theory discussed in Chapter 11 states that employees will exert greater effort if there is reason to expect that it will result in an appropriate reward. To motivate this effort, the **valence**, or attractiveness of any monetary reward, should be high.[1] Employees also must believe that good performance is valued by the

1. Edward E. Lawler, III, *Pay and Organizational Effectiveness: A Psychological View* (New York: McGraw-Hill Book Company, 1971), p. 91.

employer and will result in their receiving the expected reward. Employee perception of compensation thus can be an important factor in determining the motivational value of compensation.

The effective communication of pay information together with an organizational environment which generates employee trust in management can contribute to more accurate employee perceptions of their pay. Personal characteristics of employees can also affect their pay perceptions. One study, for example, reveals that employees who are higher performers, less educated, higher paid, and older were likely to perceive their pay as equitable. Such employees, more than others, view the organization as doing a better job in setting standards for pay increases.[2]

Also, there is evidence that pay and its role mean different things to different groups within the working population.[3] In one study, for example, pay decisions based upon performance evaluation were found to be perceived as inequitable, whereas those based heavily upon seniority were perceived as equitable.[4] These and other perceptions employees develop concerning their pay are influenced, of course, by the accuracy of their knowledge and understanding of the compensation program.

The Impact of Pay Secrecy. Misperceptions on the part of employees concerning the equity of their pay and its relationship to performance can be created by pay secrecy. According to Lawler, there is reason to believe that secrecy can generate distrust in the compensation system, reduce employee motivation, and inhibit organizational effectiveness. Yet pay secrecy seems to be an accepted practice in many organizations in both the private sector and the public sector.[5] However, a recent survey by The Bureau of National Affairs indicates a trend toward greater disclosure of pay information. More than 50 percent of the respondents to this survey now give their nonmanagement employees access to wage schedule/rates for jobs other than their own. This compares with only 34 percent that reported doing so in a 1972 survey.[6]

Managers may justify secrecy on the grounds that employees prefer to have their pay kept secret. Furthermore, research by Lawler indicates that, where secrecy prevails, there is no great demand for pay rates to be publicized; but where pay has been made public, employees tend to favor this practice.[7] Probably one of the reasons for pay secrecy that managers may be unwilling to admit is that it provides them greater freedom in compensation management since pay decisions are not disclosed and there is less need to justify or defend them. When an employee is not supposed to know what others are being paid, it is difficult for this employee to have an objective basis for pursuing grievances concerning his or her own pay.

2. Jay R. Schuster and Thomas J. Atchinson, "Examining Feelings of Pay Equity," *Business Perspectives,* Vol. 9, No. 3 (Spring, 1973), p. 19.

3. Paul F. Wernimont and Susan Fitzpatrick, "The Meaning of Money," *Journal of Applied Psychology,* Vol. 56, No. 3 (June, 1972), p. 226.

4. R. H. Finn and Sang M. Lee, "Salary Equity: Its Determination, Analysis, and Correlates," *Journal of Applied Psychology,* Vol. 56, No. 4 (August, 1972), pp. 292–293.

5. Edward E. Lawler, III, *Pay and Organization Development* (Reading, MA: Addison-Wesley Publishing Company, 1981), pp. 43–48.

6. "Wage and Salary Administration," *Personnel Policies Forum Survey No. 131* (Washington, DC: The Bureau of National Affairs, Inc., July, 1981), p. 24.

7. Lawler, *op. cit.,* pp. 44–45.

Secrecy also serves to cover up inequities existing within the pay structure. Before the veil of secrecy can be lifted in such situations, however, managers first must move toward the creation of an objective and defensible salary structure. Otherwise the disclosure of pay rates could prove disastrous to employee performance and morale.

The Bases for Compensation

Work performed in blue-collar jobs traditionally has been paid on an hourly basis. It sometimes is referred to as **hourly or day work**, in contrast to **piecework** in which employees are paid according to the number of units they produce. Day work, however, is far more prevalent than piece work as a basis for compensating employees.

Employees compensated on an hourly basis are classified as hourly employees, or wage earners. Those whose compensation is computed on the basis of weekly, biweekly, or monthly pay periods are classified as salaried employees. Hourly employees traditionally were paid only for the time they worked. Salaried employees, by contrast, were compensated for each pay period even though they occasionally may have worked less than the regular number of hours comprising the period. They also generally received certain benefits not provided to hourly employees. More recently, however, most hourly employees also have been able to acquire additional fringe benefits such as paid holidays, vacations, and sick leave. As a result of these developments, the distinction between hourly and salaried employee classifications has been reduced considerably.

Some companies, such as IBM, Hewlett-Packard, and Polaroid, have gone so far as to establish a one-class system in which all employees are paid a salary. Their pay is guaranteed even though, on a particular day, they may be tardy or fail to report for work. The one-class system thus assumes that employees are mature and responsible people who should be treated as such. It constitutes a demonstration of confidence in and a respect for employees that is intended to invite favorable reciprocation from them.[8]

Components of the Wage Mix

A combination of factors can influence, directly or indirectly, the rates at which employees are paid. Through their interaction these factors comprise the **wage mix**. A major factor in this mix is the worth of the job. Another major factor is the employee's relative worth in terms of meeting the requirements of the job. Other components of the wage mix are the condition of the labor market, the area wage rates, the cost of living, the employer's ability to pay, and collective bargaining if the employer is unionized.

Worth of the Job. Organizations without a formal compensation program generally base the worth of jobs upon the subjective opinions of those familiar with

---

8. Robert D. Hulme and Richard B. Beva, "The Blue-Collar Worker Goes on Salary," *Harvard Business Review*, Vol. 53, No. 2 (March-April, 1975), pp. 104–112.

them. In such instances, pay rates may be influenced heavily by the labor market or by collective bargaining in the case of unionized employers. Organizations with formal compensation programs, however, are more likely to rely upon a system of job evaluation to aid in rate determination. Even when rates are subject to collective bargaining, job evaluation can assist the organization in maintaining some degree of control over its wage structure.

The use of job evaluation is widespread in the private sector. According to one survey, 85 percent of the respondents in nonmanufacturing and 73 percent in manufacturing used some form of job evaluation in establishing wage structures in their plants. The jobs covered most frequently by job evaluation were those comprising the technical and office groups; those jobs covered least frequently were for top managers and plant workers.[9] The systems for evaluating jobs and for establishing rate structures will be discussed later.

Employee's Relative Worth.

It is common practice in some industries, notably construction, for unions to negotiate a single rate for jobs in a particular occupation. This egalitarian practice is based on the argument that employees who possess the same qualifications should receive the same rate of pay. Furthermore, the itinerant nature of work in the construction industry usually prevents the accumulation of employment seniority upon which pay differentials might be based. Even so, it is not uncommon for employers in the trades to seek to retain their most competent employees by paying them more than the union scale.

In industrial and office jobs, differences in employee performance can be recognized and rewarded through promotion and through various incentive systems. (Those incentive systems which are used most commonly will be discussed in the next chapter.) Superior performance also can be rewarded by granting merit raises on the basis of steps within a rate range established for a job class. If merit raises are to have their intended value, however, they must be determined by an effective performance evaluation system that differentiates between those employees who deserve them and those who do not. This system, moreover, must provide a visible and creditable relationship between performance and any raises received. Unfortunately too many so-called merit systems provide for raises to be granted automatically. As a result, employees tend to be rewarded more for merely being present rather than for being productive on the job.

Individual worth is contingent upon an employee's ability to capitalize upon it. This ability includes the leverage an employee can exercise in bargaining with an employer for raises and promotions. Such leverage often is provided when the employee receives an offer of another job. When using this leverage, however, the employee takes the risk that the boss will suggest that the job offer be accepted.

Condition of the Labor Market.

The labor market reflects the forces of supply and demand for qualified labor within an area. These forces help to influence the wage rates required to recruit or retain competent employees. It must be recognized,

---

9. *BNA Policy and Practice Series—Compensation* (Washington, DC: The Bureau of National Affairs, Inc., 1979), p. 317:2.

however, that counterforces can reduce the full impact of supply and demand upon the labor market. The economic power of unions, for example, may prevent employers from lowering wage rates even when unemployment is high among union members. Government regulations also may prevent an employer from paying at a market rate less than an established minimum.

Area Wage Rates.   A formal wage structure should provide rates that are in line with those being paid by other employers for comparable jobs within the area. Data pertaining to area wage rates may be obtained by means of local wage surveys. These data will help to prevent the rates for certain jobs from drifting too far above or below those of other employers in the region. When rates drift above existing area levels, an employer's labor costs may become excessive. Conversely, if they drop too far below area levels, difficulties may be encountered in recruiting and retaining competent personnel.

Wage survey data may be obtained from a variety of sources. Many organizations conduct their own surveys. Others engage in a cooperative exchange of wage data or rely upon various associations or professional organizations for such data. Survey data also must take into account indirect wages paid in the form of fringe benefits.

Cost of Living.   Because of continuing inflation, compensation rates have had to be adjusted upward periodically in order to help employees maintain their purchasing power. One survey revealed, for example, that 49 percent of all labor agreements contain escalator clauses. These clauses provide for quarterly cost-of-living adjustments (COLA) in wages based upon changes in the Consumer Price Index (CPI). The most common adjustments are one-cent-per-hour for each 0.3 or 0.4 point change in the CPI.[10]

The CPI as a Basis for COLA.   Increases in wages and in benefit payments for social security, retirement, and welfare based upon the CPI are under attack. One criticism is that the CPI overstates the cost of living because it is based upon a fixed "market basket." This market basket, critics claim, fails to reflect reduction in the consumption of those items hardest hit by inflation such as petroleum and other forms of energy. It also fails to reflect accurately the downgrading of quality in items being purchased or the lower standard of living many consumers are experiencing.

In addition, critics claim that housing costs, which are the largest item in the CPI, are overinflated because these costs are based upon high mortgage rates and home prices in the early 1980s.[11] The CPI, therefore, does not recognize the fact that housing costs can be lower for many families that already own their homes or are paying off low mortgage rates. Neither does it take into account the capital gains home owners are realizing in the sale of their homes. On the other hand, rents being paid largely by apartment dwellers do not provide a true measure of housing costs

10. *Collective Bargaining—Negotiation and Contracts* (Washington, DC: The Bureau of National Affairs, Inc., 1979), p. 93:2.

11. Janet L. Norwood, "The CPI Controversy," *Labor Law Journal,* Vol. 31, No. 3 (March, 1980), pp. 131–138.

because they contain a serious downward bias. To resolve the CPI treatment of housing, Cagan and Moore recommend that a rental-equivalent measure be developed to reflect more accurately the true cost of owner-occupied housing.[12]

Still another inequity created by COLA is the allowance of approximately 5 percent in the CPI for medical care. Increases in medical costs help to increase COLA even though many employees do not experience these increases because they are covered by health insurance paid for entirely by their employers.

The Effect of COLA on Pay Rates.   Within a pay structure, COLA helps to compress pay rates thereby creating inequities among those who receive them. Inequities result from adjustments being made on a cent-per-hour rather than on a percentage basis. Thus, a cost-of-living adjustment of 50 cents represents a 10 percent increase for an employee earning $5 per hour, but only a 5 percent increase for one who is earning $10 per hour.[13] Unless adjustments are made periodically in employee base rates, the desired differential between higher- and lower-paying jobs will gradually be reduced. Reduced also will be the incentive to accept the more demanding jobs.

Unfortunately the inequities created by COLA are difficult to eliminate. Efforts to change the calculation of the CPI inevitably invoke vigorous political opposition from those groups likely to be affected adversely by the change. Furthermore, while unions may agree to short-term freezes in their COLA to help employers out financially, they are adamantly opposed to the elimination or modification of COLA. Meanwhile those in society whose incomes do not rise with inflation are forced to bear the burden of inflation that COLA helps to create.

Employer's Ability to Pay.   In the public sector the amount of pay and benefits employees can receive is limited by the funds budgeted for this purpose and by the willingness of taxpayers to provide them. In the private sector the pay levels are limited by the profits that employers can derive from the goods and services their employees produce. A company's ability to pay thus is determined in part by the productivity of its employees. This productivity is a result not only of their performance but also of the amount of capital the organization has invested in labor-saving equipment. Generally, increases in capital investment reduce the number of employees required to perform the work and increase the employer's ability to provide higher pay for those employed.

Economic conditions and competition experienced by an employer also can affect significantly the rates employers are able to pay. Competition and recessions can force prices down and reduce the income from which compensation payments are derived. In such situations employers have little choice but to reduce wages and/or lay off employees, or even worse, to go out of business.

The ability or inability to pay can be major issues in collective bargaining. During periods of prosperity when earnings are up, union negotiators justify their

---

12. Phillip Cagan and Geoffrey H. Moore, "How to Fix the CPI—With Considerable Emphasis on Housing," *Across the Board,* Vol. XVIII, No. 4 (April, 1981), pp. 14–17.

13. Bruce R. Ellig, "Pay Inequities: How Many Exist Within Your Organization?" *Compensation Review,* Vol. 12, No. 3 (3rd Quarter, 1980), pp. 39–40.

demands for more pay and benefits on the grounds that the company can afford to provide them. When profits are inadequate, inability to pay may provide the basis for a company's argument against providing increases demanded by the union. Employers, however, must exercise caution in claiming inability to pay unless they are prepared to offer proof of this fact by making their financial records available to the union. Refusal to substantiate such claims has been held by the courts to constitute refusal to bargain, which is an unfair labor practice.

Unfortunately as companies in the automobile, steel, rubber, farm machinery, and other industries learned during the major recession of the 1980s, union members are less impressed by inability to pay than by ability to pay. Management efforts to buy labor peace during prosperous years by agreeing to generous pay settlements have made it difficult for union members to adjust to the fact that these halcyon days are over.[14] Also, because of distrust developed over the years, management can have a difficult time trying to convince employees that, if their jobs are to survive, they must forego pay increases. Even though union leaders may recognize this economic reality, they can have a difficult task convincing their members of it.

Collective Bargaining. One of the primary functions of a labor union, as emphasized in Chapter 15, is to bargain collectively over conditions of employment, the most important of which is compensation. The union's goal in each new agreement is to achieve increases in the **real wages,** or purchasing power, of its members. This goal includes gaining wage settlements that equal if not exceed the pattern established by other unions within the area. In obtaining a settlement, union negotiators focus on those elements of the wage mix that support their demands and attempt to play down those elements that may favor the employer's position. The agreements negotiated by unions tend to establish rate patterns within the labor market. As a result, wages generally are higher in areas where organized labor is strong.

In order to recruit and retain competent personnel and avoid unionization, nonunion employers must either meet or exceed these rates. The "union scale" also becomes the prevailing rate which all employers must pay for work performed under government contract. The impact of collective bargaining, therefore, affects considerably more than that segment of the labor force which is unionized.

JOB EVALUATION SYSTEMS

The relative worth of a job may be determined by comparing it with others within the organization or by comparing it with a scale that has been constructed for this purpose. Each method of comparison, furthermore, may be made on the basis of the jobs as a whole or on the basis of the parts comprising the jobs. Four methods of comparison are shown in Figure 17-3. They provide the basis for the principal systems of job evaluation. In the order of their popularity, these systems include the point, factor comparison, grade, and ranking systems.

---

14. "U.S. Steel's Get-Tough Policy," *Business Week* (August 20, 1981), pp. 73–74.

Figure 17–3 Comparison of Job Evaluation Systems

Basis for Comparison	SCOPE OF COMPARISON	
	Job as a Whole (Nonquantitative)	Job Parts or Factors (Quantitative)
Job v. Job	(1) Job Ranking System	(4) Factor Comparison System
Job v. Scale	(2) Job Grade System	(3) Point System

Point System

The **point system** was developed initially by Western Electric and adopted by the National Electrical Manufacturers Association (NEMA) and the National Metal Trades Association (NMTA). It has been successfully used by the United States Steel Corporation, the Johnson Wax Company, and many other companies both large and small. The principal advantage of the point system is that it is relatively simple to understand and to use. It also provides a more refined basis for making judgments than either the ranking or grade systems and thereby can produce results that are more valid and less easy to manipulate. This system permits jobs to be evaluated quantitatively on the basis of the factors or elements that comprise the demands of the job. The skills, efforts, responsibilities, and working conditions that a job usually entails are typical of the more common major factors that serve to make one job more or less important than another. The point system requires the use of a **point manual** that contains a description of the factors and the degrees to which these factors may exist within the jobs. A manual also must indicate—usually by means of a table (see Table 17-1)—the number of points that are allocated to each factor and to each of the degrees into which these factors are divided.

Developing a Point Manual.   A variety of point manuals have been developed by companies, trade associations, and management consultants. An organization that seeks to use one of these or other manuals should make certain that the manual is suited to its particular jobs and conditions of operation. If necessary, the organization should modify the manual to fit its needs. In many instances it may be preferable for the organization to develop a manual of its own.

The job factors and subfactors that are illustrated in Table 17–1 represent those covered by one particular point manual. Each of the factors listed in this manual has been divided into five degrees. The number of degrees into which the factors comprising a manual is to be divided, however, can be more or less than this number, depending upon the relative weight assigned to each factor and upon the ease with which the individual degrees can be defined or distinguished.

Table 17–1 **Point Values for Job Factors**

FACTORS	1st DEGREE	2nd DEGREE	3rd DEGREE	4th DEGREE	5th DEGREE
Skill					
1. Job Knowledge...............	14	28	42	56	70
2. Experience	22	44	66	88	110
3. Initiative and Ingenuity........	14	28	42	56	70
Effort					
4. Physical Demand	10	20	30	40	50
5. Mental or Visual Demand	5	10	15	20	25
Responsibility					
6. Equipment or Process	5	10	15	20	25
7. Material or Product	5	10	15	20	25
8. Safety of Others	5	10	15	20	25
9. Work of Others	5	10	15	20	25
Job Conditions					
10. Working Conditions	10	20	30	40	50
11. Hazards.....................	5	10	15	20	25

SOURCE: Developed by the National Metal Trades Association. Reproduced with permission.

After the job factors comprising the point manual have been divided into degrees, a statement must be prepared defining each of these degrees, as well as each factor as a whole. The definitions should be concise and yet distinguish the factors and each of their degrees. Figure 17–4 represents a portion of a point manual used by the Allis-Chalmers Manufacturing Company to describe each of the degrees for the factors of experience and of initiative and ingenuity. These descriptions enable those persons conducting an evaluation to determine the degrees of the factors that exist in each job being evaluated.

The final step in developing a point manual is that of determining the number of points to be assigned to each factor and to each degree within these factors. Although 500 points quite often is the maximum point value for a manual, there is nothing to prevent the figure from being 400, 800, 1,000, or some other point total. Using the Point Manual. Job evaluation under the point system is accomplished by comparing the job specifications, factor by factor, against the various factor degree descriptions contained in the manual. Each factor within the job being evaluated is then assigned the number of points that is appropriate on the basis of the degree descriptions contained in the manual. When the points for each factor (or subfactor) have been determined from the manual, the total point value for the job as a whole

Figure 17–4 Sample Manual Descriptions for Job Factors and for Their Degrees

EXPERIENCE

This factor measures the length of time, with the specified job knowledge, that is required to obtain and develop the skills necessary to effectively perform the work. Where previous experience is required, time spent in related work or lesser classifications, either within the Company or other organizations, will be considered as contributing to the total experience required to effectively perform the work. Consideration must be given to continuous progress by the average individual, allowing sufficient practice time to encounter and satisfactorily resolve representative deviation in the work assignments that could normally be expected.

First Degree: Up to and including three months.

Second Degree: Over three months up to one year.

Third Degree: Over one year up to three years.

Fourth Degree: Over three years up to five years.

Fifth Degree: Over five years.

INITIATIVE AND INGENUITY

This factor measures the complexity of job duties in terms of the amount of initiative and ingenuity required for successful job performance. Consider the variation and involvement of the methods, procedures, and practices; the degree of independent action and original thought required; the extent of supervision received; and the availability of standards, precedents, and shop practices.

FIRST DEGREE: Instructions are received orally or written in nontechnical terms which can be understood and carried out with a minimum of initiative and judgment. Work is of such a nature that details left to the control of the employee are limited; operations are highly repetitive and minimum of responsibility for maintaining tolerances exists.

SECOND DEGREE: Instructions may require explanation to the extent of using a single view or plan drawing. Procedures are normally detailed; the majority of work is similar in its overall requirement; however, minor variations exist in completing individual details which require the use of some judgment or initiative. Tolerances are easy to maintain, using scales, gauges, solid frame micrometers, templates, and related means of checking.

THIRD DEGREE: Instructions may require explanation to the point of using multiple view or related part drawings. Work is of a varied nature within a well-defined field under standard practices and precedents. Operations can normally be accomplished by several methods or procedures requiring a selection to fit individual variations. Judgment and initiative are required within the limits of established standards. Tolerances are considered close and somewhat difficult to maintain.

FOURTH DEGREE: Instructions available for job performance are few and of a general nature. Basic planning of successive steps together with consideration for related operations is necessary. Duties vary to the extent that assignments normally require drawing upon past parallel solutions for general guidance. Mental resourcefulness, initiative, and judgment are required to solve problems. Tolerances, sizes, clearances and balancing, testing, and related procedures are considered difficult to maintain.

FIFTH DEGREE: Instructions, precedents, and standards for performance of the job are seldom available. Considerable planning and consideration of a variety of factors difficult to evaluate are necessary for successful completion of work. Duties involve the development of new procedures, processes, or methods with a minimum of technical guidance. Requires a high degree of imagination, ingenuity, and independent action.

SOURCE: Reproduced with the permission of the Allis-Chalmers Manufacturing Co.

can be calculated. The relative worth of the job is then determined by the total points that have been assigned to it.[15]

Factor Comparison System

The **factor comparison system** was originated by Eugene Benge about 1926.[16] Like the point system, it permits the job evaluation process to be accomplished on a factor-by-factor basis. It differs from the point system, however, in that the specifications of the jobs to be evaluated are compared against the specifications of key jobs within the organization which serve as the job evaluation scale. Thus, instead of beginning with an established point scale, a factor comparison scale must be developed as a part of the job evaluation process.

Developing a Factor Comparison Scale. The first step in the development of a factor comparison scale is to select the key jobs with which the remaining jobs are to be compared. These key jobs should include jobs of varying difficulty for which complete and accurate descriptions and specifications have been developed. The wage rates for these jobs, furthermore, should be consistent both internally and externally and not be the subject of any grievance action. Usually 15 to 20 key jobs are a sufficient number for a factor comparison scale.

The next step is to determine the proportion of a key job's current wage being paid to each of the factors of which this job is comprised. Thus, the proportion of a key job's wage rate that is allocated to the skill factor will depend on the importance of skill in comparison with mental effort, physical effort, responsibility, and working conditions. Table 17–2 illustrates how the rate for six key jobs has been allocated according to the relative importance of the basic factors that comprise these jobs.

Table 17–2   Wage Apportionment

JOB	TOTAL	SKILL	MENTAL EFFORT	PHYSI-CAL EFFORT	RESPON-SIBILITY	WORK-ING CONDI-TIONS
Machinist Planner	$13.00	$6.50	$3.50	$0.50	$1.60	$0.90
Punch Press Operator	11.30	6.20	1.00	0.70	1.20	2.20
Tank Sealer	10.60	3.00	2.10	1.60	1.00	2.90
Storekeeper	9.10	4.90	1.20	1.00	0.80	1.20
Tank Cleaner	7.30	2.70	0.70	1.20	0.90	1.80
Oiler, Maintenance	6.90	2.60	0.80	0.80	0.80	1.90

15. For further descriptions of the point method, see Henry A. Sargent, "Using the Point Method to Measure Jobs," *Handbook of Wage and Salary Administration,* edited by Milton L. Rock (New York: McGraw-Hill Book Company, 1972), pp. 2-31–2-41.

16. For further information about the factor comparison system, see Herbert G. Zollitsch and Adolph Langsner, *Wage and Salary Administration* (2d ed.; Cincinnati; South-Western Publishing Co., 1970), pp. 179-184, and Eugene J. Benge (ed.), "Using Factor Methods to Measure Jobs," *Handbook of Wage and Salary Administration* (New York: McGraw-Hill Book Company, 1972), pp. 2-42–2-55.

Using the Factor Comparison Scale. The locations of the key jobs on the factor comparison scale and the specifications for these jobs provide the bench marks against which the other jobs are evaluated. As an example of how the scale is used, let us assume that the job of *screw machine operator* is to be evaluated through the use of the factor comparison scale shown in Figure 17–5 on pages 420–421. By comparing the specifications covering the skill requirement for *screw machine operator* with the skill requirements of the other jobs on the table, it was decided that the skill demands of the job placed it about half way between those of a storekeeper and a punch press operator. The job therefore was placed at the $5.60 point on the scale. The same procedure was used in locating the job at the appropriate point on the scales for the remaining factors. As additional non-key jobs are added to the scale and are available for comparison, it is possible that minor adjustments, upward or downward, may be made in the location of certain jobs on the scale. Further, as more non-key jobs are added to the scale, the jobs to be evaluated become easier to place on the scale because there are more jobs on the scale against which comparisons can be made.

The evaluated worth of the jobs added to the scale is computed by adding up the money values for each factor as determined by where the job has been placed on the scale for each factor. Thus, the evaluated worth of *screw machine operator* of $10.10 would be determined by totaling the monetary value for each factor as follows:

Skill . . . . $ 5.60
Mental Effort 90
Physical Effort 90
Responsibility 1.30
Working Conditions 1.40
$10.10

Job Grade System

In the **job grade or classification system**, jobs are classified and grouped according to a series of predetermined wage classes or grades. While this system has the advantage of simplicity, it is less precise than the point and factor comparison systems because the job is evaluated as a whole. The federal civil service job classification system is probably the best known system of this type. The descriptions for each of the job classes constitute the scale against which the specifications for the various jobs are compared.

Job Ranking System

The simplest and oldest system of job evaluation is the **job ranking system** by which jobs are arrayed on the basis of their relative worth. One technique that is used to rank jobs consists of having the raters arrange cards containing the specifications for each job in the order of importance of the jobs that the cards represent. Differences in the rankings made by the raters can then be reconciled into a single rating.

The basic weakness of the job ranking system is that it does not provide a very refined measure of each job's worth. Since the comparisons must be made on the basis of the job as a whole, it is quite easy for one or more of the factors of a job to bias the ranking that the evaluator gives to a job, particularly if the job is complex. Furthermore, the rankings merely indicate the relative importance of the jobs but not the differences in the degree of importance that may exist between jobs.

Union Reactions to Job Evaluation

Unlike wage rates that are determined by negotiation and reflect the bargaining achievements of the union officers, those rates established through job evaluation are based upon a system. Because of this fact, the role of the union negotiators in wage determination is reduced. Thus, in the opinion of many union leaders, job evaluation serves to restrict bargaining on wage adjustments and to freeze the wage structure.[17] Other complaints of union officers concerning job evaluation are that it often is used as the sole criterion in establishing wage scales rather than as a guide. They claim also that job evaluation plans are not kept current, are not understood by employees, fail to give equitable evaluation to "human elements" of the job, and are based upon "ideal" rather than normal performance. The results of one study, however, have indicated that dissatisfaction among union officials toward job evaluation has decreased from that revealed in a study four years earlier, with some officials even expressing their acceptance of it. This change, among other things, probably stems from improved communication between management and unions concerning wage and salary administration.[18]

Job Evaluation for Management Positions

Because management positions are more complicated and involve certain demands not found in jobs at the lower levels, some organizations do not attempt to include them in their job evaluation programs. Those that do evaluate these positions, however, may extend their regular system of evaluation to include such positions, or they may develop a separate evaluation system for management positions.

Several systems have been developed especially for the evaluation of management positions. One of the better known of those which are gaining acceptance is the **profile method**. This method combines certain features of the point, factor comparison, and ranking systems. The three basic factors or components that comprise the evaluation "profile" in one system include knowledge (or know-how), mental activity (or problem solving), and accountability. The profile for each position is developed by determining the percentage value to be given to each of the three broad factors. Jobs are then ranked on the basis of each factor, and point values that go to make up the profile are then assigned to each job on the basis of the percentage-value level at which the job is ranked.[19]

---

17. Harold D. Janes, "Issues in Job Evaluation: The Union View," *Personnel Journal*, Vol. 51, No. 9 (September, 1972), p. 677.

18. *Ibid.*, p. 679.

19. Charles W. G. VanHorn, "The Hay Guide Chart—Profile Method," *Handbook of Wage and Salary Administration*, edited by Milton L. Rock (New York: McGraw-Hill Book Company, 1972), pp. 2-86—2-97.

Figure 17–5 Factor Comparison Scale (page 1)

HOURLY RATE $	SKILL	MENTAL EFFORT	PHYSICAL EFFORT	RESPONSIBILITY	WORKING CONDITIONS
6.50	Machinist Planner				
6.40					
6.30					
6.20	Punch Press Oper.				
6.10					
6.00					
5.90					
5.80					
5.70					
5.60	**Screw Mach. Oper.**				
5.50					
5.40					
5.30					
5.20					
5.10					
5.00					
4.90	Storekeeper				
4.80					
4.70					
4.60					
4.50					
4.40					
4.30					
4.20					
4.10					
4.00					
3.90					
3.80					
3.70					
3.60					

Note: If this scale contained the 15 to 20 key jobs that typically comprise a factor comparison scale, the gaps between jobs on the skill scale would be reduced substantially.

Figure 17–5 Factor Comparison Scale (page 2)

HOURLY RATE $	SKILL	MENTAL EFFORT	PHYSICAL EFFORT	RESPONSIBILITY	WORKING CONDITIONS
3.50		Machinist Planner			
3.40					
3.30					
3.20					
3.10					
3.00	Tank Sealer				
2.90					Tank Sealer
2.80					
2.70	Tank Cleaner				
2.60	Oiler, Maintenance				
2.50					
2.40					
2.30					
2.20					Punch Press Oper.
2.10		Tank Sealer			
2.00					
1.90					Oiler, Maintenance
1.80					Tank Cleaner
1.70					
1.60			Tank Sealer	Machinist Planner	
1.50					
1.40					**Screw Mach. Oper.**
1.30				**Screw Mach. Oper.**	
1.20		Storekeeper	Tank Cleaner	Punch Press Oper.	Storekeeper
1.10					
1.00		Punch Press Oper.	Storekeeper	Tank Sealer	
.90		**Screw Mach. Oper.**	**Screw Mach. Oper.**	Tank Cleaner	Machinist Planner
.80		Oiler, Maintenance	Oiler, Maintenance	Storekeeper / Oiler, Maintenance	
.70		Tank Cleaner	Punch Press Oper.		
.60					
.50			Machinist Planner		

THE COMPENSATION STRUCTURE

Job evaluation systems do not determine the wage rate. They only provide the basis for wage rate determination. The evaluated worth of each job in terms of its rank, class, points, or monetary worth must be converted into an hourly, daily, weekly, or monthly wage rate. Figure 17–6 provides a schematic chart showing the processes that may be involved in wage determination and the sources of data that may be utilized.

The Wage Curve

The relationship between the relative worth of the jobs and their wage rates can be represented by means of a **wage curve or conversion line**. This curve may

Figure 17–6 A Wage Administration System

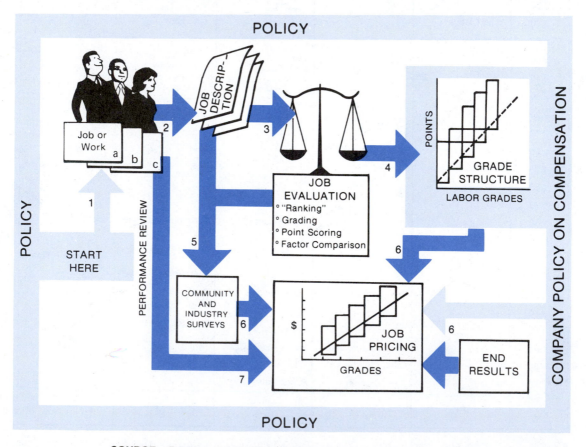

SOURCE: Bureau of Industrial Relations Seminar (Ann Arbor, Michigan: University of Michigan). Reproduced with permission of Dr. Gerard Carhalvo.

Figure 17–7 **Freehand Wage Curve**

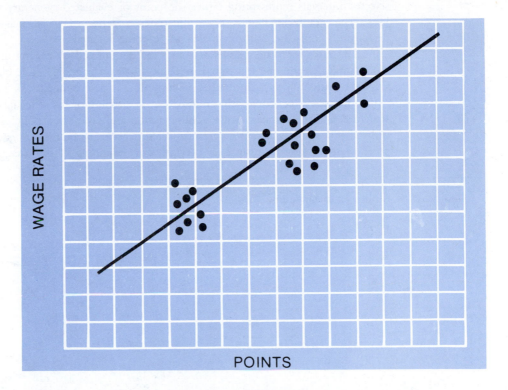

indicate the rates currently paid for jobs within the organization, the new rates resulting from job evaluation, or the rates for similar jobs currently being paid by other organizations within the community. A curve may be constructed graphically by preparing a scattergram consisting of a series of dots that represent the current wage rates. A freehand curve is then drawn through the cluster of dots in such a manner as to leave approximately an equal number of dots above and below the curve, as illustrated by Figure 17–7. This wage curve will then determine the relationship between the value of a job and its wage rate at any given point on the line. The curve also can be constructed by means of an algebraic formula using what is known as the least squares method.[20]

Wage Classes

Generally it is preferable from an administrative standpoint to group jobs into **wage classes or grades,** and to pay all jobs within a particular class the same rate

---

20. A description of the least squares method may be obtained from any basic textbook in business statistics.

or rate range. When the grade or classification system of job evaluation is used, jobs are grouped into classes as a part of the evaluation process. When the point and factor comparison systems are used, however, wage classes must be established at selected intervals representing either the point or evaluated monetary value of these jobs. The graph in Figure 17–8 illustrates a series of wage classes which are designated along the horizontal axis at 50-point intervals.

The rates for wage classes also may be determined by means of a conversion table similar to the one illustrated in Table 17–3 on page 425. The classes within a wage structure may vary in number. The number is determined by such factors as the slope of the wage curve, the number and distribution of the jobs within the structure, and the company wage administration and promotion policies. The number utilized should be sufficient to permit difficulty levels to be distinguished but not so great as to make the distinction between two adjoining classes insignificant.

Figure 17–8 Single Rate Structure

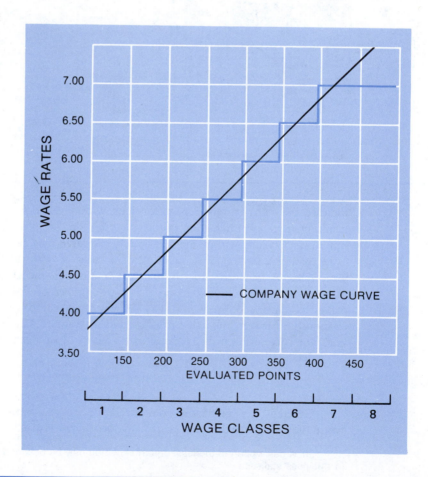

Table 17–3   **Point Conversion Table**

WAGE CLASS	POINT RANGE	HOURLY RATE RANGE
1	101-150	$3.50-4.25
2	151-200	4.00-4.75
3	201-250	4.50-5.25
4	251-300	5.00-5.75
5	301-350	5.50-6.25
6	351-400	6.00-6.75
7	401-450	6.50-7.25
8	451-500	7.00-7.75

Rate Ranges

Although a single rate may be created for each wage class as shown in Figure 17–8, it is more common to provide a rate range for each of them. The rate ranges may be the same for each class or proportionately greater for each successive class as shown in Figure 17–9. Rate ranges constructed on the latter basis provide a greater incentive for employees to accept a promotion to a job in a higher class.

Rate ranges generally are divided into a series of steps that permit employees to receive increases up to the maximum rate for the range on the basis of merit or seniority or a combination of the two. Most salary structures provide for the ranges of adjoining wage classes to overlap. The purpose of the overlap is to permit an employee with experience to earn as much as or more than a person with less experience in the next higher job classification.

Classifying Jobs

The final step in the wage determination process is to determine the appropriate wage class into which each job should be placed on the basis of its evaluated worth. Traditionally this evaluated worth is determined on the basis of the job without regard to the performance of the person in the job. Under this system the performance of those who exceed the requirements of a job may be acknowledged through merit increases within the class range or through a promotion to a job in the next higher wage class. Unfortunately such a system often fails to reward employees for the skills they possess or to encourage them to learn new job-related skills. It tends to consider employees as job holders rather than as individuals.[21] In an attempt to correct these weaknesses, some organizations have introduced **skill-evaluation plans.** Under these plans employees are paid according to the number of jobs within the organization that they can perform. This approach encourages

---

21. Edward E. Lawler, III, "New Approaches to Pay: Innovations That Work," *Personnel*, Vol. 53, No. 5 (September-October, 1976), p. 14.

Figure 17–9 Wage Structure with Increasing Rate Ranges

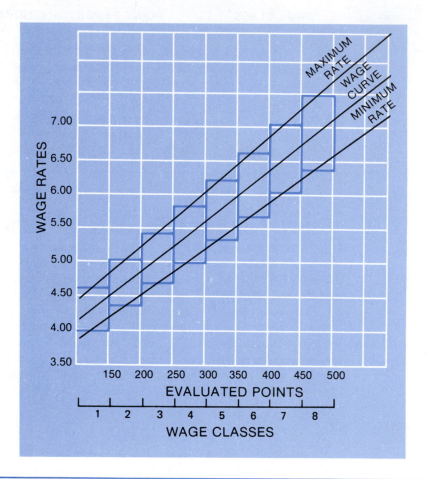

employees to acquire additional skills and is particularly well-suited to work situations where employees are rotated among a number of jobs.

Controlling the Rate Structure

The primary purpose of the pay differentials between the wage classes is to provide an incentive for employees to prepare for and accept more demanding jobs. Unfortunately this incentive is being significantly reduced by **wage rate compression**—the compression of differentials between job classes—particularly the differential between hourly workers and their supervisors. The prevalence of wage rate compression is indicated by the fact that 90 percent of the 845 companies responding to one survey admitted that it was common in their organizations. Because of this trend toward an egalitarian pay structure, getting ahead may no longer mean getting more.[22]

In addition to supervisory personnel, white-collar employees often have become victims of wage rate compression. Across-the-board increases negotiated by unions for blue-collar groups but not granted to white-collar employees have created some frustrating inequities for the latter. Such increases have come in a large part from COLA provided for in labor agreements. Other inequities have resulted from the scarcity of applicants in the computer, engineering, and other technical fields. As a result, job applicants in these fields frequently have been offered starting salaries not far below those paid to employees with considerable experience and seniority.

Companies today are encountering severe difficulties in trying to maintain differentials within their pay structure. One compensation executive describes this problem as follows:

> Fundamentally there isn't a great deal that we compensation managers can do about it. Companies can't reverse the long-term trend toward the leveling of incomes and we can't solve the problem by throwing money at the middle and upper levels of the organization; competitive pressures won't let us.[23]

Unfortunately for compensation managers, mid-level employees in the white-collar and professional jobs who have become victims of the pay rate compression are joining labor organizations to gain equitable pay.

GOVERNMENTAL REGULATION OF COMPENSATION

Compensation management, like the other areas of human resources management, is subject to state and federal regulations. A majority of states have minimum wage laws or wage boards which fix minimum wage rates on an industry-by-industry basis. Most of them also regulate hours of work and overtime payments. Table 17–4 lists the minimum wage rates required by state law.

The three principal federal laws affecting wages are the Fair Labor Standards Act, the Walsh-Healy Act, and the Davis-Bacon Act. These laws were enacted during the 1930s to prevent the payment of abnormally low wage rates and to encourage the spreading of work among a greater number of workers. The latter objective was accomplished by forcing companies to pay a premium rate for overtime work, that is, for all hours worked in excess of a prescribed number.

Fair Labor Standards Act

The Fair Labor Standards Act (FLSA), which is commonly referred to as the Wage and Hour Act, was passed in 1938 and subsequently has been amended many times. It covers those employees who are engaged in the production of goods for

---

22. Katherine Christensen, "White-Collar Blues: Middle-Rank Workers Often Find Pay Gains Trailing Subordinates," *The Wall Street Journal*, June 23, 1980, p. 1.
23. *Ibid.*

Table 17—4   Basic Hourly Minimum Wage Rates Under State Laws*

1. Alabama	None		27. Montana	$2.75
2. Alaska	$3.85		28. Nebraska	$1.60
3. Arizona	None		29. Nevada	$2.75
4. Arkansas	$2.70		30. New Hampshire	$3.35
5. California	$3.35		31. New Jersey	$3.35
6. Colorado	$1.90		32. New Mexico	$3.35
7. Connecticut	$3.37		33. New York	$3.35
8. Delaware	$2.00		34. North Carolina	$3.10
9. D.C.	$2.50-$3.90		35. North Dakota	$2.55-$3.10
10. Florida	None		36. Ohio	$2.30
11. Georgia	$1.25		37. Oklahoma	$3.10
12. Hawaii	$3.35		38. Oregon	$3.10
13. Idaho	$2.30		39. Pennsylvania	$3.35
14. Illinois	$2.30		40. Puerto Rico	50¢-$3.35
15. Indiana	$2.00		41. Rhode Island	$3.35
16. Iowa	None		42. South Carolina	None
17. Kansas	$1.60		43. South Dakota	$2.80
18. Kentucky	$2.15		44. Tennessee	None
19. Louisiana	None		45. Texas	$1.40
20. Maine	$3.35		46. Utah	$2.50-$2.75
21. Maryland	$3.35		47. Vermont	$3.35
22. Massachusetts	$3.35		48. Virginia	$2.65
23. Michigan	$3.35		49. Washington	$2.30
24. Minnesota	$3.35		50. West Virginia	$3.05
25. Mississippi	None		51. Wisconsin	$3.25
26. Missouri	None		52. Wyoming	$1.60

*Rates in effect in 1982.

SOURCE: Reprinted by permission from *BNA Policy and Practice Series*, copyright 1982 by *The Bureau of National Affairs, Inc., Washington, DC.*

interstate and foreign commerce, including those whose work is closely related to or directly essential to such production. The act's coverage also includes employees of certain retail and service establishments whose sales volumes exceed a prescribed amount and, most recently, agricultural workers. The major provisions of the FLSA are concerned with minimum wage rates and overtime payments, child labor, and equal rights.[24]

Wage and Hour Provisions.

The minimum wage prescribed by federal law has been raised many times from its original figure of 25 cents per hour to a scheduled

24. Because the act is likely to be subject to future amendments, an employer should consult the appropriate publications of one of the labor services previously mentioned or the Wage and Hour Division of the United States Department of Labor in order to obtain the latest information regarding its current provisions, particularly the minimum wage rate.

rate of $3.10 per hour, effective in 1980, and $3.35 per hour, effective in 1981. This minimum rate applies to the actual earning rate before any overtime premiums have been added. An overtime rate of $1^1/_2$ times the base rate must be paid for all hours worked in excess of 40 during a given week. The base wage rate from which the overtime rate is computed must include incentive payments or bonuses that are received during the period. For example, if a person employed at a base rate of $4 an hour works a total of 45 hours in a given week and receives a bonus of $45, that person actually is working at the rate of $5 an hour. (The $45 bonus divided by the 45 hours required to earn it equals $1 per hour which, when added to the base rate of $4 per hour, increases the employee's earning rate to $5 per hour for the week.) Earnings for the week would total $237.50, computed as follows:

Regular time	40 × $5.00 =	$200.00
Overtime	5 × $7.50 =	37.50
Total earnings		$237.50

If the bonus is paid on a monthly or quarterly basis, earnings for the period must be recalculated to include this bonus in the hourly rate for overtime payments. When employees are given time off in return for overtime work, it must be granted at $1^1/_2$ times the number of hours that were worked as overtime. Employees who are paid on a piece-rate basis also must receive a premium for overtime work. The hourly rate upon which overtime is to be based is computed by dividing earnings from piecework by the total number of hours of work required to earn this amount. For example, if an employee produced 1,250 units of work at 20 cents per unit during a 50-hour week, the earning rate would be $5.00 per hour computed as follows:

$$\frac{1,250 \text{ units} \times 20¢}{50 \text{ hours}} = \$5.00 \text{ per hour}$$

Since the 10 hours in excess of a 40-hour week constitute overtime at $1^1/_2$ times the regular rate, total earnings for the week would be $275.00 computed as follows:

Regular time	40 × $5.00 =	$200.00
Overtime	10 × $7.50 =	75.00
Total earnings		$275.00

Child Labor Provisions. The FLSA forbids the employment of minors between 16 and 18 years of age in hazardous occupations such as mining, logging, woodworking, meat-packing, and certain types of manufacturing. Minors under 16 cannot be employed in any work destined for interstate commerce except that which is performed in a nonhazardous occupation for a parent or guardian or for an employer under a temporary permit issued by the Department of Labor.

The "Teenwage" Issue. The continuing increases in the minimum wage have made it more difficult for high school youth to obtain employment. Many employers who might otherwise be willing to hire them are unwilling to pay them the same rate as adults because of their lack of experience. In an effort to reduce chronically high unemployment in this age group, proposals have been submitted to Congress for a **teenwage.** These proposals, which would permit employers to hire 16 to 19-year-olds at a rate 15 percent less than the minimum wage, so far have been rejected. The debate over this wage concept, however, is far from over.[25]

Exemptions Under the Act.   The feature of the FLSA that perhaps creates the most confusion concerns the exemption of certain groups of employees from coverage by the act or from certain of its provisions. The act now provides more than 40 separate exemptions, some of which apply only to a certain group of personnel or to certain provisions of the act such as those relating to child labor or to overtime.[26] One of the most common exemptions concerns the overtime provision of the act. Since management personnel in any organization are exempt from these provisions, they often are referred to as exempt employees. Nonmanagement personnel are referred to as nonexempt employees.

Equal Rights Provisions.   One of the most significant amendments to the FLSA was the Equal Pay Act passed in 1963. This act states:

> No employer shall discriminate between employees on the basis of sex by paying wages to employees less than the rate at which he pays wages to employees of the opposite sex for equal work on jobs which require equal *skill, effort,* and *responsibility,* and *similar working conditions.*

The federal Age Discrimination Act of 1967, as amended, extends the equal rights provisions by forbidding wage discrimination based upon age for employees in the 40 to 70-year-old age group. Neither of these acts, however, prohibits wage differentials based on factors other than age or sex, such as seniority, merit, or a measure of performance.

In spite of the Equal Pay Act, the achievement of parity by women in the labor market has been slow in coming. Women still are concentrated in the lower-paying jobs, particularly in jobs of a clerical nature. In fact, according to a Conference Board study, some 35 percent of all female employees today work in clerical jobs compared with only 30 percent about 20 years ago. Another Conference Board study has revealed that women are being paid 43 percent less than men.[27] A study by the Department of Labor has produced similar evidence indicating that the weekly earnings of women in full-time jobs was 40 percent less than men.[28] Even in white-collar jobs within the federal government, as Table 17–5 indicates, women receive lower pay than men performing the same job.

25. "Would the 'Teenwage' Cut Unemployment?" *Business Week* (Sept. 19, 1977), pp. 106–107.

26. Many employers find the major labor reference services—such as those published by The Bureau of National Affairs, Inc., by Prentice-Hall, Inc., and by the Commerce Clearing House—to be helpful sources of information concerning these exemptions and other provisions of the Act.

27. Froma Joselow, "Women and Money," *New Dawn for Women* (September, 1977), p. 33.

28. *U.S. Working Women: A Databook* (Washington, DC: U.S. Department of Labor, Bureau of Labor Statistics, 1977), p. 29.

Table 17—5 **Comparison of Occupational Salaries of Men v. Women**

AVERAGE ANNUAL SALARIES OF FEDERAL WHITE-COLLAR WORKERS BY SEX[1]

Occupational Group	Men	Women
Accounting and Budget	$26,481	$16,606
Biological Sciences	23,152	16,630
Business and Industry	27,780	18,337
Copyright, Patent, Trademark	41,747	29,804
Education	24,095	17,384
Engineering & Architecture	30,098	18,117
Equipment, Facilities, Service	26,829	19,003
General Administrative, Clerical, and Office Services	25,373	14,716
Information and Arts	27,147	20,201
Investigation	27,628	19,119
Legal and Kindred	30,740	18,145
Library and Archives	23,964	19,992
Mathematics and Statistics	33,148	20,801
Medical, Hospital, Dental & Public Health	24,323	17,811
Personnel Management, Industrial Relations	28,544	18,278
Physical Sciences	30,609	21,328
Quality Assurance, Inspection, Grading	23,631	17,277
Social Science, Psychology, Welfare	29,890	23,437
Supply	20,794	15,596
Transportation	30,917	16,968
Veterinary Medical Science	30,118	24,379

[1]Data are for full-time workers only.
SOURCE: U.S. Office of Personnel Management, *Occupations of Federal White-Collar Workers,* October 1980.

Walsh-Healy Act

The Walsh-Healy Act, which is officially called the Public Contracts Act, was passed in 1936 and covers workers employed on government contract work for supplies, equipment, and materials worth in excess of $10,000. The act requires contractors to pay employees at least the prevailing wage rates established by the Secretary of Labor for the area and overtime of 1½ times the regular rate for all work performed in excess of 8 hours in one day or 40 hours in one week, depending upon which basis provides the larger premium. For example, an employee working 4 days of 12 hours each during a given week would be entitled to receive 16 hours of overtime and 32 hours of regular time for the week. In computing overtime payments under the Walsh-Healy Act, as under the FLSA, the wage rate used must include any bonuses or incentive payments that may be a part of the employee's total earnings. The Walsh-Healy Act also contains restrictions covering the use of child and convict labor.

Davis-Bacon Act

The Davis-Bacon Act, which is also referred to as the Prevailing Wage Law, was passed in 1931 and is the oldest of the three federal wage laws. It requires that the minimum wage rates paid to persons employed on federal public works projects worth more than $2,000 be at least equal to the prevailing rates and that overtime be paid at $1\frac{1}{2}$ times this rate.

There have been efforts in Congress to repeal the act on the grounds that the need which prevailed in the 1930s at the time of its passage no longer exists. The act is also criticized for contributing to inflation because the minimum pay can be based upon the rate paid to only 30 percent of the workers in an area. This "30 percent rule" usually results in forcing contractors on federal construction projects to pay rates negotiated by unions (union scale), as long as their workers represent at least 30 percent of workers within the area. These rates are often higher than the average rate prevailing within the area. Failing to get the act repealed, its opponents have sought to eliminate the 30 percent rule as a basis for establishing the prevailing rate on federal public works projects.

The Issue of Equal Pay for Comparable Work

By far the greatest compensation management issue of the 1980s is that concerning equal pay for comparable work. The issue stems from the fact that jobs which are performed predominantly by women are paid less than those performed by men. This practice results in what critics term **institutionalized sex discrimination** and causes women to receive less pay for jobs which may be different but comparable in worth to those performed by men. As Figure 17–10 indicates, women earn about 59 cents for every dollar earned by men. The issue of comparable work goes beyond that of providing equal pay for jobs which involve the same duties for women as for men. It is not concerned with whether or not a female secretary should receive the same pay as a male secretary. Rather, the issue is concerned with whether or not secretaries should receive pay equal to that paid for jobs of comparable worth performed primarily by males. Such jobs, for example, might include those of mechanic or truck driver.

Problem of Measuring Comparability.
Unfortunately the question which the comparable work issue leaves unanswered is how the comparability of jobs involving completely different qualifications and perfomance demands is to be determined. This question may prove about as easy to answer as, "Who was worth most to society: Ludwig van Beethoven, Marie Curie, Florence Nightingale, or William Shakespeare?"

Within a particular organization it may be possible to develop some system for evaluating the worth of dissimilar jobs. The city of San Jose, CA, with the aid of consultants, has developed such a system which was acceptable to unions striking for a comparable worth pay structure. Determining the comparable worth of dissimilar jobs in different organizations where rates may be dictated by collective bargaining or by labor market conditions, however, can prove to be a much more difficult task. Currently the National Academy of Science (NAS), under contract with the EEOC,

Figure 17–10 **The Issue of Comparable Worth**

SOURCE: © Doug Marlette, 1982, The Charlotte Observer. Distributed by King Features Syndicate, Inc.

is studying whether or not existing job evaluation systems are sophisticated enough to compare widely different jobs. One respected authority, Graf S. Crystal, predicts that they will find they are not. In his opinion, "There isn't one such plan that can't be torn to pieces by an impartial observer, and I doubt the NAS can come up with a good one."[29]

Impact of the Labor Market and Collective Bargaining. Even if comparable worth eventually can be determined with acceptable accuracy, consideration also must be given to the labor market and collective bargaining forces which are a part of our economic system. A shortage of applicants for certain jobs can help to increase the rates for these jobs and, in turn, reduce their shortage. To eliminate the impact of the labor market, wage rates would have to be determined by the courts or by commissions established for this purpose. It is doubtful, however, whether those making the determination of comparable worth would be better qualified than those currently performing the task. Nor would the judgments of the former be any less free of bias. Collective bargaining which affects the labor market can be a source of

29. Graf S. Crystal, "The Managers Journal: Comparable Worth?" *The Wall Street Journal,* November 5, 1979, Editorial Page.

many pay inequities. To prevent these inequities, wage determination also would have to be subject to government control, to the detriment of our free economic society.

One of the reasons that the labor market has produced inequities in pay for women is that discrimination has denied women the opportunity for employment in male-dominated jobs. The solution to their dilemma thus involves comparable job *opportunity* as much as it does comparable job worth. There also is the factor of the comparable desirability of employment in different jobs. The fact that many men, as well as women, prefer to accept desirable working conditions in offices in lieu of higher pay for blue-collar work helps to depress the pay for white-collar jobs.

Position of Congress and the Courts.   When the Equal Pay Act was being debated, proponents of comparable worth attempted to have equal pay based upon this criterion rather than upon equal work. A majority in Congress, however, deliberately chose to avoid the use of the comparable worth criterion. Thus, as Supreme Court Justice Rehnquist concluded in a dissenting opinion involving a suit by jail matrons at the county jail in Washington County, OR:

> Congress realized that the adoption of the comparable worth doctrine would ignore the economic relations of supply and demand, and would involve both government agencies and the courts in the impossible task of ascertaining the worth of comparable work in an area in which they have little expertise.[30]

In this case, however, the majority opinion held that the jail matron who performed similar but not identical work to that performed by male jailers could sue for equal pay.[31] (The county settled out of court by paying each matron $3500, after which it abolished the job of jail matron.) This opinion may encourage similar suits as proponents of equal worth attempt to gain from the courts what they have been unable to gain from Congress.

RÉSUMÉ

Compensation is a key function of human resources management. The basis upon which compensation payments are determined and the way in which they are administered can have a significant impact upon employee productivity and upon the achievement of organizational goals. While the worth of the job and the performance of an individual in the job are major factors in determining an employee's rate of pay, this rate may be affected also by other factors such as labor market conditions, area wage rates, cost of living, employer's ability to pay, and collective bargaining.

Rate structures based upon the relative worth of the jobs within organizations can be developed through the job evaluation systems. Data gained through these systems provide the basis for establishing wage classes in which jobs can be grouped

---

30. "Review and Outlook: Pandora's Worth," *The Wall Street Journal*, July 16, 1981, p. 22.

31. Washington County *v.* Gunther. 101 Sup. Ct. 2242 (1981). 452 US 161.

according to their relative worth. Rate ranges can then be constructed for jobs in each class to recognize differences in performance and/or seniority among employees in these jobs.

Systems currently used to determine pay rates are being criticized by certain individuals and groups for perpetuating the lower rates existing for jobs performed predominantly by women. These jobs, they charge, should receive pay equal to that received by men in jobs which may involve different duties but which are determined to be of comparable worth. Unfortunately for women, difficulties in measuring comparable worth and in getting Congress and the courts to require that equal pay be based upon it have prevented the "equal pay for comparable work" issue from being resolved.

TERMS TO IDENTIFY

valence
hourly or day work
piecework
wage mix
real wages
point system
point manual
factor comparison system
job grade or classification system

job ranking system
profile method
wage curve or conversion line
wage classes or grades
skill-evaluation plans
wage rate compression
teenwage
institutionalized sex discrimination

DISCUSSION QUESTIONS

1. What are the disadvantages of pay secrecy? In spite of its disadvantages, why do some managers prefer pay secrecy?
2. Since employees may differ in terms of their job performance, would it not be more feasible to determine the wage rate for each employee on the basis of his or her relative worth?
3. What are some of the criticisms being raised concerning COLA and the CPI upon which COLA is based?
4. During collective bargaining, unions sometimes have responded to a company claim of inability to pay with the statement that the union should not be expected to subsidize inefficient management. To what extent do you feel that a union response of this type has or does not have merit?

5. One of the objections to granting wage increases on a percentage basis is that the lowest paid employees who are having the most trouble "making ends meet" get the smallest increase, while the highest paid employees get the largest increase. Is this objection a valid one?
6. An employee covered by the FLSA earns $4.00 per hour, works 50 hours during a given week, and receives a production bonus of $10.00. What are this employee's gross earnings for the week?
7. What are some of the problems to be encountered in developing a pay system based upon equal pay for comparable work?

THE IMPRACTICAL PHYSICIST

Dr. Carla Schiller, a specialist in solid state physics, possessed a Ph.D. degree from one of the nation's leading universities. She was considered to be outstanding in the field and fully worth the $50,000 per year she received from her employer, the Space Age Corporation. Although a brilliant scientist, Dr. Schiller lacked common sense in coping with practical problems, particularly those of a financial nature. Typical was the purchase of a home at a price considerably beyond that which she could afford. This financial problem was aggravated when she received a transfer from the company's Houston location to Boston. To minimize an employee's problem of disposing of a house upon being transferred, the company has established a policy of buying the houses of employees who did not choose to dispose of them personally. The price paid by the company is based upon an average of the two highest appraisals out of three made. Employees who believe that they can get a higher price by selling it themselves are free to exercise this option. However, an employee who is unsuccessful in selling the house personally cannot later request the company to buy the house.

When Dr. Schiller was transferred, several friends told her that she could get considerably more than the price offered by the company if she attempted to sell it herself. Accordingly, she put the house on the market but was unable to sell it prior to the move to Boston. Upon arrival at Boston, Dr. Schiller purchased another home which was priced beyond her means. For the next seven months she was forced to make payments not only on the new home, but also on the old one which she had not sold. At the end of that time, her personal savings had been practically exhausted and the resulting strain was beginning to affect her job performance adversely.

Dr. Schiller's superiors decided that something had to be done to help her out of the financial problem she had created for herself. The corporate human resources department was approached to see if an exception could be made to the policy of not permitting employees to change their minds after they had committed themselves to selling their homes personally. After some discussion it was decided that perhaps in Dr. Schiller's case an exception might be made on the grounds that she had not been properly counseled on the company's house-purchasing policy. Using this loophole, the company purchased Dr. Schiller's former house, thus helping to relieve her financial dilemma. Unfortunately she was still minus the $15,000 she had spent in attempting to maintain two homes at the same time.

a. Was the company correct in making an exception for Dr. Schiller in agreeing to purchase her house after she had previously declined to have the company do so?

b. How far should an employer go in helping employees like Dr. Schiller cope with their personal financial affairs?

MAKING UP FOR TIME LOST

Ethel Perkins was the owner of a small business which she chose to operate in a rather informal manner without too much concern for "red tape originating in Washington." Her employees, who were treated like members of the family, were paid on a weekly basis. If they were absent during a week when work was slow, when they were ill, or when they had to attend to personal business, they would still receive their full pay. The employees made up for their absences by working a few more hours extra when their services were needed. One employee even accumulated extra hours in advance to cover the week he took off each year during the deer-hunting season. Because this informal time-off arrangement accommodated the employees' personal needs, they appeared happy with it.

Everything was fine until Mr. Gross, a Department of Labor representative, paid a visit and requested the opportunity to make what Mrs. Perkins perceived to be a routine inspection of her payroll records. Upon completion of this inspection, Mrs. Perkins was informed that she owed five employees a total of about $5,000.00 in back wages for the overtime they had worked. Mr. Gross informed her that, under the FLSA, any time worked to make up for hours lost during a week had to be worked the same week. Three of the employees who were held to be due the overtime pay stated they would refuse to accept payment. The other two had quit, owing money to Mrs. Perkins on personal loans that were greater than the amount of overtime alleged to be due them.

a. How should this problem involving overtime be resolved?

b. What dilemma do problems such as this one create for law enforcement agencies? For owners of small businesses?

SUGGESTED READINGS

Belcher, David W. *Compensation Administration.* Englewood Cliffs, NJ: Prentice-Hall, Inc., 1974.

Berg, J. Gary. *Compensation.* New York: AMACOM, American Management Associations, 1976.

Bird, Caroline. *Everything a Woman Needs to Know to Get Paid What She's Worth.* New York: David McKay Company, Inc., 1973.

Henderson, Richard. *Compensation Management,* 3d ed. Reston, VA: Reston Publishing Company, 1982.

Marshall, Don R. *Successful Techniques for Solving Employee Compensation Problems.* New York: John Wiley & Sons, Inc., 1978.

Nash, Allan N., and Stephen J. Carroll, Jr. *The Management of Compensation.* Monterey, CA: Brooks/Cole Publishing Company, 1975.

Porter, Lyman W., Edward E. Lawler, III, and J. Richard Hackman. *Behavior in Organizations.* New York: McGraw-Hill Book Company, 1975. Chapter 12.

Rock, Milton L. (ed.). *Handbook of Wage and Salary Administration.* New York: McGraw-Hill Book Company, 1972.

Sibson, Robert E. *Compensation,* revised ed. New York: AMACOM, American Management Associations, 1982.

Treiman, Donald J., and Heidi I. Hartman. *Women, Work, and Wages: Equal Pay for Jobs of Equal Value.* Washington, DC: National Academy Press, 1981.

Chapter Objectives:

- To describe the characteristics of piecework and the advantages and disadvantages of using it to motivate employees.
- To reveal why merit raises may fail to motivate employees adequately and explain the ways in which the motivational value of merit raises may be increased.
- To identify the principal methods for compensating salespersons and the advantages of each method.
- To describe the different methods by which executive bonuses may be determined and paid.
- To recognize the objectives of Employee Stock Ownership Plans, the reasons for their growth, and the possible abuses in using them.
- To cite the objectives of gains-sharing plans and the methods by which these gains may be paid to employees.

18

Incentive Compensation

In the previous chapter we emphasized that the worth of a job is a significant factor in determining the pay rate for that job. However, pay based solely upon the worth of the job may fail to motivate employees to perform according to their full capacity. Instead, employees are likely to meet only minimum performance standards. Because of this fact, more organizations are attempting to derive greater motivational value from employee compensation by relating it more closely to employee performance. Increasing attention is thus being focused upon identifying the many variables which help to determine the effectiveness of pay as a motivator. Through the knowledge being acquired by researchers and practitioners, financial incentive plans are being constructed to meet more closely the needs of both employees and employers.

In this chapter we will discuss incentive plans in terms of the objectives they are to achieve and the various factors that may affect their success. We also will attempt to identify those plans that are most effective in motivating different categories of employees in the achievement of these objectives.

REQUIREMENTS FOR A SUCCESSFUL INCENTIVE PLAN

Whether or not an incentive plan is successful in realizing its intended goal will depend upon the environment that exists within the organization. A plan is more likely to succeed in an organization where morale is high, where employees believe they are being treated fairly, and where there is an absence of labor strife. When the opposite situation exists, an incentive plan may serve to make conditions worse.

Employee Acceptance of the Plan

For a plan to succeed, there must be some desire for it on the part of the employees.[1] This desire can be contingent in part upon how well management is able to introduce the plan and convince employees of its benefits. Encouraging employees to suggest ways of improving performance by participating in administering the plan is likely to increase their acceptance of it.

Employees must be able to perceive a positive relationship between the outcome they receive in the form of incentive payments and the job input required to earn these payments. Such perception is more likely to occur if there are objective standards by which they may judge their performance. Commitment on the part of employees to meet these standards also is essential for effective motivation. It requires mutual understanding and confidence between employees and their supervisors that only open channels of two-way communication can provide.[2] Incentive payments must never be permitted to become a guarantee that bears little

---

1. Edward E. Lawler, III, *Pay and Organizational Effectiveness* (New York: McGraw-Hill Book Company, 1971), p. 159.
2. A. W. Charles, "Theory Y Compensation," *Personnel Journal*, Vol. 52, No. 1 (January, 1973), pp. 12–18.

relationship to input. Instead, they should be perceived as a reward that must be earned. This perception can be strengthened by paying the incentive money in a separate check.

Recognition of Differences in Employee Needs

Employees tend to differ in their needs for money and in their willingness to contribute the time and effort necessary to earn it. Attitudes toward money may be affected by employees' levels of income, by the size of their families, and by their life-styles. When some employees have achieved sufficient income to satisfy their economic needs, they would rather devote their time and energies to recreational or other pursuits than to additional work on the job. Furthermore, as income levels increase, so does the amount of tax paid on these incomes. As a result, the value of incentive pay is reduced.

The amount of extra pay an employee is able to earn under an incentive plan will also affect the motivational value of the incentives received. Generally, the larger the payment, the more willing employees will be to put forth the effort necessary to earn it. However, as Lawler points out, if the financial reward is too large, it may lower the valence, or influence, that money has upon the individual's efforts.[3] The probability of earning it also affects the motivational value of incentive pay. If the probability of earning an incentive payment is too high or too low, it may provide less inducement for employees to work harder.[4]

Control of Costs

While incentive plans based upon productivity can reduce direct labor costs, they may cause certain overhead costs to increase. These overhead costs may include the cost of establishing performance standards and the added cost of record keeping that the plan will entail. The time consumed in communicating with employees about the plan, answering questions, and resolving any grievances about it also must be added to these costs. If effective performance standards are not established and enforced, employees may be able to earn more pay for an equal or lesser amount of work. Even worse, if the plan proves unsuccessful, it can precipitate a decline in employee productivity and a corresponding loss of profits. In addition, the dissatisfaction that it may create can generate problems with the union that can further increase labor costs.

INCENTIVES FOR NONMANAGEMENT PERSONNEL

Surveys indicate that the use of financial incentives differs considerably among industries and among geographic regions. These differences suggest that tradition and

---

3. Lawler, *op. cit.*, p. 175.
4. David C. McClelland, "Money as a Motivator: Some Research Insights," *The Mackenzie Quarterly* (Fall, 1967), pp. 17–18.

ideology, as well as economics and technology, help to govern the popularity of incentive plans.[5] Differences also exist in the types of plans that are used for various categories of nonmanagement personnel. Financial incentive payments for hourly personnel may provide the sole source of compensation, or they may supplement a basic wage. Incentives for salaried personnel generally involve bonuses and/or merit raises. The various gains-sharing plans discussed later in this chapter typically include both hourly and salaried personnel.

Incentives for Hourly Personnel

Incentive payments for hourly employees may be determined by the number of units produced, by the achievement of specific performance goals, or by improvements in the organization as a whole. In the majority of incentive plans, incentive payments serve to supplement the employee's basic wages.

Piecework. One of the oldest incentive plans is piecework. Under *straight* piecework, employees receive a certain rate for each unit produced. Their compensation is determined by the number of units they produce during a pay period. An advocate of piecework, Frederick W. Taylor, whose contributions to scientific management were mentioned in Chapter 1, devised a **differential piece rate**. Under this rate, employees whose production exceeds the standard amount of output receive a higher rate for *all* of their work than the rate paid to those who do not exceed the standard amount.

Piecework can provide financial motivation for employees who have a strong desire to increase their earnings. This is because the amount of wages that they receive is directly proportionate to their output. The wage payment for each employee is simple to compute. And the plan will permit a company to predict its labor costs with considerable accuracy since these costs are the same for each unit of output. The piecework system is more likely to be successful when units of output can be measured readily, when the quality of the product is less critical, when the job is fairly standardized, and when a constant flow of work can be maintained.

Employees normally are not paid for the time that they are idle unless the idleness is due to conditions for which the company is responsible such as delays in work flow, defective materials, inoperative equipment, or power failures. When the delay is not the fault of employees, they are paid for the time they are idle. There is a difference of opinion, however, as to the rate they should receive during such idleness. In one arbitration case it was held that employees should be paid on the basis of their average hourly earnings on piecework.[6] In another it was ruled that the employer need pay employees only the base wage rate for the idle period.[7] (This would be the hourly rate from which the piece rate had been calculated.)

---

5. David W. Belcher, *Compensation Administration* (Englewood Cliffs, NJ: Prentice-Hall, Inc., 1974), p. 301.
6. Pantasote Company, 3LA545.
7. Kensington Steel Company, 13LA545.

Computing the Piece Rate.   Although time standards establish the amount of time required to perform a given amount of work, they do not by themselves determine what the incentive rate should be. The incentive rates must be based upon hourly wage rates that would otherwise be paid for the type of work being performed under the incentive system. If, for example, the standard time for producing one unit of work in a job paying $4.50 per hour were computed to be 10 minutes, the piece rate would be 75 cents per unit. This piece rate is computed as follows:

$$\frac{60 \text{ (minutes per hour)}}{10 \text{ (standard time per unit)}} = 6 \text{ units per hour}$$

$$\frac{\$4.50 \text{ (hourly rate)}}{6 \text{ (units per hour)}} = 75¢ \text{ per unit}$$

Declining Use of Piecework.   In spite of its incentive value, the use of piecework is declining. One reason for the decline is that production standards upon which piecework must be based can be difficult to develop for many types of jobs. In some instances the cost of determining and maintaining this standard may exceed the benefits to be gained from piecework. Jobs in which individual contributions are difficult to distinguish or measure, or in which the work is mechanized to the point that the individual exercises very little control over output, also may be unsuited to the use of piecework. The same is true of those jobs in which employees are learning the work or in which high standards of quality are of paramount importance.

One of the most significant weaknesses of piecework, as well as other incentive plans based upon individual effort, is that it may not be always effective as a motivator. If employees believe that an increase in their output will provoke disapproval from fellow workers, they may avoid exerting maximum effort because their desire for peer approval outweighs their desire for more money.

Over a period of time, the standards upon which piece rates are based tend to loosen. This condition can result from employee pressures to loosen the standards or from employees discovering ways to perform their jobs in less than standard time. In either case, employees are not required to exert as much effort to receive the same amount of incentive pay, thereby reducing its incentive value.

Union Reaction to Piecework.   Some union leaders have feared that management will use piecework or systems similar to it to achieve a **speedup** (gaining more production from the workers for the same amount of money). Another fear is that the system may induce employees to compete against one another and thereby cause a loss of jobs for those who are revealed to be less productive. There also is the belief that the system will cause employees to work themselves out of a job or cause craft standards of workmanship to suffer.

In spite of opposition by some unions, piecework has had a history of success in the garment, leather goods, and cigar-making industries where it has been used to the mutual benefit and satisfaction of management and the union. It should not be assumed, therefore, that union leaders as a group are opposed to the use of piecework. If the union has confidence in and a good working relationship with management and if it feels that its members stand to gain from the system, it will accept piecework.

Figure 18–1 **What Is Time Bonus?**

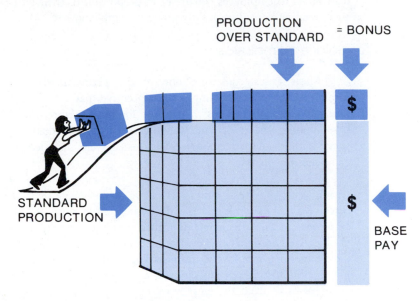

PRODUCTION
OVER STANDARD = BONUS

$

STANDARD
PRODUCTION

$

BASE
PAY

SOURCE: Reproduced with permission of the Procter & Gamble Company.

Individual Bonuses. A **bonus**, as Figure 18–1 illustrates, is an incentive payment that is supplemental to the basic wage. It has the advantage of providing employees with more pay for exerting greater effort while, at the same time, providing them the security of a basic wage. A bonus payment may be based upon the number of units that an individual produces, as in the case of piecework. For example, at the basic wage rate of $4 an hour plus a bonus of 10 cents per unit, an employee who produces 100 units during an 8-hour period is paid $42, computed as follows:

$$(\text{hours} \times \text{time rate}) + (\text{number of units} \times \text{unit rate}) = \text{wages}$$
$$(\quad 8 \quad \times \quad \$4 \quad) + (\quad 100 \quad \times \quad 10\text{¢} \quad) = \$42$$

Bonuses also may be determined on the basis of cost reduction, of quality improvement goals, or of performance criteria that may be established.

Group Bonuses. Group bonuses are most desirable when the contributions of individual employees are either difficult to distinguish or depend upon group cooperation. Thus, as production has become more automated, as teamwork and coordination among workers has become more important, and as the contribution of those engaged indirectly in production work has increased, group bonuses have become more popular. Most group bonuses that have been developed in recent years, furthermore, base the incentive payments on such factors as improvement in company profits or efficiency or upon reductions in labor costs. Group bonuses, in contrast with incentive plans based solely upon output, can broaden the scope of the contributions that employees are motivated to make. The group bonus may be distributed to employees equally or in proportion to their base pay, or on the basis of their relative contributions to group accomplishment.

Incentives for Salaried Employees

Merit raises constitute one of the financial incentive systems used most commonly for salaried employees. Incentive pay may be provided also through different types of bonuses. Like those for hourly employees, these bonuses may be based upon a variety of criteria involving either individual or group performance. As stated earlier, salaried employees also usually are included in the different types of gains-sharing plans.

Merit Raises.
Merit raises can serve to motivate employees if the employees perceive the raises to be related to the performance required to earn them. For employees to gain this perception, their performance may be evaluated upon the basis of objective criteria. If this evaluation also includes the use of subjective judgment by their superiors, employees must have confidence and trust in the validity of this judgment. Most important, any increases granted on the basis of merit should be distinguishable from the employees' regular pay and from any cost-of-living or other general increases. To achieve this distinction, Lawler recommends that the merit portion of a salary increase be separated from the employees' regular pay. He also recommends that the merit portion be withheld when a decline in an employee's performance warrants such action.[8]

In order to make merit increases more flexible and visible, some companies, such as B. F. Goodrich, Timex, and Westinghouse, have initiated **Lump Sum Increase Programs (LSIP)**. Under this program employees have the option of taking the increase in a lump sum or having it divided up among their regular paychecks. If advanced as a lump sum, the increase is considered as a loan and the unearned portion of it must be repaid if the employee quits before the end of the year. Some companies charge interest on the money advanced to offset its effect upon their cash flow.[9]

Problems with Merit Raises.
It should be recognized that merit raises may not achieve their intended purpose. Unlike a bonus, a merit raise is usually perpetuated year after year even when the performance upon which it is based is not.[10] Furthermore, according to research, a majority of employees in many organizations is opposed to merit raises because of, among other reasons, a lack of trust in management.[11] What are referred to as merit raises often turn out to be increases

8. Lawler, *op cit.*, p. 161.

9. Edward C. Lawler, III, *Pay and Organization Development* (Reading, MA: Addison-Wesley Publishing Company, 1981), p. 70.

10. Mayles H. Goldberg, "Another Look at Merit Pay Programs," *Compensation Review* (Third Quarter, 1977), p. 24.

11. Lawler, *Pay and Organizational Effectiveness, op. cit.*, p. 167.

based on seniority or raises to accommodate increases in cost of living or in area wage rates. Even when merit raises are determined by performance, the employees' gains are offset by inflation and the increased income taxes. As one employee lamented, "Last year's 7 percent inflation ate up my 9 percent merit increase. It looks like all I got is a 2 percent reward for busting my tail."[12]

Probably one of the major weaknesses of merit raises lies in the performance evaluation system upon which the increases are based. Even with an effective system, performance may be difficult to measure. Furthermore, any of the deficiencies in performance evaluation programs that were mentioned in Chapter 10 can impair the operation of a merit pay plan. The performance evaluation objectives of the employees and of the supervisors, moreover, often are at odds. Whereas employees typically want to maximize their pay increases, the supervisor may seek to reward the employee in an equitable manner based upon performance. In some instances employee pressures for pay increases actually may play a major role in determining the performance evaluation that is reported.

Incentives for Sales Personnel

The enthusiasm and drive that must be exerted in most types of sales work require that sales personnel be highly motivated. This fact, as well as the competitive nature of selling, explains why financial incentives for salespeople are utilized widely. The incentive plans for them must provide a source of motivation that will enlist greater cooperation and trust than the sales manager in Figure 18–2 is receiving. Motivation is particularly important for personnel in the field who cannot be supervised closely and who, as a result, must exercise a high degree of self-discipline.

Unique Needs of Sales Incentive Plans.

Incentive systems for salespeople are complicated by the wide differences in the types of sales jobs. These may range from order-taking to providing consultation and other services of a highly technical nature. A salesperson's performance may be measured by the dollar volume of sales and by the ability to gain new accounts. Other measures are the ability to promote new products or services and to provide various forms of service and assistance to customers which do not produce sales revenues immediately.

Performance standards for sales personnel, however, are difficult to develop because their performance often is affected by external influences which are beyond their control. Economic and seasonal conditions, sales competition, changes in customer demands, and the nature of the sales territory each can affect an individual's sales record. Sales volume alone, therefore, may not be an accurate indicator of the effort salespeople have expended.

In developing incentive plans for salespeople, employers are confronted also with the problem of how to reward extra sales effort and at the same time compensate for activities that do not contribute directly or immediately to sales achievement. Furthermore, employees in sales must be able to enjoy some degree of income stability.

---

12. "Compensation Currents," *Compensation Review*, Vol. 11, No. 1 (1st Quarter, 1979), p. 7.

Figure 18—2

"My advice to you, Hawkins, is to take the pins
out of the map and stick them into the salesmen."

SOURCE: Reprinted by permission of Chon Day.

Types of Sales Incentive Plans.   Compensation plans for sales personnel may consist of a salary, a commission, or a combination salary and commission plan. The trend is toward the use of a combination plan involving a salary and incentive bonus (usually based upon a percentage of sales).

A **straight salary plan** permits salespeople to be paid for performing various duties that are not reflected immediately in their sales volume. It enables them to devote more time to providing services and building up the goodwill of customers without jeopardizing their income. The principal limitation of the straight salary is that it may not motivate employees to exert sufficient effort in maximizing their sales volume.

On the other hand, the **straight commission plan**, based upon a percentage of sales, provides maximum incentive and is easy to compute and understand. However, its usage is limited by the following disadvantages cited by Smyth and Murphy:

1. Emphasis is on sales volume rather than on profits (except in those rare cases where the commission rate is a percentage of the profit on the sale).
2. Salespeople are too independent of the company and have very little feeling of company loyalty.
3. Territories tend to be milked rather than worked.

4. It is difficult to get missionary work and special selling tasks performed.
5. Customer service after the sale is likely to be neglected.
6. Earnings are often excessive in good business periods.
7. Earnings tend to fluctuate widely between good and poor business periods, and turnover of trained sales personnel tends to increase in periods of poor business.
8. Salespeople are tempted to grant price concessions.
9. Salespeople are tempted to overload their customers with inventory.

By way of contrast, Smyth and Murphy cite the following advantages for the **combination salary and commission plan** which indicate why it is utilized so widely:

1. The right kind of incentive compensation, if linked to salary in the right proportion, has most of the advantages of both the straight salary and the straight commission forms of compensation.
2. A salary-plus-incentive compensation plan offers greater design flexibility and therefore can be more readily designed to help maximize company profits.
3. The plan can develop the most favorable ratio of selling expense to sales.
4. The field sales force can be motivated to achieve specific company marketing objectives in addition to sales volume.[13]

INCENTIVES FOR MANAGEMENT PERSONNEL

A major function of financial incentive plans for executives is to motivate them to develop and utilize their abilities and to contribute their energies to the maximum extent possible. Incentive plans also should encourage the recruitment and retention of competent executive personnel. This can be accomplished by creating plans that will enable them to accumulate a financial estate and to shelter a portion of their compensation from current income taxes.

Incentives Related to Individual Performance

It is common for companies to have more than one incentive plan for executives in order to serve different organizational goals and executive needs. In creating an incentive plan related to individual performance, certain decisions must be made. These decisions may include determining which executives are to be covered by the plan, what will be the basis for the incentive bonus, and in what form will the bonus be paid.

Coverage of the Plan.   Theoretically the incentive plan should include key executives whose duties and responsibilities give them an opportunity to contribute substantially to the attainment of organizational goals. Because of overlapping responsibilities among executive positions, these contributions may be difficult to

13. Reprinted by permission of the publisher from Richard C. Smyth and Matthew J. Murphy, *Compensating and Motivating Salesmen* (New York: American Management Associations, © 1969), pp. 22–24.

determine exactly.[14] Although pressures to expand the number of positions covered by a plan are likely to exist, coverage preferably should be restricted to those positions that demonstrably contribute to company profits. According to Patton, when more than 1 percent of a company's total work force is included in an incentive program, the credibility of individual performance evaluation tends to suffer. Ideally, in his opinion, the optimum number to be included should not exceed one half of 1 percent.[15] Incentives for the remaining executives, however, may be provided through merit raises or gain-sharing incentive plans.

Bases for Bonuses.

Incentive bonuses for executives should be based upon the contributions they render to the organization. A variety of formulas has been developed for this purpose. Incentive bonuses may be based upon a percentage of a company's total profits or a percentage of profits in excess of a specific return on stockholders' investments. Some formulas also seek to adjust the payments to reflect a company's performance relative to the industry. In other instances the payments may be tied to an annual profit plan whereby the amount is determined by the extent to which an agreed-upon profit level is exceeded. Payments also may be based upon performance ratings or upon the achievement of specific objectives agreed upon between executives and the board of directors.

Incentives for executives, as for other personnel, should not be permitted to become a guarantee. Those executives whose performance is deserving should be able to receive up to the maximum reward, and those who are less deserving should receive smaller rewards or even none at all. In order for rewards to have maximum motivational value, Crystal recommends that they range up to as much as 50 to 60 percent of an executive's regular salary. He also suggests that the amount of the bonuses be permitted to rise sharply as the company closes in on its objective, thus recognizing the fact that the last increments of performance are the hardest to achieve and also the most profitable.[16]

Form of Bonus Payments.

The payment of a bonus may be in cash or deferred until a later date. In some companies the deferral of a portion of the bonus is required, whereas in others it is voluntary. The trend, however, is toward voluntary deferrals.[17]

Cash Bonus. By providing a reward that is fairly immediate and can be associated with the performance upon which it is based, a cash bonus can provide significant motivation. This form of payment also best serves those executives who must satisfy immediate financial needs. If the money is not needed immediately, an executive may invest it elsewhere and gain a greater return than the interest it otherwise would earn in a deferred plan.

---

14. Graef S. Crystal, *Financial Motivation for Executives* (New York: American Management Associations, 1972), pp. 28–40.

15. Arch Patton, "Why Incentive Plans Fail," *Harvard Business Review,* Vol. 50, No. 3 (May-June, 1972), p. 65.

16. Crystal, *op. cit.,* p. 128.

17. Thomas H. Paine, "Trends in Executive Benefits and Deferred Compensation," *Compensation Review,* Vol. 11, No. 3 (Fourth Quarter, 1979), p. 20.

Deferred Bonus. A deferred bonus can be used to provide the sole source of retirement benefits or to supplement a regular pension plan. If the executive is in a lower tax bracket when the deferred benefits ultimately are received—which is not always the case—income tax savings can be realized. In addition, interest on the deferred amount can cause it to appreciate without being taxed until it is received. To the company's advantage, deferred bonuses are not subject to the reporting requirement of the Employee Retirement Income Security Act (ERISA). Moreover, the company can have the use of the money during this period.

A disadvantage of deferred incentive plans is that the deferred compensation under IRS regulations cannot be used as a part of the base salary upon which retirement benefits are calculated. Furthermore, any interest that the company earns on deferred compensation funds is taxable to the company. Deferred income funds also become a part of the company's indebtedness—a part or all of which might be lost should the company become insolvent. If these funds do not appreciate with inflation, participants also stand to suffer a loss from inflation.[18]

When the employer requires that bonus payments be deferred, the bonuses can provide the **golden handcuffs** with which to retain executives.[19] In order to receive the bonus, the executives must remain with the company for a certain number of years—frequently until retirement. However, such practices can work to the detriment of both a company and an executive. Highly competent executives are likely to get other employers seeking their services to reimburse them for the loss of any bonus that the move might cause them to suffer. Thus, the "golden handcuffs" may result in retaining the less competent executives who are unable to obtain such reimbursements. The recognition of this fact, together with competitive pressures to offer cash bonuses, is causing fewer companies to require bonuses to be deferred.[20]

Incentives Related to Company Performance

While incentive payments for executives may be based upon the achievement of specific goals relating to their positions, they must also take into account the performance of the company as a whole. Important to its stockholders are such performance results as growth in earnings per share, return on stockholders' equity, and, ultimately, stock price appreciation. A variety of incentive plans, therefore, has been developed to relate rewards to these performance results, particularly over the long term.

Stock Options. A **stock option** is a right to purchase a certain number of shares of stock at a certain price within a stated period of time. The option price normally is less than the prevailing market price. The difference between the option price and the market price for the stock at any given time is the value of the option. Some company stock option plans permit supervisors and middle-level managers to participate. Generally, only upper-level executives are likely to have the income and/

18. James T. Brinks, "Executive Compensation: Crossroads of the 80s," *Personnel Administrator,* Vol. 26, No. 12 (December, 1981), p. 26.

19. Crystal, *loc. cit.*

20. Paine, *loc. cit.*

or the capital necessary to exercise an option and to benefit from any income tax advantages that the option may provide. High interest rates, however, can make the borrowing of such capital difficult or uneconomical. Furthermore, declining stock prices may prevent executives from benefiting from the option in spite of outstanding performance on their part. Changes in tax regulations governing stock options also can reduce their attractiveness as an incentive.

Incentive Stock Options (ISO).

An **Incentive Stock Option,** authorized by Congress in 1981, permits executives to purchase at some future date a block of their company stock at today's prices. Even though the actual market price may be higher than the purchase price at the time of the purchase, tax is not due on the appreciation until the stock is sold. If the stock is held more than one year and then sold, the appreciation can qualify for capital gains treatment.[21]

Stock Appreciation Rights (SAR).

The **Stock Appreciation Right (SAR)** is a right attached to a nonqualified option (an option that does not qualify for capital gains treatment). It does not require the executive to invest money in company stock. However, it allows its holder to receive directly from the company the payment of any gain in the market value of the stock without having to exercise the option. Thus, like the option holders, SAR holders are dependent upon the market performance of the stock. However, unlike the option holders, SAR holders need not invest money in the stock.[22]

Phantom Stock Rights.

Executives who are granted **phantom stock rights** are entitled to receive bonus payments equal to the appreciation in the value of the company's stock. The appreciation may be based upon market value or a formula that may include dividend equivalents over a period of years.[23]

Performance Shares/Units.

Under **performance shares/units plans**, corporate performance rather than the market value of its stock determines the bonuses executives are to receive. This single focus on corporate performance has the advantage of encouraging teamwork while allowing other incentive plans to reward individual performance. The bonus can be in the form of stock, units exchangeable for stock, or cash amounts, the full payment of which is contingent upon the company achieving its long-term goals.[24]

21. "Why Managers Covet the New Stock Option Plans," *Business Week* (March 15, 1982), p. 156.

22. John C. Perham, "Appreciation Rights: A Sure Thing," *Dun's Review,* Vol. 105, No. 3 (March, 1975), p. 46.

23. Frederick W. Cook, "Long-Term Incentives for Management, Part I: An Overview," *Compensation Review,* Vol. 12, No. 6 (Second Quarter, 1980), p. 23.

24. *Ibid.,* pp. 23, 25.

Incentives for Professional Personnel

Like others on a salary, professional personnel may be motivated through bonuses and salary increases. Unfortunately in some companies professional employees are forced to assume an administrative assignment in order to advance beyond a certain point in the salary structure. Consequently, when they are promoted, their professional talents cease to be utilized fully. In the process the company may lose a good professional employee and gain a poor administrator. To avoid this situation some companies have extended the salary range for professional positions to equal or nearly equal that for departmental administrative positions. The extension of this range provides a double-track wage system whereby professionals who do not aspire to become administrators may have an opportunity to earn comparable salaries.

There also has been a trend for companies to use **career curves or maturity curves**, as a basis for providing salary increases to professional personnel. These curves, such as the ones shown in Figure 18–3 provide for the annual salary rate to be based upon experience and performance. Separate curves are established to reflect different levels of performance and to provide for annual increases. The curves

Figure 18–3 Professional Maturity Curves

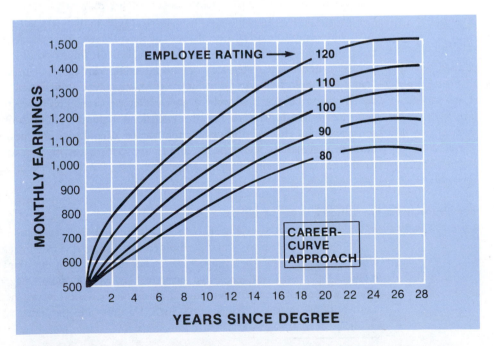

SOURCE: Robert E. Sibson, *Wages and Salaries* (New York: American Management Associations, 1960), p. 170. Reproduced with permission.

representing the higher levels of performance tend to rise to a higher level and at a more rapid rate than the curves representing lower performance levels.

Criticisms of Executive Incentive Plans

A major criticism of executive incentive plans is that they have rewarded executives handsomely for performance from which shareholders have not always derived comparable benefits. According to Brindisi, for example, the total compensation of senior executives in the Standard & Poor's 400 rose between 1971 and 1981 by 10 percent in *real dollars*. During the same period the total stockholder value of these companies, which included stock price appreciation plus dividends, declined by 2 percent in *real dollars*.[25] As Kraus points out, executive compensation tends to be based on surveys conducted by consulting firms and business publications. Salary ranges are then established that will equal or exceed the survey averages, or even anticipated increases in these averages. This practice can help to create an upward push in the salary ranges.[26]

Another criticism of some plans is that the time period upon which executive performance is measured often is too short and the rewards based upon it are too large. This situation has encouraged quarterly earnings growth at the expense of research and development and to the neglect of maintaining the firm's share of the market. In the long run, therefore, stockholders may not receive a return equal to that which might be achieved from other investments.

The complicated features of some of the plans we have discussed, as well as the tax regulations governing them, make them difficult for stockholders and the general public to understand. This lack of understanding can cause them to be perceived as "fail-safe" incentive systems which assure that executives will receive generous benefits regardless of how well or poorly they perform. Public reaction, in turn, may generate political pressure for greater federal regulation and control of executive compensation. This possibility therefore creates a challenge for industry to engage in more self-regulation, self-policing, and in some instances more restraint with respect to their compensation programs.[27]

GAINS-SHARING INCENTIVE PLANS

Gains-sharing plans enable employees to share in the benefits of improved efficiency realized by the company or major units within it. Many of these plans include supervisors and executive personnel as well as nonmanagement personnel. The plans encourage teamwork among all employees and reward them for their total contributions to the organization. Such features are particularly desirable when

---

25. Louis J. Brindisi, Jr., "Managers Journal: Why Executive Compensation Programs Go Wrong," *The Wall Street Journal*, June 14, 1981, p. 18.

26. David Kraus, "Executive Pay: Ripe for Reform?" *Harvard Business Review*, Vol. 58, No. 5 (September–October, 1980), p. 38.

27. *Ibid.*, p. 48.

working conditions make individual performance difficult if not impossible to measure. Some of the more widely used gains-sharing plans include stock ownership plans, profit-sharing plans, and the Scanlon and Rucker plans.

Stock Ownership

Stock ownership plans for employees have existed in some companies for many years. Not uncommon are plans for purchasing stock on an installment basis through payroll deductions and without the payment of brokerage fees. Over the years, the stock of some of the large "blue chip" companies, such as AT&T, Exxon, and General Electric, has proven to be a good investment for their employees. Furthermore, in the United States today about 250 companies with at least 10 employees are entirely employee owned. In most of these situations, ownership by employees is the result of their efforts to salvage a failing firm. According to the National Center for Employee Ownership, approximately 50,000 jobs have been saved through these direct ownership (D.O.) plans.[28] Ironically even employee ownership of the company may not insure labor peace. At South Bend Lathe, Inc., in Indiana, for example, workers went out on strike even though they owned the company. This occurred because the old management still made the decisions. Dissatisfaction with the management's wage proposals and inadequate employee representation on the board of directors were major reasons for the strike.[29]

Employee Stock Ownership Plans (ESOP). Favorable federal income tax provisions now encourage employers to utilize a distinctive incentive plan called the **Employee Stock Ownership Plan (ESOP)** as a means of providing retirement benefits for their employees. These provisions permit a portion of a company's earnings to be excluded from taxation if it is assigned to employees in the form of stock shares. Stock allocations can be based upon employee wages or seniority. When the employees retire, they can sell their stock back to the company or on the open market if it is traded publicly. The company also may use the stock placed in an ESOP trust as a collateral for a bank loan. As the loan is repaid, the stock used as collateral is allocated to employee accounts. Payments of the principal and interest both can be deducted from the company's income tax liabilities.

Potential Benefits of ESOPs. Through ESOPs employers can provide retirement benefits for their employees at relatively low cost because stock contributions are in effect subsidized by the federal government. ESOPs can also provide employees with an incentive to increase productivity and to help a company prosper and grow. Enthusiastic promoters of ESOPs go so far as to claim that these plans will "revitalize what is wrong with capitalism." The plans, they maintain, will increase productivity, improve labor relations, and promote economic justice.[30]

28. *Bulletin to Management: Policy Guide,* Bulletin 1659, (Washington, DC: The Bureau of National Affairs, Inc., January 7, 1982), p. 8.

29. *Ibid.*

30. Christian Hill, "Employee Stock Plans: An Economic Cure-All or a Dubious Benefit?" *The Wall Street Journal,* December 8, 1980, p. 1.

Whether or not these potential benefits are realized, however, is likely to depend upon the economic prosperity of the industry, as well as trends in company profits and in the price of its stock.

Problems with ESOPs.   Generally ESOPs are more likely to serve their intended purposes in publicly held companies rather than in the closely held ones. A major problem with the closely held company is the possible inability of the company to buy back the stock of employees when they retire. Unfortunately these employees do not have the alternative of disposing of their stock on the open market. One authority on ESOPs sees the repurchase liability as being like a time bomb waiting to go off. He believes that closely held companies should be required to establish a sinking fund, which they cannot touch, to use for repurchasing stock.

Furthermore, a study by the United States General Accounting Office concluded that, in a number of closely held companies, the value of the stock allocated to employees was being overstated. ESOPs were also being set up for purposes other than the workers' best interests, such as to fend off a take-over or to provide owners with a more lucrative way of disposing of their personal stock holdings.[31]

Disadvantages of Employee Stock Ownership.

It is doubtful whether the possession of a small amount of company stock will cause employees to feel any closer kinship with management. Furthermore, from an investment standpoint it is not considered the best practice for individuals to have both their jobs and savings invested with the same company. Another limitation is that many employees are not in a position to risk a possible loss of their equity through declining stock prices. For employees who cannot risk this loss or who have a limited understanding of corporate finances and stock market operations, the plan may create more problems than benefits.

Profit-Sharing Plans

Probably no incentive plan has been the subject of more widespread interest, attention, and misunderstanding than profit sharing. According to the Council of Profit Sharing Industries, **profit sharing** is any procedure by which an employer pays or makes available to all regular employees, in addition to good rates of regular pay, special current or deferred sums based upon the profits of the business.[32]

Profit-sharing plans are intended to provide employees with the opportunity to increase their earnings by contributing to the improvement of their company's profits. Their contributions may be directed toward improving product quality, reducing operating costs, improving work methods, and building company goodwill rather than just toward increasing their rate of production. Profit sharing can help to stimulate employees to think and feel more like partners in the business and thus to concern themselves with the welfare of the company as a whole. Its purpose,

---

31. *Ibid.* pp. 1, 22.

32. *Constitution and By-Laws of the Council of Profit Sharing Industries* (1957), Article 2, Section I.

therefore, is to motivate a total commitment from employees rather than to gain contributions from them in specific areas.

Variations in Profit-Sharing Plans.   Profit-sharing plans differ as to the proportions of profits shared with employees and as to the distribution and form of payment. The amount that is shared with employees may range from 5 to 50 percent of the net profit. Generally, however, most plans provide for the sharing of about 20 to 25 percent of the net profit. Profit distributions may be made to all employees on an equal basis or may be based on their regular salary or on some formula that takes into account seniority and/or merit. The payments may be disbursed in cash, deferred, or made on the basis of a combination of these two forms of payment.

Requirements for Successful Profit-Sharing Plans.   Most authorities in the field are agreed that in order to have a successful profit-sharing program a company must first have a sound personnel program, good labor relations, and the trust and confidence of its employees. Profit sharing thus is a refinement of a good personnel program and a supplement to an adequate wage scale rather than a substitute for either one. As in the case of all incentive plans, it is the underlying philosophy of management, rather than the mechanics of the plan, that may determine its success. Particularly essential to the success of a profit-sharing plan are the provisions that enable employees to participate in decisions affecting their jobs and their performance.

Weaknesses of Profit-Sharing Plans.   In spite of its potential advantages, profit sharing is also subject to certain weaknesses. The profits shared with employees may be the result of inventory speculation, climatic factors, economic conditions, national emergencies, or other factors over which employees have no control. Conversely, company losses may occur during years when employee contributions have been at a maximum. The fact that profit-sharing payments are made only once a year or deferred until retirement may reduce the motivational value of the plans. If a plan fails to pay off very many years in a row, the resulting situation can have an adverse effect upon productivity.

Scanlon and Rucker Plans

To provide employees with bonuses which encourage maximum effort and cooperation but are not tied to profit fluctuation, two rather unique plans are in use. These plans, which bear the names of their originators, Joe Scanlon and Alan W. Rucker, are similar philosophically. Both plans place emphasis upon participative management. Both plans encourage cost reduction by sharing with employees any savings resulting from these reductions. The formulas upon which the bonuses are based, however, differ somewhat. The Rucker Plan is the more sophisticated one.[33]

---

33. Belcher, *op. cit.*, pp. 331–333.

The Scanlon Plan.   According to one of Scanlon's associates, effective employee participation, which includes the use of committees on which employees are represented, is the most significant feature of the **Scanlon Plan**. This allows employees the opportunity to communicate their ideas and opinions and to exercise some degree of influence over decisions affecting their work and their welfare within the organization.[34] The plan thus reflects a willingness on the part of management to encourage employees to develop into organizational adults. Employees also have an opportunity to become managers of their time, energy, equipment usage, the quality and quantity of their production, and other factors relating to their work.[35] They accept changes in production methods more readily and volunteer new ideas. The Scanlon Plan encourages greater teamwork and sharing of knowledge at the lower levels. It demands more efficient management and better planning as workers try to reduce overtime and work smarter rather than harder or faster.[36]

The primary mechanisms for participation in the Scanlon Plan are the shop committees which are established in each department. These committees consider problems and make suggestions for improvements within their respective departments to an organizationwide screening committee. The function of the screening committee is to oversee the operation of the plan, to act upon suggestions received from the shop committees, and to review the data upon which monthly bonuses are to be based.[37]

The financial incentives under the Scanlon plan are normally distributed to *all* employees (a significant feature of the plan) on the basis of an established formula. This formula is based upon increases in employee productivity as determined by a "norm" that has been established for labor costs. The norm, which is subject to review, reflects the relationships of the payroll to the sales value of the company's products. The plan also provides for the establishment of a reserve into which 25 percent of any earned bonus is paid for the purpose of covering deficits encountered during the months when labor costs exceed the norm. After the portion for the reserve has been deducted, the remainder of the bonus is distributed with 25 percent going to the company and 75 percent to the employees. Any surplus that has been accumulated in the reserve at the end of a year is distributed to employees on the basis of the same formula.

In one survey of 21 plants having Scanlon Plans, opinions expressed by employees indicated that the intent of the plan was being realized. This intent is not to provide a giveaway program. Rather, it is to provide a system that defines a new set of roles for participants and a unique way of assessing organizational efficiency. The plan compensates employees for improvements in organization efficiency as a

34. Robert K. Goodman, J. H. Wakeley, and R. H. Ruh, "What Employees Think of the Scanlon Plan," *Personnel*, Vol. 49, No. 5 (September-October, 1972), p. 23.

35. Harold E. Lane, "The Scanlon Plan Revisited," *Business and Society Review*, No. 16 (Winter, 1975-76), p. 59.

36. Lawler, *Pay and Organization Development, op. cit.*, pp. 148–149.

37. Fred G. Lesieur, *The Scanlon Plan: A Frontier in Labor-Management Cooperation* (Boston: Massachusetts Institute of Technology—The Technology Press and New York: John Wiley & Sons, Inc., 1958), pp. 46–48.

result of hard work.[38] There also are indications that the plan has a positive impact upon the quality of work life, a subject of considerable current attention.[39]

The Rucker Plan. The **Share of Production Plan (SOP) or Rucker Plan** normally covers production workers but may be expanded to cover all employees. The financial incentive is based upon the historic relationship of the total earnings of hourly employees to the production values that they create. The bonus that is paid to employees is based upon any improvement in this relationship that they are able to realize. Thus, for every 1 percent increase in production value that is achieved, the workers covered by the plan receive an additional bonus of 1 percent of their total payroll costs. As in the case of the Scanlon Plan, maximum use is made of committees in administering the plan.

Lessons from the Scanlon and Rucker Plans. Perhaps the most important lesson to be gained from the Scanlon and Rucker Plans is that any management which expects to gain the cooperation of its employees in improving efficiency must permit them to become involved emotionally as well as financially in the company. If employees are to contribute maximum effort, they must be able to gain a feeling of involvement and identification with their company which is not provided under the traditional manager-employee relationship. Consequently, it is important for companies to realize that while employee cooperation is essential to the successful administration of these plans, the plans themselves do not necessarily stimulate such cooperation.

The attitude of management is of paramount importance to the success of either plan. Research, for example, indicates that managers in companies that discontinued the Scanlon Plan tended to show less confidence in their employees than the managers in firms that continued it. Where the plans were discontinued, managers also held less favorable attitudes toward participative decisions than they did in the companies where the plans were continued.[40] Like any other plan, the Scanlon and Rucker Plans are no better than the organizational environment in which they must function.

RÉSUMÉ

In an effort to relate the pay of employees more closely to their contributions, a variety of financial incentive plans is in use today. The success of a particular plan often is contingent more upon the organizational climate in which it must operate, employee confidence in it, and its suitability to organizational needs than upon the mechanics of the plan. Most important, employees must view their incentive pay as being equitable and related to their performance.

38. Goodman, *et al., op. cit.,* p. 27.
39. Lawler, *Pay and Organizational Development, op. cit.,* p. 149.
40. Lane, *op. cit.,* p. 62.

A variety of financial incentive plans has been developed to motivate nonmanagement employees working in different types and levels of jobs. These plans differ in terms of the areas of performance they are intended to motivate, the criteria by which performance is measured, and the form in which the rewards are paid to employees. Incentive payments may be based upon individual or group performance or upon the company's performance. The performance of the company may be measured in terms of its earnings, profits, return on stockholder investment, or market performance of its stock.

Incentive plans at the executive level provide for bonus payments on either a cash or deferred basis. Bonuses also may be in the form of either stock or options to purchase stock.

Gains-sharing plans, particularly those which include personnel below the executive level, are becoming quite prevalent. Favorable tax concessions offered to employers have spurred the growth of Employee Stock Ownership Plans (ESOPs). While these plans have some motivational value, they serve primarily to provide employees with a source of retirement benefits. However, in small closely held companies these benefits may never be realized by employees because there is no public market available in which they may sell their stock holdings when they retire.

TERMS TO IDENTIFY

differential piece rate
speedup
bonus
Lump Sum Increase Programs (LSIP)
straight salary plan
straight commission plan
combination salary and commission plan
golden handcuffs
stock option
Incentive Stock Option (ISO)

Stock Appreciation Right (SAR)
phantom stock rights
performance shares/units plans
career curves or maturity curves
Employee Stock Ownership Plan (ESOP)
profit sharing
Scanlon Plan
Share of Production Plan (SOP) or Rucker Plan

DISCUSSION QUESTIONS

1. A company that paid its production employees entirely on a piece rate system pointed with pride to the fact that it permitted its employees "to go into business for themselves." To what extent do you feel this claim is true or untrue?

2. If the standard time for producing one unit of a product were 4 minutes, what would the piece rate per unit be if the rate for this particular type of work were $3 an hour?

3. Suggest ways in which the motivating value of merit raises may be increased.

4. In the achievement of their objectives, are incentive plans aided or hindered by inflation?

5. What are some of the primary objectives of financial incentive plans for managers and how do these plans differ from those for nonmanagement personnel?

6. What are some of the advantages and disadvantages to employees of a deferred, as opposed to a cash, bonus plan?

7. What are some of the reasons for the rapid growth of ESOPs? Cite some of the poten-

tial problems concerning their use in closely held companies.

8. What are the reasons for the success of the Scanlon and Rucker Plans?

PROBLEM 18–1

YOU FIRST

Joe Cortez and Bill Tanner were employed as salespersons in the men's furnishings department of a large store. Cortez was 60 years old and had worked for the store for over 30 years. Childless, he lived in an apartment house which his wife managed for a small salary and a rent-free apartment. The couple's recreation consisted largely of gatherings of Spanish-speaking friends at the Hotel Español on Saturday nights and an occasional picnic at one of the local parks. Since Cortez was not a good money manager, his wife banked his weekly pay after they had lunch together on Thursdays.

Not too much was known about Tanner except that he lived alone in a room in a small hotel. He was quite active for his 67 years, and spent his days off hiking and taking pictures. He had been with the store about two years after having been employed a number of years in an outside sales position with a printing firm.

In their present positions both were paid a weekly salary plus a small commission. Cortez was the more aggressive of the two and did not hesitate to approach a prospective customer entering the department. The fact that it might have been Tanner's turn to approach a customer or that he was nearer to the customer did not seem to bother Cortez at all. Although Tanner was equally capable of making a sale when given the opportunity, his weekly commissions were only about 60 percent of those of Cortez. The reason for the difference, therefore, could be attributed to the fact that he did not try to compete with Cortez in "grabbing off" potential customers.

a. What explanations can you give for the differences between the two men in their desires to earn commissions?

b. What possible impact might a commission incentive have upon their interpersonal relations in the department where they worked?

PROBLEM 18–2

THE CHRISTMAS BONUS

During the previous eight years, the Security Investment Company had given each of its employees a year-end bonus in an amount equal to from one- to two-weeks' pay. Consequently, over the years the employees had become accustomed to using this bonus as a means of meeting their Christmas season expenses. Because of unusually poor earnings one year, the company recognized that even if it did not pay a bonus to its employees it would be fortunate to avoid encountering a deficit. Since management recognized that a majority of its employees had worked hard during the year and were counting on receiving a bonus, it was reluctant to forego the bonus payment even if a deficit had to be incurred. Management also recognized that the company's bonus record was usually mentioned during employment interviews, particularly when it hired clerical help whose salaries were not too high. As the first of December approached, management was faced with the problem of making a decision regarding the payment of the bonus.

a. What decision do you feel management should make concerning the bonus, and when and how should the information concerning it be communicated to the employees?

b. What problems may arise in connection with the use of financial incentives in this case?

c. What future policy should the company establish concerning the bonus?

SUGGESTED READINGS

Cohn, Theodore, and Roy A. Lindberg. *Compensating Key Executives in the Smaller Company.* New York: AMACOM, American Management Associations, 1979.

Crystal, Graef S. *Executive Compensation: Money, Motivation and Imagination,* 2d rev. ed. New York: AMACOM, American Management Associations, 1978.

Ellig, Bruce R. *Executive Compensation: A Total Pay Perspective.* New York: McGraw-Hill Book Company, 1982.

Fox, Harland. *Top Executive Compensation,* 1976 ed. New York: The Conference Board, 1976.

Lawler, Edward E., III. *Pay and Organization Development.* Reading, MA: Addison-Wesley Publishing Company, 1981.

Moore, Brian E., and Timothy L. Ross. *The Scanlon Way to Improved Productivity: A Practical Guide.* New York: Wiley-Interscience Publications, 1978.

Nash, Allan. *Managerial Compensation.* Scarsdale, NY: Work in America Institute, Inc., 1980.

Patten, Thomas H. Jr. *Pay: Employee Compensation and Incentive Plans.* New York: The Free Press, 1977.

Rock, Milton L. (ed.). *Handbook of Wage and Salary Administration.* New York: McGraw-Hill Book Company, 1972. Chapters 31–40.

Sibson, Robert E. *Increasing Employee Productivity.* New York: AMACOM, American Management Associations, 1976.

Chapter Objectives:

- To explain the growth of employee benefits and the problems they may create.
- To stress the requirements for a sound employee benefits program.
- To identify the categories and costs of employee benefits.
- To describe the benefits that the Social Security program provides, as well as the financial problems confronting Social Security.
- To explain the effects of economic conditions and ERISA upon pension funding.
- To cite the impact of federal regulations forbidding sex discrimination in pension benefits and age discrimination in retirement programs.

Employee Benefits

19

In the previous chapter we discussed different types of incentive compensation plans that are used to motivate employees. Some of those plans provide for deferred payment of compensation, thereby also serving as a source of retirement income. Because this deferment reduces the incentive value of such incentive compensation plans, some companies classify profit sharing, stock ownership, and similar deferred incentive plans as employee benefit plans. Whether or not an employer offers these particular plans, virtually all employers provide a variety of benefits to supplement the cash payments of wages or salaries to their employees. These benefits, some of which are required by law, must be considered a part of their total compensation. Like the money that goes directly into the paycheck, employee benefits are a growing labor cost. This is why, in employee handbooks, some companies now use the term **total compensation** to emphasize that the employee benefits are a part of an employee's actual income.

EMPLOYEE BENEFITS PROGRAM

Employee benefits constitute an indirect form of compensation that is intended to improve the quality of work life for employees. By enhancing the quality of work life, these benefits are expected to increase cooperation and productivity among the employees. If these benefits were not provided by the employer, the individual employees would be forced to pay for many of them, usually at higher costs, with net income remaining after income taxes have been deducted. It is for this reason that many employees would not be able to purchase some of the benefits they now receive.

Growth of Employee Benefits

It was not until the 1920s that employee benefits were offered by more than just a few employers. Because these benefits were supplemental to the paycheck and were of minor value, they were referred to initially as **fringe benefits or fringes**. From a rather meager beginning, they have expanded both in terms of the types of benefits offered and the costs required to provide them. Much of this expansion, furthermore, has taken place only in recent years.

Factors Contributing to Growth.   Initially employee benefits were introduced by some employers to promote and reward employee loyalty and to discourage unionization. Also, the paternalistic belief that employees were incapable of providing for their personal welfare and managing their private affairs was a reason for initiating certain benefits. In either case, the benefits were provided in a spirit of benevolence without much input from the recipients.

As unions acquired power during the 1930s, their leaders were able to gain through collective bargaining additional benefits along with higher wages. Subsequently, during World War II, a wage freeze further stimulated the growth of employee benefits. The easiest way for employers to overcome the freeze was to provide special inducements in the form of nonwage supplements such as pensions, paid vacations, sick leave, and health and life insurance. Most employers then found themselves obligated to continue these benefits after the war because employees and their unions were unwilling to give them up.

Following the removal of the wage freeze after World War II, union leaders concentrated their efforts on obtaining wage increases. As the cost of living began to level off about 1948, the union wage demands began to meet with public disfavor. However, it was generally accepted by the public that employees should have better standards of health and welfare than they were enjoying. Thus, fringe benefits became a bargaining goal that the unions could pursue realistically. Interpretations by the National Labor Relations Board and the United States Supreme Court to the effect that employers were obligated to bargain for pensions were also major factors that stimulated the growth of these particular benefits. Demands for supplemental unemployment insurance, company-paid medical insurance, and other benefits were soon to follow.

Changing Concept of Benefits.   With the growth of benefits has come a change in the concept of what actually constitutes a benefit. Such items provided to employees as food services, parking, counseling, and magazines were once considered to be benefits. Today most employers regard them as an integral part of the human resources program. Furthermore, employees no longer view benefits as a fringe that is being given to them. Rather, employees regard them as earned compensation. Union successes in bargaining for more benefits and the exemption of them from income tax has served to encourage their expansion. However, as benefits provide a larger share of an employee's total compensation, it is quite possible that some of them will be made taxable and their attractiveness may be reduced in comparison with cash compensation.

It is difficult to predict specifically what employees in the future will want and expect in the way of benefits. According to Foegen, union imagination in recognizing worker needs and in finding innovative ways to meet them should not be underestimated.[1] A Pennsylvania local of the National Hospital Union, for example, has negotiated the first day of the deer season as a paid holiday. Bargaining proposals by the Police Association in a Long Island community have included proposals for free abortions, along with holiday pay for Halloween and Valentine's Day. U.S. rubber workers are now entitled to an allowance for chiropractic treatments. Benefits provided by an Indiana manufacturer include tennis and basketball courts, a sauna, free language lessons, and instructions in such subjects as T.V. repair, music appreciation, gourmet cooking, and art.[2]

Problems Relating to Employee Benefits

Employers too often expand their benefit programs either in response to what other employers are offering or as concessions to union bargaining demands.

1. J. H. Foegen, "The High Cost of Innovative Employee Benefits," *California Management Review*, Vol. 15, No. 3 (Spring, 1973), pp. 100–104.

2. J. H. Foegen, "Employee Benefits: Imagination Unlimited," *Labor Law Journal*, Vol. 29, No. 1 (January, 1978), p. 38.

Consequently, some benefits may neither contribute to specific organizational objectives nor achieve the needs of individual employees. Furthermore, some benefits may neither improve motivation nor be cost-effective.[3] In addition to consuming funds that might be better spent on cash incentives, employee benefits can increase administrative costs and become the source of union and employee relations problems.

Rising Costs. According to a 1980 United States Chamber of Commerce study with 983 companies reporting, payments for employee benefits averaged 37.1 percent of the payroll. The average distribution of these benefit costs was $6,084 per employee. Payments varied widely among industries, and larger firms tended to pay higher benefits than smaller firms. Benefit payments also were higher in manufacturing than in nonmanufacturing companies. Among the reporting companies were 186 companies that had provided data since 1959. Data from these 186 companies indicated that benefit payments increased from 24.7 percent of the payroll in 1959 to 31.1 percent in 1969 and to 41.3 percent in 1980, as illustrated in Figure 19–1. This increase was 68 percent during the 21-year period.[4]

Figure 19–1 Growth of Employee Benefits in 186 Companies, 1959–1980

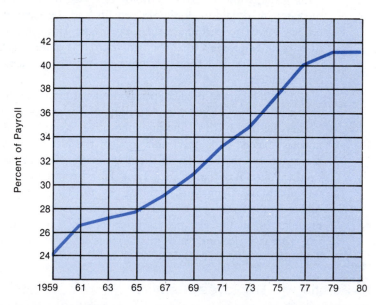

SOURCE: *Employee Benefits, 1980*, Table 19 (Washington, DC: Chamber of Commerce of the U.S., 1981).

3. Ralph L. Harris, "Let's Take the 'Fringe' Out of Fringe Benefits," *Personnel Journal*, Vol. 54, No. 2 (February, 1975), pp. 86–89.

4. *Employee Benefits, 1980* (Washington, DC: Chamber of Commerce of the United States of America, 1981), p. 27.

As benefits become an increasingly larger percentage of payroll costs, they may eventually equal the wages of employees. Since such benefits as medical, legal, and dental insurance tend to be paid across the board, the greater their cost becomes in relation to wages, the more these benefits will compress the compensation structure.

Potential Source of Complaints. Benefits can become a source of grievances or even lawsuits. Food services, parking, and similar facilities can become a magnet for complaints rather than be appreciated. A more extreme example may be suits by employees over injuries encountered during or following company social functions.

Benefits can also be a source of discrimination complaints. The EEOC, for example, ruled that it is unlawful for an employer to make benefits available for the wives and families of male employees where the same benefits are not made available to the husbands and families of female employees. The EEOC ruled also that making benefits available to employees and their spouses on the condition that the employee is the "head of household" or "principal wage earner" is in violation of Title VII since such status has no relationship to job performance.[5]

Requirements for a Sound Benefits Program

Too often a particular benefit is provided because other employers are doing it, because someone in authority believes it is a good idea, or because of union pressure. However, the type of contributions that fringe benefits will make to the personnel program will depend upon the extent to which attention is given to certain basic considerations.

Establishing Specific Objectives. Like any other phase of the personnel program, an employee benefit program should be based upon achieving specific objectives. These objectives should be concerned with satisfying employee needs and expectations while benefiting the employer, too. The objectives for a particular organization will depend upon many factors including size, location, degree of unionization, profitability, and industry patterns. Most importantly, the objectives must be compatible with the philosophy and policies of the organization.[6]

Unless an organization has a flexible benefit plan, an optimum combination or mix of benefits should be developed into a package. This involves a careful consideration of the various benefits that can be granted, the relative preference shown for each benefit by management and the employees, the estimated cost of each benefit, and the total amount of money available for the entire benefit package.

Allowing for Employee Input. Before a new benefit is introduced, the need for it should first be determined through consultations with employees. Many organizations establish committees composed of representatives of management and the employees

5. Howard J. Anderson, *Primer of Equal Employment Opportunity* (Washington, DC: The Bureau of National Affairs, Inc., 1978), pp. 25–26.

6. Robert M. McCaffery, *Managing the Employee Benefits Program* (New York: American Management Associations, 1972), p. 19.

who study needs and make recommendations concerning the benefits and services which are desired. Some organizations also utilize opinion surveys.

The fact that employees participate in designing benefit programs helps to insure that management is moving in the direction of satisfying employee wants. It also provides a basis for exchanging information about any problems associated with benefits such as abuse of sick leave privileges or overextending of the coffee break period.

Communicating Employee Benefit Information.   The true measure of a successful benefits program is the degree of trust, understanding, and appreciation which it gains from the employees. In communicating with employees about benefits, information about complicated insurance and pension plans should be made clear to them so that there will be no misunderstanding as to what the plans will and will not provide.

According to a partner of the consulting firm of Hewitt Associates, the sheer volume of materials covering employee benefits has quadrupled within the past decade or so. Employee benefit communication also has gained the attention of top managers. Rather than viewing this communication as "something nice to do," they recognize it as being something they must do, and do well.[7] Otherwise the benefits intended to attract and retain employees may, as the result of poor communication, create confusion and even resentment among them.

The communication of employee benefit information has been stimulated significantly by the passage of the Employee Retirement Income Security Act (ERISA). This act requires that employees be informed about their pension and certain other benefits "in a manner calculated to be understood by the average employee."[8] While ERISA has forced employers to communicate more effectively about their benefit programs, it has caused some of them to overreact. In doing so, Ewing indicates they "end up with materials that are really quite technical, containing all sorts of hedges, and deal with every possible contingency in breathtaking detail."[9]

Each of the various methods and media of communication discussed in Chapter 12 can and should be used to keep employees informed about the benefits they are receiving. The communication should make them fully aware of the monetary value of each benefit in terms of its equivalent rate per hour. Widely used media of communication are in-house publications and personalized annual reports. However, the method that is growing rapidly in popularity is the personalized computer-generated statement of benefits.[10] As Figure 19–2 on pages 468–469 shows, this statement can provide one of the best ways of slicing through a maze of benefit technicalities to provide concise data to employees about the status of their benefits.

7. Larry R. Ewing, "Employee Benefit Communications in the 80s," *Pension World* (February, 1980), p. 47.

8. Louis C. Kleber, "Employee Benefit Statements: The American Approach," *Pension World* (March, 1980), p. 145.

9. Ewing, *op. cit.*, p. 51.

10. Kleber, *op. cit.*, p. 145.

To assist employers with the administrative and communication functions, the International Foundation of Employee Benefit Plans in Brookfield, WI, maintains an extensive library of employee benefit publications. It also prepares publications on this subject, including the *Benefit News Spotlight.* In addition, the International Foundation sponsors seminars and has developed, in cooperation with the Wharton School, a course of study enabling a specialist in the field to become a Certified Employee Benefits Specialist (CEBS).[11] This and other developments have helped significantly to upgrade professionalism in this specialized area of human resources management.

Controlling Costs.   Since many of the benefit items represent a fixed rather than a variable cost, management must decide whether or not this cost can be met under less desirable economic conditions. It is generally recognized that, if an organization is forced to discontinue a benefit, the negative effect may exceed any positive effects that may have accrued from providing it.

Besides the actual costs of employee benefits, there are costs of administering them. For the large organization, administrative costs may not be significant. However, in the small organization the personnel costs of managing the benefit program may be sizable in proportion to the number of employees. As a matter of sound administration, as well as for collective bargaining purposes, it is important for an employer to maintain complete records of fringe benefit costs. Such costs should be communicated to employees so that they will understand that the paycheck tells only part of the total compensation story.

Modifying Employee Benefits.   To serve their intended goals, employee benefit programs must reflect the changes that are continually occurring within our society. Particularly significant are changes in the composition and life-styles of the work force. These changes make necessary new types of benefits to meet their particular needs.

Traditionally employee benefits have been designed to fit the needs of families in which the husband is the primary source of support. As we indicated in Chapter 2, the proportion of women in the work force, many of whom are working mothers, is continuing to grow. Rather than have health insurance which duplicates that of their working husbands, the working wives have need for some other benefits such as more life insurance, more time off, or even cash. Working wives may have need for pregnancy and maternal leaves and child care allowances. Provisions that enable them to separate their period of employment for child-rearing responsibilities also may be desired.

Interpersonal relations in society also are changing. Americans divorce and remarry with increasing frequency, share homes and have children without marriage, and move out of centuries-old sex roles.[12] Consequently, employers must modify their employee benefits to match these changes in the life-styles of their employees. Rising

---

11. N. Arnold Levin, "Certified Employee Benefits Specialist—A New Dimension in Employee Benefits Education," *Pension World*, Vol. 12, No. 11 (November, 1976), pp. 10–14.

12. "New Benefits for New Lifestyles," *Business Week* (February 11, 1980), p. 111.

Figure 19–2 A Computerized Benefit Statement

Peat, Marwick, Mitchell & Co.

Medical Benefits   INDIVIDUAL

Hospital   Semiprivate care for up to 120 days.

Surgical and Obstetrical   Reasonable and customary doctor's charges are covered in full.

Emergency Care   Covered in full within 72 hours of an accident or the onset of a sudden and serious illness.

Major Medical   Pays 80% of the medical expenses not covered under the Basic Hospital/Surgical section after you pay the first $150.

Disability Benefits

Sick Leave   One week at full salary for each year of service. Two weeks at one-half salary for each year of service after the first year.

Long Term Disability   After five months of disability a percentage ELECTED   of your basic salary (limited to a maximum benefit of $2,500)

- 75% for the first 12 months of disability
- 70% for the second 12 months of disability
- 65% for each month of disability thereafter up to age 65.

Note: Benefits are reduced by amounts payable from other sources such as Social Security and Workmen's Compensation.

Death Benefits

- **Life Insurance** $ 36,000
- **Survivor Benefits** (Annual income)   NOT ELECTED
- **Business Travel Accident** $100,000
- **Business Pleasure Accident** $ 50,000
- **Social Security**–lump sum payment $ 255

SOURCE: Peat, Marwick, Mitchell & Co., New York. Reproduced with permission.

Figure 19–2 **(continued)**

A personal report of estimated present and future benefits
as of August 1, 1981 for   J.A. ADAMS

Retirement Benefits– when you retire

From PMM&Co.   Based on your present compensation your projected
annual retirement income at age 65 will be $ 10,041
From Social Security   Your primary annual benefit is estimated
to add $ 7,516
Together—Your PMM&Co. and Social Security Benefits total $ 17,557
Plus—Social Security provides an annual income to your dependent
spouse (if any) of $ 3,758
To Buy the PMM&Co. Pension   you would need a lump sum
at age 65 of $ 96,971

Retirement Benefits– earned to date

You have a vested (nonforfeitable) right to a portion of your earned
PMM&Co. benefit when you have completed either a) at least five years
of service and your age plus service equals 45 or b) you have
completed 10 years of service regardless of your age.
- As of August 1, 1981, your accrued benefit payable at age 65 is $ 0
- Your vested interest of   *   in this accrued benefit
  will provide an annual income at age 65 of $ 0
* You are not currently vested, however, you will become
  50% vested on   07/01/91

Other Benefits
- **Vacation days**   10.0
- **Holidays**   9.0
- **Days off with pay for illness in family.**   3.0

What It Costs
To provide the benefits described in this Personal Statement,
PMM&Co.'s annual cost is approximately $ 5,076

incomes and heavier taxation for two-career families also are likely to create pressures for employers to provide additional benefits with pre-tax dollars. One consultant speculates that company-paid automobile and homeowners' insurance may become a reality if approved by Congress as employee benefits.[13]

Providing for Flexibility.   To accommodate differences in the individual needs of employees there is a trend toward providing **flexible benefit plans**, also known as **cafeteria plans**, **self-designated plans**, or **employee choice plans**. These plans enable individual employees to receive benefits that are best suited to their particular needs. They also prevent certain benefits from being wasted on employees who have no need for them. In the process, these plans help to control the rising cost of employee benefits.[14]

Savings also can be achieved by allowing employees to trade certain benefits for others. Thus, rather than receiving a new day-care plan as an additional benefit, some employees may prefer to shift credits to other benefits such as vacations, personal holidays, or thrift plans.[15] However, most flexible plans, such as the one pioneered successfully by the American Can Company, provide for a nonflexible core of benefits. In this company, the core includes a comprehensive medical plan, group life insurance, disability income insurance, vacations, and a pension plan.[16]

While many companies favor the concept of flexible plans, they recognize that this type of plan can be costly and complex to design and administer. Some of those considering a flexible plan have rejected it because, in the words of one executive, "It would have been an administrative nightmare."[17] There also is the concern that employees may make poor choices and then blame the company for not explaining fully the consequences.

CATEGORIES OF EMPLOYEE BENEFITS

Employee benefits may be categorized in different ways. Frequently, however, they are grouped into the following five categories: pensions and insurance; payment for time not worked; legally required benefits such as Social Security, unemployment insurance, and workers' compensation; employee services; and other miscellaneous benefits.

Pensions and Insurance

According to the United States Chamber of Commerce study cited earlier in this chapter, pensions and insurance represent the highest percentage (12.6 percent)

---

13. *Ibid.*, p. 112.
14. John Perham, "New Life for Flexible Compensation," *Compensation Review*, Vol. 11, No. 1 (First Quarter, 1979), p. 65.
15. Jane Juffer, "Firms Find Recession a Good Time to Reduce Employee Benefit Costs," *The Wall Street Journal*, August 25, 1982, p. 23.
16. Albert S. Schlachtmeyer and Robert B. Bogart, "Employee-Choice Benefits: Can Employees Handle It?" *Compensation Review*, Vol. 11, No. 3 (Third Quarter, 1979), p. 13.
17. "Fringe Benefits a la Carte," *Changing Times*, Vol. 36, No. 5 (May, 1982), p. 51.

of payroll costs. Approximately half of this amount is used to cover pension costs, and the other half is used to pay for insurance premiums.[18] Due to the complexities of pension plans, they will be discussed in a separate section later in this chapter. The various types of insurance benefits are covered briefly below.

Group Life Insurance.   One of the oldest and most popular employee benefits is group life insurance, which provides death benefits to beneficiaries and may provide also for accidental death and dismemberment benefits. It is a nearly universal employee benefit in the United States, with over $1,888 billion of group life insurance in force at the end of 1981.[19] Figure 19–3 illustrates the growth of this particular benefit.

As a rule, the amount of life insurance coverage for an individual employee depends upon salary level. However, in manufacturing industries there are many plans which provide the same amount of insurance regardless of salary. The trend toward union-negotiated, company-financed plans is continuing, but in some organizations the cost is shared by the employees and the employer.

Health Care Insurance.   The benefits that receive the greatest attention of employers today because of sharply rising costs are those for health care. In the past these benefits covered only hospital and surgical expenses. Today employers are under pressure to include prescription drugs and dental, visual, and mental health

Figure 19–3   Growth of Group Life Insurance in the United States

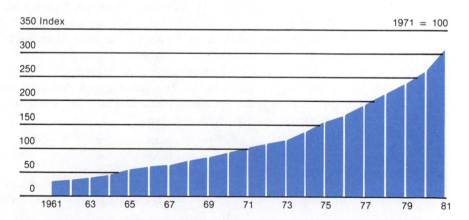

SOURCE: *Life Insurance Fact Book, 1982,* p. 29. Reproduced with the permission of the American Council of Life Insurance.

18. *Employee Benefits, 1980, op. cit.,* p. 8.
19. *Life Insurance Fact Book* (Washington, DC: American Council of Life Insurance, 1982), p. 27.

care. In a 1980 survey by the Conference Board, 48 percent of the companies reporting paid the total cost of health insurance coverage for both nonoffice employees and their dependents. At one time most companies contributed only to employees' insurance premiums which did not include dependents. Of the companies surveyed, only 25 percent require employees to contribute to the cost of premiums for their dependents and only 27 percent require employees to contribute to insurance premiums covering both their dependents and themselves.[20]

Dental insurance is the health care benefit that has grown very rapidly in the past decade. Among companies surveyed in the sample, those providing dental insurance increased from 8 percent in 1973 to 19 percent in 1975 and 41 percent in 1980. Most dental insurance is provided through a separate plan, but some companies included it as a part of their major medical coverage, with deductibles applying to that plan.[21] Since preventive dental care contributes to dental health, many plans provide for this care routinely by covering the full cost of it.

Employers also are being forced to cope with rising costs resulting from inflation and the use of increasingly expensive medical technology. These conditions have encouraged more companies to install comprehensive major medical plans, with employees sharing part of their health care costs. In the Conference Board survey cited above, 45 percent of the companies require cost sharing as compared with only 32 percent in 1973.[22] Some companies also are turning to health maintenance organizations (HMOs). These organizations, which put particular stress on preventive health care, charge members a flat monthly fee regardless of the treatment they receive. To gain better control over their health care programs, some large companies such as F. W. Woolworth, Goodyear, and Reynolds Metals have chosen to self-insure rather than contract the service out.[23]

Another recent trend is the development of sick leave banks. A sick leave bank allows employees to pool some of their compensated sick leave days in a common fund. They may then draw upon the fund if extensive illness uses up their remaining time off. Sick leave banks are fairly common among teachers, police, and firefighters. Such banks discourage absenteeism because everyone is intent on protecting the jointly owned days in the banks. To avoid the risk that conscientious workers will wind up supporting those who squander their time off, a committee generally passes on each request to draw from the bank.[24]

Payment for Time Not Worked

This category of benefits includes paid vacations, bonuses given in lieu of paid vacations, payments for holidays not worked, paid sick leave, military and jury duty,

20. Mitchell Meyer, *Profile of Employee Benefits: 1981 Edition*, Report No. 813 (New York: The Conference Board, Inc., 1981), p. 8.

21. *Ibid.*, p. 13.

22. *Ibid.*, p. 6.

23. John Perham, "Putting a Lid on Corporate Health Costs," *Dun's Review*, Vol. 116, No. 3 (September, 1980), p. 96, 98.

24. "A Low Cost Fringe That Workers Appreciate," *Business Week* (March 13, 1978), p. 79.

and payments for time lost due to death in the family or for other personal reasons. Their costs are roughly 10 percent of payroll costs.[25] Interestingly, giving up certain paid personal holidays was one of the concessions the United Auto Workers were willing to make so that the auto manufacturers' labor costs could be reduced during the 1980 recession.

There are several ways in which employees may be compensated during periods when they are unable to work because of illness or injury. Most of those in public employment, as well as many in private industry, particularly in white-collar jobs, receive a set number of sick leave days each year to cover absences for physical reasons. Where it is provided, unused sick leave generally can be accumulated up to at least a given amount to cover prolonged absences. Accumulated annual vacation leave may be used as a source of income when sick leave benefits have been exhausted. Group insurance which provides for income protection is also becoming more common. Loss of income during absences resulting from job-incurred injuries can be reimbursed, at least partially, by means of workers' compensation insurance, discussed later in this chapter.

Employee Benefits Required by Law

The legally required employee benefits constitute nearly a quarter of the benefit package that employers provide. As we indicated earlier, these benefits include employer contributions to Social Security, unemployment insurance, and workers' compensation insurance. Altogether such benefits represent about 9 percent of payroll costs.

Social Security Insurance. The Social Security Act was passed in 1935, providing an insurance plan designed to indemnify covered individuals against loss of earnings resulting from various causes. This loss of earnings may result from retirement, unemployment, disability, or, in the case of dependents, from the death of the person supporting them. Thus, as in the case of any type of casualty insurance, Social Security does not pay off except in the case where a loss of income through loss of employment actually is incurred.

In order to be eligible for old age and survivors insurance (OASI), as well as disability and unemployment insurance, under the Social Security Act, an individual must have been engaged in employment covered by it. Most employment in private enterprise, most types of self-employment, active military service after 1956, and employment in certain nonprofit organizations and governmental agencies are subject to coverage under the act.[26] Railroad workers and United States civil service employees who are covered by their own systems and some occupational groups, under certain conditions, are exempted from the act.[27]

---

25. *Employee Benefits, 1980, op. cit.,* p. 8.

26. Active military service completed between 1940 and 1956 inclusive was granted Social Security credit gratuitously based upon monthly earnings of $160 per month. If this credit is used for Social Security benefits, however, it cannot be counted toward any other federal service pension.

27. For a more detailed account of exempted groups, see the current editions of *Labor Course* or *Tax Course* (Englewood Cliffs, NJ: Prentice-Hall, Inc.).

The Social Security program is supported by means of a tax levied against an employee's earnings which must be matched by the employer. Self-employed persons are required to pay a tax on their earnings at a rate which is higher than that paid by employees but less than the combined rates paid by employees and their employers.[28]

Old Age Insurance Benefits. In order to receive old age insurance benefits, a person must have reached retirement age and be fully insured. A **fully insured person** is one who must have earned at least $50 in a quarter for a period of 40 quarters. (A calendar quarter is a three-month period beginning on the first day of January, April, July, or October.) It is possible, however, for an individual who dies or becomes totally disabled at an early age to be classified as fully insured with less than 40 quarters. To be fully insured, self-employed persons must have earned at least $400 per year (for which they receive 4 quarters of coverage) for 40 quarters.

To receive old age insurance benefits, covered individuals must also meet the **test of retirement**. To meet this test, persons under 70 cannot be earning more than an established amount through gainful employment. This limitation on earnings does not include income from sources other than gainful employment such as investments or pensions.

Because Social Security retirement benefits are computed on the basis of average monthly earnings, they are reduced by each year in which an individual does not work in covered employment. In determining this average, however, the five years in which there has been the least or no earnings may be excluded.

Since 1977, the average of actual earnings has been adjusted annually for inflation to provide an **Average Indexed Monthly Earnings (AIME)**. Benefits are now calculated on the basis of AIME rather than on the actual average of monthly earnings.[29]

Social Security retirement benefits consist of those benefits which individuals are entitled to receive in their own behalf, called the **Primary Insurance Amount (PIA)**, plus supplemental benefits for eligible dependents. These benefits can be determined from a prepared benefit table. There are also both minimum and maximum limits to the amount that individuals and their dependents can receive. Dependents for whom supplemental benefits may be claimed include the following:

1. Wife over 65 (or 62 at a reduced amount).
2. Wife caring for an unmarried child who is under 18 years of age or disabled.
3. Unmarried child who is under 18 or disabled.
4. Parents who are dependent upon a covered individual for more than 50 percent of their support.

It should be recognized that the calculation of benefits favors recipients who have had lower average earnings. For example, the difference in benefits between a

---

28. Since the Social Security Act is subject continually to amendment, readers should refer to the literature provided by the nearest Social Security office for the most current details pertaining to the tax rates and benefit provisions of the Act. The current edition of the booklet *Your Social Security*, prepared by the Social Security Administration, is an excellent general source of information.

29. J. W. Van Gorkom, "Social Security I," *Across the Board*, Vol. XVI, No. 3 (March, 1979), p. 42.

recipient with an AIME of $200 as compared to one with an AIME of $1,000 would be as follows:

AIME of $200		*AIME of $1,000*	
90% of first $180 .... $162.00		90% of first $180 .... $162.00	
+ 32% of remainder		+32% of remainder	
(32% of $20) 6.00		(32% of $820) 262.00	
Total PIA	$168.00	Total PIA	$424.00

Thus, an individual with an AIME of $1,000 will contribute five times as much as one with an AIME of $200, but will receive only two-and-one-half as much in benefits.[30]

Disability Benefits. The Social Security program provides benefit payments to workers who are too severely disabled to engage in gainful employment. In order to be eligible for such benefits, however, an individual's disability must have existed for at least 6 months and must be expected to continue for at least 12 months. Those eligible for disability benefits, furthermore, must have worked under Social Security for at least 5 out of the 10 years before becoming disabled. Disability benefits, which include auxiliary benefits for dependents, are computed on the same basis as retirement benefits and are converted to retirement benefits when the individual reaches the age of 65.

Survivors Insurance Benefits. The survivors insurance benefits represent the form of life insurance that is paid to members of a deceased person's family who meet the requirements for eligibility. As in the case of life insurance, the benefits that the survivors of a covered individual receive may be far in excess of their cost to this individual. Survivors of individuals who were currently insured, as well as those who were fully insured at the time of death, are eligible to receive certain benefits, provided that the survivors meet other eligibility requirements. A **currently insured person** is one who has been covered during at least 6 out of the 13 quarters prior to death.

Problems Confronting Social Security. Like many private and public pension plans, Social Security is confronted with the problem of mounting liabilities. These liabilities result from the fact that current taxes are being used to provide far greater benefits to retired workers than their past contributions earned for them. Retired workers are thus dependent upon the taxes to be paid by current and future workers. Even more critical are the basic flaws in the system which stem primarily from the system having been forced to serve more purposes than it can handle. According to Van Gorkom:

> This has escalated the costs of the system to the point where the low-paid individual cannot carry his (or her) full share of the tax burden. In attempting to lighten

---

30. *Ibid*, pp. 43—44.

his (or her) load, the system has gradually acquired many of the characteristics of a welfare program, and has moved away from the basic concept on which it should be based.[31]

Thus, benefits under the original act were a right, determined by the contribution paid by the recipients without regard to need. Certain benefits subsequently added to the Social Security system are determined on the basis of the beneficiaries' needs rather than upon their contributions. These benefits include those provided under the Supplementary Security Income (SSI) and the Aid to Families with Dependent Children (AFDC) programs. Although these programs are administered by the Social Security Administration, they are financed from general revenues.

Perhaps the greatest future problem confronting the Social Security program will be the growing burden being placed upon those currently paying Social Security taxes. In 1950, there were 16 workers paying Social Security taxes for each beneficiary. This number declined to 5 in 1960, to 4 in 1970, and to 3 in the 1980s. If population trends continue, it is predicted that by the year 2030 there will be only 2 workers per beneficiary.[32] Social Security thus has become an "intergenerational transfer payment system" which younger generations eventually may refuse to support.

Unemployment Insurance.   Employees who have been working in employment covered by the Social Security Act and who are laid off may be eligible for **unemployment insurance** benefits during their unemployment for a period up to 26 weeks. Eligible persons must submit an application for unemployment compensation with their state employment agency, register for available work, and be willing to accept any suitable employment that may be offered to them. However, the term "suitable" permits individuals to enjoy considerable discretion in accepting or rejecting job offers.

The amount of the compensation that workers are eligible to receive, which varies among states, is determined by their previous wage rates and previous periods of employment. Funds for unemployment compensation are derived from a federal payroll tax based upon the wages paid to each employee, up to an established maximum. The major portion of this tax is refunded to the individual states which, in turn, operate their unemployment compensation programs in accordance with minimum standards prescribed by the federal government.

In some industries unemployment compensation is augmented by **Supplemental Unemployment Benefits (SUB)**, financed by the company. These benefits were introduced in 1955 when the United Auto Workers successfully negotiated a SUB plan with the auto industry which established a pattern for other industries. This plan enables an employee who is laid off to draw, in addition to state unemployment compensation, weekly benefits from the company that are paid from a fund created for this purpose. Many SUB plans in recent years have been liberalized to permit employees to receive weekly benefits when the length of their workweek is reduced

31. J. W. Van Gorkom, "Social Security II," *Across the Board*, Vol. XVI, No. 4 (April, 1979), p. 69.

32. "Your Social Security Benefits—The Outlook Now," *U.S. News & World Report* (June 7, 1982), p. 36.

and to receive a lump sum payment if their employment is terminated permanently. The amount of these benefits is determined by length of service and wage rate. Employer liability under the plan is limited to the amount of money that has been accumulated within the fund from employer contributions based on the total hours of work performed by union members.

Workers' Compensation Insurance. State and federal **workers' compensation insurance** is based on the theory that the costs of industrial accidents should be considered as one of the costs of production and should ultimately be passed on to the consumer. Individual employees should neither be required to stand the expense of their treatment or loss of income nor be required to be subjected to complicated, delaying, and expensive legal procedures.

In most states workers' compensation insurance is compulsory. Only in New Jersey, South Carolina, and Texas is it elective.[33] When compulsory, every employer subject to it is required to comply with the law's provisions for the compensation of work injuries. The law is compulsory for the employee also. When elective, the employers have the option of either accepting or rejecting the law. However, if they reject it, they lose the customary common law defenses—assumed risk of employment, negligence of a fellow servant, and contributory negligence.[34]

Employee Services and Other Miscellaneous Benefits

A variety of miscellaneous benefits includes paid rest periods, lunch periods, travel time, and get-ready time. These comprise about 3.5 percent of payroll costs.

Employee services provided by employers are generally not included in the data compiled by the United States Chamber of Commerce. However, these services, like other benefits, also constitute a cost. Food services and free parking represent employee services that are often included in the employer's overhead costs. Other employee services described below are included in the employer's labor costs.

Van Pooling Services. Employer-organized van pooling was started by 3M in 1973 and is now being adopted by other companies. This service offers employees transportation without requiring any capital investment on their part. Aetna, for example, estimates that van-pool participation costs its employees an average of only $420 annually. This contrasts with an average cost of $3,120 for operating a six-cylinder car to commute to work 250 days per year. Transportation specialists maintain that van-pooling increases employee productivity by reducing tardiness and

---

33. BNA Policy and Practice Series—Compensation, Vol. 2 (Washington DC: The Bureau of National Affairs, Inc., 1978), pp. 365:17–365:19.

34. These three defenses are defined as follows: (1) the *doctrine of contributory negligence* states that the employer would not be liable if the injury of the employee was due wholly or in part to negligence, (2) *the doctrine of the assumption of risk* holds that when employees accept a job, they assume the ordinary risks of the job, and (3) the *fellow-servant rule* provides that if the employee was injured as a result of the negligence of a fellow employee, the employer would not be liable for the injury.

absenteeism.[35] It also saves companies the cost of parking space that otherwise would be required. This cost, depending on the cost of land and construction, can be considerable. Van pooling, of course, also renders an important contribution to society by reducing traffic congestion, air pollution, and energy consumption.[36]

Health Services.   Almost all organizations of any size provide some form of health services. The extent of these services will vary considerably but they are generally designed to handle minor illnesses and injuries. Health services may also include alcohol and drug abuse referral services, in-house counseling programs, fitness clinics, and advice on nutrition. We will discuss these and related programs in detail in the next chapter.

Counseling Services.   While most organizations expect supervisors to counsel subordinates, it is recognized that some employees may have problems that require the services of professional counselors. A large percentage of organizations refers such individuals to outside counseling services such as church organizations, family counseling services or marriage counselors, and mental health clinics. Some organizations have a qualified person, such as a clinical psychologist, a counselor, or a comparable specialist to whom employees may be referred. The types of problems and the ways in which they are handled will be examined more thoroughly in the next chapter.

Legal and Accounting Services.   Many organizations make the services of professional persons on the staff available to employees at no expense. Attorneys can contribute by providing help in drawing up wills, giving advice on contracts, and assisting employees in locating qualified personnel to handle legal cases. Similarly, the talents of accountants can be made available to help employees to some extent in connection with tax returns.

In 1973 Congress amended the Taft-Hartley Act to permit unions to bargain for legal insurance as an employer-shared benefit. Group legal plans bring legal services to millions of people who otherwise would not be able to afford them.[37]

PENSION PLANS AND PENSION FUNDING

The first pension plan in the United States was established in 1759 by "The Corporation for the Relief of Poor and Distressed Presbyterian Ministers, and for the Poor and Distressed Widows and Children of Presbyterian Ministers." This plan is still in operation. The first employer-sponsored pension plan was started by the American Express Company over 100 years later in 1875. It provided benefits equal

---

35. "Van-Pooling Takes U.S. by Storm," *San Francisco Sunday Examiner and Chronicle*, September 26, 1982, p. D-12.

36. Steven L. Wartick, "Employer-Organized Vanpooling: A Program for the 1980s," *Business Horizons*, Vol. 23, No. 6 (December, 1980), pp. 53–54.

37. "New Fringe Benefit: Prepaid Legal Service," *Business Week* (January 12, 1974), p. 34.

to 50 percent of the average pay earned in the final 10 years, not to exceed $500 annually.[38] Railroad employees and personnel in the civil and the armed services of the federal government also were early recipients of pension benefits.

Pension Philosophies

The philosophy underlying pensions has undergone a substantial change. Originally pensions were based upon a **reward philosophy** which viewed their primary purpose as that of retaining personnel by rewarding them for remaining with the organization until they retired. Those employees who quit or who were terminated prior to retirement age were not considered deserving of such rewards. As a result of the vesting requirements negotiated into most union contracts and more recently required by law, pensions are now based upon an **earnings philosophy**. Under this philosophy a pension is regarded as deferred income which employees accumulate during their working lives and which belongs to them after a specified number of years of service, whether or not they remain with the employer until retirement.

Types of Pension Plans

In a **contributory plan** contributions to a pension plan are provided jointly by employees and employers. In a **noncontributory plan** the contributions are provided solely by the employer. Most of the plans existing in industry (79 percent according to one survey) are of the noncontributory type, whereas those in government are of the contributory type.[39] The noncontributory plans have an advantage for employees in sheltering from current income taxes that portion of their income which otherwise would be required to pay their contributions.

When classified according to the amount of pension benefits to be paid, the two basic types are the defined benefit pension plan and the defined contribution plan.[40] Under the **defined benefit pension plan**, the amount of payment the employee is to receive upon retirement is specifically set forth. This amount may be based upon such factors as the employee's years of service, average earnings during a specific period of time, and age at time of retirement. While a variety of formulas exists for determining pension benefits, the one most widely used is based upon the employee's average earnings (usually over a three- to five-year period immediately preceding retirement), multiplied by the number of years of service with the organization.

The **defined contribution (or money purchase) plan** establishes the basis upon which the employer is to contribute to the pension fund. These contributions may be made through profit-sharing, thrift plans, employer-sponsored individual

---

38. Hewitt Associates, ''Employee Retirement Systems: How It All Began,'' *Pension World*, Vol. 12, No. 7 (July, 1976), p. 6.

39. *BNA Policy and Practice Series—Compensation* (Washington, DC: The Bureau of National Affairs, Inc., 1980), p. 343:4.

40. S. Travis Pritchett, ''Cost-Conscious Design and Management of Defined Benefit Pension,'' *Personnel*, Vol. 52, No. 5 (September-October, 1975), pp. 51–52.

retirement accounts, and various other contribution formulas. The amount of benefits employees are to receive upon retirement is then determined by the funds accumulated in their behalf at the time of retirement and what these funds will purchase in the way of retirement benefits. These plans, however, do not offer the benefit-security predictability which is highly desirable from the employees' point of view. However, even under defined benefit plans, employees may not receive the benefits promised upon their retirement if the plan has not been adequately funded.

Federal Regulation of Pension Plans

Private pension plans are subject to federal regulations under the Employee Retirement Income Security Act of 1975 (ERISA). Although this act does not require employers to establish a pension plan, it provides certain controls and vesting-requirement standards governing pension plans. It also establishes minimum funding standards to assure that benefits will be available when an employee retires. Furthermore, the soundness of the actuarial assumptions upon which the funding is based must be certified by an actuary at least every three years.

A Pension Benefit Guaranty Corporation (PBGC) has been formed, supported by premiums from employers, to assure that employees will receive at least a portion of their pensions even if the fund to provide it becomes insolvent. This premium, which began at a modest $1.00 per year per participant, rose in 1981 to $2.60. The PBGC is now asking for a further increase to $6.00.[41] These increases are probably only a beginning. Unfortunately it is the stockholders of the companies with the strong pension plans who must bear the burden of any increases in insurance rates needed to "bail out" companies with weaker plans.

The Tax Equity and Fiscal Responsibility Act of 1982 (TEFRA) also has had a major impact upon company pension contributions and benefits. Space limitation, however, prevents a discussion of this act as it relates to pension plans because of the highly technical nature of its provisions.

Pension Portability

A weakness of most private pension plans is that they lack the portability which would enable employees, when changing employment, to maintain equity in a single pension. Even when employees acquire **vested rights**—an irrevocable interest or equity in the benefits they had earned through their years of service—several changes in employment over their working life can result in the accumulation of equity in more than one fund.

Unions have sought to reduce this problem by encouraging the development of **multiple employer plans** in which pension liabilities are shared by participating employers. It is predicted that these plans will cover 13 million employees by 1990.[42] Employees also have the opportunity to establish their own **Individual Retirement Accounts (IRAs)** as a source of retirement benefits. The Congress of the United

---

41. "Pensions: High Anxiety," *The Wall Street Journal*, Aug. 16, 1982, p. 12.
42. *BNA Policy and Practice Series—Compensation, op. cit.*, p. 343:5.

States has encouraged the use of IRAs by permitting an employee to shelter the amount contributed to an IRA from income tax up to an annual maximum of $2,000 (or $2,250) where the employee's spouse is not employed outside the home).

Pension Funds

Pension funds may be administered through either a trusteed or an insured plan. In a **trusteed plan**, pension contributions are placed in a trust fund. The investment and administration of the fund is handled by trustees appointed by either the employer or the union, or both. Contributions to an **insured plan** are used to purchase insurance annuities. The responsibility for administering these funds rests with the insurance company providing the annuities.

Inadequate Funding.

A great problem concerning pension plans in both the public and private sectors is that many of them are not funded adequately. For some companies, the portion of their pension obligations that is underfunded may be nearly equal to or greater than the company's worth. Referring to private pension plans, one authority testifying before a congressional committee had this to say: "It appears we have a time bomb on our hands waiting to go off—and we do not know how large the explosion will be."[43] Unfortunately for public employees, many of their pension plans also are underfunded.

Current pension fund difficulties have been caused in part by the fact that the current wages upon which pensions are based today drastically exceed the wage rates upon which the contributions into the pension funds were determined in earlier years. Furthermore, employees also are exceeding the life expectancies upon which their pension benefits were funded. Some employers also have given in to union bargaining demands for higher pensions without taking a hard look at what the future costs of these demands might require.

Social Investment Issues.

Added to the problem of inadequate pension funding have been union demands for a greater voice in determining where pension funds are to be invested. There also is a movement to have more pension funds diverted to investments that they consider to be "socially desirable." The agreement between the UAW and Chrysler, for example, requires that 10 percent of all new pension fund contributions be placed in home mortgages, health centers, child care centers, hospitals, and similar investments in areas where members live.[44] Unions also seek to avoid having their pension funds invested in companies or construction projects where nonunion labor is employed. Working out an agreement as to which investments are socially desirable at times can be difficult. For example, some unions wanted to exclude investments in a southern grocery chain because of its resistance to

---

43. "Analyst Sees Pension 'Time Bomb'", *The Sacramento Union* (AP), June 8, 1982, p. C–8.

44. "Risking the Funds," *Business Week* (November 12, 1979), p. 148.

union drives to organize its clerical workers. However, the building trades unions countered that stores of the chain were built with union labor.[45]

There is resistance among employers to union attempts to exercise a greater role in pension fund investments. As one management association representative states, "Unions cannot dictate where investments are made unless they assume responsibility for funding the plans and the fiduciary responsibility for the assets. Of course, they are willing to assume neither."[46] While there is merit in making investments that are socially desirable, the primary objective of pension investments should be one of protecting employee pension funds.

Any policy of investing in socially desirable projects must give consideration to the provisions of ERISA. This act requires that fiduciaries (fund managers) must act "solely in the interest of the participants and beneficiaries—for the exclusive purpose of providing benefits." It does, however, permit a consideration of incidental features of investments, provided that they are equal in economic terms.[47]

Problems with Pension Benefits

Two significant types of problems are associated with the pension benefits themselves. One is related to inflation, and the other has its basis in sex discrimination.

Inflation-Eroded Benefits.
The purchasing power that pension benefits provide is continually being eroded by inflation. What might have been an adequate retirement annuity 20 years ago, for example, very likely would be inadequate in terms of today's living costs. Employers, therefore, are finding themselves under union, as well as moral, pressure to provide supplemental benefits to employees who retired a few years ago and whose pensions are now inadequate.

According to a survey by Hewitt Associates, employees working for major companies are most likely to receive pension increases after retirement. However, in a Hay/Huggins survey, only 8 percent of the respondents had provisions for indexing pensions to the cost of living whereas 44 percent granted increases on an ad hoc basis. The remaining 48 percent provided no adjustments in pensions to offset inflation.[48]

Sex-Based Pension Benefits.
As in other areas of human resources management, sex discrimination has become an issue concerning pension benefits. This issue stems from the actuarial reality that the extended life expectancy at retirement age, on the average, is longer for women than for men. Therefore, the cost of providing the same pension benefits is greater for women than for men. For example, the cost of

---

45. "Joann S. Lublin, "Unions Step Up Use of Pension Cash to Push 'Socially Desirable' Projects," *The Wall Street Journal*, July 23, 1980, pp. 25, 35.
46. "Unions Bid for Bigger Voice in Pension Funds,"*U.S. News & World Report* (June 18, 1981), p. 86.
47. Ian D. Lanoff, "The Social Investment of Private Pension Plan Assets: May It Be Done Lawfully Under ERISA?" *Labor Law Journal*, Vol. 31, No. 7 (July, 1980), pp. 389, 392.
48. *BNA Policy and Practice Series—Compensation, op. cit.*, pp. 343:33−89.

providing a monthly benefit of one dollar for life for employees retiring at age 65 is about $162 for men and $182 for women.[49] On the other hand, an equal amount of money in an employee's pension fund at the time of retirement will provide smaller pension payments for a woman than for a man of the same age. Women's interest groups charge that this constitutes sex discrimination.

In the landmark Manhart Case, the United States Supreme Court prohibited the payment of sex-based pension benefits as well as unequal pension contributions based upon sex.[50] However, the courts have not challenged the offering of sex-differentiated annuities in the marketplace.[51] Until the issue has been clarified further by the courts, in order to avoid sex-discrimination charges employers may be advised to consider lump-sum pension payments, defined contribution, profit sharing, and ESOP plans as a means of providing pension benefits.

RETIREMENT PROGRAMS

Many employers offer assistance in helping employees to prepare for retirement and to cope with the adjustments it may require. Others, however, leave it up to their employees to make their own preparations for retirement and to support themselves financially on whatever Social Security benefits and savings they have been able to accumulate.

Preretirement Planning

While retirement generally is eagerly anticipated, many people are bitterly disappointed once they enter this stage of life.[52] Preretirement planning programs, therefore, should help employees gain an early awareness of the various types of adjustments they may be required to make upon retirement. Such adjustments may include learning to live on a reduced fixed income and to cope with the problems of lost prestige, marital friction, or idleness that retirement may create.[53] Unfortunately, according to the national director of Action for Independent Maturity (AIM), if left to their own resources most employees spend more time planning a two-week vacation than they do planning for their retirement.[54]

Individuals who have enjoyed and have been absorbed in their work often experience the greatest difficulty in adjusting to retirement. This fact is especially

---

49. This rate will vary somewhat among insurance companies.

50. *City of Los Angeles, Department of Water and Power et al. v. Manhart et al.*, 435 US 702 (US S.Ct., 1978), 16 EPD ¶8250.

51. Linda H. Kistler and Richard C. Healy, "Sex Discrimination in Pension Plans Since Manhart," *Labor Law Journal*, Vol. 32, No. 4 (April, 1981), pp. 229, 237.

52. Patrick J. Montana, "Preretirement Counseling: Three Corporate Case Studies," *Personnel Administrator*, Vol. 27, No. 6 (June, 1982), p. 51.

53. "How to Help Employees Prepare for Retirement," *Business Week* (April 24, 1978), p. 137.

54. John C. Perham, "The Newest Employee Benefit," *Dun's Review*, Vol. 115, No. 5 (May, 1980), p. 72.

Figure 19–4 Adjustment to Retirement

"Well, Morton, your first day of retirement...
now you're one of the powers that were!"

SOURCE: Reprinted by permission. © 1980 NEA, Inc.

true for managers and professional people. Like the man in Figure 19–4, it was their work that enabled these individuals to feel "worth something"—a feeling that helped them to cope with the challenges of daily life and the problems of survival.[55] The following statement by one retired executive typifies this feeling:

> Retirement to me is a disappointment. I feel useless; unasked to do the things I worked so hard to learn to do in my work years. I have lost a lot of the old zest I had for living when I went to work every day.[56]

Unfortunately most employees must encounter retirement without the benefit of prior experience or the chance for a second time around. All they can do is to try and profit from the knowledge and experiences of others made available to them through preretirement programs.

55. Morton D. Bogdonoff, "The Human Need for an Appointment with Tomorrows," *Archives of International Medicine* (1969), pp. 635–636.

56. Harry W. Hepner, "Corporate Executives Who Retire," *Michigan Business Review*, Vol. XXII, No. 3 (May, 1970), p. 13.

Preretirement programs may be viewed as a "rehearsal for retirement." Ideally the programs should encourage people to practice ahead of time living on their retirement income and replacing their work with meaningful activities. One study of retirees indicates that the problems they may encounter in rank order of seriousness are as follows: (1) health, (2) money and financial matters, (3) too much free time, (4) lack of personal and social contacts, (5) food and nutrition, (6) transportation, and (7) housing.[57] A primary objective of preretirement programs, therefore, is to assist employees in recognizing the fact that they too may have to cope with these problems. Furthermore, a preretirement program should help to provide an answer to the question in the minds of many older employees today: "With inflation what it is today, can I really afford to retire?"

Determining the Retirement Age

Prior to 1979, employers were able to determine the age (generally 65) at which their employees would be required to retire. An amendment to the Age Discrimination in Employment Act (ADEA) now forbids mandatory retirement under the age of 70 in private employment and at any age in federal employment. The amendment does not prevent the termination of employees under 70 who are unable to perform their jobs satisfactorily. However, some of these terminations are likely to be challenged, forcing employers to provide proof of unsatisfactory performance. This fact should encourage them to have an effective program for evaluating performance which is conducted on a career-long basis.[58]

Although the issue of mandatory retirement has been the subject of considerable attention, Rones suggests that this ADEA amendment will not affect retirement programs significantly. The reason is that most workers do not choose to work beyond 65 when they become eligible for full Social Security benefits. Furthermore, studies indicate that prior to the ADEA amendment, only 5 to 10 percent of those retiring were forced to do so.[59] While employees can now work until age 70, they have no legal right to accrue pension benefits beyond age 65. However, nearly half of the companies participating in a survey conducted by Hewitt Associates provide for the accrual of pension benefits beyond age 65.

Case Against Mandatory Retirement.
Opponents of mandatory retirement view it as a form of discrimination, comparable to racism or sexism, which violates the constitutional rights of those affected. However, in the Murgia Case this argument was rejected by the Supreme Court which ruled that the issue of mandatory retirement is primarily one of social policy and not of constitutional rights.[60] According to MacDonald, opponents of mandatory retirement argue that "it

57. William H. Holley, Jr., and Hubert S. Field, Jr., "The Design of a Retirement Preparation Program: A Case History," *Personnel Journal*, Vol. 53, No. 7 (July, 1974), p. 529.

58. John Perham, "Retirement Revolution Brewing," *Dun's Review*, Vol. 113, No. 5 (May, 1979), p. 96.

59. Philip L. Rones, "The Retirement Decision: A Question of Opportunity?" *Monthly Labor Review*, Vol. 103, No. 11 (November 1980), p. 15.

60. *Massachusetts Board of Retirement v. Murgia*, 427US307 (1976).

is injurious both to the individual and society, stripping the former of livelihood, dignity, and purpose and depriving the latter of contributions sorely needed to help defray the rising costs of old age dependency." These opponents conclude that mandatory retirement thus is contrary to the public interests and therefore should be unlawful. And to a large extent it was outlawed in 1979.[61]

Case for Mandatory Retirement. In the past it was not uncommon for organizations to carry on the payroll, until age 65, employees who could not perform their jobs effectively. These employees were thus spared the demeaning experience of being forced to quit because of poor performance. Since organizations no longer can force employees under 70 to retire on the basis of age, they are more likely to terminate employees when their performance justifies doing so.

Other arguments favoring mandatory retirement are that it clears the way for younger persons to move up within the organization and creates new openings which meet affirmative-action goals. Further, mandatory retirement can provide employment opportunities for individuals who otherwise might remain on the unemployment rolls. Finally, it can facilitate long-term human resources planning, particularly as it applies to development programs and pension planning.

Trend Toward Early Retirement

To avoid layoffs, particularly of the more recently hired members of protected groups, many corporations such as Sears, United Airlines, and B. F. Goodrich Company have encouraged early retirements.[62] This encouragement has been in the form of increased pension benefits for several years, or cash bonuses which sometimes are referred to as the **silver handshake**. The cost of these retirement incentives often can be offset by the lower compensation that is paid to replacements.

One of the major factors affecting the decision to retire early and the satisfaction to be gained from it is the individual's personal financial condition. Consequently, a major obstacle to early retirement today is inflation, which threatens to seriously erode the purchasing power of an employee's income following retirement. In spite of this deterrent and federal regulations guaranteeing them the right to work longer, a growing number of older workers is choosing to retire early. The latest government figures indicate that only 12.5 percent remain in the labor force after reaching 65 as compared with 26.7 percent in the 1950s.[63] The possibility of future layoffs, failing health, frustration, and inability to meet the demands of their jobs, together with attractive Social Security benefits, are among the reasons for their retirement.

61. Ronald M. MacDonald, *Mandatory Retirement and the Law* (Washington, DC: American Enterprise Institute for Public Policy Research, 1978), p. 9.

62. Joann S. Lublin and Michael L. King, "Invited Out—More Employers Offer an Early Retirement: Some Workers Decline," *The Wall Street Journal*, November 12, 1980, p. 1.

63. "No Letup in the Trend to Retire Early," *U.S. News & World Report* (February 15, 1982), p. 55.

RÉSUMÉ

The trend today is for employees to receive an increasing proportion of their compensation in the form of benefits rather than as cash payments. There is every indication that this trend will continue. As inflation pushes employees into higher income tax brackets, the tax sheltering advantages of compensation received as benefits will continue to make this form of compensation attractive to them. Increases in the cost of the benefits required by law, as well as increases in costs resulting from federal regulations, also are likely to cause employee benefits to constitute a large percentage of an employer's labor costs each year. Furthermore, the inability of unionized employers to avoid collective bargaining pressures for increases in benefits, together with the inability of other employers to resist the pattern established by collective bargaining agreements, also make the upward trend in benefits most likely.

The growth of employee benefits has created some significant problems in managing human resources. Additional benefits can give rise to new sources of grievances and charges of discrimination. They can result also in compensation costs that contribute less than they should to the achievement of organization objectives. The reason for this fact is that rises in these costs often go unrecognized and unappreciated by employees and contribute very little to motivating performance. The most costly of employee benefits (and also the oldest) are those involving insurance and pension plans. The next most significant, in terms of cost, include payment for time not worked (including holidays and various paid leaves), followed by those benefits required by law.

The area of human resources management that has become the subject of greatest attention and concern during the past decade is that relating to retirement. The enactment of ERISA and the amendment to the Age Discrimination in Employment Act outlawing mandatory retirement have forced management to reevaluate their retirement and pension policies. ERISA has forced employers to comply with standards concerning the administration and actuarial soundness of their pension plans. It requires that employees be provided with a vested right in their pension funds. Court decisions also force employers to avoid sex discrimination in determining pension benefits. Restrictions on mandatory retirement which have affected retention and retirement policies have had a definite impact upon human resources planning. Sharp increases in Social Security taxes have also affected such planning as it relates to pension benefits.

TERMS TO IDENTIFY

total compensation
fringe benefits or fringes
flexible benefit plans (or cafeteria plans, self-
   designated plans, employee choice plans)
fully insured person
test of retirement
Average Indexed Monthly Earnings (AIME)
Primary Insurance Amount (PIA)

currently insured person
unemployment insurance
Supplemental Unemployment Benefits (SUB)
workers' compensation insurance
reward philosophy
earnings philosophy
contributory plan
noncontributory plan

defined benefit pension plan
defined contribution (or money purchase)
  plan
vested rights
multiple employer plans

Individual Retirement Accounts (IRAs)
trusteed plan
insured plan
silver handshake

DISCUSSION QUESTIONS

1. Many companies are concerned about the rising cost of employee benefits and question their value to the company and to the employees.
   a. In your opinion what benefits are of greatest value to employees? To the company? Why?
   b. What can management do to increase the value to the company of the benefits provided to employees?

2. Employee benefits were found to cost over $6,084 a year per employee in 983 United States companies surveyed by the United States Chamber of Commerce.
   a. What would you think of a plan that called for removing all benefits except those required by law, and giving the employees this amount in cash as part of wages?
   b. Discuss the advantages and disadvantages of such a plan.

3. What are some of the reasons for the greater attention companies are devoting to the communication of benefit information to employees?

4. Some organizations offer their employees a choice of selecting certain benefits in a self-designed benefit plan. What are the advantages and disadvantages of this type of plan to the employee? To the employer?

5. What is your opinion of the Social Security program? If you were a member of Congress, what changes in the program, if any, would you support? Why hasn't Congress initiated the changes you recommend?

6. Why are many private and public pension funds in severe financial difficulty?

7. Explain the reasons for the demands of some unions for a greater role in determining pension fund investments. What problems may these demands create for employers and employees?

8. With mandatory retirement now at age 70, why are the majority of employees still retiring at age 65 or earlier?

PROBLEM 19–1

THE REBELLIOUS RETIREES

Changes in the National Distributing Corporation's marketing strategy, together with the reorganization of its marketing department, created a surplus of middle management personnel within the department. Unfortunately there were no other positions within the corporation to which the surplus managers could be transferred. In order to avoid terminating managers, the company sought to encourage the older ones to take early retirement. As an inducement, the company offered to provide a special retirement allowance to offset a portion of the reduction in pension benefits that normally resulted from early retirement. Unfortunately only a few managers accepted this offer. Failing to get enough volunteers, the company forced a number of the senior managers to take early retirement. These managers were granted the same special retirement allowance that had been granted to the voluntary retirees. However, the allowances did not curb their resentment at being forced to retire early, particularly since some of those managers retained were less competent. Furthermore, performance records verified this fact.

Rebelling against the company's action, the group of involuntary retirees took its case to court in a suit filed against the company. The court ordered that the plaintiffs be reinstated in their former jobs. Having been burned once in its efforts to reduce the ranks of its middle managers in the marketing department, the company decided to tolerate the surplus until it could be reduced through regular retirement and other forms of attrition.

a. What are some of the lessons to be learned from this incident?

b. What factors other than age may complicate an organization's efforts to get rid of surplus personnel?

c. What effect would current federal law governing retirement have had upon the company's action in this case?

PROBLEM 19-2

A QUESTION OF BEREAVEMENT LEAVE PAY

A few months after Joe Lopez suffered the loss of his wife, a brother of his late wife also died. Lopez, who had always enjoyed a close relationship with this particular brother-in-law, took a three-day leave to assist with funeral arrangements. The employer's agreement with the union granted employees the right to three days off and paid leave to attend the funeral of a brother- or sister-in-law. To receive pay for such leaves, however, the employee was required to furnish satisfactory evidence of the relationship, death, and attendance at the funeral. Lopez complied with these conditions. When the company refused to pay him for the three days he was absent, Lopez filed a grievance that eventually went to arbitration. The arbitrator ruled in favor of the company.

a. What is your opinion with respect to the company's action?

b. Do you agree with the arbitrator's decision? Why or why not?

SUGGESTED READINGS

Adler, Joan. *The Retirement Book: A Complete Early-Planning Guide to Finances, New Activities, and Where to Live.* New York: William Morrow & Co., 1975.

Bradford, Leland P., and Martha I. Bradford. *Retirement: Coping with Emotional Upheavals.* Chicago: Nelson Hall, Inc., 1979.

Chruden, Herbert J., and Arthur W. Sherman, Jr. *Readings in Managing Human Resources,* 6th ed. Cincinnati: South-Western Publishing Co., 1984. Part 6.

Gordus, Heanne Prial. *Leaving Early: Perspectives and Policies in Current Retirement Practice and Policy.* Kalamazoo, MI: W.E. Upjohn Institute for Employment Research, 1980.

Hepner, Harry W. *Retirement—A Time to Live Anew.* New York: McGraw-Hill Book Company, 1976.

McCaffery, Robert M. *Managing the Employee Benefits Program.* New York: AMACOM, American Management Associations, 1972.

Sheppard, Harold L., and Sara E. Rix. *The Graying of Working America: The Coming Crisis of Retirement Age Policy.* New York: Free Press, MacMillan Publishing Co., Inc., 1977.

- To summarize the general provisions of the Occupational Safety and Health Act (OSHA).
- To explain how OSHA standards are developed.
- To describe what management can do to create a safe work environment.
- To cite the measures that should be taken to control and eliminate health hazards.
- To list the different types of health problems that typically require action by employers.
- To summarize the sources of job stress and the possible remedies for them.

20

Safety and Health

In the preceding chapters we examined the various compensation and benefit programs that are designed to meet the needs of employees for economic security. Their needs for physical and emotional security demand equal attention. Employers are expected to provide working conditions that do not impair the safety or health of their employees. They must, therefore, provide a work environment that protects employees from physical hazards, unhealthy conditions, and unsafe acts of other personnel. Through effective safety and health programs the physical and emotional well-being, as well as the economic security, of employees may be preserved and even enhanced.

LEGAL REQUIREMENTS FOR SAFETY AND HEALTH

In the late 1960s Congress became increasingly concerned that each year job-related accidents accounted for more than 14,000 worker deaths and nearly 2.5 million worker disabilities. Ten times as many personnel-days were lost from job-related disabilities as from strikes. In addition, the estimated new cases of occupational diseases total 300,000. As a result of lost production and wages, medical expenses, and disability compensation, the burden on the nation's commerce was staggering. Human cost was beyond calculation. These conditions led to the passage of the Occupational Safety and Health Act (OSHA) in 1970. The act is designed "to assure so far as possible every working man and woman in the Nation safe and healthful working conditions and to preserve our human resources."[1]

Under the provisions of the act, the Occupational Safety and Health Administration was created within the United States Department of Labor to reduce hazards at the workplace through the development and enforcement of mandatory job safety and health standards. In all of its procedures, from standards development through implementation and enforcement, the Occupational Safety and Health Administration guarantees employers and employees the right to be fully informed, to participate actively, and to appeal its actions.

In general, the Occupational Safety and Health Act extends to all employers and their employees with only a few exceptions. Exceptions include the federal government, any state or political subdivision of a state, and miners.[2] Each federal agency, however, is required to establish and maintain a safety and health program that is monitored by the Occupational Safety and Health Administration. Likewise, a state that desires to gain OSHA approval for the safety and health program of its private sector must provide a similar program which covers its state and local government employees and which is at least as effective as its program for private employers.

OSHA Standards

One of the responsibilities of the Occupational Safety and Health Administration is to develop and enforce mandatory job safety and health standards. OSHA

---

1. U.S. Department of Labor, Occupational Safety and Health Administration, *All About OSHA* (rev. ed.; Washington, DC: U.S. Government Printing Office, 1980), p. 1.
2. Miners are covered by the Federal Coal Mine Health and Safety Act.

standards fall into four major categories: general industry, maritime, construction, and agriculture. These standards cover the workplace, machinery and equipment, material, power sources, processing, protective clothing, first aid, and administrative requirements.

It is the responsibility of employers to become familiar with those standards that are applicable to their establishments. The *Federal Register* is the principal source of information on adopted or amended OSHA standards. Larger employers usually subscribe to it and/or the OSHA loose-leaf subscription service.[3]

The Occupational Safety and Health Administration can begin standards-setting procedures on its own initiative or on petitions from other parties, including the Secretary of Health and Human Services and the National Institute for Occupational Safety and Health (NIOSH). Other bodies that may also begin standards-setting procedures are state and local governments and any nationally recognized standards-producing organization, employer, or labor representative. NIOSH, however, is a major source of standards. As an agency of the Department of Health and Human Services, it is responsible for conducting research on various safety and health problems, including the psychological factors involved.

Employer Compliance with OSHA

The Secretary of Labor is authorized by the Occupational Safety and Health Act to conduct workplace inspections, to issue citations, and to impose penalties upon employers. Inspections have been delegated to the Occupational Safety and Health Administration.

Workplace Inspections.
A system of priorities for workplace inspections has been established by OSHA as follows:

1. Inspection of imminent danger situations.
2. Investigation of catastrophes, fatalities, and accidents resulting in hospitalization of five or more employees.
3. Investigation of valid employee complaints of alleged violation of standards or of unsafe or unhealthful working conditions.
4. Special emphasis inspections aimed at specific high-hazard industries, occupations, or substances that are injurious to health.

Random inspections are conducted in establishments of all sizes and types.

Citations and Penalties.
Citations may be issued immediately following the inspection or later by mail. Citations inform the employer and employees of the regulations and standards which have been violated and of the time set for their abatement. The employer must post a copy of each citation at or near the place the violation occurred for the duration of three days or until the violation is abated, whichever is longer.

---

3. This service is available from the Superintendent of Documents.

A wide range of penalties for violations exists. Penalties of as much as $1,000 are imposed on serious violations. For willful or repeated violations, penalties of up to $10,000 for each violation are imposed.

On-Site Consultation. OSHA provides a free on-site consultation service. Consultants from the state government or private contractors help employers identify hazardous conditions and determine corrective measures. A clear separation is maintained between consultative and enforcement staffs. No citations are issued and the consultant's files cannot be used to trigger an OSHA inspection. However, in accepting a consultation visit, employers must agree to eliminate any hazardous condition where death or serious physical harm could result.

Responsibilities and Rights Under OSHA

Both employers and employees have certain responsibilities and rights under OSHA. In this text only those that relate more directly to the management of human resources are discussed briefly.

Employers' Responsibilities and Rights. In addition to providing a hazard-free workplace and complying with the applicable standards, employers must inform all of their employees about the safety and health requirements of OSHA. Employers are also required to display the OSHA poster which informs employees of their rights and responsibilities (see Figure 20–1), to keep certain records, and to compile and post an annual summary of work-related injuries and illnesses. It is the employer's responsibility to make employees wear safety equipment when necessary. Employers, therefore, must engage in safety training and be prepared to discipline employees for noncompliance with safety rules.

Employers must not discriminate against employees who exercise their rights under the act by filing complaints. Employers are afforded many rights under the law. Most of them pertain to receiving information, applying for variances in standards, and contesting citations.

Employees' Responsibilities and Rights. Employees are required to comply with all applicable OSHA standards, report hazardous conditions, and follow all employer safety and health rules and regulations, including the use of prescribed protective equipment. They have a right to demand safety and health on the job without fear of punishment. Employees also have many rights relative to requesting and receiving information about safety and health conditions.

Impact of OSHA

Compliance with OSHA standards often requires extensive changes that add considerably to the costs of doing business. In addition, employers deplore the additional time and expense necessitated by paperwork. While employers may complain, there is evidence that the act has had a very positive effect. The Bureau of Labor Statistics (BLS) reports a change in the overall injury rate from 10.6 per 100 workers in 1973 to 9.2 per 100 workers in 1978—an improvement of 13 percent. In

Figure 20–1 OSHA Safety Poster

job safety and health protection

The Occupational Safety and Health Act of 1970 provides job safety and health protection for workers through the promotion of safe and healthful working conditions throughout the Nation. Requirements of the Act include the following:

Employers:

Each employer shall furnish to each of his employees employment and a place of employment free from recognized hazards that are causing or are likely to cause death or serious harm to his employees; and shall comply with occupational safety and health standards issued under the Act.

Employees:

Each employee shall comply with all occupational safety and health standards, rules, regulations and orders issued under the Act that apply to his own actions and conduct on the job.

The Occupational Safety and Health Administration (OSHA) of the Department of Labor has the primary responsibility for administering the Act. OSHA issues occupational safety and health standards, and its Compliance Safety and Health Officers conduct jobsite inspections to ensure compliance with the Act.

Inspection:

The Act requires that a representative of the employer and a representative authorized by the employees be given an opportunity to accompany the OSHA inspector for the purpose of aiding the inspection.

Where there is no authorized employee representative, the OSHA Compliance Officer must consult with a reasonable number of employees concerning safety and health conditions in the workplace.

Complaint:

Employees or their representatives have the right to file a complaint with the nearest OSHA office requesting an inspection if they believe unsafe or unhealthful conditions exist in their workplace. OSHA will withhold, on request, names of employees complaining.

The Act provides that employees may not be discharged or discriminated against in any way for filing safety and health complaints or otherwise exercising their rights under the Act.

An employee who believes he has been discriminated against may file a complaint with the nearest OSHA office within 30 days of the alleged discrimination.

Citation:

If upon inspection OSHA believes an employer has violated the Act, a citation alleging such violations will be issued to the employer. Each citation will specify a time period within which the alleged violation must be corrected.

The OSHA citation must be prominently displayed at or near the place of alleged violation for three days, or until it is corrected, whichever is later, to warn employees of dangers that may exist there.

Proposed Penalty:

The Act provides for mandatory penalties against employers of up to $1,000 for each serious violation and for optional penalties of up to $1,000 for each nonserious violation. Penalties of up to $1,000 per day may be proposed for failure to correct violations within the proposed time period. Also, any employer who willfully or repeatedly violates the Act may be assessed penalties of up to $10,000 for each such violation.

Criminal penalties are also provided for in the Act. Any willful violation resulting in death of an employee, upon conviction, is punishable by a fine of not more than $10,000 or by imprisonment for not more that six months, or by both. Conviction of an employer after a first conviction doubles these maximum penalties.

Voluntary Activity:

While providing penalties for violations, the Act also encourages efforts by labor and management, before an OSHA inspection, to reduce injuries and illnesses arising out of employment.

The Department of Labor encourages employers and employees to reduce workplace hazards voluntarily and to develop and improve safety and health programs in all workplaces and industries.

Such cooperative action would initially focus on the identification and elimination of hazards that could cause death, injury, or illness to employees and supervisors. There are many public and private organizations that can provide information and assistance in this effort, if requested.

More Information:

Additional information and copies of the Act, specific OSHA safety and health standards, and other applicable regulations may be obtained from your employer or from the nearest OSHA Regional Office in the following locations:

Atlanta, Georgia
Boston, Massachusetts
Chicago, Illinois
Dallas, Texas
Denver, Colorado
Kansas City, Missouri
New York, New York
Philadelphia, Pennsylvania
San Francisco, California
Seattle, Washington

Telephone numbers for these offices, and additional Area Office locations, are listed in the telephone directory under the United States Department of Labor in the United States Government listing.

Washington, D.C.
1981
OSHA 2203

DEPARTMENT OF LABOR · UNITED STATES OF AMERICA

Raymond J. Donovan

Raymond J. Donovan
Secretary of Labor

U. S. Department of Labor
Occupational Safety and Health Administration

GPO878 195

other words, there were nearly 4 million fewer injuries between 1973 and 1978 than would have occurred had the 1973 rate remained constant.[4]

It is recognized that factors other than OSHA may influence these statistics. However, in another study to examine the effects of OSHA independently of other factors, it was found that OSHA inspections may reduce injury rates by as much as 16 percent among the firms that have been inspected. Enforcement alone cannot eliminate all of the hazards, but the possibility of inspection of the workplace is a very effective incentive for compliance.[5] However, some safety professionals advise that, in the need to meet OSHA standards, the fact that "safety is a people problem" should not be overlooked.

Employers rightfully complained of the enforcement approach that was used in the years immediately following the enactment of the law. Citations were issued for violations of minor rules, and major problems were ignored. In the past several years the administrative agency has given attention to serious infractions and is increasing the inspection rate for industries with the most serious safety and health problems. Construction, manufacturing, transportation, and petrochemicals are in this category.

Because of the demands made upon employers, one may expect that there will be continued employer concern over OSHA standards and inspections. It appears, however, that the agency is moving toward allowing businesses with good safety records to oversee their own safety and health performance. The agency is devising programs that will place responsibility for inspections on committees of labor and management representatives.[6]

CREATING A SAFE WORK ENVIRONMENT

We have seen that employers are required by law to provide safe working conditions for their employees. Over 80 percent of the organizations surveyed by The Bureau of National Affairs reported having a formal safety program in order to meet this requirement.[7] In almost half of them, the human resources department or the industrial relations department is reported to be responsible for the safety program. One third of the surveyed respondents have a separate department for administering the safety program. Where there is a separate department, 26 percent of the safety directors report to the top personnel officer. In 78 percent of the organizations, the safety officer has the authority to stop operations considered to be hazardous.

The BNA survey also showed that nine out of ten companies with formal safety programs have a safety committee which includes representatives from each department or manufacturing unit. In some of the organizations, union representatives are on the safety committee. Committees not only provide for representation but also help to publicize the importance of safety rules and their enforcement.

---

4. Basil J. Whiting, "OSHA's Enforcement Policy," *Labor Law Journal,* Vol. 31, No. 5 (May, 1980), pp. 259–282.

5. *Ibid.*

6. "OSHA's Controversial Do-it-Yourself Approach," *Business Week* (July 19, 1982), p. 62.

7. *Safety Policies and the Impact of OSHA,* Personnel Policies Forum Survey No. 117 (Washington, DC: The Bureau of National Affairs, Inc., May, 1977), p. 4.

Safety Motivation and Knowledge

Probably the most important requirement of safety management is that managers, supervisors, and employees be motivated to promote safety. If managers and supervisors are not motivated, employees can hardly be expected to be highly motivated. In referring to managers and supervisors, Petersen notes that "in most cases their 'safety hat' is worn far less often than their 'production,' 'quality control,' and 'methods improvement' hats." In addition to motivation, safety knowledge and an understanding of where one's efforts should be placed are important. Safety knowledge can be acquired through training, which leads to an understanding of management's policy on safety, company safety procedures, and the systems used to fix accountability.[8]

Safety Awareness Programs

Most organizations have a safety awareness program that includes the use of posters, warning signs, safety talks, and other media including pamphlets (see Figure 20–2) for instructing and motivating employees in the use of safe work methods. Safety awareness efforts are usually coordinated by a safety director whose primary function is to enlist the interest and cooperation of all personnel. However, the safety director is largely dependent upon managerial and supervisory personnel for the success of the program.

Communication Role of the Supervisor.   One of the major responsibilities of the supervisor is to motivate the employee to work in a safe manner. Beginning with the orientation of the new employee, safety should be emphasized continually. Proper work procedures, the use of protective clothing and devices, and potential hazards should be explained thoroughly. Furthermore, the employee's understanding of all these should be verified during training sessions.

Gardner recognizes the barriers to communication (see Chapter 12) and advises that supervisors avoid assuming that: (1) words used in explaining have the same meaning for the employee as they have for the supervisor; (2) the employee is listening; (3) the employee is learning and will remember; and (4) the supervisors themselves have covered all phases of the subject.[9] In other words, supervisors must be aware of the possible problems in communicating safety matters to employees. Since training alone does not assure continual adherence to safe work practices, supervisors must observe employees at work and show approval for safe work practices. Where unsafe acts are detected, immediate action should be taken to find the cause.

Safety Training Programs.   The safety training programs found in many organizations include first aid, defensive driving, accident prevention techniques, handling

---

8. Dan Petersen, *Safety Management—A Human Approach* (Rivervale, NJ: Aloray, Inc., 1975), pp. 7–13.

9. James E. Gardner, *Safety Training for the Supervisor* (2d ed.; Reading, MA: Addison-Wesley Publishing Co., 1979), p. 19.

hazardous equipment, and emergency procedures. In these programs the use of emergency first-aid equipment and personal safety equipment is emphasized. The most common types of personal safety equipment are safety glasses and goggles, face protectors, safety shoes, hard hats, hair protectors, and safety belts.

Figure 20–2 **A Safety Pamphlet**

Today's machines can do almost anything we do—only better and faster. According to what we've designed them to do, they'll chew, tear, pull, squeeze, cut or rip anything that's fed to them. Even a hand or an arm. Yes, machines can do almost anything we can do—except THINK. So you think about it.

● Never operate a machine unless you've been checked out on it by a qualified person. If you have any questions, ASK. You've got to know all the machine's "ins and outs." Miss one and you could be missing a hand.

● Guards that enclose moving parts are there to protect YOU. Never remove guards unless it's to make repairs or adjustments, but shut the machine down first and lock it out. And be sure to replace guards when the repair has been made.

● You need gloves to protect your hands when handling oily, sharp or rough material. But—for work on or around machines, gloves are **taboo.** They can get snagged and pull your hands into the works.

● Don't wear rings and watch-bands around machinery or when you're handling materials. You could catch your ring on almost anything—bolt ends, nails, hooks, any projection—and tear a finger off.

● Your clothing should fit you—and your job. Loose fitting clothing can catch in moving gears. Or a dangling shirt sleeve can be pulled into spinning rollers—and your arm along with it.

SOURCE: National Safety Council. Reproduced with permission.

Safety Campaigns. In addition to organizing the regular safety training programs, safety directors often plan special safety campaigns. These campaigns typically emphasize competition among departments or plants of a company, with the department or plant having the best safety record receiving some type of award or trophy. In some companies cash bonuses are given to employees who have outstanding safety records. Contests have also been used to promote safety, and these have produced some favorable results.

Enforcement of Safety Rules

Specific rules and regulations concerning safety are found in 93 percent of the organizations surveyed by The Bureau of National Affairs. Of the organizations surveyed, 77 percent communicated these rules primarily through supervisors; 73 percent, through bulletin board notices; and 65 percent, through employee handbooks. Safety rules are also emphasized in regular shop safety meetings, at new employee orientation sessions, and in manuals of standard operating procedures.

Penalties for violation of safety rules are usually stated in the employee handbook. In a large percentage of organizations, the discipline imposed on violators is the same as that for violations of other company rules. This includes an oral or written warning for the first violation, suspension or disciplinary layoff for repeated violations, and dismissal as a last resort.[10] However, for serious violations even the first offense may be cause for discharge.

Accident Investigations and Records

Every accident, including those that are considered minor, should be investigated by the supervisor and a representative of the safety committee. Through such an investigation the causative factors may be detected and necessary corrections made before the accident is repeated. Correction may require that materials be rearranged, that safety guards or controls be installed, or, more often, that employees be given additional safety training and that their motivation for safety be re-assessed. Unsafe conditions and/or unsafe acts are a cause of every accident.

OSHA requires that a *Log and Summary of Occupational Injuries and Illnesses* (OSHA Form 200) be maintained and kept within the organization. All recordable cases are to be entered in the *Log*. A **recordable case** is any occupational death, occupational illness, and occupational injury (except for those involving only first aid).[11] Each year the Summary portion of the *Log* is to be posted for one month where notices to employees are customarily posted.

10. *Safety Policies and the Impact of OSHA, op. cit.,* p. 11.

11. OSHA defines an *Occupational Injury* as any injury, such as a cut, fracture, sprain, amputation, etc., which results from a work accident or from an exposure involving a single accident in the work environment.

An *Occupational Illness* is any abnormal condition or disorder, other than one resulting from an occupational injury, caused by exposure to environmental factors associated with employment. It includes acute and chronic illnesses or diseases which may be caused by inhalation, absorption, ingestion, or direct contact.

Not recordable are first aid cases which involve one-time treatment and subsequent observation of minor scratches, cuts, burns, splinters, etc., which do not ordinarily require medical care, even though such treatment is provided by a physician or registered professional personnel.

For every recordable case written in the *Log,* a *Supplementary Record of Occupational Injuries and Illnesses* (OSHA Form 101) is to be completed. OSHA Form 101 requires answers to questions about the case. From the records that are maintained, the Bureau of Labor Statistics and other organizations, such as the National Safety Council, compile data that an employer may use as a basis for comparison with similar organizations. The procedures for making such comparisons will be presented in the next chapter on personnel audits.

CREATING A HEALTHFUL WORK ENVIRONMENT

The Occupational Safety and Health Act was designed to protect the health, as well as safety, of employees. However, because of the dramatic impact of accidents, managers and employees alike may pay more attention to them than to job conditions that are dangerous to their health. It is essential, therefore, that health hazards be identified and controlled. Attention should also be given to nonoccupational illnesses and injuries and the impact that they have on the organization and its members. Special health programs may also be developed to provide assistance to employees with health problems.

Largely as a result of a growing awareness of the general public through the efforts of environmentalists, factors in the work environment affecting health are receiving greater attention. Pollution of water and air occurring on an unprecedented scale throughout the world has made all of us more conscious of the immediate environment in which we live and work. Articles about workers who have been exposed to potential dangers at work can be found in the current newspapers. Pressure from the federal government and the unions, as well as increased public awareness, has given employers a definite incentive to provide the safest and healthiest work environment possible.

Health Hazards at Work

Unless protective measures are taken, industrial processes can be the source of occupational hazards. Some of the more common health hazards are listed in Figure 20–3. The hazards in the list are found primarily in processing operations. Many of them have been recognized, and preventative measures have been taken. Substituting materials, altering processes, enclosing or isolating a process, issuing protective equipment, and improving ventilation are some of the common preventative measures. General conditions of health with respect to sanitation, housekeeping, cleanliness, ventilation, water supply, vermin control, and food handling are also important.[12]

Proliferating Chemicals.
An estimated 60 to 70 thousand chemical compounds are in commercial use. Many of them are harmful and lurk for years in the human

---

12. Joseph F. Follmann, Jr., *The Economics of Industrial Health—History, Theory, and Practice* (New York: AMACOM, 1978), p. 166.

Figure 20–3 **Common Health Hazards at Work**

1. Chemicals and toxic substances such as carbon monoxide, vinyl chloride, and aerosols.
2. Harmful dusts, smoke, and fumes such as coal dust, cotton dust, and asbestos.
3. Various types of gases, mists, and vapors.
4. Certain metals such as lead, beryllium, and mercury.
5. Radiation from Xrays, lasers, and uranium.
6. Infections resulting from fungi, molds, bacteria, and insects.
7. Excessive noise and vibration which may cause hearing impairment or loss, digestive disturbances, and nervous disorders.
8. Extreme temperatures which may cause respiratory ailments.

SOURCE: Reprinted, by permission of the publisher, from *The Economics of Industrial Health—History, Theory and Practice,* by John F. Follmann, Jr., pp. 163 and 164, © 1978 by AMACOM, a division of American Management Associations, New York. All rights reserved.

organism with no outward symptoms until it is too late. Cancer, for example, may develop 20 to 40 years after the original exposure. This time-bomb effect can involve government, industry, labor, and ultimately the public in controversy over how to care for victims of past exposure and how to develop preventative controls.[13] Specialists in human resources management inevitably must participate in helping to solve many specific problems that arise as a result of this controversy.

With the passage of the Toxic Substances Control Act of 1976, the 700 plus new chemicals that are marketed each year must be pretested for safety. Since 1977, OSHA has been giving greater attention to setting standards for toxic conditions created by hazardous chemicals. Up until that time, toxic substances had been a neglected area and one that showed up in OSHA statistics. It was found that the medical problem which results in the most time being lost from the job is dermatitis caused by various chemicals.[14]

Office Hazards. In the interests of conserving energy, contractors are building airtight offices and homes, thus reducing the flow of fresh air. These structures trap a variety of noxious fumes. Shortly after moving their office staff into a new building, Itel was flooded with reports from employees complaining of nausea, fatigue, and dizziness. The company finally traced the problem to a combination of cigarette smoke, formaldehyde in the furnishings, and fumes from a copying machine. Fortunately improved ventilation helped solve the problem.[15]

13. "Is Your Job Dangerous to Your Health?" *U.S. News & World Report* (February 5, 1979), pp. 38–42.
14. "Out Go 'Silly' Rules on Worker Safety," *U.S. News & World Report* (January 16, 1978), pp. 65–66.
15. "Indoor Air Pollution Raises Risks for People in New Office Buildings," *The Wall Street Journal,* July 16, 1980, p. 23.

In the first book written for a general readership about the hazards of office environments, Makower warns that, among all of the hazards, air pollution may be the most severe.[16] He lists 20 major air pollutants in offices which come from building materials, furniture and furnishings, duplicating fluids, typewriter cleaners, tobacco smoke, photocopier toners, rubber cement, correction fluids, and other items commonly found in an office. Chemicals used in an office can also cause a variety of skin problems. Like factory workers, office workers are subject to hazards such as cuts, trips, and falls, electrical shock, fires, and noise.

According to Makower, a new source of health problems has been introduced in recent years. Moderate to heavy use of the computer videodisplay terminal (VDT) leads to eye strain, loss of visual acuity, changes in color perception, back and neck pain, stomach aches, and nausea. Data processing clerks, word processing personnel, radar operators, and others using VDT on a continual basis not only have this additional health burden but are often the victims of stress—a topic that will be discussed later in this chapter.

Exposure to Smokers. The trend toward antismoking activism is on the rise. Yet 85 percent of all companies do not have an official policy regarding the rights of smokers and nonsmokers. Citing several studies, Makower notes that chronic exposure to tobacco smoke in the work environment affects the lung performance of nonsmokers, increases the need for caffeine, contributes to noise-induced hearing loss by constricting the blood flow to the inner ear, and raises the level of nicotine in the blood of nonsmoking bystanders.

While many lawsuits have been filed by employees, the issue of whether an employee has an enforceable right to a smoke-free environment has not been resolved. Blackburn notes that a Federal Indoor Clean Air Act and a Model State Smoking Pollution Prevention Act—both in the proposal stage—are needed to put the control into the hands of state enforcement agencies. Minnesota and Utah now have statutes restricting or prohibiting smoking in workplaces where smoke pollution is detrimental to the health and/or comfort of nonsmoking employees.[17]

Building Better Health

Along with improving working conditions that are hazardous to employee health, many employers provide health services and have programs that encourage employees to improve their health habits. It is recognized that better health is not only beneficial for the individual, but also will produce a payoff to the organization in terms of reduced absenteeism, increased efficiency, better morale, and other personnel savings. An increased understanding of the close relationship between physical and emotional health and job behavior has made broad health-building programs attractive to employers, as well as to employees.

---

16. Joel Makower, *Office Hazards—How Your Job Can Make You Sick* (Washington: Tilden Press, 1981), pp. 14–24.

17. John D. Blackburn, "Legal Aspects of Smoking in the Workplace," *Labor Law Journal*, Vol. 31, No. 9 (September, 1980), pp. 564–569.

Health Services. The type of health services provided by employers is primarily related to the size of the organization and the importance of such services. In some organizations only limited facilities, such as those needed to handle first-aid cases, are available. In others, complete medical diagnostic, treatment, and surgical facilities are provided. Since employers are required to provide medical services after an injury, they usually have physicians available on a prearranged basis.

We noted in Chapter 6 that nearly three fourths of all employers give preemployment physicals to prospective employees. Generally these physicals are required to assure employers that the health of applicants is adequate for the job. The preemployment physical should include a medical history with special reference to previous hazardous exposures. Those whose effects may be cumulative, such as noise, lead, and ionizing radiation, are especially relevant. For jobs involving unusual physical demands, the applicant's muscular development, flexibility, agility, range of motion, and cardiac and respiratory functions should be determined.[18] The preemployment physical which includes laboratory analyses provides an opportunity to detect those applicants who are on drugs.

Many organizations also give periodic physical examinations either on a required or voluntary basis. These subsequent physicals may be compared with the preemployment physical and interpreted accordingly. Such examinations are useful in determining the effects of potential hazards in the workplace, as well as revealing any health problems that may develop out of an individual's life-style.

Physical Fitness Programs. Many companies, such as Shaklee, Fluor, PepsiCo, and Xerox, have developed programs which emphasize regular exercise, proper nutrition, weight control, and avoidance of substances that are harmful to health.[19] The employee health management program at Xerox includes cardiovascular fitness through aerobic exercises such as jogging, rope skipping, and racquet sports. The company gives its employees a *Fitbook* that provides instructions and pictures on a variety of exercises. The *Fitbook* also has chapters on the hazards of smoking, the effects of alcohol and drug abuse, facts on nutrition and weight control, and guidelines for managing stress and learning to relax.[20]

Kimberly-Clark has a 32,000-square-foot fitness center near Madison, WI, that contains a 25-meter pool, 100-meter track, exercise equipment, sauna, and whirlpool. Participating employees have logged nearly 4,000 miles on the track in one month alone. Officials report that the center's success is being measured by computerized medical histories which reflect changes in the health status of employees. The corporation is also working with its insurance carrier to compare costs of hospitalization and incidence of major illnesses for participants with similar costs for a control group.[21]

18. May R. Mayers, *Occupational Health* (Baltimore: The Williams and Wilkins Company, 1969), Chapter 37.

19. Labor Letter, *The Wall Street Journal*, August 31, 1982, p. 1.

20. *Sacramento Bee*, November 17, 1978, p. C–1.

21. William E. Hauda, "Corporate Wellness—Cutting Costs By Developing Healthier Employees," United Press International Release, December 3, 1978.

There is mounting evidence supporting the link between certain nutritional deficiencies and various physiological and psychological disorders. Alcoholism, depression, nervousness, low energy level, perceptual inaccuracy, and lack of reasonability are but a few of them. In fact, a person's mental and emotional state is affected by the foods that he or she consumes.[22] Murray and Francis point to the need for more nutritious foods in vending machines to replace the candies, cookies, sugary pies, sweetened soft drinks, and coffee. They suggest that the potential return on a minimal investment of a sound nutritional plan is great in terms of both dollars and morale because human behavior might be more easily and quickly modified by dietary changes than by more sophisticated organizational modification techniques.[23]

Health Bonuses.   Improving one's health is a bonus in itself. Yet some employers have inaugurated plans which provide monetary rewards for individuals who follow certain health rules or who reach established goals. Merle Norman Cosmetics, for example, paid employees $10-per-quarter bonus not to smoke on the job, in storage areas, and in rest rooms. With reduced housekeeping costs, lower absenteeism, and increased productivity resulting from this plan, the company estimated that it would save more than it paid participating employees.[24] In some industries smokers will not be hired for certain jobs. The Johns Mansville Corporation, for example, banned smoking in its 14 plants in response to a finding that there is a 92 percent higher incidence of asbestiosis and related diseases in smokers than in nonsmokers.[25]

Intermatic offered employees who were 15 or more pounds overweight an opportunity to earn extra money while losing weight. Each participant listed a target weight and was paid $4 for each pound lost if the target weight was met. Failure to meet the target paid only $1 per pound lost. About 50 percent of the employees took advantage of the program.[26]

Special Health Programs for Executives.   Long before fitness programs became popular for the public, attention was being given to the health of executive personnel. It was recognized that one less heart attack a year within the executive group underwrites the cost of the fringe benefit for the entire group.[27] For an executive health program to be effective, it should include more than a periodic physical examination. It should provide services that deal with the whole person—intellect, emotions, physical well-being—and the individual's life-style. Through participation in executive health programs, executives are frequently awakened to the need for a change in attitudes and habits. Physicians who use a preventative approach with emphasis upon nutrition, exercise, and healthful living are frequently identified with such programs.

22. E. Cheraskin and W. M. Ringsdorf, Jr., with Arline Brecher, *Psychodietetics—Food As the Key to Emotional Health* (New York: Stein and Day, 1974), p. 103.

23. Stuart Murray and Jim Francis, "Nutrition and Decision Making," *Business Horizons,* Vol. 23, No. 4 (August, 1980), pp. 7–14.

24. *Oakland Tribune,* March 4, 1976.

25 "Federal Employees Get All Choked Up About Smoking," *Sacramento Bee,* November 1, 1978, p. B–5.

26. "Employer Sweetens Weight Loss Payoff," AP Release, April 23, 1978.

27. Richard L. Pyle, "Corporate Fitness Programs—How Do They Shape Up?" *Personnel,* Vol. 56, No. 1 (January-February, 1979), pp. 58–67.

Special programs, such as those offered by the Longevity Research Center of Santa Monica, CA, provide training in proper diet and exercise, primarily walking. Nathan Pritikin and his colleagues have a program known as the "2100 Program" that has been successful in helping people overcome degenerative diseases. The scientific basis for the diet is provided in Pritikin's books.[28] It involves avoiding the following items: fats, oils, sugar, salt, cholesterol, and caffeine. These food "gremlins" are responsible for heart attacks, diabetes, strokes, and other diseases associated with aging. Figure 20–4 from the book *Live Longer Now* illustrates the incidence of heart attacks for diets with different degrees of "gremlin" content. The data are for men in their forties and fifties; but according to Pritikin, no matter what your age or sex, the trend of the chart is the same.[29] Many participants at the clinic, ranging from individuals who merely wanted to lose weight to those whose physicians had "given up" on them, report a remarkable improvement in general health. One executive participant who was interviewed on the CBS "60 Minutes" program was so enthusiastic about the "2100 Program" that he offered to pay the cost for any of his employees who wished to go to the clinic.

By participating in special health programs designed for them, executives can learn how to change their life-styles so as to reduce the risk of strokes and heart attacks. Executives with Type A personalities—driving achievers with a false sense of

Figure 20–4 Incidence of Heart Attacks for Diets with Different "Gremlin" Content

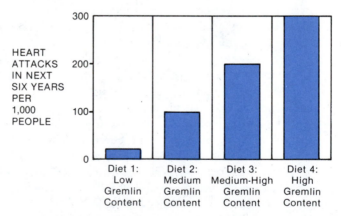

SOURCE: Jon N. Leonard, J. L. Hofer, and N. Pritikin. *Live Longer Now* (New York: Grosset and Dunlap, 1974), p. 144. Reproduced with permission.

28. The "2100 Program" is described in Jon N. Leonard, J. L. Hofer, and N. Pritikin, *Live Longer Now* (New York: Grosset and Dunlap, 1976); in Nathan Pritikin with Patrick M. McGrady, Jr., *The Pritikin Program for Diet and Exercise* (New York: Grosset and Dunlap, 1979); and in Nathan Pritikin, *The Pritikin Permanent Weight-Loss Manual* (New York: Grosset and Dunlap, 1981).

29. Leonard, Hofer, and Pritikin, *Live Longer Now, op. cit.*, pp. 143–144.

time urgency who often push themselves to destruction via heart disease—can learn to be more like Type B personalities whose emotional lives are in healthy balance. Dr. Elmer Green, a Menninger Foundation psychologist who works with executives, feels that Type A is useful to get to the top. "But you have to be able to turn off 'A' and become 'B' at will if you want to live," he advises. Dr. Meyer Friedman, the cardiologist who identified Type A and Type B personalities, advises that the trick is in knowing how to swing from A to B. Some professional guidance may be needed, but there is much that the individual can do. Some suggestions are: approaching the executive job in a more relaxed manner, delegating as much work as possible, dropping optional activities, and eliminating social affairs that do not contribute to the individual's welfare.[30]

Providing Assistance to Employees

A broad view of health includes the emotional, as well as the physical, aspects of an individual's life. While emotional problems, personal crises, alcoholism, and drug abuse are considered to be personal matters, they also become management's problems when they affect behavior at work and interfere with satisfactory job performance. There are various methods for dealing with employees who need assistance. Some employers provide opportunities for employees to consult with special in-house counselors or with outside professional persons, usually psychologists and psychiatrists. Almost 80 percent of the companies that have an *Employee Assistance Program* (EAP) report that the personnel department is responsible for the in-house counseling and for making referrals. Staff medical personnel share this responsibility in 39 percent of the counseling programs.[31] To deal with such problems, most organizations provide their supervisors with some combination of training, policy guidance, and opportunities to consult with specialized counseling or medical personnel.

Personal Crises. The most prevalent problem among employees is a personal crisis situation involving marital, family, financial, or legal problems. Such problems usually come to the supervisor's attention. With the type of counseling assistance recommended in Chapter 13, the solutions to many employee problems may be reached. In other cases, in-house counseling or referral to an outside agency may be necessary and/or desirable. In recent years crisis clinics have been established in many communities. Many of them provide counseling assistance by telephone for the person who is unable to wait for a scheduled appointment.

Emotional Problems. While crisis situations typically are fraught with emotion, most of them are resolved in a reasonable period of time and the troubled individual's equilibrium is restored. There will be, however, a small percentage of employees—roughly 3 percent on the average—who have emotional problems serious

30. "Heart Disease: New Ways to Reduce the Risk," *Business Week* (October 17, 1977), pp. 135–142.
31. *BNA Policy and Practice Series—Personnel Management* (Washington, DC: The Bureau of National Affairs, Inc., 1978), p. 245:136.

enough to require professional treatment.[32] Whether or not such individuals will be able to perform their jobs must be determined on an individual basis. Particular attention should be given to safety factors since there is general agreement that emotional disturbances are primary or secondary factors in a large proportion of industrial accidents.[33]

Managerial personnel should be aware of the fact that the behavior of some individuals is adversely affected by substances in the work environment that apparently do not affect others, or at least not as severely. Such individuals are described as being allergic to these substances. They may need to be reassigned to a different work environment rather than sent for professional help. Physicians who work in this area, called **clinical ecology**, report numerous cases of individuals whose behavior on and off the job is affected by petrochemicals, molds, cleaning substances, cosmetics and toiletries, plastics, tobacco smoke—in fact, anything that can be found in the environment. Individuals who are allergic to such items may exhibit behavioral symptoms that interfere with job effectiveness. The symptoms may range from severe depression to extreme hyperactivity. Remove the substance, or the individuals from the substance, and the symptoms disappear. Dr. Theron Randolph, an allergist, was among the first to write about the importance of environmental chemicals, in addition to foods, as the cause of many physical and emotional illnesses.[34] His work has stimulated other allergists, as well as psychiatrists, to study the phenomenon further.[35]

Alcoholism and Drug Abuse.   It is estimated that 10 percent of the American work force is affected by alcohol and drug problems which cost $28 billion in lost production.[36] The approach to handling alcoholism, which is currently recommended by many professional persons and used by a large number of employers, is to monitor the performance of all personnel regularly and systematically. Supervisors should carefully document evidence of declining performance on the job and then confront the employees concerned with unequivocal proof that their work is suffering. These employees are then assured that help will be made available without penalty. Since the evaluations are made solely in terms of lagging job performance, the supervisor can avoid any mention of alcoholism and allow such employees to seek aid as they would for any health problem. Disciplinary action may be taken against employees who refuse to take advantage of such help or whose performance does not improve with repeated warnings. It is important for employers to recognize, however, that arbitrators are looking at on-the-job alcoholism as a sickness, not as a disciplinary

32. *Ibid.*

33. Follmann, *op. cit.,* p. 80.

34. Theron G. Randolph, *Human Ecology and Susceptibility to the Chemical Environment* (Springfield, IL: Charles C. Thomas, Publisher, 1962) and Theron G. Randolph and Ralph W. Moss, *An Alternative Approach to Allergies* (New York: Lippincott and Crowell, 1980).

35. Lawrence D. Dickey (ed.), *Clinical Ecology* (Springfield, IL: Charles C. Thomas, Publisher, 1976).

36. "The EAP Works," *Alcoholism* Vol. 1, No. 4 (March-April, 1981), pp. 23–29.

case.[37] An increasing number of employers are establishing alcohol control programs to help the alcoholic employee. The National Institute on Alcohol Abuse and Alcoholism estimated 12,000 occupational programs were operating by the end of 1976, double the number existing a few years earlier.[38]The fact that approximately 75 percent of medical insurance benefits now cover part of the treatment costs for alcoholism makes it possible to receive treatment at reasonable costs.[39]

The drug problem among employees is one of the emerging societal issues of today. Contrary to popular belief, drug usage in organizations is relatively widespread and is not confined to employees in blue-collar jobs. Of the three categories—marijuana abuse, prescription drug abuse, and hard drug addiction—marijuana abuse ranges from 2 percent among managerial personnel to 5 percent among production and service personnel. Prescription drug abuse ranges from 1.8 percent among managers to 2.4 percent among production and service personnel. Hard drug addiction varies from 0.5 percent among managers to 1.5 percent among production and service personnel.[40]

A program dealing with drug abuse should be for educational and preventative purposes as well as for handling the employee who is found to be using drugs. Information about the program should be disseminated throughout the organization. Supervisory personnel should be advised to bring to the attention of the medical department any employees who are using drugs.

THE MANAGEMENT OF STRESS

Many jobs require employees to adjust to conditions that place unusual demands upon the human organism. In time these demands affect the health of employees as well as their productivity and satisfaction. Fortunately, increasing attention is being given to ways to identify and to prevent undue stress on the job.

Facts About Stress

Surveys indicate that widespread stress is adversely affecting more and more people in business. Of 2,800 managers and supervisors surveyed, almost 30 percent reported job-related health problems. Only 7 percent of these job-related health problems were classified as physical, whereas 93 percent were reported as the result of stress.[41] Physicians report similar findings from their clinical experience.[42]

It is not the individual employee alone who pays for excessive stress that is job-related. Organizational costs in the form of accidents, tardiness, absenteeism,

37. Dale E. Anderson, "Arbitral View of Alcoholism Cases," *Personnel Journal*, Vol. 58, No. 5 (May, 1979), pp. 318–322.

38. Steven H. Appelbaum, "A Human Resources Counseling Model: The Alcoholic Employee," *Personnel Administrator*, Vol. 27, No. 8 (August, 1982), pp. 35–44.

39. *BNA Policy and Practice Series—Personnel Management, op. cit.,* p. 245: 136.

40. *Ibid.,* p. 245:133.

41. *The Changing Success Ethic,* An AMA Survey Report (New York: American Management Associations, 1973).

42. Theodore Cooper with Lee Edson, "Stress, Stress, Stress," *Across the Board*, Vol. 16, No. 8 (August, 1979), pp. 10–19.

turnover, and medical claims for psychological injury also are high.[43] There are many cases on file to support the conclusion that employees more and more are initiating legal action against their employers for emotional problems that are said to be work-related.[44]

Stress is any adjustive demand that requires coping behavior. Stress comes from two basic sources: physical activity, and mental or emotional activity. The physical reaction of the body to both sources is the same. However, this should not be interpreted to mean that individuals should or can live their lives free from stress.

According to Hans Selye, dean of stress theorists, human beings thrive on stress because "stress is the spice of life."[45] Complete freedom from stress comes only with death. Selye uses two separate terms to distinguish between positive and negative life consequences of stress for the individual even though the two forms of stress are the same biochemically. **Eustress** is positive stress that accompanies achievement and exhilaration. Eustress is the stress of meeting challenges such as those found in a managerial job. Selye regards eustress as beneficial stress that forces us to forge ahead against obstacles. He is of the opinion that what is harmful is **distress.** Stress becomes distress when we begin to sense a loss of our feelings of security and adequacy. Helplessness, desperation, and disappointment turn stress into distress. Detrimental stress or distress is something that taxes us beyond our limits.

Cultural Causes of Stress. Albrecht defines stress as the 20th century disease brought about by rapid changes in five significant areas of life:

1. From rural living to urban living.
2. From stationary to mobile.
3. From self-sufficient to consuming.
4. From isolated to interconnected.
5. From physically active to sedentary.

He quotes Alvin Toffler, who coined the term *future shock,* to describe the feeling of vague, continuous anxiety that arises in people who are subjected to rapid pace of change. Thus, we all are forced to live in a state of continual adaptation.[46]

The Physiology of Stress. The stress reaction is a coordinated chemical mobilization of the entire body to meet the requirements of a fight or flight from a situation perceived to be stressful. The sympathetic nervous system activates the secretion of hormones from the endocrine glands that places the body on a "war footing." This response, commonly referred to as the **alarm reaction,** basically involves an elevated heart rate, increased respiration, elevated levels of adrenaline in the blood, and

43. James C. Quick and Jonathan D. Quick, "Reducing Stress Through Preventative Management," *Human Resource Management,* Vol. 18, No. 3 (Fall, 1979), pp. 15–22.

44. Mitchell S. Novit, "Mental Distress: Possible Implications for the Future," *Personnel Administrator,* Vol. 27, No. 8 (August, 1982), pp. 47–53.

45. Hans Selye, *Stress Without Distress* (Philadelphia: J. B. Lippincott Co., 1974), as reprinted by Signet Books (1975), p. 83.

46. Karl Albrecht, *Stress and the Manager—Making It Work for You* (Englewood Cliffs, NJ: Prentice-Hall, Inc., 1979), pp. 1–46. *See also* Alvin Toffler, *Future Shock* (New York: Random House, 1970).

increased blood pressure. It persists until one's estimate of the relative threat to well-being has been reevaluated.[47] While the alarm reaction may have made life safer for our ancestors who were confronted daily with physical peril, it lacks adaptive value for most of the invisible enemies of contemporary life.

Effects of Stress. If distress persists long enough, it can result in fatigue, exhaustion, and even physical and/or emotional breakdown. When Selye first published his experimental findings over a half century ago, many medical practitioners failed to recognize the role of stress in a wide range of illnesses for which there is no specific cause. Heart attacks, strokes, hypertension (high blood pressure), and ulcers are typically associated with prolonged distress. Even cancer may have a stress-derived component.

It is interesting to note that women are less likely to suffer stress-related illnesses than men in similar jobs. Women find it easier to vent their emotions and verbalize their frustration at work. Because of cultural conditioning, men consider it to be a sign of weakness to admit dissatisfaction and disappointment.[48]

Job-Related Stress

Although the body experiences a certain degree of stress (either eustress or distress) in all situations, we are primarily concerned with the stress that is related to the job and the work setting. It is in that setting that management can use some of the approaches of a preventative nature.

Sources of Job-Related Stress. James and Jonathan Quick have made a careful study of stress in organizational settings. In Figure 20–5 from their article, we observe that the major sources of stress in organizations—**organizational stressors**—involve role factors, job factors, physical factors, and interpersonal factors. These stressors give rise to either the fight or flight reactions described previously. Note that the effects of distress are expressed in terms of individual costs and organizational costs. In their article, the Quicks recommend some preventative methods that will be examined later in this discussion.

Examples of Job-Related Distress. Arguments with supervisors or fellow employees are a common cause of distress. A myriad of other events may also prove distressful. One individual, for example, remembers the time in the Armed Forces when he was made to rewrite a letter 13 times. "I couldn't walk off the job," he recalls, "so I went to the men's room and hit the wall so hard my co-workers came in to see what was wrong." Feeling trapped in a job for which a person is ill-suited can be equally distressing. A 28-year old airline attendant said that she was sick of "smiling when I don't want to smile" and "making excuses for the airline to furious

---

47. *Ibid.,* pp. 50–60.
48. "Job Stress—Women Cope Better," *Human Behavior,* Vol. 8, No. 1 (January, 1979), pp. 34–35.

Figure 20–5 Stress in Organizational Settings

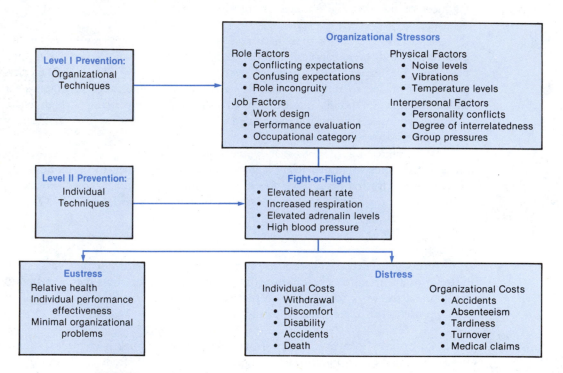

SOURCE: James C. Quick and Jonathan D. Quick, "Reducing Stress Through Prevent-ative Management," *Human Resource Management*, Vol. 18, No. 3 (Fall, 1979), pp. 15–22. Reproduced with permission.

passengers," but she did not consider herself qualified for other jobs with similar pay and benefits.[49]

Many minor irritations can also be sources of distress. Lack of privacy in offices, unappealing music, excessive smoke, and sources of other conditions can be distressful to one person or another. There are even more serious conditions that are related to the management of personnel. Potentially distressful factors include having little to say about how a job is performed, overspecialization, lack of communication on the job, and lack of recognition for a job well done.

Burnout is the most severe stage of distress. Career burnout generally occurs when a person begins questioning his or her own personal values. Quite simply, you don't feel that what you are doing is important anymore. Depression, frustration, and a loss of productivity are all symptoms of burnout. According to Maslach, burnout is

49. "How To Deal with Stress on the Job," *U.S. News & World Report* (March 13, 1978), pp. 80–81.

due primarily to a lack of personal fulfillment or positive feedback from the person's job.[50]

On the basis of death rates and admittance rates to hospitals and mental health facilities, NIOSH has rated the degree of stress to be found in a wide variety of jobs. Figure 20–6 lists the 12 jobs with the most stress and the 12 with the least. The reader who is considering a personnel staff job will be interested in the fact that, while not having the least stress, the job of personnel worker is in the category of low-stress jobs.

Other Sources of Stress

Managers and supervisors should, first of all, concern themselves with improving conditions at work that may be distressful. However, if they are to have a better understanding of their subordinates, they also should be aware of sources of stress that may not be job-related. The demands of life events constantly require one to readjust and adapt both to pleasant and unpleasant situations. From the point of view of stress-producing characteristics, it is immaterial whether the agent or situation that one faces is pleasant or unpleasant. All that counts is the intensity of the demand for readjustment or adaptation.

Demands of Life Events. Utilizing Selye's principle, Dr. Thomas Holmes undertook a study to determine the relative impact of changes that often affect

Figure 20–6 **High- and Low-Stress Jobs**

12 JOBS WITH MOST STRESS	AND 12 LOW-STRESS JOBS (In order of increasing stress)
1. Laborer	1. Clothing sewer
2. Secretary	2. Checker, examiner
3. Inspector	3. Stock handler
4. Clinical lab technician	4. Craft worker
5. Office manager	5. Maid
6. Foreman	6. Farm laborer
7. Manager/administrator	7. Heavy-equipment operator
8. Waitress/waiter	8. Freight handler
9. Machine operator	9. Child-care worker
10. Farm owner	10. Package wrapper
11. Miner	11. College professor
12. Painter	12. Personnel worker

SOURCE: National Institute for Occupational Safety and Health.

50. *BNA Bulletin to Management*, No. 1576 (Washington: The Bureau of National Affairs, Inc., May 22, 1980), p. 2.

human beings. By having a large sample of individuals assign values to the list of common events shown in Figure 20–7, Holmes arrived at a system for assigning ratings that indicate the degree of stress for each life event.[51] The following hypothetical example illustrates the application of the assigned ratings in Figure 20–7.

> John was married (50); as he had hoped, his wife became pregnant (40), stopped working (26), and bore a son (39). John, who hated his work as a soap company chemist, found a better paying job (38) as a teacher (36) in a college outside the city. After a vacation (13) to celebrate, he moved his family to the country (20), returned to the hunting and fishing (19) he had loved as a child, and began seeing a lot of his congenial·new colleagues (18). Everything was so much better that he was even able to give up smoking (24).

On the Holmes scale, these events total 323.[52]

Based upon considerable research with patients, Holmes concluded that when enough of the events listed in Figure 20–7 add up to ratings of more than 300 within a one-year period, trouble may lie ahead. He found that 80 percent of people who exceeded ratings of 300 in one year became pathologically depressed, had heart attacks, or developed other serious ailments. Of those who scored in the 150–300 range, 53 percent were similarly affected, as were 33 percent of those scoring up to 150. Holmes advises that one should avoid making too many life changes in too short a period of time.

Changes on the Job.   A few of the events listed in Figure 20–7 are job-related. In the organization of today, change is inevitable and necessary if it is to survive. Wherever feasible, employees should participate in planning for the change, and a program for communicating the details of the change and for keeping employees advised of its progress should be included. In any proposed change, employees must be convinced that they will benefit from the change or at least not be adversely affected by it. If possible, changes should be introduced gradually in order to permit employees more time to adjust to the change.

According to one proposed model, as a start on implementing change occurs, provision should be made for obtaining feedback from subordinates, which can lead to modification of the change if needed. Fundamental to this model is the provision for utilizing, rather than ignoring, the ideas and attitudes of the individuals involved and for letting feedback integration and utilization become the "pacer" of change.[53] In spite of all that may be done to develop a climate that is favorable to change, some degree of resistance may be expected.

---

51. Thomas H. Holmes and R. H. Rahe, "The Social Readjustment Rating Scale," *Journal of Psychosomatic Research*, Vol. 11, No. 4 (1967), pp. 213–218.

52. *Time*, Vol. 97, No. 9 (March 1, 1971), p. 54.

53. Joseph W. Hollis and Frank H. Krause, "Effective Development of Change," *Public Personnel Management*, Vol. 2, No. 1 (January-February, 1973), pp. 60–70.

Figure 20—7 Stress Rating Scale

RANK	LIFE EVENT	STRESS RATING	RANK	LIFE EVENT	STRESS RATING
1.	Death of spouse	100	22.	Change in responsibilities at work	29
2.	Divorce	73	23.	Son or daughter leaving home	29
3.	Marital separation	65	24.	Trouble with in-laws	29
4.	Jail term	63	25.	Outstanding personal achievement	28
5.	Death of close family member	63	26.	Wife begins or stops work	26
6.	Personal injury or illness	53	27.	Begin or end school	26
7.	Marriage	50	28.	Change in living conditions	25
8.	Fired from job	47	29.	Revision of personal habits	24
9.	Marital reconciliation	45	30.	Trouble with boss	23
10.	Retirement	45	31.	Change in work hours or conditions	20
11.	Change in health of family members	44	32.	Change in residence	20
12.	Pregnancy	40	33.	Change in schools	20
13.	Sex difficulties	39	34.	Change in recreation	19
14.	Gain of new family member	39	35.	Change in church activities	19
15.	Business adjustment	39	36.	Change in social activities	18
16.	Change in financial state	38	37.	Mortgage or loan less than $10,000	17
17.	Death of close friend	37	38.	Change in sleeping habits	16
18.	Change to different line of work	36	39.	Change in number of family get-togethers	15
19.	Change in number of arguments with spouse	35	40.	Change in eating habits	15
20.	Mortgage over $10,000	31	41.	Vacation	13
21.	Foreclosure of mortgage or loan	30	42.	Christmas	12
			43.	Minor violations of the law	11

SOURCE: Reprinted with permission from *Journal of Psychosomatic Research*, Vol. 11 No. 4, Thomas H. Holmes and R. H. Rahe, "The Social Readjustment Rating Scale," Copyright 1967, Pergamon Press, Ltd.

Coping with Stress

Everyone encounters situations that may be described as extremely distressful. Those who enjoy good physical health are generally better able to cope with the stressors that they encounter in their everyday lives. For those who wish to improve their power to cope with stress, one group of researchers who worked with 300 managers from 12 companies in London, Ontario, found that the five best coping techniques are:

1. Building resistance by regular sleep and good health habits.
2. Keeping work and nonwork life separate.
3. Getting exercise.

4. Talking things through with on-the-job peers.
5. Withdrawing physically from a situation when necessary.[54]

In addition to physical fitness programs, there are other types of formal programs offered to assist managers and employees in coping with stress. Some of the currently popular techniques include biofeedback, progressive relaxation, behavior modification, transactional analysis, and transcendental meditation. All of these techniques are designed to break the pattern of tension that accompanies stress situations and to help participants achieve greater personal control of their lives. Organizational techniques, such as clarifying the employee's work role, redesigning and enriching jobs, and performance planning also may be used.[55]

Some of the popular rituals that are found in organizations, such as the "coffee break," may be counterproductive if they lead to overconsumption of beverages containing caffeine. Many individuals, for example, develop anxiety symptoms from overdoses of caffeine. Their condition, which is often misdiagnosed as a psychological ailment, may well affect their productivity on the job and their behavior at work.[56] Instead of a coffee break, many organizations are encouraging their employees to take an "exercise break."

Before concluding this discussion, it should be observed that stress which is harmful to some employees may be healthy for others. Most executives, according to a *Business Week* article, have learned to handle distress effectively and find that it is a stimulant to better performance.[57] However, there will always be the person who is not able to handle stress and needs assistance in learning to cope with it. The increased interest of young and old alike in developing habits that will enable them to lead happier and more productive lives will undoubtedly be beneficial to them as individuals, to the organizations where they work, and to a society where people are becoming more and more interdependent.

RÉSUMÉ

The Occupational Safety and Health Act of 1970 has provided considerable impetus to the improvement of safety and health on the job. Both employers and employees have responsibilities and rights under the act. However, employers have the major burden of responsibilities. In recent years government administrators revised and simplified regulations and emphasized their enforcement for the most serious safety and health problems. The need to meet OSHA standards has caused employers to tend to overlook the human aspects of safety. Having well-publicized rules, motivating supervisors and employees to observe safety, and creating a work climate that is conducive to safety are essential requirements of a safety program.

Many processes and materials that may be hazardous to health are found in modern businesses. Not all of the hazards are acute or easily identified. As a result,

54. "Coping With Stress," *Human Behavior*, Vol. 5, No. 5 (May, 1976), p. 38.
55. Quick and Quick, *loc. cit.*
56. Cheraskin and Ringsdorf, *loc. cit.*
57. "Executive Stress May Not Be All Bad," *Business Week* (April 30, 1979), pp. 96, 103.

the onset of illnesses which may become chronic is often unnoticed. It is the responsibility of employers to identify, control, and eliminate the source of these illnesses.

The emotional, as well as physical, aspects of an employee's life are now recognized as being management problems that require facilities for providing assistance where needed. Growing attention is being given to the prevention of all types of health problems through physical fitness and health programs of various types. Creating less stressful work environments and helping employees cope with stress are preventative steps that are receiving increased attention from employers.

TERMS TO IDENTIFY

recordable case
clinical ecology
stress
eustress

distress
alarm reaction
organizational stressors
burnout

DISCUSSION QUESTIONS

1. When OSHA was enacted in 1970, it was heralded as the most important new source of protection for the U.S. worker in this half of the 20th century. What opinions about the effectiveness or the ineffectiveness of the act or its implementation have you heard from acquaintances who have been affected by it?

2. What steps should be taken by management to increase motivation for safety?

3. Many occupational health hazards that once existed no longer exist. However, industry has to remain vigilant to the possibility of new ones.
   a. What are some of the occupational health hazards that were once common but are seldom found today? What factors contributed to their elimination?
   b. What are some possible present and future hazards that did not exist in the past?
   c. What role should periodic medical examinations contribute to the detection and elimination of occupational hazards?

4. What approaches can be used to provide work areas free from tobacco smoke? How far should management go in restricting smoking at work?

5. Of what value would periodic consultations with a psychiatrist or clinical psychologist be to an executive? Who should pay for this service?

6. We observed that the field of clinical ecology relates directly to work situations.
   a. Have you noticed any chemicals that appear to affect how you feel or your behavior?
   b. On what jobs are these chemicals likely to be found?
   c. How can specialists in human resources management use this information?

7. Using the information in Figure 20–7 on page 513, compute your current stress rating. To what degree does your score coincide with the amount of pressure you feel? How can you apply management principles to your own personal life so as to keep your stress rating below the critical levels suggested by Holmes?

8. Identify the sources of stress in an organization.
   a. In what ways do they affect the individual employee? the organization?
   b. What can managers and supervisors do to make the workplace less stressful?

PROBLEM 20-1

POT POSSESSION*

Shortly after Roger Pugh drove onto the job site, he was stopped by security personnel for a routine search of his vehicle. Pugh owned the vehicle and had been issued a company parking sticker for it. The search turned up 3 marijuana cigarette butts in the ashtray, 15 marijuana seeds on the floorboards, and a package of cigarette papers in the glove compartment. After conducting a formal investigation, management decided that Pugh was in "possession" of an intoxicant on the job in violation of work rules and suspended him for ten days.

Pugh protested the suspension, asserting that the marijuana was not his and that he did not even use the substance. Pugh told his superior, Dennis James: "I lent my truck to a friend who smokes grass, and I guess that explains the joint in it. That's the only way I can figure out how that pot could have gotten into the cab, since I don't smoke the stuff."

Pugh went on to explain that he had not checked the ashtray of the vehicle upon its return to see if his friend had smoked in the cab or left any grass or dry paraphernalia. Pugh also pointed out that other workers who had been caught in possession of marijuana had received penalties less severe than ten-day suspensions.

Supervisor James was adamant. "It doesn't matter how the pot got there. What does matter is that it was in your vehicle. That means that you were in possession of drugs in violation of our work rules, which specify a ten-day suspension for the first offense. Even though you have a good work attitude and are one of our outstanding employees, we cannot tolerate this type of behavior."

The case finally went to arbitration.

a. If you were the arbitrator, how would you rule in this case?
b. What are the implications of this case for supervisory personnel?
c. What are its implications for an individual employee?

*SOURCE: Reprinted by permission from *BNA Bulletin to Management*, No. 1694, September 9, 1982, copyright 1982, by The Bureau of National Affairs, Inc., Washington, DC.

SUGGESTED READINGS

Anton, Thomas J. *Occupational Safety and Health Management.* New York: McGraw-Hill Book Company, 1979.

Chruden, Herbert J., and Arthur W. Sherman, Jr. *Readings in Managing Human Resources*, 6th ed. Cincinnati: South-Western Publishing Co., 1984. Part 6.

Ivancevich, John M., and Michael T. Matteson. *Stress and Work—A Managerial Perspective.* Glenview, IL: Scott, Foresman and Company, 1980.

Northrup, Herbert R., Richard L. Rowan, and Charles R. Perry. *The Impact of OSHA.* Philadelphia: University of Pennsylvania, Wharton School Research Unit, 1978.

Rodale, Robert. *Sane Living in a Mad World.* Emmaus, PA: Rodale Press, 1972.

Stellman, Jeanne Mager. *Women's Work, Women's Health—Myths and Realities.* New York: Pantheon Books, 1977.

Veninga, Robert L., and James P. Spadley. *The Work Stress Connection—How to Cope with Job Burnout.* Boston: Little, Brown and Company, 1981.

Human Resources Management: Looking Ahead

part

7

Chapter Objectives:

- To recognize the contributions of audits to an organization.
- To describe the approaches used in auditing the major personnel functions.
- To identify the types of information used in audits.
- To know the formulas for computing the rates for employee turnover, absenteeism, injuries, and illnesses.
- To understand the methods used to assess employee attitudes.
- To describe the methods used in analyzing audit findings.

21

Auditing the Human Resources Management Program

We have now completed our discussion of the functions comprising the program for managing human resources. It is appropriate to conclude this text by analyzing the ways in which the value of this program to the organization may be assessed. Assessing or auditing the human resources management program will be the focus of this chapter. In the final chapter, we will discuss your possible role in human resources management.

Just as financial audits are conducted, audits of the human resources management program should be conducted periodically to assure that its objectives are being accomplished. Audits typically involve analyzing data relative to the program including employee turnover, grievances, absences, accidents, and similar indicators of the effectiveness of the program. Special attention is usually given to assessing compliance with laws and regulations governing various specific areas. The most effective audit is one that provides the maximum amount of valid information concerning the overall effectiveness of the human resources program. Information from this assessment will often provide the basis for making improvements in the program.

THE HUMAN RESOURCES AUDIT

The term **human resources audit or personnel audit**, as used in this chapter, refers to a comprehensive analysis and evaluation of the human resources program. While it typically focuses on the human resources department, it is not restricted to the activities of that department. It includes a study of the functions of human resources management as they are performed in the total organization, including those performed by managerial and supervisory personnel.

Contributions of the Human Resources Audit

Traditionally, management has been concerned primarily with the efficient and economical use of material resources in the achievement of organizational goals. More recently, greater attention is being given to human resources and their contributions to the achievement of organization goals. Their contributions can best be measured by conducting audits of the human resources management program and of the personnel functions performed within it.

Among other things, the personnel audit allows management to:

1. Evaluate the effectiveness of the personnel functions.
2. Insure compliance with laws, policies, regulations, and procedures.
3. Set guidelines for establishing standards.
4. Insure that human resources management is contributing to overall organizational goals.
5. Improve the quality of the human resources staff by requiring it to assess its contributions.
6. Assist in upgrading human resources management as perceived by top management.[1]

1. Vytenis P. Kuraitis, "The Personnel Audit," *Personnel Administrator*, Vol. 26, No. 11 (November, 1981), pp. 29–34.

In essence, the human resources audit offers a method for assuring that the potential of the organization's human resources is fulfilled. In many ways it can contribute to the professionalization of the personnel functions.

If an organization is to remain competitive, it will have to undergo continual change. By auditing its human resources management program, it can help managers identify variances between actual and expected or desired conditions. Mahler refers to the audit as data-based stimuli for change. He recognizes that involvement and participation in planning, collecting, analyzing, and interpreting data about one's organizational situation can initiate a strong desire to change. Not only can the audit facilitate change, but also it can be used as an instrument of change. For example, if it is desirable that the human resources director make changes in the department, an audit can be used as a neutral medium for the views of superiors, peers, and subordinates. Thus, multiple pressures for change are brought upon the director. Mahler's philosophy is that audits must be conducted *for* and *with* an organization, not *on* them.[2]

Conducting the Audit

Audits may be conducted by internal or external professional personnel. There are advantages and disadvantages to each approach. Insiders know more about the organization and are in a better position to determine which aspects require evaluation. They are also less likely to be viewed as a threat by those being audited. How objective the insiders will be, however, is always a question. External auditors, on the other hand, are likely to be more objective and have less ego involvement. Having a breadth of experience, they can develop formal performance criteria for the organization's human resources.

Audit Coverage.

As stated earlier, a comprehensive audit of the human resources management program should encompass all aspects of the personnel functions as performed by both the human resources department and the operating or line managers. An examination of Figure 21–1 reveals the types of specific items that should be included in the audit. Several of these items will be discussed in detail later in this chapter.

With the increase of government intervention in human resources management, it is essential that audits give special attention to the analysis of **impact areas**, or those parts of the personnel system which interface with external requirements (laws, regulations, etc.) and organizational goals.[3] Figure 21-2 illustrates the interface of personnel, organizational goals, and the external requirements. Some of the major present-day impact areas are EEO/AA, safety and health, and pensions.

2. Walter R. Mahler, "Auditing PAIR," in Dale Yoder and Herbert G. Heneman, Jr. (eds.), *Planning and Auditing PAIR*, ASPA Handbook of Personnel and Industrial Relations (Washington, DC: The Bureau of National Affairs, Inc., 1976), pp. 2-91 — 2-107.

3. Kuraitis, *op. cit.*, p. 31.

Figure 21-1   Analysis of Audit Coverage

THE PERSONNEL ORGANIZATION	OPERATING OR LINE MANAGERS	SUBDIVISIONS OF PERSONNEL WORK
• Evolution of personnel organization over past ten years • Probable future evolution • Personnel organization size, reporting relationships, responsibility allocation • Role, authority, power of the personnel department in the view of the staff • Major objectives of the personnel organization • Personnel background of each professional employee in the department and his development plans • Planning process for personnel work • Control data, reporting, control system • Budget for last five years • Facilities and equipment • Manager's attitude toward department as seen by staff • Personnel policies and procedures • Critical personnel problems as seen by department • Relationships with corporate personnel	• Reason for personnel group • Own personnel objectives • Obstacles to achieving objectives • Objectives of personnel group • Role, power, and authority of personnel in view of managers • Contribution of personnel as seen by operating manager • Personnel responsibility of an operating manager (acceptance of/fulfillment of) • Changes deemed necessary in policies, procedures • Role, responsibility, and problems with compensation, employment, development, safety, communications, union relations • Critical personnel problems as seen by managers	The usual subdivisions of personnel work are communications, compensation, employment and placement, development and training, safety and medical, employee benefits, employee services, and union relations. Each of these is analyzed in relation to the following subjects: • Role and responsibility of managers and personnel • Changes needed as seen by managers and personnel • Policies and procedures as actually practiced • Positive and negative conditions as seen by managers, employees, and personnel • Future changes needed • Results desired versus results obtained

SOURCE: Dale Yoder and Herbert G. Heneman, Jr. (eds.). Reprinted by permission from *Planning and Auditing PAIR*, ASPA Handbook of Personnel and Industrial Relations, copyright 1976, by The Bureau of National Affairs, Inc., Washington, DC.

Figure 21-2   Impact Areas in an Audit

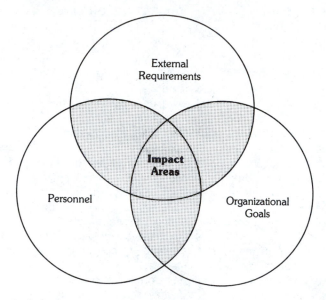

SOURCE: Vytenis P. Kuraitis, "The Personnel Audit." Reprinted from the November, 1981 issue of *Personnel Administrator*, copyright, 1981, The American Society for Personnel Administration, 30 Park Drive, Berea, OH 44017, $30 per year.

Steps in the Audit Process.   Mahler, an auditing specialist, proposes that the audit process consist of the following six steps:

1. Introduce the idea of the audit and emphasize the benefits to be derived from it.
2. Select personnel with a broad range of skills for the audit team and provide training as needed.
3. Gather data from different levels in the organization.
4. Prepare audit reports for line managers and personnel department.
5. Discuss reports with operating managers who then prepare their own evaluation.
6. Incorporate corrective actions into the regular company objective-setting process.[4]

Since auditing is a form of research, it is important that the findings be based on objective, reliable, and valid data. Personnel records of all types are available for use in audits. In addition to analyzing these records, interviews are usually conducted with managers at different levels, the human resources director, the human resources staff, and a selected number of supervisors and nonmanagement personnel.

APPROACHES TO THE HUMAN RESOURCES AUDIT

The most important function of the human resources audit is to determine the effectiveness with which the objectives of the human resources management program

---

4. Mahler, *op. cit.*, pp. 2-95 — 2-98.

are being met. Before starting the audit, the objectives and standards of the program should be stated clearly. This is especially important if external auditors are used. An audit, according to Kuraitis, should include three major approaches.[5] They are: determining compliance with laws and regulations, measuring the program's compatibility with organizational goals, and evaluating the performance of the program. In addition, policies and procedures should be examined carefully to determine their adequacy in meeting objectives.

Determining Compliance with Laws and Regulations

As we have noted throughout this book, the number of laws and regulations affecting human resources management has increased drastically in recent years. Organizations typically establish programs and procedures for achieving compliance with them. Top management needs to be aware of the manner in which managers at all levels are complying with the laws and regulations. Equal employment and affirmative-action programs, therefore, are among those compliance areas that are often made the subject of comprehensive audits.

Employers are required to maintain records for these programs in specified formats for examination by compliance investigators from federal and state agencies. In addition, many employers have learned to keep current as much information as possible about their performance in equal employment and affirmative action in order to avoid last-minute crises in data-gathering projects.

Among 26 requests an employer facing a compliance review had to meet were the following:

1. Provide a listing by ethnic group of minority promotions in a 12-month period, giving "from" and "to" position titles, along with effective dates.
2. Provide copies of seniority lists by plant, division, and department with minority members identified.
3. How were tests validated, by whom, scores used to make employment decisions?
4. Provide a listing of craftsmen jobs from the EEO-1 Report, broken down to show totals and minorities by ethnic group.
5. Who referred minority candidates, and how many?
6. How many employees by ethnic grouping in your summer employment program?[6]

The other 20 requests appear to require just as much work on the part of the human resources department as the six listed above. It is essential, therefore, that managers of human resources departments anticipate the types of information that will be required by government agencies and establish systems for maintaining such information in a computer file.

Checklists can be very useful in audit programs. Slevin devised a series of action checklists that are designed for auditing a program to utilize women more fully. His

---

5. Kuraitis, *op. cit.*, pp. 32–33.
6. George R. Wendt, "Questions Compliance Officers Ask," *Personnel Journal*, Vol. 54, No. 7 (July, 1975), pp. 385–387. *See also* Wayne K. West, "A Self-Audit for Affirmative Action Programs," *Personnel Journal*, Vol. 57, No. 12 (December, 1978), pp. 688–690, 699.

checklist for auditing promotion policies is shown in Figure 21–3. The other checklists he devised are titled as follows:

1. Top management commitment audit.
2. Administration audit.
3. Recruitment audit.
4. Selection audit.
5. Attitude audit.
6. Promotion policies audit.
7. Periodic program review.

Measuring Compatibility with Organizational Goals

For many years managers of human resources departments were viewed by top management as being out of touch with the goals of the organization. Consequently, their role, as we noted in Chapter 1, often was not considered nearly as important as that of certain other staff personnel. In the past several years, however, labor costs, government intervention, and a recognition of the need for greater productivity have caused executives to revise their view of the importance of human resources. Concurrently, managers of human resources departments have developed the expertise and have revised their orientation so as to be more in tune with the major goals of the organization.

An ASPA-BNA survey found that two thirds of the responding companies operate the human resources department on the basis of goal-setting, or management by objectives. Generally the goals are set annually, although in a few companies they are set semiannually.[7] The process of setting goals requires close coordination with top management. This insures that the policies and procedures of the department are consistent with top management's goals and objectives. The audit provides an opportunity to assess the extent to which objectives are being met and to revise policies and procedures accordingly.

Evaluating Program Performance

Each one of the functional areas of human resources management that has been described in detail throughout this book should help meet the overall objectives of a human resources management program. It is important, therefore, to audit each of these areas to determine how effectively and economically they are being operated. Since it is not possible to discuss in this text all of the details concerning the audit of each functional area, we have attempted to illustrate in Figure 21–4 (on pages 526–527) the types of specific questions that should be answered in an audit. The sources of in-house information—usually records and reports—that are available for use in the audit are also included in Figure 21–4. The questions shown are intended only to be suggestive, not comprehensive.

7. *BNA Policy and Practice Series—Personnel Management* (Washington, DC: The Bureau of National Affairs, Inc., 1979), p. 251:205.

Figure 21–3 **An Audit Checklist**

PROMOTION POLICIES AUDIT	ACTION STEPS

yes no

1. Are there instances of unequal pay for equal work? ☐ ☐
2. Are women afforded the same potential career paths as men in your organization? ☐ ☐
3. Have you developed targets for the proportion of women in each job category and done manpower planning for the next five years? ☐ ☐
4. Do you have a system (such as the assessment center) for identifying qualified women? ☐ ☐
5. Are your annual performance appraisals sexually unbiased? ☐ ☐
6. Does a woman who does not feel she is being promoted rapidly enough have an appeal procedure with her supervisor? ☐ ☐
7. Does a woman who does not feel she is being promoted rapidly enough have an appeal procedure with the action plan administrator? ☐ ☐
8. Are women participating sufficiently in attendance at management training and development seminars sponsored by your organization? ☐ ☐
9. Are women participating sufficiently in other management development efforts, such as job rotation, etc.? ☐ ☐

ACTION STEPS

If question one is answered "yes," the situation can be changed by top management mandate. If questions two through nine are answered "no," substantial long-term effort in effecting the required organizational change will be required of the administrator. Much of this may be accomplished through the attitude change techniques described in the "attitude audit." However, in many cases, specific administrative action may be taken. Some examples are:

a. review of all job classifications in which either sex is not represented in reasonable numbers.
b. review of salary and promotion progress of men and women who were hired at the same time into similar jobs to see if their progress has been dissimilar.
c. review of each employee's record to make sure that he or she has reached the highest possible level given the employee's capabilities and the organization's needs.
d. institution of a method of job posting so that all employees are aware of vacancies as they occur and that promotion into these vacancies is based on qualifications, not sex.
e. review of layoff and rehiring procedures to ascertain that they do not discriminate on the basis of sex.
f. review of all union contracts. Make sure that there are no discriminatory clauses and that there is a policy statement that discrimination is a violation of the contract.

SOURCE: Dennis Slevin, "Full Utilization of Women in Employment: The Problem and an Action Program," *Human Resource Management,* Vol. 12, No. 1 (Spring, 1973), pp. 25–32. Reproduced with permission.

Figure 21—4 Auditing the Major Functions in Human Resources Management

PERSONNEL FUNCTION	SOURCES OF INFORMATION
Planning and Recruitment • Do job specifications contain bona fide occupational qualifications? • Are job descriptions accurate, periodically reviewed, and updated? • Are there any human resources that are not being fully utilized? • Is the affirmative-action program achieving its goals? • How effective is the recruiting process? • How productive are the recruiters?	• Personnel budgets • Recruitment cost data • Job descriptions and specifications • Hiring rate
Selection • How valid are selection techniques? • Is there evidence of discrimination in hiring? • Are interviewers familiar with the job requirements? • Do interviewers understand what questions are acceptable and unacceptable to ask of job applicants? • Are tests job-related and free from bias? • How do hiring costs compare with those of other organizations?	• Employment-interview records • Applicant-rejection records • Transfer requests • EEOC complaints
Training and Development • How effective are training programs in increasing productivity and improving the quality of employee performance? • Are there sufficient opportunities for women and minorities to advance into management positions? • What is the cost of training per man-hour of instruction? • What is the relationship between training costs and accidents?	• Training cost data • Production records • Accident records • Quality-control records

Figure 21-4 (continued)

PERSONNEL FUNCTION	SOURCES OF INFORMATION
Performance Evaluation	
● Are the performance standards objective and job-related?	● Performance-appraisal records
● Do the appraisal methods emphasize performance rather than traits?	● Production records
● Are the appraisers adequately trained and thoroughly familiar with the employees' work?	● Scrap-loss records ● Appraisal-interview records ● Attendance records
● Are the appraisals documented and reviewed with employees?	● Disciplinary-action records
● Are the performance evaluation data assembled in such form that they can be used to validate tests and other selection procedures?	
Compensation	
● Does the pay system, including incentive plans, attract employees and motivate them to achieve organizational goals?	● Wages and benefits data ● Wage-survey records ● Unemployment compensation insurance rates
● Do the compensation structure and policies comply with EEO requirements, ERISA, and IRS?	● Turnover records ● Cost-of-living surveys
● Is the choice of weights and factors in job evaluation sound and properly documented?	
● Do benefit costs compare favorably with those of similar organizations?	
Labor Relations	
● Are supervisors trained to handle grievances effectively?	● Grievance records ● Arbitration-award records
● Is there continuous preparation for collective bargaining?	● Work-stoppage records ● Unfair-practice complaint records
● What is the record of the number and types of grievances, and what percentage of grievances has gone to arbitration?	
● What percentage of disciplinary discharges has been challenged?	

Most of the sources of information listed in Figure 21–4 yield statistical data that are readily available in most organizations. Where electronic data processing (EDP) facilities are being utilized, such information can be kept current for analysis and reporting, and should be used. As Fitz-Enz observes:

> The name of the game today is numbers. With ever increasing speed, computers are churning out numbers on sales volume, market penetration, production capacity, accounts receivable, and even future corporate plans. These are hard numbers. Executives manage companies on these numbers. Computer printouts do not refer to attitudes, morale, satisfaction or personal needs. They tell how much cost, how many units, how long a lead time. They are not only descriptive, they are predictive. In short, they drive the business.[8]

If the personnel functions are to receive the attention and respect of top management and if personnel is to be viewed as a professional endeavor, Fitz-Enz advises, "Being able to measure one's work in quantifiable terms is a major tool of the professional. It's time for personnel management to pick up this tool and use it."

INDICATORS FOR EVALUATING THE WORK ENVIRONMENT

Throughout this book we have emphasized that the work environment can have a significant effect upon the motivation, performance, job satisfaction, and morale of employees. It is possible to assess the quality of the environment within an organization by studying certain indicators. The indicators, which may also be used to assess the personnel functions, are widely used in all types and sizes of organizations. Among these indicators are employee turnover rates, absenteeism rates, injury and illness records, and responses from employee attitude surveys.

Employee Turnover Rates

Employee turnover refers to the movement of employees in and out of an organization. It is often cited as one of the reasons that United States industry has failed to compete effectively with foreign industries. It is also cited as one of the factors behind the failure of United States employee productivity rates to keep pace with those of our competitors.[9] Organizations that have computed employee replacement costs have come up with some rather substantial figures.[10] As a result, managers of human resources are increasing their efforts to reduce the costs of employee turnover.

---

8. J. A. Fitz-Enz, "The Measurement Imperative," *Personnel Journal*, Vol. 57, No. 4 (April, 1978), pp. 193–195. *See also* Jac Fitz-Enz, "Quantifying the Human Resources Function," *Personnel*, Vol. 57, No. 2 (March-April, 1980), pp. 41–52.

9. Thomas E. Hall, "How to Estimate Employee Turnover Costs," *Personnel*, Vol. 58, No. 4 (July-August, 1981), pp. 43–52.

10. Pamela Garretson and Kenneth S. Teel, "The Exit Interview: Effective Tool or Meaningless Gesture?" *Personnel*, Vol. 59, No. 4 (July-August, 1982), pp. 70–77.

Computing the Turnover Rate. The **turnover rate** for a department or an entire organization is an indicator of how employees respond to their work environment. The United States Department of Labor suggests the following formula for computing turnover rates:

$$\frac{\text{number of separations during the month}}{\text{total number of employees at midmonth}} \times 100$$

Thus, if there were 25 separations during a month and the total number of employees at midmonth was 500, the turnover rate would be:

$$\frac{25}{500} \times 100 = 5\%$$

Turnover rates are computed on a regular basis for more than four out of five organizations responding to a BNA survey. More than three fourths of them use the data to compare rates among specific groups within the organization such as departments, divisions, work groups, etc. In half of these organizations, comparisons are made with data provided by other organizations. The BNA's *Quarterly Report on Job Absence and Turnover* is used by the majority as a source of comparative turnover data.[11]

Another method for computing the turnover rate is one in which the rate reflects the avoidable separations. If S equals the total separations in the selection period, US equals the unavoidable separations, and M equals the midmonth work force, the formula becomes:

$$\frac{(S - US)}{M} \times 100 = T \text{ (turnover rate)}$$

Unavoidable separations include termination of temporary employment, promotions, transfers, and separations due to illness, death, or marriage.[12] This method yields what is probably the most significant measure of the effectiveness of a personnel program since it can serve to direct attention to that portion of employee turnover that can be reduced. It also represents that portion of turnover that management has the most opportunity to control by means of better selection, training, supervisory leadership, improved working conditions, better wages, and opportunities for advancement.

Ways of Determining Causes of Turnover. The quantitative rate of turnover is not the only factor to be considered. The quality of personnel who leave an organization is also important. In an effort to determine why employees leave, many organizations conduct **exit interviews** during the final week of employment. One

11. *Job Absence and Turnover Control*, PPF Survey No. 132 (Washington DC: The Bureau of National Affairs, Inc., October, 1981).
12. *BNA Policy and Practice Series—Personnel Management* (Washington, DC: The Bureau of National Affairs, Inc., 1981), pp. 241:212.

study of a limited number of organizations found that in 83 percent of them the human resources department conducts the exit interviews. In most cases the interviewers are employment recruiters. This is advantageous for two reasons. Employees are likely to be more open when speaking with someone with whom they have had previous contact. Also, recruiters are usually experienced interviewers.[13] Topics covered in exit interviews are shown in Figure 21–5.

A unique approach to the exit interview utilizes a deck of 19 cards. Each card contains a statement about the company's image regarding job security, fair salary, good relationships with supervisors, fair performance reviews, etc. The interviewee is instructed to sort the 19 cards into three piles: what is realized, what is realized in part, and what is not realized within the company. After the cards are sorted, the interviewer discusses the three piles, asks for possible reasons for the employee's choices, and solicits suggestions for improvement. The advantages of this method over other methods of conducting exit interviews are:

1. A lot of feedback information is accumulated in a very short period of time.
2. The card game is generally stimulating for the employee and increases his or her motivation to participate.
3. The objectivity of the employee's answers can be controlled.[14]

Another way to obtain information about the reasons why employees leave an organization is to mail a **post-exit questionnaire** to them after a short interval has

---

Figure 21–5 Topics Covered During Exit Interviews

- Reason for departure
- New job and salary
- Rating of:
  Job
  Supervision
  Working conditions
  Advancement opportunities
  Training
  Pay
- Would the employee return?
- Could the departure have been prevented?
- Things liked best about the job.
- Things liked least about the job.
- Suggestions

SOURCE: Reprinted, by permission of the publisher, from PERSONNEL, July-August 1982, © 1982 by AMACOM Periodicals Division. American Management Associations, New York, p. 73. All rights reserved.

---

13. Garretson and Teel, *op. cit.*, p. 71.
14. Martin Hilb, "The Standardized Exit Interview," *Personnel Journal*, Vol. 57, No. 6 (June, 1978), pp. 327–329, 336.

lapsed since the date of their termination. This approach is likely to yield a fairly honest evaluation, especially if it is requested on an anonymous basis.

Another method for determining the causes of turnover makes use of biographical data, a methodology discussed in Chapter 6. In one study of a central petroleum products credit-card issuing-and-billing office employing 700 persons, biographical information from the employees' application forms was related to turnover. Through this procedure it was possible to determine personal characteristics of the employees associated with turnover. Such factors as age, proximity to work, and military service were found to be related in one way or another. Thus, this method provided information with which to explore further the characteristics to look for in job applicants in order to maximize length of employment. Since the factors will vary from one job to another and from one organization to another, the specific information obtained in this study should *not* be generalized as to other situations.[15]

While management should be concerned with determining the causes of turnover in its organization, reference to findings from other organizations in the same industry and by type of job will provide a basis for comparison. The Bureau of National Affairs, for example, surveyed the members of its *Personnel Policies Forum* for causes of turnover among production, office, and management personnel. Their findings, as shown in Figure 21–6, indicate the relative ranking of turnover causes. The relative ranking was determined by totaling the weighted rankings given each factor by Forum companies. It should be noted that, unless such surveys include information from employees as to their reasons for leaving, the true causes of turnover may never be learned.

Costs of Turnover.   Replacing an employee can be time-consuming and expensive. Replacement costs can generally be broken down into three categories: separation costs for the departing employee, acquisition costs, and training costs for the new employee. Replacement costs are conservatively estimated to be two to three times the monthly salary of the departing employee. These estimates do not include indirect costs such as low productivity prior to quitting, lower morale, and overtime for other employees because of the job vacated. Consequently, reducing turnover could result in significant savings to an organization.[16]

Absenteeism Rates

The extent to which employees are absent from their work may also serve to indicate the state of the work environment and the effectiveness of the human resources management program. A certain amount of absenteeism is due to unavoidable causes. There will always be some who must be absent from work because of sickness, accidents, serious family problems, and other legitimate reasons.

15. Donald P. Schwab and Richard L. Oliver, "Predicting Tenure with Biographical Data: Exhuming Buried Evidence," *Personnel Psychology,* Vol. 27, No. 1 (Spring, 1974), pp. 125–128.

16. Garretson and Teel, *op. cit.* pp. 74–76.

Figure 21–6 Causes of Turnover by Weighted Averages for Three Employee Groups

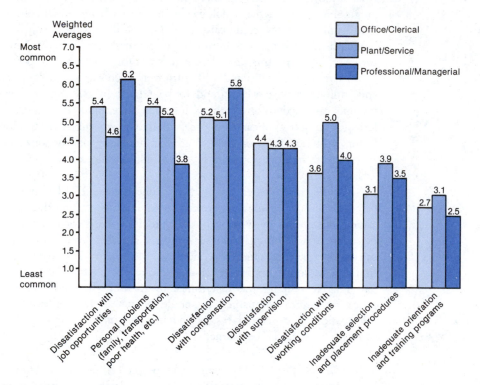

SOURCE: Reprinted by permission from *BNA Policy and Practice Series—Personnel Management,* copyright 1981, by The Bureau of National Affairs, Inc., Washington, DC.

Considerable evidence, however, indicates that there are many other absences which can be avoided.

Habitual absenteeism may be the first sign that an employee is about to quit. This was found to be true in an investigation of 127 female telephone operators in a large metropolitan area. In fact, probably much absenteeism is a way of withdrawing from the organization without taking the final step of quitting. Sometimes the factors that cause absenteeism, such as dissatisfaction with supervisors or the job or lack of opportunity, are directly under management control.[17]

Computing Absenteeism Rates.   It is advisable for management to determine the seriousness of its absenteeism problem by maintaining individual and departmental attendance records and by computing **absenteeism rates**. Neither a universally

17. "Disconnecting Operators," *Human Behavior,* Vol. 3, No. 1 (January, 1974), pp. 49–50.

accepted definition of absence nor a standard formula for computing absenteeism rates exists. However, the method of computing absenteeism rates most frequently used is that recommended by the United States Department of Labor:

$$\frac{\text{number of worker days lost through job absence during period}}{\text{average number of employees} \times \text{number of workdays}} \times 100$$

If 300 worker days are lost through job absence during one month with 25 scheduled working days at a company that employs 500 workers, the absenteeism rate for that month would be:

$$\frac{300}{500 \times 25} \times 100 = 2.4\%$$

As used by the Department of Labor, **job absence** is defined as the failure of employees to report on the job when they are scheduled to work, whether or not such failure to report is excused. Scheduled vacations, holidays, and prearranged leaves of absence are not counted as job absence.

Comparing Absenteeism Data.   The Bureau of Labor Statistics of the United States Department of Labor receives data on job absences from the Current Population Survey of Households conducted by the Bureau of the Census, and the analyses of data are published periodically. These analyses permit the identification of problem areas—industries, occupations, or groups of workers—with the highest incidence of absence or with rapidly increasing rates of absence.

Nearly six out of ten organizations responding to a BNA Survey reported that they compute absence rates on a regular basis for at least one employee group. Supervisors are encouraged to compare their department rates to those of other departments and the company average so that problems can be promptly identified and corrected.[18]

Comparison with other organizations may be made by referring to Bureau of Labor Statistics data reported in the *Monthly Labor Review* or by such personnel reporting services as The Bureau of National Affairs, Prentice-Hall, and Commerce Clearing House.

Costs of Absenteeism.   Traditional accounting and personnel information systems do not generate data which reflect the costs of absenteeism. To call management's attention to the severity of the problem, absenteeism should be translated into dollar costs. Recent estimates tag the national absence bill at between $15 billion and $20 billion a year.[19]

To encourage managers of human resources to compute absenteeism costs, Kuzmits developed a system for computing cost estimates for an individual

18. *BNA Personnel Policies Forum*, PPF Survey No. 132, *loc. cit.*
19. Frank E. Kuzmits, "How Much Is Absenteeism Costing *Your* Organization?" *Personnel Administrator*, Vol. 24, No. 6 (June, 1979), pp. 29–33.

organization. Organizations with computerized absence-reporting systems should find this additional information easy and inexpensive to generate. The cost for each man-hour lost to absenteeism is based upon the hourly weighted average salary, costs of employee benefits, supervisory costs, and incidental costs. For a hypothetical company of 1,200 employees with 78,000 man-hours lost to absenteeism, the total cost was found to be $560,886. When this figure is divided by 1,200, the cost is $467.41 per employee for the period covered.[20] (In this example the absent workers were paid. If absent workers were not paid, their salary figures were omitted from the computation.)

Occupational Injuries and Illnesses

It was noted in Chapter 20 that employers are required by OSHA to maintain a Log and Summary of Occupational Injuries and Illnesses and to prepare a Supplementary Record for every recordable injury or illness. By maintaining detailed information about accidents and illnesses, the records provide a starting point for analyzing problem areas, making changes in the working environment, and motivating personnel for safety and health.

From the records that are maintained the Bureau of Labor Statistics and other organizations, such as the National Safety Council, compile data that an employer may use as a basis for comparison with similar organizations. In order to make such comparisons, it is necessary to compute for an individual organization the incidence rate, which is the number of injuries and illnesses per 100 full-time employees during a given year. The standard formula for computing the incidence rate is shown below, where 200,000 equals the base for 100 full-time workers who work 40 hours a week, 50 weeks a year:

$$\frac{\text{Incidence}}{\text{Rate}} = \frac{\text{Number of injuries and illnesses} \times 200,000}{\text{Total hours worked by all employees during period covered}}$$

A portion of one table from a BLS publication is shown in Table 21–1. To illustrate the use of this table for comparison purposes, we can take an example cited in that publication.[21] The Jones Concrete Company, with an average number of 80 employees during 1980, experienced an incidence rate of 19.1. By examining the line printed in boldface on Table 21–1 which includes data from companies with 50–99 employees, we find that the incidence rate of 19.1 for the Jones Concrete Company is below the mean of 24.1. However, it is higher than that of 25 percent of the establishments (1st quartile = 11.5).

Incidence rates thus provide a basis for making comparisons with other companies doing similar work. These rates are also useful for making comparisons between work groups, departments, and similar units within an organization.

20. Kuzmits, *loc. cit.*

21. *Evaluating Your Firm's Injury & Illness Record, 1980—Construction Industries*, Report 659 (Washington, DC: U.S. Department of Labor, Bureau of Labor Statistics, May, 1982).

Table 21–1 **Example of Available Comparison Data for Injuries and Illnesses**

Occupational Injury and Illness Incidence rates for construction industries by employment size and quartile distribution, 1980

Industry and employment size	Incidence rates per 100 full-time workers			
	Column A	Column B	Column C	Column D
	Average incidence rates for all establishments: (mean)	One quarter of the establishments had a rate lower than or equal to: (1st quartile)	One half of the establishments had a rate lower than or equal to: (median)	Three fourths of the establishments had a rate lower than or equal to: (3rd quartile)
Special trade contractors				
Concrete work				
All sizes	14.8	0.0	0.0	0.0
1 to 19	7.8	.0	.0	.0
20 to 49	18.7	.0	15.1	28.2
50 to 99	**24.1**	**11.5**	**23.0**	**36.4**
100 to 249	25.3	12.6	19.5	32.2
250 to 499	19.8	(1)	(1)	(1)

NOTE: (1) Quartile rates were not derived because fewer than 25 establishment reports were included in the industry employment-size group.

SOURCE: *Evaluating Your Firm's Injury & Illness Record, 1980—Construction Industries,* Report 659 (Washington: U. S. Department of Labor, Bureau of Labor Statistics, May 1982), p. 3.

Employee Attitude Surveys

The influence of attitudes and values on employee behavior was discussed in Chapter 11. In the measurement of attitudes, employers are typically interested in those attitudes that relate to the job and the organization. With such information it is possible to make organizational changes that will hopefully increase employee satisfaction.

One of the most objective and economical approaches to obtaining data for use in making organizational changes is through surveys. These surveys are usually conducted on a company- or plant-wide basis and usually involve the administration of a questionnaire (or inventory) or the use of interviews.

Use of Questionnaires.

Questionnaires are intended to measure employee opinions about various aspects of their work situation. The steps in conducting a questionnaire survey are:

1. *Planning the survey.* A careful planning of the survey is essential to its success. The objectives of the survey should be clearly determined and discussed by representatives of the various groups concerned, namely, managers, supervisors, employees, and the union.

2. *Designing the questionnaire.* The questionnaire or inventory that is used in a survey should cover all phases of the employment situation that are believed to be related to employee satisfaction and dissatisfaction. One commercially available questionnaire used by several large organizations is the *SRA Attitude Survey*. It consists of a questionnaire known as the Core Survey that contains 78 items sampling 14 job categories as listed in Figure 21–7. There are also provisions for supplementary items of concern to individual organizations, as well as for use with supervisors and salespersons. A few of the typical items from this inventory are:

"If I have a complaint to make, I feel free to talk to someone up the line." "My supervisor sees that employees are properly trained for the job." "Changes are made here with little regard for welfare of employees." "Poor working conditions keep me from doing my best in my work."[22]

3. *Administering the questionnaire.* The conditions under which the attitude questionnaire is administered are of vital importance to the success of the survey and to the morale of the participants. Employees should be fully oriented in order that they understand the purpose of the survey. The usual procedure is to administer the questionnaire anonymously to large groups during working hours.

4. *Analyzing the data.* A tabulation of results broken down by departments, male versus female employees, hourly employees versus piece-rate employees, and other meaningful categories is the starting point in analyzing the data. If data are available from previous surveys, comparisons can be made. Comparisons are usually made between departments within the organization.

Once problems are identified, appropriate action should be taken. In one study of how employees viewed attitude surveys, it was found that only half of the respondents expected any action to result from the surveys.[23] These findings reinforce the admonitions about the need for feedback to employees on survey results and meaningful follow-up action.

Use of Interviews. Another approach to obtaining feedback from employees is through an interviewing program. Interviewers should make it clear that the object of the interviews is to ascertain how to make the organization a more productive and satisfying place in which to work. The emphasis is on listening and encouraging participants to speak freely. A list of action items is maintained, and concrete and prompt feedback to employees is essential.

Interview responses of thousands of blue-collar and white-collar employees from many different companies are found to fall into four categories:

1. Complaints about the working environment—30 percent.
2. Misunderstandings about company policies and procedures—10 percent.
3. Harsh, abusive, tyrannical, or inept supervision—30 percent.
4. Management sins of omission or commission—30 percent.

---

22. From the *SRA Employee Inventory.* Copyright, 1951, by the Industrial Relations Center of the University of Chicago. Reprinted by permission of the publisher, Science Research Associates, Inc.

23. William Penzer, "Employee Attitudes Toward Attitude Surveys," *Personnel*, Vol. 50, No. 3 (May-June, 1973), pp. 60–64.

Figure 21–7 Categories in the SRA Attitude Survey

Category	Questions Asked
1. Job demands	Work pressure, fatigue, boredom, work load, hours of work.
2. Working conditions	Annoyances, management's concern for conditions, equipment adequacy, safety measures, effect of these on efficiency.
3. Pay	Adequacy, comparison with pay of others in the company and in other local companies, administration of pay system.
4. Employee benefits	All benefits, comparison with benefits in other companies, knowledge of program, administration of benefits.
5. Friendliness, cooperation of fellow employees	Bossiness, friction.
6. Supervisor-employee interpersonal relations	Friendliness, fairness, treatment of suggestions, credit for good work, concern for welfare, follow-through on promises.
7. Confidence in management	Belief in management's integrity and its concern for employee welfare, adequacy of personnel policies, friendliness.
8. Technical competence of supervision	Administrative skill, knowledge of job, ability to train employees, decision making, work organization.
9. Effectiveness of administration	Competence of higher levels of management, efficiency of company operations, cooperation among departments.
10. Adequacy of communication	Freedom to express opinions and suggest improvements, complaint-handling, information about operations and plans.
11. Security of job and work relations	Security from arbitrary discharge and layoff, recognition of length of service, handling of job changes.
12. Status and recognition	Standing with the company, fair appraisal of work done, respect for judgment.
13. Identification with the company	Pride in the company, interest in its future, sense of belonging and participation with the company.
14. Opportunity for growth and advancement	Opportunities to use one's skills, to grow and develop on the job, to get ahead in the organization.

SOURCE: From *Administration and Interpretation of the SRA Attitude Survey.* © 1974, Science Research Associates, Inc. Reprinted by permission of the publisher.

Companies such as Xerox, Copperweld, Kraft Foods, and General Electric have found that the upward communication system utilizing interviews has paid off in terms of reduced absenteeism and turnover, less waste and spoilage, improved safety records, increased productivity, and increased profits.[24]

UTILIZING AUDIT FINDINGS

In the preceding discussion we observed that there are many sources and indicators from which information may be obtained about the condition of the human resources management program. This information must then be evaluated and made available to the personnel who can utilize it most effectively. Various types of corrective action are often indicated by such evaluations.

Methods of Analyzing the Findings

Several approaches may be used in analyzing the information gathered from the various sources that have been described. These approaches include the following:

1. Compare personnel programs with those of other companies, especially the successful ones.
2. Base an audit on some source of authority, such as consultant norms and behavioral science findings.
3. Rely upon some ratios or averages such as ratios of personnel staff to total employees.
4. Use a compliance audit to measure whether the activities of managers and staff in personnel management comply with policies, procedures, and rules.
5. Manage the personnel department by objectives and use a systems type of audit.[25]

Odiorne recommends approach No. 5 (management by objectives). With human resources department objectives or goals that are supportive of the organizational goals, top management is more likely to recognize the value of the department's functions and provide the support that it needs.

Other methods of analyzing the effectiveness of a program are widely used, however. As noted earlier, compliance audits are essential for determining an organization's adherence to government regulations. Increasingly senior executives and members of boards of directors are realizing that they are ultimately responsible for such compliance.

Where the comparison method is used, figures from outside sources are available. We have seen that comparison data may be obtained from government agencies, reporting services, employer associations, industry trade associations, and consulting firms.

24. Woodruff Imberman, "Letting the Employee Speak His Mind," *Personnel*, Vol. 53, No. 6 (November–December, 1976), pp. 12–22.

25. George S. Odiorne, "Evaluating the Personnel Program," in *Handbook of Modern Personnel Administration*, edited by Joseph J. Famularo (New York: McGraw-Hill Book Company, 1972), p. 8-1.

Costs of the Total Program

We noted in the discussion of absenteeism and turnover that it is important to translate audit findings wherever possible into dollar costs. Saying that turnover is "expensive" is not enough. By having specific cost data, it is possible to make intelligent decisions about how much should be spent to improve certain programs such as turnover-reduction programs. Human resources specialists should take the lead in preparing cost figures for as many of the human resources activities as possible. With such figures the cost-effectiveness or cost-benefit ratio of the activities can be clearly demonstrated.

According to one survey, the median cost for human resources activities in 1981 was approximately $361 per employee in an organization. The middle 50 percent range is from $176 to $644. As shown in Figure 21–8, the annual budget per employee is significantly lower in larger organizations than in smaller ones. This is true for both manufacturing and nonmanufacturing employers.[26]

Figure 21–8 Costs of Managing a Human Resources Management Program

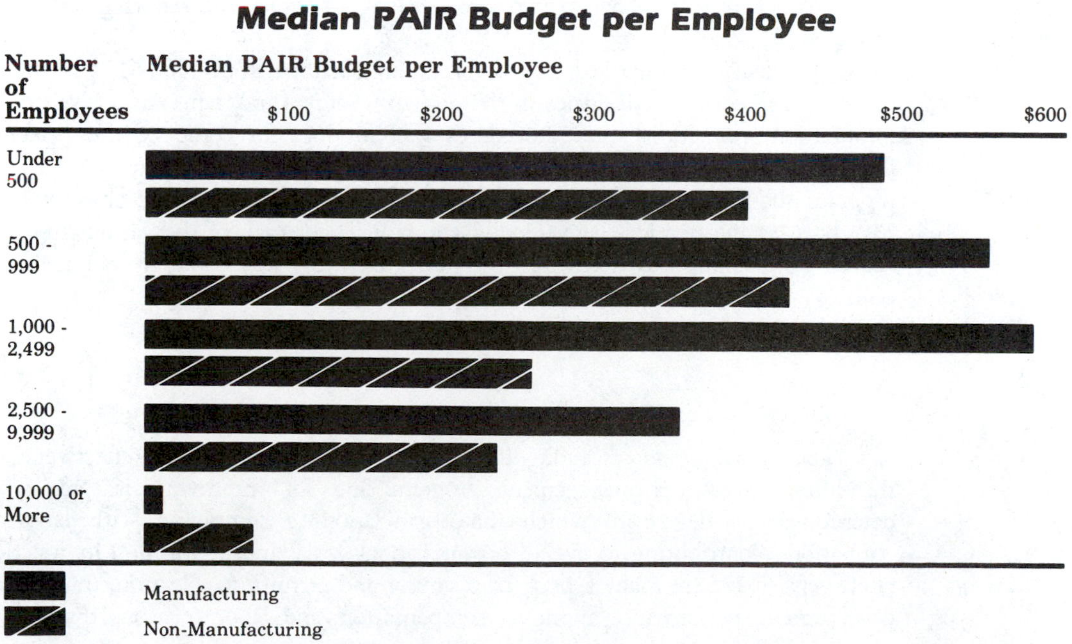

Median PAIR Budget per Employee

Number of Employees	Median PAIR Budget per Employee

SOURCE: "The Personnel and Industrial Relations Report, Part II: Budgets and Staffing," by Steven Langer, copyright July 1982. Reprinted with the permission of *Personnel Journal*, Costa Mesa, CA; all rights reserved.

26. Steven Langer, "The Personnel and Industrial Relations Report, Part 2: Budgets and Staffing," *Personnel Journal*, Vol. 61, No. 7 (July, 1982), pp. 522–527.

Surveys conducted regularly by various organizations provide information that can be used to compare costs of the total program and its parts. Data on the compensation of human resources professionals, department budgets, and personnel staff ratios are reported periodically in journals and in reporting services' publications.

The Bureau of National Affairs reports data on the **personnel staff ratios**. The ratio is the number of persons on the personnel staff per 100 employees on the company payroll. For all companies reporting in an ASPA-BNA survey, the personnel staff ratio in 1981 was one personnel department employee for every 100 employees and one professional/technical staff member for every 200 employees on the payroll.[27] As the size of the work force increases, the relative size of the human resources staff decreases. Data on the compensation for human resources specialists will be presented in the next chapter.

Preparation of Reports and Recommendations

One of the most important activities of the audit team is the preparation of reports of their findings, evaluation, and recommendations. The reports should include everything that is pertinent and will be useful to the recipients. One report is usually prepared for line managers. A special report is prepared for the human resources department manager who also receives a copy of the report given to line managers.

The value to be derived from information obtained from audits lies in the use made of it to correct deficiencies in the human resources program. An analysis of the information may reveal that procedures for carrying out some of the personnel functions need to be revised. It is even possible that certain parts of the total program should undergo a thorough revision if they are to meet the objectives that have been established for them. Finally, the policies for each of the various functions should be examined to determine their adequacy as part of the overall personnel policy.

RÉSUMÉ

The human resources audit offers a method for evaluating the effectiveness of the human resources management program and for improving its quality. It determines the degree to which the organization is complying with laws and regulations, contributing to overall organizational goals, and performing its functions effectively. There are many aspects of planning and recruiting, selection, training and development, performance appraisal, compensation, and labor relations that require study and evaluation.

By studying employee turnover, absenteeism, occupational injuries and illnesses, and employee attitudes, it is possible to evaluate the quality of the work environment. Employee attitudes, which may be assessed by interviews and/or

---

27. *BNA Policy and Practice Series—Personnel Management* (Washington, DC: The Bureau of National Affairs, Inc., 1982), p. 251:157–158.

questionnaires, provide a basis for making changes in specific areas of the work environment such as the nature of supervision, adequacy of communication, and working conditions.

There are several approaches in analyzing audit findings. These include making comparisons with personnel programs of similar organizations and relying on personnel staff ratios. Wherever possible, the cost-effectiveness of the human resources program should be assessed. Through the audit, it is possible to obtain insights that will be useful in planning for future operations.

TERMS TO IDENTIFY

human resources audit or personnel audit
impact areas
employee turnover
turnover rate
exit interviews

post-exit questionnaire
absenteeism rates
job absence
personnel staff ratios

DISCUSSION QUESTIONS

1. Why is it important to audit the human resources management program periodically?
2. Some companies employ specially trained consultants to conduct human resources audits.
   a. What are the advantages and disadvantages of using consultants for this purpose?
   b. Consultants often compare the audit findings from a company with other companies with which they are familiar. Of what value are such comparisons?
3. Many organizations have found it necessary to be prepared for compliance audits by government agencies.
   a. How can the personnel department best prepare itself for such an audit?
   b. Should all of its efforts be devoted to preparing for compliance audits?

4. What types of information should be included in audit reports to management?
5. Describe the type of information available in records and reports that can be used in auditing the major personnel functions. Give some examples of data that are easily computerized.
6. Explain the difference between an exit interview and a post-exit questionnaire. What are the advantages and disadvantages of each method?
7. Why is it important to compute absenteeism rates? What steps can management take to reduce absenteeism?
8. What are the advantages of conducting periodic employee attitude surveys? Are any problems likely to arise over a survey? Explain.

PROBLEM 21-1

ATTENDANCE BONUS PLAN

Halter Marine Services of New Orleans, a builder of off-shore support vessels, instituted an Attendance Bonus Plan to recognize and reward employees who come to work on a regular basis and to reduce absenteeism. The plan, as outlined in a letter to employees, is based upon perfect attendance Monday through Friday of each week. If the shipyard does not work for reasons beyond the employee's control, the attendance bonus is not affected, provided that the employee has punched in for that particular day. Any personal absence, excused or otherwise, will cause an employee to lose the attendance bonus for that week. The attendance bonus is 10 or 15 cents per hour depending upon the employee's hourly rate. In the letter in which the plan was announced, employees were advised that, "When you are absent, we are going to send a letter to your home showing exactly how much money you have lost. . . . Absenteeism of any kind will cause you to lose the attendance bonus. Unexcused absences may cause you to lose a raise or possibly even your job. Come to work every day and let the Attendance Bonus Plan pay you cash."

a. What effect is such a plan likely to have on production? On morale?

b. Why does the company send a letter home? Is this an advisable procedure?

c. Should such a plan include office employees as well as production employees?

SUGGESTED READINGS

Byham, William C. *The Uses of Personnel Research*. AMA Research Study 91. New York: AMACOM, American Management Associations, 1968.

Dunham, Randall B., and Frank J. Smith. *Organizational Surveys*. Glenview, IL: Scott, Foresman and Company, 1979.

Fear, Richard A. *The Evaluation Interview*. New York: McGraw-Hill Book Company, 1978.

Luck, Thomas J. *Personnel Audit and Appraisal*. New York: McGraw-Hill Book Company, 1955.

McConnell, John H. *How to Audit the Personnel Department*. New York: AMACOM, American Management Associations, 1978.

Stone, Eugene. *Research Methods in Organizational Behavior*. Santa Monica, CA: Goodyear Publishing Company, 1978.

Chapter Objectives:

- To understand what is meant by strategic human resources management.
- To identify the areas in human resources management that will be the subject of increased attention.
- To describe the changes in status of human resources managers.
- To identify the types of specialized jobs in human resources management that are available.
- To explain the preparation required for a career in human resources management.
- To describe the personal qualifications needed by those seeking a career in human resources management.

Opportunities in Human Resources Management

22

We have emphasized that human resources management is a dynamic field. It is influenced by physical, social, economic, political, and technological forces and, in turn, it influences the environment in which it is practiced. In the years to come, new and exciting challenges will require the attention of executives, managers, and personnel specialists. Many professional and technical persons whose areas of responsibility and interest involve various aspects of human resources management, as well as legislators, judges, government officials, educators, and union officials, will be required to meet the demands of our rapidly changing society.

Your enrollment in a human resources management course indicates that you have probably chosen a career path either in a human resources department or in managing subordinates so that you can practice what you have learned. If you are considering human resources management as a career, the opportunities and ways to prepare for them that are discussed in this chapter should be helpful.

LOOKING AHEAD IN HUMAN RESOURCES MANAGEMENT

Significant changes in the field of human resources management are occurring rapidly as a result of the dynamic interaction of all the forces that help to determine its role in an organization. Therefore, to obtain a true assessment of its status at a given moment is difficult. Any attempt to predict its role in the future presents similar difficulties. However, we can logically assume that the major challenges confronting human resources management that were discussed in Part 1 will continue in the future.

Major Issues and Events

As we look back over the evolution of human resources management, it is apparent that in each period there were major issues to be faced. Walker points out, for example, that in the 1960s the major problem was balancing supply and demand of different categories of personnel. In the 1970s the emphasis was upon affirmative action and equal employment opportunities. He predicted correctly that the emphasis in the 1980s would be on work and career management. In the 1990s and beyond 2000, the emphasis is predicted to be upon individual autonomy within large-scale work organizations.[1] A study of Figure 22–1, information from Walker's article, reveals many new challenges that will confront human resources departments. Such challenges require flexibility and adaptability on the part of members of these departments who will be called upon to adapt their techniques to meet the new conditions and events.

We observed in Chapter 1 that human resources management has gone through various stages of development since the turn of this century. Nkomo points out quite candidly that "the personnel function has undergone a transition from organizational

---

1. James Walker, "Human Resource Planning: An Odyssey to 2001 and Beyond," *Pittsburgh Business Review*, Vol. 47, No. 1 (March, 1978), pp. 2–8.

Figure 22–1 Human Resources Management in the Future

PERIODS AND EMPHASIS	CONDITIONS AND EVENTS	TECHNIQUES INTRODUCED OR EMPHASIZED
1980s Work and Career Management (all employees)	Consolidation of federal law governing personnel practices and administration Aging of the work force Competition among young managers for responsibility Accelerated unionization of professionals and managers Expansion of adult education Stronger pressures for egalitarian practices in pay and employment Participation in management more commonplace Increased pressures on human resources for cost control and profit contribution	Job-related criteria for personnel decisions (hires, promotions, pay, terminations, etc.) Individual career planning Activity analysis as a tool for designing jobs, forecasting needs, organization, etc. Flexible work schedules Direct access to computer systems Clarification of management commitments in human resource management; policy changes
1990s and beyond 2000 Individual Autonomy Within Large-Scale Work Organizations (all employees)	Energy, food, other resource shortages Limited work available; increased leisure time Stress on family, privacy, personal independence Extended life expectancy, improved health Legislation governing pensions, health insurance, and lifetime income security Political/social challenge to large institutions; drive for individual freedom, autonomy and recognition	Reshaping of work environments and customs Work sharing; reduced workweek Job matching/career guidance aided by government and employers New careers in emerging fields of communications, health, energy sciences, etc. Measurement and auditing of human resource changes as part of management accounting Extended vacations, sabbaticals

SOURCE: James Walker, "Human Resource Planning: An Odyssey to 2001 and Beyond," *Pittsburgh Business Review*, Vol. 47, No. 1 (March, 1978), pp. 2–8. Reproduced with the permission of the Graduate School of Business, University of Pittsburgh.

stepchild to a potentially premier force in the organization's ability to survive and grow." She notes that the personnel function has emerged into the stage that "cements the interdependent relationship between human resources capabilities and the strategic success of the organization."[2]

Strategic Human Resources Management

The current stage in human resources management with its emphasis upon strategic planning reflects the impact of government regulations, economic factors, and social changes in the work environment. Throughout this book we have stressed the influence that government regulations have on the policies and procedures for the various personnel functions (planning and recruiting, selection, training and development, performance evaluation, labor relations, and compensation). Economic factors, especially those contributing to increased labor costs and stagnating productivity, have been described as matters of concern to human resources managers. Emerging social trends involving the quality of work life, greater participation in decision making, and other employee demands have made it clear that these managers will be required to bear greater responsibilities.

To perform its strategic planning role effectively, the human resources management program must contain the following features:

1. Human resources planning must be an integral part of the organization's strategic planning process. The interrelationship between organizational goals and human resource requirements and capabilities must be made explicit.
2. Managers should be alert to internal and external threats, opportunities, and trends that may have an impact on the strategic success of the organization.
3. Human resources objectives must be specific, realistic, and measurable, and their projected date of achievement must be stated.[3]

When 93 chief executive officers were asked to indicate which areas of human resources management should receive increased attention, they said that the most important activities, in order of importance, are: productivity improvement, employee communications, management succession planning, management education and development, and performance appraisal.[4]   Other areas, as shown in Table 22–1, were indicated as needing attention but were considered to be of lesser importance. The CEOs thought that only two activities were receiving adequate attention: EEO/AA and personnel policies. Both of these subjects indeed have received considerable attention in the past few years.

2. Stella M. Nkomo, "Stage Three in Personnel Administration: Strategic Human Resources Management," *Personnel*, Vol. 57, No. 4 (July-August, 1980), pp. 69–77.
3. *Ibid.*
4. Roy Foltz, Karn Rosenberg, and Julie Foehrenbach, "Senior Management Views the Human Resource Function," *Personnel Administrator*, Vol. 27, No. 9 (September, 1982), pp. 37–51.

Table 22–1 **Areas That Should Receive Increased Attention in Human Resources Management, According to CEOs**

RANKING	SUBJECT	NUMBER	PERCENT*
1	Productivity improvement	29	31.2
2	Employee communications	26	30.0
3/4	Management succession planning	19	20.4
3/4	Management education & development	19	20.4
5	Performance appraisal	15	16.1
6/7	Career planning & development	13	14.0
6/7	Performance incentives (e.g., bonuses)	13	14.0
8	Job design	12	12.9
9	Controlling benefit costs	11	11.8
10	Forecasting staffing needs	9	9.7
11/12	Identification & evaluation of talent	7	7.5
11/12	Technical training & education	7	7.5
13/14	Maintaining a safe work environment	5	5.4
13/14	Determining competitive pay levels	5	5.4
15/16	Merit pay	4	4.3
15/16	Determining competitive benefit levels	4	4.3
15/16	Monitoring staff levels	3	3.2
17/18/19	Executive recruiting	3	3.2
17/18/19	Job evaluation & internal equity	3	3.2
20	Union-management relations	2	2.2
21/22/23	Maintaining adequate plant staffing	1	1.1
21/22/23	Outplacement	1	1.1
21/22/23	Flexible working hours	1	1.1

*Based on total number (93) responding to this question.

SOURCE: Roy Foltz, Karn Rosenberg, and Julie Foehrenbach, "Senior Management Views the Human Resource Function." Reprinted from the September, 1982 issue of *Personnel Administrator*, copyright, 1982, The American Society for Personnel Administration, 30 Park Drive, Berea, OH 44017, $30 per year.

Status of Human Resources Managers

It is being recognized more and more that the work of the human resources manager is as vital to the success of an organization as that of the line managers in production, finance, and sales who traditionally have received the primary attention of top management. For too long the human resources manager was relegated to a subordinate position that provided for little voice in important matters. This fact has often been the result of top management's attitude toward employees and their role in the organization. Sometimes it is the result of the human resources manager's inability to function as an executive. There is an increasing realization, therefore, that human resources managers must not only prepare themselves for performance of an executive quality but also be encouraged to play a more active managerial role. The nature of the role will depend largely upon top management and the individual manager's own orientation.

Role as Consultant.

By assuming a consulting role, such as that described in Chapter 3, human resources managers view themselves as being service-oriented by responding to client demands. Implicit within this role is the need for human resources professionals to perceive themselves as being accountable for their performance and that of their staffs.[5] The human resources manager, like an outside consultant, must have a total view of the organization, must be knowledgeable of all functional elements, and must be aware of the organization's strategic challenges.

Role as Change Agent.

A somewhat more assertive role for the human resources manager is to deal with confrontation and conflict and, like an organizational development (OD) specialist, assume responsibility as a change agent or innovator. Organizational development basically is a method for facilitating change and development in *people* (styles, values, skills), in *technology* (greater simplicity, complexity), and in *organizational processes* (relationships, roles). For example, if a human resources manager wants to introduce a form of participative management where a paternalistic style has traditionally existed, he or she would have to become an "inside change agent."[6]

Frame and Luthans go so far as to advocate the merger of organizational development and human resources activities when they say that:

> . . . Power and authority issues provide especially important reasons for a personnel/OD merger. The new role of the personnel manager calls for expert power and the demonstrated ability to help solve broad organizational problems rather than power based on bureaucratic authority. Integration can contribute to the desired power-authority relationship between personnel and the rest of the organization by moving it toward the consultant-client relationship found in OD.

> For example, OD can help personnel with creating and implementing techniques such as flexible working hours, early retirement, second careers, or life-planning activities. Personnel with help from OD can conduct employee surveys and other approaches such as following up on problems identified via various upward communications programs involving employees. Equal employment opportunity programs can also get help from an OD perspective for positive organizational change. An enlightened approach to affirmative action starts with the development of an organizational climate that is supportive and encouraging for minorities and women. Such a climate can be created through a combined personnel/OD effort. . . .

---

5. James W. Peters and Edward A. Mabry, "The Personnel Officer as Internal Consultant," *Personnel Administrator*, Vol. 26, No. 4 (April, 1981), pp. 29–32, 49.

6. Phillip L. Hunsaker, "Strategies for Organizational Change: The Role of the Inside Change Agent," *Personnel*, Vol. 59, No. 5 (September-October, 1982), pp. 18–28.

A merger will not only mutually benefit personnel and OD but, most importantly, meet the challenge of more effective human resource management now and in the future.[7]

Finally, in addition to being concerned with the various elements of the internal environment, the human resources manager will have to be concerned far more than ever with the impact of the external environment on the organization. There is no doubt that more will be demanded of tomorrow's executive—in study, in planning, and in action.

As human resources managers attain increased status and are successful in attacking broader and more significant problems, it will be possible for them to make even greater contributions to the organization and to society than they have made in the past. Their success and their contributions will serve to challenge managerial and supervisory personnel at all levels and will also stimulate individuals to consider staff jobs as attractive opportunities for employment.

CAREER OPPORTUNITIES IN HUMAN RESOURCES MANAGEMENT

Throughout this book we have attempted to clarify and to distinguish between the responsibilities of line managers and supervisors and those of the human resources staff in the performance of the personnel functions. It is likely that some interest in this type of activity—in either a line or staff capacity—has been stimulated by the discussions of the various functions. The available career opportunities and how to prepare for them are discussed in this section.

Line Jobs

If you are interested in the daily face-to-face contacts with employees, you should not overlook the possibilities of achieving your goals through managerial or supervisory jobs. In these jobs, opportunities are provided for creating conditions that will motivate subordinates to maximize their productivity. In addition to trying to bring out the best in each subordinate, there is the challenge of building a smoothly functioning work team. Managerial and supervisory jobs require human relations skills, as well as an understanding of the principles and practices followed in human resources management. In selecting personnel for these jobs, the focus in the past was on training and experience in production, marketing, and finance. Today companies in the United States are beginning to demand that business schools supply them with graduates who are also trained in human resources management.[8]

---

7. Robert M. Frame and Fred Luthans, "Merging Personnel and OD: A Not-So-Odd Couple," *Personnel*, Vol. 54, No. 1 (January/February, 1977), pp. 12–22.

8. "Hard times push B-schools into basics," *Business Week* (August 30, 1982), pp. 23–24.

Staff Jobs

A survey conducted by the American Society for Personnel Administration and The Bureau of National Affairs reveals that human resources departments are constantly undergoing changes in the emphasis they give to various personnel functions. Companies report that the number of new personnel functions or programs being added is greater than reductions in existing functions or programs.[9] The findings of this and other surveys indicate that there will be career opportunities for many individuals who are interested in and qualified for this challenging type of work.

Types of Staff Jobs.
Among the staff jobs in human resources management that are included or implied in various chapters of this book are the following:

Systems and Procedures Analyst	Chapter 3
Job Analyst	Chapter 4
Organizational Planning Manager	Chapter 5
Employment Interviewer, Employment Manager	Chapter 6
EEO Coordinator/Specialist, Director of Testing	Chapter 7
Training Director/Specialist, Employee Orientation Specialist, Director of Management Development	Chapter 8
Career Development Specialist	Chapter 9
Labor Relations Director/Specialist	Chapter 14
Compensation Manager/Specialist	Chapter 17
Benefits Administrator/Specialist, Recreation Director	Chapter 19
Safety Director/Specialist, Employee Counselor	Chapter 20
Employee Opinion Analyst	Chapter 21

This listing of jobs includes those that are typically found in a large organization. In smaller organizations there may be fewer jobs in human resources management. As a result, a staff employee may be responsible for performing a wider variety of functions in a small organization than in a large organization.

Predictions for Employment Opportunities.
Opportunities for employment and advancement concern all persons who are choosing a career. The following predictions for employees in human resources management were reported in the

---

9. *Bulletin to Management*, No. 1689 (Washington, DC: The Bureau of National Affairs, Inc., August 5, 1982), p. 9.

Occupational Outlook Handbook (1982–1983), a government publication widely used by career counselors and others who must have a sound basis for the information furnished to their clients:

1. The number of personnel and labor relations specialists is expected to grow about as fast as the average for all occupations through the 1980s. Most of this growth will occur in the private sector.
2. Within public personnel administration, opportunities probably will be best in state and local governments.
3. Increased record keeping and reporting requirements, as well as legal requirements, will stimulate demand for personnel and labor relations workers.
4. The amount of money spent on employee training in the public and private sectors is expected to increase in the decade ahead. Expansion in this area will contribute to the projected increase in the number of personnel and labor relations specialists during the 1980s.
5. Particularly keen competition is anticipated for jobs in labor relations. Opportunities are best for applicants with a master's degree or a strong undergraduate major in industrial relations, economics, or business. A law degree is an asset.[10]

Salaries. Most students are interested in the financial opportunities in a career. Because of changing conditions, it is not possible to quote figures on salaries that will be valid for a very long period of time. However, recent figures that are cited in Table 22–2 may be of some value for planning purposes.

Table 22–2 **Median Incomes for Human Resources Jobs**

Top Personnel/Industrial Relations Executive	$42,780
Top Employee and Community Relations Executive	38,803
Labor Relations Manager	38,341
EEO/AA Manager	31,749
Compensation and Benefits Manager	30,847
Organizational Development Manager	29,220
Recruitment Manager	28,115
Employee Services Manager	27,200
Employment Manager	26,135
Recruiter (Professional/Managerial Personnel)	24,700
Compensation Analyst	21,980
Personnel Information Systems Specialist	21,000

(Based on data from more than 1,100 organizations)

SOURCE: Abbott, Langer and Associates, 548 First Street, Crete, IL 60417. Reproduced with permission.

10. United States Department of Labor, *Occupational Outlook Handbook*, Bulletin No. 2200 (Washington, DC: U. S. Government Printing Office, 1982–1983 edition), p. 45.

Working Conditions.   Since personnel offices are usually located where outside visitors and prospective employees are free to enter, they tend to be modern and pleasant places in which to work. Personnel specialists usually work a standard 35- to 40-hour week. Labor relations specialists, however, may work longer hours, particularly when contract agreements are being prepared and negotiated. Although most personnel specialists spend their time in the office, some of them travel extensively. Recruiters, for example, regularly attend professional meetings and visit college campuses to interview prospective employees.[11]

Consulting Jobs

Human resources managers frequently go outside of the organization for professional assistance from qualified consultants. These consultants are utilized in connection with a variety of specific human resources problems. In the past, most of the consulting firms specialized in one or two areas of expertise. More recently, however, many of them have broadened their expertise to cover other fields and thus meet the needs of their clients more effectively.[12] The areas for which consultants are used most frequently are pension plans, executive recruitment, health and welfare plans, psychological assessment, wage and salary administration, job evaluation, and executive compensation.[13]

Individuals who have received general training in human resources management and who have developed expertise in one or more of the areas for which consultants are frequently used may wish to consider joining a consulting firm. Alternatively, they may offer their services on a self-employment basis after obtaining sufficient experience in the field.

Other Jobs

If you are interested in jobs involving the utilization of human resources, you may wish to consider opportunities that are available in other types of organizations. Labor unions, for example, employ several types of staff specialists who are trained in the various personnel functions to study trends and to make recommendations to union management. Pensions, benefits, and compensation plans are areas of major interest to the unions. As noted earlier, individuals with an undergraduate major in either industrial relations, economics, or business, along with a law degree, may wish to consider labor relations as a career field.

Other related jobs include those of occupational safety and health inspector, employment counselor, industrial engineer, rehabilitation counselor, college placement counselor, psychologist, and sociologist.

---

11. *Ibid.*, p. 44.
12. "The New Shape of Management Consulting," *Business Week* (May 21, 1979), pp. 97–104.
13. *BNA Policy and Practice Series—Personnel Management,* (Washington, DC: The Bureau of National Affairs, Inc., 1971), pp. 251:351–356.

PREPARING FOR A CAREER IN HUMAN RESOURCES MANAGEMENT

Students should understand the occupational world and the opportunities within it. Equally important is the fact that they understand themselves—their abilities, aptitudes, interests, and personality characteristics. Students may find it helpful to consult with professors, faculty advisers, or counselors to further their knowledge of human resources management and to gain a better understanding of themselves.

Academic Training

Most of the human resources jobs listed on page 550 usually require that an individual have training and/or experience in order to qualify for them. In recent years, college training for these jobs has been emphasized. The college training may be at the undergraduate level, the graduate level, or both.

Undergraduate Study.   In the past, many human resources professionals entered the field with degrees in liberal arts and sciences and perhaps a few basic business courses taken as electives. However, as accreditation requirements and other factors become essential for professional status, a bachelor's degree and possibly a master's degree in business will be needed to enter the field. Hoyt and Lewis recommend three broad areas of knowledge and skills for the undergraduate student: (1) general education in behavioral sciences, English, communication, psychology, and mathematics; (2) the common body of business knowledge (accounting, marketing, economics, etc.); and (3) specialized courses such as human resources management law and human relations.[14]   In addition to these courses, it is desirable for students to take courses in such specific areas as personnel and organizational psychology, industrial sociology, economics, industrial engineering, and electronic data processing.

A knowledge of computer operations is essential for processing and reporting personnel data that reflect the performance of the human resources program. Such reports are necessary for planning purposes and for determining compliance with laws and regulations. While learning about the uses of computers, it is desirable to become knowledgeable about the designing of research and the use of statistics in personnel research.[15]   The availability of computers facilitates the accomplishment of research studies. It will also inevitably stimulate more research in areas where heretofore only feeble attempts could be made to study the many complexities of human behavior in the work situation. In the final analysis, however, it is the researcher who has to do the research, not the computer.

Activities outside of the classroom and the library can provide valuable experiences. In fact, many recruiters are as interested in the extracurricular activities of prospective job applicants as they are in academic success. Positions of leadership

14. Daniel R. Hoyt and J. D. Lewis, "Planning for a Career in Human Resource Management," *Personnel Administrator*, Vol. 25, No. 10 (October, 1980), pp. 53–54, 67–68.
15. See suggested readings at the end of this chapter.

in student organizations, publication staffs, and other organizations often provide experiences that are comparable to those found on the job. Participation in a student chapter of the American Society for Personnel Administration, in Delta Sigma Pi or Alpha Kappa Psi, is especially valuable.

Graduate Study. In the past three decades, graduate degree programs in business schools have expanded considerably. Undergraduates often ask if they should pursue a graduate course of study. To obtain an answer to this question, Harper and Stephens conducted a survey among personnel practitioners who are accredited members of the ASPA. The survey asked whether a graduate degree is important for the 1980s and 1990s.

Table 22-3 summarizes the opinions of the respondents in the survey mentioned above. The results show that a master's degree is considered important by this group of practitioners in which 46 percent hold graduate degrees while 54 percent hold bachelor's degrees or less. When the same group of practitioners was asked what graduate degree is most appropriate, the MBA with expanded elective specialization in personnel and labor relations was preferred to a specialized MA or MS degree and a general MBA.[16]

Personal Qualifications

The academic training that the prospective human resources specialist acquires should provide a broad understanding of the special knowledge and skills needed for work in the field. Success, however, is dependent upon more than academic training.

Table 22–3 **Importance of a Specialized Degree in Personnel/Labor for the 1980s and 1990s**

STATEMENT: A master's in personnel and/or labor will be increasingly important in the 80s and 90s.			
Response	**No.**	**%**	**% (Cumulative)**
Strongly agree	122	40.1	40.1%
Agree	135	44.4	84.5
Slightly agree	29	9.5	94.1
Slightly disagree	17	5.6	99.7
Disagree	1	.3	100.0

SOURCE: Earl Harper and David B. Stephens, "Personnel and Labor Relations Master's Degrees for the '80s and '90s." Reprinted from the November, 1982 issue of *Personnel Administrator,* copyright, 1982, The American Society for Personnel Administration, 30 Park Drive, Berea, OH 44017, $30 per year.

16. Earl Harper and David B. Stephens, "Personnel and Labor Relations Master's Degrees for the '80s and '90," *Personnel Administrator,* Vol. 27, No. 11 (November, 1982), pp. 53–56.

Personal qualities are also important. We can have a better understanding of what personal qualities are important by referring to an American Management Associations study of 1,460 American managers. When asked what personal qualities or characteristics they look for in employees, integrity is the quality that tops the list. Determination, competency, and dependability also rank high.[17]

In addition to these qualities, we believe that it is important for the human resources specialist to be able to understand both the employee's and the management's point of view. Other important personal qualities are fairmindedness, a persuasive and congenial personality, an understanding attitude toward human behavior, and the ability to listen effectively.

Employment Experiences

Employers not only attempt to make an analysis of the applicants' personal characteristics and academic training, but also look for employment experiences that may be related to success in human resources management. While each employer has different opinions of what experiences are most desirable, many of them believe that work experience at the operating level or experience in some type of leadership position can provide a good background for human resources management. Through experiences of this type, the individual probably has learned something about the problems of motivating personnel and has developed some human relations skills.

PLANNING A CAREER IN HUMAN RESOURCES MANAGEMENT

As part of the discussion of career development programs in Chapter 9, we included a section on personal career development (see pages 221-226). You may wish to review the material on those pages where we covered such topics as making career decisions, choosing an appropriate career, and keeping a career in perspective. We also gave some suggestions on how to select an employer. When seeking employment in a human resources department, the employer's reputation or image should be considered. You should learn all that you can about that organization. It is essential to getting off to a good start in your career.

Knowledge of an Employer's Image

The word gets around about which companies have forward-looking policies and programs in human resources management. It soon spreads to campuses and affects the recruitment of college and university graduates. In one survey by Malone and Petersen, executives were asked to identify business firms that had effective or ineffective human resources departments. Of all the firms that could have been selected, nine were chosen more than once as having effective human resources

---

17. Warren H. Schmidt and Barry Z. Posner, *Managerial Values and Expectations—The Silent Power in Personal and Organizational Life,* An AMA Survey Report (New York: American Management Associations, 1982), pp. 42-46.

departments. One firm was mentioned more than once as having an ineffective department. Top management support was viewed as the key ingredient for the success of the personnel functions. The extent of participation by human resources managers in establishing company policies and plans was the second most important factor.[18]

Career Paths

The college graduate without full-time experience in human resources management who is employed by a small organization or by a branch of a large organization may be placed in the position of human resources manager. That position typically entails responsibility for handling most of the human resources functions, except perhaps those concerned with labor relations. In a medium-size organization, the same individual would not start at the manager level. He or she would probably be given an assignment in selection, in nontechnical training, or some other phase of the human resources program that is not dependent upon a broad background of experience. The initial assignment for an individual hired by a large organization employing thousands of persons would likely be that of job analyst, employment interviewer, test administrator, or human resources specialist. The title of human resources specialist may include responsibility for a wide variety of functions including the collection, tabulation, and analysis of test scores, exit interviews, and compensation.

In a large organization there are typically many opportunities to move upward in human resources management either in one location or by transferring to a different location. Figure 22-2 illustrates a typical line of advancement in the personnel area at Pfizer, a large multinational corporation.

It is desirable for individuals who aspire to become human resources managers to seek out and eagerly accept responsible rotational assignments to line management positions. Even if one has no aspiration for the executive suite, such a tour can be highly beneficial to the human resources specialist as well as to the organization.[19]

A few individuals have become chief executive officers after specializing in human resources management. However, this field is not one of the functional areas that is rated as the fastest "route to the top" at the present time or in the near future, according to a representative sample of senior-level executives.[20] It is possible, however, that more human resources executives may become chief executive officers as they assume greater responsibilities in their present roles and as their contribution to the bottom line is recognized. This possibility is likely to increase in the future.

---

18. Robert L. Malone and Donald J. Petersen, "Personnel Effectiveness: Its Dimensions and Development," *Personnel Journal,* Vol. 56, No. 10 (October, 1977), pp. 498–501.

19. Robert H. Meehan, "The Future Personnel Executive," *Personnel Administrator,* Vol. 26, No. 1 (January, 1981), pp. 25–28.

20. John Sussman, "Profile of the Successful Personnel Executive," *Personnel Administrator,* Vol. 25, No. 2 (February, 1980), pp. 77–82.

Figure 22–2 A Typical Line of Advancement in Personnel

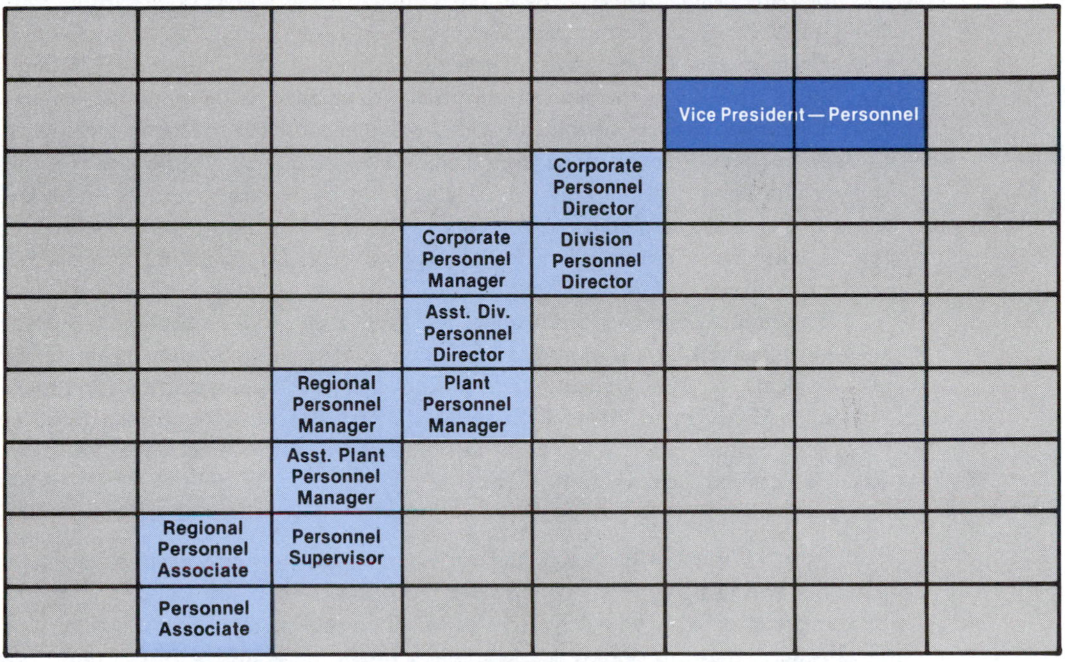

						Vice President — Personnel	
				Corporate Personnel Director			
			Corporate Personnel Manager	Division Personnel Director			
			Asst. Div. Personnel Director				
		Regional Personnel Manager	Plant Personnel Manager				
		Asst. Plant Personnel Manager					
	Regional Personnel Associate	Personnel Supervisor					
	Personnel Associate						

SOURCE: "Imagine Yourself at Pfizer," Pfizer, Inc. Reproduced with permission.

Growth with the Profession

Like all professions, human resources management is ever changing. Changes in the internal and external environments of organizations require continual study and revision of policies and procedures. The human resources practitioner must not only be alert to changes as they occur, but also must anticipate them. In order to keep current in the field, it is essential to utilize the many sources of information and assistance that are available. In addition, it is important to continue to develop one's understanding and skills that contribute to increased personal effectiveness on and off the job.

Keeping Current.   Probably the most efficient and dependable way to keep current in one's field is by reading. There are scores of journals and general business and management periodicals containing articles of concern to the human resources specialist. One should subscribe to several of the journals listed in Chapter 1, in addition to those that cover specialized areas such as training, labor law, etc. Before subscribing to a journal, it is advisable to examine several issues of it in a library. In selecting journals. for regular reading either on a subscription basis and/or in a library, it would be helpful to consult the *ASPA Handbook of Personnel and Industrial Relations—Professional PAIR*. This handbook contains an excellent chapter written by the librarians of the Industrial Relations Centers of the University of Minnesota and the University of California, Berkeley.

Herman and Lloyd provide detailed analyses of the content of 75 journals. Figure 22–3 illustrates the type of information contained in their analyses. They also provide detailed analyses of the subject coverage of looseleaf reporting services, a few of which have been cited in this book. Their chapter is filled with valuable suggestions on keeping up to date. In addition to reading journals and looseleaf reports, they advise looking for shortcuts in reading by making use of book reviews, special columns or features in journals, special abstracts including computer-based services, and newsletters.[21]

The human resources professional will find it essential to become a member of such organizations as the American Society for Personnel Administration (ASPA), the Academy of Management, and, for government employees, the International Personnel Management Association (IPMA). Attendance at the annual meetings of these organizations and participation in seminars and workshops offered by them are vital to keeping current in the field.

Improving Other Skills.

Reading skills, oral and written communication skills, planning and using time effectively, and motivating others are important for success in managerial jobs. If you perceive a need for improvement, there are many sources of assistance. It is probably best to explore self-help programs before turning to more expensive methods. Libraries and bookstores are filled with books, pamphlets, audio tapes, and video tapes that can be used on an individual basis.[22] Colleges and universities offer instruction in many subjects related to personal growth at moderate cost. Associations such as the American Management Associations, ASPA, as well as professional consultants, have programs designed to increase personal effectiveness.

Challenges and Rewards

We have attempted to present the work in human resources management as accurately as possible. This type of work, like any other, has its rewards and its deficiencies. It is, however, a type of work that presents many challenges. If you are interested in this field, you should explore its career possibilities further. Where more information is needed, a qualified counselor is likely to prove helpful. Employees who hold jobs in human resources management may also be consulted. You should make a decision only after a careful evaluation of all available information.

---

21. Georgianna Herman and Gwendolyn Lloyd, "PAIR Literature: Keeping Up To Date," *ASPA Handbook of Personnel and Industrial Relations—Professional PAIR* (Washington, DC: The Bureau of National Affairs, Inc., 1979), Chapter 8.5, pp. 8-114—8-139.

22. For an interesting discussion of this topic as well as an annotated bibliography of books, see George S. Odiorne, *Personal Effectiveness—A Strategy for Success* (Westfield, MA: MBO, Inc., 157 Pontoosic Road, Westfield, MA, 01085, 1979).

Figure 22-3 **Subject Coverage of Personnel and Industrial Relations (PAIR) Journals**

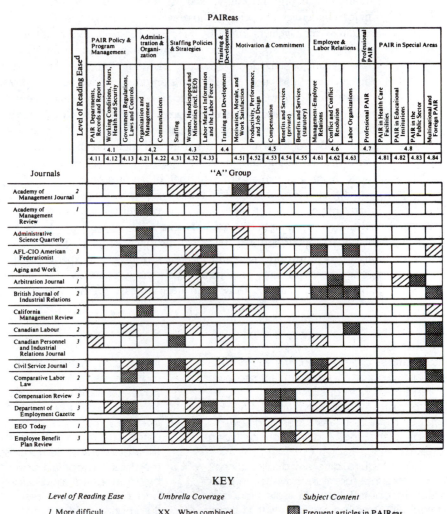

KEY

Level of Reading Ease

1 More difficult

2 Difficult

3 Less difficult

Umbrella Coverage

XX When combined, these journals provide good umbrella coverage of private-sector PAIR in the United States.

Subject Content

▨ Frequent articles in PAIReas

▧ Occasional articles

☐ Infrequent or no articles

SOURCE: Reprinted by permission from "PAIR Literature: Keeping Up To Date," *ASPA Handbook of Personnel and Industrial Relations—Professional PAIR*, copyright 1979, by The Bureau of National Affairs, Inc., Washington, DC.

RÉSUMÉ

Human resources management in the future is likely to be even more dynamic than in the past. Technological, social, and economic developments are occurring at an increasingly faster pace. As a result, the effective utilization of human resources in an individual organization, as well as in the total economy, constitutes one of the major challenges of society. Those who are engaged in the many facets of human resources management must be prepared to meet this challenge.

To perform its role effectively, human resources planning must be an integral part of an organization's strategic planning process. Areas in human resources management that need more attention are: productivity improvement, employee communications, management succession planning, management development, and performance appraisal. Human resources practitioners can expect that many phases of their work will continue to be controlled by laws and regulations. Meeting human needs and problems of a social nature will demand increasing attention. In order to perform their responsibilities most effectively, human resources managers will have to move from a consultant role to that of an innovator.

If you are interested in human resources management as a career, there are many opportunities in line, staff, and consulting positions, as well as with unions. Although the number of jobs in this field is projected to increase over the next decade, competition for these jobs is also increasing. Undergraduate specialization and graduate study are recommended. As you gain experience in personnel work, advancement to more responsible positions is generally possible. Such opportunities are likely to come to those who keep abreast of the field.

DISCUSSION QUESTIONS

1. What features are necessary for the human resources program to perform its strategic planning role most effectively?
2. In this chapter two different roles of human resources managers were described.
   a. What is the major difference between them?
   b. Do they require different qualifications?
3. Which personnel functions have been most subject to control through legislation and regulations? Describe the effects that these controls have had on human resources practitioners.
4. What steps should a college student who is interested in human resources management as a career take to prepare for it?
5. Why do individuals have to assume the initiative for keeping up to date once they qualify for a job? How can they keep up with the changes?
6. If you are interested in human resources management, what experiences could you have now that would be similar to those that you would be likely to find in a job?
7. Interview a number of people who work for different companies. Ask them to give you their opinions of human resources management as it is carried on in their companies by managerial and supervisory personnel and by the human resources department. Summarize your findings and comment on their implications for supervisory and staff personnel.
8. Make arrangements through your instructor to visit the human resources department of one or more organizations. Talk with the human resources manager and staff about their work, including its rewards and frustrations.

SUGGESTED READINGS

Douglass, Merrill E., and Donna N. Douglass. *Manage Your Time, Manage Your Work, Manage Yourself.* New York: AMACOM, American Management Associations, 1980.

Ginzberg, Eli, Daniel Quinn Mills, John D. Owen, Harold L. Sheppard, and Michael L. Wachter. *Work Decisions in the 1980s.* Boston: Auburn House Publishing Company, 1982.

London, Manuel, and Stephen A. Stumpf. *Managing Careers.* Reading, MA: Addison-Wesley Publishing Company, 1982.

Lynch, Edith M. *Decades: Lifestyle Changes in Career Expectations.* New York: AMACOM, American Management Associations, 1980.

Meyers, Lawrence S., and Neal E. Grossen. *Behavioral Research: Theory, Procedure and Design*, 2d ed. San Francisco: W. H. Freeman and Company, 1977.

Stone, Eugene. *Research Methods in Organizational Behavior.* Santa Monica, CA: Goodyear Publishing Company, 1978.

Toffler, Alvin. *The Third Wave.* New York: William Morrow and Company, Inc., 1980.

Wolf, William B. *Top Management of the Personnel Function: Current Issues and Practices.* Ithaca, NY: New York State School of Industrial and Labor Relations, 1980.

Decision Making in a Japanese Subsidiary

Helen Stein was a graduate of the University of Texas with a major in human resources management. Unable to obtain a position in her major field, she was forced to accept initial employment in the operating department of a large oil company. Eventually, however, she was successful in obtaining a position as an employment interviewer with an aerospace company. In this company she advanced to the position of assistant manager of the personnel department. When the Tormaru Electronics Company established a manufacturing plant on the West Coast, she was hired by Soji Takashima, the plant manager, as the manager of human resources for the plant.

Although Mr. Takashima was a citizen of Japan, he had worked for several years in the United States and had become familiar with American management practices. His engineering and operations managers, however, were brought directly from Japan to help open the plant. In the opinion of Ms. Stein, they were still "very Japanese." Ms. Stein was able to work well with Mr. Takashima and to establish a human resources program which reflected the management philosophies of the parent company. However, she did encounter a number of frustrations in attempting to adjust to the Japanese style of management. One such frustration perhaps can best be described in Ms. Stein's own words:

A few months after I assumed my present position, Mr. Takashima stopped by my office to tell me that additional personnel were needed on the second shift to meet a temporary backlog of orders. However, he did not want to hire new personnel and then be forced to lay them off when they no longer were needed. Company policy required that we avoid any layoffs if at all possible. The natural solution to our dilemma appeared to me to be one of using temporary employees who could be obtained through one of the local temporary help services. After all, layoffs by other electronics firms had created a pool of experienced workers within the area from which temporary help could be recruited.

Mr. Takashima agreed enthusiastically with my suggestion and I was all for making inquiries with some of the local services. However, before my proposal could be translated into action it first had to be approved by the executive committee. Since my proposal had the plant manager's approval, I considered the committee's review and approval to be only a formality. After presenting what I considered to be adequate justification of my recommendation at a special meeting of the committee, it was put to a vote. Each member voted in favor of my proposal except for Mr. Imada, the operations manager. Hoping to discover a basis for overcoming his objections, I asked him why he voted against it. His reply was, "I don't like it," and that was the only reason I could draw from him. The committee deliberated over the problem for quite some time but was unable to get Mr. Imada to agree. In spite of the fact that the majority of the committee members favored my proposal, Mr. Takashima refused to allow it to be implemented because of Mr. Imada's opposition. As a result, the plant failed to deliver some orders on schedule in spite of the extensive use of overtime.

Where I worked before, in a situation such as this one the plant manager would not have hesitated to approve a proposal supported overwhelmingly by the executive committee, even if the operations manager objected to it. When I went home that night, I was really frustrated. But I've learned to accept the fact that this is a Japanese company and they may do some things differently from what I previously had been accustomed to expect.

a. How would you explain the plant manager's action in allowing the operations manager to veto the temporary-help proposal?

b. To what extent might his decision be a reflection of Japanese culture? Of good management practice?

case

2

The Layoff Task Force

For many years the state Department of Agriculture was responsible for meat inspection under a federal-state agreement that provided for joint funding. To perform its inspection responsibilities under the terms of the agreement, the state utilized 400 civil service employees who were employed at a number of locations throughout the state.

Shortly after the election of a new governor who was making a special effort to reduce the costs of state government, the Director of Agriculture decided to take advantage of a provision of the federal-state agreement. This provision stated that the federal government would assume full responsibility for the inspection program upon being given timely notice. The new state administration thereupon decided to terminate the agreement within a four-month period, thus transferring the entire inspection function back to the federal government. This decision meant the elimination of 400 state positions. Since the federal government already had enough staff to perform part of the function, it could only utilize 300 of the state employees. Furthermore, many of the state employees were experienced only in poultry inspection and did not possess the necessary qualifications for red-meat inspection with the federal agency.

In addition to being unable to find employment with the federal government for all of its inspectors, the state Department of Agriculture also found that many inspectors who were eligible for transfer to the federal program were not eager to do so for various reasons. Among these reasons were: (1) the need to take a 10 to 25 percent cut in pay, (2) the inability to develop meaningful retirement benefits because of age, (3) the necessity in some instances to relocate, and (4) a probationary period requirement of six months during which the employee could be terminated without any rights, including appeal. (In fact, several of the individuals with experience in poultry inspection rather than red-meat inspection were later rejected by the federal program during the probationary period.)

In order to meet the department's responsibilities to employees, its personnel manager recommended to the director of the department that a task force be formed to cope with the personnel matters created by the agreement termination. Approval was immediate, and within two days ten individuals were appointed from department administration and provided with office space for the project. The assistant personnel officer of the department was designated supervisor of the task force. Each of his assistants was a specialist in a specific area of government personnel operations, including job analysis, personnel transactions, and placement activities. Clerical and other staff personnel were also included in the task force.

Each employee performing meat inspections was informed of the purpose of the task force and encouraged to consult with its members about individual concerns and problems. These members were kept busy in interviewing individuals and meeting with groups of employees, as well as representatives of the unions, the state employees association, and the federal government. Employees were kept informed of results being achieved through face-to-face contact and by written communication, including a special newsletter in which questions most frequently asked were answered.

One of the major problems encountered by the task force involved state layoff procedures designed primarily to handle individual layoffs rather than a group of 400 cases. The civil service provision for a reduction in force is for seniority to govern rights to obtain a transfer or to accept a demotion to a position "in the same line of work." These provisions usually result in a person of lesser seniority being "bumped" to a lower paying position or even laid off.

Unfortunately the meaning of "in the same line of work" was not adequately defined in the provisions governing layoff. The organization representing the employees to be laid off maintained that all inspectors in the department were "in the same line of work." (There are nine inspectors in nine different agricultural specialties.[1]) The inspectors in the other specialties, who naturally wanted to avoid being "bumped," maintained that their classifications were not "in the same line of work." In addition, the task force supervisor and his staff recognized that differences between the job tasks of meat inspectors and those of other inspectors prevented the meat inspectors from bumping inspectors in the other job classes. Furthermore, if the trained personnel for other types of agricultural inspection were bumped by the large number of meat inspectors, the effectiveness of these programs would be severely jeopardized. Finally, the matter was referred to the State Personnel Board. In spite of union arguments, the board decided in favor of the task force's narrow interpretation of what constituted "the same line of work."

---

1. The classes of inspection jobs are: Brand Inspector, Livestock Inspector I and II, Meat and Food Inspector I and II, Egg and Poultry Quality Control Inspector, Field Crop Inspector, Fruit and Vegetable Quality Control Inspector, Feed and Agricultural Chemicals Inspector, Plant Quarantine Inspector, and Supervising Meat Inspector.

When the Governor's office learned what would happen to the meat inspectors as a result of transferring the programs to the federal government, it attempted unsuccessfully to get the federal government to change its rules. The Governor's office also made an attempt to pay the moving expenses, even for those employees who left the state service, but it was discovered that such payments would constitute an unlawful expenditure of state funds.

The transfer of the inspection program to the federal government ultimately resulted in some employees obtaining federal jobs or being forced to take early retirement. There were many others, however, who were left on the layoff list. Many of these individuals wanted to go out on their own and get a job in the state Department of Agriculture in another inspection category. However, according to the rules established by the State Personnel Board, the only way in which these individuals could get a job outside of meat inspection, brand inspection, or livestock inspection was to be appointed from the meat inspector layoff list, or to take the examination for the particular inspection job and be high enough on the list to be hired. The task force supervisor believed that this rule was unfair and appealed it to the State Personnel Board. Finally, the board agreed that the individuals on the layoff list who found a job on their own could be rehired without competing with the entire list of qualified candidates for that job or taking the examination for it. This relaxation of the rule permitted several of the individuals who were to be laid off to continue to work in the department where many of them had been employed for several years.

After four months of intensive work and devotion to the outplacement of the 400 individuals, the task force mission was accomplished with a high degree of success. But there was still another problem to be faced. Removal of the meat inspection program from the state government not only affected the amount that the state paid as its share of the program's costs, but also reduced the amount received from the federal government to cover the costs of providing overhead services, including personnel to administer the program. Since the state was no longer providing these services, approximately $500,000 was withdrawn immediately. This action triggered instant layoffs in administrative jobs, including some in the personnel division.

a. What are the apparent advantages of using a task force in this type of situation?

b. What factors should be considered in determining what constitutes "the same line of work?"

c. How can employee organizations be involved most effectively in a mass layoff?

d. Do you agree with the opinion of the task force supervisor that the individuals subject to layoff should not have to compete with the list of qualified candidates or take the examination for the job for which they may apply? Why or why not?

3

The Token Woman*

The Mainstream Life Insurance Company, to forestall possible censure by the Department of Health and Human Services because of the lack of women in the insurance industry's managerial ranks, decided to actively recruit a woman to fill a recent opening in the research division of the company's trust department. The vacant Research Analyst position was one of several middle management jobs at Mainstream which traditionally had been the stepping stone for promotion to the executive rank.

The required credentials for this particular opening in the research division of the trust department were an MBA degree (or a comparable graduate degree with a major emphasis in finance), at least two years of academic or business experience, and proven research capability in the investment field. An exhaustive search and meticulous screening resulted in the insurer's hiring Claire Meredith, an attractive 27-year-old single woman whose MS degree in finance was awarded "With Distinction" (that is, with high honors) and whose master's thesis was published by a prestigious university press. Meredith was previously employed as a broker in a highly respected Wall Street investment banking firm. In addition, she had authored numerous publications which were the result of extensive theoretical and applied research projects. Mainstream was able to hire Clair Meredith only after John Forbes, her potential immediate "boss," assured her of equal opportunity on all possible levels. Additional inducement to Meredith's accepting the Mainstream offer was supplied by the starting salary which was $2,000 higher than her other recent employment offers.

At the end of her third month on the job, Meredith privately acknowledged a pervasive feeling of frustration in connection with her new position. She began reviewing the activities of the past three months in an attempt to determine the basis of her negative reaction.

During the first day on the job, each of Meredith's colleagues had expressed enthusiastic delight at having her "on board." One colleague observed that "it's high time the company hired a woman for our section—we've needed some beautification of the office for a long time now." Another chimed in with the remark that "we better tell our wives that Claire is married so they won't think we're researching monkey business!" When Claire, in reply, suggested that they all have lunch together, Roy James, a division programmer, told her that "each of the guys brings a

*This case was prepared by Linda P. Fletcher, Temple University, and Susan M. Phillips, University of Iowa. From Robert D. Hay and Edmund R. Gray (eds.), *Business and Society: Cases and Text* (Cincinnati: South-Western Publishing Co., 1981), pp. 251–254. Reproduced with permission.

brown bag for lunch and we eat and talk shop in one or the other's office."
Accordingly, Claire decided to emulate her colleagues and announced that she was
joining the brown bag league. She was surprised, therefore, when at noon the
following day Roy opened his office door and urged, "Come on, you guys, let's
research our brown bags—Frank, you and Jim get the coffee while David and I get
the ice cream, and don't forget Don wants double cream in his coffee." Since Claire's
name was not mentioned specifically, she decided, after some hesitation, to eat alone
in her office. Claire did not feel she should join the secretaries and clerks for lunch
although she knew she would be welcome. This routine, with minor variations, was
then the established pattern.

Breaks for coffee in the company cafeteria were no exception to the seemingly
established separation principle—only once in that three-month interval was Claire
invited to join her colleagues for coffee. At that particular coffee break, Claire
remembered she felt particularly uncomfortable. Although she felt she had an
excellent working relationship with her associates, she had little in common with
them outside of the work environment. In addition, it was quite obvious that the
men in the division seemed to plan social gatherings for both after work and the
weekends. Although her colleagues were very friendly in the office, they never
seemed to think to include her in their plans.

Having reviewed the informal social structure of her employment, Claire
recognized similar frustrations with respect to various functional aspects of her
position. She recalled John Forbes, the head of the research division, explaining the
operational features of the section. "We meet once a week in committee to determine
the status of current projects, discuss proposals for the future, and make individual
assignments of new research projects to be initiated. Any ideas you have, write them
up in memo form for distribution to everyone prior to the next meeting and we'll all
go over your suggestion at the earliest possible meeting to determine the feasibility
of your idea."

Because she was the most recent addition to the staff, Claire deliberately
maintained a low profile during the first few weekly committee meetings of the
research division. The other members of the committee appeared to endorse her
strategy by seeking her opinions only infrequently and by failing to draw her into
their policy deliberations. During the fourth weekly gathering, John Forbes, who
acted as chairman, noted that his secretary was unable to be present as usual to
record the minutes of the meeting. Frank Howard suggested sending for a
replacement from the secretarial pool, but John Forbes shook his head and casually
replied that "a replacement is unnecessary since the logical substitute is Claire
Meredith. Besides, brushing up on her shorthand will give her something to do
during the meeting." Claire hastened to observe that "since I do not know
shorthand, I must decline the honor of this additional responsibility." At this point,
Claire recalled, she decided to abandon her sideline role at the next conclave of the
committee by presenting a research proposal that she had been developing in the area
of commission reduction through utilization of regional exchanges.

To date, Claire's specific assignments had included responsibility for several
ongoing projects which required only infrequent attention. The major portion of her
time, however, was spent on the "cost allocation" project. Cost allocation was a

computer system which would, when completed, provide complete investment information for each of Mainstream's trust customers. All trust funds were pooled for investment purposes. The pooling was necessary since some of the trust accounts were so small that investment income would be difficult to generate for these accounts. Any income would virtually be "wiped out" by the commission expenses of such small transactions.

The current method of determining investment income for each trust account was to apply the average new investment rate to the pro rata portion of each account's share of the total investment funds. Consequently, several of Mainstream's larger trust accounts had complained that their investment income was "supporting" the smaller accounts. Threatened with the loss of these large trust accounts, the financial vice-president of Mainstream, Bill Newbit, instructed John Forbes to develop some type of allocation system within his department so that each account could be properly charged with expenses while simultaneously enjoying the investment income of the pooled fund investment mechanism.

John Forbes developed the specifications for the cost allocation system and turned over the system design and programming to the research analyst who had resigned several months before Claire Meredith joined the division. She later found out through the grapevine that he had quit because he felt he was getting nowhere with cost allocation. Claire Meredith recalled that when she was hired, she was told she would have full responsibility for the completion of the system including supervising the programming by Roy James, developing comprehensive test data, and ultimately getting the system on line. Since investment income for each account was currently calculated by hand under the supervision of Frank Howard, Claire anticipated the usual problems of employee resistance to a new computer system. She therefore had begun some system orientation classes for the personnel involved. Claire had determined that the existing personnel, with training, would be adequate to effectively utilize and run the new system. No personnel displacement would be necessary.

Claire was currently in the final stages of testing the system with Roy, the programmer assigned to her. When she took the first run of the test data into John Forbes, he expressed complete surprise. He admitted, "I can't believe that cost allocation has ever gotten off the ground. This system has been knocking around for three years—we had just about counted the $800,000 development costs spent so far as sunk. In fact, we were going to write them off this year. I guess we'll have to start thinking about moving on this thing ... human resource planning and so on."

When Meredith left Forbes's office, she was shocked and disappointed at his reaction. As she reviewed his comments, she really began to wonder just what she was supposed to be doing at Mainstream and how she could go about doing it.

   a. Describe the informal social structure of the division.
   b. Why did Claire Meredith have "nothing in common" with her colleagues, as mentioned in connection with coffee breaks?
   c. What were the forces behind Claire Meredith's "pervasive feeling of frustration"?
   d. Discuss Claire Meredith's role in weekly policy committee meetings. How might she have changed her established role in these meetings?

4 Misplaced in a Brickyard

The Thermal Brick Company, which manufactures refractory bricks for use in furnaces and other areas exposed to high temperatures, employs about 300 persons. Most of the jobs in the plant require only minimal skill and training and are monotonous in nature. This fact creates a safety problem since it causes many workers to become disinterested in their work and to be involved in accidents. Because some of the jobs also are hazardous in nature, accident prevention is of major concern to the company. Consequently, the company has an extensive safety program which includes the usual instruction courses, as well as extensive rules governing work methods and the wearing of protective clothing.

Typical of the problems relating to morale and safety within the company was one involving Harry Moss, an employee who was hired by the company after he had completed two years of college. Harry was employed initially as a laborer and after six months became a kiln helper. This latter job consists of transferring the partially cured bricks from pallets to kiln cars on which the bricks are moved slowly through the heated kilns as a final step in the curing process. After this process is completed, the bricks are transferred by the kiln helper from the cars to the pallets on which they are shipped to customers. Kiln helpers, like the other employees, are given extensive safety instruction and are required to wear safety-toed shoes, hard hats, protective goggles, and a protective apron to reduce wear on clothing.

In spite of the safety training he had received, however, Harry became careless in the performance of his work, with the result that he received two warnings and a written reprimand from his supervisor. During his third year of employment, his carelessness caused him to be injured by a moving kiln car which struck him in the lumbar region of his back.

After being absent for eight weeks as a result of the injury, Harry was cleared by the company physician to return to work. Two days after his return he complained of severe back pains and requested and received an additional 30 days' leave. On the 29th day of this leave, his supervisor received a phone call from Harry's wife requesting a two-week extension of his leave which the supervisor refused to grant without the approval of the company physician. When he failed to return at the end of his leave period, his supervisor, who had long wanted to be rid of Harry, used the continued absence as a reason for terminating him from the company. The supervisor based his action on a section of the union agreement which provided that "when an employee is on sick leave he must, before the end of the leave period, either personally notify the company that he is returning to work or personally request and receive approval for an extension of the leave." Since the request for the leave extension had been made by his wife rather than by Harry personally, and since there had been no approval of a leave extension, the plant superintendent, after noting the warning slips and low ratings in Harry's personnel file, agreed that the action taken by the supervisor was justified under the terms of the union agreement.

As might be expected, the union promptly filed a grievance demanding the reinstatement of Harry and charging that the company was being inhumane in discharging a man when he was down. The union also maintained that Harry had been in bed with the flu at the time his wife called and therefore was unable to make the call or to come in to see the plant physician. As a result of union pressure and growing unrest in the plant among employees who believed that he had received a "raw deal," the plant superintendent rescinded the discharge and permitted Harry to have an extension of leave for the remainder of the two-week period.

When Harry reported back to work and complained of being unable to do the bending and lifting required of a kiln helper, management decided that it did not want to risk having any more conflicts with the union. Consequently, he was transferred to the job of mixer which happened to be open on the graveyard shift. The job involved operating and keeping production records on a group of mixing machines and required no physical labor except for starting and stopping the machines by means of electric control buttons. Harry mastered the duties of the job quickly and soon was able to perform his job more competently than the operators on either the day or the swing shifts. After about six months on the job, however, Harry began to revert to his former work habits and to develop a record of excessive tardiness and absenteeism. The supervisor thus was forced to have a lengthy session with him at which time he reminded Harry that the entire shift operations were impaired when the mixing machines were idle during the time required to locate a replacement operator. Obtaining a replacement, furthermore, required other disrupting adjustments in work assignments to be made on the shift. Following Harry's next absence, his supervisor gave him a written warning in which he stated that any future absences would result in a three-day suspension without pay for the first absence and a discharge for the second absence. Although the warning served to prevent further absences or tardiness, it did not serve to increase Harry's enthusiasm for his work.

About two months after receiving the warning, Harry decided to seek other employment and informed his supervisor that he would have to leave an hour earlier on his next work period in order to be able to drive to a military installation about 50 miles away and take a civil service examination. He informed the shift supervisor that he had made arrangements with the group leader to have his job covered for the final hour of the shift. The supervisor, whose mind was preoccupied with production problems at the time, grunted what appeared to be his approval although he was not conscious of the fact. The next day, the plant superintendent arrived early to inspect the operation of the graveyard shift and discovered that Harry, now well known by everyone in management, had left early. Since Harry's request to leave early had never really registered with the shift supervisor, he was at a loss to explain Harry's absence and therefore replied, "I guess he just took off." Regarding such action as intolerable, the superintendent ordered that Harry be terminated immediately. When

Harry returned the next night and was handed his discharge slip, he appealed to the union, which again went to bat for him. When management refused to reinstate Harry, the union used the discharge, along with some other grievance against the company, to arouse the tensions among its members and to create a production slowdown within the plant. Again not wanting to become involved in a major confrontation with the union, management for the second time agreed to rehire Harry.

Because of its long record of difficulties with Harry and the fact that he had become somewhat of a hero in the eyes of many workers, management decided to call in a consulting psychologist to counsel Harry and see if something could be done to improve his work attitudes. The ensuing session with the psychologist proved to be quite helpful in revealing, partially at least, the basis for his attitudes. In unburdening his feelings to the psychologist, Harry revealed bitterness over the fact that he believed his education and abilities had been wasted by the company. He complained that the company had put him in jobs that could be performed by workers with far less education and ability than he possessed. Furthermore, the psychologist was able to draw from him the fact that he felt that, with his education and some training, he could qualify for work in the quality control lab or for some job in the office. The initial reaction of the superintendent and members of management to the results of the counseling session was less than enthusiastic. In the opinion of the superintendent, Harry was a grown man who had had plenty of opportunities to express his feelings about work and should have submitted a request for a job in the office or the lab on his own initiative. After some discussion, however, the psychologist managed to convince most of the management members that something had to be done if the company was to avoid continuing problems with Harry and with the union. Although it did so with some mental reservations, management agreed to give Harry a trial period of training for a position in the lab. When the reports on his progress and attitudes at the end of the first month proved favorable, his training was allowed to continue. Eventually Harry was given a permanent job in the lab. In the meantime he received notification that he had been accepted for a civil service position. Since by this time he had accumulated several years of seniority with the company and now was quite satisfied with his employment situation, Harry rejected the civil service position to remain with the company.

a. What lessons does the case have to offer in terms of employee selection, placement, and supervision?

b. What are the possible reasons why this problem was not resolved satisfactorily much sooner?

c. Should the services of an outside consultant have been utilized in this situation? What are some of the ethical considerations involved in the use of a consulting psychologist?

d. Based upon the facts given, how would you rate the personnel policies and practices of this company?

The Ambitious Staff Specialist

The Saline Chemical Corporation, with headquarters in the Midwest, was engaged primarily in the production and nationwide distribution of chemical products for industrial and retail markets. The company, like many others in its field, experienced very rapid growth both in its sales volume, number of products produced, and the size of its work force in the years following World War II. At the time that the problem for discussion arose, the company employed about 30,000 persons, including those in its subsidiaries.

In the process of its expansion, the company was continually on the lookout for opportunities to purchase mineral properties for future sources of raw materials. It was also considering the purchase of smaller companies that might enable it to diversify its line of products, to gain new channels of distribution, or to acquire nationally known brand names under which it could market certain of its existing products. Because of the rapid technological advances within the industry and the rapid expansion that had occurred within its work force, the company required a relatively large number of college-trained personnel for both line and staff positions at the executive level. Although it had had difficulty during the postwar period in recruiting adequate personnel of the caliber desired, the company had been able to develop a technical staff composed of personnel who were extremely valuable to it.

One of the members of its financial research staff was J. Clayton Hall, who was about 38 years of age and an honor graduate with an M.B.A. degree from an eastern university. He had acquired some ten years of experience with the company and was responsible for the analysis of financial data and the compilation of reports for top management that were used in making company investment decisions. His work was extremely important because it provided the basis for decisions involving the investment of millions of dollars. Hall was regarded by his superiors as an extremely hardworking and conscientious individual who was outstanding in his type of work. His salary had been advanced rapidly and was above that being paid by other companies for similar types of work. His opportunities for advancement to positions of greater income and responsibility, although contingent upon additional years of service, were definitely assured.

In spite of his successful record and his value to the company, Hall did not feel that he enjoyed prestige within the company that was commensurate with either his ability or with that accorded to persons in supervisory positions who were much less competent and less valuable to the company. His contacts with certain of his college classmates who had risen to managerial positions of major importance caused him to be extremely sensitive of the fact that he did not have authority over anyone. Hall's failure to gain supervisory responsibility was due partly to the fact that he was more valuable to the company in the type of position in which he had been working and partly to the fact that he was totally lacking in human relations skills. Most company personnel who had any contact with him considered him to be an overbearing and extremely obnoxious individual.

Although Hall did not "rub people the wrong way" intentionally, he usually was so engrossed with the technical aspects of his work that he did not have time to give much consideration to the feelings of others. Although he had been reminded of his personality deficiencies during many previous performance rating interviews with superiors, he had never been able to improve these defects to any noticeable extent. Because of his outstanding performance in his technical field, however, Hall's personality deficiencies had not impeded his progress. Furthermore, the fact that he had relatively few contacts with other people caused his unsatisfactory traits to be overlooked.

After brooding for some time over his lack of positional status, Hall approached the head of his department with the demand that he be given a position involving supervisory responsibility, or he was going to quit. His superiors were quite aware of the fact that he had received several recent offers from other companies and that he was in a position to enforce his demands. While the company did not regard any of its personnel as being indispensable, it recognized that even if it could employ another person with Hall's abilities, several years of experience would be required before the replacement could equal Hall's present contributions.

The possibility of giving Hall a position with a more prestige-lending title was considered but ruled out because it conflicted with rather rigid company policies and traditions which caused executive titles to be reserved almost entirely for positions of a managerial nature. The few senior staff positions that did carry executive rank and status were staffed by those who had at least 20 to 25 years of company service. Although Hall undoubtedly would eventually be able to achieve one of these senior positions that carried the prestige he craved, this prospect was at least ten years away. There appeared to be only two alternatives in dealing with Hall's demands. One was to disregard his personality and give him some supervisory responsibilities in which he could enjoy the title and prestige of a line executive position. Or, management could attempt to change his mind by pointing out his value to the company, the importance of his job, and the opportunities for status that would be ultimately available to him. There were strong indications, however, that Hall would not be satisfied with anything less than a supervisory position and that he would resign if he did not get one.

a. What are some of the possible underlying reasons for Hall's demands?
b. What action should his department head take?
c. Why is it that jobs involving authority over people traditionally carry more prestige and salary than technical jobs which may require more education but no authority over people?
d. Are the company's management development practices at fault?

The Many Roles of a Woman Executive

The Indian Valley Instrument Company, a manufacturer of automobile diagnostic equipment, was founded by John and Peggy Sullivan in the garage of their Ohio home at the close of World War II. Starting with an investment of $250 and a testing instrument designed by John Sullivan, the company eventually grew to employ over 100 people. John was an exceedingly talented engineer but had absolutely no interest in the financial and administrative side of the business. Consequently, the responsibility for performing the administrative duties, keeping records, and paying the bills fell on his wife's shoulders. These responsibilities she assumed in addition to maintaining a household and rearing two young children. After an initial struggle, the enterprise proved to be a success as the result of the demand for the instruments designed by John and because of Peggy Sullivan's administrative abilities. As the business continued to grow, they decided to move the plant to a recreational area in Michigan where the air was clear and the fishing excellent.

In the new plant John was able to confine himself to designing new products and to overseeing the production work. Peggy, however, was not quite so fortunate. Not only did she spend the regular workday in the office administering the business, but also in the evening she assumed the role of homemaker and mother. In addition, she was pressed into the job of entertaining company customers who came for a vacation in their home. As she stated, "When a customer to whom you sell 70 percent of your output comes to visit you, you do not suggest they stay somewhere else." Mrs. Sullivan recalled, "I would not have minded having a couple of guests, but it was a little too much when this customer brought along a couple of teenage children and two of their children's friends and stayed a week. So, during these visits I had to rush home, prepare meals, and entertain houseguests in addition to my regular work at the plant during the day."

However, Mrs. Sullivan was equal to the task and the enterprise continued to grow, experiencing none of the seasonal or cyclical fluctuations that most businesses encounter. Additional personnel brought into the business eventually included two engineers to work on product design and a plant manager to manage the production end.

While their business continued to grow and prosper, their marriage began to drift onto the rocks. Having developed the Indian Valley Instrument Company into a prosperous concern and having employed personnel to take over his engineering and production responsibilities, John decided to leave the business and move to a new home with a new wife in Mexico. Peggy Sullivan was left to hold the enterprise together and to distribute to John Sullivan, on a regular basis, his share of the profits from the business. Eventually she remarried and became the wife of Homer Jones, a retired business executive.

The new marriage forced Peggy to delegate more responsibility to the plant manager and to her son, who moved in as the president of the organization. In this capacity her son worked full time during the summer months, but during the winter months he lived in Arizona from whence he returned one week out of each month to supervise the activities of the plant. Peggy Jones, on the other hand, confined herself to being at the plant only during the summer and spent the winters in Florida. Much of the responsibility during the winter, therefore, fell upon the plant manager, who assumed his responsibilities remarkably well.

John Sullivan, co-founder of the company, continued to enjoy life in Mexico and to live quite well from his share of the profits. His only contact with the company was at the annual board of directors meeting which he attended to perform his role as chairman of the board. Although the board meeting officially lasted only one day, considerable preparatory work preceded this meeting. As Peggy recalled, "We often would meet informally for nearly a week until all our differences were ironed out." Because of these differences and her desire to spend more time with her new husband, it was decided that it would be best for all concerned to accept the offer of a large corporation to buy the business.

Looking back upon her experiences over a 34-year span as a wife and as secretary-treasurer of the company, Peggy Jones had this to recall at the time the business was being sold:

> It was hard work but I enjoyed every bit of it. There were problems along the way but no severe conflict. I guess the most serious problem, if you wish to call it that, was the generation gap that developed in later years between my plant manager and me. Much of this stemmed from the differences in our objectives. He wanted to see the growth and profits of the company continue to increase. In my own case I felt I had enough from the business already and wanted to devote more time to my personal life. So we did not see eye-to-eye on this and a number of other things.
>
> Another problem also was that in recent years I have not been at the plant enough, and the manager believed I did not see all the problems that existed there; but actually I saw a lot more than he believed I did. He is a very ambitious young man and one who wished to assume authority; and I was one who, after all those years of running the business, was not willing to relinquish as much authority as he believed I should. So, there were times when he had to back down but, unfortunately, he did not always do it gracefully. He sometimes would let me know that I was wrong in my thinking. Now that I am getting out of the business, I believe he will solve many of these problems.

When asked what were the major problems she had encountered in the business, Peggy Jones confessed that most of her problems were of a personal nature. Many of them stemmed from her relationships with her former husband and with her present husband.

> Each year John would come from Mexico with his "I wants" and we would have to spend a couple of weeks resolving all the differences in our opinions and wants. John usually wanted to take more out of the business than I thought he should, and we would go around and around over it. All of this bothered Homer who was sitting at

home waiting for me. Although he never said as much, I am sure that the presence of John bothered him. My former husband just could not understand why he couldn't take more money out of the business because he never was able to understand finances and never had anything to do with them. That was all my responsibility. When we were developing the business, he never knew whether we had 10¢ or $10,000 in cash available. When the business was growing, I took care of buying materials, keeping control of the inventory, and getting the work turned out. He was the "brains" but I was the "back" of the business.

Peggy was then asked whether or not her performance as a manager was affected by the fact that she is a woman. She had this comment to make:

I believe that perhaps women tend to be a little more emotional where family is concerned; but when it comes to handling strictly business matters, they can be as tough as anyone else. In fact, I have been tough on many occasions in the past. But, where a husband and children are concerned, a woman is likely to be more emotional than a man. I have had situations in dealing with men where they wanted to be bribed in order to ship us materials that we urgently needed, but I think I handled those problems very well. I have been lied to when I had been promised delivery week after week—I don't know whether they were trying to take advantage of me, but I have literally sworn at them. In fact, in some instances, I believe I have been tougher than a man might have been.

However, I believe that you could talk with any of the employees in our plant and none of them would say that I am hard to work with. Even when I had to come back at night and do my office work when we were in a bind, I would go out on the floor and help the people on the production line. As long as you are willing to work side by side with employees and help with an urgent order, they will not call you an S.O.B. To this day, one of the things that makes me happiest is to have one of our employees come to me, as one did about a week ago, and tell me, "This certainly is a nice place to work. You are the nicest people." Now, that is the highest compliment I can get. That comment was not asked for—no promotion for saying that, it just came from the heart. Another real compliment is that some of our employees who were the first to work for us are still working here. Still, I have no regrets for getting out of the business because I will have more time to spend with my present husband.

a. Do you believe the business could have continued to survive if John Sullivan had left the business at the end of the first five years of its existence? If Peggy had moved to Mexico instead of John?

b. What particular problems did Peggy Sullivan encounter because of being a woman?

c. Prior to leaving the business, do you believe the contributions of John and Peggy to the business were made on a 50-50 basis?

d. What effects, if any, is the sale of this business to a large corporation likely to have upon the manager and the employees within the plant? Upon the role of Mrs. Jones's son in the business?

7

Social Workers Cry for Help

Supervisor Anna Simpson exerted tight control over every function of the Brown County Department of Social Services in Collinstown. Mountains of papers relating to welfare and food stamp grants to recipients serviced by the Collinstown District Office passed over her desk for approval. In addition, she was available to the ten social workers under her supervision for consultation on any problems related to the heavy case load each of them carried. She also conferred regularly with the three unit assistants and the clerical staff about the problems requiring something other than a routine decision. Besides these responsibilities, she periodically attended executive-level meetings at the central office in Bridgetown, a 45-minute drive from Collinstown.

One day an announcement by Ms. Simpson was circulated throughout the office that she, the social workers, and the unit assistants would meet for two hours every other week with Dr. Sigmund Bergman of the Brown County Psychiatric Facility. At these meetings Dr. Bergman would counsel the social workers about difficult problems they were having with their welfare clients. The first two meetings were fruitful. Dr. Bergman established a good rapport with the group and helped several of the individuals work out procedures for dealing with some long-standing problems.

The third meeting began in the usual way, but then Minerva Aliopolis veered from a monologue on her troubles with welfare clients to an emotional speech about the difficulties she was having in trying to function effectively in the Collinstown office. Ms. Aliopolis was known to be curt and snappy in her manner and had engaged in several loud public arguments with clients on her case load. Nevertheless, as she continued her tirade, heads began to nod in agreement. Ms. Simpson sat rigid, her face growing tighter and tighter as Minerva listed the following complaints:

1. That Simpson had set unrealistically high standards for the social workers, expecting them to meet deadlines on large case loads and at the same time clearing everything through her.
2. That Simpson's desk was the bottleneck, with various forms awaiting her initials being piled up for days.
3. That policy towards clients was inconsistent, with Simpson bending the eligibility regulations one time and rigidly enforcing them the next.

At this point Gilbert Bishop, a former clergyman, interrupted Minerva, stating:

I totally agree with everything Minerva has said, and I want to add my own complaint. The social workers in this office are nothing more than glorified clerks

We're so busy figuring budgets and authorizing checks that we never have time to perform the social services that are so desperately needed. And that's the reason we have such a turnover among the social workers here! I've worked here only a year and, except for Ms. Simpson, I have seniority over every other worker.

Suddenly Ms. Simpson broke her tight-lipped silence:

And how many of you are qualified to perform social services? True, you are all college graduates, with the exception of the unit assistants. But what were your majors? Music, math, English. Your college degrees were used as screening devices, not to determine the level of your training for the job. That's why I have to watch every step of the way—because what you're getting here is on-the-job training! And to top it all off, very few of you can stand the gaff long enough to learn something so you can be of real use to the people we serve.

Mary Macy broke in, "Ha! All they care about is their welfare check. They couldn't care less about any 'services' we offer—all they want is the money." To which Washington Gomez replied, "Well, eating is a pretty important process. It's pretty difficult to concentrate on improving your character and changing your life-style when your stomach is empty!"

Dr. Bergman raised a pacifying hand:

I'm truly sorry that our time is up and I have to leave. I hesitate to leave at this point, but I have an important appointment. I suggest we all think about what has been said here today. And when I come back next time, hopefully we can begin to deal with the feelings that have been expressed. What's happened is healthy and can be the basis for some constructive changes in the way we work. I'll see you all in two weeks.

A tense silence settled over the room after Dr. Bergman left. Everyone looked at Ms. Simpson. She glared at Minerva and then rose and stalked out. Minerva fell into a deep silence while the rest of the staff talked excitedly to each other discussing Ms. Simpson's reaction and what might happen at the next meeting. They never found out. There were no more meetings. Two days before the scheduled date, a terse notice was passed around to the effect that the "experimental" project headed by Dr. Bergman had been terminated after "suitable evaluation" by the social services central office in Bridgetown.

    a. What do you see as the broad underlying causes for the difficulties between the social workers and Ms. Simpson?

    b. What changes, if any, would you make in the hiring requirements for social worker positions? Describe the effect of such changes.

    c. Can you suggest a restructuring of job content and assignments that would reduce the employee turnover, decrease the supervisors' work load, and benefit the agency clients?

    d. How do you view Dr. Bergman's handling of the meeting? Can you think of alternative courses of action that he might have followed?

case

8

Participate: It's an Order!

Prior to the appointment of Roger Hammond as chief of the Metropolitan Police Department, the management style for the organization of some 2,000 employees was highly autocratic. The style could best be described as control-oriented. Subordinates could not make decisions without approval from the next higher level in the organization. Decisions thus were made only by high-ranking officers—captains and above. Upon his appointment, Chief Hammond, who had risen through the ranks, set out to incorporate many of the newer management principles and procedures that he had learned while pursuing a master's degree in public administration. He was convinced that the time had come for the department to change its approach to human resources management.

In several of the meetings with subordinate managers, the chief discussed the more current concepts of management. Participative management, McGregor's Theory Y, and other concepts that were prominent in the literature and being adopted in other organizations were presented to these police managers who were accustomed to a Theory X leadership environment. What the chief was discussing appeared strange to them as they listened uncomfortably and in disbelief. Sensing considerable resistance from the group, the chief told the group in one of the staff meetings that participative management would be implemented immediately and accomplished within 18 months. "This is an order and there will be no exceptions," the chief stated.

A consultant was hired to perform a dual role. He worked directly with the department's top management and also with a small training team to develop a program that included presentation of the principles of participative management, discussions, and several role-playing exercises. As soon as the program was developed, classes were scheduled. The first series of training sessions, which lasted three months, was limited to captains. After all of the captains had been through the training program, the lieutenants were scheduled. Because of the larger number of lieutenants to be trained, several series of sessions were scheduled over a period of approximately five months. In the training process the officers were given unrealistic expectations for the sergeants.

Meanwhile, the sergeants who directly supervised the major part of the force were in a quandary over their role in the organization. The lieutenants were beginning to practice the principles of participative management but the sergeants didn't understand what was happening. Instead of being given orders, they were consulted about many matters and were permitted to make their own decisions. Lacking the firm direction and control that heretofore they had experienced, the sergeants were uneasy about making decisions. Consequently, they tended to approach their subordinates in a state of confusion. It was not easy for them to switch from passing along the orders from above to making independent judgments. The sergeants were not sure about just what their responsibilities were or the degree of authority that they could exercise. No one had explained to them what their new role was to be in this rapidly changing organization. Many of the sergeants adopted a permissive role with their subordinates, allowing them more freedom than was advisable. Some of the sergeants became quietly hostile and assumed a position of not doing anything in order to avoid having problems that they could not handle.

Eventually all of the officers at the rank of lieutenant and higher completed the training course. At that point the sergeants were scheduled to attend. Several series of sessions over a period of nine months were needed to train all of them in the new style of management.

After several years perceptible changes have been observed in the climate and management style of the organization. However, there are still remnants of higher ranking officers who are not used to "letting go" and who firmly believe that they should have strict control over the personnel in their units. As these individuals retire, subordinates who have adopted a more participative management style will take their places in the organization.

a. What changes could have been made in the training program that may have alleviated the problem with the sergeants?

b. Was Chief Hammond realistic in his expectations that the change be accomplished in an 18-month period? Explain your position.

c. Why should one expect varying degrees of resistance to change in an organization?

d. What are the differences between permissive management and participative management?

9

When Should Participants Participate?

As at most schools, recommendations for various changes in curriculum at the Florence Nightingale Junior High School were initiated by individual faculty members and submitted to the faculty for discussion and approval—and ultimately to the principal for approval or disapproval. To provide an orderly basis by which requests for curriculum changes might be initiated and considered by the faculty, Eloise Breen, the principal of the school, prepared and distributed to the faculty the following policy statement which previously had been submitted to and approved by the heads of each of the departments within the school.

FLORENCE NIGHTINGALE JUNIOR HIGH SCHOOL

Fall 1978

Teachers are encouraged to reevaluate programs both individually and as departments. Requests for major changes in curriculum may come from an individual teacher, a department, or a committee. Requests for major changes must be turned in to the principal one week prior to Christmas vacation. The department chairpersons and the principal will consider these requests during the month of January; if approved by the department chairpersons and the principal, they will be implemented for the following year.

A copy of requests will be circulated to the faculty so that we may benefit from all ideas. Policy adopted by department chairpersons.

Please put in guidebook.

(Signed) **ELOISE BREEN**
Principal

In accordance with the newly established policy, in December, 1978, Ms. Breen submitted to the faculty a memorandum to which was attached curriculum change proposals that included a description of each change and the rationale for making it. The memorandum also announced a January date for a faculty meeting at which time the proposals were to be discussed. At that meeting the proposals for consideration were approved by the faculty as submitted or with modification.

In February, 1979, as the schedule for the next fall semester was being developed, Ms. Breen received a request from Marcia Brown, who supervised the course titled "Cross-Age Teaching." Brown requested that this course be changed from a single- to a double-period course. (It was an advanced course established to enable the more capable students to help tutor students in a neighboring elementary school.) Because of the distance required for the students to walk to and from the elementary school, insufficient time remained of a 50-minute period to provide adequate time for the students to do much tutoring. A double period, according to Ms. Brown, would provide more time for tutoring. To compensate for the additional period, she proposed that the course be reduced from a two-semester to a one-semester course so that the total hours required for it would remain the same. After studying Brown's proposal, Ms. Breen became convinced that the change would enable the course to better accomplish its objectives and agreed to make the necessary adjustment in the 1979 fall schedule.

Because Ms. Breen considered it to be merely a change in scheduling rather than a major change in curriculum, she did not submit the proposal to the faculty for review. However, when the 1979 fall schedule was published, some of the members of the faculty perceived it to be a major curriculum change and stated so in a grievance letter submitted to the principal. In the letter it was pointed out that the double period denied those enrolled in the course the opportunity to take elective courses during the third period, some of which were being taught by signers of the grievance. Failing to get the principal to reverse her decision, the teachers contacted their association, which made the issue a formal grievance in a letter to the district superintendent. Responding to the grievance in a letter to the superintendent, with a copy to the association, Ms. Breen reaffirmed her decision and gave the following reasons for doing so:

1. That the change did not involve the addition of a new course or a change in an existing one and therefore did not constitute a major change in curriculum but rather a scheduling change.
2. That the procedure for proposing curriculum changes was a local one that had been initiated voluntarily by the principal. It was intended to provide a means of processing curriculum proposals in an orderly manner and a means for faculty input. The procedure, therefore, was not so rigid as to deprive the principal from exercising some discretion.
3. That there was nothing in the district's regulations which required the principal to discuss such a change with the faculty first. Neither was any mention made of such a requirement in the labor agreement that had been reached between the district and the association as a result of collective bargaining.

a. Do you believe the principal acted correctly in approving the change? Consider your answer from the standpoint of good management, good human relations, and good labor relations.

b. To what extent, if any, are managers in an organization obligated to follow precisely a procedure or policy that they have established?

The Association's Union

The Association of State Employees (ASE) represented over 50,000 of the individuals employed by the government of an eastern state. The primary function of the association was to engage in collective bargaining in behalf of its members and to represent them in the processing of their grievances. The association also compiled and presented to appropriate legislative committees statistical data to support requested improvement in employment conditions. As a special membership inducement, it also offered an opportunity for members to purchase group life insurance and health insurance at substantial savings in premiums.

In order to serve its members, the association maintained a staff of over 150 employees, ranging in skill from clerks to attorneys. It had always attempted to maintain a parity between the employment conditions it provided for its employees and those it achieved for state employees. In spite of this fact, the majority of its employees chose to form a local union called the Staff Employees Union (SEU). After being subjected to a one-day strike, the association agreed to recognize the union and, after a period of negotiation that was remarkably free of hostility, entered into a labor agreement with it.

One of the provisions contained in this agreement was that employees should be granted two hours off on statewide election days for the purpose of voting. The agreement also provided for the establishment of a formal grievance procedure and for an outside arbitrator to resolve any grievances that could not be settled by the two parties.

The first case to go to arbitration was one involving disciplinary action against Ron Young in the form of a three-day suspension without pay. Young was a college student employed as a part-time mail clerk from 1:00 to 5:00 p.m. Another college student was employed part-time in the mornings at the same job that had been created specifically to employ college students. In the letter of notification sent to him by Robert Yee, the association deputy general manager, Young was advised that the disciplinary action was being taken against him for the following causes: willful disobedience, insubordination, and absence without leave. Young was advised also that the basis for these charges had been set forth in the following declaration, signed by his immediate supervisor, Karen Brill:

DECLARATION

I am the immediate supervisor of Ron Young. On Tuesday, November 6, 1979, at approximately 2:00 p.m., Mr. Young informed me he would be leaving work at 3:00

p.m. to vote. Since Mr. Young is a half-time employee of ASE, I asked my supervisor, Rose Madera, if it was permissible for Mr. Young to take the time off. Ms. Madera instructed me to contact the deputy general manager for a ruling.

I attempted to contact the deputy general manager and was informed by his secretary that Mr. Young would not be permitted to take time off to vote.

At approximately 2:50 p.m., I informed Ron Young of the decision not to allow him time off. He became quite angry and subsequently stated that he would be taking two hours off on "personal leave."

Rose Madera was informed of Mr. Young's statements and she instructed Mr. Young to make a request for the time off in a written memo and that his request would then be considered.

Mr. Young left work without my authorization at approximately 3:10 p.m., and without having submitted a written request. Mr. Young's workday is from 1:00 to 5:00 p.m.

On November 6, 1979, there was an unusually large amount of work to be done. By his unauthorized absence, Mr. Young caused substantial inconvenience and additional burden to myself and other employees in getting our work completed.

I declare under penalty of perjury that the foregoing is true and correct. Executed this 9th day of November, 1979, at ———— , ———— .

(Signed) KAREN BRILL

The information contained in the Declaration submitted by Ms. Brill was supported by the following memo which Ms. Madera had sent to Mr. Yee on November 7, 1979, the day following Young's 3:00 p.m. departure:

November 7, 1979

TO: Bob Yee
FROM: Rose Madera

SUBJECT: Ron Young—Voting

On Monday, November 5, 1979, Ron Young asked Karen Brill (his supervisor) what the rule was on time off for voting. Because Ron is the job steward, we thought he was interested in getting the information for all employees. Karen asked me if I had the information. I was not sure because it was a city-county election, so I called Sherri, your secretary. You were out of town, so Sherri said she would try to find out. Later in the day, Sherri called me and said that up to two hours could be taken providing one had a ballot receipt.

On Tuesday, November 6, 1979, at about 2:00 p.m., Ron informed Karen Brill that he would be leaving at 3:00 p.m. to vote. Karen then came to me and asked if she could call you to get a ruling on part-time employees (Ron works from 1:00 to 5:00 p.m.). I told her to go ahead and call you. Karen called, but you were away from your desk—so Karen informed Sherri. Sherri then told Karen she would check with you and get back to her before 3:00 p.m. Sherri returned Karen's call about 2:50 p.m. and said that you stated Ron had enough time to vote and the answer was "no." Karen so informed Ron, and he became upset. He then informed both Karen and me that he would be taking two hours off on "personal leave." I asked Ron to write Karen a memo to this effect before he left. Ron left at about 3:10 p.m. No memo was written for Karen.

When Ron received the letter notifying him of the disciplinary action, he immediately contacted Agatha Jones, president of SEU, to request assistance in appealing the action through the newly established grievance procedure. He was asked by Ms. Jones to provide the written statement covering his version of the November 6 incident. His written statement follows:

November 12, 1979

Dear Agatha,

The following is what I remember happening last Tuesday. The times are approximate.

2:00 p.m.   I told Karen Brill that I would leave at 3:00 to vote.

2:45 p.m.   She told me I couldn't leave. I asked a few questions concerning how and why this decision had been made. I was told that she had asked Bob Yee if the two hours off applied to me and he said it didn't because I was a part-time employee.

2:55 p.m.   I asked Karen if I could have the time off using "personal leave." She said we had a lot of work and that she would ask Rose. We then went to Rose, and Karen told her about my request. I think she commented to me that it was very short notice. I explained that I had just now found out that I couldn't have the time off to vote and that it would be hard to change my plans. She paused a second, then nodded her head. She then requested that I leave a memo before I left. I believe her exact words were, "OK, but will you leave me a memo before you go?" I said that I would. She never said what she wanted it for and I didn't ask.

3:00 p.m.   At this point I left them. I decided to finish the United Parcel Service mailing before writing the memo.

3:15 p.m.   I finished the UPS mailing and left, saying goodbye to the few people standing around my work area. I forgot to write the memo.

Sincerely,

(Signed) RON YOUNG

In response to Ron Young's request, the union appealed the disciplinary action through the grievance procedure; and ultimately the case went to arbitration. Testimony presented during the hearing by witnesses representing both the union and the employer helped to provide additional information with which to judge the fairness of the disciplinary action.

Testimony by Ron Young revealed that he had insisted upon receiving the two hours off on Tuesday afternoon so that he could get home and write a term paper that was due the next morning. His wife, who worked full time as a clerk-typist for the association, had been granted the two hours off that afternoon and at 3:00 p.m. she was planning to ride home with Ron to type the paper for him. Although they both did vote, it would not have been necessary for either of them to leave work early since the polls do not close until 7:00 p.m.

Under cross-examination by the union's attorney, both Robert Yee and Ms. Madera admitted that permission to take time off in the past had often been granted to employees by their supervisors on an informal basis without requiring a written request. Furthermore, such requests were granted in only about half the instances in which time off had been requested.

During the testimony, it was revealed that besides Young's wife, at least one other employee, an elderly woman living about 25 miles from work, had been given two hours off to vote even though it was not a statewide election.

a. What action against Ron Young, if any, would you have taken in this case had you been in Robert Yee's position?

b. Are there any improvements that appear to be needed in the association's personnel program?

c. Will the newly negotiated agreement with the union increase or decrease the need for such improvements? Explain.

d. Does this case offer any clues as to why the association's employees may have chosen to unionize?

case

11

Weather and Wages

Grange County is a relatively small agricultural county in the western United States. Most personal income in the county is derived from the sale of cattle, sheep, and orchard products. Because of this fact, the extreme drought conditions that developed one year had a very severe impact upon the entire economy of the county—so much so that is was declared a disaster area. The lack of grass for grazing and the rapid rise in the price of hay forced many ranchers to sell off a large portion or, in some instances, all of their herds. These severe financial losses, as would be expected, created a significant decline in business activity and income within Grange County.

Caught in the middle of these economic repercussions were the employees of Grange County who were experiencing a decline in purchasing power and real income from inflation. Any increase in their income could come only from additional revenues which were about as likely as additional rainfall. From the standpoint of the county supervisors, the political climate was such that any supervisor voting pay raises for county employees at the same time that many of the supervisors' constituents were being wiped out financially would be committing political suicide.

In spite of the drought and the economic losses accompanying it, the Grange County Employees Association, representing the majority of the county employees, contended that it should not be required to subsidize the cost of county government by foregoing wage increases comparable to those being granted to other employees in private enterprise and in other government jurisdictions throughout the state. The association was quick to point out that during the two preceding years the cost of living had risen by 15.2 percent while wages and fringes had increased only 6 percent, thereby causing its members a loss of purchasing power equal to 9.2 percent.

Since the laws of the state did not permit public employees at any level to engage in collective bargaining or strike activity, the association was limited to presenting its proposals to the county officials and appealing to their reasonableness for fair treatment. Its proposals were discussed during "meet and confer sessions" led by professional labor relations negotiators representing each of the parties. In the course of several such discussions, the best offer that the association's negotiator was able to get from the county government negotiator was an increase in fringe benefits (mainly increased employer health insurance premiums) equal to 2.8 percent. The county board of supervisors agreed with its negotiator's recommendation of 2.8 percent and granted this increase although two supervisors voiced the opinion that there should be no increase in view of the severe losses being suffered by many of their constituents.

The County Employees Association was very dissatisfied with the county's offer and refused to accept it. Under the terms of the County Charter, a mediator mutually agreeable to both parties was to be selected to hear the position of both parties whenever an impasse between the parties developed. Following the hearing, recommendations for resolving the impasse were to be submitted to both parties. These recommendations, however, were mainly of an advisory nature and not binding on either party.

After hearing the arguments presented by each side and giving due consideration to their respective positions, the mediator recommended that an increase of only 1.8 percent in fringes be granted instead of 2.8 percent. The mediator proposed that the 1 percent thus saved be added to a proposed wage increase of 3 percent, thus providing a total wage increase of 4 percent. This wage increase, along with the 1.8 percent increase in fringes, would constitute a total package increase of 5.8 percent but short of the 9.2 percent increase sought by the association.

After reviewing the mediator's recommendations, the county board voted unanimously not to change its original offer of 2.8 percent, which was then granted to all employees. In taking such action, several supervisors expressed personal regret but reminded the association that their constituents would vote any supervisor out of office who failed to seek tax relief for them, let alone vote for any increases in these taxes.

The reaction of the association officers and members to the supervisors' action was one of anger and frustration. Several militant members urged the association to go out on strike. However, cooler heads dissuaded them from this by pointing out that a strike would be illegal and that very likely it would be lost along with their employment. The association, therefore, was left no other alternative than to accept what it could get.

a. Was the Board of Supervisors being unreasonable in their settlement with the County Employees Association? Explain why or why not.

b. Should the employees be expected to share in the economic losses of the county?

c. Would your opinion in the preceding question have been different if the county's inability to provide a raise had been due to fiscal mismanagement which had resulted in the absence of funds from which to pay the increase?

case

12

The Frustrated Personnel Director*

Personnel Director Greenleaf opened the interoffice envelope from F.L. Case, Secretary, and was surprised to see a copy of the Management Committee minutes enclosed. In the upper right-hand corner of the first page was penned: "Thought you'd be interested. A couple of items are yours. FLC." In his four years with the bank, this was only the second time that Greenleaf had been permitted to see or hold in his hand a copy of the minutes of the most important committee in the bank. To say that he was "interested" was an understatement. Case had promised that the Personnel Inventory and Appraisal recommendation would be considered at this meeting. They'd been holding it over for two months now. Greenleaf eagerly perused the minutes.

<u>MINUTES</u>

Management Committee Meeting
April

Present:	Chairman of the Board, A. B. Tateman
	President, J. C. Groming
	Executive Vice-President, D. L. Mentsen
	Controller, C. D. Perman
	Vice-President—Branches, W. H. Able
	Vice-President—Operations, R. D. Framer
	Secretary, F. L. Case
Absent:	None
Presiding:	Chairman, A. B. Tateman
Meeting called to order:	9:25 a.m.
Minutes of previous meeting:	Approved as submitted

---

*Copyright 1965, The American Bankers Association. Reproduced with permission. All names have been disguised.

1. *Statement of Condition.* Mr. Perman reported on the statistics showing the first quarter results for the bank. The committee agreed that the report reflected excellent achievements, except for the rise in interest expenses as a result of increased savings account balances and the high personnel salary and benefit costs. Mr. Perman was complimented for his presentation, his analysis of the data, and the significance of his remarks as related to the bank's statement of condition.

    Chairman Tateman reviewed comparative statistics indicating that the bank now was the fourth largest in the city as compared to fifth a year ago. He commented on the merger of the Premium National and the Metropolitan Commercial, formerly third and fourth in size, into the largest bank in the city. He expressed concern about the merger trend as evidenced in other cities and stated categorically that our bank was not a merger possibility. He noted the highly satisfactory profit picture and said that it was his intention to continue his policy of providing stockholders with an attractive return on the investments. To achieve this, he called for renewed effort to reduce expenses, the addition of new services to attract new business, and improved work procedures. He also expressed concern with personnel expenses and requested that a special effort be made to hold them down.

2. *Personnel Report.* Mr. Groming read the Personnel Director's quarterly statistical report indicating a total clerical staff of 804, an official staff of 72, total annual payroll of $6,400,000, first quarter overtime in the amount of $98,000, 92 temporary employees on payroll, first quarter turnover rate of 17 percent, and 290 salary increases for $73,890 granted during the quarter. Full discussion followed and the Secretary was instructed to obtain a complete explanation for the overtime and temporary employees.

3. *Branch Offices.* Mr. Able reported that all ten branches were performing smoothly and that applications were on file with government authorities for four additional locations in new residential neighborhoods. He noted that rapid expansion had created staffing problems which caused some of the overtime and the hiring of temporary employees reported earlier. However, he stated that he was in personal contact with a number of senior experienced people in competitive banks and that, if negotiations with them are successful, the personnel situation in the branches would be eased considerably.

4. *Check-Handling Administration.* Mr. Framer indicated that all check handling now was centralized at the main office and that negotiations were continuing with two major correspondent commercial banks to determine the feasibility of having one of them perform all checking-account bookkeeping on their computers. He stressed the necessity for culminating those negotiations as soon as possible inasmuch as the volume was increasing more rapidly than anticipated. This means that present equipment is not suitable for high-volume activity. As an alternative, Mr. Framer proposed a full study of the possibility of purchasing excess machines from Premium National to fill in the void. Such an excess exists because of their merger. Mr. Framer also thought it would be possible to hire some experienced supervisors and machine operators from both merged banks to cope with the increased check volume and the problems resulting from the centralization of check handling at the main office.

5. *New Business Activities.* A report on a recent survey of correspondent banks to determine their various customer services was made by Mr. Mentsen. Mixed reactions were given to many of the innovations now in vogue. All agreed with Chairman Tateman that the basic abilities to service checking accounts and to make

loans to assist customers were the vital services for a successful banking operation. However, since there was some interest in the small loan field, Mr. Mentsen was asked to research this area more fully. No action was taken to expand the services of the Foreign or the Fiduciary Departments because an increase in services would involve additional physical facilities and personnel.

Mr. Mentsen announced that he had obtained a new account with an opening balance of $50,000 from Kelleen Corporation.[1] This was a payroll account for Branch #6. He anticipated that approximately 300 payroll checks would be cashed at this branch every Friday and requested Mr. Able to alert his staff for the new business. Mr. Kelleen has indicated that, if he is satisfied with the service, he will consider the possibility of moving his business account to our bank.

6. *Miscellaneous Matters.* Chairman Tateman commented on a number of miscellaneous matters including:

   a. Officer Retirements—12 officers (Executive Vice-President Mentsen, Vice-President Framer, three branch managers and seven junior officers in Foreign, Fiduciary, Control, and Operations) have indicated a desire to retire as of the end of the year. He also noted that 22 clerical staff members are 64 years old or over and that some thought should now be given to a definite policy with regard to handling retirements.

   b. Banking School Enrollment—Assistant Vice-President Caufield was registered at the State School of Banking for the three-year summer course with the expectation that the exposure would help him to assume new responsibilities in the Operations Department in view of Mr. Framer's intended retirement. The registration will be at bank expense for room, board, tuition fees, and texts. Mr. Caufield will be expected to assume any personal expenses incurred.

   c. AIB (American Institute of Banking) and College Enrollments—the AIB bill for 17 students ($780) was approved for payment. In addition, 14 employees were registered in evening college courses and all have received acknowledgements of their enrollments. In the case of Mr. Hartley Junet, an executive trainee, full refund of tuition has been paid for his college courses.

   d. Maintenance of Bank Premises—in view of their unsatisfactory performance, the contract for building maintenance with Cleaner, Inc., has been terminated and additional porters will have to be hired to properly clean all bank space.

   e. Opened and Closed Accounts—ten new commercial checking accounts with opening balances of $100,000 or over were opened (three with proceeds of loans) in addition to the Kelleen Account noted earlier. Eight accounts with average balances of $10,000 or over were closed. Reasons given were "more convenient location at another bank," "inability to provide foreign facilities," "loan application rejected," and "dissatisfaction with service."

   f. Loans—the Director's Loan Committee considers the bank "loaned up" at present, and no new lines or substantial loans are to be considered without prior approval of Chairman Tateman.

   g. Personnel Inventory and Appraisal Program—the Personnel Director's recommendation that the entire staff be inventoried for the multiple purposes of evaluating performance, determining individual strengths and weaknesses,

---

1. The reader should keep in mind that the monetary figures in this case are in 1965 dollars.

and identifying areas with manpower shortages would be tabled temporarily until other pressing problems such as approval of new branch offices, correspondent bank check-processing procedure, etc., were solved.

Meeting Adjourned: 10:40 a.m.   Respectfully submitted,
F.L. Case, Secretary

Greenleaf slowly laid down the minutes and thought back to that day, four years ago, when he had accepted the appointment as Personnel Director, leaving a similar position at Premium National. Groming had talked about a dynamic bank, a major influence in the community, the tremendous opportunity to implement a broad and modern personnel program where none now existed, working with management as part of a team, a full vice-presidency within six years.

The minutes disturbed him for other reasons besides the tabling of this particular program. He saw, for the very first time, a number of new undertakings of which he had no knowledge. And there were clear-cut infringements on his responsibilities which were being approved by the committee. Further, he disliked what sounded like unethical tactics being used to recruit new personnel.

He pulled open his center drawer and removed a paper headed "Score Sheet." It was a list of all the major proposals submitted during his tenure. Opposite each proposal was noted "implemented," "pended," "rejected," or "no response." He posted "pended" against the Personnel Inventory and Appraisal Program and then reviewed the entire list.

Score Sheet

1. Orientation for new employees...................................implemented
2. Standardized vacation schedule ....implemented
3. Employee newspaper.. no response
4. Removal of time clocks .... rejected
5. Formalized, improved tuition refund program .... pended
6. Improved hospitalization and life insurance plans ....implemented
7. Centralized personnel records..................................implemented
8. Clerical recruiting and testing procedures .... no response
9. Temporary help vs. additional employees, I.....................implemented
   (with modifications)
10. Salary budgets .... pended
11. Job evaluation program.. pended
12. Morale survey... rejected
13. Implications of turnover statistics, I............................ no response
14. Supervisors' training program ....implemented
   (with modifications)
15. Organization charts.. no response
16. Discontinuance of annual bonus.................................... rejected
17. Personnel policies manual......................................implemented
   (with modifications)
18. Temporary help vs. additional employees, II .... pended
19. Pension program .... no response
20. Implications of turnover statistics, II .... pended

21. College recruiting and training program ....implemented
(with modifications)

22. Personnel inventory and appraisal program............................pended

    a. What are your reactions to the minutes of this management committee meeting? What message do they convey?

    b. What would you do if you were in Greenleaf's position?

NAME INDEX

A

Acito, Franklin, 290
Adams, J. S., 264
Adkins, Dorothy C., 154
Adler, Joan, 489
Albana, Charles, 291, 292
Alber, Antone F., 40
Albrecht, Karl, 508, 509
Alderfer, Clayton P., 262
Allan, Peter, 82
Allen, Fred T., 298
Allen, Louis A., 304
Allen, Robert F., 320
Allen, Robert W., 60, 61
Alpander, Guvenc, 102, 103
Anastasi, Anne, 154, 178
Anderson, Dale E., 507
Anderson, Howard J., 465
Anderson, John C., 341
Anthony, Richard J., 331
Anton, Thomas J., 516
Appelbaum, Steven H., 507
Appley, Lawrence A., 124
Argyris, Chris, 326
Arvey, Richard D., 137, 139, 145, 174, 241
Asher, James J., 150
Atchinson, Thomas J., 408
Atkinson, J. W., 262

B

Backhouse, Constance, 326
Baer, Walter E., 402
Baird, Lloyd E., 254
Baker, Alton W., 313
Bakke, Allan, 172
Balinsky, Benjamin, 136
Balma, Michael J., 159
Barbash, Jack, 355

Barnes-Farrell, Janet, 250
Barnett, Nona J., 231
Bass, Bernard M., 200, 306
Beach, Kenneth M., Jr., 189, 190
Beal, Edwin F., 378
Beason, George, 132
Beatty, Richard W., 241, 254
Belcher, David W., 437, 441, 455
Bellows, Roger M., 136
Belt, John A., 132
Benge, Eugene J., 417
Bennett, Amanda, 290, 349
Bennis, Warren G., 62
Benson, Philip G., 210
Berg, Eric, 210
Berg, J. Gary, 437
Berkowitz, L., 264
Berne, Eric, 291
Berwitz, Clement J., 99
Beva, Richard B., 409
Bingham, Walter Van Dyke, 8, 142
Bird, Caroline, 437
Bittel, Lester R., 310
Blackburn, John D., 501
Blackford, Katherine, 145
Blake, Robert R., 307
Block, Richard I., 399
Blundell, William E., 294
Bogart, Robert B., 470
Bogdonoff, Morton D., 484
Bok, Derek C., 340
Bolles, Richard N., 213
Bower, Donald, 291
Bowers, Mollie H., 396
Boxx, W. Randy, 187
Bradford, Leland P., 489
Bradford, Martha I., 489
Brammer, Lawrence M., 322
Brandt, Anthony, 145
Bray, Douglas W., 214
Breaugh, James A., 110, 113

Brecher, Arline, 503
Brecker, Richard L., 113
Brindisi, Louis J., Jr., 452
Brinks, James T., 449
Brown, Bob S., 317
Brown, David S., 54
Brown, James K., 47
Brown, Linda Keller, 217
Bruce, Martin M., 135, 136
Bryan, Judith F., 200
Buisman, Ben A., 41, 42
Burck, Charles G., 319
Burke, Ronald J., 238
Burns, D. Steven, 143
Buros, O. K., 148, 154
Bush, Gerald W., 234
Butterfield, D. Anthony, 317
Buzzard, R. B., 137
Byham, William C., 215, 229, 542

C

Cagen, Phillip, 412
Camden, Thomas M., 210
Campbell, J., 241
Campion, James E., 139
Campion, Michael A., 137
Carey, Ernestine Gilbreth, 7
Carhalvo, Gerard, 422
Carroll, Stephen J., Jr., 254, 437
Cascio, Wayne F., 150
Cash, Thomas F., 143
Cattell, J. McKeen, 8
Chambers, Carl D., 321
Chamot, Dennis, 350
Chao, Georgia T., 131
Chapanis, Alphonse, 82
Charles, A. W., 439
Chemers, Marvin M., 308
Cheraskin, E., 503, 514

SUBJECT INDEX

A

absenteeism, 319-320; costs of, 533-534

absenteeism rates, 531-534:
  comparing data on, 533
  computing, 532-533
  defined, 532

academic training, for career in human resources management, 19

accreditation, defined, 17

accident investigations and records, 498-499

achievement motivation theory, 262-263; defined, 262

ad hoc committee, defined, 58

adjudicator, defined, 396

adverse impact:
  bottom-line concept, 172
  defined, 171
  handling charges of, 171

advertisements, as recruiting source, 109-110

affirmative action (AA), in recruitment, 113-121

affirmative-action programs, in selection policies, 172-173

AFL-CIO, formation of, 335

Age Discrimination in Employment Act of 1967 (ADEA), 121, 167, 430, 485, 487

agency shop, defined, 374

alarm reaction, defined, 508

Albermarle Paper Company v. *Moody,* 170, 236

alcoholism, 320, 506, 507

American Federation of Labor (AFL), 335

American Society for Personnel

Administration (ASPA), 18, 290, 550, 554

anxiety, 184, 270

applicants, reliable and valid information about, 127

application forms, 130

applications, unsolicited, 113

apprenticeship training, defined, 194

appraisal by subordinates, defined, 234

arbitrating grievances, 396-400

arbitration:
  compulsory binding, 370
  criticisms of, 400
  defined, 396
  final offer, 370
  of discrimination grievances, 399
  process, the, 397-398

arbitration award, defined, 398

arbitrator, defined, 363:
  ad hoc, defined, 396
  permanent, defined, 396

arbitrators, sources of, 396

Army Alpha and Beta Tests, 12, 145

assessment center, defined, 214

attitude, defined, 259

attitude conformity, defined, 284

attitude survey, 535-538

"at will" doctrine, defined, 380

audit, human resources, 519; utilizing findings, 538-540

audit coverage, 520

audit process, steps in, 522

authority:
  defined, 52
  delegation of, 52-53
  essence of, 52

Average Indexed Monthly

Earnings (AIME), defined, 474

B

background investigations, 131

Bakke Case, 170

bargaining patterns, 356

bargaining process:
  concessionary, 366
  conducting the negotiations, 357-358
  employer's power in collective bargaining, 361-362
  preparing for negotiations, 355-357
  resolving bargaining deadlocks, 363
  union's power in collective bargaining, 358-361

bargaining strategies, 356-357

bargaining unit, defined, 333

bargaining zone, defined, 358

behaviorally anchored rating scale (BARS), defined, 240

behavioral objectives, defined, 189

behavioral sciences:
  defined, 9
  emergence of, 9-10

behavioral theories:
  defined, 305
  emphasis upon leader behavior, 306-308

behavior modeling, defined, 198

behavior modeling method, 198-199

behavior modification, defined, 201

benefits. *See* employee benefits